EDUCATION FOR DEMOCRACY

Revised Printing

D1542412

CITIZENSHIP ❖ COMMUNITY ❖ SERVICE

A Sourcebook for Students and Teachers

Benjamin R. Barber
and
Richard M. Battistoni

Editors

KENDALL/HUNT PUBLISHING COMPANY
4050 Westmark Drive   P.O. Box 1840   Dubuque, Iowa 52004-1840

Dedication

This book is dedicated to all Americans, young and old,
engaged in service to their communities.

Contents

Part One: Citizenship in a Democracy 1

Citizenship and Democratic Community

Citizenship and the Psychology of Belonging

Citizenship, Morals and Responsibility

Community, Citizenship and Service

Part Two: Challenges to Democratic Citizenship 265

Prejudice, Difference, and Inequality

The Tyranny of the Majority

To Serve or Not To Serve

Part Three: Opportunities for Citizenship and Service 493

Acknowledgments

This anthology has been in the making for several years, and owes its existence to a number of individuals. We are especially indebted to Mark B. Brown, our research assistant who not only provided intensive collaboration on the bibliography, introductions, and questions, but also served as an invaluable resource for the selection of articles to include in the volume. We would not have completed the anthology without his considerable work.

We also wish to acknowledge our students and colleagues at Rutgers and Baylor, who deserve much of the credit for this book. We express gratitude to Gregory Vafis, Karen Zivi, Herbert Caudill, Nancy Larson, and Beverly Roberts for their work in the earlier stages of the project. David Burns, Viola Van Jones, Rod Hartnett, Bryan Barnett and Sharon Grant Henry were present and active at the start of the Rutgers Civic Education and Community Service Program, the curricular experiment linking citizen education with service that serves as the source of inspiration for this volume. Our faculty colleagues with whom we worked on the linkages between citizen education and community service have contributed greatly to the ideas, selections, and questions found in this volume: Merle Alexander, Roland Anglin, Barbara Balliet, Patricia Bender, Harry Boyte, Eleanor Brilliant, Dudley Burton, Lucille Chagnon, James Dunn, Judy Francis, Michael Frisch, Claudia Gitelman, Wendy Gunther Canada, David Hendon, Christine Kelly, Muffin Lord, Jim Reed, Gary Roth, David Stricklin, Lionel Tiger, Mary Trigg, Jon Van Til, and Linda Zerilli. And our students and community partners in the Civic Education and Community Service Programs at Rutgers and Baylor constantly acted as a foil and a prod for our thinking.

Special thanks go to Peter Goldmark at the Rockefeller Foundation, Ray Chambers at the Amelior Foundation, and Bernard, Audre, and Ronald Rapoport at the Rapoport Foundation for their tremendous efforts in funding the campus community service programs at Rutgers and Baylor that make this book both possible and necessary.

Finally, we owe a debt to four presidents: to Edward Bloustein for his vision in initiating the model program at Rutgers; to Frances Lawrence at Rutgers and Herbert Reynolds at Baylor for their significant commitment in taking on a program ahead of its time; and to Bill Clinton, for his recognition of our success and of the need to connect citizen education with all national and community service initiatives. They are the model for the kind of transforming leadership essential in a democracy.

Introduction

Community service can mean many different things: to some it means charity, serving others from the goodness of one's heart. To some it means personal growth and the improvement of character: through serving others I can become a better person. To some it means a private fix to public problems: we can meet social challenges one by one and one on one, without depending on top heavy bureaucracies like the federal government. To some it is a matter of gratitude: I serve to give something back to the community that nurtured and educated me (William Buckley, Jr.'s recent book on national service was thus called Gratitude). And to some service means taking citizenship seriously: learning to take responsibility for the local and national communities from which my rights and my liberties arise. These are all valid perspectives, and most people in service experience a mixture of motives.

We start in our anthology with the special relationship between service and democratic citizenship. While service can and does mean many good things, service in a democracy must first of all be seen as a crucial aspect of social responsibility: a model of the relationship between rights bearing citizens and the many communities to which they belong. To be a citizen is not merely to have rights but to take responsibility, to see ourselves and our interests as flourishing only as our communities flourish.

Citizenship is neither a form of selfishness (what can I get for me from others!?) nor a form of altruism (how can I help others just for the sake of helping?!). It is a way of linking the self and others in a mutual web of common values and common goods. Taking responsibility for others is how we ultimately take responsibility for ourselves. To serve ourselves, we need to serve those upon whom the realization of our interests depend. Citizens are neither angels, who have no need of politics, nor egoists, who have no capacity for politics. They are ordinary women and men trying to live together cooperatively in the face of conflict and seeking commonality in spite of difference.

If service serves citizenship, education serves service. For citizenship turns out to be a set of learned skills. We may be born free but we are not born citizens, and have to acquire the traits that enable us to participate effectively in a democratic polity. That connection between education and citizenship has been a part of our tradition from the earliest times. Thomas Jefferson regarded his role in founding the University of Virginia as more significant than his two term Presidency, and many founders agreed that without common schooling, common citizenship—and thus democracy— was unlikely to survive, let alone flourish.

This connection between education and democracy explains why we have chosen so many selections in an anthology devoted to service learning that evoke themes of responsibility, community and citizenship. Which is not to say that we have ignored challenges to the preoccupation with democratic communities. After introducing our central themes in Part I, we have devoted much of Part II to the perspective of individualists, libertarians and anarchists who distrust community and the democratic majorities which speak in its name. Democracy empowers communities and enforces the will of the majority, but its ultimate concern is with the individual. Service too begins and ends with individuals even if it ties them to the communities they serve (which are also constituted by individuals!). We mean not merely to celebrate but to problematize democracy and the range of our selections make clear that many of the values we cherish are themselves in conflict.

Our anthology also exists because we want community and national service to teach experiential lessons about responsibility, citizenship and democracy, and to do this requires that the experience of the street be brought into the classroom. Service that is neither reflected upon nor refracted critically through the lens of scholarship may make us feel good but is unlikely to teach us much. Lessons on citizenship limited to the classroom may paint pretty pictures of democracy in the abstract, but will do little to help us become active and empowered and responsible citizens in the real world. The combination of acting and thinking, serving and reflecting, doing and critiquing, represents an ideal pedagogy of democracy. Perhaps that is why education based community service programs have been so spectacularly successful in the Nineties. Perhaps that is why the Clinton Administration has not only embraced the idea of service but has sought to link service through training programs and to school and university learning. It is certainly why we have devoted Part III of our anthology to readings that specifically address issues of schooling and service.

In fact, we have tried throughout to choose selections and append questions intended to bridge classroom and community. Hence, we have included fiction as well as nonfiction, literature from the humanities as well as the social sciences, conservative as well as progressive perspectives, and points of view rooted in psychology as well as in politics. The anthology should thus be usable not only in political science service learning courses, but in similar courses in the arts, the humanities, and in interdisciplinary youth corps and national service training programs. We have included pieces with a multicultural viewpoint without dismissing pertinent "canonical" writings (Tocqueville, Thoreau, or Dewey, for example), and have made originality and pertinence the key criteria of selection—along with clarity and felicity of expression. It is one of the great virtues of citizenship and service learning that they cross ideological and philosophical lines and allow those who otherwise may identify themselves as antagonists to work and to learn together.

We have also interspersed several poems among the selections, because poets often render the apparently obscure transparent while at the same time they complexify the apparently straightforward. We hope poetry will also offer another source of thought and discussion in the classroom.

In order to keep the anthology manageable in size at the same time we maximize the number and range of contributions, we have cut down and edited our selections rather ruthlessly. In some cases (as with our butchering of Melville's Billy Budd), our cuts are barely defensible; in others (as with some of the selections from political scientists like anthology coeditor Barber) the editing down may actually constitute an improvement. With social science, less is often better! But in any case no one should think a particular excerpt does more than hint at the author's complete point of view and in every case readers are urged to consult the uncut original.

Finally, although we have grouped readings according to a certain logic which some teachers and students may find useful; but others surely will not. And there is no reason why readers should not pick and choose among the many selections in a sequence which suits their own curriculum and needs, omitting selections that don't fit and incorporating others from other sources we have overlooked. Likewise, our questions are meant to be suggestive rather than definitive, and students will want to raise their own in keeping with their experiences and concerns. But since service learning is some ways a rather new pedagogy, and because we have found in our teaching that linking abstract and literary ideas to real service experience is often hard, we have offered sample questions as clues to an experiential teaching strategy.

In one sense, this anthology is a narrow contribution to a new subfield of teaching—service learning or education based community service. But in another sense, beyond its obvious substantive concerns, it raises fundamental issues about the American future. For it poses implicit questions about the nature of civic pedagogy—can it be limited to the classroom? About citizenship—can it be taught in the absence of real life experience? And about democracy—can it survive unless we transform the liberal arts back into the arts of liberty and make the teaching of citizenship an integral part of school and university curricula? To the extent the compendium of selections here does in practice manage to raise such questions, we will have achieved our goal of reestablishing the vital link between education, service, and citizenship and the life of our democracy.

Benjamin R. Barber
Richard M. Battistoni

I Hear America Singing

I hear America singing, the varied carols I hear,
Those of mechanics, each one singing his as it should be blithe and
    strong,
The carpenter singing his as he measures his plank or beam,
The mason singing his as he makes ready for work, or leaves off
    work,
The boatman singing what belongs to him in his boat, the deckhand
    singing on the steamboat deck,
The shoemaker singing as he sits on his bench, the hatter singing
    as he stands,
The wood cutter's song, the ploughboy's on his way in the morning,
    or at noon intermission or at sundown,
The delicious singing of the mother, or of the young wife at work, or
    of the girl sewing or washing,
Each singing what belongs to him or her and to none else,
The day what belongs to the day—at night the party of young fel-
    lows, robust, friendly,
Singing with open mouths their strong melodious songs.

Walt Whitman

Part One

❖

Citizenship
in a
Democracy

Introduction

W hat does it mean to be a member of the communities in which one lives or works—school, workplace, neighborhood, or nation? What does it mean to be a citizen in a democracy? What is the relationship between civil rights and civic responsibilities? And what does service have to do with democratic citizenship?

These are some of the questions we will explore in Part I, with reading selections that explore the fundamental relationship between democracy, citizenship, and service. In the first section, "Citizenship and Democratic Community," we begin with a short story by Katherine Mansfield which raises questions about the nature of family and community, and about the relationships between people who come from different communities though they live and work in the same place. We then look at several classical texts on democracy spanning the last three centuries that help define what a democratic community is and what citizens must be. This question has assumed growing significance with the "democratic revolutions" that have occurred in recent years. The selections by Arendt, Dewey, Locke, Jefferson and Whitman have in common a belief that democracy means more than just voting or democratic political institutions. All emphasize the culture of democracy—democratic values and ideals that inform a genuinely democratic society. Perhaps the reason emerging "democracies" all over the world are having so much trouble is that people have assumed that a free market and free political institutions are all it takes to make a democracy. Yet Jean-Jacques Rousseau seems closer to the mark when he writes: "There can be no patriotism without liberty; no liberty without virtue; no virtue without citizens; create citizens and you will have everything you need; without them you will have nothing but debased slaves, from the rulers of the state on downwards."

But citizenship is not just how we make democracy work: it represents a form of belonging. In the next section, we look at "Citizenship and the Psychology of Belonging." Dostoevsky's classic passage "The Grand Inquisitor" from *The Brothers Karamazov* challenges us to think hard about whether the urge to belong is compatible with freedom. Simone Weil teaches us that "the need for roots" in a larger community of belonging need not necessarily support democracy or liberty. William James uses war as a metaphor for belonging, but many will argue that war and democracy are incompatible, and that martial virtues are a poor substitute for democratic citizenship. Both Daniel Kemmis and the authors of *Habits of the Heart* take us back to earlier traditions in the United States to recapture a more benign form of community belonging. For Robert Bellah and his colleagues it is the biblical and republican traditions of small town America, and for Kemmis it is the Western phenomenon of the barnraising that discloses how we can both belong to a community and remain free. For Emerson, the balance is difficult and solitude remains an alternative to belonging—perhaps even a way to belong.

In the next section we examine the relationship between citizenship, moral values, and responsibilities. The classical Athenians Aristotle and Thucydides understood citizenship almost exclusively in terms of responsibilities and obligations. Aristotle's understanding of the citizen was one whose responsibility was to rule and be ruled in turn. In Pericles' famous funeral oration we find that the obligation to have a part in the public's business is part of what it means to be human (human beings are "political animals"). Abraham Lincoln used his moral understanding of the natural law to argue that citizens owed an obligation to preserve and maintain the values that their ancestors enshrined in the Constitution. He also held that morality and justice was the basis of the law, and that when laws were not grounded-in justice, the obligation to obey the rule of law itself was compromised. In the contemporary era, morality and responsibility have become the preserve of the individual. Citizens possess rights, their moral responsibilities are to conscience and family. Benjamin Barber contends that the American tradition of representative government has separated citizens from their lawmaking responsibilities, and produced a democratic politics where we are in constant search of leaders to follow. Harry Boyte also challenges contemporary definitions of democratic politics, and argues for the return of citizens who work together practically to solve public problems. We conclude this section with another moral political leader, former Czech President Vaclav Havel, who encourages all of us—especially public officials—to "live in truth."

The final section of Part One contains a group of short selections in which the idea of community service is linked directly to several different understandings of democracy and community. We begin this section with different stories of service, beginning with a chapter from Robert Coles' The Call of Service. This is followed by three pieces, by Mother Teresa, Millard Fuller, and Jacob Neusner, which explore faith-based understandings of service and community rooted in different religious traditions. The remaining essays in this section look at the question of national service and its relationship to citizenship and democracy. President Clinton's op ed essay sets the problem for the debate, while the selections from *Visions of Service*, many by people in or close to the national service movement, suggest the breadth of service as an organizing idea for democracy and community.

Katherine Mansfield
The Garden Party

Sometimes called the founder of the English short story, Katherine Mansfield was born in New Zealand in 1888. She had her first story accepted at age nine, and after an English education and a brief flirtation with life as a musician, began a prolific publishing career in 1910. She was most active as a writer during and immediately following World War I. She died of tuberculosis in France, at the age of 34. "The Garden-party" is a classic Mansfield story: brief and simple, it hinges on a sudden moment of insight rather than on an involved plot. The story follows a young girl's complex confrontation with death and social class, an abrupt exposure to realities from which she had been sheltered by her family "community." Laura's journey to visit the family outside the gates and down the hill from her own "community" at once exposes the great divide between different communities in a society and the opportunity a simple act of kindness brings to begin to bridge the gap between people.

We have chosen a piece of short fiction for the introductory reading to this volume. As you read this story and the excerpts from political philosophers that follow in this section, begin thinking about how you would define "community" and "citizenship." What synonyms can you think of for community? Can you think of good examples of democratic community in the world around you? How do the communities we belong to define who we are as individuals? How do questions of size and diversity affect community? Can community only exist in small, face to face settings, where people are known to one another? Or can it be approximated in larger settings? How much unity is necessary or even desirable in community? Is diversity necessary for "real" community to exist?

The Garden Party
Katherine Mansfield

And after all the weather was ideal. They could not have had a more perfect day for a garden-party if they had ordered it. Windless, warm, the sky without a cloud. Only the blue was veiled with a haze of light gold, as it is sometimes in early summer. The gardener had been up since dawn, mowing the lawns and sweeping them, until the grass and the dark flat rosettes where the daisy plants had been seemed to shine. As for the roses, you could not help feeling they understood that roses are the only flowers that impress people at garden-parties; the only flowers that everybody is certain of knowing. Hundreds, yes, literally hundreds, had come out in a single night; the green bushes bowed down as though they had been visited by archangels.

Breakfast was not yet over before the men came to put up the marquee.

"Where do you want the marquee put, mother?"

"My dear child, it's no use asking me. I'm determined to leave everything to you children this year. Forget I am your mother. Treat me as an honoured guest."

But Meg could not possibly go and supervise the men. She had washed her hair before breakfast, and she sat drinking her coffee in a green turban, with a dark wet curl stamped on each cheek. Jose, the butterfly, always came down in a silk petticoat and a kimono jacket.

"You'll have to go, Laura; you're the artistic one."

Away Laura flew, still holding her piece of bread-and-butter. It's so delicious to have an excuse for eating out of doors, and besides, she loved having to arrange things; she always felt she could do it so much better than anybody else.

From *The Short Stories of Katherine Mansfield* by Katherine Mansfield (Alfred A. Knopf, Inc., 1922).

Four men in their shirt-sleeves stood grouped together on the garden path. They carried staves covered with rolls of canvas, and they had big tool-bags slung on their backs. They looked impressive. Laura wished now that she had not got the bread-and-butter, but there was nowhere to put it, and she couldn't possibly throw it away. She blushed and tried to look severe and even a little bit short-sighted as she came up to them.

"Good morning," she said, copying her mother's voice. But that sounded so fearfully affected that she was ashamed, and stammered like a little girl, "Oh — er — have you come — is it about the marquee?"

"That's right, miss," said the tallest of the men, a lanky, freckled fellow, and he shifted his tool-bag, knocked back his straw hat and smiled down at her. "That's about it."

His smile was so easy, so friendly that Laura recovered. What nice eyes he had, small, but such a dark blue! And now she looked at the others, they were smiling too. "Cheer up, we won't bite," their smile seemed to say. How very nice workmen were! And what a beautiful morning! She mustn't mention the morning; she must be businesslike. The marquee.

"Well, what about the lily-lawn? Would that do?"

And she pointed to the lily-lawn with the hand that didn't hold the bread-and-butter. They turned, they stared in the direction. A little fat chap thrust out his under-lip, and the tall fellow frowned.

"I don't fancy it," said he. "Not conspicuous enough. You see, with a thing like a marquee," and he turned to Laura in his easy way, "you want to put it somewhere where it'll give you a bang slap in the eye, if you follow me."

Laura's upbringing made her wonder for a moment whether it was quite respectful of a workman to talk to her of bangs slap in the eye. But she did quite follow him.

"A corner of the tennis-court," she suggested. "But the band's going to be in one corner."

"H'm, going to have a band, are you?" said another of the workmen. He was pale. He had a haggard look as his dark eyes scanned the tennis-court. What was he thinking?

"Only a very small band," said Laura gently. Perhaps he wouldn't mind so much if the band was quite small. But the tall fellow interrupted.

"Look here, miss, that's the place. Against those trees. Over there. That'll do fine."

Against the karakas. Then the karaka-trees would be hidden. And they were so lovely, with their broad, gleaming leaves, and their clusters of yellow fruit. They were like trees you imagined growing on a desert island, proud, solitary, lifting their leaves and fruits to the sun in a kind of silent splendour. Must they be hidden by a marquee?

They must. Already the men had shouldered their staves and were making for the place. Only the tall fellow was left. He bent down, pinched a sprig of lavender, put his thumb and forefinger to his nose and snuffed up the smell. When Laura saw that gesture she forgot all about the karakas in her wonder at him caring for things like that — caring for the smell of lavender. How many men that she knew would have done such a thing? Oh, how extraordinarily nice workmen were, she thought. Why couldn't she have workmen for friends rather than the silly boys she danced with and who came to Sunday night supper? She would get on much better with men like these.

It's all the fault, she decided, as the tall fellow drew something on the back of an envelope, something that was to be looped up or left to hang, of these absurd class distinctions. Well, for her part, she didn't feel them. Not a bit, not an atom.... And now there came the chock-chock of wooden hammers. Some one whistled, some one sang out, "Are you right there, matey?" "Matey!" The friendliness of it, the — the — Just to prove how happy she was, just to show the tall fellow how at home she felt, and how she despised stupid conventions, Laura took a big bite of her bread-and-butter as she stared at the little drawing. She felt just like a work-girl.

"Laura, Laura, where are you? Telephone, Laura!" a voice cried from the house.

"Coming!" Away she skimmed, over the lawn, up the path, up the steps, across the veranda, and into the porch. In the hall her father and Laurie were brushing their hats ready to go to the office,

"I say, Laura," said Laurie very fast, "you might just give a squiz at my coat before this afternoon. See if it wants pressing."

"I will," said she. Suddenly she couldn't stop herself. She ran at Laurie and gave him a small, quick squeeze. "Oh, I do love parties, don't you?" gasped Laura.

"Rather," said Laurie's warm, boyish voice, and he squeezed his sister too, and gave her a gentle push. "Dash off to the telephone, old girl."

The telephone. "Yes, yes; oh yes. Kitty? Good morning, dear. Come to lunch? Do, dear. Delighted of course. It will only be a very scratch meal—just the sandwich crusts and broken meringue-shells and what's left over. Yes, isn't it a perfect morning? Your white? Oh, I certainly should. One moment—hold the line. Mother's calling." And Laura sat back. "What, mother? Can't hear."

Mrs. Sheridan's voice floated down the stairs. "Tell her to wear that *sweet* hat she had on last Sunday."

"Mother says you're to wear that sweet hat you had on last Sunday. Good. One o'clock. Bye-bye."

Laura put back the receiver, flung her arms over her head, took a deep breath, stretched and let them fall. "Huh," she sighed, and the moment after the sigh she sat up quickly. She was still, listening. All the doors in the house seemed to be open. The house was alive with soft, quick steps and running voices. The green baize door that led to the kitchen regions swung open and shut with a muffled thud. And now there came a long, chuckling absurd sound. It was the heavy piano being moved on its stiff castors. But the air! If you stopped to notice, was the air always like this? Little faint winds were playing chase,

in at the tops of the windows, out at the doors. And there were two tiny spots of sun, one on the inkpot, one on a silver photograph frame, playing too. Darling little spots. Especially the one on the inkpot lid. It was quite warm. A warm little silver star. She could have kissed it.

The front door bell pealed, and there sounded the rustle of Sadie's print skirt on the stairs. A man's voice murmured; Sadie answered, careless, "I'm sure I don't know. Wait. I'll ask Mrs. Sheridan."

"What is it, Sadie?" Laura came into the hall.

"It's the florist, Miss Laura."

It was, indeed. There, just inside the door, stood a wide, shallow tray full of pots of pink lilies. No other kind. Nothing but lilies—canna lilies, big pink flowers, wide open, radiant, almost frighteningly alive on bright crimson stems.

"O-oh, Sadie!" said Laura, and the sound was like a little moan. She crouched down as if to warm herself at that blaze of lilies; she felt they were in her fingers, on her lips, growing in her breast.

"It's some mistake," she said faintly. "Nobody ever ordered so many. Sadie, go and find mother."

But at that moment Mrs. Sheridan joined them.

"It's quite right," she said calmly. "Yes, I ordered them. Aren't they lovely?" She pressed Laura's arm. "I was passing the shop yesterday, and I saw them in the window. And I suddenly thought for once in my life I shall have enough canna lilies. The garden-party will be a good excuse."

"But I thought you said you didn't mean to interfere," said Laura. Sadie had gone. The florist's man was still outside at his van. She put her arm round her mother's neck and gently, very gently, she bit her mother's ear.

"My darling child, you wouldn't like a logical mother, would you? Don't do that. Here's the man."

He carried more lilies still, another whole tray.

"Bank them up, just inside the door, on both sides of the porch, please," said Mrs. Sheridan. "Don't you agree, Laura?"

"Oh, I *do* mother."

In the drawing-room Meg, Jose and good little Hans had at last succeeded in moving the piano.

"Now, if we put this chesterfield against the wall and move everything out of the room except the chairs, don't you think?"

"Quite."

"Hans, move these tables into the smoking-room, and bring a sweeper to take these marks off the carpet and—one moment, Hans—" Jose loved giving orders to the servants, and they loved obeying her. She always made them feel they were taking part in some drama. "Tell mother and Miss Laura to come here at once."

"Very good, Miss Jose."

She turned to Meg. "I want to hear what the piano sounds like, just in case I'm asked to sing this afternoon. Let's try over 'This life is Weary.' "

Pom! Ta-ta-ta *Tee*-ta! The piano burst out so passionately that Jose's face changed. She clasped her hands. She looked mournfully and enigmatically at her mother and Laura as they came in.

> This Life is *Wee*-ary,
> A Tear—a Sigh.
> A Love that *Chan*ges,
> This Life is *Wee*-ary,
> A Tear—a Sigh.
> A Love that *Chan*ges,
> And then...Good-bye!

But at the word "Good-bye," and although the piano sounded more desperate than ever, her face broke into a brilliant, dreadfully unsympathetic smile.

"Aren't I in good voice, mummy?" she beamed.

> This Life is *Wea*ry,
> Hope comes to Die.
> A Dream—a *Wak*ening.

But now Sadie interrupted them. "What is it, Sadie?"

"If you please, m'm, cook says have you got the flags for the sandwiches?"

"The flags for the sandwiches, Sadie?" echoed Mrs. Sheridan dreamily. And the children knew by her face that she hadn't got them. "Let me see." And she said to Sadie firmly, "Tell cook I'll let her have them in ten minutes."

Sadie went.

"Now, Laura," said her mother quickly. "Come with me into the smoking-room. I've got the names somewhere on the back of an envelope. You'll have to write them out for me. Meg, go upstairs this minute and take that wet thing off your head. Jose, run and finish dressing this instant. Do you hear me, children, or shall I have to tell your father when he comes home to-night? And—and, Jose, pacify cook if you do go into the kitchen, will you? I'm terrified of her this morning."

The envelope was found at last behind the dining-room clock, though how it had got there Mrs. Sheridan could not imagine.

"One of you children must have stolen it out of my bag, because I remember vividly—cream cheese and lemon-curd. Have you done that?"

"Yes."

"Egg and—" Mrs. Sheridan held the envelope away from her. "It looks like mice. It can't be mice, can it?"

"Olive, pet," said Laura, looking over her shoulder.

"Yes, of course, olive. What a horrible combination it sounds. Egg and olive."

They were finished at last, and Laura took them off to the kitchen. She found Jose there pacifying the cook, who did not look at all terrifying.

"I have never seen such exquisite sandwiches," said Jose's rapturous voice. "How many kinds did you say there were, cook? Fifteen?"

"Fifteen, Miss Jose."

"Well, cook, I congratulate you."

Cook swept up crusts with the long sandwich knife, and smiled broadly.

"Godber's has come," announced Sadie, issuing out of the pantry. She had seen the man pass the window.

That meant the cream puffs had come. Godber's were famous for their cream puffs. Nobody ever thought of making them at home.

"Bring them in and put them on the table, my girl," ordered cook.

Sadie brought them in and went back to the door. Of course Laura and Jose were far too grown-up to really care about such things. All the same, they couldn't help agreeing that the puffs looked very attractive. Very. Cook began arranging them, shaking off the extra icing sugar.

"Don't they carry one back to all one's parties?" said Laura.

"I suppose they do," said practical Jose, who never liked to be carried back. "They look beautifully light and feathery, I must say."

"Have one each, my dears," said cook in her comfortable voice. "Yes ma won't know."

Oh, impossible. Fancy cream puffs so soon after breakfast. The very idea made one shudder. All the same, two minutes later Jose and Laura were licking their fingers with that absorbed inward look that only comes from whipped cream.

"Let's go into the garden, out by the back way," suggested Laura. "I want to see how the men are getting on with the marquee. They're such awfully nice men."

But the back door was blocked by cook, Sadie, Godber's man and Hans.

Something had happened.

"Tuk-tuk-tuk," clucked cook like an agitated hen. Sadie had her hand clapped to her cheek as though she had toothache. Hans's face was screwed up in the effort to understand. Only

Godber's man seemed to be enjoying himself; it was his story.

"What's the matter? What's happened?"

"There's been a horrible accident," said Cook. "A man killed."

"A man killed! Where? How? When?"

But Godber's man wasn't going to have his story snatched from under his very nose.

"Know those little cottages just below here, miss?" Know them? Of course, she knew them. "Well, there's a young chap living there, name of Scott, a carter. His horse shied at a traction-engine, corner of Hawke Street this morning, and he was thrown out on the back of his head. Killed."

"Dead!" Laura stared at Godber's man.

"Dead when they picked him up," said Godber's man with relish. "They were taking the body home as I come up here." And he said to the cook, "He's left a wife and five little ones."

"Jose, come here." Laura caught hold of her sister's sleeve and dragged her through the kitchen to the other side of the green baize door. There she paused and leaned against it. "Jose!" she said, horrified, "however are we going to stop everything?"

"Stop everything, Laura!" cried Jose in astonishment. "What do you mean?"

"Stop the garden-party, of course." Why did Jose pretend?

But Jose was still more amazed. "Stop the garden-party? My dear Laura, don't be so absurd. Of course we can't do anything of the kind. Nobody expects us to. Don't be so extravagant."

"But we can't possibly have a garden-party with a man dead just outside the front gate."

That really was extravagant, for the little cottages were in a lane to themselves at the very bottom of a steep rise that led up to the house. A broad road ran between. True, they were far too near. They were the greatest possible eyesore, and they had no right to be in that neighbourhood at all. They were little mean dwellings painted a chocolate brown. In the garden patches there was nothing but cabbage stalks, sick hens and tomato cans. The very smoke coming out of their chimneys was poverty-stricken. Little rags and shreds of smoke, so unlike the great silvery plumes that uncurled from the Sheridans' chimneys. Washerwomen lived in the lane and sweeps and a cobbler, and a man whose house-front was studded all over with minute bird-cages. Children swarmed. When the Sheridans were little they were forbidden to set foot there because of the revolting language and of what they might catch. But since they were grown up, Laura and Laurie on their prowls sometimes walked through. It was disgusting and sordid. They came out with a shudder. But still one must go everywhere; one must see everything. So through they went.

"And just think of what the band would sound like to that poor woman," said Laura.

"Oh, Laura!" Jose began to be seriously annoyed. "If you're going to stop a band playing every time some one has an accident, you'll lead a very strenuous life. I'm every bit as sorry about it as you. I feel just as sympathetic." Her eyes hardened. She looked at her sister just as she used to when they were little and fighting together. "You won't bring a drunken workman back to life by being sentimental," she said softly.

"Drunk! Who said he was drunk?" Laura turned furiously on Jose. She said, just as they had used to say on those occasions, "I'm going straight up to tell mother."

"Do, dear," cooed Jose.

"Mother, can I come into your room?" Laura turned the big glass door-knob.

"Of course, child. Why, what's the matter? What's given you such a colour?" And Mrs. Sheridan turned round from her dressing-table. She was trying on a new hat.

"Mother, a man's been killed," began Laura.

"*Not* in the garden?" interrupted her mother.

"No, no!"

"Oh, what a fright you gave me!" Mrs. Sheridan sighed with relief, and took off the big hat and held it on her knees.

"But listen, mother," said Laura. Breathless, half-choking, she told the dreadful story. "Of course, we can't have our party, can we?" she pleaded. "The band and everybody arriving. They'd hear us, mother; they're nearly neighbours!"

To Laura's astonishment her mother behaved just like Jose, it was harder to bear because she seemed amused. She refused to take Laura seriously.

"But, my dear child, use your common sense. It's only by accident we've heard of it. If some one had died there normally—and I can't understand how they keep alive in those poky little holes—we should still be having our party, shouldn't we?"

Laura had to say "yes" to that, but she felt it was all wrong. She sat down on her mother's sofa and pinched the cushion frill.

"Mother, isn't it really terribly heartless of us?" she asked.

"Darling!" Mrs. Sheridan got up and came over to her, carrying the hat. Before Laura could stop her she had popped it on. "My child!" said her mother, "the hat is yours. It's made for you. It's much too young for me. I have never seen you look such a picture. Look at yourself!" And she held up her hand-mirror.

"But, mother," Laura began again. She couldn't look at herself; she turned aside.

This time Mrs. Sheridan lost patience just as Jose had done.

"You are being very absurd, Laura," she said coldly. "People like that don't expect sacrifices from us. And it's not very sympathetic to spoil everybody's enjoyment as you're doing now."

"I don't understand," said Laura, and she walked quickly out of the room into her own bedroom. There, quite by chance, the first thing she saw was this charming girl in the mirror, in her black hat trimmed with gold daisies, and a long black velvet ribbon. Never had she imagined she could look like that. Is mother right? she thought. And now she hoped her mother was right. Am I being extravagant? Perhaps it was extravagant. Just for a moment she had another glimpse of that poor woman and those little children, and the body being carried into the house. But it all seemed blurred, unreal, like a picture in the newspaper. I'll remember it again after the party's over, she decided. And somehow that seemed quite the best plan....

Lunch was over by half-past one. By half-past two they were all ready for the fray. The green-coated band had arrived and was established in a corner of the tennis-court.

"My dear!" trilled Kitty Maitland, "aren't they too like frogs for words? You ought to have arranged them round the pond with the conductor in the middle on a leaf."

Laurie arrived and hailed them on his way to dress. At the sight of him Laura remembered the accident again. She wanted to tell him. If Laurie agreed with the others, then it was bound to be all right. And she followed him into the hall.

"Laurie!"

"Hallo!" He was half-way upstairs, but when he turned round and saw Laura he suddenly puffed out his cheeks and goggled his eyes at her. "My word, Laura; You do look stunning;" said Laurie. "What an absolutely topping hat!"

Laura said faintly "Is it?" and smiled up at Laurie, and didn't tell him after all.

Soon after that people began coming in streams. The band struck up; the hired waiters ran from the house to the marquee. Wherever you looked there were couples strolling, bending to the flowers, greeting, moving on over the lawn. They were like bright birds that had alighted in the Sheridans' garden for this one afternoon, on their way to—where? Ah, what happiness it is to be with people who all are happy, to press hands, press cheeks, smile into eyes.

"Darling Laura, how well you look!"

"What a becoming hat, child!"

"Laura, you look quite Spanish. I've never seen you look so striking."

And Laura, glowing, answered softly, "Have you had tea? Won't you have an ice? The passion-fruit ices really are rather special." She ran to her father and begged him. "Daddy darling, can't the band have something to drink?"

And the perfect afternoon slowly ripened, slowly faded, slowly its petals closed.

"Never a more delightful garden-party..." "The greatest success..." "Quite the most..."

Laura helped her mother with the good-byes. They stood side by side in the porch till it was all over.

"All over, all over, thank heaven," said Mrs. Sheridan. "Round up the others, Laura. Let's go and have some fresh coffee. I'm exhausted. Yes, it's been very successful. But oh, these parties, these parties! Why will you children insist on giving parties! And they all of them sat down in the deserted marquee.

"Have a sandwich, daddy dear. I wrote the flag."

"Thanks." Mr. Sheridan took a bite and the sandwich was gone. He took another. "I suppose you didn't hear of a beastly accident that happened to-day?" he said.

"My dear," said Mrs. Sheridan, holding up her hand, "we did. It nearly ruined the party. Laura insisted we should put it off."

"Oh, mother!" Laura didn't want to be teased about it.

"It was a horrible affair all the same," said Mr. Sheridan. "The chap was married too. Lived just below in the lane, and leaves a wife and half a dozen kiddies, so they say."

An awkward little silence fell. Mrs. Sheridan fidgeted with her cup. Really, it was very tactless of father...

Suddenly she looked up. There on the table were all those sandwiches, cakes, puffs, all uneaten, all going to be wasted. She had one of her brilliant ideas.

"I know," she said. "Let's make up a basket. Let's send that poor creature some of this perfectly good food. At any rate, it will be the greatest treat for the children. Don't you agree? And she's sure to have neighbours calling in and so on. What a point to have it all ready prepared. Laura!" She jumped up. "Get me the big basket out of the stairs cupboard."

"But, mother, do you really think it's a good idea?" said Laura.

Again, how curious, she seemed to be different from them all. To take scraps from their party. Would the poor woman really like that?

"Of course! What's the matter with you today? An hour or two ago you were insisting on us being sympathetic, and now—"

Oh, well! Laura ran for the basket. It was filled, it was heaped by her mother.

"Take it yourself, darling," said she. "Run down just as you are. No, wait, take the arum lilies too. People of that class are so impressed by arum lilies."

"The stems will ruin her lace frock," said practical Jose.

So they would. Just in time. "Only the basket, then. And, Laura!"—her mother followed her out of the marquee—"don't on any account—"

"What, mother?"

No, better not put such ideas into the child's head! "Nothing! Run along."

It was just growing dusky as Laura shut their garden gates. A big dog ran by like a shadow. The road gleamed white, and down below in the hollow the little cottages were in deep shade. How quiet it seemed after the afternoon. Here she was going down the hill to somewhere where a man lay dead, and she couldn't realize it. Why couldn't she? She stopped a minute. And it seemed to her that kisses, voices, tinkling spoons, laughter, the smell of crushed grass were somehow inside her. She had no room for anything else. How strange! She looked up at the pale sky, and all she thought was, "Yes, it was the most successful party."

Now the broad road was crossed. The lane began, smoky and dark. Women in shawls and men's tweed caps hurried by. Men hung over the palings; the children played in the door-ways. A low hum came from the mean little cottages. In some of them there was a flicker of light, and a shadow, crab-like, moved across the window. Laura bent her head and hurried on. She wished now she had put on a coat. How her frock shone! And the big hat with the velvet streamer—if only it was another hat! Were the people looking at her? They must be. It was a mistake to have come; she knew all along it was a mistake. Should she go back even now?

No, too late. This was the house. It must be. A dark knot of people stood outside. Beside the gate an old, old woman with a crutch sat in a chair, watching. She had her feet on a newspaper. The voices stopped as Laura drew near. The group parted. It was as though she was expected, as though they had known she was coming here.

Laura was terribly nervous. Tossing the velvet ribbon over her shoulder, she said to a woman standing by, "Is this Mrs. Scott's house?" and the woman, smiling queerly, said, "It is, my lass."

Oh, to be away from this! She actually said, "Help me, God," as she walked up the tiny path and knocked. To be away from those staring eyes, or to be covered up in anything, one of those women's shawls even. I'll just leave the basket and go, she decided. I shan't even wait for it to be emptied.

Then the door opened. A little woman in black showed in the gloom.

Laura said, "Are you Mrs. Scott?" But to her horror the woman answered, "Walk in please, miss," and she was shut in the passage.

"No," said Laura, "I don't want to come in. I only want to leave this basket. Mother sent—"

The little woman in the gloomy passage seemed not to have heard her. "Step this way, please, miss," she said in an oily voice, and Laura followed her.

She found herself in a wretched little low kitchen, lighted by a smoky lamp. There was a woman sitting before the fire.

"Em," said the little creature who had let her in. "Em! It's a young lady." She turned to Laura. She said meaningly, "I'm 'er sister, Miss. You'll excuse 'er, won't you?"

"Oh, but of course!" said Laura. "Please, please don't disturb her. I—I only want to leave—"

But at that moment the woman at the fire turned round. Her face, puffed up, red, with swollen eyes and swollen lips, looked terrible. She seemed as though she couldn't understand why Laura was there. What did it mean? Why was this stranger standing in the kitchen with a basket? What was it all about? And the poor face puckered up again.

"All right, my dear," said the other. "I'll thank the young lady."

And again she began, "You'll excuse her, miss, I'm sure," and her face, swollen too, tried an oily smile.

Laura only wanted to get out, to get away. She was back in the passage. The door opened. She walked straight through into the bedroom, where the dead man was lying.

"You'd like a look at 'im, wouldn't you?" said Em's sister, and she brushed past Laura over to the bed. "Don't be afraid, my lass,—" and now her voice sounded fond and sly, and fondly she drew down the sheet—"'e looks a picture. There's nothing to show. Come along, my dear."

Laura came.

There lay a young man, fast asleep—sleeping so soundly, so deeply, that he was far, far away from them both. Oh, so remote, so peaceful. He was dreaming. Never wake him up again. His head was sunk in the pillow, his eyes were closed; they were blind under the closed eyelids. He was given up to his dream. What did garden-parties and baskets and lace frocks matter to him? He was far from all those things. He was wonderful, beautiful. While they were laughing and while the band was playing, this marvel had come to the lane. Happy...happy... All is well, said that sleeping face. This is just as it should be. I am content.

But all the same you had to cry, and she couldn't go out of the room without saying something to him. Laura gave a loud childish sob.

"Forgive my hat," she said.

And this time she didn't wait for Em's sister. She found her way out of the door, down the path, past all those dark people. At the corner of the lane she met Laurie.

He stepped out of the shadow. "Is that you, Laura?"

"Yes."

"Mother was getting anxious. Was it all right?"

"Yes, quite. Oh, Laurie!" She took his arm, she pressed up against him.

"I say, you're not crying, are you?" asked her brother.

Laura shook her head. She was.

Laurie put his arm round her shoulder. "Don't cry," he said in his warm, loving voice. "Was it awful?"

"No," sobbed Laura. "It was simply marvellous. But, Laurie—" She stopped, she looked at her brother. "Isn't life," she stammered, "isn't life—" But what life was she couldn't explain. No matter. He quite understood.

"*Isn't* it, darling?" said Laurie.

---❖---

John Dewey
The Search for the Great Community

---❖---

John Dewey (1859–1952), best known as a pragmatist and a philosopher of "instrumentalism," had a profound international influence on democratic philosophy and educational theory, as well as on law, psychology, and political science. Dewey was born in Burlington, Vermont and received his doctorate from Johns Hopkins University in 1884. As chairman of the philosophy department at the University of Chicago, he directed the university's laboratory school from 1896–1903, combining educational theory and practice. In 1904 Dewey left Chicago for Columbia University, becoming active in a wide variety of philosophical, educational, and political organizations.

Dewey's "learning by doing" educational theory focused on the practical, social consequences of education. In this regard, Dewey opposed the dogmatic teaching methods and rote learning popular at the time. He believed that a democratic society needed to teach its citizens to adopt a spirit of free inquiry, critical of authoritarian doctrines, and he endorsed an "experiential" approach to learning.

In the following selection, Dewey asserts that criticisms of particular democratic institutions should not be applied to the ideals of democracy, but must lead to a renewed understanding of democratic principles. The problem of democracy thus begins with the creation of the material and social conditions which will allow the development of the proper institutions. In discussing the democratic idea, Dewey equates democracy with community life itself. Democracy consists in having a share in shaping one's community. Community, for Dewey, is the necessary starting point for all other political ideas. At the same time, however, community must be consciously created and maintained. This conscious creation of community never ends, but is renewed every day and with every new generation. Community is a distinctively human creation, but we must continually teach each other how to be human.

Search for the Great Community
John Dewey

We have had occasion to refer in passing to the distinction between democracy as a social idea and political democracy as a system of government. The two are, of course, connected. The idea remains barren and empty save as it is incarnated in human relationships. Yet in discussion they must be distinguished. The idea of democracy is a wider and fuller idea than can be exemplified in the state even at its best. To be realized it must affect all modes of human association, the family, the school, industry, religion. And even as far as political arrangements are concerned, governmental institutions are but a mechanism for securing to an idea channels of effective operation. It will hardly do to say that criticisms of the political machinery leave the believer in the idea untouched. For, as far as they are justified—and no candid believer can deny that many of them are only too well grounded—they arouse him to bestir himself in order that the idea may find a more adequate machinery through which to work. What the faithful insist upon, however, is that the idea and its external organs and structures are not to be identified. We object to the common supposition of the foes of existing democratic government that the accusations against it touch the social and moral aspirations and ideas which underlie the political forms. The old saying that the cure for the ills of democracy is more democracy is not apt if it means that the evils may be remedied by introducing more machinery of the same kind as that which already exists, or by refining and perfecting that machinery. But the phrase may also indicate the need of returning to the idea itself, of clarifying and deepening our apprehension of it, and of employing our sense of its meaning to criticize and re-make its political manifestations.

Confining ourselves, for the moment, to political democracy, we must, in any case, renew

From *The Public and Its Problems* by John Dewey. Reprinted with the permission of The Ohio University Press/Swallow Press, Athens.

our protest against the assumption that the idea has itself produced the governmental practices which obtain in democratic states: General suffrage, elected representatives, majority rule, and so on. The idea has influenced the concrete political movement, but it has not caused it. The transition from family and dynastic government supported by the loyalties of tradition to popular government was the outcome primarily of technological discoveries and inventions working a change in the customs by which men had been bound together. It was not due to the doctrines of doctrinaires. The forms to which we are accustomed in democratic governments represent the cumulative effect of a multitude of events, unpremeditated as far as political effects were concerned and having unpredictable consequences. There is no sanctity in universal suffrage, frequent elections, majority rule, congressional and cabinet government. These things are devices evolved in the direction in which the current was moving, each wave of which involved at the time of its impulsion a minimum of departure from antecedent custom and law. The devices served a purpose; but the purpose was rather that of meeting existing needs which had become too intense to be ignored, than that of forwarding the democratic idea. In spite of all defects, they served their own purpose well.

Looking back, with the aid which *ex posto facto* experience can give, it would be hard for the wisest to devise schemes which, under the circumstances, would have met the needs better. In this retrospective glance, it is possible, however, to see how the doctrinal formulations which accompanied them were inadequate, one- sided and positively erroneous. In fact they were hardly more than political war-cries adopted to help in carrying on some immediate agitation or in justifying some particular practical polity struggling for recognition, even though they were asserted to be absolute truths of human nature or of morals. The doctrines served a particular local pragmatic need. But often their very adaptation to immediate circumstances unfitted them, pragmatically, to meet more enduring and more extensive needs. They lived to cumber the political ground, obstructing progress, all the more so because they were uttered and held not as hypotheses with which to direct social experimentation but as final truths, dogmas. No wonder they call urgently for revision and displacement.

Nevertheless the current has set steadily in one direction: toward democratic forms. That government exists to serve its community, and that this purpose cannot be achieved unless the community itself shares in selecting its governors and determining their policies, are a deposit of fact left, as far as we can see, permanently in the wake of doctrines and forms, however transitory the latter. They are not the whole of the democratic idea, but they express it in its political phase. Belief in this political aspect is not a mystic faith as if in some overruling providence that cares for children, drunkards and others unable to help themselves. It marks a well-attested conclusion from historic facts. We have every reason to think that whatever changes may take place in existing democratic machinery, they will be of a sort to make the interest of the public a more supreme guide and criterion of governmental activity, and to enable the public to form and manifest its purposes still more authoritatively. In this sense the cure for the ailments of democracy is more democracy. The prime difficulty, as we have seen, is that of discovering the means by which a scattered, mobile and manifold public may so recognize itself as to define and express its interests. This discovery is necessarily precedent to any fundamental change in the machinery. We are not concerned therefore to set forth counsels as to advisable improvements in the political forms of democracy. Many have been suggested. It is no derogation of their relative worth to say that consideration of these changes is not at present an affair of primary importance. The problem lies deeper; it is in the first instance an intellectual problem: the search for conditions under which the Great Society may become the Great

Community. When these conditions are brought into being they will make their own forms. Until they have come about, it is somewhat futile to consider what political machinery will suit them.

In a search for the conditions under which the inchoate public now extant may function democratically, we may proceed from a statement of the nature of the democratic idea in its generic social sense*. From the standpoint of the individual, it consists in having a responsible share according to capacity in forming and directing the activities of the groups to which one belongs and in participating according to need in the values which the groups sustain. From the standpoint of the groups, it demands liberation of the potentialities of members of a group in harmony with the interests and goods which are common. Since every individual is a member of many groups, this specification cannot be fulfilled except when different groups interact flexibly and fully in connection with other groups. A member of a robber band may express his powers in a way consonant with belonging to that group and be directed by the interest common to its members. But he does so only at the cost of repression of those of his potentialities which can be realized only through membership in other groups. The robber band cannot interact flexibly with other groups; it can act only through isolating itself. It must prevent the operation of all interests save those which circumscribe it in its separateness. But a good citizen finds his conduct as a member of a political group enriching and enriched by his participation in family life, industry, scientific and artistic associations. There is a free give-and-take: fullness of integrated personality is therefore possible of achievement, since the pulls and responses of different groups re-ënforce one another and their values accord.

Regarded as an idea, democracy is not an alternative to other principles of associated life. It is the idea of community life itself. It is an ideal in the only intelligible sense of an ideal: namely, the tendency and movement of some thing which exists carried to its final limit, viewed as completed, perfected. Since things do not attain such fulfillment but are in actuality distracted and interfered with, democracy in this sense is not a fact and never will be. But neither in this sense is there or has there ever been anything which is a community in its full measure, a community unalloyed by alien elements. The idea or ideal of a community presents, however, actual phases of associated life as they are freed from restrictive and disturbing elements, and are contemplated as having attained their limit of development. Wherever there is conjoint activity whose consequences are appreciated as good by all singular persons who take part in it, and where the realization of the good is such as to effect an energetic desire and effort to sustain it in being just because it is a good shared by all, there is in so far a community. The clear consciousness of a communal life, in all its implications, constitutes the idea of democracy.

Only when we start from a community as a fact, grasp the fact in thought so as to clarify and enhance its constituent elements, can we reach an idea of democracy which is not utopian. The conceptions and shibboleths which are traditionally associated with the idea of democracy take on a veridical and directive meaning only when they are construed as marks and traits of an association which realizes the defining characteristics of a community. Fraternity, liberty and equality isolated from communal life are hopeless abstractions. Their separate assertion leads to mushy sentimentalism or else to extravagant and fanatical violence which

---

* The most adequate discussion of this ideal with which I am acquainted is T.V. Smith's "The Democratic Way of life."

in the end defeats its own aims. Equality then becomes a creed of mechanical identity which is false to facts and impossible of realization. Effort to attain it is divisive of the vital bonds which hold men together; as far as it puts forth issue, the outcome is a mediocrity in which good is common only in the sense of being average and vulgar. Liberty is then thought of as independence of social ties, and ends in dissolution and anarchy. It is more difficult to sever the idea of brotherhood from that of a community, and hence it is either practically ignored in the movements which identify democracy with Individualism, or else it is a sentimentally appended tag. In its just connection with communal experience, fraternity is another name for the consciously appreciated goods which accrue from an association in which all share, and which give direction to the conduct of each. Liberty is that secure release and fulfillment of personal potentialities which take place only in rich and manifold association with others: the power to be an individualized self making a distinctive contribution and enjoying in its own way the fruits of association. Equality denotes the unhampered share which each individual member of the community has in the consequences of associated action. It is equitable because it is measured only by need and capacity to utilize, not by extraneous factors which deprive one in order that another may take and have. A baby in the family is equal with others, not because of some antecedent and structural quality which is the same as that of others, but in so far as his needs for care and development are attended to without being sacrificed to the superior strength, possessions and matured abilities of others. Equality does not signify that kind of mathematical or physical equivalence in virtue of which any one element may be substituted for another. It denotes effective regard for whatever is distinctive and unique in each, irrespective of physical and psychological inequalities. It is not a natural possession but is a fruit of the community when its action is directed by its character as a community.

Associated or joint activity is a condition of the creation of a community. But association itself is physical and organic, while communal life is moral, that is emotionally, intellectually, consciously sustained. Human beings combine in behavior as directly and unconsciously as do atoms, stellar masses and cells; as directly and unknowingly as they divide and repel. They do so in virtue of their own structure, as man and woman unite, as the baby seeks the breast and the breast is there to supply its need. They do so from external circumstances, pressure from without, as atoms combine or separate in presence of an electric charge, or as sheep huddle together from the cold. Associated activity needs no explanation; things are made that way. But no amount of aggregated collective action of itself constitutes a community. For beings who observe and think, and whose ideas are absorbed by impulses and become sentiments and interests, "we" is as inevitable as "I." But "we" and "our" exist only when the consequences of combined action are perceived and become an object of desire and effort, just as "I" and "mine" appear on the scene only when a distinctive share in mutual action is consciously asserted or claimed. Human associations may be ever so organic in origin and firm in operation, but they develop into societies in a human sense only as their consequences, being known, are esteemed and sought for. Even if "society" were as much an organism as some writers have held, it would not on that account be society. Interactions, transactions, occur *de facto* and the results of interdependence follow. But participation in activities and sharing in results are additive concerns. They demand *communication* as a prerequisite.

Combined activity happens among human beings; but when nothing else happens it passes as inevitably into some other mode of interconnected activity as does the interplay of iron and the oxygen of water. What takes place is wholly describable in terms of energy, or, as we say in the case of human interactions, of force. Only when there exist *signs* or *symbols* of activities and of their outcome can the flux be viewed as from without, be arrested for consideration and esteem, and be regulated. Lightning strikes and rives a tree or rock, and the resulting fragments take up and continue the process of interaction, and so on and on. But when phases of the process are represented by signs, a new medium is interposed. As symbols are related to one another, the important relations of a course of events are recorded and are preserved as meanings. Recollection and foresight are possible; the new medium facilitates calculation, planning, and a new kind of action which intervenes in what happens to direct its course in the interest of what is foreseen and desired.

Symbols in turn depend upon and promote communication. The results of conjoint experience are considered and transmitted. Events cannot be passed from one to another, but meanings may be shared by means of signs. Wants and impulses are then attached to common meanings. They are thereby transformed into desires and purposes, which, since they implicate a common or mutually understood meaning, present new ties, converting a conjoint activity into a community of interest and endeavor. Thus there is generated what, metaphorically, may be termed a general will and social consciousness: desire and choice on the part of individuals in behalf of activities that, by means of symbols, are communicable and shared by all concerned. A community thus presents an order of energies transmuted into one of meanings which are appreciated and mutually referred by each to every other on the part of those engaged in combined action. "Force" is not eliminated but is transformed in use and direction by ideas and sentiments made possible by means of symbols.

The work of conversion of the physical and organic phase of associated behavior into a community of action saturated and regulated by mutual interest in shared meanings, consequences which are translated into ideas and desired objects by means of symbols, does not occur all at once nor completely. At any given time, it sets a problem rather than marks settled achievement. We are born organic beings associated with others, but we are not born members of a community. The young have to be brought within the traditions, outlook and interests which characterize a community by means of education: by unremitting instruction and by learning in connection with the phenomena of overt association. Everything which is distinctively human is learned, not native, even though it could not be learned without native structures which mark man off from other animals. To learn in a human way and to human effect is not just to acquire added skill through refinement of original capacities.

To learn to be human is to develop through the give-and-take of communication an effective sense of being an individual distinctive member of a community; one who understands and appreciates its beliefs, desires and methods, and who contributes to a further conversion of organic powers into human resources and values. But this translation is never finished. The old Adam, the unregenerate element in human nature, persists. It shows itself wherever the method obtains of attaining results by use of force instead of by the method of communication and enlightenment.

John Locke

Second Treatise of Government

The English philosopher John Locke (1632-1704) was one of the driving influences behind the European Enlightenment and political liberalism. Locke grew up in a Puritan household, and his childhood was marked by the English Civil War and the ultimate victory of fellow Puritan Oliver Cromwell's forces. Locke attended Oxford University, where he received degrees in philosophy and medicine. Locke's close relationship with Anthony Ashley Cooper, the first Earl of Shaftesbury, brought him front and center into the emerging Whig movement, which became victorious in the Glorious Revolution of 1688.

While Locke's greatest influence may come from the epistemological empiricism found in *An Essay Concerning Human Understanding*, it is his *Two Treatises of Government*, published in 1689 to justify the Glorious Revolution, that has influenced democratic theorists for the past three centuries. In the following excerpt from the *Second Treatise of Government*, Locke examines the origins of government, and claims that all governments receive their legitimacy from the consent of the governed. In a passage that reads almost word for word like the American Declaration of Independence (contained later in this section), Locke proclaims the right of citizens to revolt against their government when "a long train of abuses, prevarications, and artifices" show to the people that the government is no longer acting in their interest.

An Essay Concerning the True Original, Extent and End of Civil Government

John Locke

❖

Of Political or Civil Society

od, having made man such a creature that, in His own judgment, it was not good for him to be alone, put him under strong obligations of necessity, convenience, and inclination, to drive him into society, as well as fitted him with understanding and language to continue and enjoy it....

Man being born, as has been proved, with a title to perfect freedom and an uncontrolled enjoyment of all the rights and privileges of the law of Nature, equally with any other man, or number of men in the world, hath by nature a power not only to preserve his property – that is, his life, liberty, and estate, against the injuries and attempts of other men, but to judge of and punish the breaches of that law in others, as he is persuaded the offence deserves, even with death itself, in crimes where the heinousness of the fact, in his opinion, requires it. But because no political society can be, nor subsist, without having in itself the power to preserve the property, and in order thereunto punish the offences of all those of that society, there, and there only, is political society where everyone of the members hath quitted this natural power, resigned it up into the hands of the community in all cases that exclude him not from appealing for protection to the law established by it. And thus all private judgment of every particular member being excluded, the community comes to be umpire, and by understanding indifferent rules and men authorised by the community for their execution, decides all the differences that may happen between any members of that society concerning any matter of right, and punishes those offences which any member hath committed against the society with such penalties as the law has established; whereby it is easy to discern who are, and are not, in political society together. Those who are united into one body, and have a common established law and judicature to appeal to, with authority to decide controversies between them and punish offenders, are in civil society one with another;

but those who have no such common appeal, I mean on earth, are still in the state of Nature, each being where there is no other, judge for himself and executioner; which is, as I have before showed it, the perfect state of Nature...

And hence it is evident that absolute monarchy, which by some men is counted for the only government in the world, is indeed inconsistent with civil society, and so can be no form of civil government at all. For the end of civil society being to avoid and remedy those inconveniences of the state of Nature which necessarily follow from every man's being judge in his own case, by setting up a known authority to which every one of that society may appeal upon any injury received, or controversy that may arise, and which every one of the society ought to obey. Wherever any persons are who have not such an authority to appeal to, and decide any difference between them there, those persons are still in the state of Nature. And so is every absolute prince in respect of those who are under his dominion....

In absolute monarchies, indeed, as well as other governments of the world, the subjects have an appeal to the law, and judges to decide any controversies, and restrain any violence that may happen betwixt the subjects themselves, one amongst another...Betwixt subject and subject, they will grant, there must be measures, laws, and judges for their mutual peace and security. But as for the ruler, he ought to be absolute, and is above all such circumstances; because he has a power to do more hurt and wrong, it is right when he does it. To ask how you may be guarded from or injury on that side, where the strongest hand is to do it, is presently the voice of faction and rebellion. As if when men, quitting the state of Nature, entered into society, they agreed that all of them but one should be under the restraint of laws; but that he should still retain all the liberty of the state of Nature, increased with power, and made licentious by impunity. This is to think that men are so foolish that they take care to avoid what mischiefs may be done them by polecats or foxes, but are content, nay, think it safety, to be devoured by lions.

Of the Beginning of Political Societies

Men being, as has been said, by nature all free, equal, and independent, no one can be put out of this estate and subjected to the political power of another without his own consent, which is done by agreeing with other men, to join and unite into a community for their comfortable, safe, and peaceable living, one amongst another, in a secure enjoyment of their properties, and a greater security against any that are not of it. This any number of men may do, because it injures not the freedom of the rest; they are left, as they were, in the liberty of the state of Nature. When any number of men have so consented to make one community or government, they are thereby presently incorporated, and make one body politic, wherein the majority have a right to act and conclude the rest.

For, when any number of men have, by the consent of every individual, made a community, they have thereby made that community one body, with a power to act as one body, which is only by the will and determination of the majority. For that which acts any community, being only the consent of the individuals of it, and it being one body, must move one way, it is necessary the body should move that way whither the greater force carries it, which is the consent of the majority, or else it is impossible it should act or continue one body, one community, which the consent of every individual that united into it agreed that it should; and so every one is bound by that consent to be concluded by the majority. And therefore we see that in assemblies empowered to act by positive laws where no number is set by that positive law which empowers them, the act of the majority passes for the act of the whole, and of course determines as having, by the law of Nature and reason, the power of the whole.

And thus every man, by consenting with others to make one body politic under one government, puts himself under an obligation to every one of that society to submit to the determination of the majority, and to be concluded by it; or else this original compact, whereby he with others incorporates into one society, would signify nothing, and be no compact if he be left free and under no other ties than he was in before in the state of Nature. For what appearance would there be of any compact? What new engagement if he were no farther tied by any decrees of the society than he himself thought fit and did actually consent to? This would be still as great a liberty as he himself had before his compact, or any one else in the state of Nature, who may submit himself and consent to any acts of it if he thinks fit.

For if the consent of the majority shall not in reason be received as the act of the whole, and conclude every individual, nothing but the consent of every individual can make anything to be the act of the whole, which, considering the infirmities of health and avocations of business, which in a number though much less than that of a commonwealth, will necessarily keep many away from the public assembly; and the variety of opinions and contrariety of interests which unavoidably happen in all collections of men, it is next impossible ever to be had. Such a constitution as this would make the mighty leviathan of a shorter duration than the feeblest creatures, and not let it outlast the day it was born in, which cannot be supposed till we can think that rational creatures should desire and constitute societies only to be dissolved. For where the majority cannot conclude the rest, there they cannot act as one body, and consequently will be immediately dissolved again.

Whosoever, therefore, out of a state of Nature unite into a community, must be understood to give up all the power necessary to the ends for which they unite into society to the majority of the community, unless they expressly agreed in any number greater than the majority. And this is done by barely agreeing to unite into one political society, which is all the compact that is, or needs be, between the individuals that enter into or make up a commonwealth. And thus, that which begins and actually constitutes any political society is nothing but the consent of any number of freemen capable of majority, to unite and incorporate into such a society. And this is that, and that only, which did or could give beginning to any lawful government in the world....

And this has generally given the occasion to the mistake in this matter; because commonwealths not permitting any part of their dominions to be dismembered, nor to be enjoyed by any but those of their community, the son cannot ordinarily enjoy the possessions of his father but under the same terms his father did, by becoming a member of the society, whereby he puts himself presently under the government he finds there established, as much as any other subject of that commonweal. And thus the consent of free men, born under government, which only makes them members of it, being given separately in their turns, as each comes to be of age, and not in a multitude together, people take no notice of it, and thinking it not done at all, or not necessary, conclude they are naturally subjects as they are men.

But it is plain governments themselves understand it otherwise; they claim no power over the son because of that they had over the father; nor look on children as being their subjects, by their fathers being so. If a subject of England have a child by an Englishwoman in France, whose subject is he? Not the King of England's; for he must have leave to be admitted to the privileges of it. Nor the King of France's, for how then has his father a liberty to bring him away, and breed him as he pleases; and whoever was judged as a traitor or deserter, if he left, or warred against a country, for being barely born in it of parents that were aliens there? It is plain, then, by the practice of governments themselves, as well as by the law of right reason, that a child is born a subject of no country nor government. He is under his father's tuition and authority till he come to age of discretion, and then he is a free man, at liberty what government he will put himself under, what body politic he will unite himself to. For if an Englishman's son born in France be at liberty, and may do so, it is evident there is no tie upon him by his father being a subject of that kingdom, nor is he bound up by any compact of his ancestors; and why then hath not his son, by the same reason, the same liberty, though he be born anywhere else? Since the power that a father hath naturally over his children is the same wherever they be born, and the ties of natural obligations are not bounded by the positive limits of kingdoms and commonwealths.

Every man being, as has been showed, naturally free, and nothing being able to put him into subjection to any earthly power, but only his own consent, it is to be considered what shall be understood to be a sufficient declaration of a man's consent to make him subject to the laws of any government. There is a common distinction of an express and a tacit consent, which will concern our present case. Nobody doubts but an express consent of any man, entering into any society, makes him a perfect member of that society, a subject of that government. The difficulty is, what ought to be looked upon as a tacit consent, and how far it binds – i.e., how far any one shall be looked on to have consented, and thereby submitted to any government, where he has made no expressions of it at all. And to this I say, that every man that hath any possession or enjoyment of any part of the dominions of any government doth hereby give his tacit consent, and is as far forth obliged to obedience to the laws of that government, during such enjoyment, as any one under it, whether this his possession be of land to him and his heirs for ever, or a lodging only for a week; or whether it be barely traveling freely on the highway; and, in effect, it reaches as far as the very being of any one within the territories of that government....

Of the Ends of Political Society and Government

If man in the state of Nature be so free as has been said, if he be absolute lord of his own person and possessions, equal to the greatest and subject to nobody, why will he part with his freedom, this empire, and subject himself to the dominion and control of any other power? To which it is obvious to answer, that though in the state of Nature he hath such a right, yet the enjoyment of it is very uncertain and constantly exposed to the invasion of others; for all being kings as much as he, every man his equal, and the greater part no strict observers of equity and justice, the enjoyment of the property he has in this state is very unsafe, very insecure. This makes him willing to quit this condition which, however free, is full of fears and continual dangers; and it is not without reason that he seeks out and is willing to join in society with others who are already united, or have a mind to unite for the mutual preservation of their lives, liberties and estates, which I call by the general name – property.

The great and chief end, therefore, of men uniting into commonwealths, and putting themselves under government, is the preservation of their property; to which in the state of Nature there are many things wanting.

Firstly, there wants an established, settled, known law, received and allowed by common consent to be the standard of right and wrong, and the common measure to decide all controversies between them. For though the law of Nature be plain and intelligible to all rational creatures, yet men, being biased by their interest, as well as ignorant for want of study of it, are not apt to allow of it as a law binding to them in the application of it to their particular cases.

Secondly, in the state of Nature there wants a known and indifferent judge, with authority to determine all differences according to the established law. For every one in that state being both judge and executioner of the law of Nature, men being partial to themselves, passion and revenge is very apt to carry them too far, and with too much heat in their own cases, as well as negligence and unconcernedness, make them too remiss in other men's.

Thirdly, in the state of Nature there often wants power to back and support the sentence when right, and to give it due execution. They who by any injustice offended will seldom fail where they are able by force to make good their injustice. Such resistance many times makes the punishment dangerous, and frequently destructive to those who attempt it.

127. Thus mankind, notwithstanding all the privileges of the state of Nature, being but in an ill condition while they remain in it are quickly driven into society. Hence it comes to pass, that we seldom find any number of men live any time together in this state. The inconveniencies that they are therein exposed to by the irregular and uncertain exercise of the power every man has of punishing the transgressions of others, make them take sanctuary under the established laws of government, and therein seek the preservation of their property. It is this that makes them so willingly give up every one his single power of punishing to be exercised by such alone as shall be appointed to it amongst them, and by such rules as the community, or those authorised by them to that purpose, shall agree on. And in this we have the original right and rise of both the legislative and executive power as well as of the governments and societies themselves....

But though men when they enter into society give up the equality, liberty, and executive power they had in the state of Nature into the hands of the society, to be so far disposed of by the legislative as the good of the society shall require, yet it being only with an intention in every one the better to preserve himself, his liberty and property (for no rational creature can be supposed to change his condition with an intention to be worse), the power of the society or legislative constituted by them can never be supposed to extend farther than the common good, but is obliged to secure every one's property by providing against those three defects above mentioned that made the state of Nature so unsafe and uneasy. And so, whoever has the legislative or supreme power of any commonwealth, is bound to govern by established standing laws, promulgated and known to the people, and not by extemporary decrees, by indifferent and upright judges, who are to decide controversies by those laws; and to employ the force of the community at home only in the execution of such laws, or abroad to prevent or redress foreign injuries and secure the community from inroads and invasion. And all this to be directed to no other end but the peace, safety, and public good of the people....

The reason why men enter into society is the preservation of their property; and the end while they choose and authorise a legislative is that there may be laws made, and rules set, as guards and fences to the properties of all the society, to limit the power and moderate the dominion of every part and member of the society. For since it can never be supposed to be the will of the society that the legislative should have a power to destroy that which every one designs to secure by entering into society, and for which the people submitted themselves to legislators of their own making: whenever the legislators endeavour to take away and destroy the property of the people, or to reduce them to slavery under arbitrary power, they put themselves into a state of war with the people, who are thereupon absolved from any farther obedience, and are left to the common refuge which God hath provided for all men against force and violence. Whensoever, therefore, the legislative shall transgress this fundamental rule of society, and either by ambition, fear, folly, or corruption, endeavour to grasp themselves, or put into the hands of any other, an absolute power over the lives, liberties, and estates of the people, by this breach of trust they forfeit the power the people had put into their hands for quite contrary ends, and it devolves to the people, who have a right to resume their original liberty, and by the establishment of a new legislative (such as they shall think fit), provide for their own safety and security, which is the end for which they are in society...

To this, perhaps, it will be said that the people being ignorant and always discontented, to lay the foundation of government in the unsteady opinion and uncertain humour of the people, is to expose it to certain ruin; and no government will be able long to subsist if the people may set up a new legislative whenever they take offence at the old one. To this I answer, quite the contrary. People are not so easily got out of their old forms as some are apt to suggest. They are hardly to be prevailed with to amend the acknowledged faults in the frame they have been accustomed to. And if there be any original defects, or adventitious ones introduced by time or corruption, it is not an easy thing to get them changed, even when all the world sees there is an opportunity for it. This slowness and aversion in the people to quit their old constitutions has in the many revolutions [that] have been seen in this kingdom, in this and former ages, still kept us to, or after some interval of fruitless attempts, still brought us back again to, our old legislative of king, lords and commons; and whatever provocations have made the crown be taken from some of our princes' heads, they never carried the people so far as to place it in another line.

Secondly: I answer, such revolutions happen not upon every little mismanagement in public affairs. Great mistakes in the ruling part, many wrong and inconvenient laws, and all the slips of human frailty will be borne by the people without mutiny or murmur. But if a long train of abuses, prevarications, and artifices, all tend-

ing the same way, make the design visible to the people, and they cannot but feel what they lie under, and see whither they are going, it is not to be wondered that they should then rouse themselves, and endeavour to put the rule into such hands which may secure to them the ends for which government was at first erected, and without which, ancient names and specious forms are so far from being better, that they are much worse than the state of Nature or pure anarchy; the inconveniencies being all as great and as near, but the remedy farther off and more difficult.

Thirdly: I answer, that this power in the people of providing for their safety anew by a new legislative when their legislators have acted contrary to their trust by invading their property, is the best fence against rebellion, and the probable means to hinder it. For rebellion being an opposition, not to persons, but authority, which is founded only in the constitutions and laws of the government: those, whoever they be, who, by force, break through, and, by force, justify their violation of them, are truly and properly rebels. For when men, by entering into society and civil government, have excluded force, and introduced laws for the preservation of property, peace, and unity amongst themselves, those who set up force again in opposition to the laws, do rebellare – that is, bring back again the state of war, and are properly rebels, which they who are in power, by the pretence they have to authority, the temptation of force they have in their hands, and the flattery of those about them being likeliest to do, the proper way to prevent the evil is to show them the danger and injustice of it who are under the greatest temptation to run into it....

To conclude. The power that every individual gave the society when he entered into it can never revert to the individuals again, as long as the society lasts, but will always remain in the community; because without this there can be no community – no commonwealth, which is contrary to the original agreement; so also when the society hath placed the legislative in any assembly of men, to continue in them and their successors, with direction and authority for providing such successors, the legislative can never revert to the people whilst that government lasts: because, having provided a legislative with power to continue for ever, they have given up their political power to the legislative, and cannot resume it. But if they have set limits to the duration of their legislative, and made this supreme power in any person or assembly only temporary; or else when, by the miscarriages of those in authority, it is forfeited; upon the forfeiture of their rulers, or at the determination of the time set, it reverts to the society, and the people have a right to act as supreme, and continue the legislative in themselves or place it in a new form, or new hands, as they think good.

Jean-Jacques Rousseau
The Social Contract, Selections

Jean-Jacques Rousseau (1712–1778), French moral and political philosopher, lived during the flowering of western individualism, science, and rational thought known as the Enlightenment. Like many Enlightenment thinkers, Rousseau attempted to find a basis for political authority in the consent of citizens—a "social contract"—rather than in the natural or divine authority of a ruler. Rousseau earned the disdain of many of his contemporaries, however, with his belief that human reason had done more to fuel greed and corruption than intellectual progress. Many misunderstood Rousseau as claiming that people should return to a "state of nature," abandoning reason and civilization. In fact, Rousseau thought human reason could be used to devise a political system which would take account of individual self-interest, but channel it into the development of virtuous citizens—a project which was taken up by the French revolutionaries a decade after Rousseau's death.

In *The Social Contract*, Rousseau attempts to develop a political theory which unites people for their common benefit, yet allows them to remain as free as when living alone. If each person surrenders his individual rights completely to everyone else, Rousseau argues, then everyone comes out with the same amount of freedom as before. They make a trade in which everyone comes out ahead: natural freedom based on instinct and physical force is exchanged for moral freedom based on reason. In a democratic society—governed by the "General Will"—we obey laws we prescribe to ourselves, thereby reconciling political authority and freedom. But for this to work there must be genuine and persistent political participation by all citizens in the law-making process. Representative government cannot achieve this.

The Social Contract
Jean-Jacques Rousseau

❖

Man is born free; and everywhere he is in chains. One thinks himself the master of others, and still remains a greater slave than they. How did this change come about? I do not know. What can make it legitimate? That question I think I can answer.

If I took into account only force, and the effects derived from it, I should say: "As long as a people is compelled to obey, and obeys, it does well; as soon as it can shake off the yoke, and shakes it off, it does still better; for, regaining its liberty by the same right as took it away, either it is justified in resuming it, or there was no justification for those who took it away." But the social order is a sacred right which is the basis of all rights. Nevertheless, this right does not come from nature, and must therefore be founded on conventions. Before coming to that, I have to prove what I have just asserted.

The Social Compact

I suppose men to have reached the point at which the obstacles in the way of their preservation in the state of nature show their power of resistance to be greater than the resources at the disposal of each individual for his maintenance in that state. That primitive condition can then subsist no longer; and the human race would perish unless it changed its manner of existence.

But, as men cannot engender new forces, but only unite and direct existing ones, they have no other means of preserving themselves than the formation, by aggregation, of a sum of forces great enough to overcome the resistance. These they have to bring into play by means of a single motive power, and cause to act in concert.

This sum of forces can arise only where several persons come together: but, as the force and liberty of each man are the chief instruments of his self-preservation, how can he pledge them without harming his own interests, and neglecting the, care he owes to himself? This difficulty, in its bearing on my present subject, may be stated in the following terms:

"The problem is to find a form of association which will defend and protect with the whole common force the person and goods of each associate, and in which each, while uniting himself with all, may still obey himself alone, and remain as free as before." This is the fundamental problem of which the *Social Contract* provides the solution.

The clauses of this contract are so determined by the nature of the act that the slightest modification would make them vain and ineffective; so that, although they have perhaps never been formally set forth, they are everywhere the same and everywhere tacitly admitted and recognized, until, on the violation of the social compact, each regains his original rights and resumes his natural liberty, while losing the conventional liberty in favour of which he renounced it.

These clauses, properly understood, may be reduced to one—the total alienation of each associate, together with all his rights, to the whole community; for, in the first place, as each gives himself absolutely, the conditions are the same for all; and, this being so, no one has any interest in making them burdensome to others.

Moreover, the alienation being without reserve, the union is as perfect as it can be, and no associate has anything more to demand: for, if the individuals retained certain rights, as there would be no common superior to decide between them and the public, each, being on one point his own judge, would ask to be so on all; the state of nature would thus continue, and the association would necessarily become inoperative or tyrannical.

Finally, each man, in giving himself to all, gives himself to nobody; and as there is no associate over which he does not acquire the same right as he yields others over himself, he gains an equivalent for everything he loses, and an increase of force for the preservation of what he has.

If then we discard from the social compact what is not of its essence, we shall find that it reduces itself to the following terms:

> *"Each of us puts his person and all his power in common under the supreme direction of the general will, and, in our corporate capacity, we receive each member as an in divisible part of the whole."*

At once, in place of the individual personality of each contracting party, this act of association creates a moral and collective body, composed of as many members as the assembly contains voters, and receiving from this act its unity, its common identity, its life, and its will. This public person, so formed by the union of all other persons, formerly took the name of *city**, and now takes that of Republic or body politic; it is called by its members *State* when passive, *Sovereign* when active, and *Power* when compared with others like itself. Those who are associated

---

* The real meaning of this word has been almost wholly lost in modern times; most people mistake a town for a city, and a townsman for a citizen. They do not know that houses make a town, but citizens a city. The same mistake long ago cost the Carthaginians dear. I have never read of the title of citizens being given to the subjects of any prince, not even the ancient Macedonians or the English of to-day, though they are nearer liberty than any one else. The French alone everywhere familiarly adopt the name of citizens, because, as can be seen from their dictionaries, they have no idea of its meaning; otherwise they would be guilty in usurping it, of the crime of *lèse-majesté*: among them, the name expresses a virtue, and not a right. When Bodin spoken of our citizens and townsmen, he fell into a bad blunder in taking the one class for the other. M. d'Alembert has avoided the error, and, in his article on Geneva, has clearly distinguished the four orders of men (or even five, counting mere foreigners) who dwell in our town, of which two only compose the Republic. No other French writer, to may knowledge, has clearly distinguised the four orders of men (or even five, counting mere foreigners) who dwell in our town, of which two only compose the Republic. No other French writer, to my knowledge, has understood the real meaning of the word citizen.

in it take collectively the name of *people*, and severally are called *citizens*, as sharing in the sovereign power, and *subjects*, as being under the laws of the State. But these terms are often confused and taken one for another: it is enough to know how to distinguish them when they are being used with precision.

The Sovereign

This formula shows us that the act of association comprises a mutual undertaking between the public and the individuals, and that each individual, in making a contract, as we may say, with himself, is bound in a double capacity; as a member of the Sovereign he is bound to the individuals, and as a member of the State to the Sovereign. But the maxim of civil right, that no one is bound by undertakings made to himself, does not apply in this case; for there is a great difference between incurring an obligation to yourself and incurring one to a whole of which you form a part.

Attention must further be called to the fact that public deliberation, while competent to bind all the subjects to the Sovereign, because of the two different capacities in which each of them may be regarded, cannot, for the opposite reason, bind the Sovereign to itself; and that it is consequently against the nature of the body politic for the Sovereign to impose on itself a law which it cannot infringe. Being able to regard itself in only one capacity, it is in the position of an individual who makes a contract with himself; and this makes it clear that there neither is nor can be any kind of fundamental law binding on the body of the people — not even the social contract itself. This does not mean that the body politic cannot enter into undertakings with others, provided the contract is not infringed by them; for in relation to what is external to it, it becomes a simple being, an individual.

But the body politic or the Sovereign, drawing its being wholly from the sanctity of the contract, can never bind itself, even to an outsider, to do anything derogatory to the original act, for instance, to alienate any part of itself, or to submit to another Sovereign. Violation of the act by which it exists would be self-annihilation; and that which is itself nothing can create nothing.

As soon as this multitude is so united in one body, it is impossible to offend against one of the members without attacking the body, and still more to offend against the body without the members resenting it. Duty and interest therefore equally oblige the two contracting parties to give each other help; and the same men should seek to combine, in their double capacity, all the advantages dependent upon that capacity.

Again, the Sovereign, being formed wholly of the individuals who compose it, neither has nor can have any interest contrary to theirs; and consequently the sovereign power need give no guarantee to its subjects, because it is impossible for the body to wish to hurt all its members. We shall also see later on that it cannot hurt any in particular. The Sovereign, merely by virtue of what it is, is always what it should be.

This, however, is not the case with the relation of the subjects to the Sovereign, which, despite the common interest, would have no security that they would fulfil their undertakings, unless it found means to assure itself of their fidelity.

In fact, each individual, as a man, may have a particular will contrary or dissimilar to the general will which he has as a citizen. His particular interest may speak to him quite differently from the common interest: his absolute and naturally independent existence may make him look upon what he owes to the common cause as a gratuitous contribution, the loss of which will do less harm to others than the payment of it is burdensome to himself; and, regarding the moral person which constitutes the State as a *persona ficta,* because not a man, he may wish to enjoy the rights of citizenship without being ready to fulfil the duties of a subject. The continuance of such an injustice could not but prove the undoing of the body politic.

In order then that the social compact may not be an empty formula, it tacitly includes the undertaking, which alone can give force to the rest, that whoever refuses to obey the general will shall be compelled to do so by the whole body. This means nothing less than that he will be forced to be free; for this is the condition which, by giving each citizen to his country, secures him against all personal dependence. In this lies the key to the working of the political machine; this alone legitimizes civil undertakings, which, without it, would be absurd, tyrannical, and liable to the most frightful abuses.

The Civil State

The passage from the state of nature to the civil state produces a very remarkable change in man, by substituting justice for instinct in his conduct, and giving his actions the morality they had formerly lacked. Then only, when the voice of duty takes the place of physical impulses and right of appetite, does man, who so far had considered only himself, find that he is forced to act on different principles, and to consult his reason before listening to his inclinations. Although, in this state, he deprives himself of some advantages which he got from nature, he gains in return others so great, his faculties are so stimulated and developed, his ideas so extended, his feelings so ennobled, and his whole soul so uplifted, that, did not the abuses of this new condition often degrade him below that which he left, he would be bound to bless continually the happy moment which took him from it for ever, and, instead of a stupid and unimaginative animal, made him an intelligent being and a man.

Let us draw up the whole account in terms easily commensurable. What man loses by the social contract is his natural liberty and an unlimited right to everything he tries to get and succeeds in getting; what he gains is civil liberty and the proprietorship of all he possesses. If we are to avoid mistake in weighing one against the other, we must clearly distinguish natural liberty, which is bounded only by the strength of the individual, from civil liberty, which is limited by the general will; and possession, which is merely the effect of force or the might of the first occupier, from property, which can be founded only on a positive title.

We might, over and above all this, add, to what man acquires in the civil state, moral liberty, which alone makes him truly master of himself; for the mere impulse of appetite is slavery, while obedience to a law which we prescribe to ourselves is liberty. But I have already said too much on this head, and the philosophical meaning of the word liberty does not now concern us.

That Sovereignty Is Inalienable

The first and most important deduction from the principles we have so far laid down is that the general will alone can direct the State according to the object for which it was instituted, i.e. the common good: for if the clashing of particular interests made the establishment of societies necessary, the agreement of these very interests made it possible. The common element in these different interests is what forms the social tie; and, were there no point of agreement between them all, no society could exist. It is solely on the basis of this common interest that every society should be governed.

I hold then that Sovereignty, being nothing less than the exercise of the general will, can never be alienated, and that the Sovereign, who is no less than a collective being, cannot be represented except by himself: the power indeed may be transmitted, but not the will.

In reality, if it is not impossible for a particular will to agree on some point with the general will, it is at least impossible for the agreement to be lasting and constant; for the particular will tends, by its very nature, to partiality, while the general will tends to equality. It is even more impossible to have any guarantee of this agreement; for even if it should always exist, it would be the effect not of art, but of chance. The Sovereign may indeed say: "I now will actually what this man wills, or at least what he says he wills"; but it cannot say: "What he wills to-morrow, I too shall will" because it is absurd for the will to bind itself for the future, nor is it incumbent on any will to consent to anything that is not for the good of the being who wills. If then the people promises simply to obey, by that very act it dissolves itself and loses what makes it a people; the moment a master exists, there is no longer a Sovereign, and from that moment the body politic has ceased to exist.

This does not mean that the commands of the rulers cannot pass for general wills, so long as the Sovereign, being free to oppose them, offers no opposition. In such a case, universal silence is taken to imply the consent of the people. This will be explained later on.

The Limits of the Sovereign Power

If the State is a moral person whose life is in the union of its members, and if the most important of its cares is the care for its own preservation, it must have a universal and compelling force, in order to move and dispose each part as may be most advantageous to the whole. As nature gives each man absolute power over all his members, the social compact gives the body politic absolute power over all its members also; and it is this power which, under the direction of the general will, bears, as I have said, the name of Sovereignty.

But, besides the public person, we have to consider the private persons composing it, whose life and liberty are naturally independent of it. We are bound then to distinguish clearly between the respective rights of the citizens and the Sovereign*, and between the duties the former have to fulfil as subjects, and the natural rights they should enjoy as men.

Each man alienates, I admit, by the social compact, only such part of his powers, goods, and liberty as it is important for the community to control; but it must also be granted that the Sovereign is sole judge of what is important.

Every service a citizen can render the State he ought to render as soon as the Sovereign demands it; but the Sovereign, for its part, cannot impose upon its subject, any fetters that are useless to the community, nor can it even wish to do so; for no more by the law of reason than by the law of nature can anything occur without a cause.

The undertakings which bind us to the social body are obligatory only because they are mutual; and their nature is such that in fulfilling them we cannot work for others without working for ourselves. Why is it that the general will is always in the right, and that all continually will the happiness of each one, unless it is because there is not a man who does not think of "each" as meaning him, and consider himself in voting for all? This proves that equality of rights and the idea of justice which such equality creates originate in the preference each man gives to himself, and accordingly in the very nature of man. It proves that the general will, to be really such, must be general in its object as well as its essence; that it must both come from all and apply to all; and that it loses its natural rectitude when it is directed to some particular and determinate object, because in such a case we are judging of something foreign to us, and have no true principle of equity to guide us...

It should be seen from the foregoing that what makes the will general is less the number of voters than the common interest uniting

---

* Attentive readers, do not, I pray, be in a hurry to charge me with contradicting myself. The terminology made it unavoidable, considering the poverty of the language; but wait and see.

them; for, under this system, each necessarily submits to the conditions he imposes on others: and this admirable agreement between interest and justice gives to the common deliberations an equitable character which at once vanishes when any particular question is discussed, in the absence of a common interest to unite and identify the ruling of the judge with that of the party.

From whatever side we approach our principle, we reach the same conclusion, that the social compact sets up among the citizens an equality of such a kind, that they all bind themselves to observe the same conditions and should therefore all enjoy the same rights. Thus, from the very nature of the compact, every act of Sovereignty, i.e. every authentic act of the general will, binds or favours all the citizens equally; so that the Sovereign recognizes only the body of the nation, and draws no distinctions between those of whom it is made up. What, then, strictly speaking, is an act of Sovereignty? It is not a convention between a superior and an inferior, but a convention between the body and each of its members. It is legitimate, because based on the social contract, and equitable, because common to all; useful, because it can have no other object than the general good, and stable, because guaranteed by the public force and the supreme power. So long as the subjects have to submit only to conventions of this sort, they obey no one but their own will; and to ask how far the respective rights of the Sovereign and the citizens extend, is to ask up to what point the latter can enter into undertakings with themselves, each with all, and all with each.

We can see from this that the sovereign power, absolute, sacred, and inviolable as it is, does not and cannot exceed the limits of general conventions, and that every man may dispose at will of such goods and liberty as these conventions leave him; so that the Sovereign never has a right to lay more charges on one subject than on another, because, in that case, the question becomes particular, and ceases to be within its competency.

When these distinctions have once been admitted, it is seen to be so untrue that there is, in the social contract, any real renunciation on the part of the individuals, that the position in which they find themselves as a result of the contract is really preferable to that in which they were before. Instead of a renunciation, they have made an advantageous exchange: instead of an uncertain and precarious way of living they have got one that is better and more secure; instead of natural independence they have got liberty, instead of the power to harm others security for themselves, and instead of their strength, which others might overcome, a right which social union makes invincible. Their very life, which they have devoted to the State, is by it constantly protected; and when they risk it in the State's defence, what more are they doing than giving back what they have received from it? What are they doing that they would not do more often and with greater danger in the state of nature, in which they would inevitably have to fight battles at the peril of their lives in defence of that which is the means of their preservation? All have indeed to fight when their country needs them; but then no one has ever to fight for himself. Do we not gain something by running, on behalf of what gives us our security, only some of the risks we should have to run for ourselves, as soon as we lost it?

Thomas Jefferson

Thomas Jefferson (1743–1826), author of the Declaration of Independence and the Virginia Bill for Establishing Religious Freedom, founder of the University of Virginia, Vice President and then two-term President of the United States (following Washington and Adams), is perhaps the leading voice for liberty, citizenship, and civic education among the founders. The son of prominent landowners in Virginia, Jefferson's ideas about democracy burst onto the scene, first in his draft of a Continental Congress petition to the British monarchy, and, at the age of 26, in his authorship of the Declaration of Independence. His bold statement "that all men are created equal…endowed by their creator with certain unalienable rights" set a standard by which all subsequent governments, both within and outside the United States, could be judged. Of course, Jefferson excluded many individuals from his vision of universal equality: he did not believe that women could be the bearers of equal civil rights, and he equivocated on questions of ultimate equality when it came to those of African ancestry, criticizing slavery but maintaining his own slaves. Still, the principles of equality and equal rights that Jefferson continuously espoused would become the quintessential feature of modern democracy. And his commitment to universal citizen education and active citizen participation caused him to oppose many less-than-democratic constitutions after 1776, and to argue that citizenship, education, and participation went hand in hand. Following his efforts in drafting and passing through the Virginia legislature the Bill for Establishing Religious Freedom, he pressed hard for the inclusion of a Bill of Rights in the U.S. Constitution.

Jefferson's commitment to democratic equality and citizen participation did not dissipate in his later years, even after as president he had pursued an aggressive politics of expansionism. In his 1813 letter to John Adams, excerpted below, he argued against any notion of aristocratic birthright, instead wishing to vest the power in the people to determine which representatives belonged to the "natural aristocracy" of talent and virtue. In his 1816 letter to Samuel Kerchival, he outlined a radically democratic proposal for decentralized "ward government," and contended that each generation had the right to choose for itself how it wished to be governed, in effect a call to re-ratify the constitution every 19 or 20 years. Shortly before his death, on the eve of the fiftieth anniversary of the signing of the Declaration, Jefferson urged people all over the world "to burst the chains under which monkish ignorance and superstition had persuaded them to bind themselves, and to assume the blessings and security of self-government." Although neither he nor any of his revolutionary colleagues were willing to extend citizenship to all, Jefferson's vision of equality and democratic citizenship still shines as a beacon to democrats everywhere.

The Declaration of Independence

July 4, 1776

When in the course of human events it becomes necessary for one people to dissolve the political bands which have connected them with another, and to assume among the powers of the earth, the separate and equal station to which the Laws of Nature and of Nature's God entitle them, a decent respect to the opinions of mankind requires that they should declare the causes which impel them to the separation.

We hold these truths to be self-evident, that all men are created equal, that they are endowed by their Creator with certain unalienable Rights, that among these are Life, Liberty and the pursuit of Happiness.—That to secure these rights, Governments are instituted among Men, deriving their just powers from the consent of the governed.—That whenever any Form of Government becomes destructive of these ends, it is the Right of the People to alter or to abolish it, and to institute new Government, laying its foundation on such principles, and organizing its powers in such form, as to them shall seem most likely to effect their Safety and Happiness. Prudence, indeed, will dictate that Govern-ments long established should not be changed for light and transient causes; and accordingly all experience hath shewn, that mankind are more disposed to suffer, while evils are sufferable, than to right themselves by abolishing the forms to which they are accustomed. But when a long train of abuses and usurpations, pursuing invariably the same Object, evinces a design to reduce them under absolute Despotism, it is their right, it is their duty to throw off such Government, and to provide new Guards for their future security.—Such has been the patient sufferance of these Colonies, and such is now the necessity which constrains them to alter their former Systems of Government. The history of the present King of Great Britain is a history of repeated injuries and usurpations, all having in direct object the establishment of an absolute Tyranny over these States. To prove this, let Facts be submitted to a candid world.

He has refused his Assent to Laws, the most wholesome and necessary for the public good.

He has forbidden his Governors to pass Laws of immediate and pressing importance, unless suspended in their operation till his Assent should be obtained; and when so suspended, he has utterly neglected to attend to them.

He has refused to pass other Laws for the accommodation of large districts of people, unless those people would relinquish the right of Representation in the Legislature, a right inestimable to them and formidable to tyrants only.

He has called together legislative bodies at places unusual, uncomfortable, and distant from the depository of their public Records, for the sole purpose of fatiguing them into compliance with his measures.

He has dissolved Representative Houses repeatedly, for opposing with manly firmness his invasions on the rights of the people.

He has refused for a long time, after such dissolutions, to cause others to be elected; whereby the Legislative powers, incapable of Annihilation, have returned to the People at large for their exercise; the State remaining in the mean time exposed to all the dangers of invasion from without, and convulsions within.

He has endeavored to prevent the population of these States; for that purpose obstructing the Laws for Naturalization of Foreigners; refusing to pass others to encourage their migrations hither, and raising the conditions of new Appropriations of Lands.

He has obstructed the Administration of Justice, by refusing his Assent to Laws for establishing Judiciary powers.

He has made Judges dependent on his Will alone, for the tenure of their offices, and the amount of payment of their salaries.

He has erected a multitude of New Offices, and sent hither swarms of Officers to harrass our people, and eat out their substance.

He has kept among us, in times of peace, Standing Armies without the Consent of our legislatures.

He has affected to render the Military independent of and superior to the Civil power.

He has combined with others to subject us to a jurisdiction foreign to our constitution, and unacknowledged by our laws; giving his Assent to their Acts of pretended Legislation:

For quartering large bodies of armed troops among us:

For protecting them, by a mock Trial, from punishment for any Murders which they should commit on the Inhabitants of these States:

For cutting off our Trade with all parts of the world:

For imposing Taxes on us without our Consent:

For depriving us in many cases, of the benefits of Trial by Jury:

For transporting us beyond Seas to be tried for pretended offences:

For abolishing the free System of English Laws in a neighbouring Province, establishing therein an Arbitrary government, and enlarging its Boundaries so as to render it at once an example and fit instrument for introducing the same absolute rule into these Colonies:

For taking away our Charters, abolishing our most valuable Laws, and altering fundamentally the Forms of our Governments:

For suspending our own Legislatures, and declaring themselves invested with power to legislate for us in all cases whatsoever.

He has abdicated Government here, by declaring us out of his Protection and waging War against us.

He has plundered our seas, ravaged our Coasts, burnt our towns, and destroyed the lives of our people.

He is at this time transporting large Armies of foreign Mercenaries to compleat the works of death, desolation and tyranny, already begun with circumstances of Cruelty & perfidy scarcely paralleled in the most barbarous ages, and totally unworthy the Head of a civilized nation.

He has constrained our fellow Citizens taken Captive on the high Seas to bear Arms against their Country, to become the executioners of their friends and Brethren, or to fall themselves by their Hands.

He has excited domestic insurrections amongst us, and has endeavored to bring on the inhabitants of our frontiers; the merciless

Indian Savages, whose known rule of warfare, is an undistinguished destruction of all ages, sexes and conditions.

In every stage of these Oppressions We have Petitioned for Redress in the most humble terms: Our repeated Petitions have been answered only by repeated injury. A Prince, whose character is thus marked by every act which may define a Tyrant, is unfit to be the ruler of a free people.

Nor have We been wanting in attentions to our British brethren. We have warned them from time to time of attempts by their legislature to extend an unwarrantable jurisdiction over us. We have reminded them of the circumstances of our emigration and settlement here. We have appealed to their native justice and magnanimity, and we have conjured them by the ties of our common kindred to disavow these usurpations, which would inevitably interrupt our connections and correspondence. They too have been deaf to the voice of justice and of consanguinity. We must, therefore, acquiesce in the necessity, which denounces our Separation, and hold them, as we hold the rest of mankind, Enemies in War, in Peace Friends.

We, therefore, the Representatives of the united States of America, in General Congress, Assembled, appealing to the Supreme Judge of the world for the rectitude of our intentions, do, in the Name, and by Authority of the good People of these Colonies solemnly publish and declare, That these United Colonies are, and of Right ought to be Free and Independent States; that they are Absolved from all Allegiance to the British Crown, and that all political connection between them and the State of Great Britain, is and ought to be totally dissolved; and that as Free and Independent States, they have full Power to levy War, conclude Peace, contract Alliances, establish Commerce, and to do all other Acts and Things which Independent States may of right do.

And for the support of this Declaration, with a firm reliance on protection of divine Providence, we mutually pledge to each other our Lives, our Fortunes and our sacred Honor.

An Act for Establishing Religious Freedom

Well aware that Almighty God hath created the mind free; that all attempts to influence it by temporal punishments or burdens, or by civil incapacitations, tend only to beget habits of hypocrisy and meanness, and are a departure from the plan of the Holy Author of our religion, who being Lord both of body and mind, yet chose not to propagate it by coercions on either, as was in his Almighty power to do; that the impious presumption of legislators and rulers, civil as well as ecclesiastical, who, being themselves but fallible and uninspired men have assumed dominion over the faith of others, setting up their own opinions and modes of thinking as the only true and infallible, and as such endeavoring to impose them on others, hath established and maintained false religions over the greatest part of the world, and through all time; that to compel a man to furnish contributions of money for the propagation of opinions which he disbelieves, is sinful and tyrannical; that even the forcing him to support this or that teacher of his own religious persuasion, is depriving him of the comfortable liberty of giving his contributions to the particular pastor whose morals he would make his pattern, and whose powers he feels most persuasive to righteousness, and is withdrawing from the ministry those temporal rewards, which proceeding from an approbation of their personal conduct, are an additional incitement to earnest and unremitting labors for the instruction of mankind; that our civil rights have no dependence on our religious opinions, more than our opinions in physics or geometry; that, therefore, the proscribing any citizen as unworthy the public confidence by laying upon him an incapacity of being called to the offices of trust and emolument, unless he profess or renounce this or that religious opinion, is depriving him injuriously of those privileges and advantages to which in common with his fellow citizens he has a natural right; that it tends also to corrupt the principles of that very religion it is meant to encourage, by bribing, with a monopoly of wordly honors and emoluments, those who will externally profess and conform to it; that though indeed these are criminal who do not withstand such temptation, yet neither are those innocent who lay the bait in their way; that to suffer the civil magistrate to intrude his powers into the field of opinion and to restrain the profession or propagation of principles on the supposition of their ill tendency, is a dangerous fallacy, which at once destroys all religious liberty, because he being of course judge of that tendency, will make his opinions the rule of judgment, and approve or condemn the sentiments of others only as they shall square with or differ from his own; that it is time enough for the rightful purposes of civil government, for its offices to interfere when principles break out into overt acts against peace and good order; and finally, that truth is great and will prevail if left to herself, that she is the proper and sufficient antagonist to error, and has nothing to fear from the conflict, unless by human interposition disarmed of her natural weapons, free argument and debate, errors ceasing to be dangerous when it is permitted freely to contradict them.

Be it therefore enacted by the General Assembly, That no man shall be compelled to frequent or support any religious worship, place or ministry whatsoever, nor shall be enforced, restrained, molested, or burthened in his body or goods, nor shall otherwise suffer on account of his religious opinions of belief; but that all men shall be free to profess, and by argument to maintain, their opinions in matters of religion, and that the same shall in nowise diminish, enlarge, or affect their civil capacities.

And though we well know this Assembly, elected by the people for the ordinary purposes of legislation only, have no power to restrain the acts of succeeding assemblies, constituted

with the powers equal to our own, and that therefore to declare this act irrevocable, would be of no effect in law, yet we are free to declare, and do declare, that the rights hereby asserted are of the natural rights of mankind, and that if any act shall be hereafter passed to repeal the present or to narrow its operation, such act will be an infringement of natural right.

To James Madison

December 20, 1787

I like much the general idea of framing a government, which should go on of itself, peaceably, without needing continual recurrence to the State legislatures. I like the organization of the government into legislative, judiciary and executive. I like the power given the legislature to levy taxes, and for that reason solely, I approve of the greater House being chosen by the people directly. For though I think a House so chosen, will be very far inferior to the present Congress, will be very illy qualified to legislate for the Union, for foreign nations, &c., yet this evil does not weigh against the good, of preserving inviolate the fundamental principle, that the people are not to be taxed but by representatives chosen immediately by themselves. I am captivated by the compromise of the opposite claims of the great and little States, of the latter to equal, and the former to proportional influence. I am much pleased too, with the substitution of the method of voting by person, instead of that of voting by States; and I like the negative given to the Executive, conjointly with a third of either House; though I should have liked it better, had the judiciary been associated for that purpose, or invested separately with a similar power. There are other good things of less moment. I will now tell you what I do not like. First, the omission of a bill of rights, providing clearly, and without the aid of sophism, for freedom of religion, freedom of the press, protection against standing armies, restriction of monopolies, the eternal and unremitting force of the habeas corpus laws, and trials by jury in all matters of fact triable by the laws of the land, and not by the laws of nations. To say, as Mr. Wilson does, that a bill of rights was not necessary, because all is reserved in the case of the general government which is not given, while in the particular ones, all is given which is not reserved, might do for the audience to which it was addressed; but it is surely a *gratis dictum*, the reverse of which might just as well be said; and it is opposed by strong inferences from the body of the instrument, as well as from the omission of the cause of our present Confederation, which had made the reservation in express terms. It was hard to conclude, because there has been a want of uniformity among the States as to the cases triable by jury, because some have been so incautious as to dispense with this mode of trial in certain cases, therefore, the more prudent States shall be reduced to the same level of calamity. It would have been much more just and wise to have concluded the other way, that as most of the States had preserved with jealousy this sacred palladium of liberty, those who had wandered, should be brought back to it; and to have established general right rather than general wrong. For I consider all the ill as established, which may be established. I have a right to nothing, which another has a right to take away; and Congress will have a right to take away trials by jury in all civil cases. Let me add, that a bill of rights is what the people are entitled to against every government on earth, general or particular; and what no just government should refuse, or rest on inference.

The second feature I dislike, and strongly dislike, is the abandonment, in every instance, of the principle of rotation in office, and most particularly in the case of the President. Reason and experience tell us, that the first magistrate will always be re-elected if he may be re-elected. He is then an officer for life. This once observed, it becomes of so much consequence to certain nations, to have a friend or a foe at the head of our affairs, that they will interfere with money and with arms. A Galloman, or an Angloman, will be supported by the nation he befriends. If once elected, and at a second or third election outvoted by one or two votes, he will pretend false votes, foul play, hold possession of the reins of government, be supported by the States voting for him, especially if they be the central ones, lying in a compact body themselves, and separating their opponents; and they will be aided by one nation in Europe, while the majority are aided by another. The election of a President of America, some years hence, will be much more interesting to certain nations of Europe, than ever the election of a King of Poland was. Reflect on all the instances in history, ancient and modern, of elective monarchies, and say if they do not give foundation for my fears; the Roman Emperors, the Popes while they were of any importance, the German Emperors till they became hereditary in practice, the Kings of Poland, the Deys of the Ottoman dependencies. It may be said, that if elections are to be attended with these disorders, the less frequently they are repeated the better. But experience says, that to free them from disorder, they must be rendered less interesting by a necessity of change. No foreign power, nor domestic party, will waste their blood and money to elect a person, who must go out at the end of a short period. The power of removing every fourth year by the vote of the people, is a power which they will not exercise, and if they were disposed to exercise it, they would not be permitted. The King of Poland is removable every day by the diet. But they never remove him. Nor would Russia, the Emperor, &c., permit them to do it. Smaller objections are, the appeals on matters of fact as well as laws; and the binding all persons, legislative, executive and judiciary by oath, to maintain that constitution. I do not pretend to decide, what would be the best method of procuring the establishment of the manifold good things in this constitution, and of getting rid of the bad. Whether by adopting it, in hopes of future amendment; or after it shall have been duly weighed and canvassed by the people, after seeing the parts they generally dislike, and those they generally approve, to say to them, "We see now what you wish. You are willing to give to your federal government such and such powers; but you wish, at the same time, to have such and such fundamental rights secured to you, and certain sources of convulsion taken away. Be it so. Send together deputies again. Let them establish your fundamental rights by a sacrosanct declaration, and let them pass the parts of the constitution you have approved. These will give powers to your federal government sufficient for your happiness."

This is what might be said, and would probably produce a speedy, more perfect and more permanent form of government. At all events, I hope you will not be discouraged from making other trials, if the present one should fail. We are never permitted to despair of the commonwealth. I have thus told you freely what I like, and what I dislike, merely as a matter of curiosity; for I know it is not in my power to offer matter of information to your judgment, which has been formed after hearing and weighing everything which the wisdom of man could offer on these subjects. I own, I am not a friend to a very energetic government. It is always oppressive. It places the governors indeed more at their ease, at the expense of the people. The late rebellion in Massachusetts has given more alarm, than I think it should have done. Calculate that one rebellion in thirteen States in the course of eleven years, is but one for each State in a century and a half. No country should be so long without one. Nor will any degree of power in the hands of government, prevent insurrections.... And say, finally, whether peace is best preserved by giving energy to the government, or information to the people. This last is the most certain, and the most legitimate engine of government. Educate and inform the whole mass of the people. Enable them to see that it is their interest to preserve peace and order, and they will preserve them. And it requires no very high degree of education to convince them

of this. They are the only sure reliance for the preservation of our liberty. After all, it is my principle that the will of the majority should prevail. If they approve the proposed constitution in all its parts, I shall concur in it cheerfully, in hopes they will amend it, whenever they shall find it works wrong. This reliance cannot deceive us, as long as we remain virtuous; and I think we shall be so, as long as agriculture is our principal object, which will be the case, while there remains vacant lands in any part of America. When we get piled upon one another in large cities, as in Europe, we shall become corrupt as in Europe, and go to eating one another as they do there...

To James Madison

Paris, January 30, 1787

A consciousness of those in power that their administration of the public affairs has been honest, may, perhaps, produce too great a degree of indignation; and those characters, wherein fear predominates over hope, may apprehend too much from these instances of irregularity. They may conclude too hastily, that nature has formed man insusceptible of any other government than that of force, a conclusion not founded in truth nor experience. Societies exist under three forms, sufficiently distinguishable. 1. Without government, as among our Indians. 2. Under governments, wherein the will of every one has a just influence; as is the case in England, in a slight degree, and in our States, in a great one. 3. Under governments of force; as is the case in all other monarchies, and in most of the other republics. To have an idea of the curse of existence under these last, they must be seen. It is a government of wolves over sheep. It is a problem, not clear in my mind, that the first condition is not the best. But I believe it to be inconsistent with any great degree of population. The second state has a great deal of good in it. The mass of mankind under that, enjoys a precious degree of liberty and happiness. It has its evils, too; the principal of which is the turbulence to which it is subject. But weigh this against the oppressions of monarchy, and it becomes nothing. *Malo periculosam libertatem quam quietam servitutem.* Even this evil is productive of good. It prevents the degeneracy of government, and nourishes a general attention to the public affairs. I hold it, that a little rebellion, now and then, is a good thing, and as necessary in the political world as storms in the physical. Unsuccessful rebellions, indeed, generally establish the encroachments on the rights of the people, which have produced them. An observation of this truth should render honest republican governors so mild in their punishment of rebellions, as not to discourage them too much. It is a medicine necessary for the sound health of government...

To John Adams

Monticello, October 28, 1813

I agree with you that there is a natural aristocracy among men. The grounds of this are virtue and talents. Formerly, bodily powers gave place among the aristoi. But since the invention of gunpowder has armed the weak as well as the strong with missile death, bodily strength, like beauty, good humor, politeness and other accomplishments, has become but an auxiliary ground of distinction. There is also an artificial aristocracy, founded on wealth and birth, without either virtue or talents; for with these it would belong to the first class. The natural aristocracy I consider as the most precious gift of nature, for the instruction, the trusts, and government of society. And indeed, it would have been inconsistent in creation to have formed man for the social state, and not to have provided virtue and wisdom enough to manage the concerns of the society. May we not even say, that form of government is the best, which provides the most effectually for a pure

selection of these natural aristoi into the offices of government? The artificial aristocracy is a mischievous ingredient in government, and provision should be made to prevent its ascendency. On the question, what is the best provision, you and I differ; but we differ as rational friends, using the free exercise of our own reason, and mutually indulging its errors. You think it best to put the pseudo-aristoi into a separate chamber of legislation, where they may be hindered from doing mischief by their co-ordinate branches, and where, also, they may be a protection to wealth against the agrarian and plundering enterprises of the majority of the people. I think that to give them power in order to prevent them from doing mischief, is arming them for it, and increasing instead of remedying the evil. For if the co-ordinate branches can arrest their action, so may they that of the co-ordinates. Mischief may be done negatively as well as positively. Of this, a cabal in the Senate of the United States has furnished many proofs. Nor do I believe them necessary to protect the wealthy; because enough of these will find their way into every branch of the legislation, to protect themselves. From fifteen to twenty legislatures of our own, in action for thirty years past, have proved that no fears of an equalization of property are to be apprehended from them. I think the best remedy is exactly that provided by all our constitutions, to leave to the citizens the free election and separation of the aristoi from the pseudo-aristoi, of the wheat from the chaff. In general they will elect the really good and wise. In some instances, wealth may corrupt, and birth blind them; but not in sufficient degree to endanger the society...

At the first session of our legislature after the Declaration of Independence, we passed a law abolishing entails. And this was followed by one abolishing the privilege of primogeniture, and dividing the lands of intestates equally among all their children, or other representatives. These laws, drawn by myself, laid the axe to the foot of pseudo-aristocracy. And had another which I prepared been adopted by the legislature, our work would have been complete. It was a bill for the more general diffusion of learning. This proposed to divide every county into wards of five or six miles square, like your townships; to establish in each ward a free school for reading, writing and common arithmetic; to provide for the annual selection of the best subjects from these schools, who might receive, at the public expense, a higher degree of education at a district school; and from these district schools to select a certain number of the most promising subjects, to be completed at an university, where all the useful sciences should be taught. Worth and genius would thus have been sought out from every condition of life, and completely prepared by education for defeating the competition of wealth and birth for public trusts. My proposition had, for a further object, to impart to these wards those portions of self-government for which they are best qualified, by confiding to them the care of their poor, their roads, police, elections, the nomination of jurors, administration of justice in small cases, elementary exercises of militia; in short, to have made them little republics, with a warden at the head of each, for all those concerns which, being under their eye, they would better manage than the larger republics of the county or State. A general call of ward meetings by their wardens on the same day through the State, would at any time produce the genuine sense of the people on any required point, and would enable the State to act in mass, as your people have so often done, and with so much effect by their town meetings. The law for religious freedom, which made a part of this system, having put down the aristocracy of the clergy, and restored to the citizen the freedom of the mind, and those of entails and descents nurturing an equality of condition among them, this on education would have raised the mass of the people to the high ground of moral respectability necessary to their own safety, and to orderly government; and would have completed the great object of qualifying them to select the

veritable aristoi, for the trusts of government, to the exclusion of the pseudalists....

With respect to the aristocracy, we should further consider, that before the establishment of the American States, nothing was known to history but the man of the old world, crowded within limits either small or overcharged, and steeped in the vices which that situation generates. A government adapted to such men would be one thing; but a very different one, that for the man of these States. Here every one may have land to labor for himself, if he chooses; or, preferring the exercise of any other industry, may exact for it such compensation as not only to afford a comfortable subsistence, but wherewith to provide for a cessation from labor in old age. Every one, by his property, or by his satisfactory situation, is interested in the support of law and order. And such men may safely and advantageously reserve to themselves a wholesome control over their public affairs, and a degree of freedom, which, in the hands of the *canaille* of the cities of Europe, would be instantly perverted to the demolition and destruction of everything public and private. The history of the last twenty-five years of France, and of the last forty years in America, nay of its last two hundred years, proves the truth of both parts of this observation.

But even in Europe a change has sensibly taken place in the mind of man. Science had liberated the ideas of those who read and reflect, and the American example had kindled feelings of right in the people. And insurrection has consequently begun, of science, talents, and courage, against rank and birth, which have fallen into contempt. It has failed in its first effort, because the mobs of the cities, the instrument used for its accomplishment, debased by ignorance, poverty, and vice, could not be restrained to rational action. But the world will recover from the panic of this first catastrophe. Science is progressive, and talents and enterprise on the alert. Resort may be had to the people of the country, a more governable power from their principles and subordination; and rank, and birth, and tinsel-aristocracy will finally shrink into insignificance, even there. This, however, we have no right to meddle with. It suffices for us, if the moral and physical condition of our own citizens qualifies them to select the able and good for the direction of their government, with a recurrence of elections at such short periods as will enable them to displace an unfaithful servant, before the mischief he meditates may be irremediable.

To Samuel Kercheval

Monticello, July 12, 1816

The true foundation of republican government is the equal right of every citizen, in his person and property, and in their management. Try this, as a tally, every provision of our Constitution, and see if it hangs directly on the will of the people. Reduce your legislature to a convenient number for full, but orderly discussion. Let every man who fights or pays, exercise his just and equal right in their election. Submit them to approbation or rejection at short intervals. Let the executive be chosen in the same way, and for the same term, by those whose agent he is to be; and leave no screen of a council behind which to skulk from responsibility. It has been thought that the people are not competent electors of judges *learned in the law*. But I do not know that this is true, and, if doubtful, we should follow principle. In this, as in many other elections, they would be guided by reputation, which would not err oftener, perhaps, than the present mode of appointment...

The organization of our county administrations may be thought more difficult. But follow principle, and the knot unties itself. Divide the counties into wards of such size as that every citizen can attend, when called on, and act in person. Ascribe to them the government of their wards in all things relating to themselves, exclusively. A justice, chosen by themselves, in each, a constable, a military company, a patrol, a school, the care of their own poor, their own portion of the public roads, the choice of one or more jurors to serve in some court, and the delivery, within their own wards, of their own votes for all elective officers of higher sphere, will relieve the county administration of nearly all its business, will have it better done, and by making every citizen an acting member of the government, and in the offices nearest and most interesting to him, will attach him by his strongest feelings to the independence of his country, and its republican Constitution. The justices thus chosen by every ward, would constitute the county court, would do its judiciary business, direct roads and bridges, levy county and poor rates, and administer all the matters of common interest to the whole country. These wards, called townships in New England, are the vital principle of their governments, and have proved themselves the wisest invention ever devised by the wit of man for the perfect exercise of self-government, and for its preservation. We should thus marshal our government into, 1, the general federal republic, for all concerns foreign and federal; 2, that of the State, for what relates to our own citizens exclusively; 3, the county republics, for the duties and concerns of the county; and 4, the ward republics, for the small, and yet numerous and interesting concerns of the neighborhood; and in government, as well as in every other business of life, it is by division and subdivision of duties alone, that all matters, great and small, can be managed to perfection. And the whole is cemented by giving to every citizen, personally, a part in the administration of the public affairs.

The sum of these amendments is, 1. General suffrage. 2. Equal representation in the legislature. 3. An executive chosen by the people. 4. Judges elective or amovable. 5. Justices, jurors, and sheriffs elective. 6. Ward divisions. And 7. Periodical amendments of the Constitution.

I have thrown out these as loose heads of amendment, for consideration and correction; and their object is to secure self-government by the republicanism of our Constitution, as well as by the spirit of the people; and to nourish and perpetuate that spirit. I am not among those who fear the people. They, and not the rich, are our dependence for continued freedom. And to preserve their independence, we must not let our rulers load us with perpetual debt. We must make our election between *economy and liberty, or profusion and servitude*. If we run into such debts, as that we must be taxed in our meat and in our drink, in our necessaries and our comforts, in our labors and our amusements, for our callings and our creeds, as the people of England are, our people, like them, must come to labor sixteen hours in the twenty-four, give the earnings of fifteen of these to the government for their debts and daily expenses; and the sixteenth being insufficient to afford us bread, we must live, as they now do, on oatmeal and potatoes; have no time to think, no means of calling the mismanagers to account; but be glad to obtain subsistence by hiring ourselves to rivet their chains on the necks of our fellow sufferers. Our land-holders, too, like theirs, retaining indeed the title and stewardship of estates called theirs, but held really in trust for the treasury, must wander, like theirs, in foreign countries, and be contented with penury, obscurity, exile, and the glory of the nation. This example reads to us the salutary lesson, that private fortunes are destroyed by public as well as by private extravagance. And this is the tendency of all human governments. A departure from principle in one instance becomes a precedent for a second; that second for a third; and so on, till the bulk of the society is reduced to be mere automatons of misery, to have no sensibilities left but for sinning and suffering. Then begins, indeed, the *bellum omnium in omnia*, which some philosophers observing to be so general in this world, have mistaken it for the natural, instead of the abusive state of man. And the fore horse of this frightful team is public debt. Taxation follows that, and in its train wretchedness and oppression.

Some men look at constitutions with sanctimonious reverence, and deem them like the ark of the covenant, too sacred to be touched. They ascribe to the men of the preceding age a wisdom more than human, and suppose what they did to be beyond amendment. I knew that age well; I belonged to it, and labored with it. It deserved well of its country. It was very like the present, but without the experience of the present; and forty years of experience in government is worth a century of book-reading; and this they would say themselves, were they to rise from the dead. I am certainly not an advocate for frequent and untried changes in laws and constitutions. I think moderate imperfections had better be borne with; because, when once known, we accommodate ourselves to them, and find practical means of correcting their ill effects. But I know also, that laws and institutions must go hand in hand with the progress of the human mind. As that becomes more developed, more enlightened, as new discoveries are made, new truths disclosed, and manners and opinions change with the change of circumstances, institutions must advance also, and keep pace with the times. We might as well require a man to wear still the coat which fitted him when a boy, as civilized society to remain ever under the regimen of their barbarous ancestors. It is this preposterous idea which has lately deluged Europe in blood. Their monarchs, instead of wisely yielding to the gradual change of circumstances, of favoring progressive accommodation to progressive improvement, have clung to old abuses, entrenched themselves behind steady habits, and obliged their subjects to seek through blood and violence rash and ruinous innovations, which, had they been referred to the peaceful deliberations and collected wisdom of the nation, would have been put into acceptable and salutary forms. Let us follow no such examples, nor weakly believe that one generation is not as capable as another of taking care of itself, and of ordering its own affairs. Let us, as our sister States have done, avail ourselves of our reason and experience, to correct the crude essays of our first and unexperienced, although wise, virtuous, and well-meaning councils. And lastly, let us provide in our Constitution for its revision at stated periods. What these periods should be, nature herself indicates. By the European tables of mortality, of the adults living at any one moment of time, a majority will be dead in about nineteen years. At the end of that period then, a new majority is come into place; or, in other words, a new generation. Each generation is as independent of the one preceding, as that of all which had gone before. It has then, like them, a right to choose for itself the form of government it believes most promotive of its own happiness; consequently, to accommodate to the circumstances in which it finds itself, that received from its predecessors; and it is for the peace and good of mankind, that a solemn opportunity of doing this every nineteen or twenty years, should be provided by the Constitution; so that it may be handed on, with, periodical repairs, from generation to generation, to the end of time, if anything human can so long endure. It is now forty years since the constitution of Virginia was formed. The same tables inform us, that, within that period, two-thirds of the adults then living are now dead. Have then the remaining third, even if they had the wish, the right to hold in obedience to their will, and to laws heretofore made by them, the other two-thirds, who, with themselves, compose the present mass of adults? If they have not, who has? The dead? But the dead have no rights. They are nothing; and nothing cannot own something. Where there is no substance, there can be no accident. This corporeal globe, and everything upon it, belong to its present corporeal inhabitants, during their generation. They alone have a right to direct what is the concern of themselves alone, and to declare the law of that direction; and this declaration can only be made by their majority. That majority, then, has a right to depute representatives to a convention, and to make the Constitution what

they think will be the best for themselves. But how collect their voice? This is the real difficulty. If invited by private authority, or county or district meetings, these divisions are so large that few will attend; and their voice will be imperfectly, or falsely, pronounced. Here, then, would be one of the advantages of the ward divisions I have proposed. The mayor of every ward, on a question like the present, would call his ward together, take the simple yea or nay of its members, convey these to the county court, who would hand on those of all its wards to the proper general authority; and the voice of the whole people would be thus fairly, fully, and peaceably expressed, discussed, and decided by the common reason of the society. If this avenue be shut to the call of sufferance, it will make itself heard through that of force, and we shall go on, as other nations are doing, in the endless circle of oppression, rebellion, reformation; and oppression, rebellion, reformation, again; and so on forever.

Notes on the State of Virginia

Query XIV: Laws

...to emancipate all slaves born after passing the act. The bill reported by the revisors does not itself contain this proposition; but an amendment containing it was prepared, to be offered to the legislature whenever the bill should be taken up, and further directing, that they should continue with their parents to a certain age, then be brought up, at the public expense, to tillage, arts or sciences, according to their geniusses, till the females should be eighteen, and the males twenty-one years of age, when they should be colonized to such place as the circumstances of the time should render most proper, sending them out with arms, implements of houshold and of the handicraft arts, seeds, pairs of the useful domestic animals, &c. to declare them a free and independent people, and extend to them our alliance and protection, till they shall have acquired strength; and to send vessels at the same time to other parts of the world for an equal number of white inhabitants; to induce whom to migrate hither, proper encouragements were to be proposed. It will probably be asked, Why not retain and incorporate the blacks into the state, and thus save the expense of supplying, by importation of white settlers, the vacancies they will leave? Deep rooted prejudices entertained by the whites; ten thousand recollections, by the blacks, of the injuries they have sustained; new provocations; the real distinctions which nature has made; and many other circumstances, will divide us into parties, and produce convulsions which will probably never end but in the extermination of the one or the other race.—To these objections, which are political, may be added others, which are physical and moral. The first difference which strikes us is that of colour. Whether the black of the negro resides in the reticular membrane between the skin and scarf-skin, or in the scarf -skin itself; whether it proceeds from the colour of the blood, the colour of the bile, or from that of some other secretion, the difference is fixed in nature, and is as real as if its seat and cause were better known to us. And is this difference of no importance? Is it not the foundation of a greater or less share of beauty in the two races? Are not the fine mixtures of red and white, the expressions of every passion by greater or less suffusions of colour in the one, preferable to that eternal monotony, which reigns in the countenances, that immoveable veil of black which covers all the emotions of the other race? Add to these, flowing hair, a more elegant symmetry of form, their own judgment in favour of the whites, declared by their preference of them, as uniformly as is the preference of the Oran-ootan for the black women over those of his own species. The circumstance of superior beauty, is thought worthy attention in the propagation of our horses, dogs, and other domestic animals; why not in that of

man? Besides those of colour, figure, and hair, there are other physical distinctions proving a difference of race. They have less hair on the face and body. They secrete less by the kidneys, and more by the glands of the skin, which gives them a very strong and disagreeable odour. This greater degree of transpiration renders them more tolerant of heat, and less so of cold, than the whites. Perhaps too a difference of structure in the pulmonary apparatus, which a late ingenious experimentalist has discovered to be the principal regulator of animal heat, may have disabled them from extricating, in the act of inspiration, so much of that fluid from the outer air, or obliged them in expiration, to part with more of it. They seem to require less sleep. A black, after hard labour through the day, will be induced by the slightest amusements to sit up till midnight, or later, though knowing he must be out with the first dawn of the morning. They are at least as brave, and more adventuresome. But this may perhaps proceed from a want of forethought, which prevents their seeing a danger till it be present. When present, they do not go through it with more coolness or steadiness than the whites. They are more ardent after their female: but love seems with them to be more an eager desire, than a tender delicate mixture of sentiment and sensation. Their griefs are transient. Those numberless afflictions, which render it doubtful whether heaven has given life to us in mercy or in wrath, are less felt, and sooner forgotten with them. In general, their existence appears to participate more of sensation than reflection. To this must be ascribed their disposition to sleep when abstracted from their diversions, and unemployed in labour. An animal whose body is at rest, and who does not reflect, must be disposed to sleep of course. Comparing them by their faculties of memory, reason, and imagination, it appears to me, that in memory they are equal to the whites; in reason much inferior, as I think one could scarcely be found capable of tracing and comprehending the investigations of Euclid; and that in imagination they are dull, tasteless, and anomalous. It would be unfair to follow them to Africa for this investigation. We will consider them here, on the same stage with the whites, and where the facts are not apocryphal on which a judgment is to be formed. It will be right to make great allowances for the difference of condition, of education, of conversation, of the sphere in which they move. Many millions of them have been brought to, and born in America. Most of them indeed have been confined to tillage, to their own homes, and their own society: yet many have been so situated, that they might have availed themselves of the conversation of their masters; many have been brought up to the handicraft arts, and from that circumstance have always been associated with the whites. Some have been liberally educated, and all have lived in countries where the arts and sciences are cultivated to a considerable degree, and have had before their eyes samples of the best works from abroad. The Indians, with no advantages of this kind, will often carve figures on their pipes not destitute of design and merit. They will crayon out an animal, a plant, or a country, so as to prove the existence of a germ in their minds which only wants cultivation. They astonish you with strokes of the most sublime oratory; such as prove their reason and sentiment strong, their imagination glowing and elevated. But never yet could I find that a black had uttered a thought above the level of plain narration; never see even an elementary trait of painting or sculpture. In music they are more generally gifted than the whites with accurate ears for tune and time, and they have been found capable of imagining a small catch. Whether they will be equal to the composition of a more extensive run of melody, or of complicated harmony, is yet to be proved. Misery is often the parent of the most affecting touches in poetry.—Among the blacks is misery enough, God knows, but no poetry. Love is the peculiar oestrum of the poet. Their love is ardent, but it kindles the senses only, not the imagination.

Religion indeed has produced a Phyllis Whatley; but it could not produce a poet. The compositions published under her name are below the dignity of criticism...

That disposition to theft with which they have been branded, must be ascribed to their situation, and not to any depravity of the moral sense. The man, in whose favour no laws of property exist, probably feels himself less bound to respect those made in favour of others. When arguing for ourselves, we lay it down as a fundamental, that laws, to be just, must give a reciprocation of right: that, without this, they are mere arbitrary rules of conduct, founded in force, and not in conscience: and it is a problem which I give to the master to solve, whether the religious precepts against the violation of property were not framed for him as well as his slave? And whether the slave may not as justifiably take a little from one, who has taken all from him, as he may slay one who would slay him?...

I advance it therefore as a suspicion only, that the blacks, whether originally a distinct race, or made distinct by time and circumstances, are inferior to the whites in the endowments both of body and mind. It is not against experience to suppose, that different species of the same genus, or varieties of the same species, may possess different qualifications. Will not a lover of natural history then, one who views the gradations in all the races of animals with the eye of philosophy, excuse an effort to keep those in the department of man as distinct as nature has formed them? This unfortunate difference of colour, and perhaps of faculty, is a powerful obstacle to the emancipation of these people....

In every government on earth is some trace of human weakness, some germ of corruption and degeneracy, which cunning will discover, and wickedness insensibly open, cultivate, and improve. Every government degenerates when trusted to the rulers of the people alone. The people themselves therefore are its only safe depositories. And to render even them safe their minds must be improved to a certain degree. This indeed is not all that is necessary, though it be essentially necessary. An amendment of our constitution must here come in aid of the public education. The influence over government must be shared among all the people. If every individual which composes their mass participates of the ultimate authority, the government will be safe; because the corrupting the whole mass will exceed any private resources of wealth: and public ones cannot be provided but by levies on the people. In this case every man would have to pay his own price. The government of Great-Britain has been corrupted, because but one man in ten has a right to vote for members of parliament. The sellers of the government therefore get nine-tenths of their price clear. It has been thought that corruption is restrained by confining the right of suffrage to a few of the wealthier of the people: but it would be more effectually restrained by an extension of that right to such numbers as would bid defiance to the means of corruption....

Walt Whitman

Democratic Vistas Selections

Walt Whitman (1819–1892), American poet and prophet, spent the first half of his life in Brooklyn and New York, working as a schoolteacher and later as editor for two Brooklyn newspapers. Both papers eventually discharged him for his frank statements on sexuality and politics. During the Civil War his humanitarian sentiments led him to serve as a volunteer nurse in Army hospitals in Washington, DC. In 1873, a apoplectic stroke forced him to retire to Camden, New Jersey where he remained for the last 15 years of his life.

Whitman based his poetry on his own mystical revelations, and the following selection, while not poetic like "I Hear America Singing" (which opens Part I), is transcendental and impressionistic rather than analytical. Whitman alternates between praise and condemnation of America, but his reflections are infused with faith in the political and spiritual potentials of democracy. Whitman's immediate purpose is to assert the need for a national literature in the United States—a literature to support the development of a New World representing the culmination of centuries of theorizing about democracy and freedom. Whitman values America's material success as a necessary fundament for the moral development of the young nation, but he voices concern over the encroachment of greed, lust, and vulgarity on spiritual values. He directly connects this concern to his evaluation of American democracy. A true democracy—which lies in America's future, but not in its present—includes much more than universal suffrage and government accountability. Democracy, for Whitman, requires a continual moral and religious education of the citizenry.

Democratic Vistas
Walt Whitman

As the greatest lessons of Nature through the universe are perhaps the lessons of variety and freedom, the same present the greatest lessons also in New World politics and progress. If a man were ask'd, for instance, the distinctive points contrasting modern European and American political and other life with the old Asiatic cultus, as lingering-bequeath'd yet in China and Turkey, he might find the amount of them in John Stuart Mill's profound essay on Liberty in the future, where he demands two main constituents, or sub-strata, for a truly grand nationality—1st, a large variety of character—and 2d, full play for human nature to expand itself in numberless and even conflicting directions—With this thought—and not for itself alone, but all it necessitates, and draws after it—let me begin my speculations....

I will not gloss over the appalling dangers of universal suffrage in the United States. In fact, it is to admit and face these dangers I am writing. To him or her within whose thought rages the battle, advancing, retreating, between democracy's convictions, aspirations, and the people's crudeness, vice, caprices, I mainly write this essay. I shall use the words America and democracy as convertible terms. Not an ordinary one is the issue. The United States are destined either to surmount the gorgeous history of feudalism, or else prove the most tremendous failure of time. Not the least doubtful am I on any prospects of their material success. The triumphant future of their business, geographic and productive departments, on larger scales and in more varieties than ever, is certain. In those respects the republic must soon (if she does not already) outstrip all examples hitherto afforded, and dominate the world.

I promulge new races of Teachers, and of perfect Women, indispensable to endow the birth-stock of a New World. For feudalism, caste, the ecclesiastic traditions, though palpably retreating from political institutions, still hold essentially, by their spirit, even in this country, entire possession of the more important fields, indeed the very subsoil, of education, and of social standards and literature.

I say that democracy can never prove itself beyond cavil, until it founds and luxuriantly grows its own forms of art, poems, schools, theology, displacing all that exists, or that has been produced anywhere in the past, under opposite influences. It is curious to me that while so many voices, pens, minds, in the press, lecture-rooms, in our Congress, &c., are discussing intellectual topics, pecuniary dangers, legislative problems, the suffrage, tariff and labor questions, and the various business and benevolent needs of America, with propositions, remedies, often worth deep attention, there is one need, a hiatus the profoundest, that no eye seems to perceive, no voice to state. Our fundamental want to-day in the United States, with closest, amplest reference to present conditions, and to the future, is of a class, and the clear idea of a class, of native authors, literatuses, far different, far higher in grade than any yet known, sacerdotal, modern, fit to cope with our occasions, lands, permeating the whole mass of American mentality, taste, belief, breathing into it a new breath of life, giving it decision, affecting politics far more than the popular superficial suffrage, with results inside and underneath the elections of Presidents or Congresses—radiating, begetting appropriate teachers, schools, manners, and, as its grandest result, accomplishing, (what neither the schools nor the churches and their clergy have hitherto accomplish'd, and without which this nation will no more stand, permanently, soundly, than a house will stand without a substratum,) a religious and moral character beneath the political and productive and intellectual bases of the States. For know you not, dear, earnest reader, that the people of our land may all read and write, and may all possess the right to vote—and yet the main things may be entirely lacking?—(and this to suggest them.)

View'd, to-day, from a point of view sufficiently over-arching, the problem of humanity all over the civilized world is social and religious, and is to be finally met and treated by literature. The priest departs, the divine literatus comes. Never was anything more wanted than, to-day, and here in the States, the poet of the modern is wanted, or the great literatus of the modern. At all times, perhaps, the central

point in any nation, and that whence it is itself really sway'd the most, and whence it sways others, is its national literature, especially its archetypal poems. Above all previous lands, a great original literature is surely to become the justification and reliance, (in some respects the sole reliance,) of American democracy....

The purpose of democracy...is, through many transmigrations, and amid endless ridicules, arguments, and ostensible failures, to illustrate, at all hazards, this doctrine or theory that man, properly train'd in sanest, highest freedom, may and must become a law, and series of laws, unto himself, surrounding and providing for, not only his own personal control, but all his relations to other individuals, and to the State; and that, while other theories, as in the past histories of nations, have proved wise enough, and indispensable perhaps for their conditions, *this*, as matters now stand in our civilized world, is the only scheme worth working from, as warranting results like those of Nature's laws, reliable, when once establish'd, to carry on themselves....

There is, in later literature, a treatment of benevolence, a charity business, rife enough it is true; but I know nothing more rare, even in this country, than a fit scientific estimate and reverent appreciation of the People—of their measureless wealth of latent power and capacity, their vast, artistic contrasts of lights and shades—with, in America, their entire reliability in emergencies, and a certain breadth of historic grandeur, of peace or war, far surpassing all the vaunted samples of book-heroes, or any *haut ton* coteries, in all the records of the world....

We have seen the alacrity with which the American born populace, the peaceablest and most good-natured race in the world, and the most personally independent and intelligent, and the least fitted to submit to the irksomeness and exasperation of regimental discipline, sprang, at the first tap of the drum, to arms—not for gain, nor even glory, nor to repel invasion—but for an emblem, a mere abstraction—for the life, the *safety of the   ag*. We have seen the unequal'd docility and obedience of these soldiers. We have seen them tried long and long by hopelessness, mismanagement, and by defeat; have seen the incredible slaughter toward or through which the armies, (as at first Fredericksburg, and afterward at the Wilderness,) still unhesitatingly obey'd orders to advance. We have seen them in trench, or crouching behind breastwork, or tramping in deep mud, or amid pouring rain or thick-falling snow, or under forced marches in hottest summer (as on the road to get to Gettysburg)—vast suffocating swarms, divisions, corps, with every single man so grimed and black with sweat and dust, his own mother would not have known him—his clothes all dirty, stain'd and torn, with sour, accumulated sweat for perfume—many a comrade, perhaps a brother, sun-struck, staggering out, dying, by the roadside, of exhaustion—yet the great bulk bearing steadily on, cheery enough, hollow-bellied from hunger, but sinewy with unconquerable resolution.

What have we here, if not, towering above all talk and argument, the plentifully-supplied, last-needed proof of democracy, in its personalities? Curiously enough, too, the proof on this point comes, I should say, every bit as much from the south, as from the north. Although I have spoken only of the latter, yet I deliberately include all. Grand, common stock! to me the accomplish'd and convincing growth, prophetic of the future; proof undeniable to sharpest sense, of perfect beauty, tenderness and pluck, that never feudal lord, nor Greek, nor Roman breed, yet rival'd. Let no tongue ever speak in disparagement of the American races, north or south, to one who has been through the war in the great army hospitals.

Meantime, general humanity, (for to that we return, as, for our purposes, what it really is, to bear in mind,) has always, in every department, been full of perverse maleficence, and is so yet. In downcast hours the soul thinks it always will be—but soon recovers from such sickly moods. I myself see clearly enough the crude, defective streaks in all the strata of the common people; the specimens and vast collections of the ignorant, the credulous, the unfit and uncouth, the incapable, and the very low and poor. The eminent person just mention'd sneeringly asks whether we expect to elevate and improve a nation's politics by absorbing such morbid collections and qualities therein. The point is a formidable one, and there will doubtless always be numbers of solid and reflective citizens who will never get over it. Our answer is general, and is involved in the scope and letter of this essay. We believe the ulterior object of political and all other government, (having, of course, provided for the police, the safety of life, property, and for the basic statute and common law, and their administration, always first in order,) to be among the rest, not merely to rule, to repress disorder, &c., but to develop, to open up to cultivation, to encourage the possibilities of all beneficent and manly outcroppage, and of that aspiration for independence, and the pride and self-respect latent in all characters. (Or, if there be exceptions, we cannot, fixing our eyes on them alone, make theirs the rule for all.)

I say the mission of government, henceforth, in civilized lands, is not repression alone, and not authority alone, not even of law, nor by that favorite standard of the eminent writer, the rule of the best men, the born heroes and captains of the race, (as if such ever, or one time out of a hundred, get into the big places, elective or dynastic)—but higher than the highest arbitrary rule, to train communities through all their grades, beginning with individuals and ending there again, to rule themselves. What Christ appear'd for in the moral-spiritual field for human-kind, namely, that in respect to the absolute soul, there is in the possession of such by each single individual, something so transcendent, so incapable of gradations, (like life,) that, to that extent, it places all beings on a common level, utterly regardless of the distinctions of intellect, virtue, station, or any height or lowliness whatever—is tallied in like manner, in this other field, by democracy's rule that men, the nation, as a common aggregate of living identities, affording in each a separate and complete subject for freedom, worldly thrift and happiness, and for a fair chance for growth, and for protection in citizenship, &c., must, to the political extent of the suffrage or vote, if no further, be placed, in each and in the whole, on one broad, primary, universal, common platform.

The purpose is not altogether direct; perhaps it is more indirect. For it is not that democracy is of exhaustive account, in itself. Perhaps, indeed, it is, (like Nature,) of no account in itself. It is that, as we see, it is the best, perhaps only, fit and full means, formulater, general caller - forth, trainer, for the million, not for grand material personalities only, but for immortal souls. To be a voter with the rest is not so much; and this, like every institute, will have its imperfections. But to become an enfranchised man, and now, impediments removed, to stand and start without humiliation, and equal with the rest; to commence, or have the road clear'd to commence, the grand experiment of development, whose end, (perhaps requiring several generations,) may be the forming of a full-grown man or woman—that *is* something. To ballast the State is also secured, and in our times is to be secured, in no other way.

We do not, (at any rate I do not,) put it either on the ground that the People, the masses, even the best of them, are, in their latent or exhibited qualities, essentially sensible and good—nor on the ground of their rights; but that good or bad, rights or no rights, the democratic formula is the only safe and preservative one for coming times. We endow the masses with the suffrage for their own sake, no doubt; then, perhaps still more, from another point of view, for community's sake. Leaving the rest to the sentimentalists, we present freedom as sufficient in its scientific aspect, cold as ice, reasoning, deductive, clear and passionless as crystal.

Democracy too is law, and of the strictest, amplest kind. Many suppose, (and often in its own ranks the error,) that it means a throwing aside of law, and running riot. But, briefly, it is the superior law, not alone that of physical force, the body, which, adding to, it supersedes with that of the spirit. Law is the unshakable order of the universe forever; and the law over all, and law of laws, is the law of successions; that of the superior law, in time, gradually supplanting and overwhelming the inferior one. (While, for myself, I would cheerfully agree—first covenanting that the formative tendencies shall be administer'd in favor, or at least not against it, and that this reservation be closely construed— that until the individual or community show due signs, or be so minor and fractional as not to endanger the State, the condition of authoritative tutelage may continue, and self-government must abide its time.) Nor is the esthetic point, always an important one, without fascination for highest aiming souls. The common ambition strains for elevations, to become some privileged exclusive. The master sees greatness and health in being part of the mass; nothing will do as well as common ground. Would you have in yourself the divine, vast, general law? Then merge yourself in it.

And, topping democracy, this most alluring record, that it alone can bind, and ever seeks to bind, all nations, all men, of however various and distant lands, into a brotherhood, a family. It is the old, yet ever-modern dream of earth, out of her eldest and her youngest, her fond philosophers and poets. Not that half only, individualism, which isolates. There is another half, which is adhesiveness or love, that fuses, ties and aggregates, making the races comrades, and fraternizing all. Both are to be vitalized by religion, (sole worthiest elevator of man or State,) breathing into the proud, material tissues, the breath of life. For I say at the core of democracy, finally, is the religious element. All the religions, old and new, are there. Nor may the scheme step forth, clothed in resplendent beauty and command, till these, bearing the best, the latest fruit, the spiritual, shall fully appear....

Political democracy, as it exists and practically works in America, with all its threatening evils, supplies a training-school for making first-class men. It is life's gymnasium, not of good only, but of all. We try often, though we fall back often. A brave delight, fit for freedom's athletes, fills these arenas, and fully satisfies, out of the action in them, irrespective of success. Whatever we do not attain, we at any rate attain the experiences of the fight, the hardening of the strong campaign, and throb with currents of attempt at least. Time is ample. Let the victors come after us. Not for nothing does evil play its part among us. Judging from the main portions of the history of the world, so far, justice is always in jeopardy, peace walks amid hourly pitfalls, and of slavery, misery, meanness, the craft of tyrants and the credulity of the populace, in some of their protean forms, no voice can at any time say, They are not. The clouds break a little, and the sun shines out— but soon and certain the lowering darkness falls again, as if to last forever. Yet is there an immortal courage and prophecy in every sane soul that cannot, must not, under any circumstances, capitulate. *Vive,* the attack—the perennial assault! *Vive,* the unpopular cause—the spirit that audaciously aims—the never-abandon'd efforts, pursued the same amid opposing proofs and precedents.

Once, before the war, (Alas! I dare not say how many times the mood has come!) I, too, was fill'd with doubt and gloom. A foreigner, an acute and good man, had impressively said to me, that day—putting in form, indeed, my own observations: "I have travel'd much in the United States, and watch'd their politicians, and listen'd to the speeches of the candidates, and read the journals, and gone into the public houses, and heard the unguarded talk of men. And I have found your vaunted America honeycomb'd from top to toe with infidelism, even to itself and its own programme. I have mark'd the brazen hell-faces of secession and slavery gazing defiantly from all the windows and doorways. I have everywhere found, primarily, thieves and scalliwags arranging the nominations to offices, and sometimes filling the offices themselves. I have found the north just as full of bad stuff as the south. Of the holders of public office in the Nation or the States or their municipalities, I have found that not one in a hundred has been chosen by any spontaneous selection of the outsiders, the people, but all have been nominated and put through by little or large caucuses of the politicians, and have got in by corrupt rings and electioneering, not capacity or desert. I have noticed how the millions of sturdy farmers and mechanics are thus the helpless supple-jacks of comparatively few politicians. And I have noticed more and more, the alarming spectacle of parties usurping the government, and openly and shamelessly wielding it for party purposes."

Sad, serious, deep truths. Yet are there other, still deeper, amply confronting, dominating truths. Over those politicians and great and little rings, and over all their insolence and wiles, and over the powerfulest parties, looms a power, too sluggish maybe, but ever holding decisions and decrees in hand, ready, with stern process, to execute them as soon as plainly needed—and at times, indeed, summarily crushing to atoms the mightiest parties, even in the hour of their pride.

In saner hours far different are the amounts of these things from what, at first sight, they appear. Though it is no doubt important who is elected governor, mayor, or legislator, (and full of dismay when incompetent or vile ones get elected, as they sometimes do,) there are other, quieter contingencies, infinitely more important. Shams, &c., will always be the show, like ocean's scum; enough, if waters deep and clear make up the rest. Enough, that while the piled embroider'd shoddy gaud and fraud spreads to the superficial eye, the hidden warp and weft are genuine, and will wear forever. Enough, in short, that the race, the land which could raise such as the late rebellion, could also put it down.

The average man of a land at last only is important. He, in these States, remains immortal owner and boss, deriving good uses, somehow, out of any sort of servant in office, even the basest; (certain universal requisites, and their settled regularity and protection, being first secured,) a nation like ours, in a sort of geological formation state, trying continually new experiments, choosing new delegations, is not served by the best men only, but sometimes more by those that provoke it—by the combats they arouse. Thus national rage, fury, discussion, &c., better than content. Thus, also, the warning signals, invaluable for after times.

What is more dramatic than the spectacle we have seen repeated, and doubtless long shall see—the popular judgment taking the successful candidates on trial in the offices—standing off, as it were, and observing them and their doings for a while, and always giving, finally, the fit, exactly due reward? I think, after all, the sublimest part of political history, and its culmination, is currently issuing from the American people. I know nothing grander, better exercise, better digestion, more positive proof of the past, the triumphant result of faith in human kind, than a well-contested American national election....

Democracy, in silence, biding its time, ponders its own ideals, not of literature and art only—not of men only, but of women. The idea of the women of America, (extricated from this daze, this fossil and unhealthy air which hangs about the word *lady*,) develop'd, raised to become the robust equals, workers, and, it may be, even practical and political deciders with the men—greater than man, we may admit, through their divine maternity, always their towering, emblematical attribute—but great, at any rate, as man, in all departments; or, rather, capable of being so, soon as they realize it, and can bring themselves to give up toys and fictions, and launch forth, as men do, amid real, independent, stormy life.

Then, as towards our thought's finalé, (and, in that, overarching the true scholar's lesson,) we have to say there can be no complete or epical presentation of democracy in the aggregate, or anything like it, at this day, because its doctrines will only be effectually incarnated in any one branch, when, in all, their spirit is at the root and centre. Far, far, indeed, stretch, in distance, our Vistas! How much is still to be disentangled, freed! How long it takes to make this American world see that it is, in itself, the final authority and reliance!

Did you, too, O friend, suppose democracy was only for elections, for politics, and for a party name? I say democracy is only of use there that it may pass on and come to its flower and fruits in manners, in the highest forms of interaction between men, and their beliefs—in religion, literature, colleges, and schools—democracy in all public and private life, and in the army and navy. I have intimated that, as a paramount scheme, it has yet few or no full realizers and believers. I do not see, either, that it owes any serious thanks to noted propagandists or champions, or has been essentially help'd, though often harm'd, by them. It has been and is carried on by all the moral forces, and by trade, finance, machinery, intercommunications, and, in fact, by all the developments of history, and can no more be stopp'd than the tides, or the earth in its orbit. Doubtless, also, it resides, crude and latent, well down in the hearts of the fair average of the American-born people, mainly in the agricultural regions. But it is not yet, there or anywhere, the fully-receiv'd, the fervid, the absolute faith.

I submit, therefore, that the fruition of democracy, on aught like a grand scale, resides altogether in the future....

We have frequently printed the word Democracy. Yet I cannot too often repeat that it is a word the real gist of which still sleeps, quite unawaken'd, notwithstanding the resonance and the many angry tempests out of which its syllables have come, from pen or tongue. It is a great word, whose history, I suppose, remains unwritten, because that history has yet to be enacted.

Hannah Arendt
The Public Realm

Hannah Arendt (1906–1975) was born in Germany and studied in Heidelberg under Karl Jaspers. In 1933 she fled from Germany, eventually coming to the United States where she was executive director of Jewish Cultural Reconstruction in New York City, the author of many books, including *Eichmann in Jerusalem* and *On Revolution*, and a visiting professor at the University of Chicago and the New School for Social Research. Her views on democracy and citizenship were shaped by her admiration for ancient Athens where citizens honored political activity above everything else. In modern economics, science, and introspective philosophy, she saw an alienation form the public world—a "twofold flight from the earth into the universe and from the world into the self."

The following excerpt comes from her 1958 book, *The Human Condition*. In it, Arendt articulates an understanding of politics that goes far beyond today's frequent equation of politics with the activities of politicians or occasional voters. For Arendt, political activity is essential for anyone who wants to lead a truly human life. In this regard, one needs to remember that she is not referring to the "politicking" that goes on behind the closed doors of government committees or corporate boardrooms. As the following selection makes evident, Arendt sees political activity as distinctive from other types of activity specifically because it occurs in public. Arendt questions whether this kind of politics remains possible in today's society, where mass culture has made an experience of the public impossible. Arendt laments the lack of concern in modern societies for achievements which will be publicly remembered. The capacity for original, creative action represents the distinguishing feature of humanity, and the demise of the public realm where such acts must occur signifies the loss of what makes us truly human.

The Public Realm

Hannah Arendt

The term "public" signifies two closely interrelated but not altogether identical phenomena: It means, first, that everything that appears in public can be seen and heard by everybody and has the widest possible publicity. For us, appearance—something that is being seen and heard by others as well as by ourselves—constitutes reality. Compared with the reality which comes from being seen and heard, even the greatest forces of intimate life—the passions of the heart, the thoughts of the mind, the delights of the senses—lead an uncertain, shadowy kind of existence unless and until they are transformed, deprivatized and deindividualized, as it were, into a shape to fit them for public appearance. The most current of such transformations occurs in storytelling and generally in artistic transposition of individual experiences. But we do not need the form of the artist to witness this transfiguration. Each time we talk about things that can be experienced only in privacy or intimacy, we bring them out into a sphere where they will assume a kind of reality which, their intensity notwithstanding, they never could have had before. The presence of others who see what we see and hear what we hear assures us of the reality of the world and ourselves, and while the intimacy of a fully developed private life, such as had never been known before the rise of the modern age and the concomitant decline of the public realm, will always greatly intensify and enrich the whole scale of subjective emotions and private feelings, this intensification will always come to pass at the expense of the assurance of the reality of the world and men.

Indeed, the most intense feeling we know of, intense to the point of blotting out all other experiences, namely, the experience of great bodily pain, is at the same time the most private and least communicable of all. Not only is it perhaps the only experience which we are unable to transform into a shape fit for public appearance, it actually deprives us of our feeling for reality to such an extent that we can forget it more quickly and easily than anything else.

There seems to be no bridge from the most radical subjectivity, in which I am no longer "recognizable," to the outer world of life. Pain, in other words, truly a borderline experience between life as "being among men" (*inter homines esse*) and death, is so subjective and removed from the world of things and men that it cannot assume an appearance at all.

Since our feeling for reality depends utterly upon appearance and therefore upon the existence of a public realm into which things can appear out of the darkness of sheltered existence, even the twilight which illuminates our private and intimate lives is ultimately derived from the much harsher light of the public realm. Yet there are a great many things which cannot withstand the implacable, bright light of the constant presence of others on the public scene; there, only what is considered to be relevant, worthy of being seen or heard, can be tolerated, so that the irrelevant becomes automatically a private matter. This, to be sure, does not mean that private concerns are generally irrelevant; on the contrary, we shall see that there are very relevant matters which can survive only in the realm of the private. For instance, love, in distinction from friendship, is killed, or rather extinguished, the moment it is displayed in public. ("Never seek to tell thy love / Love that never told can be.") Because of its inherent worldlessness, love can only become false and perverted when it is used for political purposes such as the change or salvation of the world.

What the public realm considers irrelevant can have such an extraordinary and infectious charm that a whole people may adopt it as their way of life, without for that reason changing its essentially private character. Modern enchantment with "small things," though preached by early twentieth century poetry in almost all European tongues, has found its classical presentation in the *petit bonheur* of the French people. Since the decay of their once great and glorious public realm, the French have become masters in the art of being happy among "small things," within the space of their own four walls, between chest and bed, table and chair, dog and cat and flowerpot, extending to these things a care and tenderness which, in a world where rapid industrialization constantly kills off the things of yesterday to produce today's objects, may even appear to be the world's last, purely humane corner. This enlargement of the private, the enchantment, as it were, of a whole people, does not make it public, does not constitute a public realm, but, on the contrary, means only that the public realm has almost completely receded, so that greatness has given way to charm everywhere; for while the public realm may be great, it cannot be charming precisely because it is unable to harbor the irrelevant.

Second, the term "public" signifies the world itself, in so far as it is common to all of us and distinguished from our privately owned place in it. This world, however, is not identical with the earth or with nature, as the limited space for the movement of men and the general condition of organic life. It is related, rather, to the human artifact, the fabrication of human hands, as well as to affairs which go on among those who inhabit the man-made world together. To live together in the world means essentially that a world of things is between those who have it in common, as a table is located between those who sit around it; the world, like every in-between, relates and separates men at the same time.

The public realm, as the common world, gathers us together and yet prevents our falling over each other, so to speak. What makes mass society so difficult to bear is not the number of people involved, or at least not primarily, but the fact that the world between them has lost its power to gather them together, to relate and to separate them. The weirdness of this situation resembles a spiritualistic séance where a number of people gathered around a table might suddenly, through some magic trick, see the table vanish from their midst, so that two persons sitting opposite each other were no longer separated but also would be entirely unrelated to each other by anything tangible.

Historically, we know of only one principle that was ever devised to keep a community of people together who had lost their interest in the common world and felt themselves no longer related and separated by it. To find a bond between people strong enough to replace the world was the main political task of early Christian philosophy, and it was Augustine who proposed to found not only the Christian "brotherhood" but all human relationships on charity. But this charity, though its worldlessness clearly corresponds to the general human experience of love, is at the same time clearly distinguished from it in being something which, like the world, is between men: "Even robbers have between them [*inter se*] what they call charity." This surprising illustration of the Christian political principle is in fact very well chosen, because the bond of charity between people, while it is incapable of founding a public realm of its own, is quite adequate to the main Christian principle of worldlessness and is admirably fit to carry a group of essentially worldless people through the world, a group of saints or a group of criminals, provided only it is understood that the world itself is doomed and that every activity in it is undertaken with the proviso *quamdiu mundus durat* ("as long as the world lasts"). The unpolitical, nonpublic character of the Christian community was early defined in the demand that it should form a *corpus*, a "body," whose members were to be related to each other like brothers of the same family. The structure of communal life was modeled on the relationships between the members of a family because these were known to be nonpolitical and even antipolitical. A public realm had never come into being between the members of a family, and it was therefore not likely to develop from Christian community life if this life was ruled by the principle of charity and nothing else. Even then, as we know from the history and the rules of the monastic orders—the only communities in which the principle, of charity as a political device was ever tried—the danger that the activities undertaken

under "the necessity of present life" (*necessities vitae praesentis*) would lead by themselves, because they were performed in the presence of others, to the establishment of a kind of counterworld, a public realm within the orders themselves, was great enough to require additional rules and regulations, the most relevant one in our context being the prohibition of excellence and its subsequent pride.

Worldlessness as a political phenomenon is possible only on the assumption that the world will not last; on this assumption, however, it is almost inevitable that worldlessness, in one form or another, will begin to dominate the political scene. This happened after the downfall of the Roman Empire and, albeit for quite other reasons and in very different, perhaps even more disconsolate forms, it seems to happen again in our own days. The Christian abstention from worldly things is by no means the only conclusion one can draw from the conviction that the human artifice, a product of mortal hands, is as mortal as its makers. This, on the contrary, may also intensify the enjoyment and consumption of the things of the world, all manners of intercourse in which the world is not primarily understood to be the *koinon*, that which is common to all. Only the existence of a public realm and the world's subsequent transformation into a community of things which gathers men together and relates them to each other depends entirely on permanence. If the world is to contain a public space, it cannot be erected for one generation and planned for the living only; it must transcend the life span of mortal men.

Without this transcendence into a potential earthly immortality, no politics, strictly speaking, no common world and no public realm, is possible. For unlike the common good as Christianity understood it—the salvation of one's soul as a concern common to all—the common world is what we enter when we are born and what we leave behind when we die. It transcends our life span into past and future alike; it was there before we came and will outlast our brief sojourn in it. It is what we have in common not only with those who live with us, but also with those who were here before and with those who will come after us. But such a common world can survive the coming and going of the generations only to the extent that it appears in public. It is the publicity of the public realm which can absorb and make shine through the centuries whatever men may want to save from the natural ruin of time. Through many ages before us—but now not any more—men entered the public realm because they wanted something of their own or something they had in common with others to be more permanent than their earthly lives. (Thus, the curse of slavery consisted not only in being deprived of freedom and of visibility, but also in the fear of these obscure people themselves "that from being obscure they should pass away leaving no trace that they have existed.") There is perhaps no clearer testimony to the loss of the public realm in the modern age than the almost complete loss of authentic concern with immortality, a loss somewhat overshadowed by the simultaneous loss of the metaphysical concern with eternity. The latter, being the concern of the philosophers and the *vita contemplativa*, must remain outside our present considerations. But the former is testified to by the current classification of striving for immortality with the private vice of vanity. Under modern conditions, it is indeed so unlikely that anybody should earnestly aspire to an earthly immortality that we probably are justified in thinking it is nothing but vanity.

The famous passage in Aristotle, "Considering human affairs, one must not...consider man as he is and not consider what is mortal in mortal things, but think about them [only] to the extent that they have the possibility of immortalizing," occurs very properly in his political writings. For the *polis* was for the Greeks, as the *res publica* was for the Romans, first of all their guarantee against the futility of individual life, the space protected against this futility and reserved for the relative permanence, if not immortality, of mortals.

What the modern age thought of the public realm, after the spectacular rise of society to public prominence, was expressed by Adam Smith when, with disarming sincerity, he mentions "that unprosperous race of men commonly called men of letters" for whom "public admiration...makes always a part of their reward, ...a considerable part...in the profession of physic; a still greater perhaps in that of law; in poetry and philosophy it makes almost the whole." Here it is self-evident that public admiration and monetary reward are of the same nature and can become substitutes for each other. Public admiration, too, is something to be used and consumed, and status, as we would say today, fulfills one need as food fulfills another: public admiration is consumed by individual vanity as food is consumed by hunger. Obviously, from this viewpoint the test of reality does not lie in the public presence of others, but rather in the greater or lesser urgency of needs to whose existence or nonexistence nobody can ever testify except the one who happens to suffer them. And since the need for food has its demonstrable basis of reality in the life process itself, it is also obvious that the entirely subjective pangs of hunger are more real than "vainglory," as Hobbes used to call the need for public admiration. Yet, even if these needs, through some miracle of sympathy, were shared by others, their very futility would prevent their ever establishing anything so solid and durable as a common world. The point then is not that there is a lack of public admiration for poetry and philosophy in the modern world, but that such admiration does not constitute a space in which things are saved from destruction by time. The futility of public admiration, which daily is consumed in ever greater quantities, on the contrary, is such that monetary reward, one of the most futile things there is, can become more "objective" and more real.

As distinguished from this "objectivity," whose only basis is money as a common denominator for the fulfillment of all needs, the reality of the public realm relies on the simultaneous presence of innumerable perspectives and aspects in which the common world presents itself and for which no common measurement or denominator can ever be devised. For though the common world is the common meeting ground of all, those who are present have different locations in it, and the location of one can no more coincide with the location of another than the location of two objects. Being seen and being heard by others derive their significance from the fact that everybody sees and hears from a different position. This is the meaning of public life, compared to which even the richest and most satisfying family life can offer only the prolongation or multiplication of one's own position with its attending aspects and perspectives. The subjectivity of privacy can be prolonged and multiplied in a family, it can even become so strong that its weight is felt in the public realm; but this family "world" can never replace the reality rising out of the sum total of aspects presented by one object to a multitude of spectators. Only where things can be seen by many in a variety of aspects without changing their identity, so that those who are gathered around them know they see sameness in utter diversity, can worldly reality truly and reliably appear.

Under the conditions of a common world, reality is not guaranteed primarily by the "common nature" of all men who constitute it, but rather by the fact that, differences of position and the resulting variety of perspectives notwithstanding, everybody is always concerned with the same object. If the sameness of the object can no longer be discerned, no common nature of men, least of all the unnatural conformism of a mass society, can prevent the destruction of the common world, which is usually preceded by the destruction of the many aspects in which it presents itself to human plurality. This can happen under conditions of radical isolation, where nobody can any longer agree with anybody else, as is usually the case in tyrannies. But it may also happen under conditions of mass society or mass hysteria, where we see all people suddenly behave as though they were members of one family, each multiplying and prolonging the perspective of his neighbor. In both instances, men have become entirely private, that is, they have been deprived of seeing and hearing others, of being seen and being heard by them. They are all imprisoned in the subjectivity of their own singular experience, which does not cease to be singular if the same experience is multiplied innumerable times. The end of the common world has come when it is seen only under one aspect and is permitted to present itself in only one perspective.

Fyodor Dostoevsky
The Grand Inquisitor

Fyodor Dostoyevsky (1821–1881), with Tolstoy perhaps Russia's greatest "realist" novelist, wrote *The Brothers Karamazov* as the culmination of a long battle against the materialism of western civilization. At the age of twenty-five, having left the Army Engineering Corps and devoted himself to literature, Dostoyevsky joined a group of utopian socialists, disciples of Francois Fourier. He was arrested three years later and sentenced to death. Moments before the planned execution, Dostoyevsky was informed that his sentence had been commuted to four years hard labor at a Siberian prison, described in his *House of the Dead*. After his release, Dostoyevsky returned to St. Petersburg and edited a series of literary and political journals. He published a number of stories, noted for their minute descriptions of everyday life and profound explorations of life's tragic element, exemplified in his novel *Crime and Punishment*.

The following excerpt from *The Brothers Karamazov* (1878) consists of a profound and eloquent parable exploring human freedom in the context of human nature, spirituality, and the meaning of knowledge. It was written as an attack against utilitarianism and the modern attempt to replace religion with scientific discovery, and calls into question the idea that we can really be free.

The Grand Inquisitor

Fyodor Dostoevsky

E ven this must have a preface—that is, a literary preface," laughed Ivan, "and I am a poor hand at making one. You see, my action takes place in the sixteenth century, and at that time, as you probably learnt at school, it was customary in poetry to bring down heavenly powers on earth. Not to speak of Dante, in France, clerks, as well as the monks in the monasteries, used to give regular performances in which the Madonna, the saints, the angels, Christ, and God Himself were brought on the stage. In those days it was done in all simplicity. In Victor Hugo's 'Notre Dame de Paris' an edifying and gratuitous spectacle was provided for the people in the Hotel de Ville of Paris in the reign of Louis XI. in honour of the birth of the dauphin. It was called *Le bon jugement de la très sainte et gracieuse Vierge Marie*, and she appears herself on the stage and pronounces her *bon jugement*. Similar plays, chiefly from the Old Testament, were occasionally performed in Moscow too, up to the times of Peter the Great. But besides plays there were all sorts of legends and ballads scattered about the world, in which the saints and angels and all the powers of Heaven took part when required. In our monasteries the monks busied themselves in translating, copying, and even composing such poems—and even under the Tatars. There is, for instance, one such poem (of course, from the Greek), 'The Wanderings of Our Lady through Hell,' with descriptions as bold as Dante's. Our Lady visits Hell, and the Archangel Michael leads her through the torments. She sees the sinners and their punishment. There she sees among others one noteworthy set of sinners in a burning lake; some of them sink to the bottom of the lake so that they can't swim out, and 'these God forgets'—an expression of extraordinary depth and force. And so Our Lady, shocked and weeping, falls before the throne of God and begs for mercy for all in Hell—for all she has seen there, indiscriminately. Her conversation with God is immensely interesting.

From *The Brothers Karamazov*, translated by Constance Garnett (New York: Macmillan, 1923).

She beseeches Him, she will not desist, and when God points to the hands and feet of her Son, nailed to the Cross, and asks, 'How can I forgive His tormentors?' she bids all the saints, all the martyrs, all the angels and archangels to fall down with her and pray for mercy on all without distinction. It ends by her winning from God a respite of suffering every year from Good Friday till Trinity day, and the sinners at once raise a cry of thankfulness from Hell, chanting, 'Thou art just, O Lord, in this judgment.' Well, my poem would have been of that kind if it had appeared at that time. He comes on the scene in my poem, but He says nothing, only appears and passes on. Fifteen centuries have passed since He promised to come in His glory, fifteen centuries since His prophet wrote, 'Behold, I come quickly;' 'Of that day and that hour knoweth no man, neither the Son, but the Father,' as He Himself predicted on earth. But humanity awaits him with the same faith and with the same love. Oh, with greater faith, for it is fifteen centuries since man has ceased to see signs from Heaven.

No signs from Heaven come to-day
To add to what the heart doth say.

There was nothing left but faith in what the heart doth say. It is true there were many miracles in those days. There were saints who performed miraculous cures; some holy people, according to their biographies, were visited by the Queen of Heaven herself. But the devil did not slumber, and doubts were already arising among men of the truth of these miracles. And just then there appeared in the north of Germany a terrible new heresy. 'A huge star like to a torch' (that is, to a church) 'fell on the sources of the waters and they became bitter.' These heretics began blasphemously denying miracles. But those who remained faithful were all the more ardent in their faith. The tears of humanity rose up to Him as before, awaiting His coming, loved Him, hoped for Him, yearned to suffer and die for Him as before.

And so many ages mankind had prayed with faith and fervour, 'O Lord our God, hasten Thy coming,' so many ages called upon Him, that in His infinite mercy He deigned to come down to His servants. Before that day He had come down, He had visited some holy men, martyrs and hermits, as is written in their 'Lives.' Among us, Tyutchev, with absolute faith in the truth of his words, bore witness that

Bearing the Cross, in slavish dress
Weary and worn, the Heavenly King
Our mother, Russia, came to bless,
And through our land went wandering.
And that certainly was so, I assure you.

"And behold, He deigned to appear for a moment to the people, to the tortured, suffering people, sunk in iniquity, but loving Him like children. My story is laid in Spain, in Seville, in the most terrible time of the Inquisition, when fires were lighted every day to the glory of God, and 'in the splendid *auto da fé* the wicked heretics were burnt.' Oh, of course, this was not the coming in which He will appear according to His promise at the end of time in all His heavenly glory, and which will be sudden 'as lightning flashing from east to west.' No, He visited His children only for a moment, and there where the flames were crackling round the heretics. In His infinite mercy He came once more among men in that human shape in which He walked among men for three years fifteen centuries ago. He came down to the 'hot pavements' of the southern town in which on the day before almost a hundred heretics had, *ad majorem gloriam Dei*, been burnt by the cardinal, the Grand Inquisitor, in a magnificent *auto da fé*, in the presence of the king, the court, the knights, the cardinals, the most charming ladies of the court, and the whole population of Seville.

"He came softly, unobserved, and yet, strange to say, every one recognised Him. That might be one of the best passages in the poem. I mean, why they recognised Him. The people are irresistibly drawn to Him, they surround Him, they flock about Him, follow Him. He moves silently in their midst with a gentle smile of infinite compassion. The sun of love burns in His heart, light and power shine from His eyes, and their radiance, shed on the people, stirs their hearts with responsive love. He holds out His hands to them, blesses them, and a healing virtue comes from contact with Him, even with His garments. An old man in the crowd, blind from childhood, cries out, 'O Lord, heal me and I shall see Thee!' and, as it were, scales fall from his eyes and the blind man sees Him. The crowd weeps and kisses the earth under His feet. Children throw flowers before Him, sing, and cry hosannah. 'It is He—it is He!' all repeat. 'It must be He, it can be no one but Him!' He stops at the steps of the Seville cathedral at the moment when the weeping mourners are bringing in a little open white coffin. In it lies a child of seven, the only daughter of a prominent citizen. The dead child lies hidden in flowers. 'He will raise your child,' the crowd shouts to the weeping mother. The priest, coming to meet the coffin, looks perplexed, and frowns, but the mother of the dead child throws herself at His feet with a wail. 'If it is Thou, raise my child!' she cries, holding out her hands to Him. The procession halts, the coffin is laid on the steps at His feet. He looks with compassion, and His lips once more softly pronounce, 'Maiden, arise!' and the maiden arises. The little girl sits up in the coffin and looks round, smiling with wide-open wondering eyes, holding a bunch of white roses they had put in her hand.

"There are cries, sobs, confusion among the people, and at that moment the cardinal himself, the Grand Inquisitor, passes by the cathedral. He is an old man, almost ninety, tall and erect, with a withered face and sunken eyes, in which there is still a gleam of light. He is not dressed in his gorgeous cardinal's robes, as he was the day before, when he was burning the enemies of the Roman Church—at that moment he was wearing his coarse, old, monk's cassock. At a distance behind him come his gloomy assis-tants and slaves and the 'holy guard.' He stops at the sight of the crowd and watches it from a distance. He sees everything; he sees them set the coffin down at His feet, sees the child rise up, and his face darkens. He knits his thick grey brows and his eyes gleam with a sinister fire. He holds out his finger and bids the guards take Him. And such is his power, so completely are the people cowed into submission and trembling obedience to him, that the crowd immediately make way for the guards, and in the midst of deathlike silence they lay hands on Him and lead Him away. The crowd instantly bows down to the earth, like one man, before the old inquisitor. He blesses the people in silence and passes on. The guards lead their prisoner to the close, gloomy vaulted prison in the ancient palace of the Holy Inquisition and shut Him in it. The day passes and is followed by the dark, burning 'breathless' night of Seville. The air is 'fragrant with laurel and lemon.' In the pitch darkness the iron door of the prison is suddenly opened and the Grand Inquisitor himself comes in with a light in is hand. He is alone; the door is closed at once behind him. He stands in the doorway and for a minute or two gazes into His face. At last he goes up slowly, sets the light on the table and speaks.

" 'Is it Thou? Thou?' but receiving no answer, he adds at once. 'Don't answer, be silent. What canst Thou say, indeed? I know too well what Thou wouldst say. And Thou hast no right to add anything to what Thou hadst said of old. Why, then, art Thou come to hinder us? For Thou hast come to hinder us, and Thou knowest that. But dost Thou know what will be to-morrow? I know not who Thou art and care not to know whether it is Thou or only a semblance of Him, but to-morrow I shall condemn Thee and burn Thee at the stake as the worst of heretics. And the very people who have to-day kissed Thy feet to-morrow at the faintest sign from me will rush to heap up the embers of Thy fire. Knowest Thou that? Yes, maybe Thou knowest it,' he added with thoughtful penetration, never for a moment taking his eyes off the Prisoner."

"I don't quite understand, Ivan. What does it mean?" Alyosha, who had been listening in silence, said with a smile. "Is it simply a wild fantasy, or a mistake on the part of the old man—some impossible *qui pro quo*?"

"Take it as the last," said Ivan, laughing, "if you are so corrupted by modern realism and can't stand anything fantastic. If you like it to be a case of mistaken identity, let it be so. It is true," he went on, laughing, "the old man was ninety, and he might well be crazy over his set idea. He might have been struck by the appearance of the Prisoner. It might, in fact, be simply his ravings, the delusion of an old man of ninety, overexcited by the *auto da fé* of a hundred heretics the day before. But does it matter to us after all whether it was a mistake of identity or a wild fantasy? All that matters is that the old man should speak out, should speak openly of what he has thought in silence for ninety years."

"And the Prisoner too is silent? Does He look at him and not say a word?"

"That's inevitable in any case," Ivan laughed again. "The old man has told Him He hasn't the right to add anything to what He has said of old. One may say it is the most fundamental feature of Roman Catholicism, in my opinion at least. 'All has been given by Thee to the Pope,' they say, 'and all, therefore, is still in the Pope's hands, and there is no need for Thee to come now at all. Thou must not meddle for the time, at least.' That's how they speak and write too—the Jesuits, at any rate. I have read it myself in the works of their theologians. 'Hast Thou the right to reveal to us one of the mysteries of that world from which Thou hast come?' my old man asks Him, and answers the question for Him. 'No, Thou hast not; that Thou mayest not add to what has been said of old, and mayest not take from men the freedom which Thou didst exalt when Thou wast on earth. Whatsoever Thou revealest anew will encroach on men's freedom of faith; for it will be manifest as a miracle, and the freedom of their faith was dearer to Thee than anything in those days

fifteen hundred years ago. Didst Thou not often say then, "I will make you free"? But now Thou has seen these "free" men,' the old man adds suddenly, with a pensive smile. 'Yes, we've paid dearly for it,' he goes on, looking sternly at Him, 'but at last we have completed that work in Thy name. For fifteen centuries we have been wrestling with Thy freedom, but now it is ended and over for good. Dost Thou not believe that it's over for good? Thou lookest meekly at me and deignest not even to be wroth with me. But let me tell Thee that now, to-day, people are more persuaded than ever that they have perfect freedom, yet they have brought their freedom to us and laid it humbly at our feet. But that has been our doing. Was this what Thou didst? Was this Thy freedom?' "

"I don't understand again," Alyosha broke in. "Is he ironical, is he jesting?"

"Not a bit of it! He claims it as a merit for himself and his Church that at last they have vanquished freedom and have done so to make men happy. 'For now' (he is speaking of the Inquisition, of course) 'for the first time it has become possible to think of the happiness of men. Man was created a rebel; and how can rebels be happy? Thou wast warned,' he says to Him. 'Thou hast had no lack of admonitions and warnings, but Thou didst not listen to those warnings; Thou didst reject the only way by which men might be made happy. But, fortunately, departing Thou didst hand on the work to us. Thou has promised, Thou hast established by Thy word, Thou has given to us the right to bind and to unbind, and now, of course, Thou canst not think of taking it away. Why, then, hast Thou come to hinder us?' "

"And what's the meaning of 'no lack of admonitions and warnings'?" asked Alyosha.

"Why, that's the chief part of what the old man must say."

" 'The wise and dread Spirit, the spirit of self-destruction and non-existence,' the old man goes on, 'the great spirit talked with Thee in the wilderness, and we are told in the books that he "tempted" Thee. Is that so? And could anything truer be said than what he revealed to Thee in three questions and what Thou didst reject, and what in the books is called "the temptation"? And yet if there has ever been on earth a real stupendous miracle, it took place on that day, on the day of the three temptations. The statement of those three questions was itself the miracle. If it were possible to imagine simply for the sake of argument that those three questions of the dread spirit had perished utterly from the books, and that we had to restore them and to invent them anew, and to do so had gathered together all the wise men of the earth—rulers, chief priests, learned men, philosophers, poets—and had set them the task to invent three questions, such as would not only fit the occasion, but express in three words, three human phrases, the whole future history of the world and of humanity—dost Thou believe that all the wisdom of the earth united could have invented anything in depth and force equal to the three questions which were actually put to Thee then by the wise and mighty spirit in the wilderness? From those questions alone, from the miracle of their statement, we can see that we have here to do not with the fleeting human intelligence, but with the absolute and eternal. For in those three questions the whole subsequent history of mankind is, as it were, brought together into one whole, and foretold, and in them are united all the unsolved historical contradictions of human nature. At the time it could not be so clear, since the future was unknown; but now that fifteen hundred years have passed, we see that everything in those three questions was so justly divined and foretold, and has been so truly fulfilled, that nothing can be added to them or taken from them.

" 'Judge Thyself who was right—Thou or he who questioned Thee then? Remember the first question; its meaning, in other words, was this: "Thou wouldst go into the world, and art going with empty hands, with some promise of freedom which men in their simplicity and their natural unruliness cannot even understand, which they fear and dread—for nothing has ever been more insupportable for a man and a human society than freedom. But seest Thou these stones in this parched and barren wilderness? Turn them into bread, and mankind will run after Thee like a flock of sheep, grateful and obedient, though forever trembling, lest Thou withdraw Thy hand and deny them Thy bread." But Thou wouldst not deprive man of freedom and didst reject the offer, thinking, what is that freedom worth, if obedience is bought with bread? Thou didst reply that man lives not by bread alone. But dost Thou know that for the sake of that earthly bread the spirit of the earth will rise up against Thee and will strive with Thee and overcome Thee, and all will follow him, crying, "Who can compare with this beast? he has given us fire from heaven!" Dost Thou know that the ages will pass, and humanity will proclaim by the lips of their sages that there is no crime, and therefore no sin; there is only hunger? "Feed men, and then ask of them virtue!" that's what they'll write on the banner, which they will raise against Thee, and with which they will destroy Thy temple. Where Thy temple stood will rise a new building; the terrible tower of Babel will be built again, and though, like the one of old, it will not be finished, yet Thou mightest have prevented that new tower and have cut short the sufferings of men for a thousand years; for they will come back to us after a thousand years of agony with their tower. They will seek us again, hidden underground in the catacombs, for we shall be again persecuted and tortured. They will find us and cry to us, "Feed us, for those who have promised us fire from heaven haven't given it!" And then we shall finish building their tower, for he finishes the building who feeds them. And we alone shall feed them in Thy name, declaring falsely that it is in Thy name. Oh, never, never can they feed themselves without us! No science will give them bread so long as they remain free. In the end they will lay their freedom at our feet, and say to us, "Make us your slaves, but feed us." They will understand themselves, at last, that freedom and bread enough for all are inconceivable together, for never, never will they be able to share between them! They will be convinced, too, that they can never be free, for they are weak, vicious, worthless and rebellious. Thou didst promise them the bread of Heaven, but, I repeat again, can it compare with earthly bread in the eyes of the weak, ever sinful and ignoble race of man? And if for the sake of the bread of Heaven thousands and tens of thousands shall follow Thee, what is to become of the millions and tens of thousands of millions of creatures who will not have the strength to forego the earthly bread for the sake of the heavenly? Or dost Thou care only for the tens of thousands of the great and strong, while the millions, numerous as the sands of the sea, who are weak but love Thee, must exist only for the sake of the great and strong? No, we care for the weak too. They are sinful and rebellious, but in the end they too will become obedient. They will marvel at us and look on us as gods, because we are ready to endure the freedom which they have found so dreadful and to rule over them—so awful it will seem to them to be free. But we shall tell them that we are Thy servants and rule them in Thy name. We shall deceive them again, for we will not let Thee come to us again. That deception will be our suffering, for we shall be forced to lie.

" 'This is the significance of the first question in the wilderness, and this is what Thou hast rejected for the sake of that freedom which Thou hast exalted above everything. Yet in this question lies hid the great secret of this world. Choosing "bread," Thou wouldst have satisfied the universal and everlasting craving of humanity—to find some one to worship. So long as man remains free he strives for nothing so incessantly and so painfully as to find some one to worship. But man seeks to worship what is established beyond dispute, so that all men would agree at once to worship it. For these pitiful creatures are concerned not only to find what one or the other can worship, but to find something that all would believe in and worship; what is essential is that all may be *together* in

it. This craving for *community* of worship is the chief misery of every man individually and of all humanity from the beginning of time. For the sake of common worship they've slain each other with the sword. They have set up gods and challenged one another, "Put away your gods and come and worship ours, or we will kill you and your gods!" And so it will be to the end of the world, even when gods disappear from the earth; they will fall down before idols just the same. Thou didst know, Thou couldst not but have known, this fundamental secret of human nature, but Thou didst reject the one infallible banner which was offered Thee to make all men bow down to Thee alone—the banner of earthly bread; and Thou hast rejected it for the sake of freedom and the bread of Heaven. Behold what Thou didst further. And all again in the name of freedom! I tell Thee that man is tormented by no greater anxiety than to find some one quickly to whom he can hand over that gift of freedom with which the ill-fated creature is born. But only one who can appease their conscience can take over their freedom. In bread there was offered Thee an invincible banner; give bread, and man will worship Thee, for nothing is more certain than bread. But if some one else gains possession of his conscience—oh! then he will cast away Thy bread and follow after him who has ensnared his conscience. In that Thou wast right. For the secret of man's being is not only to live but to have something to live for. Without a stable conception of the object of life, man would not consent to go on living, and would rather destroy himself than remain on earth, though he had bread in abundance. That is true. But what happened? Instead of taking men's freedom from them, Thou didst make it greater than ever! Didst Thou forget that man prefers peace, and even death, to freedom of choice in the knowledge of good and evil? Nothing is more seductive for man than his freedom of conscience, but nothing is a greater cause of suffering. And behold, instead of giving a firm foundation for setting the conscience of man at rest forever, Thou didst choose all that is exceptional, vague and enigmatic; Thou didst choose what was utterly beyond the strength of men, acting as though Thou didst not love them at all—Thou who didst come to give Thy life for them! Instead of taking possession of men's freedom, Thou didst increase it, and burdened the spiritual kingdom of mankind with its sufferings for ever. Thou didst desire man's free love, that he should follow Thee freely, enticed and taken captive by Thee. In place of the rigid ancient law, man must hereafter with free heart decide for himself what is good and what is evil, having only Thy image before him as his guide. But didst Thou not know he would at last reject even Thy image and Thy truth, if he is weighed down with the fearful burden of free choice? They will cry aloud at last that the truth is not in Thee, for they could not have been left in greater confusion and suffering than Thou hast caused, laying, upon them so many cares and unanswerable problems.

" 'So that, in truth, Thou didst Thyself lay the foundation for the destruction of Thy kingdom, and no one is more to blame for it. Yet what was offered Thee? There are three powers, three powers alone, able to conquer and to hold captive for ever the conscience of these impotent rebels for their happiness—those forces are *miracle*, *mystery* and *authority*. Thou hast rejected all three and hast set the example for doing so. When the wise and dread spirit set Thee on the pinnacle of the temple and said to Thee, "If Thou wouldst know whether Thou art the Son of God then cast Thyself down, for it is written: the angels shall hold him up lest he fall and bruise himself, and Thou shalt know then whether Thou art the Son of God and shalt prove then how great is Thy faith in Thy Father." But Thou didst refuse and wouldst not cast Thyself down. Oh! of course, Thou didst proudly and well, like God; but the weak, unruly race of men, are they gods? Oh, Thou didst know then that in taking one step, in making one movement to cast Thyself down, Thou wouldst be tempting God and have lost all Thy faith in Him, and wouldst have been dashed to

pieces against that earth which Thou didst come to save. And the wise spirit that tempted Thee would have rejoiced. But I ask again, are there many like Thee? And couldst Thou believe for one moment that men, too, could face such a temptation? Is the nature of men such, that they can reject miracle, and at the great moments of their life, the moments of their deepest, most agonising spiritual difficulties, cling only to the free verdict of the heart? Oh, Thou didst know that Thy deed would be recorded in books, would be handed down to remote times and the utmost ends of the earth, and Thou didst hope that man, following Thee, would cling to God and not ask for a miracle. But Thou didst not know that when man rejects miracle he rejects God too; for man seeks not so much God as the miraculous. And as man cannot bear to be without the miraculous, he will create new miracles of his own for himself, and will worship deeds of sorcery and witchcraft, though he might be a hundred times over a rebel, heretic and infidel. Thou didst not come down from the Cross when they shouted to Thee, mocking and reviling Thee, "Come down from the cross and we will believe that Thou art He." Thou didst not come down, for again Thou wouldst not enslave man by a miracle, and didst crave faith given freely, not based on miracle. Thou didst crave for free love and not the base raptures of the slave before the might that has overawed him for ever. But Thou didst think too highly of men therein, for they are slaves, of course, though rebellious by nature. Look round and judge; fifteen centuries have passed, look upon them. Whom hast Thou raised up to Thyself? I swear, man is weaker and baser by nature than Thou hast believed him! Can he, can he do what Thou didst? By showing him so much respect, Thou didst, as it were, cease to feel for him, for Thou didst ask far too much from him—Thou who hast loved him more than Thyself! Respecting him less, Thou wouldst have asked less of him. That would have been more like love, for his burden would have been lighter. He is weak and vile. What though he is everywhere now rebelling against our power, and proud of his rebellion? It is the pride of a child and a schoolboy. They are little children rioting and barring out the teacher at school. But their childish delight will end; it will cost them dear. They will cast down temples and drench the earth with blood. But they will see at last, the foolish children, that, though they are rebels, they are impotent rebels, unable to keep up their own rebellion. Bathed in their foolish tears, they will recognise at last that He who created them rebels must have meant to mock at them. They will say this in despair, and their utterance will be a blasphemy which will make them more unhappy still, for man's nature cannot bear blasphemy, and in the end always avenges it on itself. And so unrest, confusion and unhappiness—that is the present lot of man after Thou didst bear so much for their freedom! Thy great prophet tells in vision and in image, that he saw all those who took part in the first resurrection and that there were of each tribe twelve thousand. But if there were so many of them, they must have been not men but gods. They had borne Thy cross, they had endured scores of years in the barren, hungry wilderness, living upon locusts and roots—and Thou mayest indeed point with pride at those children of freedom, of free love, of free and splendid sacrifice for Thy name. But remember that they were only some thousands; and what of the rest? And how are the other weak ones to blame, because they could not endure what the strong have endured? How is the weak soul to blame that it is unable to receive such terrible gifts? Canst Thou have simply come to the elect and for the elect? But if so, it is a mystery and we cannot understand it. And if it is a mystery, we too have a right to preach a mystery, and to teach them that it's not the free judgment of their hearts, not love that matters, but a mystery which they must follow blindly, even against their conscience. So we have done. We have corrected Thy work and have founded it upon *miracle*, *mystery* and *authority*. And men rejoiced that they were again led like sheep, and that the terrible gift that had brought them such

suffering, was, at last, lifted from their hearts. Were we right teaching them this? Speak! Did we not love mankind, so meekly acknowledging their feebleness, lovingly lightening their burden, and permitting their weak nature even sin with our sanction? Why hast Thou come now to hinder us? And why dost Thou look silently and searchingly at me with Thy mild eyes? Be angry. I don't want Thy love, for I love Thee not. And what use is it for me to hide anything from Thee? Don't I know to Whom I am speaking? All that I can say is known to Thee already. And is it for me to conceal from Thee our mystery? Perhaps it is Thy will to hear it from my lips. Listen, then. We are not working with Thee, but with *him*—that is our mystery. It's long—eight centuries—since we have been on *his* side and not on Thine. Just eight centuries ago, we took from him what Thou didst reject with scorn, that last gift he offered Thee, showing Thee all the kingdoms of the earth. We took from him Rome and the sword of Caesar, and proclaimed ourselves sole rulers of the earth, though hitherto we have not been able to complete our work. But whose fault is that? Oh, the work is only beginning, but it has begun. It has long to await completion and the earth has yet much to suffer, but we shall triumph and shall be Caesars, and then we shall plan the universal happiness of man. But Thou mightest have taken even then the sword of Caesar. Why didst Thou reject that last gift? Hadst Thou accepted that last counsel of the mighty spirit, Thou wouldst have accomplished all that man seeks on earth—that is, some one to worship, some one to keep his conscience, and some means of uniting all in one unanimous and harmonious ant-heap, for the craving for universal unity is the third and last anguish of men. Mankind as a whole has always striven to organise a universal state. There have been many great nations with great histories, but the more highly they were developed the more unhappy they were, for they felt more acutely than other people the craving for worldwide union. The great conquerors, Timours and Ghenghis-

Khans, whirled like hurricanes over the face of the earth striving to subdue its people, and they too were but the unconscious expression of the same craving for universal unity. Hadst Thou taken the world and Caesar's purple, Thou wouldst have founded the universal state and have given universal peace. For who can rule men if not he who holds their conscience and their bread in his hands. We have taken the sword of Caesar, and in taking it, of course, have rejected Thee and followed *him*. Oh, ages are yet to come of the confusion of free thought, of their science and cannibalism. For having begun to build their tower of Babel without us, they will end, of course, with cannibalism. But then the beast will crawl to us and lick our feet and spatter them with tears of blood. And we shall sit upon the beast and raise the cup, and on it will be written, "Mystery." But then, and only then, the reign of peace and happiness will come for men. Thou art proud of Thine elect, but Thou hast only the elect, while we give rest to all. And besides, how many of those elect, those mighty ones who could become elect, have grown weary waiting for Thee, and have transferred and will transfer the powers of their spirit and the warmth of their heart to the other camp, and end by raising their *free* banner against Thee. Thou didst Thyself lift up that banner. But with us all will be happy and will no more rebel nor destroy one another as under Thy freedom. Oh, we shall persuade them that they will only become free when they renounce their freedom to us and submit to us. And shall we be right or shall we by lying? They will be convinced that we are right, for they will remember the horrors of slavery and confusion to which Thy freedom brought them. Freedom, free thought and science, will lead them into such straits and will bring them face to face with such marvels and insoluble mysteries, that some of them, the fierce and rebellious, will destroy themselves, others, rebellious but weak, will destroy one another, while the rest, weak and unhappy, will crawl fawning to our feet and whine to us: "Yes, you were right, you alone possess His mystery, and we come back to you, save us from ourselves!"

" 'Receiving bread from us, they will see clearly that we take the bread made by their hands from them, to give it to them, without any miracle. They will see that we do not change the stones to bread, but in truth they will be more thankful for taking it from our hands than for the bread itself! For they will remember only too well that in old days, without our help, even the bread they made turned to stones in their hands, while since they have come back to us, the very stones have turned to bread in their hands. Too, too well they know the value of complete submission! And until men know that, they will be unhappy. Who is most to blame for their not knowing it, speak? Who scattered the flock and sent it astray on unknown paths? But the flock will come together again and will submit once more, and then it will be once for all. Then we shall give them the quiet humble happiness of weak creatures such as they are by nature. Oh, we shall persuade them at last not to be proud, for Thou didst lift them up and thereby taught them to be proud. We shall show them that they are weak, that they are only pitiful children, but that childlike happiness is the sweetest of all. They will become timid and will look to us and huddle close to us in fear, as chicks to the hen. They will marvel at us and will be awe-stricken before us, and will be proud at our being so powerful and clever, that we have been able to subdue such a turbulent flock of thousands of millions. They will tremble impotently before our wrath, their minds will grow fearful, they will be quick to shed tears like women and children, but they will be just as ready at a sign from us to pass to laughter and rejoicing, to happy mirth and childish song. Yes, we shall set them to work, but in their leisure hours we shall make their life like a child's game, with children's songs and innocent dance. Oh, we shall allow them even sin, they are weak and helpless, and they will love us like children because we allow them to sin. We shall tell them that every sin will be expiated, if it is done with our permission, that we allow them to sin because we love them, and the punishment for these sins we take upon ourselves. And we shall take it upon ourselves, and they will adore us as their saviours who have taken on themselves their sins before God. And they will have no secrets from us. We shall allow or forbid them to live with their wives and mistresses, to have or not to have children—according to whether they have been obedient or disobedient—and they will submit to us gladly and cheerfully. The most painful secrets of their conscience, all, all they will bring to us, and we shall have an answer for all. And they will be glad to believe our answer, for it will save them from the great anxiety and terrible agony they endure at present in making a free decision for' themselves. And, all will be happy, all the millions of creatures except the hundred thousand who rule over them. For only we, we who guard the mystery, shall be unhappy. There will be thousands of millions of happy babes and a hundred thousand sufferers who have taken upon themselves the curse of the knowledge of good and evil. Peacefully they will die, peacefully they will expire in Thy name, and beyond the grave they will find nothing but death. But we shall keep the secret, and for their happiness we shall allure them with the reward of heaven and eternity. Though if there were anything in the other world, it certainly would not be for such as they. It is prophesied that Thou wilt come again in victory, Thou wilt come with Thy chosen, the proud and strong, but we will my that they have only saved themselves, but we have saved all. We are told that the harlot who sits upon the beast, and holds in her hands the *mystery*, shall be put to shame, that the weak will rise up again, and will rend her royal purple and will strip naked her loathsome body. But then I will stand up and point out to Thee the thousand millions of happy children who have known no sin. And we who have taken their sins upon us for their happiness will stand up before Thee and say: "Judge us if Thou canst and darest." Know that I fear Thee not. Know that I too

have been in the wilderness, I too have lived on roots and locusts, I too prized the freedom with which Thou hast blessed men, and I too was striving to stand among Thy elect, among the strong and powerful, thirsting "to make up the number." But I awakened and would not serve madness. I turned back and joined the ranks of those *who have corrected Thy work*. I left the proud and went back to the humble, for the happiness of the humble. What I say to Thee will come to pass, and our dominion will be built up. I repeat, to-morrow Thou shalt see that obedient flock who at a sign from me will hasten to heap up the hot cinders about the pile on which I shall burn Thee for coming to hinder us. For if any one has ever deserved our fires, it is Thou. To-morrow I shall burn Thee. Dixi.' "

Ivan stopped. He was carried away as he talked and spoke with excitement; when he had finished, he suddenly smiled.

Alyosha had listened in silence; towards the end he was greatly moved and seemed several times on the point of interrupting, but restrained himself. Now his words came with a rush.

"But...that's absurd!" he cried, flushing. "Your poem is in praise of Jesus, not in blame of Him—as you meant it to be. And who will believe you about freedom? Is that the way to understand it? That's not the idea of it in the Orthodox Church...That's Rome, and not even the whole of Rome, it's false—those are the worst of the Catholics, the Inquisitors, the Jesuits!... And there could not be such a fantastic creature as your Inquisitor. What are these sins of mankind they take on themselves? Who are these keepers of the mystery who have taken some curse upon themselves for the happiness of mankind? When have they been seen? We know the Jesuits, they are spoken ill of, but surely they are not what you describe? They are not that at all, not at all.... They are simply the Romish army for the earthly sovereignty of the world in the future, with the Pontiff of Rome for Emperor...that's their ideal, but there's no sort of mystery or lofty melancholy about it.... It's simple lust of power, of filthy earthly gain, of domination—something like a universal serf-dom with them as masters—that's all they stand for. They don't even believe in God perhaps. Your suffering inquisitor is a mere fantasy."

"Stay, stay," laughed Ivan, "how hot you are! A fantasy you say, let it be so! Of course it's a fantasy. But allow me to say: do you really think that the Roman Catholic movement of the last centuries is actually nothing but the lust of power, of filthy earthly gain? Is that Father Païssy's teaching?"

"No, no, on the contrary, Father Païssy did once say something rather the same as you…but of course it's not the same, not a bit the same," Alyosha hastily corrected himself.

"A precious admission, in spite of your 'not a bit the same.' I ask you why your Jesuits and Inquisitors have united simply for vile material gain? Why can there not be among them one martyr oppressed by great sorrow and loving humanity? You see, only suppose that there was one such man among all those who desire nothing but filthy material gain—if there's only one like my old inquisitor, who had himself eaten roots in the desert and made frenzied efforts to subdue his flesh to make himself free and perfect. But yet all his life he loved humanity, and suddenly his eyes were opened, and he saw that it is no great moral blessedness to attain perfection and freedom, if at the same time one gains the conviction that millions of God's creatures have been created as a mockery, that they will never be capable of using their freedom, that these poor rebels can never turn into giants to complete the tower, that it was not for such geese that the great idealist dreamt his dream of harmony. Seeing all that he turned back and joined—the clever people. Surely that could have happened?"

"Joined whom, what clever people?" cried Alyosha, completely carried away. "They have no such great cleverness and no mysteries and secrets…. Perhaps nothing but Atheism, that's all their secret. Your inquisitor does not believe in God, that's his secret!"

"What if it is so! At last you have guessed it. It's perfectly true that that's the whole secret, but isn't that suffering, at least for a man like that, who has wasted his whole life in the desert and yet could not shake off his incurable love of humanity? In his old age he reached the clear conviction that nothing but the advice of the great dread spirit could build up any tolerable sort of life for the feeble, unruly 'incomplete, empirical creatures created in jest.' And so, convinced of this, he sees that he must follow the council of the wise spirit, the dread spirit of death and destruction, and therefore accept lying and deception, and lead men consciously to death and destruction, and yet deceive them all the way so that they may not notice where they are being led, that the poor blind creatures may at least on the way think themselves happy. And note, the deception is in the name of Him in Whose ideal the old man had so fervently believed all his life long. Is not that tragic? And if only one such stood at the head of the whole army 'filled with the lust of power only for the sake of filthy gain'—would not one such be enough to make a tragedy? More than that, one such standing at the head is enough to create the actual leading idea of the Roman Church with all its armies and Jesuits, its highest idea. I tell you frankly that I firmly believe that there has always been such a man among those who stood at the head of the movement. Who knows, there may have been some such even among the Roman Popes. Who knows, perhaps the spirit of that accursed old man who loves mankind so obstinately in his own way, is to be found even now in a whole multitude of such old men, existing not by chance but by agreement, as a secret league formed long ago for the guarding of the mystery, to guard it from the weak and the unhappy, so as to make them happy. No doubt it is so, and so it must be indeed. I fancy that even among the Masons there's something of the same mystery at the bottom, and that that's why the Catholics so detest the Masons as their rivals breaking up the unity of the idea, while it is so essential that there should be one flock and one shepherd.... But from the way I defend my idea I might be in author impatient of your criticism. Enough of it."

"You are perhaps a Mason yourself!" broke suddenly from Alyosha. "You don't believe in God," he added, speaking this time very sorrowfully. He fancied besides that his brother was looking at him ironically. "How does your poem end?" he asked, suddenly looking down. "Or was it the end?"

"I meant to end it like this. When the Inquisitor ceased speaking he waited some time for his Prisoner to answer him. His silence weighed down upon him. He saw that the Prisoner had listened intently all the time, looking gently in his face and evidently not wishing to reply. The old man longed for Him to say something, however bitter and terrible. But He suddenly approached the old man in silence and softly kissed him on his bloodless aged lips. That was all his answer. The old man shuddered. His lips moved. He went to the door, opened it, and said to Him: 'Go, and come no more...come not at all, never, never!' And he let Him out into the dark alleys of the town. The Prisoner went away."

"And the old man?"

"The kiss glows in his heart, but the old man adheres to his idea."

"And you with him, you too?" cried Alyosha, mournfully. Ivan laughed.

"Why, it's all nonsense, Alyosha. It's only a senseless poem of a senseless student, who could never write two lines of verse. Why do you take it so seriously? Surely you don't suppose I am going straight off to the Jesuits, to join the men who are correcting His work? Good Lord, it's no business of mine. I told you, all I want is to live on to thirty, and then...dash the cup to the ground!"

"But the little sticky leaves, and the precious tombs, and the blue sky, and the woman you love! How will you live, how will you love them?" Alyosha cried sorrowfully. "With such

a hell in your heart and your head, how can you? No, that's just what you are going away for, to join them...if not, you will kill yourself, you can't endure it!"

"There is a strength to endure everything," Ivan said with a cold smile.

"What strength?"

"The strength of the Karamazovs—the strength of the Karamazov baseness."

"To sink into debauchery, to stifle your soul with corruption, yes?"

"Possibly even that...only perhaps till I am thirty I shall escape it, and then."

"How will you escape it? By what will you escape it? That's impossible with your ideas."

"In the Karamazov way, again."

" 'Everything is lawful,' you mean? Everything is lawful, is that it?"

Ivan scowled, and all at once turned strangely pale.

"Ah, you've caught up yesterday's phrase, which so offended Miüsov—and which Dmitri pounced upon so naïvely and paraphrased!" he smiled queerly. "Yes, if you like, 'everything is lawful' since the word has been said. I won't deny it. And Mitya's version isn't bad."

Alyosha looked at him in silence.

"I thought that going away from here I have you at least," Ivan said suddenly, with unexpected feeling; "but now I see that there is no place for me even in your heart, my dear hermit. The formula, 'all is lawful,' I won't renounce—will you renounce me for that, yes?"

Alyosha got up, went to him and softly kissed him on the lips.

"That's plagiarism," cried Ivan, highly delighted. "You stole that from my poem. Thank you though. Get up, Alyosha, it's time we were going, both of us."

They went out, but stopped when they reached the entrance of the restaurant.

"Listen, Alyosha," Ivan began in a resolute voice, "if I am really able to care for the sticky little leaves I shall only love them, remembering you. It's enough for me that you are somewhere

here, and I shan't lose my desire for life yet. Is that enough for you? Take it as a declaration of love if you like. And now you go to the right and I to the left. And it's enough, do you hear, enough. I mean even if I don't go away to-morrow (I think I certainly shall go) and we meet again, don't say a word more on these subjects. I beg that particularly. And about Dmitri too, I ask you specially never speak to me again," he added, with sudden irritation; "it's all exhausted, it has all been said over and over again, hasn't it? And I'll make you one promise in return for it. When at thirty, I want to 'dash the cup to the ground,' wherever I may be I'll come to have one more talk with you, even though it were from America, you may be sure of that. I'll come on purpose. It will be very interesting to have a look at you, to see what you'll be by that time. It's rather a solemn promise, you see. And we really may be parting for seven years or ten. Come, go now to your Pater Seraphicus, he is dying. If he dies without you, you will be angry with me for having kept you. Good-bye, kiss me once more; that's right, now go."

Ivan turned suddenly and went his way without looking back. It was just as Dmitri had left Alyosha the day before, though the parting had been very different. The strange resemblance flashed like an arrow through Alyosha's mind in the distress and dejection of that moment. He waited a little, looking after his brother. He suddenly noticed that Ivan swayed as he walked and that his right shoulder looked lower than his left. He had never noticed it before. But all at once he turned too, and almost ran to the monastery. It was nearly dark, and he felt almost frightened; something new was growing up in him for which he could not account. The wind had risen again as on the previous evening, and the ancient pines murmured gloomily about him when he entered the hermitage copse. He almost ran. "Pater Seraphicus—he got that name from somewhere—where from?" Alyosha wondered. "Ivan, poor Ivan, and when shall I see you again?... Here is the hermitage. Yes, yes, that he is, Pater Seraphicus, he will save me—from him and for ever!"

Several times afterwards he wondered how he could on leaving Ivan so completely forget his brother Dmitri, though he had that morning, only a few hours before, so firmly resolved to find him and not to give up doing so, even should he be unable to return to the monastery that night.

Simone Weil

The Need for Roots

Simone Weil died at the age of 33, before any of her work was published. At the time she was working with the provisional French government in London during the Nazi occupation of France. A devout Christian who all her life tried to identify with the oppressed (she worked as a factory worker, as an unarmed soldier, and as a farm hand), she died because she refused to take more food than the official ration of ordinary people in France. She wrote The Need For Roots, from which the following piece is excerpted, in the context of the destruction of culture and community wrought by the Second World War. It was published in 1952.

What Weil calls "rootedness" is a "real, active and natural participation in the life of a community." She names three factors that sever people from their roots: colonialism, war, and money—the last two of which have assumed importance on an unprecedented scale in today's society. Aside from spreading destruction and greed, they have damaged our ability to even understand the importance of community. For Weil, "uprootedness" represents much more than an unwillingness to remain in the same city or town for a lifetime; it describes a condition in which people feel morally lost, psychologically disconnected from their homes and the people around them.

The sense of uprootedness is particularly intense in America, she argues, by the country's very nature: this is a land of immigrants. Weil argues that society needs to return to tradition and to develop a reverence for history. Education plays a major role in creating a sense of rootedness in one's community, especially education concerning one's past. Without an understanding of the past, we have nothing to give the future. Rather than focusing on contemporary popular culture, or preparing students for the job market, education needs to encourage an appreciation for tradition as the fundamental nourishment for the roots of community.

The Need for Roots
Simone Weil

Uprootedness

To be rooted is perhaps the most important and least recognized need of the human soul. It is one of the hardest to define. A human being has roots by virtue of his real, acti ve, and natural participation in the life of a community, which preserves in living shape certain particular treasures of the past and certain particular expectations for the future. This participation is a natural one, in the sense that it is automatically brought about by place, conditions of birth, profession, and social surroundings. Every human being needs to have multiple roots. It is necessary for him to draw well nigh the whole of his moral, intellectual, and spiritual life by way of the environment of which he forms a natural part.

Reciprocal exchanges by which different sorts of environment exert influence on one another are no less vital than to be rooted in natural surroundings. But a given environment should not receive an outside influence as something additional to itself, but as a stimulant intensifying its own particular way of life. It should draw nourishment from outside contributions only after having digested them, and the human beings who compose it should receive such contributions only from its hands. When a really talented painter walks into a picture gallery, his own originality is thereby confirmed. The same thing should apply to the various communities throughout the world and the different social environments.

Uprootedness occurs whenever there is a military conquest, and in this sense conquest is nearly always an evil. There is the minimum of uprootedness when the conquerors are migrants who settle down in the conquered country, intermarry with the inhabitants, and take root themselves. Such was the case with the Hellenes in Greece, the Celts in Gaul, and the Moors in Spain. But when the conqueror remains a stranger in the land of which he has tak-

---

en possession, uprootedness becomes an almost mortal disease among the subdued population. It reaches its most acute stage when there are deportations on a massive scale, as in Europe under the German occupation, or along the upper loop of the Niger, or where there is any brutal suppression of all local traditions, as in the French possessions in the Pacific (if Gauguin and Alain Gerbault are to be believed).

Even without a military conquest, money power and economic domination can so impose a foreign influence as actually to provoke this disease of uprootedness.

Finally, the social relations existing in any one country can be very dangerous factors in connection with uprootedness. In all parts of our country at the present time—and setting aside the question of the conquest—there are two poisons at work spreading this disease. One of them is money. Money destroys human roots wherever it is able to penetrate, by turning desire for gain into the sole motive. It easily manages to outweigh all other motives, because the effort it demands of the mind is so very much less. Nothing is so clear and so simple as a row of figures.

Uprootedness in the Towns

There are social conditions in which an absolute and continuous dependence on money prevails—those of the wage-earning class, especially now that work by the piece obliges each workman to have his attention continually taken up with the subject of his pay. It is in these social conditions that the disease of uprootedness is most acute. Bernanos has said that our workmen are not, after all, immigrants like those of Mr. Ford. The major social difficulty of our age proceeds from the fact that in a certain sense they *are* like them. Although they have remained geographically stationary, they have been morally uprooted, banished, and then reinstated, as it were on sufferance, in the form of industrial brawn. Unemployment is, of

course, an uprootedness raised to the second power. They are unable to feel themselves at home whether it be in the factories, their own dwellings, the parties and trade-unions ostensibly created on their behalf, places of amusement, or in intellectual activities if they attempt to acquire some culture.

For the second factor making for uprootedness is education as it is understood nowadays. The Renaissance everywhere brought about a break between people of culture and the mass of the population; but while abstracting culture from national tradition, it did at least cause it to be steeped in Greek tradition. Since then, links with the national traditions have not been renewed, but Greece has been forgotten. The result has been a culture which has developed in a very restricted medium, removed from the world, in a stovepipe atmosphere—a culture very strongly directed toward and influenced by technical science, very strongly tinged with pragmatism, extremely broken up by specialization, entirely deprived both of contact with this world and, at the same time, of any window opening onto the world beyond.

Nowadays a man can belong to so-called cultured circles without, on the one hand, having any sort of conception about human destiny or, on the other hand, being aware, for example, that all the constellations are not visible at all seasons of the year. A lot of people think that a little peasant boy of the present day who goes to primary school knows more than Pythagoras did, simply because he can repeat parrotwise that the earth moves round the sun. In actual fact, he no longer looks up at the heavens. This sun about which they talk to him in class hasn't, for him, the slightest connection with the one he can see. He is severed from the universe surrounding him, just as little Polynesians are severed from their past by being forced to repeat, "Our ancestors, the Gauls, had fair hair."

What is called today educating the masses is taking this modern culture, evolved in such a closed, unwholesome atmosphere, and one so indifferent to the truth, removing whatever it may still contain of intrinsic merit—an operation known as popularization—and shoveling the residue as it stands into the minds of the unfortunate individuals desirous of learning, in the same way as you feed birds with a stick.

Moreover, the desire to learn for the sake of learning, the desire for truth has become very rare. The prestige of culture has become almost exclusively a social one, as much for the peasant who dreams of having a schoolteacher son, or the schoolteacher who dreams of having a son at the *Ecole Normale Supérieure**, as for the society people who fawn upon savants and well-known writers.

The youth of our schools are as much obsessed by their examinations as our workmen engaged in piecework are by their pay checks. There is something woefully wrong with the health of a social system, when a peasant tills the soil with the feeling that, if he is a peasant, it is because he wasn't intelligent enough to become a schoolteacher.

The mixture of confused and more or less false ideas known under the name of Marxism—a mixture to which, since Marx's day, it is, generally speaking, only very ordinary middle-class intellectuals who have contributed—is also for the working class a completely outlandish doctrine, which they are incapable of assimilating, and which is, besides, devoid of any nutritive value, for it has been emptied of nearly all the truth contained in Marx's writings. From time to time, a scientific presentation for popular consumption is added. The effect of all this can only be to bring about the most intense uprootedness among the working class.

Uprootedness is by far the most dangerous malady to which human societies are exposed, for it is a self-propagating one. For people who are really uprooted there remain only two possible sorts of behavior: either to fall into a spiritual lethargy resembling death, like the majority of the slaves in the days of the Roman Empire, or to hurl themselves into some form of activity necessarily designed to uproot, often by the most violent methods, those who are not yet uprooted, or only partly so.

The Romans were a handful of fugitives who banded themselves together artificially to form a city, and deprived the Mediterranean peoples of their individual manner of life, their country, traditions, past history to such an extent that posterity has taken them, at their own valuation, for the founders of civilization in these conquered territories. The Hebrews were escaped slaves, and they either exterminated or reduced to servitude all the peoples of Palestine. The Germans, at the time Hitler assumed command over them, were really—as he was never tired of repeating—a nation of proletarians, that is to say, uprooted individuals. The humiliation of 1918, inflation, overindustrialization, and above all the extreme gravity of the unemployment crisis had infected them with the moral disease to the acute point where irresponsibility takes possession. The Spaniards and Englishmen, who, from the sixteenth century onward, massacred or enslaved colored peoples, were adventurers almost without any contact with the fundamental life of their own respective countries. The same may be said in regard to a part of the French Empire, which moreover was built up at a time when the French tradition was suffering from a decline. Whoever is uprooted himself uproots others. Whoever is rooted in himself doesn't uproot others.

Under the same name of revolution, and often using identical slogans and subjects for propaganda, lie concealed two conceptions entirely opposed to one another. One consists in transforming society in such a way that the working class may be given roots in it; while the other

* *Ecole Normale Supérieure*, situated rue d'Ulm in Paris. Institution created by the Convention in 1794, reorganized under the Empire in 1808. Its object is to form an *élite* of teachers for secondary schools, and, in practice, teachers for all the higher branches of education are drawn from it.[Translator.]

consists in spreading to the whole of society the disease of uprootedness, which has been inflicted on the working class. It must not be said or supposed that the second operation can ever form a prelude to the first; that is false. They are two opposite roads which do not meet.

The second conception is nowadays much more frequently met with than the first both among militants and among the mass of the workers. It is obvious that it tends more and more to gain ground in proportion as uprootedness continues and increases its ravages. It can easily be realized that, from one day to another, the harm may become irreparable.

On the conservative side, a similar ambiguity prevails. A few really want the workers to become rooted again; only this desire of theirs is accompanied by imaginary pictures most of which, instead of having reference to the future, are borrowed from a past which is, moreover, partly fictitious. The rest want purely and simply to see maintained or reinforced that category of human material to which the proletariat has been reduced.

Thus those who really desire the good—and they are not very numerous—weaken their position still further by distributing themselves among two hostile camps with which they have nothing in common.

The sudden collapse of France in June, 1940, which surprised every one all over the world, simply showed to what extent the country was uprooted. A tree whose roots are almost entirely eaten away falls at the first blow. If France offered a spectacle more painful than that of any other European country, it is because modern civilization with all its toxins was in a more advanced stage there than elsewhere, with the exception of Germany. But in Germany, uprootedness had taken on an aggressive form, whereas in France it was characterized by inertia and stupor. The difference is due to more or less hidden causes, some of which could no doubt be discovered were one to undertake the necessary search. On the other hand, the country which in face of the first wave of German terror behaved far and away the best was the one where tradition is strongest and most carefully nurtured, that is to say England....

As for the American continent, since its population has for several centuries been founded above all on immigration, the dominating influence which it will probably exercise greatly increases the danger.

In this almost desperate situation, all we can look to for encouragement here below is in those historical atolls of the living past left upon the surface of the earth. Not that we should approve the fuss started by Mussolini over the Roman Empire, or try to make use of Louis XIV for the same sort of purpose. Conquests are not of life, they are of death at the very moment they take place. It is the distillations from the living past that should be jealously preserved, everywhere, whether it be in Paris or Tahiti, for there are not too many such on the entire globe.

It would be useless to turn one's back on the past in order simply to concentrate on the future. It is a dangerous illusion to believe that such a thing is even possible. The opposition of future to past or past to future is absurd. The future brings us nothing, gives us nothing; it is we who in order to build it have to give it everything, our very life. But to be able to give, one has to possess; and we possess no other life, no other living sap, than the treasures stored up from the past and digested, assimilated, and created afresh by us. Of all the human soul's needs, none is more vital than this one of the past....

For several centuries now, men of the white race have everywhere destroyed the past, stupidly, blindly, both at home and abroad. If in certain respects there has been, nevertheless, real progress during this period, it is not because of this frenzy, but in spite of it, under the impulse of what little of the past remained alive.

The past once destroyed never returns. The destruction of the past is perhaps the greatest of all crimes. Today the preservation of what little of it remains ought to become almost an obsession. We must put an end to the terrible uprootedness which European colonial methods always produce, even under their least cruel aspects. We must abstain, once victory is ours, from punishing the conquered enemy by uprooting him still further; seeing that it is neither possible nor desirable to exterminate him, to aggravate his lunacy would be to show oneself more of a lunatic than he. We must also keep, above all, well to the fore in any political, legal, or technical innovations likely to have social repercussions, some arrangement whereby human beings may once more be able to recover their roots.

William James

The Moral Equivalent of War

William James (1842–1910), the great pragmatist philosopher and psychologist best known for his works *The Meaning of Truth and The Varieties of Religious Experience,* wrote this short essay at the end of his life. It was shortly before World War I, when combat was still relatively unmechanized and personal, and the numbing and anonymous slaughter of the "Great War" had not yet occurred.

James was a pacifist, but was fascinated by the power of military life and of war itself to foster values that he thought were essential to a democratic society: patriotism, a sense of service, fellowship, community, honor, and physical toughness. He abjorred the costs of war in brutalization and human life but recognized its impact on moral character. James worried that the "utopians" (the socialists, pacifists, and idealists who aspired to forge a perfect society without injustice or poverty or war) risked making women and men soft and selfish. The soldier is tougher, more altruistic, and has a more rewarding sense of membership in a community than ordinary people engaged in business and private life; indeed, the soldier may have the very qualities that "idealists" lack, the qualities needed to create a more ideal society.

James ended up recommending a form of national citizen service—something the New Deal Administration actually tried in the 1930s with the Civilian Conservation Corps (See Part III, Section B). He thought such a program could capture the exhilarating feeling of fraternity and service that comes with war without its devastation.

The Moral Equivalent of War

William James

The war against war is going to be no
holiday excursion or camping party.
The military feelings are too deeply
grounded to abdicate their place among our
ideals until better substitutes are offered than
the glory and shame that come to nations as
well as to individuals from the ups and downs
of politics and the vicissitudes of trade. There
is something highly paradoxical in the modern
man's relation to war. Ask all our millions,
north and south, whether they would vote now
(were such a thing possible) to have our war for
the Union expunged from history, and the record of a peaceful transition to the present time
substituted for that of its marches and battles,
and probably hardly a handful of eccentrics
would say yes. Those ancestors, those efforts,
those memories and legends, are the most ideal
part of what we now own together, a sacred
spiritual possession worth more than all the
blood poured out. Yet ask those same people
whether they would be willing in cold blood
to start another civil war now to gain another
similar possession, and not one man or woman
would vote for the proposition. In modern eyes,
precious though wars may be, they must not be
waged solely for the sake of the ideal harvest.
Only when forced upon one, only when an
enemy's injustice leaves us no alternative, is a
war now thought permissible.

It was not thus in ancient times. The earlier
men were hunting men, and to hunt a neighboring tribe, kill the males, loot the village and
possess the females, was the most profitable, as
well as the most exciting, way of living. Thus
were the more martial tribes selected, and in
chiefs and peoples a pure pugnacity and love of
glory came to mingle with the more fundamental appetite for plunder.

Modern war is so expensive that we feel
trade to be a better avenue to plunder; but
modern man inherits all the innate pugnacity
and all the love of glory of his ancestors. Showing war's irrationality and horror is of no effect
upon him. The horrors make the fascination.
War is the *strong* life; it is life *in extremis*; war-
taxes are the only ones men never hesitate to
pay, as the budgets of all nations show us.

History is a bath of blood. The Iliad is one long recital of how Diomedes and Ajax, Sarpedon and Hector *killed*. No detail of the wounds they made is spared us, and the Greek mind fed upon the story. Greek history is a panorama of jingoism and imperialism—war for war's sake, all the citizens being warriors. It is horrible reading, because of the irrationality of it all—save for the purpose of making "history"—and the history is that of the utter ruin of a civilization in intellectual respects perhaps the highest the earth has ever seen.

Those wars were purely piratical. Pride, gold, women, slaves, excitement, were their only motives. In the Peloponnesian war for example, the Athenians ask the inhabitants of Melos (the island where the "Venus of Milo" was found), hitherto neutral, to own their lordship. The envoys meet, and hold a debate which Thucydides gives in full, and which, for sweet reasonableness of form, would have satisfied Matthew Arnold. "The powerful exact what they can," said the Athenians, "and the weak grant what they must." When the Meleans say that sooner than be slaves they will appeal to the gods, the Athenians reply: "Of the gods we believe and of men we know that, by a law of their nature, wherever they can rule they will. This law was not made by us, and we are not the first to have acted upon it; we did but inherit it, and we know that you and all mankind, if you were as strong as we are, would do as we do. So much for the gods; we have told you why we expect to stand as high in their opinion as you." Well, the Meleans still refused, and their town was taken. "The Athenians," Thucydides quietly says, "thereupon put to death all who were of military age and made slaves of the women and children. They then colonized the island, sending thither five hundred settlers of their own."

Alexander's career was piracy pure and simple, nothing but an orgy of power and plunder, made romantic by the character of the hero. There was no rational principle in it, and the moment he died his generals and governors attacked one another. The cruelty of those times is incredible. When Rome finally conquered Greece, Paulus Æmilius was told by the Roman Senate to reward his soldiers for their toil by "giving" them the old kingdom of Epirus. They sacked seventy cities and carried off a hundred and fifty thousand inhabitants as slaves. How many they killed I know not; but in Etolia they killed all the senators, five hundred and fifty in number. Brutus was "the noblest Roman of them all," but to reanimate his soldiers on the eve of Philippi he similarly promises to give them the cities of Sparta and Thessalonica to ravage, if they win the fight.

Such was the gory nurse that trained societies to cohesiveness. We inherit the warlike type; and for most of the capacities of heroism that the human race is full of we have to thank this cruel history. Dead men tell no tales, and if there were any tribes of other type than this they have left no survivors. Our ancestors have bred pugnacity into our bone and marrow, and thousands of years of peace won't breed it out of us. The popular imagination fairly fattens on the thought of wars. Let public opinion once reach a certain fighting pitch, and no ruler can withstand it. In the Boer war both governments began with bluff but couldn't stay there, the military tension was too much for them. In 1898 our people had read the word "war" in letters three inches high for three months in every newspaper. The pliant politician McKinley was swept away by their eagerness, and our squalid war with Spain became a necessity.

At the present day, civilized opinion is a curious mental mixture. The military instincts and ideals are as strong as ever, but are confronted by reflective criticisms which sorely curb their ancient freedom. Innumerable writers are showing up the bestial side of military service. Pure loot and mastery seem no longer morally avowable motives, and pretexts must be found for attributing them solely to the enemy. England and we, our army and navy authorities repeat without ceasing, arm solely for peace, Germany and Japan it is who are bent on loot and glory. "Peace" in military mouths to-day is a synonym for "war expected." The word has become a pure provocative, and no government wishing peace sincerely should allow it ever to be printed in a newspaper. Every up-to date dictionary should say that "peace" and "war" mean the same thing, now *in posse*, now *in actu*. It may even reasonably be said that the intensely sharp competitive *preparation* for war by the nations i*s the real war*, permanent, unceasing; and that the battles are only a sort of public verification of the mastery gained during the "peace" interval.

It is plain that on this subject civilized man has developed a sort of double personality. If we take European nations, no legitimate interest of any one of them would seem to justify the tremendous destructions which a war to compass it would necessarily entail. It would seem as though common sense and reason ought to find a way to reach agreement in every conflict of honest interests. I myself think it our bounden duty to believe in such international rationality as possible. But, as things stand, I see how desperately hard it is to bring the peace-party and the war-party together, and I believe that the difficulty is due to certain deficiencies in the program of pacificism which set the militarist imagination strongly, and to a certain extent justifiably, against it. In the whole discussion both sides are on imaginative and sentimental ground. It is but one utopia against another, and everything one says must be abstract and hypothetical. Subject to this criticism and caution, I will try to characterize in abstract strokes the opposite imaginative forces, and point out what to my own very fallible mind seems the best utopian hypothesis, the most promising line of conciliation.

In my remarks, pacificist though I am, I will refuse to speak of the bestial side of the war-*régime* (already done justice to by many writers) and consider only the higher aspects of militaristic sentiment. Patriotism no one thinks discreditable; nor does any one deny that war is the romance of history. But inordinate ambitions are the soul of every patriotism, and the possibility of violent death the soul of all romance. The militarily patriotic and romantic-minded everywhere, and especially the professional military class, refuse to admit for a moment that war may be a transitory phenomenon in social evolution. The notion of a sheep's paradise like that revolts, they say, our higher imagination. Where then would be the steeps of life? If war had ever stopped, we should have to re-invent it, on this view, to redeem life from flat degeneration.

Reflective apologists for war at the present day all take it religiously. It is a sort of sacrament. Its profits are to the vanquished as well as to the victor; and quite apart from any question of profit, it is an absolute good, we are told, for it is human nature at its highest dynamic. Its "horrors" are a cheap price to pay for rescue from the only alternative supposed, of a world of clerks and teachers, of coeducation and zoophily, of "consumer's leagues" and "associated charities," of industrialism unlimited, and femininism unabashed. No scorn, no hardness, no valor any more! Fie upon such a cattleyard of a planet!

So far as the central essence of this feeling goes, no healthy minded person, it seems to me, can help to some degree partaking of it. Militarism is the great preserver of our ideals of hardihood, and human life with no use for hardihood would be contemptible. Without risks or prizes for the darer, history would be insipid indeed; and there is a type of military character which every one feels that the race should never cease to breed, for every one is sensitive to its superiority. The duty is incumbent on mankind, of keeping military characters in stock—of keeping them, if not for use, then as ends in themselves and as pure pieces of perfection,—so that Roosevelt's weaklings and mollycoddles may not end by making everything else disappear from the face of nature.

This natural sort of feeling forms, I think, the innermost soul of army-writings. Without any exception known to me, militarist authors take a highly mystical view of their subject, and regard war as a biological or sociological necessity, uncontrolled by ordinary psychological checks and motives. When the time of development is ripe the war must come, reason or no reason, for the justifications pleaded are invariably fictitious. War is, in short, a permanent human *obligation*. General Homer Lea, in his recent book "The Valor of Ignorance," plants himself squarely on this ground. Readiness for war is for him the essence of nationality, and ability in it the supreme measure of the health of nations.

Nations, General Lea says, are never stationary—they must necessarily expand or shrink, according to their vitality or decrepitude. Japan now is culminating; and by the fatal law in question it is impossible that her statesmen should not long since have entered, with extraordinary foresight, upon a vast policy of conquest—the game in which the first moves were her wars with China and Russia and her treaty with England, and of which the final objective is the capture of the Philippines, the Hawaiian Islands, Alaska, and the whole of our Coast west of the Sierra Passes. This will give Japan what her ineluctable vocation as a state absolutely forces her to claim, the possession of the entire Pacific Ocean; and to oppose these deep designs we Americans have, according to our author, nothing but our conceit, our ignorance, our commercialism, our corruption, and our feminism. General Lea makes a minute technical comparison of the military strength which we at present could oppose to the strength of Japan, and concludes that the islands, Alaska, Oregon, and Southern California, would fall almost without resistance, that San Francisco must surrender in a fortnight to a Japanese investment, that in three or four months the war would be over, and our republic, unable to regain what it had heedlessly neglected to protect sufficiently, would then "disintegrate," until perhaps some Cæsar should arise to weld us again into a nation.

A dismal forecast indeed! Yet not unplausible, if the mentality of Japan's statesmen be of the Cæsarian type of which history shows so many examples, and which is all that General Lea seems able to imagine. But there is no reason to think that women can no longer be the mothers of Napoleonic or Alexandrian characters; and if these come in Japan and find their opportunity, just such surprises as "The Valor of Ignorance" paints may lurk in ambush for us. Ignorant as we still are of the innermost recesses of Japanese mentality, we may be foolhardy to disregard such possibilities.

Other militarists are more complex and more moral in their considerations. The "Philosophie des Krieges," by S. R. Steinmetz is a good example. War, according to this author, is an ordeal instituted by God, who weighs the nations in its balance. It is the essential form of the State, and the only function in which peoples can employ all their powers at once and convergently. No victory is possible save as the resultant of a totality of virtues, no defeat for which some vice or weakness is not responsible. Fidelity, cohesiveness, tenacity, heroism, conscience, education, inventiveness, economy, wealth, physical health and vigor—there isn't a moral or intellectual point of superiority that doesn't tell, when God holds his assizes and hurls the peoples upon one another. *Die Weltgeschichte ist das Weltgericht*; and Dr. Steinmetz does not believe that in the long run chance and luck play any part in apportioning the issues.

The virtues that prevail, it must be noted, are virtues anyhow, superiorities that count in peaceful as well as in military competition; but the strain on them, being infinitely intenser in the latter case, makes war infinitely more searching as a trial. No ordeal is comparable to its winnowings. Its dread hammer is the welder of men into cohesive states, and nowhere but in such states can human nature adequately develop its capacity. The only alternative is "degeneration."

Dr. Steinmetz is a conscientious thinker, and his book, short as it is, takes much into account. Its upshot can, it seems to me, be summed up in Simon Patten's word, that mankind was nursed in pain and fear, and that the transition to a "pleasure-economy" may be fatal to a being wielding no powers of defence against its disintegrative influences. If we speak of the *fear of emancipation from the fear-régime*, we put the whole situation into a single phrase; fear regarding ourselves now taking the place of the ancient fear of the enemy.

Turn the fear over as I will in my mind, it all seems to lead back to two unwillingnesses of the imagination, one aesthetic, and the other moral; unwillingness, first to envisage a future in which army-life, with its many elements of charm, shall be forever impossible, and in which the destinies of peoples shall nevermore be decided quickly, thrillingly, and tragically, by force, but only gradually and insipidly by "evolution"; and, secondly, unwillingness to see the supreme theatre of human strenuousness closed, and the splendid military aptitudes of men doomed to keep always in a state of latency and never show themselves in action. These insistent unwillingnesses, no less than other æsthetic and ethical insistencies, have, it seems to me, to be listened to and respected. One cannot meet them effectively by mere counter-insistency on war's expensiveness and horror. The horror makes the thrill; and when the question is of getting the extremist and supremest out of human nature, talk of expense sounds ignominious. The weakness of so much merely negative criticism is evident — pacificism makes no converts from the military party. The military party denies neither the bestiality nor the horror, nor the expense; it only says that these things tell but half the story. It only says that war is *worth* them; that, taking human nature as a whole, its wars are its best protection against its weaker and more cowardly self, and that mankind cannot *afford* to adopt a peace-economy.

Pacificists ought to enter more deeply into the aesthetical and ethical point of view of their opponents. Do that first in any controversy, says J. J. Chapman, *then move the point*, and your opponent will follow. So long as anti-militarists propose no substitute for war's disciplinary function, no *moral equivalent* of war, analogous, as one might say, to the mechanical equivalent of heat, so long they fail to realize the full inwardness of the situation. And as a rule they do fail. The duties, penalties, and sanctions pictured in the utopias they paint are all too weak and tame to touch the military-minded. Tolstoï's pacificism is the only exception to this rule, for it is profoundly pessimistic as regards all this world's values, and makes the fear of the Lord furnish the moral spur provided elsewhere by the fear of the enemy. But our socialistic peace-advocates all believe absolutely in this world's values; and instead of the fear of the Lord and the fear of the enemy, the only fear they reckon with is the fear of poverty if one be lazy. This weakness pervades all the socialistic literature with which I am acquainted. Even in Lowes Dickinson's exquisite dialogue, high wages and short hours are the only forces invoked for overcoming man's distaste for repulsive kinds of labor. Meanwhile men at large still live as they always have lived, under a pain-and-fear economy — for those of us who live in an ease-economy are but an island in the stormy ocean — and the whole atmosphere of present-day utopian literature tastes mawkish and dishwatery to people who still keep a sense for life's more bitter flavors. It suggests, in truth, ubiquitous inferiority.

Inferiority is always with us, and merciless scorn of it is the keynote of the military temper. "Dogs, would you live forever?" shouted Frederick the Great. "Yes," say our utopians, "let us live forever, and raise our level gradually." The best thing about our "inferiors" to-day is that they are as tough as nails, and physically and morally almost as insensitive. Utopianism would see them soft and squeamish, while militarism would keep their callousness, but transfigure it into a meritorious characteristic, needed by "the service," and redeemed by that from the suspicion of inferiority. All the qualities of a man acquire dignity when he knows that the service of the collectivity that owns him needs them. If proud of the collectivity, his own pride rises in proportion. No collectivity is like an army for nourishing such pride; but it has to be confessed that the only sentiment which the image of pacific cosmopolitan industrialism is capable of arousing in countless worthy breasts is shame at the idea of belonging to *such* a collectivity. It is obvious that the United States of America as they exist to-day impress a mind like General Lea's as so much human blubber. Where is the sharpness and precipitousness, the contempt for life, whether one's own, or another's? Where is the savage "yes" and "no," the unconditional duty? Where is the conscription? Where is the blood-tax? Where is anything that one feels honored by belonging to?

Having said thus much in preparation, I will now confess my own utopia. I devoutly believe in the reign of peace and in the gradual advent of some sort of a socialistic equilibrium. The fatalistic view of the war-function is to me nonsense, for I know that war-making is due to definite motives and subject to prudential checks and reasonable criticisms, just like any other form of enterprise. And when whole nations are the armies, and the science of destruction vies in intellectual refinement with the sciences of production, I see that war becomes absurd and impossible from its own monstrosity. Extravagant ambitions will have to be replaced by reasonable claims, and nations must make common cause against them. I see no reason why all this should not apply to yellow as well as to white countries, and I look forward to a future when acts of war shall be formally outlawed as between civilized peoples.

All these beliefs of mine put me squarely into the anti-militarist party. But I do not believe that peace either ought to be or will be permanent on this globe, unless the states pacifically organized preserve some of the old elements of army-discipline. A permanently successful peace-economy cannot be a simple pleasure-economy. In the more or less socialistic future towards which mankind seems drifting we must still subject ourselves collectively to those severities which answer to our real position upon this only partly hospitable globe. We must make new energies and hardihoods continue the manliness to which the military mind so faithfully clings. Martial virtues must be the enduring cement; intrepidity, contempt of softness, surrender of private interest, obedience to command, must still remain the rock upon which states are built—unless, indeed, we wish for dangerous reactions against commonwealths fit only for contempt, and liable to invite attack whenever a centre of crystallization for military-minded enterprise gets formed anywhere in their neighborhood.

The war-party is assuredly right in affirming and reaffirming that the martial virtues, although originally gained by the race through war, are absolute and permanent human goods. Patriotic price and ambition in their military form are, after all, only specifications of a more general competitive passion. They are its first form, but that is no reason for supposing them to be its last form. Men now are proud of belonging to a conquering nation, and without a murmur they lay down their persons and their wealth, if by so doing they may fend off subjection. But who can be sure that *other aspects of one's country* may not, with time and education and suggestion enough, come to be regarded with similarly effective feelings of pride and shame? Why should men not some day feel that it is worth a blood-tax to belong to a collectivity superior in *any* ideal respect? Why should they not blush with indignant shame if the community that owns them is vile in any way whatsoever? Individuals, daily more numerous, now feel this civic passion. It is only a question of blowing on the spark till the whole population gets incandescent, and on the ruins of the old morals of military honor, a stable system of morals of civic honor builds itself up. What the whole community comes to believe in grasps the individual as in a vise. The war-function has grasped us so far; but constructive interests may some day seem no less imperative, and impose on the individual a hardly lighter burden.

Let me illustrate my idea more concretely. There is nothing to make one indignant in the mere fact that life is hard, that men should toil and suffer pain. The planetary conditions once for all are such, and we can stand it. But that so many men, by mere accidents of birth and opportunity, should have a life of *nothing else* but toil and pain and hardness and inferiority imposed upon them, should have *no* vacation, while others natively no more deserving never get any taste of this campaigning life at all—*this* is capable of arousing indignation in reflective minds. It may end by seeming shameful to all of us that some of us have nothing but campaigning, and others nothing but unmanly ease. If now—and this is my idea—there were, instead of military conscription, a conscription of the whole youthful population to form for a certain number of years a part of the army enlisted against *Nature*, the injustice would tend to be evened out, and numerous other goods to the commonwealth would follow. The military ideals of hardihood and discipline would be wrought into the growing fibre of the people; no one would remain blind as the luxurious classes now are blind, to man's relations to the globe he lives on, and to the permanently sour and hard foundations of his higher life. To coal and iron mines, to freight trains, to fishing fleets in December, to dish-washing, clothes-washing, and window-washing, to road-building and tunnel-making, to foundries and stoke-holes, and to the frames of sky-scrapers, would our gilded youths be drafted off, according to their choice, to get the childishness knocked out of them, and to come back into society with healthier sympathies and soberer ideas. They would have paid their blood-tax, done their own part in the immemorial human warfare against nature; they would tread the earth more proudly, the women would value them more highly, they would be better fathers and teachers of the following generation.

Such a conscription, with the state of public opinion that would have required it, and the many moral fruits it would bear, would preserve in the midst of a pacific civilization the manly virtues which the military party is so afraid of seeing disappear in peace. We should get toughness without callousness, authority with as little criminal cruelty as possible, and painful work done cheerily because the duty is temporary, and threatens not, as now, to degrade the whole remainder of one's life. I spoke of the "moral equivalent" of war. So far, war has been the only force that can discipline a whole community, and until an equivalent discipline is organized, I believe that war must have its way. But I have no serious doubt that the ordinary prides and shames of social man, once developed to a certain intensity, are capable of organizing such a moral equivalent as I have sketched, or some other just as effective for preserving manliness of type. It is but a question of time, of skilful propagandism, and of opinion-making men seizing historic opportunities.

The martial type of character can be bred without war. Strenuous honor and disinterestedness abound elsewhere. Priests and medical men are in a fashion educated to it, and we should all feel some degree of it imperative if we were conscious of our work as an obligatory service to the state. We should be *owned*, as soldiers are by the army, and our pride would rise accordingly. We could be poor, then, without humiliation, as army officers now are. The only thing needed henceforward is to inflame the civic temper as past history has inflamed the military temper. H. G. Wells, as usual, sees the centre of the situation. "In many ways," he says, "military organization is the most peaceful of activities. When the contemporary man steps from the street, of clamorous insincere advertisement, push, adulteration, underselling and intermittent employment into the barrack-yard, he steps on to a higher social plane, into an atmosphere of service and cooperation and of infinitely more honorable emulations. Here at least men are not flung out of employment to degenerate because there is no immediate work for them to do. They are fed and drilled and trained for better services. Here at least a man is supposed to win promotion by self-forgetfulness and not by self-seeking. And beside the feeble and irregular endowment of research by commercialism, its little short-sighted snatches at profit by innovation and scientific economy, see how remarkable is the steady and rapid development of method and appliances in naval and military affairs! Nothing is more striking than to compare the progress of civil conveniences which has been left almost entirely to the trader, to the progress in military apparatus during the last few decades. The house-appliances of to-day for example, are little better than they were fifty years ago. A house of to-day is still almost as ill-ventilated, badly heated by wasteful fires, clumsily arranged and furnished as the house of 1858. Houses a couple of hundred years old are still satisfactory places of residence, so little have our standards risen. But the rifle or battleship of fifty years ago was beyond all comparison inferior to those we possess; in power, in speed, in convenience alike. No one has a use now for such superannuated things."

Wells adds that he thinks that the conceptions of order and discipline, the tradition of service and devotion, of physical fitness, unstinted exertion, and universal responsibility, which universal military duty is now teaching European nations, will remain a permanent acquisition, when the last ammunition has been used in the fireworks that celebrate the final peace. I believe as he does. It would be simply preposterous if the only force that could work ideals of honor and standards of efficiency into English or American natures should be the fear of being killed by the Germans or the Japanese. Great indeed is Fear; but it is not, as our military enthusiasts believe and try to make us believe, the only stimulus known for awakening the higher ranges of men's spiritual energy. The amount of alteration in public opinion which my utopia postulates is vastly less than the difference between the mentality of those black warriors who pursued Stanley's party on the Congo with their cannibal war-cry of "Meat! Meat!" and that of the "general-staff" of any civilized nation. History has seen the latter interval bridged over: the former one can be bridged over much more easily.

Robert Bellah

Habits of the Heart

Beginning in 1979, Robert Bellah and his associates Richard Madsen, William Sullivan, Ann Swidler, and Steven Tipton began a lengthy, interdisciplinary study of how contemporary Americans understand and define the nature of the good life, how we answer the questions, "Who are we?" and "How ought we to live?" The study interviewed 200 people over the next five years, and the findings and interpretations of these interviews, which draw on the fields of sociology, history, religion, philosophy, and social theory, were published in 1985. The title of the book, from which the following excerpts come, is taken from Alexis de Tocqueville's study of *Democracy in America* 150 years earlier (see excerpts in Part II, Section B and Part III, Section B). Tocqueville used the term "habits of the heart" to describe the mores and values he found on his journey across the United States.

In their interviews, Bellah and his associates found this paradox: American society is more interdependent than ever, and shares a common life to a greater extent than ever before; but instead of encouraging community and commitment to others around us, it encourages each citizen to retreat from community—to privatize our existence and make our life a "small world of its own." Tocqueville predicted that "individualism" could be the undoing of the United States. *Habits of the Heart* follows up on Tocqueville's critique of individualism, warning that by abandoning the sense of community.that comes from our biblical and republican traditions, Americans will lose "the language needed to make moral sense of their life."

Habits of the Heart
Robert Bellah

How ought we to live? How do we think about how to live? Who are we, as Americans? What is our character? These are questions we have asked our fellow citizens in many parts of the country. We engaged them in conversations about their lives and about what matters most to them, talked about their families and communities, their doubts and uncertainties, and their hopes and fears with respect to the larger society. We found them eager to discuss the right way to live, what to teach our children, and what our public and private responsibilities should be, but also a little dismayed by these subjects. These are important matters to those to whom we talked, and yet concern about moral questions is often relegated to the realm of private anxiety, as if it would be awkward or embarrassing to make it public. We hope this book will help transform this inner moral debate, often shared only with intimates, into public discourse. In these pages, Americans speak with us, and, indirectly, with one another, about issues that deeply concern us all. As we will see, many doubt that we have enough in common to be able mutually to discuss our central aspirations and fears. It is one of our purposes to persuade them that we do.

The fundamental question we posed, and that was repeatedly posed to us, was how to preserve or create a morally coherent life. But the kind of life we want depends on the kind of people we are—on our character. Our inquiry can thus be located in a long-standing discussion of the relationship between character and society. In the eighth book of the *Republic*, Plato sketched a theory of the relationship between the moral character of a people and the nature of its political community, the way it organizes and governs itself. The founders of the American republic at the time of the Revolution adopted a much later version of the same theory. Since for them, as for the Americans with whom we talked, freedom was perhaps the most important value, they were particularly concerned with the qualities of character necessary for the creation of a free republic.

In the 1830s, the French social philosopher Alexis de Tocqueville offered the most comprehensive and penetrating analysis of the relationship between character and society in America that has ever been written. In his book *Democracy in America*, based on acute observation and wide conversation with Americans, Tocqueville described the mores—which he on occasion called "habits of the heart"—of the American people and showed how they helped to form American character. He singled out family life, our religious traditions, and our participation in local politics as helping to create the type of person who could sustain a connection to a wider political community and thus ultimately support the maintenance of free institutions. He also warned that some aspects of our character—what he was one of the first to call "individualism"—might eventually isolate Americans one from another and thereby undermine the condition of freedom.

The central problem of our book concerns the American individualism that Tocqueville described with a mixture of admiration and anxiety. It seems to us that it is individualism, and not equality, as Tocqueville thought, that has marched inexorably through our history. We are concerned that this individualism may have grown cancerous—that it may be destroying those social integuments that Tocqueville saw as moderating its more destructive potentialities, that it may be threatening the survival of freedom itself. We want to know what individualism in America looks and feels like, and how the world appears in its light.

We are also interested in those cultural traditions and practices that, without destroying individuality, serve to limit and restrain the destructive side of individualism and provide alternative models for how Americans might live. We want to know how these have fared since Tocqueville's day, and how likely their renewal is.

While we focus on what people say, we are acutely aware that they often live in ways they cannot put into words. It is particularly here, in the tension between how we live and what our culture allows us to say, that we have found both some of our richest insights into the dilemmas our society faces and hope for the reappropriation of a common language in which those dilemmas can be discussed.

Taking our clue from Tocqueville, we believe that one of the keys to the survival of free institutions is the relationship between private and public life, the way in which citizens do, or do not, participate in the public sphere. We therefore decided to concentrate our research on how private and public life work in the United States: the extent to which private life either prepares people to take part in the public world or encourages them to find meaning exclusively in the private sphere, and the degree to which public life fulfills our private aspirations or discourages us so much that we withdraw from involvement in it....

The Entrepreneur

The citizen perceived by Tocqueville was indeed closer to being an individual "shut up in the solitude of his own heart" than earlier Americans of religious and republican stripe had been. Yet he was a considerably less isolated and self-regarding figure than the entrepreneurs of the Gilded Age of the late nineteenth-century or the bureaucratic managers and therapists of the twentieth.

Tocqueville voiced great misgivings about two phenomena that he thought threatened the moral balance of Jacksonian democracy. One was the slave society of the South, which not only treated blacks inhumanely but, as Tocqueville, like Jefferson, noted, degraded whites as well. The second danger lay in the industrial system, which first made its appearance in the Northeast. Factories had concentrated great numbers of poor and dependent workers, often women and immigrants, into rapidly growing mill towns, and Tocqueville feared the rise of a new form of aristocracy that would make owners and managers into petty despots and reduce workers to mechanically organized, dependent operatives, a condition incompatible with full democratic citizenship. Just as the plantation system subordinated the yeoman farmer in the South, so the spread of industrial organization both concentrated economic control in the hands of relatively few owners and threatened to displace the independent artisans so central to nineteenth century democratic life. Ironically, the traumatic Civil War that destroyed the slave civilization enormously furthered the growth of the industrial structures that would fatally unbalance the original American pattern of decentralized, self-governing communities.

Between the period of rapid westward expansion and industrial growth that followed the Civil War and the entry of the United States onto the world scene in World War I, American society passed through the most rapid and profound transformation in its history, not excluding our own time. Nothing less than a new national society came into being in those years, a society within whose structure we still live, and one markedly unlike that of most of the nineteenth century. By the end of that century, new technologies, particularly in transport, communications, and manufacturing, pulled the many semi-autonomous local societies into a vast national market. Though fostered in many ways by the federal government, the new expansion was largely carried out by private individuals and financial groups, who generated private wealth and control on a previously unheard-of scale.

The new economically integrated society emerging at the turn of the century developed its own forms of social organization, political control, and culture, including new representative characters. The new social form, capable of extending the control of a group of investors over vast resources, huge numbers of employees and, often, great distances, was the business corporation. The Pennsylvania Railroad, with its tentacular reach, its supervised, graded, and uniformed army of workers, its mechanical precision of operation and monopolistic ambitions, became the model of a new institution destined eventually to affect the lives of almost all Americans. The steel, oil, banking and finance, and insurance industries rapidly adopted the new bureaucratic form of the corporation.

The old local governments and organizations lacked the capacity to deal with the problems that were increasingly national in scope. Under these conditions, the traditional forms of social and economic life of the town lost their dominant position, in fact, if not in symbol, and the traditional idea of American citizenship was called into question. The new industrial order was focussed on large cities that seemed the antithesis of the order and decency of the town. Factories, slums, immigrants, and wardbosses seemed "foreign" and frightening. In those years, a new politics of interest developed, with the powerful national economic interests of the corporations, banks, and their investors, and, eventually, the labor movement, competing with the old regional, ethnic, and religious interests. These developments changed the workings of the political parties in the national government. By the early decades of the twentieth century, the Progressive movement was calling for a smoother partnership between large-scale economic organizations and government at all levels to "rationalize" the tumultuous process of social and political change. If all generations of Americans have had to confront "future shock," surely the turn-of-the-century generation faced the most severe challenge.

The eclipse of the old economic and social patterns brought stormy political conflicts and complex cultural changes in its wake. One was the acceleration of a possibility always available to some in American society, the emancipation of the successful entrepreneur from the confining ties of the old town morality. The Gilded Age was the era of the spectacular "self-made" economic success: captains of industry who could ignore the clamor of public opinion and rise to truly national power and prestige by economic means alone. In the predatory capitalists the age dubbed robber barons, some of the worst fears of earlier republican moralists seemed confirmed: that by releasing the untrammeled pursuit of wealth without regard to the demands of social justice, industrial capitalism was destroying the fabric of a democratic society, threatening social chaos by pitting class against class. Where, many wondered, could new limits and directions for individual initiative be found beyond the broken bounds of the local self-governing community? The inability of the old moral order effectively to encompass the new social developments set the terms of a cultural debate in which we as a nation are still engaged.

The most distinctive aspect of twentieth-century American society is the division of life into a number of separate functional sectors: home and workplace, work and leisure, white collar and blue collar, public and private. This division suited the needs of the bureaucratic industrial corporations that provided the model for our preferred means of organizing society by the balancing and linking of sectors as "departments" in a functional whole, as in a great business enterprise. Particularly powerful in molding our contemporary sense of things has been the division between the various "tracks" to achievement laid out in schools, corporation, government, and the professions, on the one hand, and the balancing life-sectors of home, personal ties, and "leisure," on the other. All this is in strong contrast to the widespread nineteenth-century pattern in which, as on the often-sentimentalized family farm, these functions had only indistinct boundaries. Domesticity, love, and intimacy increasingly became "havens" against the competitive culture of work.

With the industrialization of the economy, working life became more specialized and its organization tighter. Simultaneously, industrialization made functional sectors of the economy—various industries, whole geographical regions—more interdependent than before. Yet the sectoral form of organization and the competitive pressures of the national market made this interdependence difficult to perceive. While the pressures to compete and the network of private life were immediately perceptible, the interrelationships of society as a whole were largely abstractions. The sectoral pattern of modern American society has thus often been able to contain potential conflicts by separating those who are different without impairing the economic linkages of sectors within the larger economy.

Under such conditions, it is not surprising that the major problems of life appear to be essentially individual matters, a question of negotiating a reliable and harmonious balance among the various sectors of life to which an individual has access. As its points of reference contracted from an economically and occupationally diverse local community to the geographically spread, but functionally homogeneous, sector within which a person competes, success came to be defined in professional terms. The concept of one's "peers" concomitantly underwent a subtle, but important, shift of meaning. It came to signify those who share the same specific mix of activities, beginning with occupation and economic position, but increasingly implying the same attitudes, tastes, and style of life. The responses to all this that were articulated around the turn of the century have continued to shape our ways of conceiving and relating to American society. Those responses have all along been closely interwoven with new character types that, like the earlier ones, have come to seem representative approaches to the common conditions of life, giving moral meaning and direction to the lives of individuals.

The Manager

The self-sufficient entrepreneur, competitive, tough, and freed by wealth from external constraints, was one new American character. Certainly much of the moral appeal of the self-made man is his apparent freedom, not only from traditional restraints, but from the tight organization, the drudgery and banality, of so much of modern industrial life. The irony, of course, is that the entrepreneur's major historical role has been to create the modern industrial context. Celebrating the economic struggle, the self-made man of means became the legitimizing symbol for some of the aspiring middle class. Yet in practice the recurrent American dream of success has often continued to approximate the old image of the businessman as family provider and citizen. The turn-of-the-century nabobs themselves frequently sought legitimation through public philanthropy and national service, drawing on models more deferential—their critics said "feudal"—than American republican tradition countenanced. But the activist individual entrepreneur, though a continuing feature of American life and still a powerful symbol, has not represented the dominant direction of economic and social development.

The bureaucratic organization of the business corporation has been the dominant force in this century. Within the corporation, the crucial character has been the professional manager. The competitive industrial order with its sectoral organization and its push toward profitability has been the indisputable reality of modern life for the manager, rather than the object of a passionate faith in "progress," as for the entrepreneur. Although the manager in effect builds upon the work of the entrepreneur and shares with him the drive to achieve and problem-solving activism that are old American traits, the social positions and outlooks of the two types differ importantly.

The essence of the manager's task is to organize the human and nonhuman resources available to the organization that employs him so as to improve its position in the marketplace. His role is to persuade, inspire, manipulate, cajole, and intimidate those he manages so that his organization measures up to criteria of effectiveness shaped ultimately by the market but specifically by the expectations of those in control of his organization—finally, its owners. The manager's view of things is akin to that of the technician of industrial society par excellence, the engineer, except that the manager must admit interpersonal responses and personalities, including his own, into the calculation of effectiveness.

Like the entrepreneur, the manager also has another life, divided among spouse, children, friends, community, and religious and other nonoccupational involvements. Here, in contrast to the manipulative, achievement-oriented practices of the workplace, another kind of personality is actualized, often within a social pattern that shows recognizable continuity with earlier American forms of family and community. But it is an outstanding feature of industrial life that these sectors have become radically discontinuous in the kinds of traits emphasized and the moral understandings that guide individuals within them. "Public" and "private" roles often contrast sharply, as symbolized by the daily commute from green suburban settings reminiscent of rural life to the industrial, technological ambience of the workplace.

The split between public and private life correlates with a split between utilitarian individualism, appropriate in the economic and occupational spheres, and expressive individualism, appropriate in private life. For a long time such a split was incipient in American life. Early in the nineteenth century, indeed already in the eighteenth-century, an appeal to calculating utility was complemented by an appeal to sentiment or emotion. Jefferson, following the eighteenth century Scottish philosophers, believed in an innate "moral sentiment" that impelled men toward benevolence. The Puritan theologian Jonathan Edwards (1703–58) had seen religion, too, as located in the "affections." When science seemed to have dominated the explanatory schemas of the external world, morality and religion took refuge in human subjectivity, in feeling and sentiment. Morality and religion were related to aesthetics, the realm of feeling par excellence, as we saw in the case of Whitman. When morality came to be associated with the role of women and the family, and religion to be largely a matter of revivalistic emotion, the split between the utilitarian and the expressive spheres in nineteenth-century America widened. Nonetheless, theologians and moralists believed feeling had some cognitive content, some access to the external world, and Whitman certainly believed his poetry was expressing the truth not only of himself but of the world. But with the emergence of psychology as an academic field—and, even more important, as a form of popular discourse—in the late nineteenth and early twentieth-centuries, the purely subjective grounding of expressive individualism became complete.

The town had provided a metaphor of a moral ecology in which the polarities of public and private, masculine and feminine, were integrated by means of generally shared codes of behavior. Preindustrial American character surely oscillated between the instrumental orientation of the "masculine" world of work achievement and the values of the "feminine" spheres of nurturing domesticity. But the cultural framework made that oscillation, including its conflicts, intelligible.

With the coming of the managerial society, the organization of work, place of residence, and social status came to be decided by criteria of economic effectiveness. Those same economic criteria further facilitated the growth of national mass marketing and, with it, expanded consumer choice. The older social and moral standards became in many ways less relevant to the lives of those Americans most directly caught up in the new system. The manager could reorganize resources for greater effectiveness in economic life. Similarly, the relatively affluent twenti-

eth-century American could reorganize habits and styles of life experimentally to achieve a more gratifying private life. In this process, Americans learned to become more efficient in adapting to new sets of expectations and styles of consumption.

The Therapist

Like the manager, the therapist is a specialist in mobilizing resources for effective action, only here the resources are largely internal to the individual and the measure of effectiveness is the elusive criterion of personal satisfaction. Also like the manager, the therapist takes the functional organization of industrial society for granted, as the unproblematical context of life. The goal of living is to achieve some combination of occupation and "lifestyle" that is economically possible and psychically tolerable, that "works." The therapist, like the manager, takes the ends as they are given; the focus is upon the effectiveness of the means.

Between them, the manager and the therapist largely define the outlines of twentieth century American culture. The social basis of that culture is the world of bureaucratic consumer capitalism, which dominates, or has penetrated, most older, local economic forms. While the culture of manager and therapist does not speak in the language of traditional moralities, it nonetheless proffers a normative order of life, with character ideals, images of the good life, and methods of attaining it. Yet it is an understanding of life generally hostile to older ideas of moral order. Its center is the autonomous individual, presumed able to choose the roles he will play and the commitments he will make, not on the basis of higher truths but according to the criterion of life-effectiveness as the individual judges it.

The moral language and images of this culture of utilitarian and expressive individualism have influenced the lives of most of the characters in this book, and one of our chief tasks in the chapters that follow will be to delineate and understand its forms. As we shall see, the effects of this managerial and therapeutic understanding are not always benign; it does not always succeed, even by its own standards. Indeed, the very term *therapeutic* suggests a life focussed on the need for cure. But cure of what? In the final analysis, it is cure of the lack of fit between the present organization of the self and the available organization of work, intimacy, and meaning. And this cure is to take the form of enhancing and empowering the self to be able to relate successfully to others in society, achieving a kind of satisfaction without being overwhelmed by their demands. In its own understanding, the expressive aspect of our culture exists for the liberation and fulfillment of the individual. Its genius is that it enables the individual to think of commitments—from marriage and work to political and religious involvement—as enhancements of the sense of individual well-being rather than as moral imperatives.

The culture of the manager and the therapist is thus both recognizably continuous with earlier American cultural forms and yet different from them. The obvious point of similarity is the emphasis on the independence of the individual. As we have seen, self-reliance is an old American value, but only one strand of the complex cultural weft we have inherited. The expressive culture, now deeply allied with the utilitarian, reveals its difference from earlier patterns by its readiness to treat normative commitments as so many alternative strategies of self-fulfillment. What has dropped out are the old normative expectations of what makes life worth living. With the freedom to define oneself anew in a plethora of identities has also come an attenuation of those common understandings that enable us to recognize the virtues of the other.

In fact, the new culture is deeply ambiguous. It represents both the easing of constraints and dogmatic prejudices about what others should be and an idealization of the coolly manipula-

tive style of management. In our society, with its sharply divided spheres, it provides a way for the beleaguered individual to develop techniques for coping with the often-contradictory pressures of public and private life. Yet it does so by extending the calculating managerial style into intimacy, home, and community, areas of life formerly governed by the norms of a moral ecology....

American Culture Today

Perhaps the crucial change in American life has been that we have moved from the local life of the nineteenth century—in which economic and social relationships were visible and, however imperfectly, morally interpreted as parts of a larger common life—to a society vastly more interrelated and integrated economically, technically, and functionally. Yet this is a society in which the individual can only rarely and with difficulty understand himself and his activities as interrelated in morally meaningful ways with those of other, different Americans. Instead of directing cultural and individual energies toward relating the self to its larger context, the culture of manager and therapist urges a strenuous effort to make of our particular segment of life a small world of its own.

However, the cultural hegemony of the managerial and therapeutic ethos is far from complete. It is rooted in the technological affluence of postwar society, a prosperity that has been neither equitably shared nor universally accepted. Challenges to that ethos have arisen from a variety of quarters, from those left out of that prosperity, as well as from those who, while its beneficiaries, criticize it for moral defects. Sometimes the criticism seems to be motivated by a desire to hold on to the last vestiges of the autonomous community and its ideal of the independent citizen. Sometimes it is motivated by a desire to transform the whole society, and particularly its economy, so that a more effectively functioning democracy may emerge. In either case, there is a powerful rejection of the managerial-therapeutic ethos, in which we can see not only the discontents of the present economic and social order, but also reminders of the continuing importance of the biblical and republican cultural traditions in American politics....

Private and Public

Sometimes Americans make a rather sharp dichotomy between private and public life. Viewing one's primary task as "finding oneself" in autonomous self-reliance, separating oneself not only from one's parents but also from those larger communities and traditions that constitute one's past, leads to the notion that it is in oneself, perhaps in relation to a few intimate others, that fulfillment is to be found. Individualism of this sort often implies a negative view of public life. The impersonal forces of the economic and political worlds are what the individual needs protection against. In this perspective, even occupation, which has been so central to the identity of Americans in the past, becomes instrumental—not a good in itself, but only a means to the attainment of a rich and satisfying private life. But on the basis of what we have seen in our observation of middle-class American life, it would seem that this quest for purely private fulfillment is illusory: it often ends in emptiness instead. On the other hand, we found many people, some of whom we introduced earlier in this chapter, for whom private fulfillment and public involvement are not antithetical. These people evince an individualism that is not empty but is full of content drawn from an active identification with communities and traditions. Perhaps the notion that private life and public life are at odds is incorrect. Perhaps they are so deeply involved with each other that the impoverishment of one entails the impoverishment of the other. Parker Palmer is probably right when he says that "in a healthy society the private and

the public are not mutually exclusive, not in competition with each other. They are, instead, two halves of a whole, two poles of a paradox. They work together dialectically, helping to create and nurture one another."

Certainly this dialectical relationship is clear where public life degenerates into violence and fear. One cannot live a rich private life in a state of siege, mistrusting all strangers and turning one's home into an armed camp. A minimum of public decency and civility is a precondition for a fulfilling private life. On the other hand, public involvement is often difficult and demanding. To engage successfully in the public world, one needs personal strength and the support of family and friends. A rewarding private life is one of the preconditions for a healthy public life.

For all their doubts about the public sphere, Americans are more engaged in voluntary associations and civic organizations than the citizens of most other industrial nations. In spite of all the difficulties, many Americans feel they must "get involved." In public life as in private, we can discern the habits of the heart that sustain individualism and commitment, as well as what makes them problematic....

A Change of Eras?

In the course of this book, we have documented the latest phase of that process of separation and individuation that modernity seems to entail. John Donne, in 1611, at the very beginning of the modern era, with the prescience that is sometimes given to great poets, vividly described that process:

Tis all in peeces, all cohaerence gone;
All just supply, and all Relation:
Prince, Subject, Father, Sonne, are things forgot,
For every man alone thinkes he hath got
To be a Phoenix, and that then can bee
None of that kinde, of which he is, but hee.

Donne lived in a world where the ties of kinship and village and feudal obligation were already loosening, though only a few perceived how radical the consequences would be.

America was colonized by those who had come loose from the older European structures, and so from the beginning we had a head start in the process of modernization. Yet the colonists brought with them ideas of social obligation and group formation that disposed them to recreate in America structures of family, church, and polity that would continue, if in modified form, the texture of older European society. Only gradually did it become clear that every social obligation was vulnerable, every tie between individuals fragile. Only gradually did what we have called ontological individualism, the idea that the individual is the only firm reality, become widespread. Even in our day, when separation and individuation have reached a kind of culmination, their triumph is far from complete. The battles of modernity are still being fought.

But today the battles have become half-hearted. There was a time when, under the battle cry of "freedom," separation and individuation were embraced as the key to a marvelous future of unlimited possibility. It is true that there were always those, like Donne, who viewed the past with nostalgia and the present with apprehension and who warned that we were entering unknown and dangerous waters. It is also true that there are still those who maintain their enthusiasm for modernity, who speak of the third wave or the Aquarian Age or the new paradigm in which a dissociated individuation will reach a final fulfillment. Perhaps most common today, however, is a note of uncertainty, not a desire to turn back to the past but an anxiety about where we seem to be headed. In this view, modernity seems to be a period of enormously rapid change, a transition from something relatively fixed toward something not yet clear. Many might find still applicable Matthew Arnold's assertion that we are

Wandering between two worlds, one dead,
The other powerless to be born.

There is a widespread feeling that the promise of the modern era is slipping away from us. A movement of enlightenment and liberation that was to have freed us from superstition and tyranny has led in the twentieth century to a world in which ideological fanaticism and political oppression have reached extremes unknown in previous history. Science, which was to have unlocked the bounties of nature, has given us the power to destroy all life on the earth. Progress, modernity's master idea, seems less compelling when it appears that it may be progress into the abyss. And the globe today is divided between a liberal world so incoherent that it seems to be losing the significance of its own ideals, an oppressive and archaic communist statism, and a poor, and often tyrannical, Third World reaching for the very first rungs of modernity. In the liberal world, the state, which was supposed to be a neutral nightwatchman that would maintain order while individuals pursued their various interests, has become so overgrown and militarized that it threatens to become a universal policeman.

Yet in spite of those daunting considerations, many of those we talked to are still hopeful. They realize that though the processes of separation and individuation were necessary to free us from the tyrannical structures of the past, they must be balanced by a renewal of commitment and community if they are not to end in self-destruction or turn into their opposites. Such a renewal is indeed a world waiting to be born if we only had the courage to see it....

The Culture of Coherence

But that is not the whole story. It could not be the whole story, for the culture of separation, if it ever became completely dominant, would collapse of its own incoherence. Or, even more likely, well before that happened, an authoritarian state would emerge to provide the coherence the culture no longer could. If we are not entirely a mass of interchangeable fragments within an aggregate, if we are in part qualitatively distinct members of a whole, it is because there are still operating among us, with whatever difficulties, traditions that tell us about the nature of the world, about the nature of society, and about who we are as people. Primarily biblical and republican, these traditions are, as we have seen, important for many Americans and significant to some degree for almost all. Somehow families, churches, a variety of cultural associations, and, even if only in the interstices, schools and universities, do manage to communicate a form of life, a *paideia*, in the sense of growing up in a morally and intellectually intelligible world.

The communities of memory of which we have spoken are concerned in a variety of ways to give a qualitative meaning to the living of life, to time and space, to persons and groups. Religious communities, for example, do not experience time in the way the mass media present it—as a continuous flow of qualitatively meaningless sensations. The day, the week, the season, the year are punctuated by an alternation of the sacred and the profane. Prayer breaks into our daily life at the beginning of a meal, at the end of the day, at common worship, reminding us that our utilitarian pursuits are not the whole of life, that a fulfilled life is one in which God and neighbor are remembered first. Many of our religious traditions recognize the significance of silence as a way of breaking the incessant flow of sensations and opening our hearts to the wholeness of being. And our republican tradition, too, has ways of giving form to time, reminding us on particular dates of the great events of our past or of the heroes who helped to teach us what we are as a free people. Even our private family life takes on a shared rhythm with a Thanksgiving dinner or a Fourth of July picnic.

In short, we have never been, and still are not, a collection of private individuals who, except for a conscious contract to create a minimal government, have nothing in common. Our lives make sense in a thousand ways, most of which we are unaware of, because of traditions that are centuries, if not millennia, old. It is these traditions that help us to know that it does make a difference who we are and how we treat one another. Even the mass media, with their tendency to homogenize feelings and sensations, cannot entirely avoid transmitting such qualitative distinctions, in however muted a form.

But if we owe the meaning of our lives to biblical and republican traditions of which we seldom consciously think, is there not the danger that the erosion of these traditions may eventually deprive us of that meaning altogether? Are we not caught between the upper millstone of a fragmented intellectual culture and the nether millstone of a fragmented popular culture? The erosion of meaning and coherence in our lives is not something Americans desire. Indeed, the profound yearning for the idealized small town that we found among most of the people we talked to is a yearning for just such meaning and coherence. But although the yearning for the small town is nostalgia for the irretrievably lost, it is worth considering whether the biblical and republican traditions that small town once embodied can be reappropriated in ways that respond to our present need. Indeed, we would argue that if we are ever to enter that new world that so far has been powerless to be born, it will be through reversing modernity's tendency to obliterate all previous culture. We need to learn again from the cultural riches of the human species and to reappropriate and revitalize those riches so that they can speak to our condition today.

We may derive modest hope from the fact that there is a restlessness and a stirring in the intellectual culture itself. Stephen Toulmin tells us that "our own natural science today is no longer 'modern' science." It is a "postmodern" science in which disciplinary boundaries are beginning to appear as the historical accidents they are and the problems that are necessarily "transdisciplinary" are beginning to be addressed. This recognition is based on the realization that we cannot, after all, finally separate who we are from what we are studying. As Toulmin puts it, "We can no longer view the world as Descartes and Laplace would have us do, as 'rational onlookers,' from outside. Our place is within the same world that we are studying, and whatever scientific understanding we achieve must be a kind of understanding that is available to participants within the processes of nature, i.e., from inside." Perhaps nature as perceived by the poet, the theologian, and the scientist may be the same thing after all. At least there is now room to talk about that possibility. And there are parallel developments in the social sciences. There, too, it appears that studying history and acting in it are not as different as we had thought. If our high culture could begin to talk about nature and history, space and time, in ways that did not disaggregate them into fragments, it might be possible for us to find connections and analogies with the older ways in which human life was made meaningful. This would not result in a neotraditionalism that would return us to the past. Rather, it might lead to a recovery of a genuine tradition, one that is always self-revising and in a state of development. It might help us find again the coherence we have almost lost....

Reconstituting the Social World

The transformation of our culture and our society would have to happen at a number of levels. If it occurred only in the minds of individuals (as to some degree it already has), it would be powerless. If it came only from the initiative of the state, it would be tyrannical. Personal transformation among large numbers is essential, and it must not only be a transformation of

consciousness but must also involve individual action. But individuals need the nurture of groups that carry a moral tradition reinforcing their own aspirations. Implicitly or explicitly, a number of the communities of memory we have discussed in this book hold ethical commitments that require a new social ecology in our present situation. But out of existing groups and organizations, there would also have to develop a social movement dedicated to the idea of such a transformation. We have several times spoken of the Civil Rights movement as an example. It permanently changed consciousness, in the sense of individual attitudes toward race, and it altered our social life so as to eliminate overt expressions of discrimination. If the Civil Rights movement failed fundamentally to transform the position of black people in our society, it was because to do that would have required just the change in our social ecology that we are now discussing. So a movement to transform our social ecology would, among other things, be the successor and fulfillment of the Civil Rights movement. Finally, such a social movement would lead to changes in the relationship between our government and our economy. This would not necessarily mean more direct control of the economy, certainly not nationalization. It would mean changing the climate in which business operates so as to encourage new initiatives in economic democracy and social responsibility, whether from "private" enterprise or autonomous small- and middle-scale public enterprises. In the context of a moral concern to revive our social ecology, the proposals of the proponents of the Administered Society and Economic Democracy that we discussed in the preceding chapter could be considered and appropriate ones adopted.

To be truly transformative, such a social movement would not simply subside after achieving some of its goals, leaving the political process much as it found it. One of its most important contributions would be to restore the dignity and legitimacy of democratic politics. We have seen in earlier chapters how suspicious

Americans are of politics as an area in which arbitrary differences of opinion and interest can be resolved only by power and manipulation. The recovery of our social ecology would allow us to link interests with a conception of the common good. With a more explicit understanding of what we have in common and the goals we seek to attain together, the differences between us that remain would be less threatening. We could move to ameliorate the differences that are patently unfair while respecting differences based on morally intelligible commitments. Of course, a political discourse that could discuss substantive justice and not only procedural rules would have to be embodied in effective political institutions, probably including a revitalized party system.

It is evident that a thin political consensus, limited largely to procedural matters, cannot support a coherent and effective political system. For decades that has become ever clearer. We have been afraid to try for a more substantial consensus for fear that the effort may produce unacceptable levels of conflict. But if we had the courage to face our deepening political and economic difficulties, we might find that there is more basic agreement than we had imagined. Certainly, the only way to find out is to raise the level of public political discourse so that the fundamental problems are addressed rather than obscured.

If we are right in our stress on a revitalized social ecology, then one critically important action that government could take in a new political atmosphere would be, in Christopher Jencks's words, to reduce the "punishments of failure and the rewards of success." Reducing the inordinate rewards of ambition and our inordinate fears of ending up as losers would offer the possibility of a great change in the meaning of work in our society and all that would go with such a change. To make a real difference, such a shift in rewards would have to be a part of a reappropriation of the idea of vocation or calling, a return in a new way to the idea of work as a contribution to the good

of all and not merely as a means to one's own advancement.

If the extrinsic rewards and punishments associated with work were reduced, it would be possible to make vocational choices more in terms of intrinsic satisfactions. Work that is intrinsically interesting and valuable is one of the central requirements for a revitalized social ecology. For professionals, this would mean a clearer sense that the large institutions most of them work for really contribute to the public good. A bright young lawyer (or a bright old lawyer, for that matter) whose work consists in helping one corporation outwit another is intelligent enough to doubt the social utility of what he or she is doing. The work may be interesting—even challenging and exciting—yet its intrinsic meaninglessness in any larger moral or social context necessarily produces an alienation that is only partly assuaged by the relatively large income of corporate lawyers. Those whose work is not only poorly rewarded but boring, repetitive, and unchallenging are in an even worse situation. Automation that turns millions of our citizens into mere servants of robots is already a form of despotism, for which the pleasures of private life—modest enough for those of minimum skill and minimum wage—cannot compensate. The social wealth that automation brings, if it is not siphoned into the hands of a few, can be used to pay for work that is intrinsically valuable, in the form of a revival of crafts (that already flourish in supplying goods for the wealthy) and in the improvement of human services. Where routine work is essential, its monotony can be mitigated by including workers in fuller participation in their enterprises so that they understand how their work contributes to the ultimate product and have an effective voice in how those enterprises are run.

Undoubtedly, the satisfaction of work well done, indeed "the pursuit of excellence," is a permanent and positive human motive. Where its reward is the approbation of one's fellows more than the accumulation of great private wealth, it can contribute to what the founders of our republic called civic virtue. Indeed, in a revived social ecology, it would be a primary form of civic virtue. And from it would flow a number of positive consequences. For one thing, the split between private and public, work and family, that has grown for over a century, might begin to be mended. If the ethos of work were less brutally competitive and more ecologically harmonious, it would be more consonant with the ethos of private life and, particularly, of family life. A less frantic concern for advancement and a reduction of working hours for both men and women would make it easier for women to be full participants in the workplace without abandoning family life. By the same token, men would be freed to take an equal role at home and in child care. In this way, what seemed at first to be a change only in the nature of work would turn out to have major consequences for family life as well.

Another consequence of the change in the meaning of work from private aggrandizement to public contribution would be to weaken the motive to keep the complexity of our society invisible. It would become part of the ethos of work to be aware of our intricate connectedness and interdependence. There would be no fear of social catastrophe or hope of inordinate reward motivating us to exaggerate our own independence. And with such a change, we might begin to be better able to understand why, though we are all, as human beings, morally deserving of equal respect, some of us begin with familial or cultural advantages or disadvantages that others do not have. Or perhaps, since we would not conceive of life so much in terms of a race in which all the prizes go to the swiftest, we might begin to make moral sense of the fact that there are real cultural differences among us, that we do not all want the same thing, and that it is not a moral defect to find other things in life of interest besides consuming ambition. In short, a restored social ecology might allow us to mitigate the harm that has been done to disadvantaged groups without blaming the vic-

tims or trying to turn them into carbon copies of middle-class high achievers.

It should be clear that we are not arguing, as some of those we criticized in chapter 10 have done, that a few new twists in the organization of the economy would solve all our problems. It is true that a change in the meaning of work and the relation of work and reward is at the heart of any recovery of our social ecology. But such a change involves a deep cultural, social, and even psychological transformation that is not to be brought about by expert fine-tuning of economic institutions alone. On the contrary, at every point, institutional changes, educational changes, and motivational changes would go hand in hand. For example, part of our task might well involve a recovery of older notions of the corporation. As Alan Trachtenberg has written:

> The word [corporation] refers to any association of individuals bound together into a *corpus*, a body sharing a common purpose in a common name. In the past, that purpose had usually been communal or religious; boroughs, guilds, monasteries, and bishoprics were the earliest European manifestations of the corporate form.... It was assumed, as it is still in nonprofit corporations, that the incorporated body earned its charter by serving the public good.... Until after the Civil War, indeed, the assumption was widespread that a corporate charter was a privilege to be granted only by a special act of a state legislature, and then for purposes clearly in the public interest. Incorporation was not yet thought of as a right available on application by any private enterprise.

As late as 1911...a leading Boston businessman, Henry Lee Higginson, could say, following earlier Protestant notions of stewardship, that corporate property "belongs to the community."

Reasserting the idea that incorporation is a concession of public authority to a private group *in return for* service to the public good, with effective public accountability, would change what is now called the "social responsibility of the corporation" from its present status, where it is often a kind of public relations whipped cream decorating the corporate pudding, to a constitutive structural element in the corporation itself. This, in turn, would involve a fundamental alteration in the role and training of the manager. Management would become a profession in the older sense of the word, involving not merely standards of technical competence but standards of public obligation that could at moments of conflict override obligations to the corporate employer. Such a conception of the professional manager would require a deep change in the ethos of schools of business administration, where "business ethics" would have to become central in the process of professional formation. If the rewards of success in business management were not so inordinate, then choice of this profession could arise from more public-spirited motives. In short, personal, cultural, and structural change all entail one another.

Signs of the Times

Few of those with whom we talked would have described the problems facing our society in exactly the terms we have just used. But few have found a life devoted to "personal ambition and consumerism" satisfactory, and most are seeking in one way or another to transcend the limitations of a self-centered life. If there are vast numbers of a selfish, narcissistic "me generation" in America, we did not find them, but we certainly did find that the language of individualism, the primary American language of self-understanding, limits the ways in which people think.

Many Americans are devoted to serious, even ascetic, cultivation of the self in the form of a number of disciplines, practices, and "trainings," often of great rigor. There is a question as to whether these practices lead to

the self-realization or self-fulfillment at which they aim or only to an obsessive self-manipulation that defeats the proclaimed purpose. But it is not uncommon for those who are attempting to find themselves to find in that very process something that transcends them. For example, a Zen student reported: "I started Zen to get something for myself, to stop suffering, to get enlightened. Whatever it was, I was doing it for myself. I had hold of myself and I was reaching for something. Then to do it, I found out I had to give up that hold on myself. Now it has hold of me, whatever 'it' is." What this student found is that the meaning of life is not to be discovered in manipulative control in the service of the self. Rather, through the disciplined practices of a religious way of life, the student found his self more grasped than grasping. It is not surprising that "self-realization" in this case has occurred in the context of a second language, the allusive language of Zen Buddhism, and a community that attempts to put that language into practice.

Many Americans are concerned to find meaning in life not primarily through self-cultivation but through intense relations with others. Romantic love is still idealized in our society. It can, of course, be remarkably self-indulgent, even an excuse to use another for one's own gratification. But it can also be a revelation of the poverty of the self and lead to a genuine humility in the presence of the beloved. We have noted in the early chapters of this book that the therapeutically inclined, jealous though they are of their personal autonomy, nonetheless seek enduring attachments and a community within which those attachments can be nurtured. As in the case of self-cultivation, there is in the desire for intense relationships with others an attempt to move beyond the isolated self, even though the language of individualism makes that sometimes hard to articulate.

Much of what is called "consumerism," and often condemned as such, must be understood in this same ambiguous, ambivalent context. Attempts to create a beautiful place in which to live, to eat well and in a convivial atmosphere, to visit beautiful places where one may enjoy works of art, or simply lie in the sun and swim in the sea, often involve an element of giving to another and find their meaning in a committed relationship. Where the creation of a consumption-oriented lifestyle, which may resemble that of "the beautiful people" or may simply involve a comfortable home and a camper, becomes a form of defense against a dangerous and meaningless world, it probably takes on a greater burden than it can bear. In that case, the effort to move beyond the self has ended too quickly in the "little circle of family and friends" of which Tocqueville spoke, but even so the initial impulse was not simply selfish.

With the weakening of the traditional forms of life that gave aesthetic and moral meaning to everyday living, Americans have been improvising alternatives more or less successfully. They engage, sometimes with intense involvement, in a wide variety of arts, sports, and nature appreciation, sometimes as spectators but often as active participants. Some of these activities involve conscious traditions and demanding practices, such as ballet. Others, such as walking in the country or jogging, may be purely improvisational, though not devoid of some structure of shared meaning. Not infrequently, moments of intense awareness, what are sometimes called "peak experiences," occur in the midst of such activities. At such moments, a profound sense of well-being eclipses the usual utilitarian preoccupations of everyday life. But the capacity of such experiences to provide more than a momentary counterweight to pressures of everyday life is minimal. Where these activities find social expression at all, it is apt to be in the form of what we have called the lifestyle enclave. The groups that form around them are too evanescent, too inherently restricted in membership, and too slight in their hold on their members' loyalty to carry much public weight. Only at rare moments do such largely expressive solidarities create anything like a civic consciousness, as when a local pro-

fessional sports team wins a national championship and briefly gives rise to a euphoric sense of metropolitan belongingness.

Many of those with whom we talked were locked into a split between a public world of competitive striving and a private world supposed to provide the meaning and love that make competitive striving bearable. Some, however, were engaged in an effort to overcome this split, to make our public and our private worlds mutually coherent—in a word, to recover our social ecology. Cecilia Dougherty, Mary Taylor, Ed Schwartz, and Paul Morrison, whom we met near the end of chapters 6, 7, 8, and 9, are examples of those engaged in such efforts. Cecilia Dougherty is working for a society in which the "have-nots" can have voice and participation, and in which her children and grandchildren can safely lead their lives. Mary Taylor is trying to think about the long haul, at least the next twenty-five years and not just the next one or two years that preoccupy most politicians. She is concerned to repair the damage that has been done both to our natural ecology and to our social ecology. Ed Schwartz is concerned with the dehumanizing aspect of the way we organize work and is trying to bring the moral concerns of the biblical and republican traditions into our economic structures. Paul Morrison is attempting to build a strong parish life so that the members of his congregation can carry out vocations in the world that will really make a difference.

All of these people are drawing on our republican and biblical traditions, trying to make what have become second languages into our first language again. We have spoken of "reappropriating tradition"—that is, finding sustenance in tradition and applying it actively and creatively to our present realities. These people give us specific examples of what that means. We may ask what help they receive in their reappropriation of traditions from the major cultural institutions of our society. Here the story is mixed. In spite of the fragmentation of our intellectual culture, work done in the universities did provide assistance to some of those to whom we talked. For example, Ed Schwartz has been influenced significantly by one strand of contemporary American political philosophy that is trying to rethink the republican tradition. Paul Morrison draws on contemporary theology and theological ethics for help in thinking through his positions. It may not always be easy to find, but among the fragments of our intellectual culture there is clearly significant work being done.

And while our universities are under greater pressure than ever to emphasize pragmatic results—technological achievements and career-oriented skills—there are voices calling for a reaffirmation of the classic role of education as a way to articulate private aspirations with common cultural meanings so that individuals simultaneously become more fully developed people and citizens of a free society. Eva Brann has recently given an eloquent defense of this understanding of education in her *Paradoxes of Education in a Republic*. She argues that in education at present, the choice is either tradition or technique, and that technique has become far too dominant. The result is that in the multiversities of today, it is hard to find a single book, even a single play of Shakespeare's, that all the students in a large class know. When education becomes an instrument for individual careerism, it cannot provide either personal meaning or civic culture. And yet, somehow, the tradition does get transmitted, at least to students who seek it out.

Tradition gets transmitted because there are still teachers who love it and who cannot help transmitting it. Helen Vendler, in her 1980 presidential address to the Modern Language Association, took as her text a passage at the end of Wordsworth's *The Prelude*:

> *What we have loved,*
> *Others will love, and we will teach them how.*

She sums up her argument by saying:

> It is not within our power to reform the primary and secondary schools, even if we have a sense of how that reform might begin. We do have it within our power, I believe, to reform ourselves, to make it our own first task to give, especially to our beginning students, that rich web of associations, lodged in the tales of majority and minority cultures alike, by which they could begin to understand themselves as individuals and as social beings.... All freshman English courses, to my mind, should devote at least half their time to the reading of myth, legend and parable; and beginning language courses should do the same.... We owe it to ourselves to show our students, when they first meet us, what we are: we owe their dormant appetites, thwarted for so long in their previous schooling, that deep sustenance that will make them realize that they too, having been taught, love what we love.

If college education, and probably more than a few secondary schools as well, are still providing us with some of the help we need to make tradition a vital resource in our lives, it is hard to see how that other great cultural institution, television, which competes with the schools for the education of our youth and for the continuing education of adults, succeeds in doing so. Except for some notable contributions from public television, most programming is devoid of any notion of coherent tradition.

On the basis of our interviews, and from what we can observe more generally in our society today, it is not clear that many Americans are prepared to consider a significant change in the way we have been living. The allure of the packaged good life is still strong, though dissatisfaction is widespread. Americans are fairly ingenious in finding temporary ways to counteract the harsher consequences of our damaged social ecology. Livy's words about ancient Rome also apply to us: "We have reached the point where we cannot bear either our vices or their cure." But, as some of the more perceptive of the people to whom we talked believe, the time may be approaching when we will either reform our republic or fall into the hands of despotism, as many republics have done before us.

Daniel Kemmis

Barn Raising

D aniel Kemmis, who is currently mayor of Missoula, Montana, has combined careers as a public official and a democratic theorist. He grew up in a rural community in eastern Montana, but went on to earn a law degree from Harvard and to run a campaign for the Montana Supreme Court. In his 1990 book, *Community and the Politics of Place* Kemmis notes that the challenges of life on the frontier have long led the people of Montana to identify themselves closely with the landscape they share. The "public" in Montana takes much of its character and its meaning from the concrete qualities of its "place." Kemmis discusses this understanding of the public in the context of a quote from Hannah Arendt: "To live together in the world means essentially that a world of things is between those who have it in common, as a table is located between those who sit around it…." Both a table and the Montana high plains are concrete, objective "places"—they do not depend on the values or preferences of individuals for their meaning. This objectivity makes them something that everyone shares, i.e., something "public."

By recognizing the importance of "place," Kemmis explains, we can get beyond our individual preferences and begin to speak about our common commitments. Such an awareness can lead to a sense of mutual responsibility for preserving and enhancing the shared place. This represents a way to get beyond the gridlock of contemporary individualistic politics where one side argues for maximum individual freedom and the other argues for maximum bureaucratic control of individual greed.

Barn Raising
Daniel Kemmis

In many instances in which public undertakings or community development initiatives are blocked, there is a latent public consensus that would be more satisfying to most of the participants than what finally emerges. But in fact this consensus rarely sees the light of day. Another way to say this is that in most of these cases there is more common ground, and higher common ground, than the people involved ever succeed in discovering. The common ground is there (just as it was in the stock sale or the trace race), but our prevailing way of doing things blocks us from realizing it. Our failure to realize is twofold: we do not recognize the common ground (a failure to realize its existence), and we do not make it a reality (a failure to realize its potential). This twofold failure leaves our communities poorer than they need to be.

What is it that could block us from realizing common ground? To a certain extent it is a problem of language—of how we speak publicly....

In this spirit, I will tell one brief story about some men and women who have helped me understand what "cooperation" might mean. Most of us could tell different versions of this same story.

By the time I was eight or nine years old, the wind that blew almost ceaselessly across the high plains of eastern Montana had taken its toll on our barn. We planned to tear down the old one and from its remnants build a new barn in the swale of a dry creek bank, high enough to avoid the torrents that roared through every year or two. It never would have occurred to us, in the early 1950s, to tackle this massive job without calling on the neighbors for help.

Since my brother and I were too young to be of much help to the builders, we spent most of the day down among the box elders on the creek bottom playing with the neighbor children. That day stands out clear in my mind, not so much for the image of the new barn rising out of the old, but for the fact that our neighbor, Albert Volbrecht, had brought his children along. We didn't exactly play with Albert's children; we listened to them tell dirty stories that would have made our mother, Lilly, frying chicken up in the house, cry with rage. What fascinated me was the fact that the little Volbrecht girl was the one in the family with the best stock of stories. Her younger brothers revered her, at least on that score, for her prowess.

Though my mother did not know the exact wording of the stories the Volbrecht girl was entertaining us with, she did know the kind of language the child used under other circumstances, and she heartily disapproved. She would have done anything in her power to deny my brother and me that part of our education. But there was nothing she could do about it. The Volbrechts had to be at the barn raising, just as they had to be there when we branded calves. They were neighbors, and that was that. Albert's presence loomed large on the scene no matter the situation. His hat was the biggest in the corral, his voice the loudest, his language the foulest, his intake of beer the most prodigious. His influence was pervasive. I saw my father drink a can of beer once after the last calf was branded. I was astonished to see him do such a thing, and so was my mother. The blame for my father's indiscretion came to rest on Albert. Like his children, Albert was too fond of off-color stories for my mother's taste. The simplest event became colorful, wild, when Albert retold it. My mother accused him of being unable to open his mouth without storying. And Albert, for his part, delighted in watching my mother squirm at his bawdy jokes.

In another time and place, Albert and Lilly would have had nothing to do with one another. But on those Montana plains, life was still harsh enough that they had no choice. Avoiding people you did not like was not an option. Everyone was needed by everyone else in one ca-

pacity or another. If Albert and Lilly could have snubbed one another, our barn might not have been built, and neither our calves nor Albert's branded. Lilly and Albert didn't like each other much better at the end of the barn raising than at the beginning. But that day, and many others like it, taught them something important. They learned, whether they liked it or not, a certain tolerance for another slant on the world, another way of going at things that needed doing. They found in themselves an unsuspected capacity to accept one another. This acceptance, I believe, broadened them beyond the boundaries of their own likes and dislikes and made these personal idiosyncrasies seem less important. In addition, they learned that they could count on one another. If Albert said he would be there with a "farmhand" attachment on his tractor to lift the roof into place, he would be there with the "farmhand." If Lilly said she would fry the chicken, she would do it whether she was in the mood that morning or not. And because Albert and Lilly and the rest of our neighbors were able to count on one another, they experienced the satisfaction of accomplishing a big, tough job by working together.

This eastern Montana of my boyhood still echoed of the frontier. From Plymouth Rock onwards, Americans on the frontier had found themselves united with their neighbors in the face of an often hostile and precarious existence. Over the generations, the lessons of cooperation wove themselves into something that can only be called political education. People who had learned by repeated experience that they could count on each other, and in doing so accomplish difficult and important tasks together, were the people who eventually formed cooperatives to bring electricity to the most remote areas or to market wheat or beef out of those areas. This way of working together was still taken for granted in my childhood. When early in the 1950s the rural electric association lines marched across the hill to our farmstead, bringing us the magic of electricity, I was oblivious to the fact that generations of Alberts and Lillys learning to work together were behind this miracle.

The point here is not nostalgia. We cannot re-create the world of the frontier, even if we thought we wanted to. But there is something to be learned from the subtle but persistent process by which frontier families learned the politics of cooperation. They learned it the way almost anything worthwhile is learned—by practice. Republican theorists have always understood that citizens do not become capable of democratic self-determination by accident. As Bellah points out, republicans from Montesquieu to Jefferson (and we might add the populists) had recognized that the character which is required for participation in face-to-face self-government can only be instilled through repeated experiences of a very specific kind. For these democratic republicans, "...the virtuous citizen was one who understood that personal welfare is dependent on the general welfare and could be expected to act accordingly. Forming such character requires the context of practices in which the coincidence of personal concern and the common welfare can be *experienced* [emphasis added]."

From childhood, Albert and Lilly and all of their neighbors were schooled in those experiences. Because of that practical education, they could overcome many of their differences; they could recognize their need for one another and act accordingly. By contrast, the people at the comprehensive plan hearing had gone to a very different school, and they, too, acted accordingly. Their differences seemed insurmountable to them, and they seemed to see little of their mutual need for one another. The political education which had created this pessimism and isolation is exemplified by another brief story.

A group of citizens in a western town recently began making plans to initiate a major annual art and music festival. During the first summer, they wanted to hold a small one-day preview event, both to raise awareness within the community about the larger festival idea and to raise some money for the next year's festival. They settled on the idea of an old-fashioned box social, where people would be asked to bring picnic lunches, which could then be auctioned. The idea gathered momentum quickly and seemed like a nearly certain success until someone pointed out the possibility of a lawsuit. What if someone got sick from one of the lunches and filed suit? With that question, the box social was laid to rest.

How could it be that my parents and their neighbors could have box socials but we cannot? I have tried to imagine Albert suing us because my mother's fried chicken laid him up or because he got hurt in our corral. But it is truly unimaginable. He no more had that option than we had the choice of not inviting him to help with the barn because we disapproved of the way he or his kids told stories. Most of us now do have those options, and as a society, we pursue them with a vengeance. We have as little as possible to do with those whose "life-styles" make us uncomfortable. If we are injured by one of "them" (or even by one of "us"), we will not lightly shrink from a lawsuit. Short of that, we readily and regularly oppose each other at public hearings, avidly pursuing our own interests and protecting our own rights with no sense of responsibility to hear or respond to the legitimate interest of those on the "other side" or to discover common ground. More and more often, the result is deadlock—and then frustration and withdrawal from all things public. Whereas the politics of cooperation gave people a robust sense of their capacity to get big, tough jobs done together, we increasingly come to the gloomy conclusion that "anybody can wreck anything," so there is no purpose in trying anything. We have been practiced in the politics of alienation, separation, and blocked initiatives rather than any "practices of commitment" which might "give us the strength to get up and do what needs to be done."

Yet one of the lessons of *Habits of the Heart* is that even those who testified on the Missoula comprehensive plan, even those who never got to testify on the Dubois forest plan, do have some experience with "the second languages and practices of commitment." They do not have enough of that experience to change the way they behave at a public hearing, and that is a growing problem for our society. But they do have snatches of such experience, and it is there that the possibility of reform must be sought. Here, picked almost at random, are a few examples of such "practices of commitment":

- Children in a 4-H club are taught to raise and care for animals, preparing for the competition at the county fair.
- Residents of a rural community form and maintain a volunteer fire department.
- Urban residents create a neighborhood watch program for their block.
- Other urban residents form a softball league, carrying their competition through to the fall championships.

As with instances of community deadlock, these examples can also be multiplied almost endlessly. And as with those other examples, these, too, share certain common features. Those features are essential ingredients in any revitalization of public life, either in this region or in the nation itself. But because that connection is far from obvious, it will bear some deliberate looking into.

There are two basic ingredients of practices such as those listed here or the thousands of others which might have been listed instead. It is the combination of these two ingredients which give to these practices the potential for revitalizing public life. The two elements are: 1) a central concern with value, with standards of excellence, with what is good; and 2) a rigorous objectivity. What these practices promise (and what, in fact, nothing else can provide) is the kind of experience which would enable us to identify and build upon common ground. The common ground we need to find is like a high, hidden valley which we know is there but which seems always to remain beyond our reach. This hidden valley may be called common ground

because it is a place of shared values. The values are shared because they are objective; they are, in fact, public values. This is what makes this common ground valuable, but it is also what keeps it hidden from us. It is valuable because the reclaiming of a vital, effective form of public life can only happen if we can learn to say words like *value* in the same breath with words like *public* or *objective*.

But this valley of common ground remains hidden because we all inhabit a world in which values are always private, always subjective. Always, that is, except when we are engaged in practices. What barn building and violin playing, softball and steer raising all have fundamentally in common is this: all of them deal with questions of value, with what is good or excellent (a well-built barn; a well-executed double play), but they all do so in an explicitly social setting, wherein purely subjective or individualistic inclinations are flatly irrelevant, if not counterproductive. MacIntyre explains why:

> If, on starting to listen to music, I do not accept my own incapacity to judge correctly, I will never learn to hear, let alone to appreciate, Bartok's last quartets. If, on starting to play baseball, I do not accept that others know better than I when to throw a fast ball and when not, I will never learn to appreciate good pitching let alone to pitch. In the realm of practices the authority of both goods and standards operates in such a way as to rule out all subjectivist and emotivist analyses of judgment.

What MacIntyre says here of baseball or Bartok may also be said of the thousands of examples of practices which people engage in, from raising steers to running a rural fire department. No one can do these things in a "practiced" way while maintaining a purely subjectivist approach to values. People who engage in these kinds of activities experience what it is to operate within a system of shared values, in which it is clearly not enough to say,

"Well, those may be your values, but these are mine." Everyone who testifies at a public hearing may act on that occasion as if all values are subjective and may therefore contribute to the difficulty we have in acting upon shared values. But for most of those people, there is at least one part of their lives where they act, think, and talk very differently. Whether they are cross-country skiing or raising prize irises, they come into relationship with other people in a very particular way. "Every practice," according to MacIntyre, "requires a certain kind of relationship between those who participate in it." What that relationship instills, over time, are precisely the "civic virtues"—those habits which would be necessary if people were ever to relate to each other in a truly public way. Here is how MacIntyre describes how even our homeliest practices gradually instill these civic virtues:

> We have to learn to recognize what is due to whom; we have to be prepared to take whatever self-endangering risks are demanded along the way; and we have to listen carefully to what we are told about our own inadequacies and to reply with the same carefulness for the facts. In other words we have to accept as necessary components of any practice with internal goods and standards of excellence the virtues of justice, courage and honesty.

What Hannah Arendt calls the "weirdness" of our modern situation may be reduced to this: that in what we call the "public" realm, all of these virtues which might in fact enable us to be public are suddenly overshadowed. The "second language of commitment," which so many public hearing contestants speak in their softball leagues or their PTA meetings, becomes suddenly silent when these people think they are in a public setting. Instead, in that setting, they speak their "first language of individualism," with consequences which are all too familiar. The person who grew up knowing that she could not arbitrarily decide what

constitutes a prize-winning steer or a good time to bunt now accepts as utterly natural the idea that what she considers a good community is "her value" and what her opponent considers a good community is "his value." What this does to the tone of "public" discourse is predictable: "From our rival conclusions we can argue back to our rival premises, but when we do arrive at our premises argument ceases and the invocation of one premise against another becomes a matter of pure assertion and counter-assertion. Hence perhaps the slightly shrill tone of so much moral debate.

At the root of this difficulty, MacIntyre discovers the same feature which struck the authors of *Habits of the Heart* so forcibly: the feeling on the part of most people that, in the end, their position (and certainly the positions of their opponents) are a result, not of reason, but of individual inclination.

> [I]f we possess no unassailable criteria, no set of compelling reasons by means of which we may convince our opponents, it follows that in the process of making up our own minds we can have made no appeal to such criteria or such reasons. If I lack any good reasons to invoke against you, it must seem that I lack any good reasons. Hence it seems that underlying my own position there must be some non-rational decision to adopt that position. Corresponding to the interminability of public argument there is at least the appearance of a disquieting private arbitrariness. It is small wonder if we become defensive and therefore shrill.

We are faced, then, with a considerable paradox. While many people do receive training in civic virtues, and are therefore capable of at least a halting fluency in the "second language of commitment," the place that they are least likely to use that language is in what we call public settings. Our public discourse is couched almost entirely in the framework which MacIntyre identifies as the dichotomy of regulated versus unregulated individuality. If people think of public choices only in these terms, it is not surprising that they use in any public setting the "first language of individualism." This, then, is where people "have difficulty articulating the richness of their commitments"; this is where "their lives sound more isolated and arbitrary than...they actually are"; here, where the capacity to identify shared values is most acutely needed, it is most consistently lacking. So what can be done about this deadly paradox? If it is true that people attain civic virtues through practices, and if it is true that many people gain such education outside the public arena, the obvious question is: "What can be done to establish practices which would teach people to act and speak in a truly public way in public?"

There is no simple answer to that question. But one part of the answer may emerge from understanding how important to practices is the concrete, the specific, the tangible. It is precisely that element of concreteness which gives to practices their capacity to present values as something objective, and therefore as something public. Again, we need to recall Arendt's table—that actual, physical thing, the *res* which makes the public (the common unity or community) possible at all. Lawrence Haworth has perhaps best understood the essential connection between the concepts of community and objectivity: "In any genuine community there are shared values: the members are united through the fact that they fix on some object as preeminently valuable. And there is a joint effort, involving all members of the community, by which they give overt expression to their mutual regard for that object."

In the case of my parents and their neighbors, this matter of objectivity may be viewed on several levels. The barn itself was an "object" which, being a straightforward matter of life and death, seems to qualify as being "preeminently valuable." The barn was as real, as objective, as anything could be, but it only acquired its urgency within the context of the broader and even more compelling objectivity

of the land and the weather to which it was a response. However Albert and Lilly may have differed in some of their personal values, they differed not at all in their experience of winter on the high plains. For both of them alike, the prairie winter was cold and deadly, and it absolutely required a good barn.

Strangely enough, that objective requirement of a good barn meant that they were not free to treat their values as being purely subjective. In some things they could afford to be subjective, to be sure. Albert could value beer and salty language in a way that Lilly never would. But when it came to values like reliability, perseverance, or even a certain level of conviviality, they found themselves dealing in something much more objective than we generally think of "values" as being. In fact, those people could no more do without those values than they could do without their barns, simply because they could not get the barns built without the values. The shaping of their values was as much a communal response to their place as was the building of their barns.

The kinds of values which might form the basis for a genuinely public life, then, arise out of a context which is concrete in at least two ways. It is concrete in the actual things or events—the barns, the barn dances—which the practices of cooperation produce. But it is also concrete in the actual, specific places within which those practices and that cooperation take place. Clearly, the practices which shaped the behavior and the character of frontier families did not appear out of thin air; they grew out of the one thing those people had most fundamentally in common: the effort to survive in hard country. And when the effort to survive comes to rely upon shared and repeated practices like barn raising, survival itself is transformed; it becomes inhabitation. To in*habit* a place is to dwell there in a practiced way, in a way which relies upon certain regular, trusted habits of behavior.

Our prevailing, individualistic frame of mind has led us to forget this root sense of the concept of "inhabitation." We take it for grant-ed that the way we live in a place is a matter of individual choice (more or less constrained by bureaucratic regulations). We have largely lost the sense that our capacity to live well in a place might depend upon our ability to relate to neighbors (especially neighbors with a different life-style) on the basis of shared habits of be-havior. Our loss of this sense of inhabitation is exactly parallel to our loss of the "republican" sense of what it is to be public.

In fact, no real public life is possible except among people who are engaged in the project of inhabiting a place. If there are not habituated patterns of work, play, grieving, and celebra-tion designed to enable people to live well in a place, then those people will have at best a lim-ited capacity for being public with one another. Conversely, where such inhabitory practices are being nurtured, the foundation for public life is also being created or maintained. This suggests a fairly intimate connection between two potent strains of contemporary American thought. One is the revival of interest in civic republicanism. The other appears frequently under the title of "bioregionalism." That word raises issues of definition which need not detain us here. (I mean specifically the challenge of defining any particular bioregion with lines on a map.) What is of particular interest in this context is the tendency of bioregionalists to identify their work by the word *re-inhabitation*. In a talk with that title, Gary Snyder evokes the connection between "coming into the country" and the habituated ways which make it possible to stay there: "Countless local ecosystem habitation styles emerged. People developed specific ways to *be* in each of those niches: plant knowledge, boats, dogs, traps, nets, fishing—the smaller animals, and smaller tools." These "habitation styles" carried with them precisely the element of objectivity which MacIntyre and Haworth emphasize. Habitation, in other words, implies right and wrong ways of doing things: "Doing things right means living as though your grand-children would also be alive, in this land, car-

rying on the work we're doing right now, with deepening delight."

In this talk, as elsewhere, Snyder acknowl-edges his debt to Wendell Berry's teachings about practiced ways of living in places. Berry makes clear to us why the concept of inhabita-tion is broader and deeper than "environmental-ism":

> The concept of country, homeland, dwell-ing place becomes simplified as "the environment"—that is, what surrounds us. Once we see our place, our part of the world, as *surrounding* us, we have already made a profound division between it and ourselves. We have given up the under-standing—dropped it out of our language and so out of our thought—that we and our country create one another, depend on one another, are literally part of one another; that our land passes in and out of our bod-ies just as our bodies pass in and out of our land; that as we and our land are part of one another, so all who are living as neighbors here, human and plant and animal, are part of one another, and so cannot possibly flourish alone; that, therefore, our culture must be our response to our place, our cul-ture and our place are images of each other and inseparable from each other, and so neither can be better than the other.

Berry and Snyder present some of the best thinking and writing about this intimate relationship of place and culture, including, crucially, the awareness of how places, by de-veloping practices, create culture. The civic re-publicans, in a sense, take up where these writ-ers leave off. That is, they recognize the crucial role of practices, not only in the development of culture, but also in the revitalization of public life. Here is how Bellah speaks of what he calls "practices of commitment":

> People growing up in communities of memory not only hear the stories that tell how the community came to be, what its

hopes and fears are, and how its ideals are exemplified in outstanding men and women; they also participate in the practices—ritual, aesthetic, ethical—that define the community as a way of life. We call these "practices of commitment" for they define the patterns of loyalty and obligation that keep the community alive.

There is considerable room for more mutual reinforcement of these two strains of understanding. The political philosophy of the bioregionalists tends to be vague, uncertain, often more than a little precious and utopian. A more solid, and therefore more confident understanding of how place-centered practices could transform public life would do much to make re-inhabitory politics more credible. The civic republicans are developing very valuable insights into this potentially transformative power of homely practices; what they tend to underemphasize is precisely what the bioregionalists understand so well: the essential role of place in developing those practices.

It is in what Bellah calls "communities of memory" that these "second languages and practices of commitment" have been most carefully preserved. Because of this, it has seemed appropriate to take the occasion of centennial (and bicentennial) celebrations to help us recall how cooperation could once have become such an important part of our culture. But of course there comes a time for turning from what was to what may be. If public life needs to be revitalized, if its renewal depends upon more conscious and more confident ways of drawing upon the capacity of practices to make values objective and public, if those practices acquire that power from the efforts of unlike people to live well in specific places, then we need to think about specific places, and the real people who now live in them, and try to imagine ways in which their efforts to live there might become more practiced, more inhabitory, and therefore more public.

There are two arenas within which this move toward a more inhabitory and more public life must occur if it is to sustain itself. One is the arena of economics; the other, that of politics. The final two chapters will explore the concept of re-inhabitation in those two contexts.

Ralph Waldo Emerson
Society and Solitude

Ralph Waldo Emerson (1803–1882), American poet and essayist, was the leading figure of a group of New England idealist thinkers known as the transcedentalists. Emerson believed that individuals should approach political problems by seeking the truth within themselves, rather than in the analysis of history. While the human mind is merely an imperfect copy of the mind of God, the human soul is part of the divine spirit. The political theories of the mind will always be contested by future generations, but the lessons of the soul—or the lessons of Nature—remain true for all time.

In the following selection, Emerson begins with a portrait of a "humorist," an overbred, eccentric intellectual incapable of speaking to the common people. In discussing this person's radically solitary life, Emerson develops a theory asserting that all intellectual achievement tragically and necessarily leads to a lonely life, isolated from the corrupting influences of society. Most great men in history have been social outcasts, Emerson observes. But then, halfway through the essay, Emerson catches himself and rejects these conclusions as overly intellectual and contradictory of experience. Observation shows that social life fulfills a psychological need. Furthermore, in society people can cooperate in order to achieve more than when alone. Only the "friction of society" can free the "animal spirits" or creative passions of the soul, without which rational knowledge of "facts" remains powerless. Everyone has these creative passions, but most need contact with others to stimulate their non-rational side. Emerson thus finds value in social contact, but he also remains suspicious of society's corrupting influences. Our sympathy for others can either improve or corrupt us, depending on with whom we associate. Emerson thus presents life in society as a balancing act: we need society to support and stimulate us, but we must retain a rigorous independent capacity for insight into our individual principles about the type of society we desire.

Society and Solitude
Ralph Waldo Emerson

I fell in with a humorist on my travels, who had in his chamber a cast of the Rondanini Medusa, and who assured me that the name which that fine work of art bore in the catalogues was a misnomer, as he was convinced that the sculptor who carved it intended it for Memory, the mother of the Muses. In the conversation that followed, my new friend made some extraordinary confessions. "Do you not see," he said, "the penalty of learning, and that each of these scholars whom you have met at S—, though he were to be the last man, would, like the executioner in Hood's poem, guillotine the last but one?" He added many lively remarks, but his evident earnestness engaged my attention, and in the weeks that followed we became better acquainted. He had good abilities, a genial temper and no vices; but he had one defect,—he could not speak in the tone of the people. There was some paralysis on his will, such that when he met men on common terms he spoke weakly and from the point, like a flighty girl. His consciousness of the fault made it worse. He envied every drover and lumberman in the tavern their manly speech. He coveted Mirabeau's *don ter-* *rible de la familiarité*, believing that he whose sympathy goes lowest is the man from whom kings have the most to fear. For himself he declared that he could not get enough alone to write a letter to a friend. He left the city; he hid himself in pastures. The solitary river was not solitary enough; the sun and moon put him out. When he bought a house, the first thing he did was to plant trees. He could not enough conceal himself. Set a hedge here; set oaks there,—trees behind trees; above all, set evergreens, for they will keep a secret all the year round. The most agreeable compliment you could pay him was to imply that you had not observed him in a house or a street where you had met him. Whilst he suffered at being seen where he was, he consoled himself with the delicious thought of the inconceivable number of places where he was not. All he wished of his tailor was to provide that sober mean of color and cut which would never detain the eye for a moment. He went to Vienna, to Smyrna, to London. In all the variety of costumes, a carnival, a kaleidoscope of clothes, to his horror he could never discover a man in the street who wore anything like his own dress. He would have given his soul for the ring of Gyges. His dismay at his visibility had blunted the fears of mortality. "Do you think," he said, "I am in such great terror of being shot,—I, who am only waiting to shuffle off my corporeal jacket to slip away into the back stars, and put diameters of the solar system and sidereal orbits between me and all souls,—there to wear out ages in solitude, and forget memory itself, if it be possible?" He had a remorse running to despair of his social *gaucheries*, and walked miles and miles to get the twitchings out of his face, the starts and shrugs out of his arms and shoulders. God may forgive sins, he said, but awkwardness has no forgiveness in heaven or earth. He admired in Newton not so much his theory of the moon as his letter to Collins, in which he forbade him to insert his name with the solution of the problem in the Philosophical Transactions: "It would perhaps increase my acquaintance, the thing which I chiefly study to decline."

These conversations led me somewhat later to the knowledge of similar cases, and to the discovery that they are not of very infrequent occurrence. Few substances are found pure in nature. Those constitutions which can bear in open day the rough dealing of the world must be of that mean and average structure such as iron and salt, atmospheric air and water. But there are metals, like potassium and sodium, which, to be kept pure, must be kept under naphtha. Such are the talents determined on some specialty, which a culminating civilization fosters in the heart of great cities and in royal chambers. Nature protects her own work. To the culture of the world an Archimedes, a Newton is indispensable; so she guards them by a certain aridity. If these had been good fellows, fond of dancing, port and clubs, we should have had no Theory of the Sphere and no Principia. They had that necessity of isolation which genius feels. Each must stand on his glass tripod if he would keep his electricity. Even Swedenborg, whose theory of the universe is based on affection, and who reprobates to weariness the

danger and vice of pure intellect, is constrained to make an extraordinary exception: "There are also angels who do not live consociated, but separate, house and house; these dwell in the midst of heaven, because they are the best of angels."

We have known many fine geniuses with that imperfection that they cannot do anything useful, not so much as write one clean sentence. 'T is worse, and tragic, that no man is fit for society who has fine traits. At a distance he is admired, but bring him hand to hand, he is a cripple. One protects himself by solitude, and one by courtesy, and one by an acid, worldly manner,—each concealing how he can the thinness of his skin and his incapacity for strict association. But there is no remedy that can reach the heart of the disease but either habits of self-reliance that should go in practice to making the man independent of the human race, or else a religion of love. Now he hardly seems entitled to marry; for how can he protect a woman, who cannot protect himself?

We pray to be conventional. But the wary Heaven takes care you shall not be, if there is anything good in you. Dante was very bad company, and was never invited to dinner. Michel Angelo had a sad, sour time of it. The ministers of beauty are rarely beautiful in coaches and saloons. Columbus discovered no isle or key so lonely as himself. Yet each of these potentates saw well the reason of his exclusion. Solitary was he? Why, yes; but his society was limited only by the amount of brain nature appropriated in that age to carry on the government of the world. "If I stay," said Dante, when there was question of going to Rome, "who will go? and if I go, who will stay?"

But the necessity of solitude is deeper than we have said, and is organic. I have seen many a philosopher whose world is large enough for only one person. He affects to be a good companion; but we are still surprising his secret, that he means and needs to impose his system on all the rest. The determination of each is *from* all the others, like that of each tree up into free space. 'T is no wonder, when each has his whole head, our societies should be so small. Like President Tyler, our party falls from us every day, and we must ride in a sulky at last. Dear heart! take it sadly home to thee,—there is no coöperation. We begin with friendships, and all our youth is a reconnoitring and recruiting of the holy fraternity they shall combine for the salvation of men. But so the remoter stars seem a nebula of united light, yet there is no group which a telescope will not resolve; and the dearest friends are separated by impassable gulfs. The coöperation is involuntary, and is put upon us by the Genius of Life, who reserves this as a part of his prerogative. 'T is fine for us to talk; we sit and muse and are serene and complete; but the moment we meet with anybody, each becomes a fraction.

Though the stuff of tragedy and of romances is in a moral union of two superior persons whose confidence in each other for long years, out of sight and in sight, and against all appearances, is at last justified by victorious proof of probity to gods and men, causing joyful emotions, tears and glory,—though there be for heroes this *moral union*, yet they too are as far off as ever from an intellectual union, and the moral union is for comparatively low and external purposes, like the coöperation of a ship's company or of a fire-club. But how insular and pathetically solitary are all the people we know! Nor dare they tell what they think of each other when they meet in the street. We have a fine right, to be sure, to taunt men of the world with superficial and treacherous courtesies!

Such is the tragic necessity which strict science finds underneath our domestic and neighborly life, irresistibly driving each adult soul as with whips into the desert, and making our warm covenants sentimental and momentary. We must infer that the ends of thought were peremptory, if they were to be secured at such ruinous cost.

They are deeper than can be told, and belong to the immensities and eternities. They reach down to that depth where society itself originates and disappears; where the question is, Which is first, man or men? where the individual is lost in his source.

But this banishment to the rocks and echoes no metaphysics can make right or tolerable. This result is so against nature, such a half-view, that it must be corrected by a common sense and experience. "A man is born by the side of his father, and there he remains." A man must be clothed with society, or we shall feel a certain bareness and poverty, as of a displaced and unfurnished member. He is to be dressed in arts and institutions, as well as in body garments. Now and then a man exquisitely made can live alone, and must; but coop up most men and you undo them. "The king lived and ate in his hall with men, and understood men," said Selden. When a young barrister said to the late Mr. Mason "I keep my chamber to read law,"— "Read law!" replied the veteran, "'t is in the court-room you must read law." Nor is the rule otherwise for literature. If you would learn to write, 't is in the street you must learn it. Both for the vehicle and for the aims of fine arts you must frequent the public square. The people, and not the college, is the writer's home. A scholar is a candle which the love and desire of all men will light. Never his lands or his rents, but the power to charm the disguised soul that sits veiled under this bearded and that rosy visage is his rent and ration. His products are as needful as those of the baker or the weaver. Society cannot do without cultivated men. As soon as the first wants are satisfied, the higher wants become imperative.

'T is hard to mesmerize ourselves, to whip our own top; but through sympathy we are capable of energy and endurance. Concert fires people to a certain fury of performance they can rarely reach alone. Here is the use of society: it is so easy with the great to be great; so easy to come up to an existing standard;—as easy as it is to the lover to swim to his maiden through waves so grim before. The benefits of affection are immense; and the one event which never loses its romance is the encounter with superior persons on terms allowing the happiest intercourse.

It by no means follows that we are not fit for society, because *soirèes* are tedious and because the *soirèe* finds us tedious. A backwoodsman, who had been sent to the university, told me that when he heard the best-bred young men at the law-school talk together, he reckoned himself a boor; but whenever he caught them apart, and had one to himself alone, then they were the boors and he the better man. And if we recall the rare hours when we encountered the best persons, we then found ourselves, and then first society seemed to exist. That was society, though in the transom of a brig or on the Florida Keys.

A cold sluggish blood thinks it has not facts enough to the purpose, and must decline its tome in the conversation. But they who speak have no more,—have less. 'T is not new facts that avail, but the heat to dissolve everybody's facts. Heat puts you in right relation with magazines of facts. The capital defect of cold, arid natures is the want of animal spirits. They seem a power incredible, as if God should raise the dead. The recluse witnesses what others perform by their aid, with a kind of fear. It is as much out of his possibility as the prowess of Coeur-de-Lion, or an Irishman's day's work on the railroad. 'T is said the present and the future are always rivals. Animal spirits constitute the power of the present, and their feats are like the structure of a pyramid. Their result is a lord, a general, or a boon companion. Before these what a base mendicant is Memory with his leathern badge! But this genial heat is latent in all constitutions, and is disengaged only by the friction of society. As Bacon said of manners, "To obtain them, it only needs not to despise them," so we say of animal spirits that they are the spontaneous product of health and of a social habit. "For behavior, men learn it, as they take diseases, one of another."

But the people are to be taken in very small doses. If solitude is proud, so is society vulgar. In society, high advantages are set down to the individual as disqualifications. We sink as easily as we rise, through sympathy. So many men whom I know are degraded by their sympathies; their native aims being high enough, but their relation all too tender to the gross people about them. Men cannot afford to live together on their merits, and they adjust themselves by their demerits,—by their love of gossip, or by sheer tolerance and animal good nature. They untune and dissipate the brave aspirant.

The remedy is to reinforce each of these moods from the other. Conversation will not corrupt us if we come to the assembly in our own garb and speech and with the energy of health to select what is ours and reject what is not. Society we must have; but let it be society, and not exchanging news or eating from the same dish. Is it society to sit in one of your chairs? I cannot go to the houses of my nearest relatives, because I do not wish to be alone. Society exists by chemical affinity, and not otherwise.

Put any company of people together with freedom for conversation, and a rapid self-distribution takes place into sets and pairs. The best are accused of exclusiveness. It would be more true to say they separate as oil from water, as children from old people, without love or hatred in the matter, each seeking his like; and any interference with the affinities would produce constraint and suffocation. All conversation is a magnetic experiment. I know that my friend can talk eloquently; you know that he cannot articulate a sentence: we have seen him in different company. Assort your party, or invite none. Put Stubbs and Coleridge, Quintilian and Aunt Miriam, into pairs, and you make them all wretched. 'T is an extempore Sing-Sing built in a parlor. Leave them to seek their own mates, and they will be as merry as sparrows.

A higher civility will reëstablish in our customs a certain reverence which we have lost. What to do with these brisk young men who break through all fences, and make themselves at home in every house? I find out in an instant if my companion does not want me, and ropes cannot hold me when my welcome is gone. One would think that the affinities would pronounce themselves with a surer reciprocity.

Here again, as so often, nature delights to put us between extreme antagonisms, and our safety is in the skill with which we keep the diagonal line. Solitude is impracticable, and society fatal. We must keep our head in the one and our hands in the other. The conditions are met, if we keep our independence, yet do not lose our sympathy. These wonderful horses need to be driven by fine hands. We require such a solitude as shall hold us to its revelations when we are in the street and in palaces; for most men are cowed in society, and say good things to you in private, but will not stand to them in public. But let us not be the victims of words. Society and solitude are deceptive names. It is not the circumstance of seeing more or fewer people, but the readiness of sympathy, that imports; and a sound mind will derive its principles from insight, with ever a purer ascent to the sufficient and absolute right, and will accept society as the natural element in which they are to be applied.

Aristotle

The Politics

Aristotle (384–322 BC) was born in northern Greece and studied at Plato's Academy in Athens, well after the "golden Age" of Periclean Athens to which Socrates and then Plato had borne witness. Aristotle served as tutor to Alexander the Great, eventually returning to Athens where he founded his own school of philosophy. Aristotle thought political theory should always take existing conditions as its starting point, and much of *The Politics* stems from his observations of the institutions of over 150 Greek states. Although his travels rarely gave him the opportunity to enjoy the life of a citizen, he believed that the fulfillment of human nature lies in political activity. He defined man as a "political animal," though he excluded women, slaves, and foreigners ("barbarians") from citizenship.

In the following selection from *The Politics*, Aristotle considers whether "mechanics"—common workers, artisans, farmers, etc.—can be citizens. Mechanics provide the material foundations of the state, but have little time or ability to hold state offices. This prevents them from gaining the experience of both ruling and being ruled that Aristotle considers essential for good citizenship. Aristotle's conclusions on this question reflect his pragmatic attitude toward political diversity, coupled with his view that we are "political animals" and can only enjoy "the good life" as citizens of a state.

The Politics
Aristotle

Citizenship and Constitutions

§ I. There is still a question which remains to be considered in regard to citizenship. Is citizenship in the true sense to be limited to those who have the right of sharing in office, or must mechanics be also included in the ranks of citizens? If we hold that mechanics, who have no share in the offices of the state are also to be included, we shall have some citizens who can never achieve the excellence of the good citizen [which requires an experience of ruling as well as of being ruled]. If, on the other hand, mechanics should not be called citizens, in what class are they to be placed? They are not resident aliens, neither are they foreigners: what is their class? § 2. It is difficult to say; but may we not hold **1278** a that the difficulty does not involve us in any absurdity? [If mechanics cannot be placed in any of the classes mentioned] neither can slaves, nor freedmen. The truth is that we cannot include as citizens all who are 'necessary conditions' [without being 'integral parts'] of the state's existence*. Similarly, too, children [though they come nearer to being citizens] are not citizens in the same sense as adults. Adults are citizens absolutely; children are citizens only in a qualified sense and with a reservation—the reservation that they are undeveloped. § 3. There were some

From *The Politics of Aristotle* edited and translated by Ernest Barker. Copyright 1946. Reprinted by permission of Oxford University Press.

* Aristotle here draws, by implication, a distinction between (1) those members of a polis who are 'integral parts' and actively share in its life, thus enjoying the status of *polites* or citizen, and (2) those members of the polis who are 'necessary conditions' or *sine quibus non*, and whose share in its life is not that of active participation in its political activity, but only that of providing the material basis (of housing, food, commodities, and services) which is a condition of that activity.

states, in ancient times, where the class of mechanics was actually composed of slaves or foreigners only, and this explains why a great number of mechanics are slaves or foreigners even to-day. The best form of state [will not go so far, but at the same time it] will not make the mechanic a citizen. In states where mechanics *are* admitted to citizenship we shall have to say that the citizen excellence of which we have spoken [that of the good citizen who has experience of ruling as well as of being ruled] cannot be attained by every citizen, or by all who are simply free men, but can only be achieved by those who are free from menial duties.... § 4. Those who do menial duties may be divided into two classes—slaves, who do them for individuals, and mechanics and labourers, who do them for the community....

If we start from this basis, and carry our inquiry a little further, the position of these mechanics and labourers will soon become evident; in fact, enough has already been said to make it clear, once the bearing of the argument is grasped.* § 5. Constitutions are various: there must thus be various kinds of citizens; more especially, there must be various kinds of citizens who are subjects. In one variety of constitution it will be necessary that mechanics and labourers should be citizens: in other varieties it will be impossible. It will be impossible, for example, where there is a constitution of the type termed 'aristocratic', with offices distributed on the basis of worth and excellence; for a man who lives the life of a mechanic or labourer cannot pursue the things which belong to excellence. § 6. The case is different in oligarchies. Even there, it is true, a labourer cannot be a citizen (participation in office depending on a high property qualification); but a mechanic

may, for the simple reason that craftsmen often become rich men. § 7. Yet in Thebes [even when it was an oligarchy] there was a law that no man could share in office who had not abstained from selling in the market for a period of ten years. On the other hand there are many constitutions where the law goes to the length of admitting aliens to citizenship. There are, for example, some democracies where a man who has only a citizen-mother is admitted; and there are many states where the same privilege is given to persons of illegitimate birth. § 8. But the policy of extending citizenship so widely is [generally a temporary policy] due to a dearth of genuine citizens; and it is only a decrease of numbers which produces such legislation. When the population increases again [a different policy is gradually followed]: first sons of a slave-father or slave-mother are disqualified; then those who are born of a citizen-mother but an alien father; and finally citizenship is confined to those who are of citizen parentage on both sides.

§ 9. These considerations prove two things—that there are several different kinds of citizens, and that the name of citizen is particularly applicable to those who share in the offices and honours of the state. Homer accordingly speaks in the *Iliad* of a man being treated like an alien man, *without honour*; and it is true that those who do not share in the offices and honours of the state are just like resident aliens. To deny men a share [may sometimes be justified, but] when it is done by subterfuge its only object is merely that of hoodwinking others. § 10. Two conclusions also emerge from our discussion of the question, 'Is the excellence **1278 b** of the good man identical with that of the good citizen, or different from it?' The first is that there

---

*'Enough has already been said' is a reference to c. I, § 9 of this book, where it was noticed that constitutions differed and were of different qualities. It follows naturally from these differences that citizenship differs from constitution to constitution, and that under some constitutions the position of mechanics and hired labourers may be that of citizens, though it will not be such under other constitutions.

are some states in which the good man and the good citizen are identical, and some in which they are different. The second is that, in states of the former type, it is not all good citizens who are also good men, but only those among them who hold the position of statesmen—in other words those who direct or are capable of directing, either alone or in conjunction with others, the conduct of public affairs.

Thucydides

The Peloponnesian War

Thucydides' *History of the Peloponnesian* War may be western civilization's first war-time journalism. The Athenian historian began his narrative account at the outbreak of war in 431 BC. between the Athenians and the Spartan led Laecedæmonians. The two leagues had previously been allies, but according to Thucydides, the growth of the Athenian empire threatened the Laecedæmonians and made war inevitable. Thucydides took great pains to present an impartial account of the war, basing his reconstruction of events on both his own impressions and those of others. The *History*, however, represents more than documentation for its own sake. Thucydides wrote with the intent that his work be "judged useful by those inquirers who desire an exact knowledge of the past as an aid to the interpretation of the future."

In the following selection, known as the "The Funeral Oration," Thucydides reconstructs a speech by the Athenian leader Pericles given to honor the first Athenians killed in the war. Pericles' aim is the "comfort…not condolence" of the Athenians— friends and relatives can consider the dead fortunate to have heroically given their lives in defense of their city. He reminds them that in Athens political discussion precedes action, that the politically inactive are considered useless, and that Athens serves as a model for all of Greece. In this way, he places the mourners' loss in a larger context and gives both the dead and the living a common purpose. Rather than dwelling on private grief, Pericles reminds his listeners that their Athenian citizenship unites them in a public bond which will always bring them honor and happiness.

The Peloponnesian War
Thucydides

The Funeral Oration

In the course of this winter the Athenians, in accordance with the custom of their forefathers, buried at the public expense those who had first fallen in this war, after the following manner. Having erected a tent, they lay out the bones of the dead three days before, and each one brings to his own relative whatever [funeral offering] he pleases. When the funeral procession takes place, cars convey coffins of cypress wood, one for each tribe; in which are laid the bones of every man, according to the tribe to which he belonged; and one empty bier is carried, spread in honour of the missing, whose bodies could not be found to be taken up. Whoever wishes, both of citizens and strangers, joins in the procession; and their female relatives attend at the burial to make the wailings. They lay them then in the public sepulchre, which is in the fairest suburb of the city, and in which they always bury those who have fallen in the wars (except, at least, those who fell at Marathon; but to them, as they considered their valour distinguished above that of all others, they gave a burial on the very spot). After they have laid them in the ground, a man chosen by the state—one who in point of intellect is considered talented, and in dignity is pre-eminent—speaks over them such a panegyric as may be appropriate; after which they all retire. In this way they bury them: and through the whole of the war, whenever they had occasion, they observed the established custom. Over these who were first buried at any rate, Pericles son of Xanthippus was chosen to speak. And when the time for doing so came, advancing from the sepulchre on to a platform, which had been raised to some height, that he might be heard over as great a part of the crowd as possible, he spoke to the following effect:

"The greater part of those who ere now have spoken in this place, have been accustomed to praise the man who introduced this oration into the law; considering it a right thing that it should be delivered over those who are buried after falling in battle. To me, however, it would have appeared sufficient, that when men had shown themselves brave by deeds, their honours also should be displayed by deeds—as you now see in the case of this burial, prepared at the public expense—and not that the virtues of many should be perilled in one individual, for credit to be given him according as he expresses himself well or ill. For it is difficult to speak with propriety on a subject on which even the impression of one's truthfulness is with difficulty established. For the hearer who is acquainted [with the facts], and kindly disposed [towards those who performed them], might perhaps think them somewhat imperfectly set forth, compared with what he both wishes and knows; while he who is unacquainted with them might think that some points were even exaggerated, being led to this conclusion by envy, should he hear any thing surpassing his own natural powers. For praises spoken of others are only endured so far as each one thinks that he is himself also capable of doing any of the things he hears; but that which exceeds their own capacity men at once envy and disbelieve. Since, however, our ancestors judged this to be a right custom, I too, in obedience to the law, must endeavour to meet the wishes and views of every one, as far as possible.

"I will begin then with our ancestors first: for it is just, and becoming too at the same time, that on such an occasion the honour of being thus mentioned should be paid them. For always inhabiting the country without change, through a long succession of posterity, by their valour they transmitted it free to this very time. Justly then may they claim to be commended; and more justly still may our own fathers. For in addition to what they inherited, they acquired the great empire which we possess, and by painful exertions bequeathed it to us of the present day: though to most part of it have additions been made by ourselves here, who are still, generally speaking, in the vigour of life; and we have furnished our city with every thing, so as to be most self-sufficient both for peace and for war. Now with regard to our military achievements, by which each possession was gained, whether in any case it were ourselves, or our fathers, that repelled with

spirit hostilities brought against us by barbarian or Greek; as I do not wish to enlarge on the subject before you who are well acquainted with it, I will pass them over. But by what a mode of life we attained to our power, and by what form of government and owing to what habits it became so great, I will explain these points first, and then proceed to the eulogy of these men; as I consider that on the present occasion they will not be inappropriately mentioned, and that it is profitable for the whole assembly, both citizens and strangers, to listen to them.

"For we enjoy a form of government which does not copy the laws of our neighbors; but we are ourselves rather a pattern to others than imitators of them. In name, from its not being administered for the benefit of the few, but of the many, it is called a democracy; but with regard to its laws, all enjoy equality, as concerns their private differences; while with regard to public rank, according as each man has reputation for any thing, he is preferred for public honours, not so much from consideration of party, as of merit; nor, again, on the ground of poverty, while he is able to do the state any good service, is he prevented by the obscurity of his position. We are liberal then in our public administration; and with regard to mutual jealousy of our daily pursuits, we are not angry with our neighbor, if he does any thing to please himself; nor wear on our countenance offensive looks, which though harmless, are yet unpleasant. While, however, in private matters we live together agreeably, in public matters, under the influence of fear, we most carefully abstain from transgression, through our obedience to those who are from time to time in office, and to the laws; especially such of them as are enacted for the benefit of the injured, and such as, though unwritten, bring acknowledged disgrace [on those who break them].

"Moreover, we have provided for our spirits the most numerous recreations from labours, by celebrating games and sacrifices through the whole year, and by maintaining elegant private establishments, of which the daily gratification drives away sadness. Owing to the greatness too of our city, every thing from every land is imported into it; and it is our lot to reap with no more peculiar enjoyment the good things which are produced here, than those of the rest of the world likewise.

"In the studies of war also we differ from our enemies in the following respects. We throw our city open to all, and never, by the expulsion of strangers, exclude any one from either learning or observing things, by seeing which unconcealed any of our enemies might gain an advantage; for we trust not so much to preparations and stratagems, as to our own valour for daring deeds. Again, as to our modes of education, *they* aim at the acquisition of a manly character, by laborious training from their very youth; while *we*, though living at our ease, no less boldly advance to meet equal dangers. As a proof of this, the Lacedæmonians never march against our country singly, but with all [their confederates] together: while we, generally speaking, have no difficulty in conquering in battle upon hostile ground those who are standing up in defence of their own. And no enemy ever yet encountered our whole united force, through our attending at the same time to our navy, and sending our troops by land on so many different services: but wherever they have engaged with any part of it, if they conquer only some of us, they boast that we were all routed by them; and if they are conquered, they say it was by all that they were beaten. And yet if with careless ease rather than with laborious practice, and with a courage which is the result not so much of laws as of natural disposition, we are willing to face danger, we have the advantage of not suffering beforehand from coming troubles, and of proving ourselves, when we are involved in them, no less bold than those who are always toiling; so that our country is worthy of admiration in these respects, and in others besides.

"For we study taste with economy, and philosophy without effeminacy; and employ wealth rather for opportunity of action than for boastfulness of talking; while poverty is noth-

ing disgraceful for a man to confess, but not to escape it by exertion is more disgraceful. Again, the same men can attend at the same time to domestic as well as to public affairs; and others, who are engaged with business, can still form a sufficient judgment on political questions. For we are the only people that consider the man who takes no part in these things, not as unofficious, but as useless; and we ourselves judge rightly of measures, at any rate, if we do not originate them; while we do not regard words as any hindrance to deeds, but rather [consider it a hindrance] not to have been previously instructed by word, before undertaking in deed what we have to do. For we have this characteristic also in a remarkable degree, that we are at the same time most daring and most calculating in what we take in hand; whereas to other men it is ignorance that brings daring, while calculation brings fear. Those, however, would deservedly be deemed most courageous, who know most fully what is terrible and what is pleasant, and yet do not on this account shrink from dangers. As regards beneficence also we differ from the generality of men; for we make friends, not by receiving, but by conferring kindness. Now he who has conferred the favour is the firmer friend, in order that he may keep alive the obligation by good will towards the man on whom he has conferred it; whereas he who owes it in return feels less keenly, knowing that it is not as a favour, but as a debt, that he will repay the kindness. Nay, we are the only men who fearlessly benefit any one, not so much from calculations of expediency, as with the confidence of liberality.

"In short, I say that both the whole city is a school for Greece, and that, in my opinion, the same individual would amongst us prove himself qualified for the most varied kinds of action, and with the most graceful versatility. And that this is not mere vaunting language for the occasion, so much as actual truth, the very power of the state, which we have won by such habits, affords a proof. For it is the only country at the present time that, when brought to the test, proves superior to its fame; and the only one that neither gives to the enemy who has attacked us any cause for indignation at being worsted by such opponents, nor to him who is subject to us room for finding fault, as not being ruled by men who are worthy of empire. But we shall be admired both by present and future generations as having exhibited our power with great proofs, and by no means without evidence; and as having no further need, either of Homer to praise us, or any one else who might charm for the moment by his verses, while the truth of the facts would mar the idea formed of them; but as having compelled every sea and land to become accessible to our daring, and every where established everlasting records, whether of evil or of good. It was for such a country then that these men, nobly resolving not to have it taken from them, fell fighting; and every one of their survivors may well be willing to suffer in its behalf.

"For this reason, indeed, it is that I have enlarged on the characteristics of the state; both to prove that the struggle is not for the same object in our case as in that of men who have none of these advantages in an equal degree; and at the same time clearly to establish by proofs [the truth of] the eulogy of those men over whom I am now speaking. And now the chief points of it have been mentioned; for with regard to the things for which I have commended the city, it was the virtues of these men, and such as these, that adorned her with them; and few of the Greeks are there whose fame, like these men's, would appear but the just counterpoise of their deeds. Again, the closing scene of these men appears to me to supply an illustration of human worth, whether as affording us the first information respecting it, or its final confirmation. For even in the case of men who have been in other respects of an inferior character, it is but fair for them to hold forth as a screen their military courage in their country's behalf; for, having wiped out their evil by their good, they did more service collectively, than harm by their individual offences. But of these men

there was none that either was made a coward by his wealth, from preferring the continued enjoyment of it; or shrank from danger through a hope suggested by poverty, namely, that he might yet escape it, and grow rich; but conceiving that vengeance on their foes was more to be desired than these objects, and at the same time regarding this as the most glorious of hazards, they wished by risking it to be avenged on their enemies, and so to aim at procuring those advantages; committing to hope the uncertainty of success, but resolving to trust to action, with regard to what was visible to themselves; and in that action, being minded rather to resist and die, than by surrendering to escape, they fled from the shame of [a discreditable] report, while they endured the brunt of the battle with their bodies; and after the shortest crisis, when at the very height of their fortune, were taken away from their glory rather than their fear.

"Such did these men prove themselves, as became the character of their country. For you that remain, you must pray that you may have a more successful resolution, but must determine not to have one less bold against your enemies; not in word alone considering the benefit [of such a spirit], (on which one might descant to you at great length—though you know it yourselves quite as well—telling you how many advantages are contained in repelling your foes;) but rather day by day beholding the power of the city as it appears in fact, and growing enamoured of it, and reflecting, when you think it great, that it was by being bold, and knowing their duty, and being alive to shame in action, that men acquired these things; and because, if they ever failed in their attempt at any thing, they did not on that account think it right to deprive their country also of their valour, but conferred upon her a most glorious joint-offering. For while collectively they gave her their lives, individually they received that renown which never grows old, and the most distinguished tomb they could have; not so much that in which they are laid, as that in which their glory is left behind them, to be everlastingly recorded on every occasion for doing so, either by word or deed, that may from time to time present itself. For of illustrious men the whole earth is the sepulchre; and not only does the inscription upon the columns in their own land point it out, but in that also which is not their own there dwells with every one an unwritten memorial of the heart, rather than of a material monument. Vieing then with these men in your turn, and deeming happiness to consist in freedom, and freedom in valour, do not think lightly of the hazards of war. For it is not the unfortunate, [and those] who have no hope of any good, that would with most reason be unsparing of their lives; but those who, while they live, still incur the risk of a change to the opposite condition, and to whom the difference would be the greatest, should they meet with any reverse. For more grievous, to a man of high spirit at least, is the misery which accompanies cowardice, than the unfelt death which comes upon him at once, in the time of his strength and of his hope for the common welfare.

"Wherefore to the parents of the dead—as many of them as are here among you—I will not offer condolence, so much as consolation. For they know that they have been brought up subject to manifold misfortunes; but that happy is *their* lot who have gained the most glorious—death, as these have,—sorrow, as you have; and to whom life has been so exactly measured, that they were both happy in it, and died in [that happiness]. Difficult, indeed, I know it is to persuade you of this, with regard to those of whom you will often be reminded by the good fortune of others, in which you yourselves also once rejoiced; and sorrow is felt, not for the blessings of which one is bereft without full experience of them, but of that which one loses after becoming accustomed to it. But you must bear up in the hope of other children, those of you whose age yet allows you to have them. For to yourselves individually those who are subsequently born will be a reason for your forgetting those who are no more; and to the state it will be beneficial in two ways, by its not being depopulated, and by the enjoyment of security; for it is not possible that those should offer any fair and just advice, who do not incur equal risk with their neighbours by having children at stake. Those of you, however, who are past that age, must consider that the longer period of your life during which you have been prosperous is so much gain, and that what remains will be but a short one; and you must cheer yourselves with the fair fame of these [your lost ones]. For the love of honour is the only feeling that never grows old; and in the helplessness of age it is not the acquisition of gain, as some assert, that gives greatest pleasure, but the enjoyment of honour.

"For those of you, on the other hand, who are sons or brothers of the dead, great, I see, will be the struggle of competition. For every one is accustomed to praise the man who is no more; and scarcely, though even for an excess of worth, would you be esteemed, I do not say equal to them, but only slightly inferior. For the living are exposed to envy in their rivalry; but those who are in no one's way are honoured with a good will free from all opposition. If, again, I must say any thing on the subject of woman's excellence also, with reference to those of you who will now be in widowhood, I will express it all in a brief exhortation. Great will be your glory in not falling short of the natural character that belongs to you; and great is hers, who is least talked of amongst the men, either for good or evil.

"I have now expressed *in word*, as the law required, what I had to say befitting the occasion; and, *in deed*, those who are here interred, have already received part of their honours; while, for the remaining part, the state will bring up their sons at the public expense, from this time to their manhood; thus offering both to these and to their posterity a beneficial reward for such contests; for where the greatest prizes for virtue are given, there also the most virtuous men are found amongst the citizens. And now, having finished your lamentations for your several relatives, depart."

James Madison
Alexander Hamilton
Federalist Papers No. 10 and No. 51

The Federalist Papers were written fast and furiously in the aftermath of the Constitutional Convention in Philadelphia in 1787. James Madison, the future President, who had played a critical role in Philadelphia, worked with Alexander Hamilton and John Jay (under the psuedonym "Publius") to explain the philosophy and purposes of the new constitution to newspaper readers in New York whose vote for ratification would be needed. Originating as a kind of campaign document, the Papers have become a kind of deep journalistic version of America's founding political philosophy.

They are important for us because they offer a glimpse of how historically Americans have distrusted the voluntary political associations that, as political parties, have become the bridge between civil society and our democratic governing institutions. The Founders thought of parties as "factions" whose divisive interests could obscure both common good and republican virtues, and they engineered a system of government which set power against rival power ("ambition must be made to counteract ambition") in the hope that private interests would cancel one another out. Just as today we worry about "special interest politics" and turn to community service to seek common ground, the Federalists worried about the "latent causes of faction that are sown into the nature of man."

At the same time, although the Federalists thought the Articles of Confederation had conferred too little power on government and hence catalyzed factionalism, they continued to distrust centralized power as well. They began with the premise that men are not angels and that government must protect men from men and protect men from government, and at the same time protect government from the vices of men. Madison's aim was seemingly to empower a government that could unify America and overcome its factions, and then protect the American people from government's potential for abuse—a liberal democracy in which liberal principles prevented democracy from getting out of hand, a limited government in which constitutional limits (like the Bill of Rights) prevented government from getting out of hand.

The Federalist No. 10
James Madison

To the People of the State of New York:

Among the numerous advantages promised by a well-constructed Union, none deserves to be more accurately developed than its tendency to break and control the violence of faction. The friend of popular governments never finds himself so much alarmed for their character and fate as when he contemplates their propensity to this dangerous vice. He will not fail, therefore, to set a due value on any plan which, without violating the principles to which he is attached, provides a proper cure for it. The instability, injustice, and confusion introduced into the public councils have, in truth, been the mortal diseases under which popular governments have everywhere perished, as they continue to be the favorite and fruitful topics from which the adversaries to liberty derive their most specious declamations. The valuable improvements made by the American constitutions on the popular models, both ancient and modern, cannot certainly be too much admired; but it would be an unwarrantable partiality to contend that they have as effectually obviated the danger on this side, as was wished and expected. Complaints are everywhere heard from our most considerate and virtuous citizens, equally the friends of public and private faith and of public and personal liberty, that our governments are too unstable, that the public good is disregarded in the conflicts of rival parties, and that measures are too often decided, not according to the rules of justice and the rights of the minor party, but by the superior force of an interested and overbearing majority. However anxiously we may wish that these complaints had no foundation, the evidence of known facts will not permit us to deny that they are in some degree true. It will be found, indeed, on a candid review of our situation, that some of the distresses under which we labor have been erroneously charged on the operation of our governments; but it will be found, at the same time, that other causes will not alone account for many of our heaviest misfortunes; and, particularly, for that prevailing and increasing distrust of public engagements and alarm for private rights which are echoed from one end of the continent to the other. These must be chiefly, if not wholly, effects of the unsteadiness and injustice with which a factious spirit has tainted our public administrations.

By a faction I understand a number of citizens, whether amounting to a majority or minority of the whole, who are united and actuated by some common impulse of passion, or of interest, adverse to the rights of other citizens, or to the permanent and aggregate interests of the community.

There are two methods of curing the mischiefs of faction: the one, by removing its causes; the other, by controlling its effects.

There are again two methods of removing the causes of faction: the one, by destroying the liberty which is essential to its existence; the other, by giving to every citizen the same opinions, the same passions, and the same interests.

It could never be more truly said than of the first remedy that it was worse than the disease. Liberty is to faction what air is to fire, an ailment without which it instantly expires. But it could not be a less folly to abolish liberty, which is essential to political life, because it nourishes faction than it would be to wish the annihilation of air, which is essential to animal life, because it imparts to fire its destructive agency.

The second expedient is as impracticable as the first would be unwise. As long as the reason of man continues fallible, and he is at liberty to exercise it, different opinions will be formed. As long as the connection subsists between his reason and his self-love, his opinions and his passions will have a reciprocal influence on each other; and the former will be objects to which the latter will attach themselves. The diversity in the faculties of men, from which the rights of property originate, is not less an insuperable obstacle to a uniformity of interests. The protection of these faculties is the first object of government. From the protection of different and unequal faculties of acquiring property, the possession of different degrees and kinds of property immediately results; and from the influence of these on the sentiments and views of the respective proprietors ensues

a division of the society into different interests and parties.

The latent causes of faction are thus sown in the nature of man; and we see them everywhere brought into different degrees of activity, according to the different circumstances of civil society. A zeal for different opinions concerning religion, concerning government, and many other points, as well of speculation as of practice; an attachment to different leaders ambitiously contending for pre-eminence and power; or to persons of other descriptions whose fortunes have been interesting to the human passions, have, in turn, divided mankind into parties, inflamed them with mutual animosity, and rendered them much more disposed to vex and oppress each other than to co-operate for their common good. So strong is this propensity of mankind to fall into mutual animosities that where no substantial occasion presents itself the most frivolous and fanciful distinctions have been sufficient to kindle their unfriendly passions and excite their most violent conflicts. But the most common and durable source of factions has been the various and unequal distribution of property. Those who hold and those who are without property have ever formed distinct interests in society. Those who are creditors, and those who are debtors, fall under a like discrimination. A landed interest, a manufacturing interest, a mercantile interest, a moneyed interest, with many lesser interests, grow up of necessity in civilized nations, and divide them into different classes, actuated by different sentiments and views. The regulation of these various and interfering interests forms the principal task of modern legislation and involves the spirit of party and faction in the necessary and ordinary operations of government.

No man is allowed to be a judge in his own cause, because his interest would certainly bias his judgment, and, not improbably, corrupt his integrity. With equal, nay with greater reason, a body of men are unfit to be both judges and parties at the same time; yet what are many of the most important acts of legislation but so many judicial determinations, not indeed concerning the rights of single persons, but concerning the rights of large bodies of citizens? And what are the different classes of legislators but advocates and parties to the causes which they determine Is a law proposed concerning private debts? It is a question to which the creditors are parties on one side and the debtors on the other. Justice ought to hold the balance between them. Yet the parties are, and must be, themselves the judges; and the most numerous party, or in other words, the most powerful faction must be expected to prevail. Shall domestic manufacturers be encouraged, and in what degree, by restrictions on foreign manufacturers? are questions which would be differently decided by the landed and the manufacturing classes, and probably by neither with a sole regard to justice and the public good. The apportionment of taxes on the various descriptions of property is an act which seems to require the most exact impartiality; yet there is, perhaps, no legislative act in which greater opportunity and temptation are given to a predominant party to trample on the rules of justice. Every shilling with which they overburden the inferior number is a shilling saved to their own pockets.

It is in vain to say that enlightened statesmen will be able to adjust these clashing interests and render them all subservient to the public good. Enlightened statesmen will not always be at the helm. Nor, in many cases, can such an adjustment be made at all without taking into view indirect and remote considerations, which will rarely prevail over the immediate interest which one party may find in disregarding the rights of another or the good of the whole.

The inference to which we are brought is that the *causes* of faction cannot be removed and that relief is only to be sought in the means of controlling its *effects*.

If a faction consists of less than a majority, relief is supplied by the republican principle, which enables the majority to defeat its sinister views by regular vote. It may clog the administration, it may convulse the society; but it

will be unable to execute and mask its violence under the forms of the Constitution. When a majority is included in a faction, the form of popular government, on the other hand, enables it to sacrifice to its ruling passion or interest both the public good and the rights of other citizens. To secure the public good and private rights against the danger of such a faction, and at the same time to preserve the spirit and the form of popular government, is then the great object to which our inquiries are directed. Let me add that it is the great desideratum by which alone this form of government can be rescued from the opprobrium under which it has so long labored and be recommended to the esteem and adoption of mankind.

By what means is this object attainable? Evidently by one of two only. Either the existence of the same passion or interest in a majority at the same time must be prevented, or the majority, having such coexistent passion or interest, must be rendered, by their number and local situation, unable to concert and carry into effect schemes of oppression. If the impulse and the opportunity be suffered to coincide, we well know that neither moral nor religious motives can be relied on as an adequate control. They are not found to be such on the injustice and violence of individuals, and lose their efficacy in proportion to the number combined together, that is, in proportion as their efficacy becomes needful.

From this view of the subject it may be concluded that a pure democracy, by which I mean a society consisting of a small number of citizens who assemble and administer the government in person, can admit of no cure for the mischiefs of faction. A common passion or interest will, in almost every case, be felt by a majority of the whole; a communication and concert results from the form of government itself; and there is nothing to check the inducements to sacrifice the weaker party or an obnoxious individual. Hence it is that such democracies have ever been spectacles of turbulence and contention; have ever been found incompatible with personal security or the rights of property; and have in general been as short in their lives as they have been violent in their deaths. Theoretic politicians, who have patronized this species of government, have erroneously supposed that by reducing mankind to a perfect equality in their political rights, they would at the same time be perfectly equalized and assimilated in their possessions, their opinions, and their passions.

A republic, by which I mean a government in which the scheme of representation takes place, opens a different prospect and promises the cure for which we are seeking. Let us examine the points in which it varies from pure democracy, and we shall comprehend both the nature of the cure and the efficacy which it must derive from the Union.

The two great points of difference between a democracy and a republic are: first, the delegation of the government, in the latter, to a small number of citizens elected by the rest; secondly, the greater number of citizens and greater sphere of country over which the latter may be extended.

The effect of the first difference is, on the one hand, to refine and enlarge the public views by passing them through the medium of a chosen body of citizens, whose wisdom may best discern the true interest of their country and whose patriotism and love of justice will be least likely to sacrifice it to temporary or partial considerations. Under such a regulation it may well happen that the public voice, pronounced by the representatives of the people, will be more consonant to the public good than if pronounced by the people themselves, convened for the purpose. On the other hand, the effect may be inverted. Men of factious tempers, of local prejudices, or of sinister designs, may, by intrigue, by corruption, or by other means, first obtain the suffrages, and then betray the interests of the people. The question resulting is, whether small or extensive republics are most favorable to the election of proper guardians of

the public weal; and it is clearly decided in favor of the latter by two obvious considerations.

In the first place it is to be remarked that however small the republic may be the representatives must be raise to a certain number in order to guard against the cabals of a few; and that however large it may be they must be limited to a certain number in order to guard against the confusion of a multitude. Hence, the number of representatives in the two cases not being in proportion to that of the constituents, and being proportionally greatest in the small republic, it follows that if the proportion of fit characters be not less in the large than in the small republic, the former will present a greater option, and consequently a greater probability of a fit choice.

In the next place, as each representative will be chosen by a greater number of citizens in the large than in the small republic, it will be more difficult for unworthy candidates to practice with success the vicious arts by which elections are too often carried; and the suffrages of the people being more free, will be more likely to center on men who possess the most attractive merit and the most diffusive and established characters.

It must be confessed that in this, as in most other cases, there is a mean, on both sides of which inconveniences will be found to lie. By enlarging too much the number of electors, you render the representative too little acquainted with all their local circumstances and lesser interests; as by reducing it too much, you render him unduly attached to these, and too little fit to comprehend and pursue great wad national objects. The federal Constitution forms a happy combination in this respect; the great and aggregate interests being referred to the national, the local and particular to the State legislatures.

The other point of difference is the greater number of citizens and extent of territory which may be brought within the compass of republican than of democratic government; and it is this circumstance principally which renders factious combinations less to be dreaded in the former than in the latter. The smaller the society, the fewer probably will be the distinct parties and interests composing it; the fewer the distinct parties and interests, the more frequently will a majority be found of the same party; and the smaller the number of individuals composing a majority, and the smaller the compass within which they are placed, the more easily will they concert and execute their plans of oppression. Extend the sphere and you take in a greater variety of parties and interests; you make it less probable that a majority of the whole will have a common motive to invade the rights of other citizens; or if such a common motive exists, it will be more difficult for all who feel it to discover their own strength and to act in unison with each other. Besides other impediments, it may be remarked that, where there is a consciousness of unjust or dishonorable purposes, communication is always checked by distrust in proportion to the number whose concurrence is necessary.

Hence, it clearly appears that the same advantage which a republic has over a democracy in controlling the effects of faction is enjoyed by a large over a small republic—is enjoyed by the Union over the States composing it. Does this advantage consist in the substitution of representatives whose enlightened views and virtuous sentiments render them superior to local prejudices and to schemes of injustice? It will not be denied that the representation of the Union will be most likely to possess these requisite endowments. Does it consist in the greater security afforded by a greater variety of parties, against the event of any one party being able to outnumber and oppress the rest? In an equal degree does the increased variety of parties comprised within the Union increase this security. Does it, in fine, consist in the greater obstacles opposed to the concert and accomplishment of the secret wishes of an unjust and interested majority? Here again the extent of the Union gives it the most palpable advantage.

The influence of factious leaders may kindle a flame within their particular States but will be unable to spread a general conflagration through the other States. A religious sect may degenerate into a political faction in a part of the Confederacy; but the variety of sects dispersed over the entire face of it must secure the national councils against any danger from that source. A rage for paper money, for an abolition of debts, for an equal division of property, or for any other improper or wicked project, will be less apt to pervade the whole body of the Union than a particular member of it, in the same proportion as such a malady is more likely to taint a particular county or district than an entire State. In the extent and proper structure of the Union, therefore, we behold a republican remedy for the diseases most incident to republican government. And according to the degree of pleasure and pride we feel in being republicans ought to be our zeal in cherishing the spirit and supporting the character of Federalists.

Publius

The Federalist No. 51
Alexander Hamilton or James Madison

To the People of the State of New York:

To what expedient, then, shall we finally resort, for maintaining in practice the necessary partition of power among the several departments as laid down in the Constitution? The only answer that can be given is that as all these exterior provisions are found to be inadequate the defect must be supplied, by so contriving the interior structure of the government as that its several constituent parts may, by their mutual relations, be the means of keeping each other in their proper places. Without presuming to undertake a full development of this important idea I will hazard a few general observations which may perhaps place it in a clearer light, and enable us to form a more correct judgment of the principles and structure of the government planned by the convention.

In order to lay a due foundation for that separate and distinct exercise of the different powers of government, which to a certain extent is admitted on all hands to be essential to the preservation of liberty, it is evident that each department should have a will of its own; and consequently should be so constituted that the members of each should have as little agency as possible in the appointment of the members of the others. Were this principle rigorously adhered to, it would require that all the appointments for the supreme executive, legislative, and judiciary magistracies should be drawn from the same fountain of authority, the people, through channels having no communication whatever with one another. Perhaps such a plan of constructing the several departments would be less difficult in practice than it may in contemplation appear. Some difficulties, however, and some additional expense would attend the execution of it. Some deviations, therefore, from the principle must be admitted. In the constitution of the judiciary department in particular, it might be inexpedient to insist rigorously on the principle: first, because peculiar qualifications being essential in the members, the primary consideration ought to be to select that mode of choice which best secures these qualifications; second, because the permanent tenure by which the appointments are held in that department must soon destroy all sense of dependence on the authority conferring them.

It is equally evident that the members of each department should be as little dependent as possible on those of the others for the emoluments annexed to their offices. Were the executive magistrate, or the judges, not independent of the legislature in this particular, their independence in every other would be merely nominal.

But the great security against a gradual concentration of the several powers in the same department consists in giving to those who administer each department the necessary constitutional means and personal motives to resist encroachments of the others. The provision for defense must in this, as in all other cases, be made commensurate to the danger of attack. Ambition must be made to counteract ambition. The interest of the man must be connected with the constitutional rights of the place. It may be a reflection on human nature that such devices should be necessary to control the abuses of government. But what is government itself but the greatest of all reflections on human nature? If men were angels, no government would be necessary. If angels were to govern men, neither external nor internal controls on government would be necessary. In framing a government which is to be administered by men over men, the great difficulty lies in this: you must first enable the government to control the governed; and in the next place oblige it to control itself. A dependence on the people is, no doubt, the primary control on the government; but experience has taught mankind the necessity of auxiliary precautions.

This policy of supplying, by opposite and rival interests, the defect of better motives, might be traced through the whole system of human affairs, private as well as public. We see it particularly displayed in all the subordinate distributions of power, where the constant aim is to divide and arrange the several offices in such a manner as that each may be a check on the other—that the private interest of every individual may be a sentinel over the public rights. These inventions of prudence cannot be less requisite in the distribution of the supreme powers of the State.

But it is not possible to give to each department an equal power of self-defense. In republican government, the legislative authority necessarily predominates. The remedy for this inconvenience is to divide the legislature into different branches; and to render them, by different modes of election and different principles of action, as little connected with each other as the nature of their common functions and their common dependence on the society will admit. It may even be necessary to guard against dangerous encroachments by still further precautions. As the weight of the legislative authority requires that it should be thus divided, the weakness of the executive may require, on the other hand, that it should be fortified. An absolute negative on the legislature appears, at first view, to be the natural defense with which the executive magistrate should be armed. But perhaps it would be neither altogether safe nor alone sufficient. On ordinary occasions it might not be exerted with the requisite firmness, and on extraordinary occasions it might be perfidiously abused. May not this defect of an absolute negative be supplied by some qualified connection between this weaker department and the weaker branch of the stronger department, by which the latter may be led to support the constitutional rights of the former, without being too much detached from the rights of its own department?

If the principles on which these observations are founded be just, as I persuade myself they are, and they be applied as a criterion to the several State constitutions, and to the federal Constitution, it will be found that if the latter does not perfectly correspond with them, the former are infinitely less able to bear such a test.

There are, moreover, two considerations particularly applicable to the federal system of America, which place that system in a very interesting point of view.

First. In a single republic, all the power surrendered by the people is submitted to the administration of a single government; and the usurpations are guarded against by a division of the government into distinct and separate departments. In the compound republic of America, the power surrendered by the people is first divided between two distinct governments, and then the portion allotted to each subdivided among distinct and separate departments. Hence a double security arises to the rights of the people. The different governments will control each other, at the same time that each will be controlled by itself.

Second. It is of great importance in a republic not only to guard the society against the oppression of its rulers, but to guard one part of the society against the injustice of the other part. Different interests necessarily exist in different classes of citizens. If a majority be united by a common interest, the rights of the minority will be insecure. There are but two methods of providing against this evil: the one by creating a will in the community independent of the majority—that is, of the society itself; the other, by comprehending in the society so many separate descriptions of citizens as will render an unjust combination of a majority of the whole very improbable, if not impracticable. The first method prevails in all governments possessing an hereditary or self-appointed authority. This, at best, is but a precarious security; because a power independent of the society may as well espouse the unjust views of the major as the rightful interests of the minor party, and may possibly be turned against both parties. The second method will be exemplified in the federal republic of the United States. Whilst all authority in it will be derived from and dependent on the society, the society itself will be broken into so many parts, interests and classes of citizens, that the rights of individuals, or of the minority, will be in little danger from interested combinations of the majority. In a free government the security for civil rights must be the same as that for religious rights. It consists

in the one case in the multiplicity of interests, and in the other in the multiplicity of sects. The degree of security in both cases will depend on the number of interests and sects; and this may be presumed to depend on the extent of country and number of people comprehended under the same government. This view of the subject must particularly recommend a proper federal system to all the sincere and considerate friends of republican government, since it shows that in exact proportion as the territory of the Union may be formed into more circumscribed Confederacies, or States, oppressive combinations of a majority will be facilitated; the best security, under the republican forms, for the rights of every class of citizen, will be diminished; and consequently the stability and independence of some member of the government, the only other security, must be proportionally increased. Justice is the end of government. It is the end of civil society. It ever has been and ever will be pursued until it be obtained, or until liberty be lost in the pursuit. In a society under the forms of which the stronger faction can readily unite and oppress the weaker, anarchy may as truly be said to reign as in a state of nature, where the weaker individual is not secured against the violence of the stronger; and as, in the latter state, even the stronger individuals are prompted, by the uncertainty of their condition, to submit to a government which may protect the weak as well as themselves; so, in the former state, will the more powerful factions or parties be gradually induced, by a like motive, to wish for a government which will protect all parties, the weaker as well as the more powerful. It can be little doubted that if the State of Rhode Island was separated from the Confederacy and left to itself, the insecurity of rights under the popular form of government within such narrow limits would be displayed by such reiterated oppression of factious majorities that some power altogether independent of the people would soon be called for by the voice of the very factions whose misrule had proved the necessity of it. In the extended republic of the United States, and among the great variety of interests, parties, and sects which it embraces, a coalition of a majority of the whole society could seldom take place on any other principles than those of justice and the general good; whilst there being thus less danger to a minor from the will of a major party, there must be less pretext, also, to provide for the security of the former, by introducing into the government a will not dependent on the latter, or, in other words, a will independent of the society itself. It is no less certain than it is important, notwithstanding the contrary opinions which have been entertained, that the larger the society, provided it lie within a practicable sphere, the more duly capable it will be of self-government. And happily for the *republican cause*, the practicable sphere may be carried to a very great extent by a judicious modification and mixture of the *federal principle*.

Publius

Abraham Lincoln

Springfield Boys' Lyceum, First Inaugural, Second Inaugural, Gettysburg Address

Abraham Lincoln (1809–1865), Civil War President of the United States, was self-educated and raised on the frontier, never acquiring much training in social or diplomatic conventions. He based his career on an intense commitment to the ideals of American democracy, combined with a pragmatic attitude toward the realities of democratic politics. In his moral sentiments, as well as his politics, Lincoln was a lawyer and a cautious man; he was acutely aware of the dangers presented by the success of American democracy. His was the first generation to come of age under a firmly established system of democratic government, and Lincoln saw that the task of preserving this system often posed greater difficulties than those faced by the Revolutionaries in creating it. Lincoln took a gradualist approach to slavery, disagreeing with radical abolitionists like William Lloyd Garrison. At the same time, he boldly reasserted the natural law foundations of human equality at a time when many people, among them the powerful Illinois Senator Stephen Douglas, advocated a "neutral" government stance on slavery. Lincoln did not fight the Civil War to end slavery, but to defend a political system based on the natural right to self-government, and to preserve national union. Only after the conflict was under way did this objective become identified with the abolition of slavery.

Springfield Boys' Lyceum
Abraham Lincoln

January 27, 1838

As a subject for the remarks of the evening, *the perpetuation of our political institutions*; is selected.

In the great journal of things happening under the sun, we, the American People, find our account running, under date of the nineteenth century of the Christian era. We find ourselves in the peaceful possession, of the fairest portion of the earth, as regards extent of territory, fertility of soil, and salubrity of climate. We find ourselves under the government of a system of political institutions, conducing more essentially to the ends of civil and religious liberty, than any of which the history of former times tells us. We, when mounting the stage of existence, found ourselves the legal inheritors of these fundamental blessings. We toiled not in the acquirement or establishment of them—they are a legacy bequeathed us, by a *once* hardy, brave, and patriotic, but *now* lamented and departed race of ancestors. Their's was the task (and nobly they performed it) to possess themselves, and through themselves, us, of this goodly land; and to uprear upon its hills and its valleys, a political edifice of liberty and equal rights; 'tis ours only, to transmit these, the former, unprofaned by the foot of an invader; the latter, undecayed by the lapse of time, and untorn by [usurpation—to the latest generation that fate shall permit the world to know. This task of gratitude to our fathers, justice to] ourselves, duty to posterity, and love for our species in general, all imperatively require us faithfully to perform.

How, then, shall we perform it? At what point shall we expect the approach of danger? By what means shall we fortify against it? Shall we expect some transatlantic military giant, to step the Ocean, and crush us at a blow? Never! All the armies of Europe, Asia and Africa combined, with all the treasure of the earth (our own excepted) in their military chest; with a Buonaparte for a commander, could not by force, take a drink from the Ohio, or make a track on the Blue Ridge, in a trial of a thousand years.

At what point then is the approach of danger to be expected? I answer, if it ever reach us, it must spring up amongst us. It cannot come from abroad. If destruction be our lot, we must ourselves be its author and finisher. As a nation of freemen, we must live through all time, or die by suicide.

I hope I am over wary; but if I am not, there is, even now, something of ill-omen amongst us. I mean the increasing disregard for law which pervades the country; the growing disposition to substitute the wild and furious passions, in lieu of the sober judgement of Courts; and the worse than savage mobs, for the executive ministers of justice. This disposition is awfully fearful in any community; and that it now exists in ours, though grating to our feelings to admit, it would be a violation of truth, and an insult to our intelligence, to deny. Accounts of outrages committed by mobs, form the every-day news of the times....

I know the American people are *much* attached to their Government;—I know they would suffer *much* for its sake;—I know they would endure evils long and patiently, before they would ever think of exchanging it for another. Yet, notwithstanding all this, if the laws be continually despised and disregarded, if their rights to be secure in their persons and property, are held by no better tenure than the caprice of a mob, the alienation of their affections from the Government is the natural consequence; and to that, sooner or later, it must come.

Here then, is one point at which danger may be expected.

The question recurs "how shall we fortify against it?" The answer is simple. Let every American, every lover of liberty, every well wisher to his posterity, swear by the blood of the Revolution, never to violate in the least particular, the laws of the country; and never to tolerate their violation by others. As the patriots of seventy-six did to the support of the Declaration of Independence, so to the support of the Constitution and Laws, let every American pledge his life, his property, and his sacred honor;—let every man remember that to violate the law, is to trample on the blood of his father, and to tear the character [charter?] of his own,

and his children's liberty. Let reverence for the laws, be breathed by every American mother, to the lisping babe, that prattles on her lap—let it be taught in schools, in seminaries, and in colleges;—let it be written in Primmers, spelling books, and in Almanacs;—let it be preached from the pulpit, proclaimed in legislative halls, and enforced in courts of justice. And, in short, let it become the *political religion* of the nation; and let the old and the young, the rich and the poor, the grave and the gay, of all sexes and tongues, and colors and conditions, sacrifice unceasingly upon its altars.

While ever a state of feeling, such as this, shall universally, or even, very generally prevail throughout the nation, vain will be every effort, and fruitless every attempt, to subvert our national freedom.

When I so pressingly urge a strict observance of all the laws, let me not be understood as saying there are no bad laws, nor that grievances may not arise, for the redress of which, no legal provisions have been made. I mean to say no such thing. But I do mean to say, that, although bad laws, if they exist, should be repealed as soon as possible, still while they continue in force, for the sake of example, they should be religiously observed. So also in unprovided cases. If such arise, let proper legal provisions be made for them with the least possible delay; but, till then, let them if not too intolerable, be borne with.

There is no grievance that is a fit object of redress by mob law. In any case that arises, as for instance, the promulgation of abolitionism, one of two positions is necessarily true; that is, the thing is right within itself, and therefore deserves the protection of all law and all good citizens; or, it is wrong, and therefore proper to be prohibited by legal enactments; and in neither case, is the interposition of mob law, either necessary, justifiable, or excusable.

But, it may be asked, why suppose danger to our political institutions? Have we not preserved them for more than fifty years? And why may we not for fifty times as long?

We hope there is no *sufficient* reason. We hope all dangers may be overcome; but to conclude that no danger may ever arise, would itself be extremely dangerous. There are now, and will hereafter be, many causes, danger-ous in their tendency, which have not existed heretofore; and which are not too insignificant to merit attention. That our government should have been maintained in its original form from its establishment until now, is not much to be wondered at. It had many props to support it through that period, which now are decayed, and crumbled away. Through that period, it was felt by all, to be an undecided experiment; now, it is understood to be a successful one. Then, all that sought celebrity and fame, and distinc-tion, expected to find them in the success of that experiment. Their *all* was staked upon it: —their destiny was *inseparably* linked with it. Their ambition aspired to display before an ad-miring world, a practical demonstration of the truth of a proposition, which had hitherto been considered, at best no better, than problemati-cal; namely, *the capability of a people to govern themselves.* If they succeeded, they were to be immortalized; their names were to be transferred to counties and cities, and rivers and mountains; and to be revered and sung, and toasted through all time. If they failed, they were to be called knaves and fools, and fanatics for a fleeting hour; then to sink and be forgotten. They suc-ceeded. The experiment is successful; and thou-sands have won their deathless names in making it so. But the game is caught; and I believe it is true, that with the catching, end the pleasures of the chase. This field of glory is harvested, and the crop is already appropriated. But new reap-ers will arise, and *they*, too, will seek a field. It is to deny, what the history of the world tells us is true, to suppose that men of ambition and talents will not continue to spring up amongst us. And, when they do, they will as naturally seek the gratification of their ruling passion, as others have *so* done before them. The question then, is, can that gratification be found in sup-porting and maintaining an edifice that has been erected by others? Most certainly it cannot. Many great and good men sufficiently qualified for any task they should undertake, may ever be found, whose ambition would aspire to nothing beyond a seat in Congress, a gubernatorial or a presidential chair; *but such belong not to the family of the lion, or the tribe of the eagle*[.] What! think you these places would satisfy an Alexander, a Caesar, or a Napoleon? Never! Towering genius disdains a beaten path. It seeks regions hitherto unexplored. It sees *no distinc-tion* in adding story to story, upon the monu-ments of fame, erected to the memory of others. It *denies* that it is glory enough to serve under any chief. It *scorns* to tread in the footsteps of *any* predecessor, however illustrious. It thirsts and burns for distinction; and, if possible, it will have it, whether at the expense of emancipating slaves, or enslaving freemen. Is it unreasonable then to expect, that some man possessed of the loftiest genius, coupled with ambition sufficient to push it to its utmost stretch, will at some time, spring up among us? And when such a one does, it will require the people to be united with each other, attached to the government and laws, and generally intelligent, to successfully frustrate his designs.

Distinction will be his paramount object; and although he would as willingly, perhaps more so, acquire it by doing good as harm; yet, that opportunity being past, and nothing left to be done in the way of building up, he would set boldly to the task of pulling down.

Here then, is a probable case, highly dan-gerous, and such a one as could not have well existed heretofore.

Another reason which *once was*; but which, to the same extent, is *now no more*, has done much in maintaining our institutions thus far. I mean the powerful influence which the inter-esting scenes of the revolution had upon the *passions* of the people as distinguished from their judgment. By this influence, the jealousy, envy, and avarice, incident to our nature, and so common to a state of peace, prosperity, and conscious strength, were, for the time, in a great measure smothered and rendered inactive; while the deep rooted principles of *hate*, and the powerful motive of *revenge*, instead of being turned against each other, were directed exclusively against the British nation. And thus, from the force of circumstances, the basest principles of our nature, were either made to lie dormant, or to become the active agents in the advancement of the noblest of cause—that of establishing and maintaining civil and religious liberty.

But this state of feeling *must fade, is fading, has faded*, with the circumstances that produced it.

I do not mean to say, that the scenes of the revolution *are now or ever will be* entirely forgotten; but that like every thing else, they must fade upon the memory of the world, and grow more and more dim by the lapse of time. In history, we hope, they will be read of, and recounted, so long as the bible shall be read;—but even granting that they will, their influence *cannot be* what it heretofore has been. Even then, they *cannot be* so universally known, nor so vividly felt, as they were by the generation just gone to rest. At the close of that struggle, nearly every adult male had been a participator in some of its scenes. The consequence was, that of those scenes, in the form of a husband, a father, a son or a brother, a *living history was* to be found in every family-a history bearing the indubitable testimonies of its own authenticity, in the limbs mangled, in the scars of wounds received, in the midst of the very scenes related—a history, too, that could be read and understood alike by all, the wise and the ignorant, the learned and the unlearned. But *those* histories are gone. They *can* be read no more forever. They *were* a fortress of strength; but, what invading foemen could *never* do, the silent artillery of time *has done*; the levelling of its walls. They are gone. They *were* a forest of giant oaks; but the all-resistless hurricane has swept over them, and left only, here and there, a lonely trunk, despoiled of its verdure, shorn of its foliage; unshading and unshaded, to murmur in a few more gentle breezes, and to combat with its mutilated limbs, a few more ruder storms, then to sink, and be no more.

They *were* the pillars of the temple of liberty; and now, that they have crumbled away, that temple must fall, unless we, their descendants, supply their places with other pillars, hewn from the solid quarry of sober reason. Passion has helped us; but can do so no more. It will in future be our enemy. Reason, cold, calculating, unimpassioned reason, must furnish all the materials for our future support and defence. Let those [materials] be moulded into *general intelligence*, [*sound*] *morality* and, in particular, a *reverence for the constitution and laws*; and, that we improved to the last; that we remained free to the last; that we revered his name to the last; [tha]t, during his long sleep, we permitted no hostile foot to pass over or desecrate [his] resting place; shall be that which to le[arn the last] trump shall awaken our Wash[ington.

Upon these] let the proud fabric of freedom r[est, as the] rock of its basis; and as truly as has been said of the only greater institution, "*the gates of hell shall not prevail against it.*"

The Momentous Issue of Civil War
First Inaugural Address, 1861
Abraham Lincoln

March 4, 1861

I take the official oath to-day, with no mental reservations, and with no purpose to construe the Constitution or laws, by any hypercritical rules. And while I do not choose now to specify particular acts of Congress as proper to be enforced, I do suggest, that it will be much safer for all, both in official and private stations, to conform to, and abide by, all those acts which stand unrepealed, than to violate any of them, trusting to find impunity in having them held to be unconstitutional.

It is seventy-two years since the first inauguration of a President under our national Constitution. During that period fifteen different and greatly distinguished citizens, have, in succession, administered the executive branch of the government. They have conducted it through many perils; and, generally, with great success. Yet, with all this scope for precedent, I now enter upon the same task for the brief constitutional term of four years, under great and peculiar difficulty. A disruption of the Federal Union heretofore only menaced, is now formidably attempted.

I hold, that in contemplation of universal law, and of the Constitution, the Union of these States is perpetual. Perpetuity is implied, if not expressed, in the fundamental law of all national governments. It is safe to assert that no government proper, ever had a provision in its organic law for its own termination. Continue to execute all the express provisions of our national Constitution, and the Union will endure forever—it being impossible to destroy it, except by some action not provided for in the instrument itself.

Again, if the United States be not a government proper, but an association of States in the nature of contract merely, can it, as a contract, be peaceably unmade, by less than all the parties who made it? One party to a contract may violate it—break it, so to speak; but does it not require all to lawfully rescind it?

Descending from these general principles, we find the proposition that, in legal contemplation, the Union is perpetual, confirmed by the history of the Union itself. The Union is much older than the Constitution. It was formed in fact, by the Articles of Association in 1774. It was matured and continued by the Declaration of Independence in 1776. It was further matured and the faith of all the then thirteen States expressly plighted and engaged that it should be perpetual, by the Articles of Confederation in 1778. And finally, in 1787, one of the declared objects for ordaining and establishing the Constitution, was "*to form a more perfect union.*"

But if destruction of the Union, by one, or by a part only, of the States, be lawfully possible, the Union is *less* perfect than before the Constitution, having lost the vital element of perpetuity.

It follows from these views that no State, upon its own mere motion, can lawfully get out of the Union,—that *resolves* and *ordinances* to that effect are legally void, and that acts of violence within any State or States, against the authority of the United States, are insurrectionary or revolutionary, according to circumstances.

I therefore consider that, in view of the Constitution and the laws, the Union is unbroken; and, to the extent of my ability, I shall take care, as the Constitution itself expressly enjoins upon me, that the laws of the Union be faithfully executed in all the States. Doing this I deem to be only a simple duty on my part; and I shall perform it, so far as practicable, unless my rightful masters, the American people, shall withhold the requisite means, or, in some authoritative manner, direct the contrary. I trust this will not be regarded as a menace, but only as the declared purpose of the Union that it *will* constitutionally defend, and maintain itself....

That there are persons in one section, or another who seek to destroy the Union at all events, and are glad of any pretext to do it, I will neither affirm or deny; but if there be such, I need address no word to them. To those,

however, who really love the Union, may I not speak?

Before entering upon so grave a matter as the destruction of our national fabric, with all its benefits, its memories, and its hopes, would it not be wise to ascertain precisely why we do it? Will you hazard so desperate a step, while there is any possibility that any portion of the ills you fly from, have no real existence? Will you, while the certain ills you fly to, are greater than all the real ones you fly from? Will you risk the commission of so fearful a mistake?

All profess to be content in the Union, if all constitutional rights can be maintained. Is it true, then, that any right, plainly written in the Constitution, has been denied? I think not. Happily the human mind is so constituted, that no party can reach to the audacity of doing this. Think, if you can, of a single instance in which a plainly written provision of the Constitution has ever been denied. If, by the mere force of numbers, a majority should deprive a minority of any clearly written constitutional right, it might, in a moral point of view, justify revolution-certainly would, if such right were a vital one. But such is not our case. All the vital rights of minorities, and of individuals, are so plainly assured to them, by affirmations and negations, guaranties and prohibitions, in the Constitution, that controversies never arise concerning them. But no organic law can ever be framed with a provision specifically applicable to every question which may occur in practical administration. No foresight can anticipate, nor any document of reasonable length contain express provisions for all possible questions. Shall fugitives from labor be surrendered by national or by State authority? The Constitution does not expressly say. *May* Congress prohibit slavery in the territories? The Constitution does not expressly say. *Must* Congress protect slavery in the territories? The Constitution does not expressly say.

From questions of this class spring all our constitutional controversies, and we divide upon them into majorities and minorities. If the minority will not acquiesce, the majority must, or the government must cease. There is no other alternative; for continuing the government, is acquiescence on one side or the other. If a minority, in such case, will secede rather than acquiesce, they make a precedent which, in turn, will divide and ruin them; for a minority of their own will secede from them, whenever a majority refuses to be controlled by such minority. For instance, why may not any portion of a new confederacy, a year or two hence, arbitrarily secede again, precisely as portions of the present Union now claim to secede from it. All who cherish disunion sentiments, are now being educated to the exact temper of doing this. Is there such perfect identity of interests among the States to compose a new Union, as to produce harmony only, and prevent renewed secession?

Plainly, the central idea of secession, is the essence of anarchy. A majority, held in restraint by constitutional checks, and limitations, and always changing easily, with deliberate changes of popular opinions and sentiments, is the only true sovereign of a free people. Whoever rejects it, does, of necessity, fly to anarchy or to despotism. Unanimity is impossible; the rule of a minority, as a permanent arrangement, is wholly inadmissable; so that, rejecting the majority principle, anarchy, or despotism in some form, is all that is left....

Physically speaking, we cannot separate. We cannot remove sections from each other, nor build an impassable wall between them. A husband and wife may be divorced, and go out of the presence, and beyond the reach of each other; but the different parts of our country cannot do this. They cannot but remain face to face; and intercourse, either amicable or hostile, must continue between them. Is it possible then to make that intercourse more advantageous, or more satisfactory, *after* separation than *before*? Can aliens make treaties easier than friends can make laws? Can treaties be more faithfully enforced between aliens, than laws can among friends? Suppose you go to war, you cannot fight always; and when, after much loss on both sides, and no gain on either, you cease fighting, the identical old questions, as to terms of intercourse, are again upon you....

Why should there not be a patient confidence in the ultimate justice of the people? Is there any better, or equal hope, in the world? In our present differences, is either party without faith of being in the right? If the Almighty Ruler of nations, with his eternal truth and justice, be on your side of the North, or on yours of the South, that truth, and that justice, will surely prevail, by the judgment of this great tribunal, the American people.

By the frame of the government under which we live, this same people have wisely given their public servants but little power for mischief; and have, with equal wisdom, provided for the return of that little to their own hands at very short intervals.

While the people retain their virtue, and vigilance, no administration, by any extreme of wickedness or folly, can very seriously injure the government, in the short space of four years.

My countrymen, one and all, think calmly and *well*, upon this whole subject. Nothing valuable can be lost by taking time. If there be an object to *hurry* any of you, in hot haste, to a step which you would never take d*eliberately*, that object will be frustrated by taking time; but no good object can be frustrated by it. Such of you as are now dissatisfied, still have the old Constitution unimpaired, and, on the sensitive point, the laws of your own framing under it; while the new administration will have no immediate power, if it would, to change either. If it were admitted that you who are dissatisfied, hold the right side in the dispute, there still is no single good reason for precipitate action. Intelligence, patriotism, Christianity, and a firm reliance on Him, who has never yet forsaken this favored land, are still competent to adjust, in the best way, all our present difficulty.

In *your* hands, my dissatisfied fellow countrymen, and not in *mine*, is the momentous issue of civil war. The government will not assail *you*. You can have no conflict, without being yourselves the aggressors. *You* have no oath registered in Heaven to destroy the government, while *I* shall have the most solemn one to "preserve, protect and defend" it.

I am loth to close. We are not enemies, but friends. We must not be enemies. Though passion may have strained, it must not break our bonds of affection. The mystic chords of memory, stre[t]ching from every battle-field, and patriot grave, to every living heart and hearthstone, all over this broad land, will yet swell the chorus of the Union, when again touched, as surely they will be, by the better angels of our nature.

Second Inaugural Address, 1865
Abraham Lincoln

March 4, 1865

At this second appearing to take the oath of the presidential office, there is less occasion for an extended address than there was at the first. Then a statement, somewhat in detail, of a course to be pursued, seemed fitting and proper. Now, at the expiration of four years, during which public declarations have been constantly called forth on every point and phase of the great contest which still absorbs the attention, and engrosses the energies of the nation, little that is new could be presented. The progress of our arms, upon which all else chiefly depends, is as well known to the public as to myself; and it is, I trust, reasonably satisfactory and encouraging to all. With high hope for the future, no prediction in regard to it is ventured.

On the occasion corresponding to this four years ago, all thoughts were anxiously directed to an impending civil-war. All dreaded it—all sought to avert it. While the inaugural address was being delivered from this place, devoted altogether to saving the Union without war, insurgent agents were in the city seeking to destroy it without war—seeking to dissol[v]e the Union, and divide effects, by negotiation. Both parties deprecated war; but one of them would make war rather than let the nation survive; and the other would *accept* war rather than let it perish. And the war came.

One eighth of the whole population were colored slaves—not distributed generally over the Union, but localized in the Southern part of it. These slaves constituted a peculiar and powerful interest. All knew that this interest was, somehow, the cause of the war. To strengthen, perpetuate, and extend this interest was the object for which the insurgents would rend the Union, even by war; while the government claimed no right to do more than to restrict the territorial enlargement of it. Neither party expected for the war, the magnitude, or the duration, which it has already attained. Neither anticipated that the *cause* of the conflict might cease with, or even before, the conflict itself should cease. Each looked for an easier triumph, and a result less fundamental and astounding. Both read the same Bible, and pray to the same God; and each invokes His aid against the other. It may seem strange that any men should dare to ask a just God's assistance in wringing their bread from the sweat of other men's faces; but let us judge not that we be not judged. The prayers of both could not be answered; that of neither has been answered fully. The Almighty has His own purposes. "Woe unto the world because of offences! for it must needs be that offences come; but woe to that man by whom the offence cometh!" If we shall suppose that American Slavery is one of those offences which, in the providence of God, must needs come, but which, having continued through His appointed time, He now wills to remove, and that He gives to both North and South, this terrible war, as the woe due to those by whom the offence came, shall we discern therein any departure from those divine attributes which the believers in a Living God always ascribe to Him? Fondly do we hope—fervently do we pray—that this mighty scourge of war may speedily pass away. Yet, if God wills that it continue, until all the wealth piled by the bond-man's two hundred and fifty years of unrequited toil shall be sunk, and until every drop of blood drawn with the lash, shall be paid by another drawn with the sword, as was said three thousand years ago, so still it must be said "the judgments of the Lord, are true and righteous altogether."

With malice toward none; with charity for all; with firmness in the right, as God gives us to see the right, let us strive on to finish the work we are in; to bind up the nation's wounds; to care for him who shall have borne the battle, and for his widow, and his orphan—to do all which may achieve and cherish a just, and a lasting peace, among ourselves, and with all nations.

Gettysburg Address, 1863

Abraham Lincoln

November 19, 1863

Four score and seven years ago our fathers brought forth on this continent, a new nation, conceived in Liberty, and dedicated to the proposition that all men are created equal.

Now we are engaged in a great civil war, testing whether that nation, or any nation so conceived and so dedicated, can long endure. We are met on a great battle-field of that war. We have come to dedicate a portion of that field, as a final resting place for those who here gave their lives that nation might live. It is altogether fitting and proper that we should do this.

But, in a larger sense, we can not dedicate — we can not consecrate — we can not hallow — this ground. The brave men, living and dead, who struggled here, have consecrated it, far above our poor power to add or detract. The world will little note, nor long remember what we say here, but it can never forget what they did here. It is for us the living, rather, to be dedicated here to the unfinished work which they who fought here have thus far so nobly advanced. It is rather for us to be here dedicated to the great task remaining before us — that from these honored dead we take increased devotion to that cause for which they gave the last full measure of devotion — that we here highly resolve that these dead shall not have died in vain — that this nation, under God, shall have a new birth of freedom — and that government of the people, by the people, for the people, shall not perish from the earth.

Benjamin R. Barber

Neither Leaders nor Followers: Citizenship Under Strong Democracy

In the following essay, Benjamin Barber looks at a lagging American democracy and asks, "Alright, who's in charge here?" His answer: "We citizens sure aren't, but we ought to be." Rather than calling for better leaders to solve America's problems, Barber argues that the most admired leaders contribute more than anyone to creating a passive and irresponsible citizenry. Those leaders whose power, charm, and eloquence allow them to dazzle the world with their brilliance leave average citizens with little to do. Like over-protective parents, once such leaders are gone, their children-citizens are left without the skills to take care of themselves. The basic skills of politics, however, are not so difficult. An active citizen requires an ability to make informed common-sense judgments with an eye to the public good. Jurors, senators, and even presidents make decisions in this way all the time. Rather than showcasing their problem-solving abilities, politicians need to provide citizens with the education, information, and institutions necessary to discuss and decide upon the issues themselves.

Neither Leaders nor Followers: Citizenship Under Strong Democracy

Benjamin R. Barber

Strong leaders make a weak people. (Emile Zapata)

Some say pity the "country that has no heroes"; I say "pity the country that needs heroes." (Bertolt Brecht)

At the heart of democratic theory lies a profound dilemma that has afflicted democratic practice at least since the eighteenth century. Democracy requires both effective leadership and vigorous citizenship; yet the conditions and consequences of leadership often seem to undermine civic vigor. Although it cries out for both, democracy must customarily make do either with strong leadership or with strong citizens. For the most part, depending on devices of representation in large-scale societies, democracy in the West has settled for strong leaders and correspondingly weak citizens....

Woodrow Wilson's stewardship of daring has in fact set the standard for strong presidential leadership in the twentieth century. It asks little of Americans but focuses anxiously on what Americans might ask of their president. "This is not a day of triumph," Wilson intoned in his first inaugural address, "it is a day of dedication. Here muster not the forces of party, but the forces of humanity. Men's hearts wait upon us; men's lives hang in the balance; men's hopes call on us to say what we will do. Who shall live up to the great trust? Who dares fail to try."

This stewardship of daring has become the hallmark of our presidential politics. In 1940, after several terms of the bracing but caution-

By permission of the author. This selection is adapted from M. Beschloss and Thomas E. Cronin, eds., *Essays in Honor of James MacGregor Burns*, Prentice Hall, Englewood Cliffs, NJ 07632, 1989.

inducing leadership of Franklin Delano Roosevelt, Harold Laski was still crying out in his *The American Presidency* for leadership and more leadership. "Power is also opportunity," he wrote, "and to face danger with confidence is the price of its fulfillment." Twenty years further down the road, Richard Neustadt was still arguing in his *Presidential Power* that power used was power enhanced, that presidents became powerful not by conserving and husbanding their power for a rainy day as if it were in a jar in the cupboard but by employing it with energy and zeal, knowing that it reproduced itself as it was expended. John F. Kennedy was received as a glittering knight on a white horse who might restore America to itself. Although he told Americans to ask what they could do for their government rather than what it might do for them, his presidency has been discussed exclusively in terms of what he did (or, as the revisionists argue, did not do) for his country....

Nowadays we continue to bemoan not the absence of civic competence but the absence of leaders and the fear to lead that characterized presidents in the 1970s. Ronald Reagan, although more popular than genuinely powerful as a president, was universally celebrated for returning dignity and force to the office of the presidency and even President Clinton has thought him worthy of emulation....

The argument I wish to make here is that strong leaders have on the whole made Americans weak citizens; that representative institutions have...distanced the citizenry from the government to which representation is meant to tie it. As a consequence, when faced by crisis—when leadership has failed them—the American people have turned not to themselves or the civic resourcefulness of their fellow citizens, but to a futile and self-exonerating quest for new and better leaders. Presidents such as Jimmy Carter, who have made prudent noises about the limits of leadership and about the responsibilities a people must assume for their own destiny, have been ridiculed and turned out of office. Democrats who offer to assume full responsibility for the welfare of Americans, who insist they will do it all for their constituents, and Republicans who insist they will get government off the backs of the people by liquidating government altogether are making the same argument—and have been rewarded accordingly by a politically lazy people. The struggle to improve the quality of democracy has thus become a search for leadership, a quest for excellence, a hunt for better delegates, more effective representatives, wiser surrogates, more grandiloquent mouthpieces. Civic responsibility has in turn ceased to mean self-government and come to mean electing governors to govern in the public stead. Democracy means simply to enlist, to choose, to elect, and to reward (or to punish) representatives—and, of course, to keep them accountable via future elections.

It is not simply that Americans have gone astray in substituting leadership for citizenship. It is that the very virtues that make for leadership have attenuated the skills and capacities that constitute citizenship. A too responsible leadership can make for an irresponsible citizenry; an overly vigorous executive can reduce citizens to passive observers whose main public activity is applause. Public officials displaying an omnicompetent mastery of their public responsibilities unburden private men and women of their public responsibilities and leave them with a feeling of civic incompetence or civic indifference. Incompetence is what makes otherwise enfranchised citizens powerless in a democracy.

Thus, legislators and executives who arrogate to themselves the responsibilities of political judgment, the adjudication of public interests, and the bargaining and exchange of public goods in the name of the public interest leave citizens only with the responsibility to articulate and fight for private interests. Modern political science has in fact ascribed to the public at large only functions of private interest interaction, leaving it to representatives to force from these private interests such minimal common ends as a pluralistic democracy may be said to possess.

In the same fashion, knowledgeable leadership—prudent bureaucrats, fiscal experts, foreign policy professionals, defense specialists, and so forth—relieve citizens of the need to understand their public world, domestic or foreign. To call an issue technical is to excuse the general public from responsibility for it, even though almost all public policy rests on issues of a technical nature, even though their technicality is well within the grasp of intelligent lay politicians and bureaucrats and thus, presumably, of intelligent lay citizens. Expressions such as "the experts know better," and "they must know what they are doing" point to a vocabulary of exoneration by which the modern citizen eschews competence to govern his world. Yet again and again we see effective politicians rendering prudent judgments about complex matters on the basis of general value positions. President Reagan was certainly not a careful student of the technical sides of the policy issues he faces, but this made him no less effective a judge of crucial political issues. For civic competence, whether in leaders or citizens, is finally a matter of good political judgment and the application to particular cases of general value systems, not of technical expertise. Advocates of strong leadership pretend otherwise, but in fact good citizens require no more expertise than presidents and senators, and need not be economists or nuclear scientists to reach intelligent positions on trade policy or arms negotiations. Minimally, it might be said that a citizen need be no more technically knowledgeable than was Ronald Reagan to be an effective citizen—for surely we need not ask more of citizens than of presidents.

In traditional political theory, we customarily speak of the act of sovereign authorization by which a people empower a sovereign to govern in its name. The trouble with representative institutions is that they often turn the act of sovereign authorization into an act of civic deauthorization. They do not authorize but transfer authority, depriving the authorizing people of its own generic sovereignty and thus of its right to rule. A people that empowers leaders to govern for it can end by disenfranchising itself. As one nineteenth-century French critic of representation put it, the equality with which voters enter the polling booth disappears into the ballot box along with their vote. Electoral activity reduces citizens to alienated spectators—at best, watchdogs with residual and wholly passive functions of securing the accountability of those to whom they have turned over their sovereignty. Under the representative system, leaders turn electors into followers; and the correct posture for followers is deference. Democracy becomes a system that defines how elites are chosen—in Joseph Schumpeter's classical definition, elective oligarchy, in which the subjugated public from time to time selects the elites who otherwise govern it. Democratic politics thus becomes a matter of what leaders do, something that citizens watch rather than something they do. Civic spectacles like the party nominating conventions are little different than such spectator sports as the Super Bowl—watched but not participated in by a lazy and privatized public. Indeed, were it not to do an injury to the English language, one would be tempted nowadays to refer to Americans collectively as "the Privates" rather than "the Public."

"Lead or follow or get the hell out of the way," reads a popular corporate desk sign. It goes to the heart of what is wrong with contemporary approaches to leadership under democracy. The pair to which the term leader belongs is not leader-follower as the aphorism suggests, but leader-citizen. Leader-follower leaves no room for the mutuality and sense of collective responsibility implicit in the idea of citizenship. The citizen is a self-sufficient and autonomous being, who is nonetheless defined by engagement in a self-governing community. Strong leaders can impair autonomy, and thus mutuality and self-government. An old saw made popular by President Ford has it that a government powerful enough to give us everything we want is a government powerful enough to take away everything we have. We might paraphrase Ford by suggesting that a leader strong enough to do everything we would like done for us is strong enough to deprive us of the capacity to do anything at all for ourselves.

Leaders lead—both for good and ill, lead us aright and lead us astray. As Garry Wills has noticed in his study of the Kennedy Presidency (*The Kennedy Imprisonment*), "we do the most damage under the presidents we love most." The test of democratic leadership is found in its passing. If the death of Roosevelt and the assassination of Kennedy demoralized America more than they energized it, if their passing left Americans wistful and uncertain rather than focused and decisive, then—however effective their leadership in the short run—we must judge their stewardships corrupting to democracy in the long run.

Lao-tse had a prescription for leadership which the Western democracies are unlikely to be able to live up to. "A leader is best," he advised, "when people barely know he exists. Not so good when people obey and acclaim him, worse when they despise him...but of a good leader, who talks little, when his work is done, his aim fulfilled, they will say 'we did this ourselves.'" Our leaders cultivate and flaunt their charisma (which is how they get elected in the media age) and are either much acclaimed or much despised for it. Leaders who talk little and scarcely exist for their constituents are unlikely candidates for office in a modern representative democracy where power is won by packaging and imagery.

Yet the aim of genuinely democratic leadership must not be merely to create the illusion of a people noisily taking the credit for what the leadership has in reality quietly achieved on its own, but to create genuine civic engagement and civic competence. Strong democratic leadership is leadership that leaves a citizenry more capable when the leader departs than before he

arrives. It is leadership that can boast: "Now that he is gone, we can do this ourselves."

The question is whether such leadership is possible. Conventional leadership operates successfully by creating loyal followers rather than self-sufficient citizens. Are there leaders who arrive on foot rather than astride magnificent white horses? who modestly catalyze a people to self-government rather than governing on their behalf? who are scarcely noticed, let alone missed when they go? Are there delegates who facilitate popular sovereignty instead of stealing the sovereign's mantle? H.G. Wells recommended leaders who could "guide us as far as they can and then vanish."

There are, I will argue, three kinds of leadership that are compatible with strong democracy: they are what I will call founding leadership, moral leadership, and facilitating (or enabling) leadership. While leadership in its current manifestation under representative democracy bears little resemblance to any of the three, suggestive models for each can be found elsewhere in modern society.

Both founding and moral leadership can be regarded as apolitical or extrapolitical forms of leadership. Both kinds of leader guide by inspiration, moving others to political engagement without themselves being politically engaged. The founding leader may institute a constitution or a movement or a political cause, but if he conforms to classical republican strictures about the limited role of the Great Legislator, he will permit his duties to extend only to the creation of a framework or an ideology or a point of view within which others will engage actively in politics. The founder is an empowerer....

Eugene Debs was painfully aware of the dangers that a too-competent leadership could pose to a popular movement. To his adoring would-be followers he issued this warning:

> Too long have the workers of the world
> waited for some Moses to lead them out

of bondage. He has not come; he will not come. I would not lead you out if I could; for if you could be led out, you could be led back again.

Debs is a model of what can be called extrapolitical moral leadership. Like founding leadership, moral leadership sets an example and creates a moral zeal for engagement and self-responsibility. Because it is aimed at democracy, it refuses to act in place of those it would inspire. The step from moral catalyst to moral surrogate is a tiny one, and the moral leader must exert extraordinary self-control, as Martin Luther King, on the whole, did....

The third model of leadership noted above—facilitating or enabling leadership—embodies a kind of leadership that is not only fully compatible with democracy but formulated to strengthen it by reenforcing citizenship.

Facilitating leadership empowers people. It functions modestly to enhance the quality and intensity of civic participation, and simultaneously guards the rights of all citizens to equal participation. Inverting the customary relationship between vigorous leaders and passive, watchdog followers, the facilitating leader subordinates himself to his constituents, making himself the vigilant watchdog of his community's civic activity and the guarantor of equitable participation. He holds the people accountable to standards of civic engagement and mutual respect. He holds but does not exercise power. Rather, he facilitates its exercise by those to whom it rightfully belongs. He assures equity among participants without throwing himself into the political balance. He resembles more the teacher than the administrator, the judge than the legislator, the therapist than the surgeon, the moderator than the chairman. Indeed, we may define facilitating leadership by the qualities attached to role models of this sort.

Take the teacher—a person who is poised to have a profound impact on students. As mentor, propagandist, indoctrinator, socializer, shaper of character, he can mold disciplines and as-

sure himself abject followers—clones who will learn not how to think but how to think as he thinks. Yet the measure of the great teacher is not discipleship, but critical self-sufficiency and the ability to think independently. The teacher who has discharged the liberal pedagogic function properly is the teacher who has become superfluous. The student who has been well taught is the student who no longer needs the teacher, who can argue with him as an equal and who demonstrates his debt to the teacher's skills by displaying his independence from the teacher's beliefs. The successful tutor boasts "I am superfluous! I will not be missed." The facilitating political leader must be capable of just this boast.

The judge in a jury trial plays an analogous role. She must instruct the jury in the substance of the law, preserve decorum in the courtroom, and guarantee that evidence is fairly presented, that witnesses are properly interrogated, and that the cases for plaintiff and defendant are judiciously argued. Yet the judge who has done her job well will secure conditions under which a jury can reach an independent verdict of which they can say "it is truly our decision, it is the people's verdict" and not some manipulated reflection of the judge's covert will. Like the teacher, the judge must be a facilitator who enables a jury to undertake its vital duties fairly and effectively. A thoughtful and just jury verdict attests to a competent and democratic judge, who glories not in her own but the jury's wisdom....

A second model for the facilitating leader is the therapist or, more accurately, the group therapist. On first glance, this may seem to be a rather farfetched example. Yet the therapist is above all an enabler whose success is measured by the degree to which his patients become self-sufficient life actors, able to function without him. The therapist restores men and women to good health, and his success is marked by the termination of his involvement. The patient does the hard labor, while the therapist only provides the conditions under which that labor is possible. He is an aid to a process in which the patient's own activity is crucial. In a successful therapy, the therapist is passive ("nondirective") and the patient is active. Many therapists will argue that the patient's will to get well is the single indispensable factor in a therapy and that the therapist does little more than witness and reenforce that will. Not "physician heal thyself" but "patient heal thyself, is an apt motto for the patient and, it seems, the citizen.

Our political doctors have created a society of dependent hypochondriacs who think themselves capable of being healthy only when they are under the doctor's care. No wonder they remain permanently incapacitated while their political doctors come to bear an odd resemblance to witches. The witch doctor, of course, aspires not to cure but to subjugate the bewitched. If there are analogs in politics to abusive therapists who profit from their patients' incapacities and toil to enhance rather than diminish their dependency, there are also analogs in politics to corrupt judges who exploit their special knowledge of the law and their authority in the courtroom to wring premeditated verdicts from juries that are autonomous only in name. There are also political versions of the teachers who prefer disciples to critics among their students, and who use their brilliance to intimidate rather than emancipate their best pupils....

To this point in the argument, our three examples are drawn from nonpolitical analogies that instruct only by inference. But there is one example of enabling leadership that does not depend on analogy, since it is inherently political: the example of the town moderator. The moderator is splendidly named, for his function is precisely to provide the moderating conditions under which citizens can interact, debate, listen to one another, deliberate, and eventually arrive at common decisions that do not radically alienate individuals or minorities of the small, neighborly townships where all must live together. The moderator is not a chairperson or a presiding officer who directs a meeting in accordance with his own agenda or acts as *primus inter pares* to weld together a committee into a functioning unit. On the contrary, he remains an outsider to the actual proceedings, listening, watching, and intervening only to assure equity, to guarantee fairness, and to secure the orderliness and moderation of the meeting. A well-moderated meeting will not notice its moderator; it will know only that its business is conducted and that participants are satisfied whether they emerge as winners or losers....

The moderator's skills are as much skills of listening as talking. Like the wise teacher, the moderator will impart to his constituents something of his own artfulness. For listening is equity's best ally in participatory meetings where garrulousness is always unequally distributed. Leaders typically speak well, and skillfulness in speech divides communities into the eloquent and the mute. Citizens typically listen well, and the capacity to hear unites communities through an art all can master. To be a citizen is not merely to express but to receive opinions, not merely to articulate one's own interests but to empathize with the interests of others. In representative societies, talk is vertically structured: leaders talk *to* citizens, though citizens rarely talk to or among one another. There is little lateral interaction.

Too often in representative democracies, speech means only talk *by* leaders. The institutions that are most valued are those that most benefit talkers: thus, the parliament or talk-assembly, which places a premium on the eloquent articulation of interests, or the representative political party that becomes a mouthpiece for otherwise inarticulate constituencies. However, it is far easier for representatives to speak on our behalf than to listen on our behalf. There are many human activities where representation is inappropriate: the World Series, a church communion, a sing-along, for example. Or politics.

The moderator does not pretend to represent anyone; he neither speaks nor acts for the town. He is rather a scrupulous listener. His task is to ensure that participants in the political process listen as well as they talk, or that the usual talkers are made to listen, and the usual listeners get a chance to talk. "I will listen" means to the moderator not to scan an adversary's position for weaknesses or potential trade-offs, nor even to permit every speaker his or her moment on the floor. Rather it means to encourage each to put himself in place of the other, to empathize with the other, to discover in the babble of voices a consensus that is audible only to the scrupulous auditor. The effective moderator wishes to transform all the He's and She's who come into the meeting with their own interests into a single We with a common interest. He will insist that every citizen be heard, but by that he will mean not only that all can speak but that all must listen.

Good listeners are not necessarily charismatic leaders, but they turn out to be excellent neighbors and trustworthy citizens. Where talking focuses on inequalities in the capacity to speak with clarity or eloquence, listening is a mutualistic art that by its very practice enhances equality—the equality of silence. The empathetic listener becomes more like his interlocutor as a consequence of sensitive listening. Indeed, one measure of healthy political talk is the amount of silence it permits, for silence is the precious medium in which reflection is nurtured and empathy can grow. In listening there is no cacophony, in silence no competition. The adept moderator will cultivate silence with the same assiduousness the adept leader cultivates eloquence. He will not be able to turn political discourse into a Quaker meeting, but the lesson of Quaker meetings for the attainment of concord and public good will not be lost on him.

If we are to have facilitating leaders on the model of the sensitive and modest moderator, we obviously require participatory institutions organized around his talents. Great Communicators do well in our great political talkshops and flourish in the kind of electoral politics where television is a dominant instrument. Citizens, on the other hand, do well where their energies are enlisted on behalf of direct political responsibility and where they can deliberate, interact, and legislate together....

If these remarks on leadership carry conviction, then Americans concerned with democracy and with the nature of democratic leadership need to shift their focus away from heads of state and towards the body politic that is the citizenry. Citizens are neither leaders nor followers: they embody a form of civic activity that precludes such radical forms of polarization. Our current weak form of democracy, relying on representation and preoccupied with leadership, permits us to choose who governs us but does not allow us to be self-governing. It makes our rulers accountable to the people but does not make the people citizens. Instead, it turns them into passive spectators, sometime watchdogs and grasping clients of leaders who are cynical bureaucrats and expert manipulators of popular prejudice. As the chasm between leaders and followers grows wider, democracy grows frailer.

The remedy is not better leaders but better citizens; and we can become better citizens only if we reinvigorate the tradition of strong democracy that focuses on citizenship and civic competence. This calls for participation as well as accountability; for civic duty as well as individual rights. It demands that we add the constructive use of public judgment and power to the already well established protection of private rights and interests. I have called this tradition *strong democracy*, to distinguish it from its "thin" representative cousin.

To reorient democracy away from leadership and representation and towards stronger forms of citizenship and participation, we need to foster institutional and practical experimentation with participatory institutions—many of which are already in place at the state and local level. These institutions, which I have elaborated in some detail in my *Strong Democracy: Participatory Politics for a New Age*, would include the following:

- A nationwide system of neighborhood assemblies of approximately 5000 citizens that would meet weekly and permit discussion and eventually voting on issues of local, regional, and national significance. These forums could be linked together by regional television networks and provide the setting for less parochial inter-regional debates as well. Their aim would be to enhance lateral communication among citizens and lessen the importance of national leaders.

- A communications cooperative that would oversee and regulate civic uses of new telecommunication technologies and distribute free civic information through a civic videotex service; the aim here would be more informed, self-sufficient, and thus competent citizens, less in need of expert leadership.

- Selective use of a lottery system of election, like the system used for jury service, but modeled on the lottery representation device use to fill a majority to political offices in ancient Athens. This system would be employed to fill some local and regional political offices—on school boards, local finance committees, or zoning boards, for example—and to select a limited number of delegates at large to state assemblies. By permitting citizens to actually serve in public office, and making every citizen a potential public servant, the chasm between leaders and followers would be significantly narrowed.

- Local "common-work" volunteer programs. These could include sweat equity projects, housing renovation, urban neighborhood farms, crime-watch programs, service to sick and elderly shut-ins, and rural reconstruction; by involving citizens in the actual work of democracy, the distinction between "us" and "them" would be reduced, and the responsibility of neighbors for the welfare of their own neighborhoods would be enhanced.

- A program of universal citizen service, including but not limited to a military option for all women and men between 18 and 26 for a two-year period. Citizen service restores the linkage between rights and duties and gives the young an introduction to citizenship rooted in participation and responsibility rather than mere voting.

These and other similar measures (spelled out in *Strong Democracy*) together create a powerful program of civic reorientation. They would not reconstitute America as a direct democracy—which is government by all of the people all of the time in all public affairs; but they would constitute the country as a strong democracy, which is government by all of the people some of the time in some public affairs. And they would reenforce an understanding of citizenship that permits citizens to give as well as to take, to serve as well as to be served, to cooperate as well as to contest, to act as well as to vote. Above all, it would demonstrate that democracy thrives neither when it possesses powerful leaders, nor when it breeds loyal followers, but only when it creates competent citizens who—in governing themselves—follow their own lead. We will know we have succeeded in our democratic aspirations not when we have found great leaders, but when we can boast that we no longer need great leaders.

Harry Boyte
Practical Politics

Along with Benjamin Barber, Harry Boyte is one of the most prominent advocates of a new and revitalized citizenship in America. The author of *Commonwealth*, and, with Sara Evans, the co-author of *Free Spaces* (see excerpt in Part III, Section B), Boyte currently directs a citizenship training program called Project Public Life at the Hubert Humphrey Institute at the University of Minnesota.

In the following essay, Boyte echoes Barber's concerns about the current decline in citizen participation. Boyte sees a rise in the last generation in "professional politics," exemplified by media-centered, candidate-packaged election campaigns, and a corresponding sense among Americans that they are the "clients" of a government from which they receive benefits, not participants in a politics "of and by the people." Furthermore, Boyte contends that the two main alternatives to electoral politics: advocacy and protest politics on the one hand; and a "therapeutic politics of intimacy" on the other, heighten the sense of distance between citizens and their governments. Boyte calls on the long tradition of "citizen politics" found in a variety of voluntary, civic, and reform efforts ranging from the women's suffrage organizations in the 19th century to the civil rights movement in the 20th, to argue for a reinvigoration of a spirit of practical politics.

Practical Politics
Harry Boyte

America faces a paradox. Citizen participation no longer produces many citizens.

Over the past several years, voluntary involvements—from work in food shelfs to issue advocacy efforts—have notably increased. Simultaneously democracy has largely become a spectator sport. Politics is more popular after the 1992 elections than in the recent past, but people's main role is call-in radio critic, with Rush Limbaugh emceeing.

The decline of people's involvement in politics means that people lose a sense of their stake and ownership in the nation. They become outsiders and tourists of the age. The politics of serious democracy is the give and take, messy, everyday public work through which citizens set about dealing with problems, the general issues of our common existence. Politics is the way people *become* citizens: accountable players and contributors to the country.

In place of government of the people, by the people, and for the people—a politics in which we have a role and personal stake—we see government as "for" the people, providing us services and giving us answers. In place of citizens, we have become a nation of clients.

The erosion of widespread experience with practical politics does not mean that people have become inactive. It means that activism is not understood in public ways: it denies its political nature and its impact on the larger world. Citizen participation today reflects the resurfacing of an older tradition that is anti-political, utopian, and personalized.

Activists simultaneously assert their particular and narrow perogatives even while they imagine themselves as pure and noble. "Not in my backyard" forms a familiar rallying cry in every community. But the poorly understood subtext is that activists believe that their values are far superior to those of the sinister world outside.

We are also in danger of becoming a nation of "idiots" in the Greek sense of the word, *idion*—people locked into private worlds, who have no experience with the creation of a common environment....

Politics after Mediating Institutions

The collapse in mediating political institutions and the spread everywhere of the professional-client pattern created a vacuum that has had disastrous consequences for both officeholders and citizens. The vacuum has been filled over the last generation by the rise of an insular, professionalized politics, on the one hand. On the other hand, it is populated by utopian, righteous strands of activism.

Since the late 1960s, immense energy has gone into the creation of countercultural organizations from communes to natural food co-ops. These, moreover, find counterparts in a distinctive politics of protest that comes at issues—and politics itself—from the outside, as victimized, righteous crusaders facing an evil, all-powerful, all encompassing establishment. Protest politics echoes in our time in everything from issue advocacy to movies like "JFK." The message of protest politics is the ironic combination of a condemnation of those in power with the demand that they solve our problems.

Advocacy and protest today merge with a politics of intimacy: the highly personalized approach that emerged as companion piece to sixties activism and came into its own in the 1970s and 1980s. Weekend therapy sessions and television talk shows, self-help groups and varieties of New Age phenomena, all have the effect of expanding a language of private experience and shared vulnerabilities into a personalized utopianism writ large. The ultimate logic of intimate politics is to refashion the nation as a limitless encounter group session, where everyone is expected to share things with the largest possible audience that they would rarely discuss in the privacy of their own homes.

Having been raised in therapeutic environments which stress self-esteem and emotional expressiveness, young people *take* everything in politics personally. In my graduate classes at the Humphrey Institute of Public Affairs, I find that students preparing for careers in public service combine a morally charged vocabulary about issues with striking vulnerability. Students vigorously argue for their positions, but they simultaneously feel personally assaulted if other students disagree with them. They look upon arguments as a challenge to their being—a sign that others don't think they are a "good person"—rather than as indications of different experiences, histories, and values.

The result of the utopian, intimate, and sentimental quality of citizen activism is that people see themselves as aggrieved, righteous, and misunderstood outsiders. Countless variations on the theme of "send them a message" have, in consequence, become the main way in which many people are connected to the larger world. People ask to be heard in politics and to receive things from government. They rarely imagine themselves as creators or producers *of* politics.

Public figures from Amitai Etzioni to Bill Clinton propose that America needs a renewed spirit of community, shared values, and service to strengthen citizenship. For communitarians, community forms both the precondition and also the end of civic involvements.

Calls for community usefully remind us of the need to reengage each other in productive fashion and highlight the important local dimensions of problem-solving which traditional liberalism slights. But the language of community is too idealized and hortatory to form an adequate basis for citizenship in our fragmented, professionalized and moralized age. If we are to do much about the disconnection of ordinary people from democracy, we need a practical politics in which citizens learn to claim and develop their public work in a world of diverse communities, values, and points of view. Americans need to relearn the skills of everyday problem-solving—how to work with others with whom we may not desire at all to share life in community.

To renew a politics of the citizen is a difficult and challenging task because it means shifting from righteous clienthood to an understanding that we are all inevitably implicated in the world's ambiguities and compromises. In Project Public Life, our civic and political education initiative at the University of Minnesota, we regularly ask groups of young people and adults what to do about critical issues they see in society. Almost invariably, they look to professionals and government to solve their problems. They have never been asked—nor have they imagined—what they might do about significant public issues, even those with immediate consequences for themselves. In one session, a group of deaf youngsters listed dozens of problems, from discrimination to phones that were unusable and teachers who did not know sign language. Afterwards, the two social workers with the group told our workshop leader that in more than 20 years of combined work with the deaf, they had never heard *anyone* ask hearing impaired teenagers what they themselves could do about the problems that they experienced in their lives.

Most mechanisms for citizen political action aside from voting involve learning the techniques of lobbying, pressuring officials, and gaining access to policy makers. But in fact, these techniques are in many ways a distraction. They assume that the citizens' main role is to pressure government officials to act, rather than to take action.

The first step in deprofessionalizing politics thus requires rethinking the *who* of politics. It involves the recognition that government officials and professional politicians have important but also specific and limited roles in solving major public problems. Government can fix pot holes and pick up garbage (even here, recycling has added a citizen dimension). To deal with teenage pregnancy, crime, school reform, racial conflict, and a host of other complex issues, however, will require far more extensive, responsible citizen effort than we have today.

Politics must be redefined from something we look to for benefits and solutions by professionals to the work that we as citizens do to address our problems. We need to see government as an instrument to which we delegate responsibilities and which we hold accountable, after citizens have discussed and argued about how problems are defined and how they might best be addressed.

Thus, in reengaging people with the public world, a starting point for any group is the challenge to citizens to repossess politics, to define politics as not something we watch but as our own work. We find that people generally respond well to the idea of redefining politics as public problem-solving—work by "the public," on public problems. Indeed, this is a much more effective approach than the exhortation to civic virtue—"good citizenship"—which generally characterizes civic education, or than the focus on "deliberation" and discussion which has recently been advanced as an alternative. The work of public problem-solving explicitly recognizes the role of self-interest, understood as those things that strongly motivate people to act in the public arena. The difficulties of politics emerge in learning the practice.

This shift means developing new approaches for educating citizens generally and young people in particular in politics. More than a dozen training centers now teach citizens how to access and impact professional politicians. But almost no education develops the capacities that citizens need to act effectively themselves on problems.

Learning practical politics means a shift from moralized posturing and advocacy to a more pragmatic viewpoint that sees the need for diverse points of view and contributions to address significant issues.

One striking consequence of the contemporary professionalization of politics is an inflamed vocabulary on virtually every issue. As E.J. Dionne has demonstrated in his recent book, *Why Americans Hate Politics*, politicians make their cases in polarities: pro-life versus pro-choice; for or against the death penalty; in favor or against taxes on the rich; pro-environment or pro-jobs.

Despite the widespread distaste for politicians' posturings, in many ways they reflect the moral flavor of the professional advocacy organizations which speak in the name of citizens. Issue advocacy groups across the political spectrum characteristically use a highly charged language in which proponents for a particular position are high-minded and virtuous, and their opponents are evil, corrupt stooges for the powers that be. This good and evil pattern is reinforced by modern technologies of fund-raising and communications like direct mail appeals, door to door fund-raising canvasses, and television news shows. All depend on simplistic emotional arousal and an outsider stance.

Some problems have an intrinsically moral cast. Americans, for instance, came to recognize racial segregation as a profound injustice. Child abuse has come to be seen as morally reprehensible in recent years.

But most public problems are far more complex than can be encompassed by a simplistic language of good and evil, and practical work to resolve the issues of our common existence gets lost in such polarizations. The dilemmas of teen age pregnancy are left unaddressed by confrontations between different sides of the abortion issue. Crime rates remain largely unaffected by debates about the death penalty. The troubles besetting our economy are not solved by fights about middle class tax cuts.

To reclaim politics as our own work, we need to reintegrate and hold in combination our ideals and the "real world"—a division which allows us to see ourselves as virtuous outsiders, rather than responsible participants.

We can create a non idealized and practical citizen politics by reversing the environmentalist and New Age phrase, "think globally and act locally." The phrase should be, instead, something like "think locally and learn to act with impact on the larger world." Effective citizen education needs to teach people to filter their ideals through a self-consciousness about the political and public dimensions of everyday life, where the work of getting things done inevitably involves compromise and ambiguity.

This entails a head-on challenge to the assumption, typical of educational philosophy, that most people are uninterested in and perhaps incapable of conceptual thinking. Today, most education, including civic education, focuses on conveying bodies of knowledge, information, and discrete skills. In contrast, I argue that civic education must combine systematic reflection on political ideas with practical experience in applying such concepts. Conceptual abilities are vital to preparing youth to participate creatively and effectively in complex, information-rich environments, where the capacity to make explicit, reflect upon, debate, and develop underlying principles of institutional practice is essential to constructive change.

Young children have an instinctive interest in the political aspects of their environments. They simply have today very few ways to develop their skills in political observation and action. Yet people can learn these skills. They can map settings such as schools, voluntary associations, government agencies, or workplaces according to the diversity of interests present, the dynamics of power and decision making that operate, the existing rules for being effective, and the ways such rules might be reworked. Skills of politics that can be taught include developing problem-solving relationships with others, listening and speaking well, understanding and practicing power, negotiating and bargaining, practicing judgment, holding people accountable, and the arts of self-evaluation. Learning to apply such political perspectives and skills to everyday life, in turn, teaches the lesson that our ideals always need to be connected to practical, difficult, messy realities.

Democratic politics involves norms of inclusiveness, openness, and equal access that challenge the way we do political business today. Practical politics is never a utopian or idealized arena; real differences in power, capacity, and organization are part of life. Every setting has flaws, even tragic dimensions. But a public world awash in special interest money, engineered by political consultants, and organized around media spectacles makes a mockery of the idea of a public realm of free citizens, joined together in serious action on public issues. Citizen-centered politics requires reforms to make official politics a more open and equal terrain.

Reworking politics also involves multiplying the number of locations where public problem-solving occurs. Government has appropriate roles, but many public functions can best be accomplished through nongovernmernmental organizations—nonprofits, community groups, private firms—as long as citizens insist on standards of public accountability.

Neither professional-dominated service programs nor the dismantling of government programs is the answer. Rather, the evidence of three decades on many issues is that citizens need *particular sorts* of government aid: tools of self-help that they can use to rebuild communities and create linkages with the political system. In inner cities, for instance, programs like Headstart, community policing, community-controlled job training, housing, and health initiatives have catalyzed action on a scale disproportionate to cost. A tragedy of the Reagan years is that inexpensive civic resources were specifically targeted for elimination or radical cutbacks, from the Office of Neighborhood Self-Help Development to VISTA Volunteers.

Multiplying the locations of public problem-solving also requires the partial deprofessionalization of mediating political institutions which remain. Unions, settlement houses, service agencies, schools, and other organizations continue to connect people's lives to the larger arena of public policy and governance, but they

have become recast in a professional-client pattern. Yet in Project Public Life, we have found that Extension Services, Headstart, public health departments, schools, and health providers organizations are usually aware of the inadequacy of excessively professionalized delivery approaches in which experts simply deliver information or services to client populations.

Extension agents and public health workers using the conceptual map of a public-minded citizen politics, for instance have changed their approach when communities ask for aid on issues like teenage suicide or alcohol use. Instead of simply delivering "expert advice," they pose the problem as a public issue connected to other issues about which citizens, including young people, must come to grips, talk through, and take action.

To develop strategies for deprofessionalizing service environments, we have found it essential to draw out the public dimensions of settings that have become excessively personalized. This means making distinctions between the public world and environments of friends, family, and small, homogeneous communities. Groups like 4-H, for instance, have traditionally described themselves with a "family" metaphor that no longer works well in a complex, diverse society. Schools suffer even more from the vocabulary of personal development which permeates K-12 education today, reflecting the ascendancy of psychology in schools of education. Self-expressiveness is useful in smaller settings of friendship or communities of belonging. But the language of "expressing feelings," "being understood," and "feeling okay about yourself" disarms youth in addressing the tough problems they worry about in the larger public world, from drugs, suicide, and racial discord to failing schools nd pollution.

A language of "publicness" gives people a way to see themselves as serious public actors. Effective citizen politics recognizes the appropriate roles of professionals but is not overawed by professional expertise; in the phrase from community organizing, it puts experts "on tap, not on top." Public spaces are open, accessible, and involve a mix of different people and groups. Moreover, the aim of politics is action on significant public problems—not bonding, or intimacy, or communal consensus. This means people must be able to work pragmatically with a variety of others, whether or not they like each other. In private, we want love and loyalty. In public, principles such as recognition, respect, and accountability are more useful bases for action.

Clarifying these dimensions of the public world creates new possibilities for developing workable public relationships. It allows people with different histories, backgrounds, and understandings of controversial issues like abortion or affirmative action to work together on problems that otherwise create unbridgeable divisions, if one imagines the end to be consensus or a shared way of life in community.

We will have to learn to be more than outsiders, innocents, and supplicants. "They" are neither the problem nor the solution. There is no they in this case. As Pogo put it, we have met the enemy and he is us. To do much about the challenges facing the nation, citizens will have to reenter the arena that we hate, rediscover its rewards, and take up its challenges. We need to become political again, if we are to become participants in the creation of our common world.

Václav Havel

Politics, Morality, and Civility

Vaclav Havel (1936—), was the last President of Czechoslovakia and the first President of the Czech Republic. Born in Prague of a prominent and wealthy family, Havel became a playwright and author, one who increasingly spoke out against the repressive communist regime in his home country during the 1960s and 1970s. He was repeatedly arrested during the 1970s and 1980s, serving a total of almost five years in prison. When Civic Forum, the movement for democratic political reform, emerged in 1989, Havel became one of its leading figures. The "Velvet Revolution" led to the dissolution of the communist regime, and Havel was elected president, first on an interim basis, and then in nationwide elections in 1990. After Slovakia established independence in 1992, Havel was elected to serve as the first President of the Czech Republic in 1993, a position he held for ten years.

In "Politics, Morality, and Civility," Havel emphasizes the role moral values play in political life, and the responsibility of leaders in fostering the linkage between morality and politics. He lays out the ways political leaders can instill values-based democratic action among the people, by simply "living in truth." As you read excerpts from this essay, think about the kind of community you are engendering through your own actions and decision-making, and what it means to "live in truth" in the context of your own work in the community.

Politics, Morality, and Civility
Václav Havel

As RIDICULOUS or quixotic as it may sound these days, one thing seems certain to me: that it is my responsibility to emphasize, again and again, the moral origin of all genuine politics, to stress the significance of moral values and standards in all spheres of social life, including economics, and to explain that if we don't try, within ourselves, to discover or rediscover or cultivate what I call "higher responsibility", things will turn out very badly indeed for our country.

The return of freedom to a society that was morally unhinged has produced something it clearly had to produce, and something we therefore might have expected, but which has turned out to be far more serious than anyone could have predicted: an enormous and dazzling explosion of every imaginable human vice. A wide range of questionable or at least morally ambiguous human tendencies, subtly encouraged over the years and, at the same time, subtly pressed to serve the daily operation of the totalitarian system, have suddenly been liberated, as it were, from their straitjacket and given freedom at last. The authoritarian regime imposed a certain order—if that is the right expression for it—on these vices (and in doing so "legitimized" them, in a sense). This order has now been shattered, but a new order that would limit rather than exploit these vices, an order based on freely accepted responsibility to and for the whole of society, has not yet been built—nor could it have been, for such an order takes years to develop and cultivate.

Thus we are witnesses to a bizarre state of affairs: society has freed itself, true, but in some ways it behaves worse than when it was in chains. Criminality has grown rapidly, and the familiar sewage that in times of historical reversal always wells up from the nether regions of the collective psyche has overflowed into the mass media, especially the gutter press.

But there are other, more serious and dangerous symptoms: hatred among nationalities, suspicion, racism, even signs of Fascism; politicking, an unrestrained, unheeding struggle for purely particular interests, unadulterated ambition, fanaticism of every conceivable kind, new and unprecedented varieties of robbery, the rise of different mafias; and a prevailing lack of tolerance, understanding, taste, moderation, and reason. There is a new attraction to ideologies, too—as if Marxism had left behind it a great, disturbing void that had to be filled at any cost.

It is enough to look around our political scene (whose lack of civility is merely a reflection of the more general crisis of civility). Mutual accusations, denunciations, and slander among political opponents know no bounds. One politician will undermine another's work only because they belong to different political parties. Partisan considerations still visibly take precedence over pragmatic attempts to arrive at reasonable and useful solutions to problems. Analysis is pushed out of the press by scandal mongering. Supporting the government in a good cause is practically shameful; kicking it in the shins, on the other hand, is praiseworthy. Sniping at politicians who declare their support for another political group is a matter of course. Anyone can accuse anyone else of intrigue or incompetence, or of having a shady past and shady intentions.

Demagogy is rife, and even something as important as the natural longing of a people for autonomy is exploited in power plays, as rivals compete in lying to the public. Many members of the party elite, the so-called *nomenklatura* who, until very recently, were faking concern about social justice and the working class, have cast aside their masks and, almost overnight, openly become speculators and thieves. Many a once-feared Communist is now an unscrupulous capitalist, shamelessly and unequivocally laughing in the face of the same worker whose interests he once allegedly defended.

Citizens are becoming more and more disgusted with all this, and their disgust is un-derstandably directed against the democratic government they themselves elected. Making the most of this situation, some characters with suspicious backgrounds have been gaining popular favour with ideas such as, for instance, the need to throw the entire government into the Vltava River.

And yet, if a handful of friends and I were able to bang our heads against the wall for years by speaking the truth about Communist totalitarianism while surrounded by an ocean of apathy, there is no reason why I shouldn't go on banging my head against the wall by speaking *ad nauseam*, despite the condescending smiles, about responsibility and morality in the face of our present social marasmus. There is no reason to think that this struggle is a lost cause. The only lost cause is one we give up on before we enter the struggle.

TIME and time again I have been persuaded that a huge potential of goodwill is slumbering within our society. It's just that it's incoherent, suppressed, confused, crippled and perplexed—as though it does not know what to rely on, where to begin, where or how to find meaningful outlets.

In such a state of affairs, politicians have a duty to awaken this slumbering potential, to offer it direction and ease its passage, to encourage it and give it room, or simply hope. They say a nation gets the politicians it deserves. In some senses this is true: politicians are indeed a mirror of their society, and a kind of embodiment of its potential. At the same time—paradoxically—the opposite is also true: society is a mirror of its politicians. It is largely up to the politicians which social forces they choose to liberate and which they choose to suppress, whether they rely on the good in each citizen or on the bad. The former regime systematically mobilized the worst human qualities, like selfishness, envy, and hatred. That regime was far more than just something we deserved; it was also responsible for what we became. Those who find themselves in politics therefore bear a heightened responsibility for the moral state of society, and it is their responsibility to seek out the best in that society, and to develop and strengthen it.

By the way, even the politicians who often anger me with their short-sightedness and their malice are not, for the most part, evil-minded. They are, rather, inexperienced, easily infected with the particularisms of the time, easily manipulated by suggestive trends and prevailing customs; often they are simply caught up, unwillingly, in die swirl of bad politics, and find themselves unable to extricate themselves because they are afraid of the risks this would entail.

SOME say I'm a naive dreamer who is always trying to combine the incompatible: politics and morality.

COMMUNISM WAS OVERTHROWN BY LIFE, BY THOUGHT, BY HUMAN DIGNITY. Those who still claim that politics is chiefly the manipulation of power and public opinion, and that morality has no place in it, are just as wrong. Political intrigue is not really politics, and, although you can get away with superficial politics for a time, it does not bring much hope of lasting success. Through intrigue one may easily become prime minister, but that will be the extent of one's success; one can hardly improve the world that way.

I am happy to leave political intrigue to others; I will not compete with them, certainly not by using their weapons.

Genuine politics—politics worthy of the name, and the only politics I am willing to devote myself to—is simply a matter of serving those around us: serving the community, and serving those who will come after us. Its deepest roots are moral because it is a responsibility, expressed through action, to and for the whole, a responsibility that is what it is—a "higher" responsibility—only because it has a metaphysical grounding: that is, it grows out of a conscious or subconscious certainty that our death ends nothing, because everything is forever being recorded and evaluated somewhere else, somewhere "above us", in what I have called

"the memory of Being"—an integral aspect of the secret order of the cosmos, of nature, and of life, which believers call God and to whose judgement everything is subject. Genuine conscience and genuine responsibility are always, in the end, explicable only as an expression of the silent assumption that we are observed "from above", that everything is visible, nothing is forgotten, and so earthly time has no power to wipe away the sharp disappointments of earthly failure: our spirit knows that it is not the only entity aware of these failures.

What can I do, as president, not only to remain faithful to that notion of politics, but also to bring it to at least partial fruition? (After all, the former is unthinkable without the latter. Not to put at least some of my ideas into practice could have only two consequences: either I would eventually be swept from office or I would become a tolerated eccentric, sounding off to an unheeding audience—not only a less dignified alternative, but a highly dishonest one as well, because it would mean another form of resignation, both of myself and of my ideals.)

As in everything else, I must start with myself. That is: in all circumstances try to be decent, just, tolerant, and understanding, and at the same time try to resist corruption and deception. In other words, I must do my utmost to act in harmony with my conscience and my better self. For instance, I am frequently advised to be more "tactical" not to say everything right away, to dissimulate gently, not to fear wooing someone more than my nature commands, or to distance myself from someone against my real will in the matter. In the interests of strengthening my hand, I am advised at times to assent to someone's ambition for power, to flatter someone merely because it pleases him, or to reject someone even though it goes against my convictions, because he does not enjoy favour with others.

I constantly hear another kind of advice, as well: I should be tougher, more decisive, more authoritative. For a good cause, I shouldn't be afraid to pound the table occasionally, to shout at people, to try to rouse a little fear and trembling. Yet, if I wish to remain faithful to myself and my notion of politics, I mustn't listen to advice like this—not just in the interests of my personal mental health (which could be seen as a private, selfish desire), but chiefly in the interests of what most concerns me: the simple fact that directness can never be established by indirection, or truth through lies, or the democratic spirit through authoritarian directives. Of course, I don't know whether directness, truth, and the democratic spirit will succeed. But I do know how *not* to succeed, which is by choosing means that contradict the ends. As we know from history, that is the best way to eliminate the very ends we set out to achieve.

In other words, if there is to be any chance at all of success, there is only one way to strive for decency, reason, responsibility, sincerity, civility, and tolerance, and that is decently, reasonably, responsibly, sincerely, civilly, and tolerantly. I'm aware that, in everyday politics, this is not seen as the most practical way of going about it. But I have one advantage: among my many bad qualities there is one that happens to be missing—a longing or a love for power. Not being bound by that, I am essentially freer than those who cling to their power or position, and this allows me to indulge in the luxury of behaving untactically.

I see the only way forward in that old, familiar injunction: "live in truth".

But how is this to be done, practically speaking, when one is president? I see three basic possibilities.

The first possibility: I must repeat certain things aloud over and over again. I don't like repeating myself, but in this case it's unavoidable. In my many public utterances, I feel I must emphasize and explain repeatedly the moral dimensions of all social life, and point out that morality is, in fact, hidden in everything. And this is true: whenever I encounter a problem in my work and try to get to the bottom of it, I always discover some moral aspect, be it apathy, unwillingness to recognize personal error or guilt, reluctance to give up certain positions and the advantages flowing from them, envy, an excess of self-assurance, or whatever.

I feel that the dormant goodwill in people needs to be stirred. People need to hear that it makes sense to behave decently or to help others, to place common interests above their own, to respect the elementary rules of human coexistence. They want to be told about this publicly. They want to know that those "at the top" are on their side. They feel strengthened, confirmed, hopeful. Goodwill longs to be recognized and cultivated. For it to develop and have an impact it must hear that the world does not ridicule it.

The second possibility: I can try to create around me, in the world of so-called high politics, a positive climate, a climate of generosity, tolerance, openness, broadmindedness, and a kind of elementary companionship and mutual trust. In this sphere I am far from being the decisive factor. But I can have a psychological influence.

The third possibility: There is a significant area in which I do have direct political influence in my position as president. I am required to make certain political decisions. In this, I can and must bring my concept of politics to bear, and inject into it my political ideals, my longing for justice, decency, and civility, my notion of what, for present purposes, I will call "the moral state". Whether I am successful or not is for others to judge, of course, but the results will always be uneven, since, like everyone else, I am a fallible human being.

JOURNALISTS, and in particular foreign correspondents, often ask me how the idea of "living in truth", the idea of "anti-political politics", or the idea of politics subordinated to conscience can, in practice, be carried out. They are curious to know whether, finding myself in high office, I have not had to revise much of what I once wrote as an independent critic of politics and politicians. Have I not been compelled to lower my former "dissident" expectations of politics, by which they mean the standards I derived from the "dissident experience", which are therefore scarcely applicable outside that sphere?

There may be some who won't believe me, but in my second term as president in a land full of problems that presidents in stable countries never even dream of, I can safely say that I have not been compelled to recant anything of what I wrote earlier, or to change my mind about anything. It may seem incredible, but it is so: not only have I not had to change my mind, but my opinions have been confirmed.

Despite the political distress I face every day, I am still deeply convinced that politics is not essentially a disreputable business; and to the extent that it is, it is only disreputable people who make it so. I would concede that it can, more than other spheres of human activity, tempt one to disreputable practices, and that it therefore places higher demands on people. But it is simply not true that a politician must lie or intrigue. That is utter nonsense, spread about by people who — for whatever reasons — wish to discourage others from taking an interest in public affairs.

Of course, in politics, as elsewhere in life, it is impossible and pointless to say everything, all at once, to just anyone. But that does not mean having to lie. All you need is tact, the proper instincts, and good taste. One surprising experience from "high politics" is this: I have discovered that good taste is more useful here than a post-graduate degree in political science. It is largely a matter of form: knowing how long to speak, when to begin and when to finish; how to say something politely that your opposite number may not want to hear; how to say, always, what is most significant at a given moment, and not to speak of what is not important or relevant; how to insist on your own position without offending; how to create the kind of friendly atmosphere that makes complex negotiations easier; how to keep a conversation going without prying or being aloof; how to balance serious political themes with lighter, more relaxing topics; how to plan your official

journeys judiciously and to know when it is more appropriate not to go somewhere, when to be open and when reticent and to what degree.

But more than that, it means having a certain instinct for the time, the atmosphere of the time, the mood of people, the nature of their worries, their frame of mind—that too can perhaps be more useful than sociological surveys. An education in political science, law, economics, history, and culture is an invaluable asset to any politician, but I have been persuaded, again and again, that it is not the most essential asset. Qualities like fellow-feeling, the ability to talk to others, insight, the capacity to grasp quickly not only problems but also human character, the ability to make contact, a sense of moderation: all these are immensely more important in politics. I am not saying, heaven forbid, that I myself am endowed with these qualities; not at all! These are merely my observations.

To sum up: if your heart is in the right place and you have good taste, not only will you pass muster in politics, you are destined for it. If you are modest and do not lust after power, not only are you suited to politics, you absolutely belong there. The *sine qua non* of a politician is not the ability to lie; he need only be sensitive and know when, what, to whom, and how to say what he has to say. It is not true that a person of principle does not belong in politics; it is enough for his principles to be leavened with patience, deliberation, a sense of proportion, and an understanding of others. It is not true that only the unfeeling cynic, the vain, the brash, and the vulgar can succeed in politics; such people, it is true, are drawn to politics, but, in the end, decorum and good taste will always count for more.

My experience and observations confirm that politics as the practice of morality is possible. I do not deny, however, that it is not always easy to go that route, nor have I ever claimed that it was.

I want to do everything I can to contribute, in a specific way, to a program for raising the general level of civility, or at least do everything

I can to express my personal interest in such an improvement, whether I do so as president or not. I feel this is both an integral part and a logical consequence of my notion of politics as the practice of morality and the application of a "higher responsibility". After all, is there anything that citizens — and this is doubly true of politicians — should be more concerned about, ultimately, than trying to make life more pleasant, more interesting, more varied, and more bearable?

IF I TALK here about my political — or, more precisely, my civil — program, about my notion of the kind of politics and values and ideals I wish to struggle for, this is not to say that I am entertaining the naive hope that this struggle may one day be over. A heaven on earth in which people all love each other and everyone is hard-working, well-mannered, and virtuous, in which the land flourishes and everything is sweetness and light, working harmoniously to the satisfaction of God: this will never be. On the contrary, the world has had the worst experiences with utopian thinkers who promised all that. Evil will remain with us, no one will ever eliminate human suffering, the political arena will always attract irresponsible and ambitious adventurers and charlatans. And man will not stop destroying the world. In this regard, I have no illusions.

Neither I nor anyone else will ever win this war once and for all. At the very most, we can win a battle or two — and not even that is certain. Yet I still think it makes sense to wage this war persistently. It has been waged for centuries, and it will continue to be waged — we hope — for centuries to come. This must be done on principle, because it is the right thing to do. Or, if you like, because God wants it that way. It is an eternal, never-ending struggle waged not just by good people (among whom I count myself, more or less) against evil people, by honourable people against dishonourable people, by people who think about the world and eternity against people who think only of themselves and the moment. It takes place

inside everyone. It is what makes a person a person, and life, life.

So anyone who claims that I am a dreamer who expects to transform hell into heaven is wrong. I have few illusions. But I feel a responsibility to work towards the things I consider good and right. I don't know whether I'll be able to change certain things for the better, or not at all. Both outcomes are possible. There is only one thing I will not concede: that it might be meaningless to strive in a good cause.

WE ARE building our country anew. Fate has thrust me into a position in which I have a somewhat greater influence on that process than most of my fellow citizens do. It is appropriate, therefore, that I admit to my notions about what kind of country it should be, and articulate the vision that guides me—or rather, the vision that flows naturally from politics as I understand it.

Perhaps we can all agree that we want a state based on rule of law, one that is democratic (that is, with a pluralistic political system), peaceful, and with a prospering market economy. Some insist that this state should also be socially just. Others sense in the phrase a hangover from socialism and argue against it. They object to the notion of "social justice" as vague, claiming that it can mean anything at all, and that a functioning market economy can never guarantee any genuine social justice. They point out that people have, and always will have, different degrees of industriousness, talent, and, last but not least, luck. Obviously, social justice in the sense of social equality is something the market system cannot, by its very nature, deliver. Moreover, to compel the marketplace to do so would be deeply immoral. (Our experience of socialism has provided us with more than enough examples of why this is so.)

I do not see, however, why a democratic state, armed with a legislature and the power to draw up a budget, cannot strive for a certain fairness in, for example, pension policies or tax policies, or support to the unemployed, or salaries to public employees, or assistance to the elderly living alone, people who have health problems, or those who, for various reasons, find themselves at the bottom of society. Every civilized state attempts, in different ways and with different degrees of success, to come up with reasonable policies in these areas, and not even the most ardent supporters of the market economy have anything against it in principle. In the end, then, it is a conflict not of beliefs, but rather of terminology.

I am repeating these basic, self-evident, and rather general facts for the sake of completeness and order. But I would like to say more about other aspects of the state that may be somewhat less obvious and are certainly much less talked about, but are no less important — because they qualify and make possible everything that is considered self-evident.

I am convinced that we will never build a democratic state based on rule of law if we do not at the same time build a state that is — regardless of how unscientific this may sound to the ears of a political scientist — humane, moral, intellectual and spiritual, and cultural. The best laws and the best-conceived democratic mechanisms will not in themselves guarantee legality or freedom or human rights — anything, in short, for which they were intended — if they are not underpinned by certain human and social values. What good, for instance, would a law be if no one respected it, no one defended it, and no one tried responsibly to follow it? It would be nothing but a scrap of paper. What use would elections be in which the voter's only choice was between a greater and a lesser scoundrel? What use would a wide variety of political parties be if not one of them had the general interest of society at heart?

No state — that is, no constitutional, legal, and political system — is anything in and of itself, outside historical time and social space. It is not the clever technical invention of a team of experts, like a computer or a telephone. Every state, on the contrary, grows out of specific intellectual, spiritual, and cultural traditions that breathe substance into it and give it meaning.

So we are back to the same point: without commonly shared and widely entrenched moral values and obligations, neither the law, nor democratic government, nor even the market economy will function properly. They are all marvellous products of the human spirit, mechanisms that can, in turn, serve the spirit magnificently — assuming that the human spirit wants these mechanisms to serve it, respects them, believes in them, guarantees them, understands their meaning, and is willing, if necessary, to fight for them or make sacrifices for them.

Again I would use law as an illustration. The law is undoubtedly an instrument of justice, but it would be an utterly meaningless instrument if no one used it responsibly. From our own recent experience we all know too well what can happen to even a decent law in the hands of an unscrupulous judge, and how easily unscrupulous people can use democratic institutions to introduce dictatorship and terror. The law and other democratic institutions ensure little if they are not backed up by the willingness and courage of decent people to guard against their abuse. That these institutions can help us become more human is obvious; that is why they were created, and why we are building them now. But if they are to guarantee anything to us, it is we, first of all, who must guarantee them.

In the somewhat chaotic provisional activity around the technical aspects of building the state, it will do us no harm occasionally to remind ourselves of the meaning of the state, which is, and must remain, truly human — which means it must be intellectual, spiritual, and moral.

How ARE we to go about building such a state? What does such an ambition bind us to or offer us, in practical terms?

There is no simple set of instructions on how to proceed. A moral and intellectual state cannot be established through a constitution, or through law, or through directives, but only through complex, long-term, and never-ending work involving education and self-education.

What is needed is lively and responsible consideration of every political step, every decision; a constant stress on moral deliberation and moral judgement; continued self-examination and self-analysis; an endless rethinking of our priorities. It is not, in short, something we can simply declare or introduce. It is a way of going about things, and it demands the courage to breathe moral and spiritual motivation into everything, to seek the human dimension in all things. Science, technology, expertise, and so-called professionalism are not enough. Something more is necessary. For the sake of simplicity, it might be called spirit. Or feeling. Or conscience.

Community, Citizenship and Service
Selected Essays

Community service has become the talk of the nation and common practice in local communities, churches, and schools at all levels. More and more Americans are engaged in government-sponsored service, through the Americorps program and other federally-funded national service policy initiatives that have been in place for the past decade. Of course, the federal government has funded various schemes for citizen service in this century, from the Civilian Conservation Corps to the Peace Corps to VISTA. But in recent years the community service movement has gained momentum, especially among young people.

Section D begins with four essays grounding community service in a moral fabric that motivates individuals to work for the common good or on behalf of those disadvantaged by society. The famous Harvard child psychologist and author Robert Coles, in an excerpt from his book *The Call of Service*, tells two stories—his own and that of one of the children who desegregated New Orleans' public schools in 1961—that place "service" in the broader context of the civil rights movement. The following three articles provide the religious foundation for service as understood by three representative pieces in the Judeo-Christian tradition. The story of Mother Teresa (1910–1997), whose poetry and prayers connecting faith, love, and service to others we excerpt here, is well known. Born with the name Gonxha Bojaxhiu, to a prosperous Albanian family that had moved to Macedonia, she was "seized with devotion to God and to the poor" at age 18. She left everything behind, following in the footsteps of St. Francis by taking vows of poverty. From then on, she spent the bulk of her life in Calcutta, India, working among the "poorest of the poor," particularly its children, and founding an international religious order—the Missionaries of Charity—to carry on a variety of efforts on behalf of the poor and abandoned internationally. Before her death last year, she received worldwide acclaim for her work, winning virtually all the great international prizes, including the Nobel Peace Prize in 1979. An excerpt from Millard Fuller's *Theology of the Hammer* follows Mother Teresa. Fuller's story is almost as compelling, and is recounted in part of the narrative in this volume. Raised Protestant in small town Alabama, Fuller became a lawyer and reached his goal of amassing a great deal of wealth at an early age. Precipitated by his wife Linda, the Fullers decided to give their wealth away and founded Habitat for Humanity, an international organization dedicated to eliminating inadequate and poverty housing throughout the world as a witness to the teachings of Jesus. Finally, Jacob Neusner's short essay explores the Jewish roots of service in the concept of *tzedaka*h. As the essay indicates, in Hebrew there is no word for charity. *Tzedakah*, which Neusner translates as "righteousness," conveys a more obligatory connotation than the word charity does. When you combine the four essays, in a variety of ways and expressions, the reader will get a sense of the strong strain of thought within the Judeo-Christian tradition that regards service to others as a duty of one's humanity and one's faith in a Supreme Being.

The essays that follow the first four place community service in the context of the larger national service effort. President Clinton's essay is an editorial promoting national service, published on the eve of his first major policy address on the subject at Rutgers University in March, 1993 (see Part III, Section A, for excerpts from this address). Jon Van Til, professor of Urban Studies at Rutgers University-Camden, is the author of *Mapping the Third Sector: Voluntarism in a Changing Social Economy*. He has written an essay especially for this volume which addresses a series of questions raised by the national service movement. Amitai Etzioni, University Professor of Sociology and Director of the Center for Policy Research at The George Washington University, is the author of many books, most recently *The New Golden Rule*: *Community and Morality in a Democratic Society*. He is also founder and editor of The Responsive Community, the quarterly of the communitarian network. He writes here about opportunities and concerns created by large-scale national service. This is also the focus of Donald Eberly's article. Executive director of the National Service

Secretariat, Eberly has been at the forefront of the push for national service since his 1958 proposal "National Service for Peace" was a source of the Peace Corps legislation.

A few of the writers highlight the educational purposes of community service. Rev. Theodore Hesburgh, C.S.C., former president of the University of Notre Dame, sees federal resources as an encouragement for all young people, including the indigent, to serve and learn about voluntarism and altruism. Allen Wutzdorff, former Executive Director of the National Society for Experiential Education, writes about the importance of combining community service with an intentional educational program so that those who do national service actually learn from the experience. Benjamin Barber's essay ties community service and service-learning more specifically to citizenship and civic education.

Several of the essays emphasize the ways in which community service programs can use young people as resources in solving public problems and in their own self-empowerment. This is the overwhelming spirit behind the essay by Jack Calhoun, former Executive Director of the National Crime Prevention Council. Bernadette Chi, a graduate student at the University of California, Berkeley who continues to work on community service projects for the California Department of Education, wants to better structure national service initiatives in order to lead young people into lives of public service and community improvement. And Maura Wolf, former Board Chair for the Campus Outreach Opportunities League (COOL) and program director for Boston Do Something, sees young people serving as a resource to the needs of children across the country.

Still others view national service as a method for achieving institutional and social change. Kathleen Kennedy Townsend currently serves as Lieutenant Governor for the State of Maryland, where community service has been mandated as a requirement for graduation from high school. In her essay, she explores the connection between education-based community service and school reform. Ira Harkavy, Professor of History and Director of the Center for Community Partnerships at the University of Pennsylvania, argues that national service can be a catalyst in transforming our institutions of higher education into neighborly, community-connected organizations.

As you read these thoughtful essays, think about your own service work and how it connects to some of the larger issues of community, faith, and national service raised by these writers.

The Call of Service
Robert Coles

By November 1961 I had come to know for a year the four black six-year-old girls who initiated school desegregation in New Orleans at the behest of Federal Judge J. Skelly Wright. I have many times described the ordeal of Ruby Bridges, who had to fight her way through angry, threatening mobs every day for months. Federal marshals escorted her to and from the Frantz School because the city police and the state police were unwilling to protect her. Obscenities were her everyday fare, and often she heard grown men and women, mothers and fathers, tell her she was going to die one day soon. She withstood this ordeal with remarkable resilience and even managed to find time occasionally to pray for her tormentors.

I have also described, though in less detail, the three other girls, who went through a similarly harrowing trial at the McDonogh 19 School. One of them, Tessie, figured promi-nently in some of my first writing, three decades ago, as I tried to understand her stoic courage. Like Ruby, she was a mystery and a challenge to a young pediatrician and child psychiatrist. I was in the midst of psychoanalytic training and was all too eagerly on the prowl for psychopa-thology. I was especially interested in Tessie's maternal grandmother, Martha, a tall, hand-some woman with gray hair, carefully groomed, and large, warm eyes that often settled on her granddaughter. Tessie's eyes, in turn, sought out her grandmother's, as if she was thereby nourished and strengthened. This woman of fifty had lived a life of poverty and pain (she had fairly severe rheumatoid arthritis), but she had never lost her sense of humor, her capac-ity to laugh and laugh—she had a big laugh that shook her ample body and was sometimes punctuated by a clap or two of her hands and a two-word exclamation: "*Lord Almighty!*"

She spoke those words in church repeatedly, of course. I would sit with Martha and her daughter and son-in-law and Tessie and her sister and brothers, and when one of the Hebrew prophets—Isaiah or Jeremiah or Micah or Amos—was quoted, she would commonly add her affirmation to their pleas for justice, to their denunciations of iniquity and arrogance and self-indulgence. In conversation she seemed to be aware of the "culture of narcissism" long before it was the subject of popular analysis: "There's so much selfishness in us, and we have to fight it this whole life long." After the slightest pause, she would raise her voice, exclaiming, "Lord Almighty." On occasion in church, she raised her voice higher still—and when the words of Jesus were spoken, she really gave forth her *Lord Almighty!*

She was often the one who delivered Tessie to the federal marshals. They arrived in their cars promptly at eight in the morning, and as they approached her door, she would fling it open, greet the men, and greet the day: "Lord Almighty, another gift!" She was referring to the hours ahead, I soon learned—no matter the travail she knew to be in store for her granddaughter. Tessie would emerge from behind her, lunch pail in hand, and go off with those tall, white, dark-suited men, who carried revolvers underneath their jackets.

On one such morning I heard Martha use a phrase that was almost identical to the title of this book. Her amplification of that phrase has rung in my ears over the years as a rationale of sorts for a way of being, and even for the kind of research described in a chapter that takes up the somewhat pompous matter of "methodology"—how we do what we do. On that day Tessie was not so much reluctant to go to school as tired and weary. She was emerging from a bout of the flu; she had slipped and fallen while playing in a nearby back yard; and she didn't like her substitute teacher. The grandmother, privy as always to the child's worries, doubts, and difficulties, knew full well her granddaughter's state of mind that early

morning. Tessie had suggested, over a breakfast that included her grandmother's homemade corn bread (celebrated by friends and relatives, many of whom received now and then what Martha always called "a little something"), that perhaps, for the first time, she would stay home from school.

As I arrived and sat down to some of that "little something" myself, Tessie once more, shyly and guardedly, suggested that she might stay home. The grandmother said yes, that would be fine if Tessie truly wasn't well. But if she was more discouraged than sick, that was quite another matter. Then came a disquisition which my old bulky tape recorder fortunately was prepared to receive.

"It's no picnic, child—I know that, Tessie— going to that school. Lord Almighty, if I could just go with you, and stop there in front of that building, and call all those people to my side, and read to them from the Bible, and tell them, remind them, that He's up there, Jesus, watching over all of us—it don't matter who you are and what your skin color is. But I stay here, and you go—and your momma and your daddy, they have to leave the house so early in the morning that it's only Saturdays and Sundays that they see you before the sun hits the middle of its traveling for the day. So I'm not the one to tell you that you should go, because here I am, and I'll be watching television and eating or cleaning things up while you're walking by those folks. But I'll tell you, you're doing them a great favor; you're doing them a service, a big service."

She stopped briefly to pick up a fly swatter and go after a bee that had noisily appeared in the kitchen. She hit it and watched it fall to the floor, then she plucked a tissue from a box on a counter, picked up the bee, still alive, and took it outside, where it flew off. I was surprised; I'd expected her to kill the bee and put its remains in a wastebasket. She resumed speaking and, again to my surprise, connected her rescue of the bee to what she had started to say.

"You see, my child, you have to help the good Lord with His world! He puts us here—and He calls us to help Him out. That bee doesn't belong here; it belongs out there. You belong in that McDonogh School, and there will be a day when everyone knows that, even those poor folks—Lord, I pray for them!—those poor, poor folks who are out there shouting their heads off at you. You're one of the Lord's people; He's put His Hand on you. He's given a call to you, a call to service in His name! There's all those people, scared out of their minds, and by the time you're ready to leave the McDonogh School they'll be calmed down, and they won't be paying you no mind at all, child, and I'll guarantee you, that's how it will be!"

As she was speaking, Tessie finished her breakfast, marched confidently to the sink with her dishes, put them in a neat pile, and went to get her raincoat and empty lunch pail from her room—all without saying a word. She was going to school, I realized. No further words on the subject were exchanged. The grandmother told Tessie what she was putting in the lunch pail, and Tessie expressed her thanks. In no time, it seemed, the girl was out the door and walking with the marshals, who had waited near their car.

Later that day, playing that tape, Jane and I tried to understand what had taken place. Tessie had tried to beg off just a bit—not to escape from her educational (and personal) fate, but simply out of a moment's queasiness. Her grandmother was by no means insensitive to Tessie's daily ups and downs, nor was she a stern taskmaster—indeed, Tessie's parents worried sometimes that she was spoiled a bit by her granny. Yet that morning she was obviously urging her granddaughter on, and with biblical sanction. This approach was quite familiar to Tessie—she may have even expected the miniature sermon she received.

Weeks later, sitting with Tessie as she drew a picture of the McDonogh School and then one of Martha, I asked whether she had followed her grandmother's meaning. "I wasn't sure what your granny meant that morning. I wasn't sure how you should be of 'service' to those people out there on the street."

The girl had no trouble at all in seeing what was on my mind and in helping me out. She hesitated only a second, then told me, "If you just keep your eyes on what you're supposed to be doing, then you'll get there—to where you want to go. The marshals say, 'Don't look at them; just walk with your head up high, and you're looking straight ahead.' My granny says that there's God, He's looking too, and I should remember that it's a help to Him to do this, what I'm doing; and if you serve Him, then that's important. So I keep trying."

She was getting to the heart of what she had learned that mattered. For her, service meant serving, and not only on behalf of those she knew and liked or wanted to like. Service meant an alliance with the Lord Himself on behalf of people who were obviously unfriendly. Service was not an avocation or something done to fulfill a psychological need, not even an action that would earn her any great immediate or long-term reward. Service was itself a challenge—maybe a bigger one than the challenge of getting by a truculent, agitated mob twice a day.

"If I can help the good Lord and do a good job, then it'll all be okay, and I won't be wasting my time," Tessie announced once, as she tried to divert me from my interest in her responses to what she heard on the street. She had told me often how awful those men and women were and how upset she was by their stubbornly persistent attention to her. "They never seem to give up," she said one day, four months into the experience of being in the school with only two other black students, while a mob stayed outside much of the time, especially to greet her in the morning. But those segregationist voices of hateful outrage and bitterness, of deep disappointment, even of threats, were not enough to deflect her abiding concern for the voices of her parents, of the minister who visited her home once a week, and, not least, of her grandmother. "You have to listen to the right people; otherwise you get yourself into trouble!"

I agreed, of course—and I could hear her trying to strengthen her resolve, lest she become further prey to the anxiety and apprehension with which she had to contend. But she was letting me know that without losing sight of the danger, she had turned her attention away from that trouble and toward something else. She wasn't resorting to a valiant, desperate effort at "denial" to get through a most scary time. She was fully aware of what was happening, but also fully aware of why she was going through this ordeal. Here was a major crisis in America's history of desegregation, and children had become the adversary of an entire city, it seemed.

Yet Tessie had learned to regard herself not as a victim, not as an outsider trying hard to enter a world bent on keeping her out, not as a mere six-year-old black girl from a poor family with no clout and no connections but rather as an emissary from on high, a lucky one designated to lead an important effort, a child given the errand of rendering service to a needy population. She had connected a civic moment in her life with a larger ideal, and in so doing had learned to regard herself as a servant, as a person "called to service."

The elders in her life, especially her grandmother Martha, use those words or phrases insistently as they tried hard to give her not only reassurance and affection (the "support" many of us today talk about so much), but also something else. What they were giving her was most powerfully expressed one day toward the end of that long first year of school when the mob was still holding fast to its daily vigil. Martha said, "We're the lucky ones to be called, and we've got to prove we can do what the Lord wants, that we're up to it."

A grandmother was prepared not only to say that—a rhetoric of urgent, even desperate survival—but prepared to give of herself and ask of others in the interest, finally, of something

(Someone) larger than herself. No wonder, then, that at certain moments when I thought Tessie vulnerable—a passing flu, a hard lesson at school, a fight with her brother—and in need of a little extra consideration, Tessie's grandmother became sterner, more exhortative than usual. I eventually realized that what I interpreted as a somewhat strained, even overbearing declaration was for an entire family quite something else: it was a rationale for a life, a pronouncement with enormous moral and emotional significance for young and old alike.

Tessie knew that service meant offering oneself to others as an example, a teacher; one bears a message and hopes that it will, in time, be understood and accepted. When white children at last began to return to the McDonogh School—when their parents tired of seeing them get no education at all—Tessie was glad for the company (not to mention the disappearance of the mob); but she was happy for another reason, as I found out one afternoon, much to my astonishment, when she told me that she wondered what her "next thing to do" would be.

I couldn't figure out what she meant, so I asked. She said, "Those people have gone back home, and they don't mind their kids coming here to school with us anymore. So that's what we were supposed to do." She stopped abruptly, as I waited, wondering where she was headed. Rather soon, with no prodding from me, she resumed. "We were supposed to get them to stop being so angry; then they'd quiet down, and we'd have the desegregation and now it's happening. So we did the service we were supposed to for New Orleans, and Granny says, 'Next it'll be some other thing to do,' because you always should be trying to help out God somehow."

Tessie was, in her own mind, a missionary, deputized by no less than God—a first-grader doing service on behalf of her own people but also on behalf of those who railed and ranted against her. I mention Tessie's ideas about herself, as well as the origins of those ideas in a family's life and in a people's cultural and moral life, at the start of this book because the very definition or notion of service has to do with the ethical and spiritual assumptions that inform a family's life.

As a pediatrician and child psychiatrist, I was trained to discern symptom formation, both medical and psychiatric, as I talked with Tessie and the other children in New Orleans. I was trained to take stock of a crisis in a child's life, then work with the child and his or her family and teacher to develop relationships, achieve insights, make interpretations, and establish communication. The first time I discussed this work with my New Orleans medical colleagues (at a meeting of Tulane psychiatrists) I heard a lot about the sociological and anthropological side of the research. I was warned to keep in mind cultural differences in habits, customs, and traditions.

But none of us was quite prepared for Tessie or her grandmother (or for others whose ways of seeing things were similarly challenging). Tessie and her grandmother turned many of my ideas and assumptions upside down. Where I expected trouble, they saw great opportunity; where I waited for things to break down, they anticipated a breakthrough of sorts; where I saw a child bravely shouldering the burden of a divided, troubled society, they saw a blessed chance for a child to become a teacher, a healer, an instrument, maybe, of the salvation of others.

To listen to Tessie carefully turning a word on its head, taking the notion of service so seriously that her tormentors, she hoped, would become her beneficiaries, was to engage in research, all right. A child's idiosyncratic and utterly spiritual notion of service was a key. If you want to understand me, do your research in my home with my family, she was letting me know, you had best pay the closest attention to what I say, because the meaning I give to a word such as "service" may not at all resemble your sense of that word. Many times, as I have heard men and women talk about the service they "do," the volunteer effort they are making, I think of the standard Tessie held up to herself,

though it was not necessarily one that others would consider desirable or germane.

After spending time with Tessie and the other six-year-olds, I began to view the nature of my research somewhat differently. My job had always been to listen, but now I was aware that at times we can be deaf listeners, thoroughly unable to hear some remarks while all too attentive to others. We can even take what we don't want to hear—what we are unprepared to acknowledge because of our own preconceptions—and turn it into what we're expecting to hear. Tessie's talk about offering her city, her tormentors a service could be heard as evidence of denial, as a rationalization or a maneuver of a beleaguered ego trying to mobilize various mechanisms of defense. That's how I heard her, at least for a while. Tessie's account of her purposes was surely evidence of anxiety and fear concealed by high-flown pronouncements connected to religion.

In time, ironically, the influential people who vehemently opposed school desegregation came around to Tessie's point of view. She and her three fellow pioneers received the begrudging acknowledgment of the city's leaders: these little girls *had* done the city a service, its mayor finally admitted, as did some of the segregationists I was getting to know in the mob that awaited Tessie with such rancor. "Those [three] girls, they're not the real problem," I heard one of the hecklers, a parent, say in front of the McDonogh School. "They're just trying to do what they think is right, what they've been *told* is right—trying to be of help to their people. I suppose they've done something for us. We had our fight, and we've lost it, and now we've got to put it all behind and try to get an education for our kids, because if we don't, we'll be in worse shape than having a few Negroes there at school with our white children."

This mother was beginning to recast her judgment and even find evidence of assistance offered, a service done: Tessie was no longer a devil (as she had often been called) but a hapless victim, maybe, or, on a more upbeat note, someone who helped "clear the air." That was the phrase the woman used two years later, as she looked back with some awkwardness, even a growing disbelief, at what had occurred "back then," as she put it—as if the subject were ancient history.

Sometimes, unfortunately, attentive listening (so that one hears one's own constraints as well as those of the people one is studying) doesn't quite work because there seems to be no way to agree upon a conversation. I spent years talking with Tessie and other children, and gradually some of them began to wear me down, even as they had worn down the street mobs. At last I began to fathom some new definitions of words I thought I knew backward and forward (maybe words I thought I owned), such as "service" and its variations.

In 1962, however, I found myself in a situation where I was anxious to be all ears, but no one was interested in talking. I had by then expanded my study of school desegregation to include Atlanta, where a federal judge had sent ten black youths into four of the city's high schools. I came to know these youths fairly well, and I have described that work at some length. One consequence of that work was that one of the high schoolers became involved with the sit-in movement and regularly went to the office in downtown Atlanta of the Student Non-Violent Coordinating Committee. There he helped plan and later implement sit-ins, and there he learned how to work with his own people to persuade young blacks to become politically awakened and energized. When this young man, Lawrence Jefferson, went to the Ebenezer Baptist Church to hear Dr. Martin Luther King, Jr., Jane and I often went with him. When he told me he was working at SNCC headquarters, I also wanted to accompany him—and one day I did so.

When we arrived, he went off to his regular tasks, but I was taken to another room, where I was questioned and questioned with considerable intensity. I well remember noticing my watch at one point—and being noticed doing

so. My questioners were James Foreman and Stokely Carmichael, two black leaders of the young organization, and Bob Zellner, a white Alabamian. The three, already veterans of southern jails, sat near one another in chairs; I sat on a sagging couch. By the time I looked at my watch and discovered that over two hours had passed, I felt as if the couch had collapsed altogether and I was sitting on the floor. That thought turned out to be rather prophetic.

I was asking these young men for permission to interview various members of SNCC. I spoke of my work with children in New Orleans and Atlanta and mentioned the Southern Regional Council, a group of black and white Southerners much interested in working toward desegregation throughout the eleven states of tile old Confederacy. I offered to obtain letters of support from the officers of that council and from the distinguished black psychologist Kenneth Clark, who had been quite helpful to me in my research in New Orleans, and even from Thurgood Marshall and Jack Greenberg, then important members of the NAACP Legal Defense Fund, which had been arguing one desegregation case after another through the courts. The three youths were vastly uninterested in this mobilization of affirmative reassurance. The more I spelled out my credentials and training, the less interested they seemed.

What was I trying to learn? Again and again they posed that question, and each time I tried to answer with as much intelligence, tact, and sensitivity as I could summon. I talked of the youthful idealism I would no doubt be witnessing and of my wish to understand the motivations for it and the manner in which the mind struggled with the threats and dangers and stresses and strains that go with such an idealism. I used some psychiatric and psychoanalytic terms, but by then I had learned to be a bit skeptical of such language—partially because I was seeing its limitations. Psychoanalytic jargon sometimes closed off avenues of inquiry, and overwrought, self-serving, parochial shop talk put people off.

I tried to relax, share my convictions, and indicate my strong enthusiasm for what the SNCC workers were trying to do. Whereas two years earlier I was very much the eager psychiatric researcher, now I was a somewhat shaken and perplexed doctor, trying to get my bearings and learning, almost daily, it sometimes seemed, what I didn't know and hadn't even thought to want to know about. But my three hosts, or interrogators, were singularly unimpressed. Eventually they told me they had to leave—and said that they were not at all inclined to let me interview anyone at SNCC.

I can still feel the floor falling away. I sat there in silence. Part of me wanted to summon the old, familiar retaliatory reflex, to go on and on to myself about their suspiciousness, even paranoia—a peculiar naming or name-calling habit that is rather congenial to my kind. Part of me wanted to continue with my self-presentation a bit longer, to *somehow* convince these three that I was truly on the up and up. I wanted to tell them that my heart was with them and that in no way would my inquiries be disruptive or rude or unsettling. Part of me was fuming: they weren't really asking me the right questions, and they were being rude, even patronizing. I felt sad because it was very important (so every researcher feels) to know more about the lives of these young activists, about the origins of their attitudes, about the kind of work they did, about their accomplishments, and about the psychological costs.

As all of this ran through my head, I was brought up short. Almost in unison all three men stood, and I, reluctantly, stood up with them. We chatted only a minute or two as we walked out of the room. Just as we were saying good-bye, I blurted out, "I'd still like to help—any way you'd want." Silence—and then I said, "Isn't there something I can do that you need done?" More silence, and then Jim Foreman's response (one all of us would recall years later with smiles and laughter): "You can help us keep this place clean!"

Foreman was at the time the nominal head of SNCC, and the day before he had complained (I later learned) how "messy" the offices were getting. I was initially surprised by his words, but I was quick to accept the offer. Within minutes I was sweeping floors, dusting, scrubbing down the bathroom, washing dishes in the small room that served as a kitchen. In my mind, of course, I was being tested; soon they would permit me to talk with these young people, to observe and interview them rather than clean up after them. I have to confess I felt no small amount of pride at how persuasive I had been and how resourceful and flexible I'd turned out to be: the effective, persistent field worker.

Days of sweeping a suite of offices in an old, dusty downtown building turned into weeks, then months. I had an official position with SNCC: I was the janitor. I even bought us a vacuum cleaner and did such unexpected extras as cleaning the windows. Gradually I was greeted by my first name, was offered coffee or food, and was invited to evening meetings and parties. Sometimes a young man or woman asked to talk with me, and I obliged with great interest, of course.

It would have been easy, I realized after two or three weeks, to stop my janitoring work and carve out, gradually and informally, one of those "roles" that social scientists describe. Less pompously, I could join "the movement" and take care to learn all I could through casual exchanges and attendance at strategy meetings or discussions where ideas were debated. Yet as I mastered my janitorial routine, I felt increasingly secure with the position, and I reminded myself that a good half of the black parents I knew did similar work as a full-time career.

I also began to be aware of all that was happening as I did my work—the comments I heard and overheard, the thoughts that crossed my mind and, not least, the range of feelings that I experienced. Even today, when I do volunteer teaching in a school and see the janitor or see children seeing the janitor, I realize that I was not being rebuffed or shortchanged by those

SNCC members. For some time I kept thinking that they were testing me, maybe cutting me down to size a little, and letting me know who was boss. In fact, they were teaching me—or, better, enabling me to learn, putting me in a situation where I had plenty to do, yet could listen to my heart's content. I was constantly learning by experience rather than through abstract discussions.

A year later, when I'd held on to the job so long that everyone (myself included) simply took for granted that I would continue, I stumbled into a memorable talk with Jim Foreman. The year was 1963, and the civil rights struggle was becoming increasingly strenuous, even fierce. It was a week after Labor Day, and the schools had just reopened. The weather was quite hot, and the fans didn't do enough to make us comfortable. I'd finished my morning chores, and Jim asked me if I wanted a cup of coffee. Sure—and soon we were talking away. At one point he changed the subject abruptly with a brief question, somewhat coldly, even provocatively asked, "So, what have you learned from all this?" A second's silence, and then, to make clear what "this" meant, "The janitorial research."

Surprised, I fell silent. We'd been exchanging small talk, and now I wondered what to do. Should I turn that question into an excuse for a bantering, self-mocking continuation of small talk? I was tempted in that direction, but a glance at Jim's face told me of his seriousness. I lowered my head and heard myself grasping for words, fumbling incoherently. Jim finally spoke for me, told me he thought I had come to like the work and not feel demeaned by it, indeed, to take a certain pleasure in it.

I concurred. By accident, at a particular moment in the life of SNCC and in the lives of its members and in my own life, all of us had acted in such a way that I was able to connect with a group of young people bent on connecting with impoverished, voteless, legally segregated blacks. In doing my everyday tasks, I was able to observe, learn, and come to some understanding of how life went for the SNCC workers and for people in the communities where they were living and "organizing."

With Tessie, I had learned very slowly what service meant for her and her grandmother. With my SNCC friends, I slowly learned to abandon my reliance on questionnaires and structured interviews and instead to *do*, to experience service, and thereby learn something about what those young people had in mind as they went about their activist lives. I learned that the "methodology" for a research project had to do with *definition*, first, and then *vantage point*, meaning the way a word such as "service" is variously interpreted and the manner in which an observer looks and listens.

Words to Love By

Mother Teresa

The fruit of prayer is a deepening of faith.
And the fruit of faith is love.
And the fruit of love is service.
But to be able to pray we need silence
silence of the heart.
The soul needs time to go away and pray
to use the mouth
to use the eyes
to use the whole body.
And if we don't have that silence
then we don't know how to pray.

I think if we can spread this prayer, if we can translate it into our lives, it will make all the difference. It is so full of Jesus. It has made a great difference in the lives of the Missionaries of Charity.

Dear Jesus,
Help us to spread your fragrance everywhere we go.
Flood our souls with your spirit and life.
Penetrate and possess our whole being so utterly
that our lives may only be a radiance of yours.
Shine through us
and be so in us
that every soul we come in contact with
may feel your presence in our soul.
Let them look up and see no longer us
but only Jesus.
Stay with us
and then we shall begin to shine as you shine,
so to shine as to be light to others.
The light, O Jesus, will be all from you.
None of it will be ours.

It will be you shining on others through us.
Let us thus praise you in the way you love best
by shining on those around us.
Let us preach you without preaching
not by words, but by our example
by the catching force
the sympathetic influence of what we do
the evident fullness of the love our hearts bear
to you

                             Amen.

We all want to love God, but how?

The Little Flower is a most wonderful example.
She did small things with great love. Ordinary
things with extraordinary love. That is why she
became a great saint.
I think we can bring this beautiful thing into
our lives.

Love cannot remain by itself—it has no meaning.
Love has to be put into action
and that action is service.

How do we put the love for God in action?
By being faithful to our family
to the duties that God has entrusted to us.
Whatever form we are
able or disabled
rich or poor
it is not how much we do
but how much love we put in the doing
—a lifelong sharing of love with others.

I never look at the masses as my responsibility.
I look at the individual. I can love only one
person at a time.

I can feed only one person at a time.
Just one, one, one.
You get closer to Christ by coming closer to each
other. As Jesus said, "Whatever you do to the
least of my brethren, you do to me."
So you begin.... I begin.
I picked up one person—
maybe if I didn't pick up that one person I wouldn't
have picked up 42,000.
The whole work is only a drop in the ocean.
But if I
didn't put the drop in, the ocean would be one
drop less.
Same thing for you
same thing in your family
same thing in the church where you go
just begin...one, one, one.

At the end of life we will not be judged by
how many diplomas we have received
how much money we have made
how many great things we have done.

We will be judged by
"I was hungry and you gave me to eat
I was naked and you clothed me
I was homeless and you took me in."

Hungry not only for bread
—but hungry for love
Naked not only for clothing
—but naked of human dignity and respect
Homeless not only for want of a room of bricks
—but homeless because of rejection.
This is Christ in distressing disguise.

A Theology of Enough
Millard Fuller

A rich man in Atlanta recently built for himself and his family a huge house on a large parcel of land. The amenities included an attached carriage house, a swimming pool, a lake, extensive flower gardens, and many other wonderful features. People compared this awesome layout to the palace in Versailles, France. When asked why he built such an extravagant place he exclaimed, "Because I'm a born-again Christian and I wanted to glorify God."

Is God glorified when a family builds for itself housing that is vastly in excess of what the legitimate needs are for that family? Or, is God glorified more when a wealthy family exercises restraint, builds more modestly for its needs, and uses the excess funds to build additional modest houses for less fortunate families?

What do you think? What does the Bible have to say on this subject?

Reflect on these pertinent words from Deuteronomy:

> Be careful that you do not forget the Lord your God, failing to observe his commands, his laws, and his decrees that I am giving you this day. Otherwise, when you eat and are satisfied, when you build fine houses and settle down, and when your herds and your flocks grow large and your silver and gold increase and all you have is multiplied, then your heart will become proud, and you will forget the Lord your God. (8:11–14)

Isaiah minced no words in railing against those who want more and more, bigger and bigger, until they crowd everybody else out:

> Woe to you who add house to house and join field to field, till no space is left and

you live alone in the land. The Lord Almighty has declared in my hearing: "Surely the great houses will become desolate, the fine mansions left without occupants." (5:8–9)

Amos was even sharper in his condemnation of the rich and their big houses:

> "I will tear down the winter house
> along with the summer house;
> the houses adorned with ivory will be destroyed
> and the mansions will be demolished,"
> declares the Lord....
> Therefore, though you have built stone mansions, you will not live in them;
> though you have planted lush vineyards, you will not drink their wine.
> For I know how many are your offenses and how great your sins.
> You oppress the righteous and take bribes and you deprive the poor of justice in the courts.
> (3:15; 5:11b-12)

Jeremiah also heaped condemnation on the person who builds a roomy house but does not concern himself with justice and righteousness. Then, he concluded with a clear admonition that "defending the cause of the poor and needy" is what it means to know the Lord:

> Woe to him who builds his palace by unrighteousness, his upper rooms by injustice, making his countrymen work for nothing, not paying them for their labor. He says, "I will build myself a great palace with spacious upper rooms." So he makes large windows in it, panels it with cedar, and decorates it in red. Does it make you a king to have more and more cedar? Did not your father have food and drink? He did what was right and just, so all went well with him. He defended the cause of the poor and needy, and so all went well. "Is that not what it means to know me?" declares the Lord. (22:13–16)

Jack Abrams of Habitat for Humanity of Manasota in Sarasota, Florida, shared a remarkable story with me about a rich man who did have a heart of concern for the poor. The episode started with a letter I received from a man who was living in a very deficient garage apartment in Nokomis, a town near Sarasota. I forwarded the letter to John Schaub, president of Manasota Habitat, and asked him to investigate the matter. John passed the letter along to Jack, who related what happened:

> My wife, Audrey, and I approached the address and saw that it was a large estate right on the bay. Obviously, only a wealthy man could afford such an expansive estate, and our righteous indignation jumped to the fore. We were prepared to ask some searching questions concerning his negligence in furnishing proper living conditions for the poor man who lived in the apartment above the garage.
>
> As we drove up the long winding driveway, a man came out of the imposing house. I introduced myself and explained why we were there. Before I could ask the searching questions we had so carefully prepared, the gentleman informed us that the man who had written the letter of complaint had moved out before he, the present owner, had moved in.
>
> Realizing this was an excellent opportunity to do some missionary work for Habitat, I described our activities in the southern part of the county. The gentleman had heard of Habitat but did not know there was a local affiliate. I asked if I could come back and bring some literature about our work. He invited us to do so.
>
> We drove home and returned immediately with the material. The result was a $10,000 donation for a house we were planning to build in Nokomis only about a mile from his estate.
>
> That house has subsequently been built for a family that was living in a run-down trailer. One of the children of that family was lodged in a closet in the trailer. Their

new house is now complete and the little boy who slept in the closet has a nice big room. He hugs me constantly whenever I visit.

We need more rich people (and middle income people!) such as the man in this story. Unfortunately, not all wealthy people have that kind of a loving, caring, and sharing heart.

Jesus repeatedly warned the rich about their neglect of the poor. He clearly stated that the likelihood of a rich person getting into the kingdom of God is about as remote as that of a camel going through the eye of a needle. He told the powerful story of the rich man who did not help Lazarus, a beggar who was covered with sores and who lay at his gate. When the two men eventually died, the angels carried Lazarus to Abraham's side and the rich man went to hell. According to the story, the rich man's sin was simply that of wealth and callous unconcern for the poor.

Jesus also told a parable about a rich man who filled up his existing barns with abundant crops. Reflecting on his excess, the prosperous man decided to tear down the old barns and build bigger ones. The story, I submit, is equally applicable to houses. Hear these eternally relevant words of our Lord:

"Watch out! Be on your guard against all kinds of greed; a man's life does not consist in the abundance of his possessions." And he told them this parable: "The ground of a certain rich man produced a good crop. He thought to himself, 'What shall I do? I have no place to store my crops.' Then he said, 'This is what I'll do: I will tear down my barns and build bigger ones, and there I will store all my grain and my goods. And I'll say to myself, "You have plenty of good things laid up for many years. Take life easy; eat, drink and be merry."' But God said to him, 'You fool! This very night your life will be demanded from you. Then who will get what you have prepared for yourself?' This is how it will be with anyone who stores up things for himself, but is not rich toward God. (Luke 12:15–21)

I was raised in a Christian home in the small east Alabama cotton mill town of Lanett. Our family faithfully attended Sunday School and church. I learned the teachings of the Bible about wealth. I memorized one of the central teachings of Jesus: that one should, "seek first his kingdom and his righteousness, and all these things will be given to you as well" (Matt 6: 33). I knew that Jesus had said it was very difficult for a rich person to inherit the kingdom of God. I also knew that Jesus said, "With God, all things are possible" (Matt 19:26).

At an early age, I decided that I wanted to be a wealthy person. At the same time I wanted to remain faithful to my Christian upbringing. My ambition was to be a Christian rich man. The Bible said so very clearly that such would be difficult, but I did not mind a challenge! I would just have to keep things in proper perspective, seeking to do God's will first and foremost and then going after the other things.

This all seemed very logical. I began my business career even in elementary school: fattening and selling a pig. I went on to raising and selling more pigs, then chickens, rabbits, and cattle. I engaged in some other business ventures in high school and in undergraduate school at Auburn University. In law school at the University of Alabama, I met a fellow student named Morris Dees, Jr. The two of us formed a company that began to make some significant money. Over an eight-year period we developed the company that was eventually named Fuller and Dees Marketing Group, Inc. The last five of those eight years were spent in Montgomery, Alabama, where we had a law office and headquarters for our young company.

As time went on, I spent more and more time working. I had married Linda Caldwell of Tuscaloosa, Alabama, in my senior year of law school. At first, we were very happy; but, after moving to Montgomery, I practically made her a widow by being virtually married to the company. We drifted apart, despite the fact that I was buying more and more things for Linda and myself. She had more clothes and shoes than she could get into the closets. She had a full-time maid to clean the house and help take care of the two children born during the first three years of our marriage. Linda was continuing her education at nearby Huntingdon College.

We bought a spacious old brick house in the Cloverdale section of the city, a new Lincoln Continental automobile, and a cabin on Lake Martin, near Wetumpka, Alabama. My partner and I started buying land; soon we owned 2,000 acres with cattle, horses, and many fishing lakes. Not satisfied with the house Linda and I owned, I bought a twenty-acre lot and hired an architect to draw plans for a much larger house.

The treasurer of our company told me one day that a newly produced financial statement showed that I, personally, was worth $1,000,000. I responded that my next goal was $10,000,000.

Before I could reach that new goal, however, Linda precipitated a crisis. Sitting on the edge of our king-sized bed one Saturday evening, she told me that she did not love me anymore. She announced that she needed to leave town and to think about our future or decide if we even had one together. I was shaken to my foundation.

The complete story of this tumultuous time in our lives is told in depth in my earlier books *Bokotola* and *Love In the Mortar Joints*, but just let me recount here that we were eventually reconciled in an emotional reunion in New York City. A decision was made there to sell my interest in the company and give all the money away. We wanted to make ourselves poor again in order to rekindle our own love relationship and to put ourselves right with God. We both realized that we had strayed far from God's path for our lives. In a truly miraculous way, God led us to Koinonia Farm near Americus, Georgia, and to our magnificent encounter with Clarence Jordan.

Someone once said that when the student is ready to learn the teacher appears. Clarence Jordan was our teacher. He helped us to see the great power that possessions have over people. Our whole culture blares constantly that the totality of a person is the things he or she has. We even ask questions like, "Do you know what Mr. So-and-so is worth?" Everything is determined by one's monetary worth; nothing else counts.

Clarence once said that the emptier a person is on the inside, the more that person needs on the outside to compensate for that inward emptiness. As I more fully comprehended the great truthfulness of what my new friend was saying, the Bible came absolutely alive to me. I resonated, especially with scripture such as that found in 1 Timothy where the Apostle Paul was sharing with his young assistant about wealth and how it should be used:

> Command those who are rich in this present world not to be arrogant nor to put their hope in wealth, which is so uncertain, but to put their hope in God, who richly provides us with everything for our enjoyment. Command them to do good, to be rich in good deeds, and to be generous and willing to share. In this way they will lay up treasures for themselves as a firm foundation for the coming age, so that they may take hold of the life that is truly life. (1 Tim 6: 17–19)

I was also struck by Paul's second letter to the Corinthians in which he talked about true riches and the need of those with an abundance to share with those who have too little so that there might be equality:

> For you know the grace of our Lord Jesus Christ, that though he was rich, yet for your sakes he became poor, so that you through his poverty might become rich. And here is my advice about what is best for you in this matter: Last year you were the first not only to give but also to have the desire to do so. Now finish the work, so that your

eager willingness to do it may be matched by your completion of it, according to your means. For if the willingness is there, the gift is acceptable according to what one has, not according to what he does not have. Our desire is not that others might be relieved while you are hard pressed, but that there might be equality. At the present time your plenty will supply what they need, so that in turn their plenty will supply what you need. Then there will be equality, as it is written: "He who gathered much did not have too much, and he who gathered little did not have too little." (8:9–15)

These passages, and many more like them found throughout the Bible, are all a part of "the theology of the hammer." God has put all that is needed on the earth—in human, natural, and financial resources—to solve completely the problems of poverty housing and homelessness.

One of the big impediments to solving the problem is that too few talented and wealthy people have a developed "theology of enough." They keep striving, struggling, and scrambling for more and more things for themselves and are too short-sighted and immature spiritually to see the futility of that type of grasping lifestyle.

The Bible is not the only book that contains dire warnings about putting trust in possessions and focusing earthly existence on incessant and insatiable acquisition. Materialism has been denounced by all the sages from Buddha to Muhammad, and every world religion is rife with warnings against the evils of excess. As Arnold Toynbee observed,

These religious founders disagreed with each other in the pictures of what is the nature of the universe, the nature of the spiritual life, the nature of ultimate reality. But they all agreed in their ethical precepts.... They all said with one voice if we made material wealth our paramount aim, this would lead to disaster.

Religious historian Robert Bellah confirmed and expanded upon what Toynbee said, stating:

That happiness is to be attained through limitless material acquisition is denied by every religion and philosophy known to humankind, but is preached incessantly by every American television set.

Everything in this world is passing away, including the T.V. set! The Bible is true when it says, "All men are like grass, and all their glory is like the flowers of the field; the grass withers and the flowers fall, but the word of the Lord stands forever" (1 Pet 1:24).

The only truly safe investment one can make in life is what is given away. That can never be taken from anyone. Everything else, eventually, will be taken by trickery, fraud, deception, bad management, poor investments, bankruptcy, ruinous divorce, theft, or death. You will be separated from your possessions, one way or the other!

Poet E. M. Poteat was surely right when he penned these poignant words:

Count up your conquests of sea and land,
Heap up your gold and hoard as you may.
All you can hold in your cold dead hand Is
   what you have given away.

And so was the psalmist who wrote:

For all can see that wise men die;
The foolish and the senseless alike perish,
And leave their wealth to others.
Their tombs will remain their houses forever,
Their dwellings for endless generations,
Though they had named lands after themselves.
But man, despite his riches, does not endure;
He is like the beasts that perish.
This is the fate of those who trust in themselves,

And of their followers, who approve their
    sayings.
Like sheep they are destined for the grave,
And death will feed on them.
The upright will rule over them in the
    morning;
Their forms will decay in the grave,
Far from their princely mansions.
    (Ps 49:10–14)

True riches come from a life of service, a life
committed to doing God's work in the world.
Helping the poor is the most authentic service
to God. Recall Jesus' message in Matthew 25
about feeding the hungry, giving water to the
thirsty, inviting strangers in, providing clothing
to the naked, and visiting the sick and those in
prison.

Consider James 1:27, "True religion, pure
and undefiled is this, to minister to the widow
and orphans in their time of distress and to keep
oneself unspoiled from the world."

Jesus' inaugural sermon announced, "The
spirit of the Lord is on me, because he has
anointed me to preach good news to the poor."
During his entire ministry he went about doing
good—feeding the hungry, healing the sick,
restoring sight to the blind. How could we possibly miss the point?

Very early in the Bible, the author of Deuteronomy clearly stated how God wanted things
to be "in the land the Lord was giving to His
people."

There should be no poor among you, for in
the land the Lord your God is giving you to
possess as your inheritance, he will richly
bless you.... If there is a poor man among
your brothers in any of the towns of the
land that the Lord your God is giving you,
do not be hardhearted or tightfisted toward
your poor brother. Rather be openhanded
and freely lend him whatever he needs....
Give generously to him and do so without
a grudging heart; then because of this the
Lord your God will bless you in all your
work and in everything you put your hand

to. There will always be poor people in
the land. Therefore I command you to be
openhanded toward your brothers and toward the poor and needy in your land. (15:
4, 7–8, 10–11)

Simply put, the message is that we must have
a well developed "theology of enough." God's
order of things holds no place for hoarding
and greed. There are sufficient resources in
the world for the needs of everybody, but not
enough for the greed of even a significant minority.

The people of Habitat for Humanity in Gua-
temala surely know about generous sharing with
those in need. They freely opened their hands to
help a needy Habitat family. International Partners Charlie and Ruth Magill, serving in West
Quetzaltenango, related the following:

This is a sad story, but within it is the light
of the theology of the hammer.

Santiago Lopez, thirty-three years old,
was not only a Habitat homeowner but also
president of the local Habitat committee,
president of the regional project, representative to the national Habitat for Humanity
foundation, and member of the national directive. He had all the Habitat philosophy
in his heart as well as his head. He was also
the father of three boys aged four, ten, and
thirteen. He had finished high school three
years before and was working half-time in
a gas station and half-time as a compesino,
or field worker.

When Santiago died unexpectedly, his
remaining mortgage was just over 2,700
quetzales, or $470. Marta, his widow,
does not read or write. Her income from
weaving might be five or six dollars per
month—not enough to cover her monthly
house payments of six dollars and sixty
cents.

There are eight Habitat projects in Gua-
temala, covering eighteen towns. The local
committee in Ixchiguan, Departmento de
San Marcos, sent a letter to the local committees of each project:

"We want to tell you immediately that in our last meeting we were informed of the death of our companero Santiago Lopez, of Concepcion Chiquirichapa. Thinking about the difficult situation of his debts, we decided to help, soliciting from every Habitat homeowner two quetzales (forty cents) to be able to pay part of the debt of his house. For this, we ask each committee to do the same and to channel said help by way of the national office."

When the committee in Concepcion Chiquirichapa received the letter from Ixchiguan, there was not a dry eye in the meeting. The newly elected president, Esteban Izara, remarked that he believes "Santiago is still alive. He is in my house. I would not have this house without his help." Others made similar comments, and after a long discussion, with many words of thanks for the sentiments expressed by the Ixchiguan committee, the homeowners voted unanimously to give two quetzales each. After the vote, there was a small discussion in the back of the room; then one homeowner asked: "Is this every month?"

In Christ's kingdom we are willing to give not only from our wealth, but also from our poverty. In the community of Habitat we are willing to help our neighbor's family without reservation — one time, or every month.

Habitat for Humanity is counting on all people — especially talented and wealthy people and richly blessed churches, companies, and other organizations — to come forward and to freely open their hands and hearts so that additional resources, both material and human, will be made available to rid the world of shacks and other poor housing and homelessness. For this to happen, many hearts and minds must go through a radical transformation. With God:, all things truly are possible!

Linda and I now live modestly in Americus, Georgia. Our physical needs are being met, and our greatest joy is in helping others meet their basic needs rather than piling up more and more for ourselves. We think it is a better way to live.

Righteousness, Not Charity
Judaism's View of Philanthropy

Jacob Neusner

If in the Hebrew of the Judaic religious tradition you want to say "charity," the word you must use is the word for "righteousness": *tsedakah*.

That simple fact tells you what Judaism has to say about philanthropy: It is an act that we perform not because we feel like it, but because we are responsible human beings—in God's image, after God's likeness. It is a tax imposed by God in the Torah (the Five Books of Moses)—so Judaism maintains—and in secular terms, it is an obligation imposed by conscience. The main point is that many people think charity is voluntary, an act of good will, while in Judaism, philanthropy in all its forms constitutes an act of what is (only) right: righteousness, which is a matter of moral obligation.

How such philanthropy that is thought of as (mere) righteousness actually works can best be understood by studying the writings of Moses Maimonides (1135–1204 C.E.). Maimonides was one of a number of medieval scholars who codified the oral and written laws of Judaism for ready reference. These codes summarize the law in an accessible form. The importance of the Mishneh Torah (literally, "a repetition of the Torah"), which Mainonides wrote, is not that it gives the opinion of a great rabbi, but that it does not. It is public, not personal. The contents of the book, in general, derive from other authoritative legal literature of Judaism. The reason we turn to Maimonides' codification, therefore, is that it provides us with a reliable, accurate, and succinct picture of the Jewish law of *tsedakah*.

Maimonides treats *tsedakah* within the seventh book of his code, *The Book of Agriculture*, where he summarizes a wide range of rules governing how people conduct the business of farming. At the time that Maimonides was writing, Jews mostly were engaged in agriculture; hence, these laws address the core of economic life as it was then structured. It is appropriate to consider giving away money or goods in the very setting where wealth is formed, because resources allow people the opportunity to engage in *tsedakah*.

Maimonides does two things in his treatise on *tsedakah*: He provides a picture of the whole—the laws seen from afar, the main point of it all—and he also presents many individual rules.

The code of Maimonides presents three principles:

- The way to deal with poverty is to help the poor help themselves.
- When one gives *tsedakah* to the poor, the way to do it is so that the left hand does not know what the right is doing, so to speak. The poor are respected; the donors remain anonymous. This second point is spelled out in the following stages:
  - The poor do not know who has given; the donors do not know to whom the money goes.
  - The donors know; the poor do not.
  - The poor know; the donors do not.
- The final principle is essentially a repetition of the main point of the second: The dignity of the poor must be respected. This is spelled out in four further stages:
  - The donors give (what is required) without being asked.
  - The donors give (what is required) only when asked.
  - The donors give less than is proper but in a friendly way.
  - The donors give in an unfriendly way. In all, the Jewish law makes one fundamental point: the poor person must enjoy self-respect and dignity.

The best way to give is not to give but to lend, thus helping the poor person make his or her own livelihood. That concept stands outside of the framework of "charity," but it is central to an understanding of *tsedakah*, since this allows the poor person's dignity to be preserved. The third principle restates this in a more personal way: not being asked, being asked, giving in a friendly way, giving in an unfriendly way.

What Jewish law requires, therefore, is consideration for the humanity of the poor person, who remains no different from those of us who give. The poor are not less than us, nor are they different from us. They not only have needs, but they also have feelings. They not only want bread; they also want respect. When we give to the poor, we must do so in such a way that the equality of the giver and receiver is acknowledged. This is not an act of grace or an expression of affection. It is an act of respect, an expression of duty.

Using the word *tsedakah*, which carries the sense of doing what is right and required, is deliberate and definitive. We give not because we feel like it, but because it is our obligation. We do so in a way that will not make us feel superior, and we do so in a way that will not make the poor person feel inferior.

How does this conceptual framework translate into a contemporary approach to philanthropy? We begin with the notion that the best way to perform righteous acts—*tsedakah*—is to find work for the poor and relieve them of the need to beg. Failing that, the next best thing is to ensure that we do not discover who is receiving our charity so that we do not develop a sense of self-importance, thinking ourselves "Lord and Lady Bountifuls." It is less acceptable if the donor knows but the recipient does not know the source of the funds; the recipient still enjoys dignity. Finally, the poor person may know the source of the money, but the wealthy one not know the recipient.

In establishing as an ideal a situation in which the donor does not know who gets and the recipient does not know who gives, this code of conduct attempts to preserve the dignity of the poor even under less-than-ideal circumstances. It also emphasizes that the situation of the donor is as important as that of the recipient. How the donor thinks and feels about the act of *tsedakah* is a central concern.

It is not enough simply to give: Giving must be thoughtful; it must be marked by reflection, respect for the other party, and hence humility on the part of the donor. How the money is handed over—in the worst case, in which the giver hands it directly to the recipient—is subject to a simpler rule: it must be done with regard and in friendship. It must not be done in a mean and niggardly spirit.

The Eight Stages of *Tsedakah*

There are eight degrees of *tsedakah*, each one superior to the next.

The highest degree, than which there is none higher, is the one who upholds the hand of an Isralite reduced to poverty by handing that person a gift or loan by entering into partnership with him or her, or by finding that Israelite work, in order to strengthen that person's hand, so that she or he will have no need to beg from others. Concerning such a person it is stated, "You shell uphold that one, as a stranger and a settler shall that person live with you." That is, uphold that person, so that she or he will not lapse into want.

Below this is one who gives alms to the poor in such a way that the giver knows not to whom the alms are given, nor does the poor person know from whom the alms are received. This constitutes the fulfilling of a religious duty for its own sake, and for such there was a chamber of secrets in the Temple, where the righteous would contribute sums secretly, and where the poor of good families would draw their sustenance in equal secrecy. Close to such a person is the one who contributes directly to the charity fund. (One should not, however, give directly to the charity fund unless it has been ascertained that the person in charge of it is trustworthy, as sage, who knows how to administer it properly, as was the case [when it was directed by the hand of Rabbi Hananiah ben Teradyon.])

Below this is the person who knows the one receiving while the poor person knows not from whomt he gift comes. Such a donor is like the great among the sages who would set forth secretly, throwing money before the doors of the poor. This is an appropriate procedure, to be preferred if those administering charity funds are not behaving honorabe.

Below this is the instance in which the poor knows the identity of the donor, but remains unknown to the donor. The giver is thus like the great among the sages who would place money in the folded corner of a linen sheet, them and remove the money without being asked for it.

Below this is the one who hands charity to the poor after the poor have requested it.

Below this is the one who gives charity with a scowl.

The great among the sages used to hand a small coin to a poor person before praying and then pray, "As for me, I shall behold Your face in righteousness."

FROM THE MISHNEH TORAH

How you approach *tsedakah* thus matters at least as much as what you do; I am inclined to think it matters even more. That is the meaning of the laws of *tsedakah*, which have a high opinion of us all. The laws seek to ensure dignity and honor for all, despite one's particular need to give or to receive—in fact, not "despite," but "through *tsedakah*"!

Donor and recipient are equally in the image and likeness of God. Though the one appears powerful and the other weak, the giver "greets the Presence of God." The weakness of the poor person stands for God. We are strong so that, in giving, we may become less rich, less powerful; we are in need so that, in receiving, we may give to the giver. We seek power and wealth in order to achieve. The laws give form and body to the soul and heart. To see philanthropy as righteousness is to move from what is required of us to what we are required to become.

National Service
Bill Clinton

A pathy is dead.

Of everything I've learned in my first few weeks in the White House, that's the thing that's made me the happiest. Whether or not the people I've met outside the capital support the changes I have proposed, they're all saying they're ready to rebuild our country.

But they know, as I do, that no economic plan can do it alone. A plan can make vaccines available to children, but alone it will not administer the shots to all of them. It can put security guards in the schools, but alone it will not take gangs off the streets. And It can provide more aid for college, but alone it will not make the costs of college less daunting for the middle class.

That's why I believe we need national service — now.

If Congress acts quickly enough, just months from now more than 1,000 young people will start serving our country in a special summer effort. In four years, the successors to these pioneers will multiply a hundredfold. Imagine: an army of 100,000 young people restoring urban and rural communities and giving their labor in return for education and training.

National service is an idea as old as America. Time and again, our people have found new ways to honor citizenship and match the needs of changing times.

Lincoln's Homestead Act rewarded those who had the courage to settle the frontier with the land to raise a family. Franklin D. Roosevelt's Social Security Act insured that Americans who work a lifetime can grow old with dignity. Harry S. Truman's G.I. Bill rewarded the service of my father's generation, transforming youthful veterans into an army of educated civilians that led our nation into a new era.

For my generation, the reality of national service was born 32 years ago tomorrow, when President John F. Kennedy created the Peace Corps. At its peak, the Peace Corps enrolled only 16,000 volunteers yet it changed the way a generation of Americans look at themselves and the world.

Today, the spirit of our people once again can meet head-on the troubles of our times.

The task is as complex as our challenge is great. We must combine the intensity of the post-World War II years with the idealism of the early 1960's—and help young people afford a college education or job training.

In 1993, we'll restore the spirit of service by asking our people to serve here at home. We won't refight the wars we won, but we'll tackle the growing domestic dangers that threaten our future.

Our new initiative will embody the same principles as the old G.I. Bill. It will challenge our people to serve our country and do the work that should—and must—be done. It will give those who serve the honor and rewards they deserve. It will invest in the future of the quiet heroes who invest in the future of others.

The national service legislation that I will send to Congress shortly will give our people the chance to serve in two basic ways:

First, it will make it easier for young people to hold low-paying public service jobs and still pay off their student loans.

Under our program, Americans will be able to borrow the money they need for college and pay it back as a small percentage of their income over time. By giving graduates the chance to repay loans on an affordable, reasonable schedule, this "income-contingent" program will allow our people to do the work that our communities really need.

Second, our legislation will create new opportunities for Americans to serve our country for a year or two—and receive financial support for education or training in return.

We'll offer people of different ages and educational levels different ways to serve. And to focus our energies and get the most for our money, we'll direct special attention to a few areas:

- We'll ask thousands of young people to serve in our schools—some as teachers, others as youth mentors, reading special-

ists and math tutors. They'll join the effort to ensure that our schools offer the best education in the world.

- We'll send people into medical clinics to help immunize the nation's 2-year-olds. Some participants will be qualified to give the shots, but thousands of others can provide essential support, contacting parents and following up to make sure children get the shots they need.

- We'll help police forces across the country through a new Police Corps trained to walk beats. We'll also organize others in our communities to keep kids out of gangs and off drugs.

- We'll put still others to work controlling pollution and recycling waste, to help ensure that we pass on to our children a nation that is clean and safe for years to come.

Our national service program will offer more than benefits to individuals. We'll help pay operating costs for community groups with proved track records, providing the support they'll need to grow. And we'll let entrepreneurs compete for venture capital to develop new service programs.

While the Federal Government will provide the seed money for national service, we are determined that the participants—the individuals who serve and the groups that sponsor their service—will guide the process. Spending tens of millions of tax dollars to build a massive bureaucracy would be self-defeating; it would squash the spirit of innovation that national service demands.

By design, our national service program will not happen overnight. Instead, it will grow year by year, with funding reaching $3 billion in 1997. And as I've said many times, I believe it will be the best money we ever spend.

If Congress gives us the chance, this summer we'll create an eight-week leadership training program. We'll recruit more than 1,000 young people for special projects to meet the needs of children at risk—and to train the first class of full-year participants.

In the first full year of our initiative, we'll launch our flexible loan program and aim to put tens of thousands of people to work. By 1997, more than 100,000 citizens could be serving our country, getting education and training benefits in return. And hundreds of thousands more people could be doing invaluable work because college loans no longer block the way.

But the best planning and the most ambitious design won't make this vision of national service a reality. That responsibility ultimately rests with the American people.

I am convinced that after 12 years of drifting apart instead of working together we are ready to meet the challenge. From a 14-year-old boy in North Dakota who sent us $1,000 to help pay off the deficit, to a 92-year-old widower in Kansas who followed his example, people are demonstrating that they want to give something back to their nation.

National service will exercise our talents and rebuild our communities. It will harness the energy of our youth and attack the problems of our time. It will bring together men and women of every age and race and lift up our nation's spirit. And for all of us, it will rekindle the excitement of being Americans.

Large Scale Community Service:
Two Considerations
Amitai Etzioni

Large scale community service is an important idea whose time has come. It will do much to overcome divisiveness if it is designed to provide people from different backgrounds with the opportunity to work together in a non academic environment on intense, meaningful projects. And it will respond creatively to the fact that we will most likely be very short of resources in the 1990s, regardless of how successful national economic policies turn out to be.

We need to be concerned with two subsidiary considerations. First, we need to design community service in ways that will not absorb large amounts of resources. It has been reported that of the $26 million raised by the important Carter initiative to turn around Atlanta, initially

many of these funds were dedicated to the staff. Other programs pay their staff more than their participants. For a community service plan, we should look for ways to allow more of the allocated resources to be directed toward the front-line participants and those they serve.

One suggestion is to ask each college (and maybe each high school) in a given area to commit itself to provide a number of volunteer days each semester and to dedicate some of its personnel (e.g., an assistant dean of students) to ensure that the volunteers are properly scheduled, prepared, etc. Students attending professional schools, such as law and medicine, should be included and expected to serve in their areas of evolving expertise as part of their training requirement. This approach would al-

From Shirley Sagawa and Samuel Halperin, editors, *Visions of Service: The Future of the National and Community Service Act.* Washington, D.C.: National Women's Law Center and American Youth Policy Forum, 1993.

low the community service staff to focus on structuring the places the volunteers will go and ensuring that their efforts are meaningful.

Second, we have to guard against the diminution of the terms "voluntary service" and "community and national service." The Bush White House "Points of Light" approach high-lighted the danger of celebrating rather small efforts on behalf of the community as major achievements, entitled to presidential approbation. We may wish to recognize all efforts but focus particular praise on programs that are especially significant in scope and effort.

Toward National Service as an Institution
Donald J. Eberly

It is time to fill the vacuum in our unwritten youth policy and to reverse the growing neglect of human and environmental services. These twin goals can be met by working to establish national service as an institution early in the twenty first century.

Throughout the first half of this century, most young people were constructively (if not always happily) engaged in one or more of the established institutions of education, work, marriage, and military service. Since then, the constructive engagement of young people has eroded steadily. This erosion has not been reversed by the introduction of the all volunteer armed forces in 1973, by the economic boom of the 1980s, or by President Bush's "thousand points of light."

Combined with this growing failure of our unwritten youth policy has been an increased need for human services, particularly among the very old and the very young, and an increased deterioration of our land, water and air.

The hopelessness of present youth and service policies was suggested recently by Canadian Senator Jacques Hébert. He said that "the welfare state is at the end of its rope...the governments of the democratic countries...are dangerously reducing budget allocations for existing services. Are we going to continue reducing services in day care centers, centers for the handicapped, and even hospitals, and at the same time refuse the voluntary contributions of tens of thousands of young people who would like nothing better than to be of use?"

A national service that challenges all young people to serve, that supports all who volunteer, that gives financial aid for the further education and training of those who serve, would fill

From Shirley Sagawa and Samuel Halperin, editors, *Visions of Service: The Future of the National and Community Service Act.* Washington, D.C.: National Women's Law Center and American Youth Policy Forum, 1993.

much of the vacuum in our current youth policy and would greatly alleviate existing human and environmental needs. Studies show that more than one million young people could be usefully engaged in these areas and that nearly one million young people at any one time are ready to volunteer for service.

As a long time student of national service, I have concluded that the promise of national service can be realized most fully by a design that recognizes the importance of federal standards and financial support while allocating to the end users—such as state departments of natural resources, nonprofit literacy centers, and the young people interested in serving—the major power of decision on the work to be done. The framework of such a national service would look like this:

At the national level, a national service foundation sets guidelines for program operation. It stipulates that those in service—whom I would call Cadets—must meet human or environmental needs and that they may not displace regular employees or unpaid volunteers. The foundation makes grants to state and local organizations that direct the program. It provides a "GI Bill" for the further education and training of those who complete their service agreements, and sets aside five percent of its budget to experiment with variations on the basic national service model.

At the local level, young people register at the age of 17 and receive information about the service opportunities open to them when they reach age 18. The local grantee determines which public and nonprofit agencies qualify to sponsor national service participants and invites them to list openings. The list of openings is made available to labor unions and others who might challenge them as falling outside the guidelines. The youthful applicants examine the list and interview for those openings that interest them. When sponsor and applicant agree on an assignment, they fill out an agreement form specifying the responsibilities of each. The agreement is presented to the grantee, which approves it if everything is in order.

The Cadet receives an $8,000 annual stipend, ten percent of which is paid in cash by the sponsor. The sponsor also assumes responsibility for supervising and training the Cadets it engages. Support for the sponsor's $800 annual payment, as well as supervisory, training, and other costs, comes from the sponsor's budget and from what it can raise from outside sources.

National service is characterized by low entry standards and high performance standards. Admission is open to everyone willing to serve; continued enrollment is contingent on living up to the service agreement between the Cadet and the sponsoring agency. Should a peacetime draft be reinstituted, persons completing two years of national service would have the same draft status as those completing two years of military service.

The National and Community Service Act is a positive step in this direction and could be transformed into the recommended national service system. The Act has two serious flaws, however: It confuses proven forms of national service—notable full time youth service and conservation corps—with those still untested, and it gives to the federal government power that should reside with the private sector. Several corrections must be made to put the Act on the right course.

First, the Act's American Conservation and Youth Service Corps and National and Community Service demonstration program should be merged into a single National Youth Service limited to 18 to 24 year olds engaged in full time service for periods of nine months or more. Once the merger has taken place, these proven programs should be allowed to grow gradually over four years, so that by the end of that time all young people who want to serve are able to do so. According to my studies, this growth would involve an increase from the 8,000 18 to 24 year olds in full time service with the Peace Corps, the California Conservation Corps, and other full time, year round programs in place in 1991, to several hundred thousand by 1996.

Second, the Act should lower the age of registration for military service from 18 to 17 and extend it to include women as well as men and civilian service as well as military. This innovation will encourage young people to exercise their responsibilities of citizenship and will require the federal government to exercise its responsibility to the future by informing young people of their civilian and military service options and challenging them to volunteer. This mandatory registration and information provision would go into effect in four years, when National Youth Service has openings for several hundred thousand young people.

Third, the untested portions of the Act, such as the Governors' Innovative Service Programs, should become part of the recommended five percent allocated for experimental programs.

Fourth, the Act should be simplified to relieve the Commission on National and Community Service of responsibilities that are more appropriate to the private sector. The Points of Light Foundation, which concerns itself primarily with unpaid volunteering, should revert to the private sector, which can easily support its budget of a few million dollars a year, and where it will have the freedom it deserves.

And a word of caution: Congress should resist the temptation to require service learning of students. Part time service learning is oriented more toward educational outcomes than toward service delivery, and as such is more the domain of states and localities than of the federal government. I make this statement as one who helped to coin the phrase "service learning" in the 1960s and who, if I were a school board member and if money was available for a service learning coordinator, would vote to require service learning for high school students.

To translate the already strong public backing for the idea of national service into widespread support for a new societal institution, national service must become more visible. This breakthrough should occur when the number of Cadets reaches about 200,000. In view of the 500,000 young men who served in the Civilian Conservation Corps in 1935 and the imminent reduction of active duty military personnel from 2.0 to 1.5 million, this goal is both manageable and affordable.

Educating for Service
Rev. Theodore M. Hesburgh, C.S.C.

I applaud the National and Community Service Act and the distinguished Commission that has given it life and meaning in our society so needful of service to those less fortunate.

From my own experience working with Sarge Shriver and (now Senator) Harris Wofford at the beginning of the Peace Corps over thirty years ago, I have one suggestion to make for the future of higher education through voluntary service.

The worst virus to infect higher education a generation ago was the "me first" generation of self indulgent and self serving young people. It struck at the heart of what higher education is really about: developing the minds and hearts of young people so that they might become contributors to the general well being of our society, to make it more equitable for all, to make it a caring society for those on the fringes.

After all, society puts up most of the money to support higher education. At least society can rightly expect those it educates to be more intelligent, more capable of personal development, and willing to use this enlarged capability to benefit not only themselves but their fellow citizens as well. As John Donne said, "No man is an island." No woman, either.

I believe we successfully eliminated this "me first" virus in recent years, and we did it by stressing that service to others in need is an essential goal of all education, especially that on the college and university level.

I remember that when I entered the freshman class at Notre Dame in 1934, during the Great Depression, there was only one student I knew who was engaged in voluntary public service. I still remember his name, Vince McAloon. Vince used to pick up all the leftover food at the dining hall each night and deliver it to the

From Shirley Sagawa and Samuel Halperin, editors, *Visions of Service: The Future of the National and Community Service Act*. Washington, D.C.: National Women's Law Center and American Youth Policy Forum, 1993.

"jungles" near the railroad station where the unemployed (they were called "hobos") dropped off the freight cars and gathered around a fire to share the few scraps of food they could beg, borrow or steal. Interestingly, Vince, now over 80 years of age, has spent all these years in a variety of full time service capacities, helping thousands of unfortunate people. What he began as a young man became a way of life, here and abroad, and the world is richer for his service.

By contrast, today over two thirds of Notre Dame's 7,500 undergraduates are engaged in a wide variety of voluntary services. They serve in many ways in our local South Bend Hospitality House, which helps thousands of homeless men, women and children each year. It is not just a soup kitchen. It meets all of these people's needs, physical and spiritual, health and home finding, job training and correction of drug and substance abuse, child care and family reunion, whatever is needed and responsibly received.

The students are largely responsible for the Logan Center, which cares for hundreds of children afflicted with Downs Syndrome. This is a very demanding task, but one that the young men and women who do it will never forget.<T>Then there are the myriad other tasks that need to be done in any society, more than twenty five in number. To name some: Big Brothers and Sisters for children without family support, tutoring those who might otherwise drop out of school; helping minority children, mainly Hispanic, with a language problem; Head Start; Christmas in April; Habitat for Humanity and many more. Our students do them all.

During fall and spring break, hundreds of our students fan out across the land, living and working at established service centers of all kinds: battered women shelters, drug and alcohol rehabilitation centers, food for the poor or bedridden, juvenile criminal rehabilitation, Dismas Houses for released jail prisoners (we operate one in South Bend, too), and on and on.

There are good results from these programs. The local alumni clubs (of which we have over 200) both locate the public service centers in their locality and support the students who work there during brief vacations or through the long summer break.

Thus, both the students and the alumni and alumnae are being educated about the need out there, forgotten by most, and learning what they can do to help, in both a temporary and permanent way.

How did all this get started? First of all, it happened because the most visible leaders at Notre Dame, both administration and faculty, were concerned about social problems and engaged in serving. Secondly, when students became interested in service, the faculty either accompanied or debriefed them in groups on their return to the University to solidify the lessons learned and motivate each other to do more when possible.

This led to another development. At graduation each May, we have a special ceremony to send off more than a hundred graduates who have volunteered to spend a full year or two of their lives, right now, in various forms of special service. For those going overseas, we provide language training for two or three months. Different tasks also have appropriate orientation and training when needed.

Another reason that the student service program prospered and grew at Notre Dame is that we gave it visibility on campus. When our TV station moved to a new location, we gave the old building to what is now called the Center for Social Concerns. Everybody knows where C.S.C. is and what it is doing. Those who are doing nothing to help others feel a twinge of conscience when they walk by the Center each day.

We have also established annual awards for outstanding student and faculty service. The Center has a faculty priest director and a dozen or so staff people, some of them also volunteers. We have been asked, "Why don't you make student service required for graduation?" The day we do that the service will cease to be voluntary and generous.

In the context of this article, I must admit that all of this has been accomplished at one school (and many others) without a cent of federal money—or state money, either. However, we do have indigent students who are working all year round and unable to break free for voluntary service.

I am sure that if federal scholarship grants were available, we could enlist the services of many of our indigent and minority students, who tend to be underrepresented even in areas of service where they could have maximum impact. Also, it would be enormously helpful if our graduates who spend a year or two in service here and overseas would have graduate fellowships, federally funded, available to them on their return. As it is, they come back not only broke financially, but often in debt.

I finish where I began. Higher education has the greatest pool of young and educated potential volunteers (14 million). They are easy to locate, many right in the midst of some of the greatest social needs of our times, in the inner cities of America. It may take federal grants to start a series of programs such as we have here at Notre Dame. Campus Compact was organized to help college and university service programs develop. Still, in many impoverished areas, start up grants would help and all American higher education would be enriched.

The only addition I would suggest for the National and Community Service Act would be some support and reward (mainly educational benefits) in recognition of national and international service on the part of young Americans.

A Mandate for Liberty
Benjamin R. Barber

The extraordinary rise in public interest in community service has inspired widespread participation by the nation's young in service programs. It has also provoked a profound and telling debate about the relationship of service to voluntarism on the one hand, and to civic education and citizenship on the other. Two complementary approaches to service have emerged that are mutually supportive but also in a certain tension with one another. The first aims at attracting young volunteers, particularly students, out of the classroom and into service projects as part of a strategy designed to strengthen altruism, philanthropy, individualism, and self reliance. The second is concerned with integrating service into the classroom and into academic curricula in hopes of making civic education and social responsibility core subjects of high school and university education.

Underlying these two complementary approaches are conflicting though not altogether incompatible views of the real aim of student community service programs. The differences are exemplified by the issue of whether classroom based service programs should be voluntary or mandatory. If the aim of service is the encouragement of voluntarism and a spirit of altruism...then clearly it cannot be mandated or required. To speak of coercing voluntarism is to speak in oxymorons and hardly makes pedagogical sense. But if service is understood as a dimension of citizenship education and civic responsibility in which individuals learn the meaning of social interdependence and become empowered in the democratic arts, then to require service is to do no more in this domain than is done in curricula decisions generally.

As it turns out, the educational justification for requiring courses essential to the develop-

From Shirley Sagawa and Samuel Halperin, editors, *Visions of Service: The Future of the National and Community Service Act*. Washington, D.C.: National Women's Law Center and American Youth Policy Forum, 1993.

ment of democratic citizens is a very old one. America's colleges were founded in part to assure the civic education of the young—to foster competent citizenship and to nourish the arts of democracy. Civic and moral responsibility were goals of both colleges organized around a religious mission and secular land grant colleges. The premise was that democratic skills must be acquired. We think of ourselves as "born free," but we are, in truth, born weak and dependent and acquire equality as a concomitant of our citizenship. Liberty is learned: it is a product rather than the cause of our civic work as citizens.

Those most in need of training in the democratic arts of citizenship are, in fact, least likely to volunteer. Complacency, ignorance of interdependence, apathy, and an inability to see the relationship between self interest and broader community interests are not only the targets of civic education: they are obstacles to it, attitudes that dispose individuals against it. The problem to be remedied is here the impediment to the remedy. Education is the exercise of authority—legitimate coercion—in the name of freedom: the empowerment and liberation of the student. To make people serve others may produce desirable behavior, but it does not create responsibility and autonomous individuals. To make people participate in educational curricula that can empower them, however, does create such individuals.

Thinking that the national problem of civic apathy can be cured by encouraging voluntarism is like thinking that illiteracy can be remedied by distributing books on the importance of reading. What young people require in order to volunteer their participation in education based community service courses are the very skills and understandings that these courses are designed to provide.

There are, of course, problems with mandating education of any kind, but most educators agree that an effective education cannot be left entirely to the discretion of pupils, and schools and universities require a great many things of

students—things less important than the skills necessary to preserve American freedoms. It is the nature of pedagogical authority that it exercises some coercion in the name of liberation. Civic empowerment and the exercise of liberty are simply too important to be treated as extracurricular electives.

This account of education based service as integral to liberal education in a democracy and, thus, as an appropriate subject for mandatory educational curricula points to a larger issue: the uncoupling of rights and responsibilities in America. We live at a time when our government has to compete with industry and the private sector to attract servicemen and women to the military, when individuals regard themselves almost exclusively as private persons with responsibilities only to family and job, with endless rights against an alien government, of which they see themselves, at best, as no more than watchdogs and clients and, at worst, as adversaries or victims. The idea of service to country or an obligation to the institutions by which rights and liberty are maintained has fairly vanished. "We the People" have severed our connections with "It" the state or "They" the bureaucrats and politicians who run it. If we posit a problem of governance, it is always framed in the language of leadership—as if the preservation of democracy were merely a matter of assuring adequate leadership, surrogates who do our civic duties for us. Our solution to problems in democracy is to blame our representatives. "Throw the rascals out!"—Or place limits on the terms they can serve. Our own complicity in the health of our system is forgotten, and so we take the first fatal step in the undoing of the democratic state.

Civic education rooted in service learning can be a powerful response to civic scapegoatism and the bad habits of representative democracy (deference to authority, blaming deputies for the vices of their electors). When students use experience in the community as a basis for critical reflection in the classroom, and turn classroom reflection into a tool to examine the nature of democratic communities and the role of the citizen in them, there is an opportunity to teach liberty, to uncover the interdependence of self and other, to expose the intimate linkage between rights and responsibilities. Classroom based community service programs empower students even as they teach them. They bring the lessons of service into the classroom even as they bring the lessons of the classroom out into the community.

A number of institutions around the country have been experimenting with programs, a few have even instituted mandatory curricula. Many others, including Stanford University, Spelman College, Baylor University, Notre Dame, the University of Minnesota, and Harvard University, are beginning to explore the educational possibilities of service learning as a significant element in liberal education.

In a vigorous democracy capable of withstanding the challenges of a complex, often undemocratic, interdependent world, creating new generations of citizens is not a discretionary activity. Freedom is a hothouse plant that flourishes only when it is carefully tended. Freedom, as Rousseau once reminded us, is a food easy to eat but hard to digest and it has remained undigested more often than it has been assimilated by our democratic body politic. Without active citizens who see in service not the altruism of charity but the necessity of taking responsibility for the authority on which liberty depends, no democracy can function properly or, in the long run, even survive.

National service is not merely a good idea, or, as William Buckley has suggested in his book endorsing a service requirement, a way to repay the debt owed our "patrimony." It is an indispensable prerequisite of citizenship and thus a condition for democracy's preservation. Democracy does not just "deserve" our gratitude: it demands our participation as a price of survival.

Youth Service: Pervasive, Local, Empowered, Positively Driven, Personally Investe

Jack Calhoun

The National and Community Service Act was a beacon, challenging us to help youth understand that how our brothers and sisters are faring is a more important question than whether one owns the newest in Guess? jeans. The Act is a thrilling starting point, but we will not unleash the transforming potential of service and involve the greatest numbers unless youth themselves are actively involved in identifying issues of interest and crafting solutions to them, and unless community service is an accepted ethos in communities large and small across the nation. Will the passage of another decade see youth service embedded in the hearts and minds of each generation? Maybe. Maybe not. The redrawing of the National and Community Service Act in 1993 can lay the foundations for a sturdy community service construct for generations to come or leave an ephemeral framework that collapses into the special interest group category.

We share a common vision that foresees a society in which the issue of voluntary versus mandatory service is no longer relevant—because people not only want to serve but see community service as vital to their own well being. Teaching community service would not be a duty imposed on overburdened schools but an opportunity for all. In the bright future, people have multiple avenues for service in multiple settings in every community across the land.

From Shirley Sagawa and Samuel Halperin, editors, *Visions of Service: The Future of the National and Community Service Act*. Washington, D.C.: National Women's Law Center and American Youth Policy Forum, 1993.

If this vision is to become reality, several things must happen. The concept of youth service must become pervasive; it must be seen as empowering; it must be localized; it must encourage personal investment; it must offer a variety of positive incentives.

Pervasive: The idea of service to others needs to be a part of the warp and woof of civic life. It should be both an expectation and a resource. It is not enough that we have a tradition of volunteerism. Service cannot be confined to a few specific institutions and "special initiatives." Moreover, it cannot be seen as applying only to specific groups or kinds of people or to defined areas of work.

Empowering: Every human being wants to be able to control, as much as possible, decisions that affect life. The more empowering youth service programs are—the more that young people have a say in what gets done and how it's done—the more likely the programs are to succeed.

Localized: Left as a generalized national goal, community service will float in the policy sphere, its conceptual string clutched only in the hands of those who have deep investment in the concept. Localized—made tangible, specific, and owned at the community and even the neighborhood level—it gains constantly renewed vitality, high relevance to daily lives, and a growing body of advocates.

Grounded in personal investment: Personal conviction that community service is beneficial—especially conviction that grows out of direct experience—drives the convinced individual to seek out areas in which community service can help, people who could serve if recruited, and ways to maximize the returns of service to all.

Driven by positive incentives: Our national character tends to be repulsed by government compulsion, absent an overwhelming need for protection against disaster. If we are truly to become a serving culture, if servant leadership is to become the norm, then the servants must be willing. Mandating service is not a permanent solution, though it may be the boost that gets the movement rolling.

We know the importance of these features in community service because they are key components of the successful and growing Youth as Resources (YAR) programs. YAR was piloted in Boston, developed in three Indiana cities and spread to other sites in that state with funding from the Lilly Endowment. It is already expanding to communities across America.

It is clear to us that the pervasiveness, empowerment, personal investment, as well as the local and voluntary nature of YAR have been critical to its astonishing success. Crafters of the 1993 version of the Act must find ways to reflect such principles and to encourage them. Youth Corps efforts are promising, but not every youth is able to serve full time or away from home. College service is commendable, but not everyone goes to college and not everyone can serve if there. School based service can mean a revolution in learning—but it can also mean additional demands on an already beleaguered system. School systems have even begun to shorten their days, giving students more unoccupied time during the day. Meanwhile, communities—their streets, libraries, museums, malls and youth centers—have become de facto latchkey care programs.

YAR is grounded in pervasiveness, empowerment, local service, personal investment, and positive incentives:

Pervasiveness: YAR has attracted young people who range from drop-outs to Scouts, from barely passing to honor roll, from delinquent to model citizen. It has attracted community participation from churches, youth serving agencies, schools, juvenile detention facilities, businesses, civic groups and more. Because of YAR related experiences, community organizations ranging from the Hispanic Festival to the United Way have brought young people into active, full membership on their Boards.

Empowerment: YAR is empowerment for youth. Young people pick the issues and decide what to do about them. They develop the project plan and budget and advocate for its approval. If they get the OK, they take charge of carrying it out. And the skills and capacities that young people bring are valued. Erin, whose tangled personal history has placed her in an institution serving delinquent girls, saw how even the simple gift of a recipe could be of value: "At first I felt real bad the people in the shelter didn't have anything and I did, and then I felt good because I could give them something [food made from her mother's recipe]."

Local service: YAR is grounded in the local community. Its grant making board consists of adults and youth from that community. Organizations that sponsor the young applicants are from that community. Priorities are those of the grant seeking youth in that community. Beneficiaries are right there in the community. Equally important, YAR is flexible and can be quite inexpensive (project grants of $500 to $1,500 are the norm).

Personal investment: Youth and adults who have been involved in YAR become invested in substantial numbers in the concept of community service. One young man summed up the transformation concisely: "We got into this just to say we were doing it, and then we were going to get out. Now we wouldn't leave for anything."

Positive incentives: YAR is voluntary and open to all. Youth are not required to take part. But they are offered the opportunity for enjoyable activities and public acclaim (project kickoffs, youth celebrations, news coverage, and award ceremonies, for example), and more important, they are offered power and authority through the grantmaking process in which they, not adults, take charge.

Three more elements are important to the success of YAR. First, each youth can use his or her unique gifts: Dancers created an original work on resisting peer pressure; good listeners have mediated disputes; artists have developed murals and brochures; teen mothers developed

a play on the realities of teen pregnancy and parenting; Girl Scouts helped care for children at a shelter for battered women.

Second, youth work in contexts in which they feel comfortable, whether a community center, arts institute, school, church, Boys' and Girls' Club, or wherever. They work near home, near school, at a local playground, or across town at a shelter. They work with and in a framework they helped to create.

Third, YAR applicants design a project on something they feel is important, that they feel they can fix—or at least help improve. They are challenged to look at the community, identify problems, and figure out solutions. The problems they have dealt with—ranging from homelessness to day care, from drop out and pregnancy prevention to needs of the elderly—are at the core of today's social needs. In describing to the YAR Board the need for her Girls, Inc. sponsored project, eleven year old Kamieka explained, "Just because these people are old doesn't mean we have to set them aside. We want to show them that we care about them and make friends so they won't think kids and teenagers are self centered." The group's application was approved.

The community service movement is rich. The enthusiasm built for school based, college based, youth corps, and community based programs is a major resource. But it is one that can be too quickly and tragically squandered.

Unless the concept is woven into the very fabric of the community's normalizing and mediating institutions, unless the idea is locally owned as well as nationally stimulated, the beneficiaries of the Act will be few, its advocates fewer, and its lifespan regrettably short. We cannot afford in this reauthorization to settle for anything less than a system that makes youth service pervasive, local, empowering, positively driven, and personally invested. We won't get a second chance.

What Is Wrong with This Picture?

Bernadette Chi

Doing service as a college student was such a meaningful experience for me. I hope that my children have the opportunity to work in homeless shelters.

Educating active, responsible citizens was one of the essential reasons for establishing public schools in the 1800s. Young people are constantly blamed for being selfish, apathetic, and not voting and yet currently, there are few mechanisms for young people to learn positive citizenship. Should we label young people as "apathetic" when the institutions that affect them the most, such as families and schools, have been hardest hit in recent years? Should we blame them for not voting when they have had little or no institutional support or opportunity to exercise their citizenship skills? They cannot be held solely responsible. Perhaps we have not shown young people how to be contributing members of a participatory democracy.

Advocates for youth service claim that performing service develops citizenship. But as illustrated by the quote above, service alone does not lead its participants to *long-term solutions* for a better society. As described in the following paragraphs, well-structured youth service programs include three critical elements: to develop leadership skills in young people; to provide knowledge about pressing community issues; and to offer the experience of participating in long-term community problem-solving. To provide opportunities for all young people, we must look to the schools to revitalize their original mission with well-structured service opportunities.

From Shirley Sagawa and Samuel Halperin, editors, *Visions of Service: The Future of the National and Community Service Act*. Washington, D.C.: National Women's Law Center and American Youth Policy Forum, 1993.

As an element that is often overlooked, personal leadership skills are necessary preparation for young people in their roles as active citizens. Successful programs teach effective communication, active listening, group facilitation, sensitivity to diversity, informational interviewing, and public speaking. Young people can then identify community needs, manage projects, and lead groups in planning and mobilizing for civic action. Such skills will serve them well—now and in the future as lifelong citizens.

One important way to foster youth leadership is to view youth as resources in selecting projects and planning and implementation of programs. There are challenges and benefits. From my experience as a college student in decision-making settings, I know that extra time is required for orientation, that young people can feel intimidated and uncertain of their roles. The young person benefits by learning tremendous amounts of information as well as experiencing what it takes to make their point (with respect, of course). Through youth involvement, programs gain an honest assessment of proposed activities and greater ownership by youth in meeting the needs of youth. As a college graduate, I can no longer speak as a young person, but I realize my responsibility to include them in the process. We must invest time, energy and resources in youth to build youth leadership now and to provide experienced leaders for the future. Orient youth leaders, give them adequate preparation, and let them tell you what they really think.

The second critical element of well-structured youth service programs is providing young people with the knowledge of needs in the community. To have meaning and impact, service must meet real community needs. As a result, projects should be developed in cooperation with entities in the community, such as service agencies, local government, and the client population. Youth in particular should be involved in the identification of issues and the development of projects. By doing so, young people learn about the pressing issues in the community.

The third critical element emphasizes long-term community problem-solving and offers young people the experience of working as responsible citizens. As shown by the opening quote, service provides necessary short-term solutions and enriching experiences for individuals. But service alone does not reach for long-term solutions. Long-term community problem-solving is brought about by advocating for changes in the policies and community institutions; by lobbying for legislation; by participating in organizations; and most essentially, by voting. The student quoted missed the opportunity to examine the causes of homelessness and to realize the need for broader action. This scenario demonstrates the necessity of reflection after completing service projects to examine feelings, the causes of such pressing problems, and future steps for action. Citizenship, after all, is a lifelong process of seeking to improve our communities and our country. Young people should be guided to recognize that such long-term efforts are required to ensure that homeless shelters become unnecessary before their children's time. They could begin to learn what it takes to be active, caring citizens, and the consequences of inaction.

As evidenced today by the poverty of our inner-cities, our increasing abuse of drugs, and our overburdened prison systems, society deteriorates when responsibility does not accompany individual rights and freedoms. To begin to develop strong citizenship skills for the greatest number of youth, service proponents and educators should look to each other for support. Advocates of service should rely on the structure of schools for two reasons: in the short-term, to reach the largest number of youth; in the long-term, for institutionalization of service opportunities. Conversely, educators could view service as a means to fulfill the original mission of the schools—to prepare active citizens to participate in our democratic government. It is clear that no other institution can address this critical need of our participatory democracy. Although there are numerous challenges in establishing such programs, youth service as citizenship development can bring life to the mission of education.

The National and Community Service Act offers governmental support and much needed technical assistance to address the challenges facing schools and communities that wish to involve young people in quality youth service programs. However, to promote programs that develop active and responsible citizens and to institutionalize service in education, several issues in the Act must be addressed. As related to the three critical elements, leadership development should be emphasized as preparation for citizenship. Additionally, to offer access for all students, the need for student stipends in economically disadvantaged areas should be seriously considered. To organize service projects that meet real needs in the community, staff development for current teachers and liability constraints precluding some projects should be addressed. Finally, long-term community problem-solving should be encouraged as students could best learn true citizenship through experience. The Commission on National and Community Service should take it upon itself to promote the coordination of written resources, the collection of "exemplary programs," and the development of curricula for trainers (for youth, teachers, and agency staff) to meet the challenges of implementation.

Most importantly for the programs and the service field overall, governmental support must be sustained. We cannot have year-to-year funding that starts programs, leaves them without funding, and then evaluates them as failures. The Act should be reauthorized, perhaps for ten years, to allow programs to take hold, learn from their mistakes and demonstrate their positive impact. To counter claims that youth are "apathetic," the young people I have met have told me that they want opportunities to serve and to contribute, to get involved and to make a difference. Though they may not see themselves as "citizens," they recognize the benefits to themselves and to their communities if they act as citizens. Some believe that if service were promoted, their peers could find connections to community in positive ways, rather than turning to drugs, crime, and gangs. They say service allows young people to feel a responsibility to make their communities better. And, it "doesn't matter where you live or what race you are, as long as you work together and work hard."

Our communities and our country should support young people in their citizenship development as young people address short-term needs and attempt to find long-term solutions. Recognize youth as resources and not liabilities, as providers and not recipients. Give the power of youth service to develop citizenship a fair chance. Perhaps then we can hope for young people who seek to solve problems of homelessness, who do not expect shelters to continue to exist. It will not be easy, but if we believe in it, then we can and must make the commitment. We have few other choices.

Youth Service: The Best Solution Strategy Around

Maura Wolf

When ten people paddle a boat in four different directions, they exert a lot of energy but end up in the same place they started. If, instead, they line up strategically and work together towards an agreed-upon direction, they can exert the same amount of energy and get a lot closer to their destination.

While youth service efforts are not as unproductive as ten people going around in a circle in the middle of a river, they certainly could be more coordinated, directed and strategic. With greater focus and direction on specific social issues, young people can have a tremendous impact on the problems we face as a nation.

One problem that has an impact on so many others is the crisis of children in America. Perhaps we've seen one too many statistic and become numb to that crisis. Problems like neglect, poor education, child abuse, violence and suicide may not exist in our backyard, but they're happening in someone's and pretty soon the fence around our houses will burn down and we'll have to realize our backyards are connected. The youth service movement needs to be challenged and supported by organizations like the Commission on National and Community Service to focus its momentum on the crisis of children.

We talk often about the 400,000 kids who will drop out of school each year and the one million who will get pregnant. Many more kids are growing up without a sense of hope, self-esteem or family relationships. The 1.8 million kids who will be victims of violent crime in a year are nothing compared to the number of

---

From Shirley Sagawa and Samuel Halperin, editors, *Visions of Service: The Future of the National and Community Service Act.* Washington, D.C.: National Women's Law Center and American Youth Policy Forum, 1993.

kids scared to death to walk home from school. Perhaps the hardest task is looking at ourselves, our brothers and sisters, kids or neighbors, and realizing we are all vulnerable and at-risk. Our lives, hope and dignity can be ripped away from us by a passing car, bullet or sneer in a single moment.

While all of us are at-risk, kids are among the most vulnerable members of the population. Too many of them risk dying early, getting a poor education, not having a job and living in a world filled with racism, despair and selfish individualism. We need to recognize the crisis and realize that it affects all our children.

Kids at-risk are only half the equation. The other half is kids at-strength. Every child has the potential to be great. They may be great at finger-painting, loving their mom, selling candy bars for school, playing soccer, acting in a play, taking care of their younger sister, learning to read or organizing other kids to play fair or help out elderly people in their neighborhood.

While all children are at-risk, they can be at-strength if they have some help with their basic needs such as food, shelter, clothing, healthy moms, strong families, prenatal and early childhood health care, love, continuing education, support and opportunities as their lives go on.

The Forgotten Half, by the William T. Grant Foundation Commission on Youth and America's Future, *Beyond Rhetoric* by the National Commission on Children, and many other reports have told us that not enough kids are making it from one side of the equation to the other. More kids need the bridge to make it from surviving at-risk to developing at-strength. We need more bridges that are wide and strong and can support young people of all types—walking, running, crossing in wheelchairs or trying to find a bridge where dirt roads exist instead of paved ones.

Young people play a role in building the bridge:

- We make great role models, mentors and tutors because we are close enough to relate, but old enough to pass on the lessons.
- We have the time and energy other kids need.
- We know the urgency for our actions because the crisis of our future, community, brothers and sisters, and children depends upon the choices we make.
- We can be strong advocates for issues that are close to our lives.

There are thousands of examples of youth taking an active role in addressing issues that affect kids. Young people of all ages contribute to educational, cultural and recreational programs that operate after school, during school and during the summer. Medical students help young mothers and babies get quality health care. Many junior and senior high school students use their lunch hour to tutor and mentor younger children. A coalition of Black students works with the Children's Defense Fund on a variety of issues related to kids.

Obviously, what we are doing is not enough. What we need to do is get together with child care administrators, teachers, teen-pregnancy prevention program directors, young people who feel they have been left out, and community-leaders from business, government and the private sector who understand the problems. We need to be connected to people who can identity needs that aren't being filled and who want to discuss and support effective roles for young people as a part of the solution.

The contributions we can make include:

- Improving education by assisting with parental involvement programs; mentoring; tutoring; expanding early childhood education programs and helping to develop service-learning opportunities.
- Expanding recreation opportunities by developing and/or staffing school sports programs; building recreational and

enrichment programs around the often under-utilized summer federal food-assistance program and organizing recreational opportunities in housing projects, at parks and in local neighborhoods.

- Making good health care more accessible by organizing public health clinics and fairs; researching affordable options for health care; and developing public education campaigns for immunization, the prevention of teen pregnancy and prenatal care.
- Expanding access to quality, low-cost child-care by serving as child care staff assistants; researching options for child care that are now available and assisting in staff development activities for child-care workers.

Young people can mobilize around a wide variety of children and youth development issues by organizing community-wide forums to discuss issues and generate action; setting up community-wide clearing-houses of available youth services and educating people about them and reaching out to the media to focus them on what is working for kids.

It is obvious that this is an area in which we have a tremendous amount to learn. We need individuals and organizations to support our efforts by:

- Educating young people about issues such as child development, program evaluation, education reform and effective youth services.
- Offering young people the opportunity to give speeches, write articles, receive press attention and sit on organization boards to promote their voices for changing kids' lives.
- Funding young people directly to support efforts that address the needs of kids.
- Embracing the definition of community service that includes public education on policy issues.
- Breaking down barriers and building bridges among people of different ages, races, economic levels, education levels, organizations and government entities. We need examples that give us hope that it can happen; training to help us understand how to do it; and technical and financial support to implement efforts that can help us bridge the gaps.

Kids are in crisis. Young people are a resource. And there are many bridges that need building. The Commission on National and Community Service, as well as other entities, have the opportunity to focus community service efforts on the development of kids at-strength.

Making Service-Learning the Center of the Debate on School Reform

Kathleen Kennedy Townsend

Our challenge is to make sure that every student in the United States knows that he or she can make a difference. We want all schools to teach young people that they may use their English, math, science and social studies skills as resources in their community. A well-educated person will be defined not only by high test scores but by the ability to speak out on issues and contribute to the community.

This vision requires that we push service learning to the center of the debate on school reform. I propose that we work with the Carnegie Commission Task Force on Adolescent Development, Ted Sizer's Essential Schools, the National Education Goals Panel, the Education Commission of the States, and others who believe that young people are resources for our schools and our communities and that the best teachers coach their students to achieve.

The task we have set for ourselves is tough. Many Americans have not even heard the words service-learning. Moreover, with the nation's renewed focus on math and science, many have forgotten that the original purpose of schools was to teach citizenship. Finally, using service to achieve educational goals seems at odds with an educational system dependent on lectures and multiple choice tests.

A case in point is the storm of controversy over required service. Recently, the Maryland State Board of Education required service as a condition of graduation. The objections were

From Shirley Sagawa and Samuel Halperin, editors, *Visions of Service: The Future of the National and Community Service Act*. Washington, D.C.: National Women's Law Center and American Youth Policy Forum, 1993.

virulent, particularly from the educational establishment itself.

One member of the school board claimed that service was "feel-good, fluffy stuff." A former deputy superintendent argued that it would harm students' chances at college because admission officers would know that the service was not freely given but required. A teachers' union representative thought a service requirement inappropriate because a high school diploma represents "book learning." Another union threatened suit on the grounds that a service requirement violated the 13th amendment prohibition against "involuntary servitude" and the First Amendment strictures about separation of church and state. *A Wall Street Journal* op-ed piece contended that the requirement violated child labor laws. Testimony at the school board hearing and letters to the editor argued, among other things, that the requirement would cause a war or result in child abuse and rape.

Although ostensibly the arguments focused on the required aspect of the service, in fact, most could be used against any kind of service. The passion of the arguments shows that most educators do not value service either as a goal of education or as a teaching strategy. If every school was engaged actively in teaching students to serve others or using service to reach learning objectives, then they would not be so troubled.

With grit and imagination we should use the resources of federal and state governments as well as non-profits to support the idea that every educated person serves. We need to connect service-learning to four strands of educational reform: student learning, school structure, professionalism and school community relations.

One of the best ways to do this is to use the National and Community Service Act as a catalyst. The Act is impressive in stressing the need for preparation, action and reflection in order to achieve high-quality service programs. For instance, all our sub-grants from the local education agencies use these magic words. Five years ago they were not in their vocabulary.

Now we are poised to go further. The Act or its regulations might start to describe teachers as "coaches," and students as "resources" or "active learners." It would be helpful if the Act explicitly tied its grants to education reform. A number of states are moving to performance-based assessment, the creation of a "product" and the development of portfolios. These offer opportunities to connect service with assessment tools. A criteria for grants could be the ability to affect testing or assessment at the state or national level.

While the National and Community Service Act is important as a catalyst, other federal legislation can contribute to the expectation that everyone should serve. Job Training Partnership Act funds should be structured to reward those states that use a corps model. Chapter 2 education funds should be used to promote in-school service. The Secretary of Labor's SCANS report on the skills that will be needed for the Year 2000—leadership, higher order thinking, communication and teambuilding—should highlight service activities as one of the best ways to teach these skills.

The ability to perform excellent service should be part of any national or state test or assessment system. Certainly, the quantity of service if not the quality should be counted under Goal Three of our National Education Goals, which deals with achievement in specific subject areas, including citizenship. Once a subject is tested, the system begins to shape its curricula and techniques to success on that test.

In addition, federal monies should encourage teachers to use service-learning techniques. For instance, the Maryland Student Service Alliance will help train "Teach for America" teachers and new teachers who were part of the military. Why should not similar training occur as a matter of course?

Finally, Bill Clinton's proposals to encourage service should be implemented. Every student could go to college and pay back his or her loan by service to the community or as a percentage of his or her enhanced income. Thus, no student would be turned away from college because he or she could not afford the tuition. No graduate would reject the option of working for a non-profit because he or she needed a higher salary to meet a loan repayment schedule.

The state also has an important role to play. Maryland has been greatly aided by the Governor's leadership. His backing was crucial to getting the service requirement passed. Of course there is opposition. But, the combination of the requirement and the National and Community Service Act funds has been a major boon to service. The requirement means that local superintendents take the issue seriously and the sub-grants mean that we have the opportunity to influence positively the shape of service-learning.

Non-profits have also been important. First, their support for the requirement was significant. While a number of people testified that there were not enough service opportunities for the thousands of students who would be unleashed upon the state, many of the non-profits told how they would be eager to have this extra help. Mary Reese at the Volunteer Action Center was particularly helpful in assuring schools that her organization could provide training as well as interesting and worthwhile placements.

In sum, service can and should be encouraged at many levels. Still, our top priority is to make the ability to serve part of our definition of a well-educated person. Once that is accomplished, resources and ideas of how to educate that person will be plentiful.

Community Service and the
Transformation of the American University

Ira Harkavy

The National and Community Service Act has helped to bring the issues of responsible citizenship, youth service and community solidarity to the fore of public discourse. It has also served as a first step toward the development of a national community service movement. The Act, however, has made little contribution to solving the deep, pervasive and myriad problems afflicting American society. Indeed, since 1990 the problems of poverty, crime, unemployment, homelessness, and family and community disintegration have largely grown worse. Any revision of the 1990 Act should help the community service movement to tackle these and other problems seriously, creatively and effectively.

How the Act might do this is the really difficult question, requiring hard thought and learning from what has already been done. Part of that process involves defining the nature and extent of the problems we face. Simply put, our education, health care, human services, criminal, judicial, indeed all major societal systems, are in a state of crisis, unable to function effectively and meet their professed goals. We are burdened with nineteenth century institutions in a twenty-first century world, with institutions that are both hopelessly outdated and dysfunctional.

A continuing and accelerating failure of our institutions means that the community service movement is bound to become increasingly irrelevant and ultimately fail in its mission. Responsible citizens are significantly shaped by responsible institutions that foster values of democracy, civic-mindedness, and public con-

From Shirley Sagawa and Samuel Halperin, editors, *Visions of Service: The Future of the National and Community Service Act*. Washington, D.C.: National Women's Law Center and American Youth Policy Forum, 1993.

cern. The transformation of core institutions into responsible civic institutions, therefore, needs to be at the very top of the community service movement's agenda.

Putting something on an agenda and getting it done are two very different things. Radically changing the way our core institutions operate and are organized will not be easy or quick. A strategic place to begin to focus the energies of the community service movement is the American university. Given its prestige, worldwide networks, influence on other institutions (including schools at all levels and the professions), and its enormous human and intellectual resources, a substantial change in American higher education would have significant and enduring society-wide impacts.

Moreover, the complexity of today's problems requires a comprehensive view that transcends institutional particularism and avoids confusing institutional with societal interests. Universities, in principle, are the only modern institutions both designed to encompass the broad range of human experience and devoted to the use of reason to help deal with the enormous complexity of our society and world. As such, they are the closest approximation we have to a universal institution—an institution whose particular mission is that of societal improvement and whose resources, when appropriately organized, enable it to contribute to achieving that general mission.

Universities are, of course, a long way from realizing their professed goal. No matter how compelling the societal need, how pressing the problems that confront us, it will not be easy to reorient America's universities. But conditions in the 1990s make that change more likely than ever before. Stated directly, universities are likely to change because their institutional self-interest will compel them to do so.

If the crisis in our cities and in society at large continues to worsen at an accelerating rate, universities will suffer for it. Failing public schools, devastated neighborhoods, high crime, and a fortress mentality do little to create a positive campus ambience and to enhance faculty and student recruitment and retention.

More indirectly, as conditions in society continue to deteriorate, universities will face increased public scrutiny. That scrutiny is bound to intensify as America focuses on resolving its deep and pervasive societal problems amid continuously expanding global competition. Institutions of higher education will increasingly be held to new and demanding standards that evaluate performance on the basis of direct and short-run societal benefit. In addition, public, private, and foundation support will be more than ever based on that standard, and it will become increasingly clear to colleges and universities that "altruism pays"—that altruism is practically an imperative for institutional development and improvement.

That conditions are ripe for change is no guarantee that change will actually occur. Catalysts are needed to convert probabilities into actualities. Revisions in the 1990 Act can be the needed catalyst. A revised Act can function in this way by encouraging institutionally rooted service to place student, faculty, and staff community service at the center of the university.

Universities have three missions: research, teaching, and service. Although they are presented as a seamless web that exemplifies higher education's noble purpose, anyone associated with a university knows better. Only research generally counts in tenure and promotion decisions, and a wide division exists among the three missions. To place service at the center of the institution means linking it to the research and teaching enterprise.

A revised National and Community Service Act can help forge that link through support for school-year and summer academic internships for undergraduates. Loan forgiveness, student aid, and other forms of support could be provided to students who engage in, for example, twenty-hour-a-week internships that also serve as the basis for an intensive academic experience involving serious research and study. Rather than waiting to graduate to receive aid for service, students would be encouraged to serve in meaningful ways while they are still students. The internship would also involve the application and enhancement of academic skills as well as an opportunity for career preparation in a wide variety of areas.

For a student to receive this kind of support, his or her higher education institution would have to provide vehicles that enable students to link community service and academic study. The National and Community Service Act would, therefore, provide a strong incentive for colleges and universities to function increasingly as civic institutions.

Another provision that would increase community service and help transform higher educational institutions would focus on the establishment of structures that promote volunteer activity among *all* groups within the university—faculty, staff, and alumni, as well as students. Staff members living in a university's local community represent a particularly promising source for effective neighborly assistance to the local community. Support should be directed to those colleges and universities that have provided, or are willing to provide, their own resources for developing a comprehensive structure that stimulates and coordinates total university engagement in community service.

A third institution-changing provision could provide matching money to a select number of school districts and higher education institutions for the purpose of establishing offices to promote effective volunteer programs to help staff university-assisted community schools. Functioning as government-funded, multi-purpose community centers capable of expanding and responsibly supervising the provision of services to residents in the area, university-assisted community schools would help address and solve neighborhood problems and concerns.

This idea, as well as the other two provisions outlined above, suggest ways that the National and Community Service Act might be a catalyst for helping to transform the American university system. My more general argument has three components. First, a transformation of our core institutions is needed if American society is to solve its more pressing and fundamental problems. Second, a transformation of core institutions requires that the American university system be significantly transformed. Third, the community service movement can be an effective vehicle for transforming American universities into responsible civic universities that significantly contribute to creating a fair, decent, and just society.

Song of the Insufficiency of Human Endeavor

1

Mankind lives by its head
Its head won't see it through
Inspect your own. What lives off that?
At most a louse or two.
For this bleak existence
Man is never sharp enough.
Hence his weak resistance
To its tricks and bluff.

2

Aye, make yourself a plan
They need you at the top!
Then make yourself a second plan
Then let the whole thing drop.
For this bleak existence
Man is never bad enough
Though his sheer persistence
Can be lovely stuff.

3

Aye, race for happiness
But don't you race too fast.
When all chase after happiness
Happiness comes in last.
For this bleak existence
Man is never undemanding enough.
All his loud insistence
Is a load of guff.

Bertholt Brecht

From *Dreigroschenoper* by Bertolt Brecht, translated by Ralph Manheim and John Willet. Copyright © 1928 by Gustav Kiepenheuer Verlag renewed 1968 by Helene Weigel. English translation copyright © 1976, 1977 by Stefan S. Brecht.

Let America Be America Again.

Let America be America again.
Let it be the dream it used to be.
Let it be the pioneer on the plain
Seeking a home where he himself is free.

(America never was America to me.)

Let America be the dream the dreamers dreamed—
Let it be that great strong land of love
Where never kings connive nor tyrants scheme
That any man be crushed by one above.

(It never was America to me.)

O, let my land be a land where Liberty
Is crowned with no false patriotic wreath,
But opportunity is real, and life is free,
Equality is in the air we breathe.

(There's never been equality for me,
Nor freedom in this "homeland of the free.")

Say, who are you that mumbles in the dark?
And who are you that draws your veil across the stars?

I am the poor white, fooled and pushed apart,
I am the Negro bearing slavery's scars.
I am the red man driven from the land,
I am the immigrant clutching the hope I seek—
And finding only the same old stupid plan
Of dog eat dog, of mighty crush the weak.

I am the young man, full of strength and hope,
Tangled in that ancient endless chain
Of profit, power, gain, of grab the land!
Of grab the gold! Of grab the ways of satisfying need!
Of work the men! Of take the pay!
Of owning everything for one's own greed!

I am the farmer, bondsman to the soil.
I am the worker sold to the machine.
I am the Negro, servant to you all.
I am the people, humble, hungry, mean—
Hungry yet today despite the dream.
Beaten yet today—O, Pioneers!
I am the man who never got ahead,
The poorest worker bartered through the years.

Yet I'm the one who dreamt our basic dream
In that Old World while still a serf of kings,
Who dreamt a dream so strong, so brave, so true,
That even yet its mighty daring sings
In every brick and stone, in every furrow turned
That's made America the land it has become.
O, I'm the man who sailed those early seas
In search of what I meant to be my home—
For I'm the one who left dark Ireland's shore,
And Poland's plain, and England's grassy lea,
And torn from Black Africa's strand I came
To build a "homeland of the free."

The free?

Who said the free? Not me?
Surely not me? The millions on relief today?
The millions shot down when we strike?
The millions who have nothing for our pay?
For all the dreams we've dreamed
And all the songs we've sung
And all the hopes we've held
And all the ags we've hung,
The millions who have nothing for our pay—
Except the dream that's almost dead today.

O, let America be America again—
The land that never has been yet—
And yet must be—the land where every man is free.
The land that's mine—the poor man's, Indian's,
*   Negro's, ME—*
Who made America,
Whose sweat and blood, whose faith and pain,
Whose hand at the foundry, whose plow in the rain,
Must bring back our mighty dream again.

Sure, call me any ugly name you choose—The steel of freedom does not stain.
From those who live like leeches on the people's lives,
We must take back our land again,
America!

O, yes,
I say it plain,
America never was America to me,
And yet I swear this oath—
America will be!

Out of the rack and ruin of our gangster death,
The rape and rot of graft, and stealth, and lies,
We, the people, must redeem
The land, the mines, the plants, the rivers.
The mountains and the endless plain—
All, all the stretch of these great green states—
And make America again!

Langston Hughes

Part Two

❖

Challenges to Democratic Citizenship

Introduction

When we speak about service, community, responsibility and citizenship, it is easy to forget that pursuing these common values has costs. Democracy is always a struggle among values—which is what makes it such a difficult form of government—and it is about conflict as well as cooperation. In the struggle to privilege community and responsibilities, we may put individual rights at risk. In the search for commonality, cooperation and social consensus, we may undermine difference and unwittingly nourish a politics of exclusion. In praising democracy, we may license majorities to repress minorities as long as decisions are democratically taken. In celebrating commonality, we may suppress individualism and try to impress conformity on those who march to their own drum beat. Can a democratic community be truly inclusive? Can it tolerate or even encourage strong individualists?

In this Part we take up these challenges to democratic citizenship and community service. In the first section we are concerned with difference, and the prejudices and inequalities differences can spawn, even in (especially in?) a democracy. Communities often win their solidarity at the price of exclusion. Communities tend to spring up among those who are alike. Difference is not necessarily natural to communities and is a problem for them. The problem is how to create artificial communities which tolerate, even celebrate differences between their members in the face of natural communities which tend to be hostile to difference. The very word "fraternity" suggests men only! Yet some would argue that American democracy is based on the celebration of differences. E pluribus unum—out of many, one—is our national motto. The selections here take up issues of race, gender, class, sexual orientation, and "ability" as challenges to those who would forge genuinely democratic communities. Audre Lorde's provocative essay leads the section, asserting that the model for the democratic Citizen in the United States has been a thin, young, white, heterosexual male, excluding most from participation. From Lorde's essay we move on to two competing views of race in American society, articulated by Gloria Anzaldua and Shelby Steele. Anzaldua presents a provocative critique of "middle" American democracy and culture from the perspective of those on the margins or "borderlands," while Steele's equally provocative account challenges individuals of color to assert a moral authority against the politics of race. Carole Pateman and Susan Okm force us to confront the issue of gender inequality within a democratic community. Both argue that to bring women fully into the picture of democratic citizenship will require a rethinking of our categories of rights and responsibilities, private and public. The author bell hooks and Former Secretary of Labor Robert Reich present us with challenges to democracy based on economic class, hooks from the perspective of low-income communities and Reich from the perspective of "the fortunate fifth" in our economy. Finally, Barack Obama uses the metaphor of hope to envision a democratic community where difference is indeed celebrated.

In Section B, Alexis de Tocqueville's classic warning about the danger of tyrannical majorities is a common thread weaving together a group of selections exploring whether the freedom of individuals can be reconciled with the demands of a democratic community. It includes John Stuart Mill's classic essay On Liberty, the Bill of Rights and Post-Civil War Amendments from the U.S. Constitution, and Marge Piercy's poem on women's rights. Benjamin Barber's essay comes at the question from a different perspective, connecting a democracy's protection of rights to the individual citizen's willingness to take on civic responsibilities. Melville's telling portrait of what happens to an individual trying to live with integrity in a society demanding conformity to rules and discipline and Shirley Jackson's fearsome story suggesting how the pursuit of common goods can destroy not just individuals, but the moral basis of all good, provide us with fictional accounts of the denial of individual liberty. And the U.S. Supreme Court cases of Korematsu v. U.S. and Minersville School District v. Gobitis give us two real accounts of how far a majority will go, when afraid, to endanger the rights of individuals who live within democratic communities. Martin Luther King closes this section with justifications for civil disobedience against democratic majorities which ultimately seem rooted in the logic of democracy itself.

In the last section, we look squarely at challenges to the notion of universal citizenship as a solution to the problems of democratic community. We begin the section with the classic essay by Henry David Thoreau, which raises the question of whether citizens are really obligated to serve their country, either in the military or in any other fashion. Thoreau's essay on civil disobedience is followed by Ayn Rand's radical individualist denunciation of democracy, which similarly questions whether an individual owes anything to others. The Seeger case and the short story by Ursula Leguin in different ways raise critical concerns about the conflict between service to the community and the individual's conscience. Joe Steffan's story in "The Gay Cadet" presents us with the dilemmas of those who wish to serve their country, and are not allowed to do so. Matthew Spalding and Keith Morton close out the section with two different critiques of service. Spalding challenges the principles behind current national service policies, while Morton questions the basic assumptions underlying many community service efforts.

Audre Lorde

Age, Race, Class, and Sex: Women Redefining Difference

Audre Lorde (1934–1992), American poet, often described herself with a list of particulars: black, woman, lesbian, feminist, educator, mother of two children, daughter of Grenadian immigrants. During her fourteen-year battle against cancer, Lorde continually turned her fear of death into a source of strength for doing her work; in a paper delivered in December 1977, she said, "I was going to die, if not sooner then later, whether or not I had ever spoken myself. My silences had not protected me. Your silence will not protect you."

While many feminists have centered their energies on constructing a unified movement to combat patriarchy, the following essay questions the way we construct and prioritize unity itself. For Lorde, any "movement" that defined an "enemy" was likely to leave one or more of her multiple identities on the sidelines. A purely feminist struggle, for example, would betray Lorde's fight against racial oppression; a unified focus on her black identity would obstruct her struggle against sexism within both the black community and society as a whole. Lorde believed in learning to see difference as a source of strength rather than conflict. Beginning with our own internalized habits of rejecting everything not in accordance with the "mythical norm," Lorde argued, we can work to discover new foundations for a society supportive of equality without homogeneity and difference without oppression.

Age, Race, Class, and Sex: Women Redefining Difference

Audre Lorde

Much of Western European history conditions us to see human differences in simplistic opposition to each other: dominant/subordinate, good/bad, up/down, superior/inferior. In a society where the good is defined in terms of profit rather than in terms of human need, there must always be some group of people who, through systematized oppression, can be made to feel surplus, to occupy the place of the dehumanized inferior. Within this society, that group is made up of Black and Third World people, working-class people, older people, and women.

As a forty-nine-year-old Black lesbian feminist socialist mother of two, including one boy, and a member of an interracial couple, I usually find myself a part of some group defined as other, deviant, inferior, or just plain wrong. Traditionally, in american society, it is the members of oppressed, objectified groups who are expected to stretch out and bridge the gap between the actualities of our lives and the consciousness of our oppressor. For in order to survive, those of us for whom oppression is as american as apple pie have always had to be watchers, to become familiar with the language and manners of the oppressor, even sometimes adopting them for some illusion of protection. Whenever the need for some pretense of communication arises, those who profit from our oppression call upon us to share our knowledge with them. In other words, it is the responsibility of the oppressed to teach the oppressors their mistakes. I am responsible for educating teachers who dismiss my children's culture in school. Black and Third World people are expected to educate white people as to our humanity. Women are expected to educate men. Lesbians and gay men are expected to educate the heterosexual world. The oppressors maintain their position and evade responsibility for their own actions There is a constant drain of energy which might be better used in redefining ourselves and devising realistic scenarios for altering the present and constructing the future.

Institutionalized rejection of difference is an absolute necessity in a profit economy which needs outsiders as surplus people. As members of such an economy, we have all been programmed to respond to the human differences between us with fear and loathing and to handle that difference in one of three ways: ignore it, and if that is not possible, copy it if we think it is dominant, or destroy it if we think it is subordinate. But we have no patterns for relating across our human differences as equals. As a result, those differences have been misnamed and misused in the service of separation and confusion.

Certainly there are very real differences between us of race, age, and sex. But it is not those differences between us that are separating us. It is rather our refusal to recognize those differences, and to examine the distortions which result from our misnaming them and their effects upon human behavior and expectation.

Racism, the belief in the inherent superiority of one race over all others and thereby the right to dominance. Sexism, the belief in the inherent superiority of one sex over the other and thereby the right to dominance. Ageism. Heterosexism. Elitism. Classism.

It is a lifetime pursuit for each one of us to extract these distortions from our living at the same time as we recognize, reclaim, and define those differences upon which they are imposed. For we have all been raised in a society where those distortions were endemic within our living. Too often, we pour the energy needed for recognizing and exploring difference into pretending those differences are insurmountable barriers, or that they do not exist at all. This results in a voluntary isolation, or false and treacherous connections. Either way, we do not develop tools for using human difference as a springboard for creative change within our lives. We speak not of human difference, but of human deviance.

Somewhere, on the edge of consciousness, there is what I call a mythical norm, which each one of us within our hearts knows "that is not me." In America, this norm is usually defined as white, thin, male, young, heterosexual, Christian, and financially secure. It is with this mythical norm that the trappings of power reside within this society. Those of us who stand outside that power often identify one way in which we are different, and we assume that to be the primary cause of all oppression, forgetting other distortions around difference, some of which we ourselves may be practicing. By and large within the women's movement today, white women focus upon their oppression as women and ignore differences of race, sexual preference, class, and age. There is a pretense to a homogeneity of experience covered by the word *sisterhood* that does not in fact exist.

Unacknowledged class differences rob women of each others' energy and creative insight. Recently a women's magazine collective made the decision for one issue to print only prose, saying poetry was a less "rigorous" or "serious" art form. Yet even the form our creativity takes is often a class issue. Of all the art forms, poetry is the most economical. It is the one which is the most secret, which requires the least physical labor, the least material, and the one which can be done between shifts, in the hospital pantry, on the subway, and on scraps of surplus paper. Over the last few years, writing a novel on tight finances, I came to appreciate the enormous differences in the material demands between poetry and prose. As we reclaim our literature, poetry has been the major voice of poor, working class, and Colored women. A room of one's own may be a necessity for writing prose, but so are reams of paper, a typewriter, and plenty of time. The actual requirements to produce the visual arts also help determine, along class lines, whose art is whose. In this day of inflated prices for material, who are our sculptors, our painters, our photographers? When we speak of a broadly based women's culture, we need to be aware of the effect of class and economic differences on the supplies available for producing art.

As we move toward creating a society within which we can each flourish, ageism is another distortion of relationship which interferes without vision. By ignoring the past, we are encouraged to repeat its mistakes. The "generation gap" is an important social tool for any repressive society. If the younger members of a community view the older members as contemptible or suspect or excess, they will never be able to join hands and examine the living memories of the community, nor ask the all important question, "Why?" This gives rise to a historical amnesia that keeps us working to invent the wheel every time we have to go to the store for bread.

We find ourselves having to repeat and relearn the same old lessons over and over that our mothers did because we do not pass on what we have learned, or because we are unable to listen. For instance, how many times has this all been said before? For another, who would have believed that once again our daughters are allowing their bodies to be hampered and purgatoried by girdles and high heels and hobble skirts?

Ignoring the differences of race between women and the implications of those differences presents the most serious threat to the mobilization of women's joint power.

As white women ignore their built-in privilege of whiteness and define *woman* in terms of their own experience alone, then women of Color become "other," the outsider whose experience and tradition is too "alien" to comprehend. An example of this is the signal absence of the experience of women of Color as a resource for women's studies courses. The literature of women of Color is seldom included in women's literature courses and almost never in other literature courses, nor in women's studies as a whole. All too often, the excuse given is that the literatures of women of Color can only be taught by Colored women, or that they are too difficult to understand, or that classes cannot "get into" them because they come out of experiences that are "too different." I have heard this argument presented by white women of otherwise quite clear intelligence, women who seem to have no trouble at all teaching and reviewing work that comes out of the vastly different experiences of Shakespeare, Moliere, Dostoyefsky, and Aristophanes. Surely there must be some other explanation.

This is a very complex question, but I believe one of the reasons white women have such difficulty reading Black women's work is because of their reluctance to see Black women as women and different from themselves. To examine Black women's literature effectively requires that we be seen as whole people in our actual complexities—as individuals, as women, as human—rather than as one of those problematic but familiar stereotypes provided in this society in place of genuine images of Black women. And I believe this holds true for the literatures of other women of Color who are not Black.

The literatures of all women of Color recreate the textures of our lives, and many white women are heavily invested in ignoring the real differences. For as long as any difference between us means one of us must be inferior, then the recognition of any difference must be fraught with guilt. To allow women of Color to step out of stereotypes is too guilt provoking, for it threatens the complacency of those women who view oppression only in terms of sex.

Refusing to recognize difference makes it impossible to see the different problems and pitfalls facing us as women.

Thus, in a patriarchal power system where whiteskin privilege is a major prop, the entrapments used to neutralize Black women and white women are not the same. For example, it is easy for Black women to be used by the power structure against Black men, not because they are men, but because they are Black. Therefore, for Black women, it is necessary at all times to separate the needs of the oppressor from our own legitimate conflicts within our communities. This same problem does not exist for white women. Black women and men have shared racist oppression and still share it, although in different ways. Out of that shared oppression we have developed joint defenses and joint vulnerabilities to each other that are not duplicated in the white community, with the exception of the relationship between Jewish women and Jewish men.

On the other hand, white women face the pitfall of being seduced into joining the oppressor under the pretense of sharing power. This possibility does not exist in the same way for women of Color. The tokenism that is sometimes extended to us is not an invitation to join power; our racial "otherness" is a visible reality that makes that quite clear. For white women there is a wider range of pretended choices and rewards for identifying with patriarchal power and its tools.

Today, with the defeat of ERA, the tightening economy, and increased conservatism, it is easier once again for white women to believe the dangerous fantasy that if you are good enough, pretty enough, sweet enough, quiet enough, teach the children to behave, hate the right people, and marry the right men, then you will be allowed to coexist with patriarchy in relative peace, at least until a man needs your job or the neighborhood rapist happens along. And true, unless one lives and loves in the trenches it is difficult to remember that the war against dehumanization is ceaseless.

But Black women and our children know the fabric of our lives is stitched with violence and with hatred, that there is no rest. We do not deal with it only on the picket lines, or in dark midnight alleys, or in the places where we dare to verbalize our resistance. For us, increasingly, violence weaves through the daily tissues of our living—in the supermarket, in the classroom, in the elevator, in the clinic and the schoolyard, from the plumber, the baker, the saleswoman, the bus driver, the bank teller, the waitress who does not serve us.

Some problems we share as women, some we do not. You fear your children will grow up to join the patriarchy and testify against you, we fear our children will be dragged from a car and shot down in the street, and you will turn your backs upon the reasons they are dying.

The threat of difference has been no less blinding to people of Color. Those of us who are Black must see that the reality of our lives and our struggle does not make us immune to the errors of ignoring and misnaming difference. Within Black communities where racism is a living reality, differences among us often seem dangerous and suspect. The need for unity is often misnamed as a need for homogeneity, and a Black feminist vision mistaken for betrayal of our common interests as a people. Because of the continuous battle against racial erasure that Black women and Black men share, some Black women still refuse to recognize that we are also oppressed as women, and that sexual hostility against Black women is practiced not only by the white racist society, but implemented within our Black communities as well. It is a disease striking the heart of Black nationhood, and silence will not make it disappear. Exacerbated by racism and the pressures of powerlessness, violence against Black women and children often becomes a standard within our communities, one by which manliness can be measured. But these woman-hating acts are rarely discussed as crimes against Black women.

As a group, women of Color are the lowest paid wage earners in America. We are the primary targets of abortion and sterilization abuse, here and abroad. In certain parts of Africa, small girls are still being sewed shut between their legs to keep them docile and for men's pleasure. This is known as female circumcision, and it is not a cultural affair as the late Jomo Kenyatta insisted, it is a crime against Black women.

Black women's literature is full of the pain of frequent assault, not only by a racist patriarchy, but also by Black men. Yet the necessity for and history of shared battle have made us, Black women, particularly vulnerable to the false accusation that antisexist is anti-Black. Meanwhile, woman-hating as a recourse of the powerless is sapping strength from Black communities, and our very lives. Rape is on the increase, reported and unreported, and rape is not aggressive sexuality, it is sexualized aggression. As Kalamu ya Salaam, a Black male writer points out, "As long as male domination exists, rape will exist. Only women revolting and men made conscious of their responsibility to fight sexism can collectively stop rape.*

Differences between ourselves as Black women are also being misnamed and used to separate us from one another. As a Black lesbian feminist comfortable with the many different ingredients of my identity, and a woman committed to racial and sexual freedom from oppression, I find I am constantly being encouraged to pluck out some one aspect of myself and present this as the meaningful whole, eclipsing or denying the other parts of self. But this is a destructive and fragmenting way to live. My fullest concentration of energy is available to me only when I integrate all the parts of who I am, openly, allowing power from particular sources of my living to flow back and forth freely through all my different selves, without the restrictions of externally imposed definition. Only then can I bring myself and my energies as a whole to the service of those struggles which I embrace as part of my living.

A fear of lesbians, or of being accused of being a lesbian, has led many Black women into testifying against themselves. It has led some of

us into destructive alliances, and others into despair and isolation. In the white women's communities, heterosexism is sometimes a result of identifying with the white patriarchy, a rejection of that interdependence between women-identified women which allows the self to be, rather than to be used in the service of men. Sometimes it reflects a die-hard belief in the protective coloration of heterosexual relationships, sometimes a self-hate which all women have to fight against, taught us from birth.

Although elements of these attitudes exist for all women, there are particular resonances of heterosexism and homophobia among Black women. Despite the fact that woman-bonding has a long and honorable history in the African and African-american communities, and despite the knowledge and accomplishments of many strong and creative women-identified Black women in the political, social and cultural fields, heterosexual Black women often tend to ignore or discount the existence and work of Black lesbians. Part of this attitude has come from an understandable terror of Black male attack within the close confines of Black society, where the punishment for any female self-assertion is still to be accused of being a lesbian and therefore unworthy of the attention or support of the scarce Black male. But part of this need to misname and ignore Black lesbians comes from a very real fear that openly women-identified Black women who are no longer dependent upon men for their self-definition may well reorder our whole concept of social relationships.

Black women who once insisted that lesbianism was a white woman's problem now insist that Black lesbians are a threat to Black nationhood, are consorting with the enemy, are basically un-Black. These accusations, coming from the very women to whom we look for deep and real understanding, have served to keep

---

* From "Rape: A Radical Analysis, An African American Perspective" by Kalamu ya Salaam in Black Books Bulletin, vol. 6, no. 4 (1980).

many Black lesbians in hiding, caught between the racism of white women and the homophobia of their sisters. Often, their work has been ignored, trivialized, or misnamed, as with the work of Angelina Grimke, Alice Dunbar-Nelson, Lorraine Hansberry. Yet women-bonded women have always been some part of the power of Black communities, from our unmarried aunts to the amazons of Dahomey.

And it is certainly not Black lesbians who are assaulting women and raping children and grandmothers on the streets of our communities.

Across this country, as in Boston during the spring of 1979 following the unsolved murders of twelve Black women, Black lesbians are spearheading movements against violence against Black women.

What are the particular details within each of our lives that can be scrutinized and altered to help bring about change? How do we redefine difference for all women? It is not our differences which separate women, but our reluctance to recognize those differences and to deal effectively with the distortions which have resulted from the ignoring and misnaming of those differences.

As a tool of social control, women have been encouraged to recognize only one area of human difference as legitimate, those differences which exist between women and men. And we have learned to deal across those differences with the urgency of all oppressed subordinates. All of us have had to learn to live or work or coexist with men, from our fathers on. We have recognized and negotiated these differences, even when this recognition only continued the old dominant/subordinate mode of human relationship, where the oppressed must recognize the masters' difference in order to survive.

But our future survival is predicated upon our ability to relate within equality. As women, we must root out internalized patterns of oppression within ourselves if we are to move beyond the most superficial aspects of social change. Now we must recognize differences among women who are our equals, neither inferior nor superior, and devise ways to use each others' difference to enrich our visions and our joint struggles.

The future of our earth may depend upon the ability of all women to identify and develop new definitions of power and new patterns of relating across difference. The old definitions have not served us, nor the earth that supports us. The old patterns, no matter how cleverly rearranged to imitate progress, still condemn us to cosmetically altered repetitions of the same old exchanges, the same old guilt, hatred, recrimination, lamentation, and suspicion.

For we have, built into all of us, old blueprints of expectation and response, old structures of oppression, and these must be altered at the same time as we alter the living conditions which are a result of those structures. For the master's tools will never dismantle the master's house.

As Paulo Freire shows so well in *The Pedagogy of the Oppressed,*[*] the true focus of revolutionary change is never merely the oppressive situations which we seek to escape, but that piece of the oppressor which is planted deep within each of us, and which knows only the oppressors' tactics, the oppressors' relationships.

Change means growth, and growth can be painful. But we sharpen self-definition by exposing the self in work and struggle together with those whom we define as different from ourselves, although sharing the same goals. For

---

[*] Seabury Press, New York, 1970.

Black and white, old and young, lesbian and heterosexual women alike, this can mean new paths to our survival.

We have chosen each other
and the edge of each others battles
the war is the same

if we lose
someday women's blood will congeal
upon a dead planet
if we win
there is no telling
we seek beyond history
for a new and more possible meeting.*

---

*   From "Outlines," unpublished poem.

Gloria Anzaldúa

Borderlands/La Frontera:
The New Mestiza

In the Preface to *Borderlands/La Frontera*, Gloria Anzaldúa describes herself as a "border woman." She grew up in "the valley," on the border between Texas and Mexico, straddling the psychological border between two cultures. In addition to the cultural borderlands that represent the actual physical setting of the United States Southwest, Anzaldúa also documents the sexual, spiritual, and linguistic frontiers traversed in her own personal life journey. A poet and fiction writer, Anzaldúa uses the image of the border throughout this work to demonstrate the exclusion felt by Latinos at the hands of mainstream Anglo society and culture. For Anzaldúa, American democracy is dominated by dualities: reason/passion, objective/subjective, male/female, white/black-brown-yellow-red, matter/spirit, individual/community. In each dualism, the first is privileged over the other, denying the identity and integrity of the other. Anzaldúa uses the Spanish *amasamiento*, or ambiguity, to summarize her position, arguing for the celebration of pluralism as an answer to the exclusion she and other latinas experience. She also opposes the "linguistic terrorism" of U.S. culture and education, and switches from English to Castillian Spanish to the Aztec language Nahuatl, mixing in a variety of dialects to denote that language can also exist on the borderlands. Although not overtly a work about democratic citizenship, the following excerpt from Anzaldúa's work raises important questions about diversity and inequality within American democracy.

Borderlands/La Frontera: The New Mestiza

Gloria Anzaldúa

El otro México

El otro México que acá hemos construido
el espacio es lo que ha sido
territorio nacional.
Esté el esfuerzo de todos nuestros hermanos
y latinoamericanos que han sabido
progressar.
                        —Los Tigres del Norte

The Aztecas del norte…compose the largest single tribe or nation of Anishinabeg (Indians) found in the United States today…. Some call themselves Chicanos and see themselves as people whose true homeland is Aztlán [the U.S. Southwest]."

Wind tugging at my sleeve
feet sinking into the sand

I stand at the edge where earth touches
                ocean
where the two overlap
a gentle coming together
at other times and places a violent clash.

Across the border in Mexico
stark silhouette of houses gutted by waves,
cliffs crumbling into the sea,
silver waves marbled with spume
gashing a hole under the border fence.

Miro el mar atacar
la cerca en Border Field Park
con sus buchones de agua,
an Easter Sunday resurrection
of the brown blood in my veins.

Oigo el llorido del mar, el respiro del aire,
my heart surges to the beat of the sea.
In the gray haze of the sun
the gulls' shrill cry of hunger,
the tangy smell of the sea seeping into me.
I walk through the hole in the fence
to the other side.
Under my fingers I feel the gritty wire
rusted by 139 years
of the salty breath of the sea.

Beneath the iron sky
Mexican children kick their soccer ball
across,
run after it, entering the U.S.

I press my hand to the steel curtain—
chainlink fence crowned with rolled barbed
wire—
rippling from the sea where Tijuana touches
San Diego
unrolling over mountains
and plains
and deserts,
this "Tortilla Curtain" turning into el río
Grande
flowing down to the flatlands
of the Magic Valley of South Texas
its mouth emptying into the Gulf.

1,950 mile-long open wound
dividing a *pueblo*, a culture,
running down the length of my body,
staking fence rods in my flesh,
splits me splits me
me raja me raja

This is my home
this thin edge of
barbwire.
But the skin of the earth is seamless.
The sea cannot be fenced,
el mar does not stop at borders.
To show the white man what she thought of
his

arrogance,
Yemaya blew that wire fence down.

This land was Mexican once,
was Indian always
and is.
And will be again.

Yo soy un puente tendido
del mundo gabacho al del mojado,
lo pasado me estirá pa' 'trás
y lo presente pa' 'delante.
Que la Virgen de Guadalupe me cuide
Ay ay ay, soy mexicana de este lado.

The U.S. Mexican-border *es una herida abierta* where the Third World grates against the first and bleeds. And before a scab forms it hemorrhages again, the lifeblood of two worlds merging to form a third country—a border culture. Borders are set up to define the places that are safe and unsafe, to distinguish *us* from *them*. A border is a dividing line, a narrow strip along a steep edge. A borderland is a vague and undetermined place created by the emotional residue of an unnatural boundary. It is in a constant state of transition. The prohibited and forbidden are its inhabitants. *Los atravesados* live here: the squint-eyed, the perverse, the queer, the troublesome, the mongrel, the mulato, the half-breed, the half dead; in short, those who cross over, pass over, or go through the confines of the "normal." Gringos in the U.S. Southwest consider the inhabitants of the borderlands transgressors, aliens—whether they possess documents or not, whether they're Chicanos, Indians or Blacks. Do not enter, trespassers will be raped, maimed, strangled, gassed, shot. The only "legitimate" inhabitants are those in power, the whites and those who align themselves with whites. Tension grips the inhabitants of the borderlands like a virus. Ambivalence and unrest reside there and death is no stranger....

Shelby Steele

I'm Black, You're White, Who's Innocent?

In his 1990 book on race in America, *The Content of Our Character,* Shelby Steele describes himself as a "forty-ish, middle-class, black American male with a teaching position at a large state university in California." He goes on to explain that he was raised in an all-black community outside Chicago, but now feels quite comfortable in his white middle-class suburban neighborhood. He describes himself as a member of a growing black professional middle-class, the beneficiaries of declining racism and sustained individual effort.

According to Steele, blacks today suffer not so much from racism, but from "integration shock:" the fear of personal accountability that comes from no longer being able to use race as an excuse for failure. Steele rejects the popular "self-fulfilling prophecy theory"—which states that blacks do poorly because teachers and parents expect them to—because it sees blacks as only victims without any choices. These choices become clearer through a de-emphasis of racial and group identity. "In the 1990s," Steele writes, "we blacks are in a position where our common good will best be served by the determined pursuit of our most personal aspirations."

I'm Black, You're White, Who's Innocent?
Shelby Steele

Race and Power in an Era of Blame

It is a warm, windless California evening, and the dying light that covers the redbrick patio is tinted pale orange by the day's smog. Eight of us, not close friends, sit in lawn chairs sipping chardonnay. A black engineer and I (we had never met before) integrate the group. A psychologist is also among us, and her presence encourages a surprising openness. But not until well after the lovely twilight dinner has been served, when the sky has turned to deep black and the drinks have long since changed to scotch, does the subject of race spring awkwardly upon us. Out of nowhere the engineer announces, with a coloring of accusation in his voice, that it bothers him to send his daughter to a school where she is one of only three black children. "I didn't realize my ambi-tion to get ahead would pull me into a world where my daughter would lose touch with her blackness," he says.

Over the course of the evening we have talk-ed about money, past and present addictions, child abuse, even politics. Intimacies have been revealed, fears named. But this subject, race, sinks us into one of those shaming silences where eye contact terrorizes. Our host looks for something in the bottom of his glass. Two women stare into the black sky as if to locate the Big Dipper and point it out to us. Finally, the psychologist seems to gather herself for a challenge, but it is too late. "Oh, I'm sure she'll be just fine," says our hostess, rising from her chair. When she excuses herself to get the cof-fee, the psychologist and two sky gazers offer to help.

With four of us now gone, I am surprised to see the engineer still silently holding his ground. There is a willfulness in his eyes, an inner pride. He knows he has said something awkward, but he is determined not to give a damn. His unwavering eyes intimidate even me. At last the host's head snaps erect. He has an idea. "The hell with coffee," he says. "How about some of the smoothest brandy you've ever tasted?" An idea made exciting by the escape it offers. Gratefully, we follow him back into the house, quickly drink his brandy, and say our good-byes.

An autopsy of this party might read: death induced by an abrupt and lethal injection of the American race issue. An accurate if superficial assessment. Since it has been my fate to live a rather integrated life, I have often witnessed sudden deaths like this. The threat of them, if not the reality, is a part of the texture of integration. In the late 1960s, when I was just out of college, I took a delinquent's delight in playing the engineer's role, and actually developed a small reputation for playing it well. Those were the days of flagellatory white guilt; it was such great fun to pinion some professor or housewife or, best of all, a large group of remorseful whites, with the knowledge of both their racism and their denial of it. The adolescent impulse to sneer at convention, to startle the middle-aged with doubt, could be indulged under the guise of racial indignation. And how could I lose? My victims—earnest liberals for the most part—could no more crawl out from under my accusations than Joseph K. in Kafka's *Trial* could escape the amorphous charges brought against him. At this odd moment in history the world was aligned to facilitate my immaturity.

About a year of this was enough: the guilt that follows most cheap thrills caught up to me, and I put myself in check. But the impulse to do it faded more slowly. It was one of those petty talents that is tied to vanity, and when there were ebbs in my self-esteem the impulse to use it would come alive again. In integrated situations I can still feel the faint itch. But then there are many youthful impulses that still itch, and now, just inside the door of midlife, this one is least precious to me.

In the literature classes I teach I often see how the presence of whites all but seduces some black students into provocation. When we come to a novel by a black writer, say Toni Morrison, the white students can easily discuss the human motivations of the black characters. But, inevitably, a black student, as if by reflex, will begin to set in relief the various racial problems that are the background of these characters' lives. This student's tone will carry a reprimand: the class is afraid to confront the reality of racism. Classes cannot be allowed to die like dinner parties, however. My latest strategy is to thank that student for his or her moral vigilance and then appoint the young man or woman as the class's official racism monitor. But even if I get a laugh—I usually do, but sometimes the student is particularly indignant, and it gets uncomfortable—the strategy never quite works. Our racial division is suddenly drawn in neon. Overcaution spreads like spilled paint. And, in fact, the black student who started it all does become a kind of monitor. The very presence of this student imposes a new accountability on the class.

I think those who provoke this sort of awkwardness are operating out of a black identity that obliges them to badger white people about race almost on principle. Content hardly matters. (For example, it made little sense for the engineer to expect white people to anguish terribly much over his decision to send his daughter to school with *white* children.) Race indeed remains a source of white shame; the goal of these provocations is to put whites, no matter how indirectly, in touch with this collective guilt. In other words, these provocations I speak of are *power* moves, little shows of power that try to freeze the "enemy" in self-consciousness. They gratify and inflate the provocateur. They are the underdog's bite. And whites, far more secure in their power, respond with a self-contained and tolerant silence that is itself a show of power. What greater power than that of nonresponse, the power to let a small enemy sizzle in his own juices, to even feel a little sad at his frustration just as one is also complimented by it. Black anger always, in a way, flatters white power. In America, to know that one is not black is to feel an extra grace, a little boost of impunity.

I think the real trouble between the races in America is that the races are not just races but competing power groups—a fact that is easily minimized, perhaps because it is so obvious. What is not so obvious is that this is true quite apart from the issue of class. Even the well-situated middleclass (or wealthy) black is never completely immune to that peculiar contest of power that his skin color subjects him to. Race is a separate reality in American society, an entity that carries its own potential for power, a mark of fate that class can soften considerably but not eradicate.

The distinction of race has always been used in American life to sanction each race's pursuit of power in relation to the other. The allure of race as a human delineation is the very shallowness of the delineation it makes. Onto this shallowness—mere skin and hair—men can project a false depth, a system of dismal attributions, a series of malevolent or ignoble stereotypes that skin and hair lack the substance to contradict. These dark projections then rationalize the pursuit of power. Your difference from me makes you bad, and your badness justifies, even demands, my pursuit of power over you—the oldest formula for aggression known to man. Whenever much importance is given to race, power is the primary motive.

But the human animal almost never pursues power without first convincing himself that he is *entitled* to it. And this feeling of entitlement has its own precondition: to be entitled one must first believe in one's innocence, at least in the area where one wishes to be entitled. By innocence I mean a feeling of essential goodness in relation to others and, therefore, superiority to others. Our innocence always inflates us and deflates those we seek power over. Once inflated we are entitled; we are in fact licensed to go after the power our innocence tells us we deserve. In this sense, *innocence is power*. Of course, innocence need not be genuine or real in any objective sense, as the Nazis demonstrated not long ago. Its only test is whether or not we can convince ourselves of it.

I think the racial struggle in America has always been primarily a struggle for innocence. White racism from the beginning has been a claim of white innocence and therefore of white entitlement to subjugate blacks. And in the sixties, as went innocence so went power. Blacks used the innocence that grew out of their long subjugation to seize more power, while whites lost some of their innocence and so lost a degree of power over blacks. Both races instinctively understand that to lose innocence is to lose power (in relation to each other). To be innocent someone else must be guilty, a natural law that leads the races to forge their innocence on each other's backs. The inferiority of the black always makes the white man superior; the evil might of whites makes blacks good. This pattern means that both races have a hidden investment in racism and racial disharmony despite their good intentions to the contrary. Power defines their relations, and power requires innocence, which, in turn, requires racism and racial division.

I believe it was his hidden investment that the engineer was protecting when he made his remark—the white "evil" he saw in a white school "depriving" his daughter of her black heritage confirmed his innocence. Only the logic of power explained his emphasis—he bent reality to show that he was once again a victim of the white world and, as a victim, innocent. His determined eyes insisted on this. And the whites, in their silence, no doubt protected their innocence by seeing him as an ungracious troublemaker, his bad behavior underscoring their goodness. What none of us saw was the underlying game of power and innocence we were trapped in, or how much we needed a racial impasse to play that game....

Now the other side of America's racial impasse: How do blacks lay claim to their racial innocence?

The most obvious and unarguable source of black innocence is the victimization that blacks endured for centuries at the hands of a race that insisted on black inferiority as a means to its own innocence and power. Like all victims, what blacks lost in power they gained in innocence—innocence that, in turn, entitled them to pursue power. This was the innocence that fueled the civil rights movement of the sixties and that gave blacks their first real power in American life—victimization metamorphosed into power via innocence. But this formula carries a drawback that I believe is virtually as devastating to blacks today as victimization once was. It is a formula that binds the victim to his victimization by linking his power to his status as a victim. And this, I'm convinced, is the tragedy of black power in America today. It is primarily a victim's power, grounded too deeply in the entitlement derived from past injustice and in the innocence that Western/Christian tradition has always associated with poverty.

Whatever gains this power brings in the short run through political action, it undermines in the long run. Social victims may be collectively entitled, but they are all too often individually demoralized. Since the social victim has been oppressed by society, he comes to feel that his individual life will be improved more by changes in society than by his own initiative. Without realizing it, he makes society rather than himself the agent of change. The power he finds in his victimization may lead him to collective action against society, but it also encourages passivity within the sphere of his personal life.

Not long ago, I saw a television documentary that examined life in Detroit's inner city on the twentieth anniversary of the riots there in which forty-three people were killed. A comparison of the inner city then and now showed a decline in the quality of life. Residents feel less safe, drug trafficking is far worse, crimes by blacks against blacks are more frequent, housing remains substandard, and the teenage pregnancy rate has skyrocketed. Twenty years of decline and demoralization, even as opportunities for blacks to better themselves have increased. This paradox is not peculiar to Detroit. By many measures, the majority of blacks—those not yet in the middle class—are further behind whites today than before the victories of the civil rights movement. But there is a reluctance among blacks to examine this paradox, I think, because it suggests that racial victimization is not our real problem. If conditions have worsened for most of us as racism had receded, then much of the problem must be of our own making. To admit this fully would cause us to lose the innocence we derive from our victimization. And we would jeopardize the entitlement we've always had to challenge society. We are in the odd and self-defeating position in which taking responsibility for bettering ourselves feels like a surrender to white power.

So we have a hidden investment in victimization and poverty. These distressing conditions have been the source of our only real power, and there is an unconscious sort of gravitation toward them, a complaining celebration of them. One sees evidence of this in the near happiness with which certain black leaders recount the horror of Howard Beach, Bensonhurst, and other recent instances of racial tension. As one is saddened by these tragic events, one is also repelled at the way some black leaders—agitated to near hysteria by the scent of victim power inherent in them—leap forward to exploit them as evidence of black innocence and white guilt. It is as though they sense the decline of black victimization as a loss of standing and dive into the middle of these incidents as if they were reservoirs of pure black innocence swollen with potential power.

Seeing for innocence pressures blacks to focus on racism and to neglect the individual initiative that would deliver them from poverty—the only thing that finally delivers *anyone* from poverty. With our eyes on innocence we see racism everywhere and miss opportunity even as we stumble over it. About 70 percent of black students at my university drop out before graduation—a flight from opportunity that racism cannot explain. It is an injustice that whites can see for innocence with more impunity than blacks can. The price whites pay is a certain blindness to themselves. Moreover, for whites seeing for innocence continues to engender the bad faith of a long-disgruntled minority. But the price blacks pay is an ever-escalating poverty that threatens to make the worst off a permanent underclass. Not fair, but real.

Challenging works best for the collective, while bargaining is more the individual's suit. From this point on, the race's advancement will come from the efforts of its individuals. True, some challenging will be necessary for a long time to come. But bargaining is now—today—a way for the black individual to join the larger society, to make a place for himself or herself.

"Innocence is ignorance," Kierkegaard says, and if this is so, the claim of innocence amounts to an insistence on ignorance, a refusal to know. In their assertions of innocence both races carve out very functional areas of ignorance for themselves—territories of blindness that license a misguided pursuit of power. Whites gain superiority by not knowing blacks; blacks gain entitlement by not seeing their own responsibility for bettering themselves. The power each race seeks in relation to the other is grounded in a double-edged ignorance of the self as well as of the other.

The original sin that brought us to an impasse at the dinner party I mentioned occurred centuries ago, when it was first decided to exploit racial difference as a means to power. It was a determinism that flowed karmically from this sin that dropped over us like a net that night. What bothered me most was our helplessness. Even the engineer did not know how to go forward. His challenge hadn't worked, and he'd lost the option to bargain. The marriage of race and power depersonalized us, changed us from eight people to six whites and two blacks. The

easiest thing was to let silence blanket our situation, our impasse.

I think the civil rights movement in its early and middle years offered the best way out of America's racial impasse: in this society, race must not be a source of advantage or disadvantage for anyone. This is fundamentally a *moral* position, one that seeks to breach the corrupt union of race and power with principles of fairness and human equality: if all men are created equal, then racial difference cannot sanction power. The civil rights movement was conceived for no other reason than to redress that corrupt union, and its guiding insight was that only a moral power based on enduring principles of justice, equality, and freedom could offset the lower impulse in man to exploit race as a means to power. Three hundred years of suffering had driven the point home, and in Montgomery, Little Rock, and Selma, racial power was the enemy and moral power the weapon

An important difference between genuine and presumed innocence, I believe, is that the former must be earned through sacrifice while the latter is unearned and only veils the quest for privilege. And there was much sacrifice in the early civil rights movement. The Gandhian principle of nonviolent resistance that gave the movement a spiritual center as well as a method of protest demanded sacrifice, a passive offering of the self in the name of justice. A price was paid in terror and lost life, and from this sacrifice came a hard-earned innocence and a credible moral power.

Nonviolent passive resistance is a bargainer's strategy. It assumes the power that is the object of the protest has the genuine innocence to respond morally, and puts the protesters at the mercy of that innocence. I think this movement won so many concessions precisely because of its belief in the capacity of whites to be moral. It did not so much demand that whites change as offer them relentlessly the opportunity to live by their own morality—to attain a true innocence based on the sacrifice of their racial privilege, rather than a false innocence based on presumed racial superiority. Blacks always bargain with or challenge the larger society; but I believe that in the early civil rights years, these forms of negotiation achieved a degree of integrity and genuineness never seen before or since.

In the mid-sixties all this changed. Suddenly a sharp *racial* consciousness emerged to compete with the moral consciousness that had defined the movement up to that point. Whites were no longer welcome in the movement, and a vocal "black power" minority gained dramatic visibility. Increasingly, the movement began to seek racial as well as moral power, and thus it fell into the fundamental contradiction that plagues it to this day. Moral power precludes racial power by denouncing race as a means to power. Now suddenly the movement itself was using race as a means to power and thereby affirming the very union of race and power it was born to redress. In the end, black power can claim no higher moral standing than white power.

It makes no sense to say this shouldn't have happened. The sacrifices that moral power demands are difficult to sustain, and it was inevitable that blacks would tire of these sacrifices and seek a more earthly power. Nevertheless, a loss of genuine innocence and moral power followed. The movement, splintered by a burst of racial militancy in the late sixties, lost its hold on the American conscience and descended more and more to the level of secular interest-group politics. Bargaining and challenging once again became racial rather than moral negotiations.

You hear it asked, why are there no Martin Luther Kings around today? I think one reason is that there are no black leaders willing to resist the seductions of racial power, or to make the sacrifices moral power requires. King understood that racial power subverts moral power, and he pushed the principles of fairness and equality rather than black power because he believed those principles would bring blacks

their most complete liberation. He sacrificed race for morality, and his innocence was made genuine by that sacrifice. What made King the most powerful and extraordinary black leader of this century was not his race but his morality.

Black power is a challenge. It grants whites no innocence; it denies their moral capacity and then demands that they be moral. No power can long insist on itself without evoking an opposing power. Doesn't an insistence on black power call up white power? (And could this have something to do with what many are now calling a resurgence of white racism?) I believe that what divided the races at the dinner party I attended, and what divides them in the nation, can only be bridged by an adherence to those moral principles that disallow race as a source of power, privilege, status, or entitlement of any kind. In our age, principles like fairness and equality are ill-defined and all but drowned in relativity. But this is the fault of people, not principles. We keep them muddied because they are the greatest threat to our presumed innocence and our selective ignorance. Moral principles, even when somewhat ambiguous, have the power to assign responsibility and therefore to provide us with knowledge. At the dinner party we were afraid of so severe an accountability.

What both black and white Americans fear are the sacrifices and risks that true racial harmony demands. This fear is the measure of our racial chasm. And though fear always seeks a thousand justifications, none is ever good enough, and the problems we run from only remain to haunt us. It would be right to suggest courage as an antidote to fear, but the glory of the word might only intimidate us into more fear. I prefer the word effort—relentless effort, moral effort. What I like most about this word are its connotations of everydayness, earnestness, and practical sacrifice. No matter how badly it might have gone for us that warm summer night, we should have talked. We should have made the effort.

Susan Moller Okin

Introduction: Justice and Gender

S usan Moller Okin, contemporary political theorist, currently teaches at Stanford University. Her first book, *Women in Western Political Thought*, brought her great acclaim, and is now considered a classic text in feminist analysis of the Western tradition.

In her 1989 book *Justice, Gender, and the Familyy*, Okin shows how a series of critical social institutions: the schools, the workplace, marriage, and—most importantly—the family, continue to follow the traditional assumption that workers are men who have wives at home to care for their children. This assumption—besides contradicting contemporary fact—has no basis in nature, as some still argue, but relies on the construction of gender in society. Because gender inequality forms such a pervasive aspect of society, any theory of justice needs to account for it; most contemporary political theory fails to do this. This failure, Okin explains, lies in an understanding of the family as pre-political, not a subject for inquiries on justice. And this, in turn, rests on an ignorance of what eighteenth century political theorists still knew: the family is the first school of justice. Because the family has such a strong influence on moral development, and because just citizens do not simply pop out of nowhere, great care must be given to ensure that a child experiences just relations within his or her own family. This requires that both politicians and theorists begin to address the "private" sphere of the home as an essential aspect of their public work.

Introduction: Justice and Gender
Susan Moller Okin

We as a society pride ourselves on our democratic values. We don't believe people should be constrained by innate differences from being able to achieve desired positions of influence or to improve their well-being; equality of opportunity is our professed aim. The Preamble to our Constitution stresses the importance of justice, as well as the general welfare and the blessings of liberty. The Pledge of Allegiance asserts that our republic preserves "liberty and justice for all."

Yet substantial inequalities between the sexes still exist in our society. In economic terms, full-time working women (after some very recent improvement) earn on average 71 percent of the earnings of full-time working men. One-half of poor and three- fifths of chronically poor households with dependent children are maintained by a single female parent. The poverty rate for elderly women is nearly twice that for elderly men. On the political front, two out of a hundred U.S. senators are women, one out of nine justices seems to be considered sufficient female representation on the Supreme Court, and the number of men chosen in each congressional election far exceeds the number of women elected in the entire history of the country. Underlying and intertwined with all these inequalities is the unequal distribution of the unpaid labor of the family.

An equal sharing between the sexes of family responsibilities, especially child care, is "the great revolution that has not happened." Women, including mothers of young children, are, of course, working outside the household far more than their mothers did. And the small proportion of women who reach high-level positions in politics, business, and the professions command a vastly disproportionate amount of space in the media, compared with the millions of women who work at low-paying, dead-end jobs, the millions who do part-time work with its lack of benefits, and the millions of others who stay home performing for no pay what is frequently not even acknowledged as work. Certainly, the fact that women are doing more paid work does not imply that they are more equal. It is often said that we are living in a postfeminist era. This claim, due in part to the distorted emphasis on women who have "made it," is false, no matter which of its meanings is intended. It is certainly not true that feminism has been vanquished, and equally untrue that it is no longer needed because its aims have been fulfilled. Until there is justice within the family, women will not be able to gain equality in politics, at work, or in any other sphere.

[T]he typical current practices of family life, structured to a large extent by gender, are not just. Both the expectation and the experience of the division of labor by sex make women vulnerable. As I shall show, a cycle of power relations and decisions pervades both family and workplace, each reinforcing the inequalities between the sexes that already exist within the other. Not only women, but children of both sexes, too, are often made vulnerable by gender-structured marriage. One-quarter of children in the United States now live in families with only one parent—in almost 90 percent of cases, the mother. Contrary to common perceptions—in which the situation of never-married mothers looms largest—65 percent of single-parent families are a result of marital separation or divorce. Recent research in a number of states has shown that, in the average case, the standard of living of divorced women and the children who live with them plummets after divorce, whereas the economic situation of divorced men tends to be better than when they were married.

A central source of injustice for women these days is that the law, most noticeably in the event of divorce, treats more or less as equals those whom custom, workplace discrimination, and the still conventional division of labor within the family have made very unequal. Central to

this socially created inequality are two commonly made but inconsistent presumptions: that women are primarily responsible for the rearing of children; and that serious and committed members of the work force (regardless of class) do not have primary responsibility, or even shared responsibility, for the rearing of children. The old assumption of the workplace, still implicit, is that workers have wives at home. It is built not only into the structure and expectations of the workplace but into other crucial social institutions, such as schools, which make no attempt to take account, in their scheduled hours or vacations, of the fact that parents are likely to hold jobs.

Now, of course, many wage workers do not have wives at home. Often, they *are* wives and mothers, or single, separated, or divorced mothers of small children. But neither the family nor the workplace has taken much account of this fact. Employed wives still do by far the greatest proportion of unpaid family work, such as child care and housework. Women are far more likely to take time out of the workplace or to work part-time because of family responsibilities than are their husbands or male partners. And they are much more likely to move because of their husbands' employment needs or opportunities than their own. All these tendencies, which are due to a number of factors, including the sex segregation and discrimination of the workplace itself, tend to be cyclical in their effects: wives advance more slowly than their husbands at work and thus gain less seniority, and the discrepancy between their wages increases over time. Then, because both the power structure of the family and what is regarded as consensual 'rational' family decision making reflect the fact that the husband usually earns more, it will become even less likely as time goes on that the unpaid work of the family will be shared between the spouses. Thus the cycle of inequality is perpetuated. Often hidden from view within a marriage, it is in the increasingly likely event of marital breakdown that the socially constructed inequality of married women is at its most visible.

This is what I mean when I say that gender-structured marriage *makes* women vulnerable. These are not matters of natural necessity, as some people would believe. Surely nothing in our natures dictates that men should not be equal participants in the rearing of their children. Nothing in the nature of work makes it impossible to adjust it to the fact that people are parents as well as workers. That these things have not happened is part of the historically, socially constructed differentiation between the sexes that feminists have come to call gender. We live in a society that has over the years regarded the innate characteristic of sex as one of the clearest legitimizers of different rights and restrictions, both formal and informal. While the legal sanctions that uphold male dominance have begun to be eroded in the past century, and more rapidly in the last twenty years, the heavy weight of tradition, combined with the effects of socialization, still works powerfully to reinforce sex roles that are commonly regarded as of unequal prestige and worth. The sexual division of labor has not only been a fundamental part of the marriage contract, but so deeply influences us in our formative years that feminists of both sexes who try to reject it can find themselves struggling against it with varying degrees of ambivalence. Based on this linchpin, "gender"—by which I mean *the deeply entrenched institutionalization of sexual difference*—still permeates our society.

The Construction of Gender

Due to feminism and feminist theory, gender is coming to be recognized as a social factor of major importance. Indeed, the new meaning of the word reflects the fact that so much of what has traditionally been thought of as sexual difference is now considered by many to be largely socially produced. Feminist scholars from many disciplines and with radically different points of view have contributed to the enterprise of making gender fully visible and comprehensible. At one end of the spectrum are those whose explanations of the subordination of women focus primarily on biological difference as causal in the construction of gender, and at the other end are those who argue that biological difference may not even lie at the core of the social construction that is gender; the views of the vast majority of feminists fall between these extremes. The rejection of biological determinism and the corresponding emphasis on gender as a social construction characterize most current feminist scholarship. Of particular relevance is work in psychology, where scholars have investigated the importance of female primary parenting in the formation of our gendered identities, and in history and anthropology, where emphasis has been placed on the historical and cultural variability of gender. Some feminists have been criticized for developing theories of gender that do not take sufficient account of differences *among* women, especially race, class, religion, and ethnicity. While such critiques should always inform our research and improve our arguments, it would be a mistake to allow them to detract our attention from gender itself as a factor of significance. Many injustices are experienced by women *as women*, whatever the differences among them and whatever other injustices they also suffer from. The past and present gendered nature of the family, and the ideology that surrounds it, affects virtually all women, whether or not they live or ever lived in tradition families. Recognizing this is not to deny or de-emphasize the fact that gender may affect different subgroups of women to a different extent and in different ways.

The potential significance of feminist discoveries and conclusions about gender for issues of social justice cannot be overemphasized. They undermine centuries of argument that started with the notion that not only the distinct differentiation of women and men but the domination of women by men, being natural, was therefore inevitable and not even to be considered in discussions of justice. As I shall make clear in later chapters, despite the fact that such notions cannot stand up to rational scrutiny, they not only still survive but flourish in influential places.

During the same two decades in which feminists have been intensely thinking, researching, analyzing, disagreeing about, and rethinking the subject of gender, our political and legal institutions have been increasingly faced with issues concerning the injustices of gender and their effects. These issues are being decided within a fundamentally patriarchal system, founded in a tradition in which "individuals" were assumed to be male heads of households. Not surprisingly, the system has demonstrated a limited capacity for determining what is just, in many cases involving gender. Sex discrimination, sexual harassment, abortion, pregnancy in the workplace, parental leave, child care, and surrogate mothering have all become major and well-publicized issues of public policy, engaging both courts and legislatures. Issues of family justice, in particular—from child custody and terms of divorce to physical and sexual abuse of wives and children—have become increasingly visible and pressing, and are commanding increasing attention from the police and court systems. There is clearly a major "justice crisis" in contemporary society arising from issues of gender.

Theories of Justice and the Neglect of Gender

During these same two decades, there has been a great resurgence of theories of social justice. Political theory, which had been sparse for a period before the late 1960s except as an important branch of intellectual history, has become a flourishing field, with social justice as its central concern. Yet, remarkably, major contemporary theorists of justice have almost without exception ignored the situation I have just described. They have displayed little interest in or knowledge of the findings of feminism. They have largely bypassed the fact that the society to which their theories are supposed to pertain is heavily and deeply affected by gender, and faces difficult issues of justice stemming from its gendered past and present assumptions. Since theories of justice are centrally concerned with whether, how, and why persons should be treated differently from one another, this neglect seems inexplicable. These theories are *about* which initial or acquired characteristics or positions in society legitimize differential treatment of persons by social institutions, laws, and customs. They are *about* how and whether and to what extent beginnings should affect outcomes. The division of humanity into two sexes seems to provide an obvious subject for such inquiries. But, as we shall see, this does not strike most contemporary theorists of justice, and their theories suffer in both coherence and relevance because of it. This book is about this remarkable case of neglect. It is also an attempt to rectify it, to point the way toward a more fully humanist theory of justice by confronting the question, "How just is gender?"

Why is it that when we turn to contemporary theories of justice, we do not find illuminating and positive contributions to this question? How can theories of justice that are ostensibly about people in general neglect women, gender, and all the inequalities between the sexes? One reason is that most theorists *assume*, though they do not discuss, the traditional, gender-structured family. Another is that they often employ gender-neutral language in a false, hollow way. Let us examine these two points.

The Hidden Gender-Structured Family

In the past, political theorists often used to distinguish clearly between "private" domestic life and the "public" life of politics and the marketplace, claiming explicitly that the two spheres operated in accordance with different principles. They separated out the family from what they deemed the subject matter of politics, and they made closely related, explicit claims about the nature of women and the appropriateness of excluding them from civil and political life. Men, the subjects of the theories, were able to make the transition back and forth from domestic to public life with ease, largely because of the functions performed by women in the family. When we turn to contemporary theories of justice, superficial appearances can easily lead to the impression that they are inclusive of women. In fact, they continue the same "separate spheres" tradition, by ignoring the family, its division of labor, and the related economic dependency and restricted opportunities of most women. The judgment that the family is "nonpolitical" is implicit in the fact that it is simply not discussed in most works of political theory today. In one way or another, as will become clear in the chapters that follow, almost all current theorists continue to assume that the "individual" who is the basic subject of their theories is the male head of a fairly traditional household. Thus the application of principles of justice to relations between the sexes, or within the household, is frequently, though tacitly, ruled out from the start....

What is the basis of my claim that the family, while neglected, is *assumed* by theorists of justice? One obvious indication is that they take mature, independent human beings as the subjects of their theories without any mention of how they got to be that way. We know, of course, that human beings develop and mature only as a result of a great deal of attention and hard work, by far the greater part of it done by women. But when theorists of justice talk about "work," they mean paid work performed in the marketplace. They must be assuming that women, in the gender-structured family, continue to do their unpaid work of nurturing and socializing the young and providing a haven of intimate relations—otherwise there would be no moral subjects for them to theorize about. But these activities apparently take place outside the scope of their theories. Typically, the family

itself is not examined in the light of whatever standard of justice the theorist arrives at.

The continued neglect of the family by theorists of justice flies in the face of a great deal of persuasive feminist argument. Scholars have clearly revealed the interconnections between the gender structure inside and outside the family and the extent to which the personal is political. They have shown that the assignment of primary parenting to women is crucial, both in forming the gendered identities of men and women and in influencing their respective choices and opportunities in life. Yet, so far, the simultaneous assumption and neglect of the family has allowed the impact of these arguments to go unnoticed in major theories of justice.

False Gender Neutrality

Many academics in recent years have become aware of the objectionable nature of using the supposedly generic male forms of nouns and pronouns. As feminist scholars have demonstrated, these words have most often *not* been used, throughout history and the history of philosophy in particular, with the intent to include women. *Man, mankind,* and *he* are going out of style as universal representations, though they have by no means disappeared. But the gender-neutral alternatives that most contemporary theorists employ are often even more misleading than the blatantly sexist use of male terms of reference. For they serve to disguise the real and continuing failure of theorists to confront the fact that the human race consists of persons of two sexes. They are by this means able to ignore the fact that there are *some* socially relevant physical differences between women and men, and the even more important fact that the sexes have had very different histories, very different assigned social roles and "natures," and very different degrees of access to power and opportunity in all human societies up to and including the present.

False gender neutrality is not a new phenomenon. Aristotle, for example, used *anthropos*—"human being"—in discussions of "the human good" that turn out not only to exclude women but to depend on their subordination. Kant even wrote of "all rational beings as such" in making arguments that he did not mean to apply to women. But it was more readily apparent that such arguments or conceptions of the good were not about all of us, but only about male heads of families. For their authors usually gave at some point an explanation, no matter how inadequate, of why what they were saying did not apply to women and of the different characteristics and virtues, rights, and responsibilities they thought women ought to have. Nevertheless, their theories have often been read as though they pertain (or can easily be applied) to all of us. Feminist interpretations of the last fifteen years or so have revealed the falsity of this "add women and stir" method of reading the history of political thought.

The falseness of the gender-neutral language of contemporary political theorists is less readily apparent. Most, though not all, contemporary moral and political philosophers use "men and women," "he or she," "persons," or the increasingly ubiquitous "self." Sometimes they even get their computers to distribute masculine and feminine terms of reference randomly. Since they do not explicitly exclude or differentiate women, as most theorists in the past did, we may be tempted to read their theories as inclusive of all of us. But we cannot. Their merely terminological responses to feminist challenges, in spite of giving a superficial impression of tolerance and inclusiveness, often strain credulity and sometimes result in nonsense. They do this in two ways: by ignoring the irreducible biological differences between the sexes, and/or by ignoring their different assigned social roles and consequent power differentials, and the ideologies that have supported them. Thus gender-neutral terms frequently obscure the fact that so much of the real experience of "persons," so

long as they live in gender-structured societies, *does* in fact depend on what sex they are.

False gender neutrality is by no means confined to the realm of theory. Its harmful effects can be seen in public policies that have directly affected large numbers of women adversely. It was used, for example, in the Supreme Court's 1976 decision that the exclusion of pregnancy-related disabilities from employers' disability insurance plans was "not a gender-based discrimination at all." In a now infamous phrase of its majority opinion, the Court explained that such plans did not discriminate against women because the distinction drawn by such plans was between pregnant women and "non-pregnant *persons*."…

The combined effect of the omission of the family and the falsely gender-neutral language in recent political thought is that most theorists are continuing to ignore the highly political issue of gender. The language they use makes little difference to what they actually do, which is to write about men and about only those women who manage, in spite of the gendered structures and practices of the society in which they live, to adopt patterns of life that have been developed to suit the needs of men. The fact that human beings are born as helpless infants—not as the purportedly autonomous actors who populate political theories—is obscured by the implicit assumption of gendered families, operating outside the range of the theories. To a large extent, contemporary theories of justice, like those of the past, are about men with wives at home.

Gender as an Issue of Justice

For three major reasons, this state of affairs is unacceptable. The first is the obvious point that women must be fully included in any satisfactory theory of justice. The second is that equality of opportunity, not only for women but for children of both sexes, is seriously undermined by the current gender injustices of our society.

And the third reason is that, as has already been suggested, the family—currently the linchpin of the gender structure—must be just if we are to have a just society, since it is within the family that we first come to have that sense of ourselves and our relations with others that is at the root of moral development.

Counting Women In

When we turn to the great tradition of Western political thought with questions about the justice of the treatment of the sexes in mind, it is to little avail. Bold feminists like Mary Astell, Mary Wollstonecraft, William Thompson, Harriet Taylor, and George Bernard Shaw have occasionally challenged the tradition, often using its own premises and arguments to overturn its explicit or implicit justification of the inequality of women. But John Stuart Mill is a rare exception to the rule that those who hold central positions in the tradition almost never question the justice of the subordination of women. This phenomenon is undoubtedly due in part to the fact that Aristotle, whose theory of justice has been so influential, relegated women to a sphere of "household justice"—populated by persons who are not fundamentally equal to the free men who participate in political justice, but inferiors whose natural function is to serve those who are more fully human. The liberal tradition, despite its supposed foundation of individual rights and human equality, is more Aristotelian in this respect than is generally acknowledged. In one way or another, almost all liberal theorists have assumed that the "individual" who is the basic subject of the theories is the male head of a patriarchal household. Thus they have not usually considered applying the principles of justice to women or to relations between the sexes.

When we turn to contemporary theories of justice, however, we expect to find more illuminating and positive contributions to the subject of gender and justice. As the omission of the family and the falseness of their gender-neutral language suggest, however, mainstream contemporary theories of justice do not address the subject any better than those of the past. Theories of justice that apply to only half of us simply won't do; the inclusiveness falsely implied by the current use of gender-neutral terms must become real. Theories of justice must apply to all of us, and to all of human life, instead of *assuming* silently that half of us take care of whole areas of life that are considered outside the scope of social justice. In a just society, the structure and practices of families must afford women the same opportunities as men to develop their capacities, to participate in political power, to influence social choices, and to be economically as well as physically secure.

Unfortunately, much feminist intellectual energy in the 1980s has gone into the claim that "justice" and "rights" are masculinist ways of thinking about morality that feminists should eschew or radically revise, advocating a morality of care. The emphasis is misplaced, I think, for several reasons. First, what is by now a vast literature on the subject shows that the evidence for differences in women's and men's ways of thinking about moral issues is not (at least yet) very clear; neither is the evidence about the source of whatever differences there might be. It may well turn out that any differences can be readily explained in terms of roles, including female primary parenting, that are socially determined and therefore alterable. There is certainly no evidence—nor could there be, in such a gender-structured society—for concluding that women are somehow naturally more inclined toward contextuality and away from universalism in their moral thinking, a false concept that unfortunately reinforces the old stereotypes that justify separate spheres. The capacity of reactionary forces to capitalize on the "different moralities" strain in feminism is particularly evident in Pope John Paul II's recent Apostolic Letter, "On the Dignity of Women," in which he refers to women's special capacity to care for others in arguing for confining them to motherhood or celibacy....

Gender and Equality of Opportunity

The family is a crucial determinant of our opportunities in life, of what we "become." It has frequently been acknowledged by those concerned with real equality of opportunity that the family presents a problem. But though they have discerned a serious problem, these theorists have underestimated it because they have seen only half of it. They have seen that the disparity among families in terms of the physical and emotional environment, motivation, and material advantages they can give their children has a tremendous effect upon children's opportunities in life. We are not born as isolated, equal individuals in our society, but into family situations: some in the social middle, some poor and homeless, and some superaffluent; some to a single or soon-to-be-separated parent, some to parents whose marriage is fraught with conflict, some to parents who will stay together in love and happiness. Any claims that equal opportunity exists are therefore completely unfounded. Decades of neglect of the poor, especially of poor black and Hispanic households, accentuated by the policies of the Reagan years, have brought us farther from the principles of equal opportunity. To come close to them would require, for example, a high and uniform standard of public education and the provision of equal social services—including health care, employment training, job opportunities, drug rehabilitation, and decent housing—for all who need them. In addition to redistributive taxation, only massive reallocations of resources from the military to social services could make these things possible.

But even if all these disparities were somehow eliminated, we would still not attain equal opportunity for all. This is because what has not been recognized as an equal opportunity problem, except in feminist literature and circles, is the disparity *within* the family, the fact that its gender structure is itself a major obstacle to equality of opportunity. This is very important in itself, since one of the factors with most influence on our opportunities in life is the social significance attributed to our sex. The opportunities of girls and women are centrally affected by the structure and practices of family life, particularly by the fact that women are almost invariably primary parents. What nonfeminists who see in the family an obstacle to equal opportunity have *not* seen is that the extent to which a family is gender-structured can make the sex we belong to a relatively insignificant aspect of our identity and our life prospects or an all-pervading one. This is because so much of the social construction of gender takes place in the family, and particularly in the institution of female parenting.

Moreover, especially in recent years, with the increased rates of single motherhood, separation, and divorce, the inequalities between the sexes have *compounded* the first part of the problem. The disparity among families has grown largely because of the impoverishment of many women and children after separation or divorce. The division of labor in the typical family leaves most women far less capable than men of supporting themselves, and this disparity is accentuated by the fact that children of separated or divorced parents usually live with their mothers. The inadequacy—and frequent nonpayment—of child support has become recognized as a major social problem. Thus the inequalities of gender are now directly harming many children of both sexes as well as women themselves. Enhancing equal opportunity for women, important as it is in itself, is also a crucial way of improving the opportunities of many of the most disadvantaged children....

The Family as a School of Justice

One of the things that theorists who have argued that families need not or cannot be just, or who have simply neglected them, have failed to explain is how, within a formative social environment that is *not* founded upon principles of justice, children can learn to develop that sense of justice they will require as citizens of a just society. Rather than being one among many co-equal institutions of a just society, a just family is its essential foundation.

It may seem uncontroversial, even obvious, that families must be just because of the vast influence they have on the moral development of children. But this is clearly not the case. I shall argue that unless the first and most formative example of adult interaction usually experienced by children is one of justice and reciprocity, rather than one of domination and manipulation or of unequal altruism and one-sided self-sacrifice, and unless they themselves are treated with concern and respect, they are likely to be considerably hindered in becoming people who are guided by principles of justice. Moreover, I claim, the sharing of roles by men and women, rather than the division of roles between them, would have a further positive impact because the experience of *being* a physical and psychological nurturer—whether of a child or of another adult—would increase that capacity to identify with and fully comprehend the viewpoints of others that is important to a sense of justice. In a society that minimized gender this would be more likely to be the experience of all of us.

Almost every person in our society starts life in a family of some sort or other. Fewer of these families now fit the usual, though by no means universal, standard of previous generations, that is, wage-working father, homemaking mother, and children. More families these days are headed by a single parent; lesbian and gay parenting is no longer so rare; many children have two wage-working parents, and receive at least some of their early care outside the home. While its forms are varied, the family in which a child is raised, especially in the earliest years, is clearly a crucial place for early moral development and for the formation of our basic attitudes to others. It is, potentially, a place where we can *learn to be just*. It is especially important for the development of a sense of justice that grows from sharing the experiences of others and becoming aware of the points of view of others who are different in some respects from

ourselves, but with whom we clearly have some interests in common....

Contemporary theorists of justice, with few exceptions, have paid little or no attention to the question of moral development—of how we are to *become* just. Most of them seem to think, to adapt slightly Hobbes's notable phrase, that just men spring like mushrooms from the earth. Not surprisingly, then, it is far less often acknowledged in recent than in past theories that the family is important for moral development, and especially for instilling a sense of justice. As I have already noted, many theorists pay no attention at all to either the family or gender. In the rare case that the issue of justice within the family is given any sustained attention, the family is not viewed as a potential school of social justice. In the rare case that a theorist pays any sustained attention to the development of a sense of justice or morality, little if any attention is likely to be paid to the family. Even in the rare event that theorists pay considerable attention to the family *as* the first major locus of moral socialization, they do not refer to the fact that families are almost all still thoroughly gender-structured institutions....

...[T]he family in the specific forms in which it exists in our society is not just...gender-structured marriage and family life as practiced in the United States today are far from meeting most currently accepted standards of social justice.... gender-structured marriage is an institutuion that make women economically and socially vulnerable.... My proposals, centered on the family but also on the workplace and other social institutions that currently reinforce the gender structure, will suggest some ways in which we might make our way toward a society much less structured by gender, and in which any remaining, freely chosen division of labor by sex would not result in injustice. In such a society, in all the spheres of our lives, from the most public to the most personal, we would strive to live in accordance with truly humanist principles of justice.

Peggy McIntosh

White Privilege: Unpacking the Invisible Knapsack

Dr. Peggy McIntosh is the Associate Director of the Wellesley College Center for Research on Women. She is also the founder and co-director of the National S.E.E.D. (Seeking Educational Equity and Diversity) Project on Inclusive Curricula. She has taught at a number of higher education institutions, including Harvard University and the University of Durham. McIntosh is most famous for her articles on systems of unearned privilege, and how they must be changed to create more inclusive and multicultural environments.

In *White Privilege: Unpacking the Invisible Knapsack*, McIntosh examines the various advantages in everyday life that people privileged by their race, gender, or sexual orientation take for granted. She ends by discussing the ways that dominant groups in society can use their "arbitrary awarded power" to construct a more just world. As you read through her lists of "unearned advantages" gained by people based on their skin color or gender, think about your own position in society and your own socialization around race, gender, and sexual orientation.

White Privilege and Male Privilege: A Personal Account of Coming to See Correspondences Through Work in Women's Studies

Peggy McIntosh

Through work to bring materials and perspectives from Women's Studies into the rest of the curriculum, I have often noticed men's unwillingness to grant that they are overprivileged in the curriculum, even though they may grant that women are disadvantaged. Denials that amount to taboos surround the subject of advantages that men gain from women's disadvantages. These denials protect male privilege from being fully recognized, acknowledged, lessened, or ended.

Thinking through unacknowledged male privilege as a phenomenon with a life of its own, I realized that since hierarchies in our society are interlocking, there was most likely a phenomenon of white privilege that was similarly denied and protected, but alive and real in its effects. As a white person, I realized I had been taught about racism as something that puts others at a disadvantage, but had been taught not to see one of its corollary aspects, white privilege, which puts me at an advantage.

I have appreciated commentary on this paper from the Working Papers Committee of the Wellesley College Center for Research on Women, from members of the Dodge seminar, and from many individuals, including Margaret Andersen, Sorel Berman, Joanne Braxton, Johnnella Bulter, Sandra Dickerson, Marnie Evans, Beverly Guy-Sheftall, Sandra Harding, Eleanor Hinton Hoytt, Pauline Houston, Paul Lauter, Joyce Miller, Mary Norris, Gloria Oden, Beverly Smith, and John Walter.

White Privilege and Male Privilege by Peggy McIntosh. Reprinted by permission of The National SEED Project, Wellesley Centers for Women, Wellesley, MA.

I think whites are carefully taught not to recognize white privilege, as males are taught not to recognize male privilege. So I have begun in an untutored way to ask what it is like to have white privilege. This paper is a partial record of my personal observations and not a scholarly analysis. It is based on my daily experiences within my particular circumstances.

I have come to see white privilege as an invisible package of unearned assets that I can count on cashing in each day, but about which I was "meant" to remain oblivious. White privilege is like an invisible weightless knapsack of special provisions, assurances, tools, maps, guides, codebooks, passports, visas, clothes, compass, emergency gear, and blank checks.

Since I have had trouble facing white privilege, and describing its results in my life, I saw parallels here with men's reluctance to acknowledge male privilege. Only rarely will a man go beyond acknowledging that women are disadvantaged to acknowledging that men have unearned advantage, or that unearned privilege has not been good for men's development as human beings, or for society's development, or that privilege systems might ever be challenged and *changed*.

I will review here several types or layers of denial that I see at work protecting, and preventing awareness about, entrenched male privilege. Then I will draw parallels, from my own experience, with the denials that veil the facts of white privilege. Finally, I will list forty-six ordinary and daily ways in which I experience having white privilege, by contrast with my African American colleagues in the same building. This list is not intended to be generalizable. Others can make their own lists from within their own life circumstances.

Writing this paper has been difficult, despite warm receptions for the talks on which it is based.[1] For describing white privilege makes one newly accountable. As we in Women's Studies work reveal male privilege and ask men to give up some of their power, so one who writes about having white privilege must ask, "Having described it, what will I do to lessen or end it?"

The denial of men's overprivileged state takes many forms in discussions of curriculum change work. Some claim that men must be central in the curriculum because they have done most of what is important or distinctive in life or in civilization. Some recognize sexism in the curriculum but deny that it makes male students seem unduly important in life. Others agree that certain *individual* thinkers are male oriented but deny that there is any *systemic* tendency in disciplinary frameworks or epistemology to overempower men as a group. Those men who do grant that male privilege takes institutionalized and embedded forms are still likely to deny that male hegemony has opened doors for them personally. Virtually all men deny that male overreward alone can explain men's centrality in all the inner sanctums of our most powerful institutions. Moreover, those few who will acknowledge that male privilege systems have overempowered them usually end up doubting that we could dismantle these privilege systems. They may say they will work to improve women's status, in the society or in the university, but they can't or won't support the idea of lessening men's. In curricular terms, this is the point at which they say that they regret they cannot use any of the interesting new scholarship on women because the syllabus is full. When the talk turns to giving men less cultural room, even the most thoughtful and fair-minded of the men I know will tend to reflect, or fall back on, conservative assumptions about the inevitability of present gender relations and

---

1. This paper was presented at the Virginia Women's Studies Association conference in Richmond in April, 1986, and the American Educational Research Association conference in Boston in October, 1986, and discussed with two groups of participants in the Dodge seminars for Secondary School Teachers in New York and Boston in the spring of 1987.

distributions of power, calling on precedent or sociobiology and psychobiology to demonstrate that male domination is natural and follows inevitably from evolutionary pressures. Others resort to arguments from "experience" or religion or social responsibility or wishing and dreaming.

After I realized, through faculty development work in Women's Studies, the extent to which men work from a base of unacknowledged privilege, I understood that much of their oppressiveness was unconscious. Then I remembered the frequent charges from women of color that white women whom they encounter are oppressive. I began to understand why we are justly seen as oppressive, even when we don't see ourselves that way. At the very least, obliviousness of one's privileged state can make a person or group irritating to be with. I began to count the ways in which I enjoy unearned skin privilege and have been conditioned into oblivion about its existence, unable to see that it put me "ahead" in any way, or put my people ahead, overrewarding us and yet also paradoxically damaging us, or that it could or should be changed.

My schooling gave me no training in seeing myself as an oppressor, as an unfairly advantaged person, or as a participant in a damaged culture. I was taught to see myself as an individual whose moral state depended on her individual moral will. At school, we were not taught about slavery in any depth; we were not taught to see slaveholders as damaged people. Slaves were seen as the only group at risk of being dehumanized. My schooling followed the pattern which Elizabeth Minnich has pointed out: whites are taught to think of their lives as morally neutral, normative, and average, and also ideal, so that when we work to benefit others, this is seen as work that will allow "them" to be more like "us." I think many of us know how obnoxious this attitude can be in men.

After frustration with men who would not recognize male privilege, I decided to try to work on myself at least by identifying some of the daily effects of white privilege in my life. It is crude work, at this stage, but I will give here a list of special circumstances and conditions I experience that I did not earn but that I have been made to feel are mine by birth, by citizenship, and by virtue of being a conscientious law-abiding "normal" person of goodwill. I have chosen those conditions that I think in my case *attach somewhat more to skin-color privilege* than to class, religion, ethnic status, or geographical location, though these other privileging factors are intricately intertwined. As far as I can see, my Afro-American co-workers, friends, and acquaintances with whom I come into daily or frequent contact in this particular time, place, and line of work cannot count on most of these conditions.

1. I can, if I wish, arrange to be in the company of people of my race most of the time.
2. I can avoid spending time with people whom I was trained to mistrust and who have learned to mistrust my land or me.
3. If I should need to move, I can be pretty sure of renting or purchasing housing in an area which I can afford and in which I would want to live.
4. I can be reasonably sure that my neighbors in such a location will be neutral or pleasant to me.
5. I can go shopping alone most of the time, fairly well assured that I will not be followed or harassed by store detectives.
6. I can turn on the television or open to the front page of the paper and see people of my race widely and positively represented.
7. When I am told about our national heritage or about "civilization," I am shown that people of my color made it what it is.
8. I can be sure that my children will be given curricular materials that testify to the existence of their race.

9. If I want to, I can be pretty sure of finding a publisher for this piece on white privilege.

10. I can be fairly sure of having my voice heard in a group in which I am the only member of my race.

11. I can be casual about whether or not to listen to another woman's voice in a group in which she is the only member of her race.

12. I can go into a book shop and count on finding the writing of my race represented, into a supermarket and find the staple foods that fit with my cultural traditions, into a hairdresser's shop and find someone who can deal with my hair.

13. Whether I use checks, credit cards, or cash. I can count on my skin color not to work against the appearance that I am financially reliable.

14. I could arrange to protect our young children most of the time from people who might not like them.

15. I did not have to educate our children to be aware of systemic racism for their own daily physical protection.

16. I can be pretty sure that my children's teachers and employers will tolerate them if they fit school and workplace norms; my chief worries about them do not concern others' attitudes toward their race.

17. I can talk with my mouth full and not have people put this down to my color.

18. I can swear, or dress in secondhand clothes, or not answer letters, without having people attribute these choices to the bad morals, the poverty, or the illiteracy of my race.

19. I can speak in public to a powerful male group without putting my race on trial.

20. I can do well in a challenging situation without being called a credit to my race.

21. I am never asked to speak for all the people of my racial group.

22. I can remain oblivious to the language and customs of persons of color who constitute the world's majority without feeling in my culture any penalty for such oblivion.

23. I can criticize our government and talk about how much I fear its policies and behavior without being seen as a cultural outsider.

24. I can be reasonably sure that if I ask to talk to "the person in charge," I will be feeing a person of my race.

25. If a traffic cop pulls me over or if the IRS audits my tax return, I can be sure I haven't been singled out because of my race.

26. I can easily buy posters, postcards, picture books, greeting cards, dolls, toys, and children's magazines featuring people of my race.

27. I can go home from most meetings of organizations I belong to feeling somewhat tied in, rather than isolated, out of place, outnumbered, unheard, held at a distance, or feared.

28. I can be pretty sure that an argument with a colleague of another race is more likely to jeopardize her chances for advancement than to jeopardize mine.

29. I can be fairly sure that if I argue for the promotion of a person of another race, or a program centering on race, this is not likely to cost me heavily within my present setting, even if my colleagues disagree with me.

30. If I declare there is a racial issue at hand, or there isn't a racial issue at hand, my race will lend me more credibility for either position than a person of color will have.

31. I can choose to ignore developments in minority writing and minority activist programs, or disparage them, or learn from them, but in any case, I can find ways to be more or less protected from negative consequences of any of these choices.

32. My culture gives me little fear about ignoring the perspectives and powers of people of other races,

33. I am not made acutely aware that my shape, bearing, or body odor will be taken as a reflection on my race.

34. I can worry about racism without being seen as self-interested or self-seeking.

35. I can take a job with an affirmative action employer without having my co-workers on the job suspect that I got it because of my race.

36. If my day, week, or year is going badly, I need not ask of each negative episode or situation whether it has racial overtones.

37. I can be pretty sure of finding people who would be willing to talk with me and advise me about my next steps, professionally.

38. I can think over many options, social, political, imaginative, or professional, without asking whether a person of my race would be accepted or allowed to do what I want to do.

39. I can be late to a meeting without having the lateness reflect on my race.

40. I can choose public accommodation without fearing that people of my race cannot get in or will be mistreated in the places I have chosen.

41. I can be sure that if I need legal or medical help, my race will not work against me.

42. I can arrange my activities so that I will never have to experience feelings of rejection owing to my race.

43. If I have low credibility as a leader, I can be sure that my race is not the problem.

44. I can easily find academic courses and institutions that give attention only to people of my race.

45. I can expect figurative language and imagery in all of the arts to testify to experiences of my race.

46. I can choose blemish cover or bandages in "flesh" color and have them more or less match my skin.

I repeatedly forgot each of the realizations on this list until I wrote it down. For me, white privilege has turned out to be an elusive and fugitive subject. The pressure to avoid it is great, for in facing it I must give up the myth of meritocracy. If these things are true, this is not such a free country; one's life is not what one makes it: many doors open for certain people through no virtues of their own. These perceptions mean also that my moral condition is not what I had been led to believe. The appearance of being a good citizen rather than a troublemaker comes in large part from having all sorts of doors open automatically because of my color.

A further paralysis of nerve comes from literary silence protecting privilege. My clearest memories of finding such analysis are in Lillian Smith's unparalleled *Killers of the Dream* and Margaret Andersen's review of Karen and Mamie Fields' *Lemon Swamp*. Smith, for example, wrote about walking toward black children on the street and knowing they would step into the gutter; Andersen contrasted the pleasure that she, as a white child, took on summer driving trips to the south with Karen Fields' memories of driving in a closed car stocked with all necessities lest, in stopping, her black family should suffer "insult, or worse." Adrienne Rich also recognizes and writes about daily experiences of privilege, but in my observation, white women's writing in this area is far more often on systemic racism than on our daily lives as light-skinned women.[2]

---

2. Andersen, Margaret, "Race and the Social Science Curriculum: A Teaching and Learning Discussion." *Radical Teacher*, November, 1984, pp. 17-20. Smith, Lillian, *Killers of the Dream*, New York: W. W. Norton, 1949.

In unpacking this invisible knapsack of white privilege, I have listed conditions of daily experience that I once took for granted, as neutral, normal, and universally available to everybody, just as I once thought of a male-focused curriculum as the neutral or accurate account that can speak for all. Nor did I think of any of these perquisites as bad for the holder. I now think that we need a more finely differentiated taxonomy of privilege, for some of these varieties are only what one would want for everyone in a just society, and others give license to be ignorant, oblivious, arrogant, and destructive. Before proposing some more finely tuned categorization, I will make some observations about the general effects of these conditions on my life and expectations.

In this potpourri of examples, some privileges make me feel at home in the world. Others allow me to escape penalties or dangers that others suffer. Through some, I escape fear, anxiety, insult, injury, or a sense of not being welcome, not being real. Some keep me from having to hide, to be in disguise, to feel sick or crazy, to negotiate each transaction from the position of being an outsider or, within my group, a person who is suspected of having too close links with a dominant culture. Most keep me from having to be angry.

I see a pattern running through the matrix of white privilege, a pattern of assumptions that were passed on to me as a white person. There was one main piece of cultural turf; it was my own turf, and I was among those who could control the turf. I could measure up to the cultural standards and take advantage of the many options I saw around me to make what the culture would call a success of my life. *My skin color was an asset for any move I was educated to want to make.* I could think of myself as "belonging" in major ways and of making social systems work for me. I could freely disparage, fear, neglect, or be oblivious to anything outside of the dominant cultural forms. Being of the main culture, I could also criticize it fairly freely. My life was reflected back to me frequently enough so that I felt, with regard to my race, if not to my sex, like one of the real people.

Whether through the curriculum or in the newspaper, the television, the economic system, or the general look of people in the streets, I received daily signals and indications that my people counted and that *others either didn't exist or must be trying, not very successfully, to be like people of my race.* I was given cultural permission not to hear voices of people of other races or a tepid cultural tolerance for hearing or acting on such voices. I was also raised not to suffer seriously from anything that darker-skinned people might say about my group, "protected," though perhaps I should more accurately say *prohibited*, through the habits of my economic class and social group, from living in racially mixed groups or being reflective about interactions between people of differing races.

In proportion as my racial group was being made confident, comfortable, and oblivious, other groups were likely being made unconfident, uncomfortable, and alienated. Whiteness protected me from many kinds of hostility, distress, and violence, which I was being subtly trained to-visit in turn upon people of color.

For this reason, the word "privilege" now seems to me misleading. Its connotations are too positive to fit the conditions and behaviors which "privilege systems" produce. We usually think of privilege as being a favored state, whether earned, or conferred by birth or luck. School graduates are reminded they are privileged and urged to use their (enviable) assets well. The word "privilege" carries the connotation of being something everyone must want. Yet some of the conditions I have described here work to systemically overempower certain groups. Such privilege simply *confers dominance*, gives permission to control, because of one's race or sex. The kind of privilege that gives license to some people to be, at best, thoughtless and, at worst, murderous should not continue to be referred to as a desirable attribute. Such "privilege" may be widely desired without being in any way beneficial to the whole society.

Moreover, though "privilege" may confer power, it does not confer moral strength. Those who do not depend on conferred dominance have traits and qualities that may never develop in those who do. Just as Women's Studies courses indicate that women survive their political circumstances to lead lives that hold the human race together, so "underprivileged" people of color who are the world's majority have survived their oppression and lived survivors' lives from which the white global minority can and must learn. In some groups, those dominated have actually become strong through *not* having all of these unearned advantages, and this gives them a great deal to teach the others. Members of so-called privileged groups can seem foolish, ridiculous, infantile, or dangerous by contrast.

I want, then, to distinguish between earned strength and unearned power conferred systemically. Power from unearned privilege can look like strength when it is, in fact, permission to escape or to dominate. But not all of the privileges on my list are inevitably damaging. Some, like the expectation that neighbors will be decent to you, or that your race will not count against you in court, should be the norm in a just society and should be considered as the entitlement of everyone. Others, like the privilege not to listen to less powerful people, distort the humanity of the holders as well as the ignored groups. Still others, like finding one's staple foods everywhere, may be a function of being a member of a numerical majority in the population. Others have to do with not having to labor under pervasive negative stereotyping and mythology.

We might at least start by distinguishing between positive advantages that we can work to spread, to the point where they are not advantages at all but simply part of the normal civic and social fabric, and negative types of advantage that unless rejected will always reinforce our present hierarchies. For example, the positive "privilege" of belonging, the feeling that one belongs within the human circle, as Native Americans say, fosters development and should not be seen as privilege for a few. It is, let us say, an entitlement that none of us should have to earn; ideally it is an *unearned entitlement*. At present, since only a few have it, it is an *unearned advantage* for them. The negative "privilege" that gave me cultural permission not to take darker-skinned-Others seriously can be seen as arbitrarily conferred dominance and should not be desirable for anyone. This paper results from a process of coming to see that some of the power that I originally saw as attendant on being a human being in the United States consisted in *unearned advantage* and *conferred dominance*, as well as other kinds of special circumstance not universally taken for granted.

In writing this paper I have also realized that white identity and status (as well as class identity and status) give me considerable power to choose whether to broach this subject and its trouble. I can pretty well decide whether to disappear and avoid and not listen and escape the dislike I may engender in other people through this essay, or interrupt, answer, interpret, preach, correct, criticize, and control to some extent what goes on in reaction to it. Being white, I am given considerable power to escape many kinds of danger or penalty as well as to choose which risks I want to take.

There is an analogy here, once again, with Women's Studies. Our male colleagues do not have a great deal to lose in supporting Women's Studies, but they do not have a great deal to lose if they oppose it either. They simply have the power to decide whether to commit themselves to more equitable distributions of power. They will probably feel few penalties whatever choice they make; they do not seem, in any obvious short-term sense, the ones at risk, though they and we are all at risk because of the behaviors that have been rewarded in them.

Through Women's Studies work I have met very few men who are truly distressed about systemic, unearned male advantage and conferred dominance. And so one question for me and others like me is whether we will be like them, or whether we will get truly distressed, even outraged, about unearned race advantage and conferred dominance and if so, what we will do to lessen them. In any case, we need to do more work in identifying how they actually affect our daily lives. We need more down-to-earth writing by people about these taboo subjects. We need more understanding of the ways in which white "privilege" damages white people, for these are not the same ways in which it damages the victimized. Skewed white psyches are an inseparable part of the picture, though I do not want to confuse the kinds of damage done to the holders of special assets and to those who suffer the deficits. Many, perhaps most, of our white students in the United States think that racism doesn't affect them because they are not people of color; they do not see "whiteness" as a racial identity. Many men likewise think that Women's Studies does not bear on their own existences because they are not female; they do not see themselves as having gendered identities. Insisting on the universal "effects" of "privilege" systems, then, becomes one of our chief tasks, and being more explicit about the *particular* effects in particular contexts is another. Men need to join us In this work.

In addition, since race and sex are not the only advantaging systems at work, we need to similarly examine the daily experience of having age advantage, or ethnic advantage, or physical ability, or advantage related to nationality, religion, or sexual orientation. Professor Mamie Evans suggested to me that in many ways the list I made also applies directly to heterosexual privilege. This is a still more taboo subject than race privilege: the daily ways in which heterosexual privilege makes some persons comfortable or powerful, providing supports, assets, approvals, and rewards to those who live or expect to live in heterosexual pairs.

Unpacking that content is still more difficult, owing to the deeper imbeddedness of heterosexual advantage and dominance and stricter taboos surrounding these.

But to start such an analysis I would put this observation from my own experience: The fact that I live under the same roof with a man triggers all kinds of societal assumptions about my worth, politics, life, and values and triggers a host of unearned advantages and powers. After recasting many elements from the original list I would add further observations like these:

1. My children do not have to answer questions about why I live with my partner (my husband).
2. I have no difficulty finding neighborhoods where people approve of our household.
3. Our children are given texts and classes that implicitly support our kind of family unit and do not turn them against my choice of domestic partnership.
4. I can travel alone or with my husband without expecting embarrassment or hostility in those who deal with us.
5. Most people I meet will see my marital arrangements as an asset to my life or as a favorable comment on my likability, my competence, or my mental health.
6. I can talk about the social events of a weekend without fearing most listeners' reactions.
7. I will feel welcomed and "normal" in the usual walks of public life, institutional and social.
8. In many contexts, I am seen as "all right" in daily work on women because I do not live chiefly with women.

Difficulties and dangers surrounding the task of finding parallels are many. Since racism, sexism, and heterosexism are not the same, the advantages associated with them should not be seen as the same. In addition, it is hard to isolate aspects of unearned advantage that derive chiefly from social class, economic class, race, religion, region, sex, or ethnic identity. The oppressions are both distinct and interlocking, as the Combahee River Collective statement of 1977 continues to remind us eloquently.[3]

One factor seems clear about all of the interlocking oppressions. They take both active forms that we can see and embedded forms that members of the dominant group are taught not to see. In my class and place, I did not see myself as racist because I was taught to recognize racism only in individual acts of meanness by members of my group, never in invisible systems conferring racial dominance on my group from birth. Likewise, we are taught to think that sexism or heterosexism is carried on only through intentional, individual acts of discrimination, meanness, or cruelty, rather than in invisible systems conferring unsought dominance on certain groups. Disapproving of the systems won't be enough to change them. I was taught to think that racism could end if white individuals changed their attitudes; many men think sexism can be ended by individual changes in daily behavior toward women. But a man's sex provides advantage for him whether or not he approves of the way in which dominance has been conferred on his group. A "white" skin in the United States opens many doors for whites whether or not we approve of the way dominance has been conferred on us. Individual acts can palliate, but cannot end, these problems. To redesign social systems, we need first to acknowledge their colossal unseen dimensions. The silences and denials surrounding privilege are the key political tool here. They keep the thinking about equality or equity incomplete, protecting unearned advantage and conferred dominance by making these taboo subjects. Most talk by whites about equal opportunity seems to me now to be about equal opportunity to try to get into a position of dominance while denying that *systems* of dominance exist.

Obliviousness about white advantage, like obliviousness about male advantage, is kept strongly inculturated in the United States so as to maintain the myth of meritocracy, the myth that democratic choice is equally available to all. Keeping most people unaware that freedom of confident action is there for just a small number of people props up those in power and serves to keep power in the hands of the same groups that have most of it already. Though systemic change takes many, decades, there are pressing questions for me and I imagine for some others like me if we raise our daily consciousness on the perquisites of being light-skinned. What will we do with such knowledge? As we know from watching men, it is an open question whether we will choose to use unearned advantage to weaken invisible privilege systems and whether we will use any, of our arbitrarily awarded power to try to reconstruct power systems on a broader base.

---

3. "A Black Feminist Statement," The Combahee River Collective, pp. 13–22 in G. Hull, P. Scott, B. Smith, Eds., All the Women Are White, *All the Blacks Are Men, But Some of Us Are Brave: Black Women's Studies*, Old Westbury, NY: The Feminist Press, 1982.

bell hooks
Representing the Poor

b ell hooks, born Gloria Jean Watkins in 1952, is a professor at the City University of New York and a well-known writer, poet, and feminist scholar. Early in her career, she adopted and lowercased her *nom de plume* from that of her courageous great-grandmother, Bell Hooks. She is the author of numerous books and essays, including *Teaching to Transgress* and *Outlaw Culture*, from which the essay which follows is taken. In it, hooks complicates our understanding of social class differences by comparing the way "the poor" are represented by U.S. society with her own personal understanding of poverty based on her life in small-town Kentucky. She urges us to change the way we "see" poor people at the same time as we attempt to eradicate poverty, to understand that individuals can live lives of dignity and integrity in the midst of poverty.

Representing the Poor

bell hooks

Cultural critics rarely talk about the poor. Most of us use words such as "underclass" or "economically disenfranchised" when we speak about being poor. Poverty has not become one of the new hot topics of radical discourse. When contemporary Left intellectuals talk about capitalism, few if any attempts are made to relate that discourse to the reality of being poor in America. In his collection of *essays Prophetic Thought in Postmodern Times*, black philosopher Cornel West includes a piece entitled "The Black Underclass and Black Philosophers" wherein he suggests that black intellectuals within the "professional-managerial class in U.S. advanced capitalist society" must "engage in a kind of critical self-inventory, a historical situating and positioning of ourselves as persons who reflect on the situation of those more disadvantaged than us even though we may have relatives and friends in the black underclass." West does not speak of poverty or being poor in his essay. And I can remember once in conversation with him referring to my having come from a "poor" background; he corrected me and stated that my family was "working class." I told him that technically we *were* working class, because my father worked as a janitor at the post office, however the fact that there were seven children in our family meant that we often faced economic hardship in ways that made us children at least think of ourselves as p oor. Indeed, in the segregated world of our small Kentucky town, we were all raised to think in terms of the haves and the have-nots, rather than in terms of class. We acknowledged the existence of four groups: the poor, who were destitute; the working folks, who were poor because they made just enough to make ends meet; those who worked and had extra money; and the rich. Even though our family was among the working folks, the economic struggle to make ends meet for such a large family always gave us a sense that there was not enough money to take care of the basics. In our house, water was a luxury and using too much could be a cause for punishment. We never talked about being poor. As children we knew we were not supposed to see ourselves as poor but we felt poor.

I began to *see* myself as poor when I went away to college. I never had any money. When I told my parents that I had scholarships and loans to attend Stanford University, they wanted to know how I would pay for getting there, for buying books, for emergencies. We were not poor, but there was no money for what was perceived to be an individualistic indulgent desire; there were cheaper colleges closer to family. When I went to college and could not afford to come home during breaks, I frequently spent my holidays with the black women who cleaned in the dormitories. T heir world was my world. They, more than other folks at Stanford, knew where I was coming from. They supported and affirmed my efforts to be educated, to move past and beyond the world they lived in, the world I was coming from.

To this day, even though I am a well-paid member of what West calls the academic "professional-managerial class," in everyday life, outside the classroom, I rarely think of myself in relation to class. I mainly think about the world in terms of who has money to spend and who does not. Like many technically middle-class folks who are connected in economic responsibility to kinship structures where they provide varying material support for others, the issue is always one of money. Many middle-class black folks have no money because they regularly distribute their earnings among a larger kinship group where folks are poor and destitute, where elder parents and relatives who once were working class have retired and fallen into poverty.

Poverty was no disgrace in our household. We were socialized early on, by grandparents and parents, to assume that nobody's value could be measured by material standards. Value was connected to integrity, to being honest and hardworking. One could be hardworking and still be poor. My mother's mother Baba, who did not read or write, taught us—against the wishes of our parents—that it was better to be poor than to compromise one's dignity, that it was better to be poor than to allow another person to assert power over you in ways that were dehumanizing or cruel.

I went to college believing there was no connection between poverty and personal integrity. Entering a world of class privilege which compelled me to think critically about my economic background, I was shocked by representations of the poor learned in classrooms, as well as by the comments of professors and peers that painted an entirely different picture. They were almost always portrayed the poor as shiftless, mindless, lazy, dishonest, and unworthy. Students in the dormitory were quick to assume that anything missing had been taken by the black and Filipina women who worked there. Although I went through many periods of shame about my economic background, even before I educated myself for critical consciousness about class by reading and studying Marx, Gramsci, Memmi, and the like, I contested stereotypical negative representations of poverty. I was especially disturbed by the assumption that the poor were without values. Indeed one crucial value that I had learned from Baba, my grandmother, and other family members was not to believe that "schooling made you smart." One could have degrees and still not be intelligent or honest. I had been taught in a culture of poverty to be intelligent, honest, to work hard, and always to be a person of my word. I had been taught to stand up for what I believed was right, to be brave and courageous. These lessons were the foundation that made it possible for me to succeed, to become the writer I always wanted to be, and to make a living in my job as an academic. They were taught to me by the poor, the disenfranchised, the underclass.

Those lessons were reinforced by liberatory religious traditions that affirmed identification with the poor. Taught to believe that poverty could be the breeding ground of moral integrity, of a recognition of the significance of communion, of sharing resources with others in the black church, I was prepared to embrace the teachings of liberatory theology, which emphasized solidarity with the poor. That solidarity was meant to be expressed not simply through charity, the sharing of privilege, but in the assertion of one's power to change the world so that the poor would have their needs met, would have access to resources, would have justice and beauty in their lives.

Contemporary popular culture in the United States rarely represents the poor in ways that display integrity and dignity. Instead, the poor are portrayed through negative stereotypes. When they are lazy and dishonest, they are consumed with longing to be rich, a longing so intense that it renders them dysfunctional. Willing to commit all manner of dehumanizing and brutal acts in the name of material gain, the poor are portrayed as seeing themselves as always and only worthless. Worth is gained only by means of material success.

Television shows and films bring the message home that no one can truly feel good about themselves if they are poor. In television sitcoms the working poor are shown to have a healthy measure of self-contempt; they dish it out to one another with a wit and humor that we can all enjoy, irrespective of our class. Yet it is clear that humor masks the longing to change their lot, the desire to "move on up" expressed in the theme song of the sitcom *The Jeffersons*. Films which portray the rags-to-riches tale continue to have major box-office appeal. Most contemporary films portraying black folks—*Harlem Nights*, *Boomerang*, *Menace II Society*, to name only a few—have as their primary theme the lust of the poor for material plenty and their willingness to do anything to

satisfy that lust. *Pretty Woman* is a perfect example of a film that made huge sums of money portraying the poor in this light. Consumed and enjoyed by audiences of all races and classes, it highlights the drama of the benevolent, ruling-class person (in this case a white man, played by Richard Gere) willingly sharing his resources with a poor white prostitute (played by Julia Roberts). Indeed, many films and television shows portray the ruling class as generous, eager to share, as unattached to their wealth in their interactions with folks who are not materially privileged. These images contrast with the opportunistic avaricious longings of the poor.

Socialized by film and television to identify with the attitudes and values of privileged classes in this society, many people who are poor, or a few paychecks away from poverty, internalize fear and contempt for those who are poor. When materially deprived teenagers kill for tennis shoes or jackets they are not doing so just because they like these items so much. They also hope to escape the stigma of their class by appearing to have the trappings of more privileged classes. Poverty, in their minds and in our society as a whole, is seen as synonymous with depravity, lack, and worthlessness. No one wants to be identified as poor. Teaching literature by African American women writers at a major urban state university to predominantly black students from poor and working-class families, I was bombarded by their questioning as to why the poor black women who were abused in families in the novels we read did not "just leave." It was amazing to me that these students, many of whom were from materially disadvantaged backgrounds, had no realistic sense about the economics of housing or jobs in this society. When I asked that we identify our class backgrounds, only one student—a young single parent—was willing to identify herself as poor. We talked later about the reality that although she was not the only poor person in the class, no one else wanted to identify with being poor for fear this stigma would mark them, shame them in ways that would go beyond our class. Fear of shame-based humiliation is a primary factor leading no one to want to identify themselves as poor. I talked with young black women receiving state aid, who have not worked in years, about the issue of representation. They all agree that they do not want to be identified as poor. In their apartments they have the material possessions that indicate success (a VCR, a color television), even if it means that they do without necessities and plunge into debt to buy these items. Their self-esteem is linked to not being seen as poor.

If to be poor in this society is everywhere represented in the language we use to talk about the poor, in the mass media, as synonymous with being nothing, then it is understandable that the poor learn to be nihilistic. Society is telling them that poverty and nihilism are one and the same. If they cannot escape poverty, then they have no choice but to drown in the image of a life that is valueless. When intellectuals, journalists, or politicians speak about nihilism and the despair of the underclass, they do not link those states to representations of poverty in the mass media. And rarely do they suggest by their rhetoric that one can lead a meaningful, contented, and fulfilled life if one *is* poor. No one talks about our individual and collective accountability to the poor, a responsibility that begins with the politics of representation.

When white female anthropologist Carol Stack looked critically at the lives of black poor people more than twenty years ago and wrote her book *The Culture of Poverty*, she found a value system among them which emphasized the sharing of resources. That value system has long been eroded in most communities by an ethic of liberal individualism, which affirms that it is morally acceptable not to share. The mass media has been the primary teacher bringing into our lives and our homes the logic of liberal individualism, the idea that you make it by the privatized hoarding of resources, not by sharing them. Of course, liberal individualism works best for the privileged classes. But it has worsened the lot of the poor who once depended on an ethic of communalism to provide affirmation, aid, and support.

To change the devastating impact of poverty on the lives of masses of folks in our society we must change the way resources and wealth are distributed. But we must also change the way the poor are represented. Since many folks will be poor for a long time before those changes are put in place that address their economic needs, it is crucial to construct habits of seeing and being that restore an oppositional value system affirming that one can live a life of dignity and integrity in the midst of poverty. It is precisely this dignity Jonathan Freedman seeks to convey in his book *From Cradle to Grave: The Human Face of Poverty in America*, even though he does not critique capitalism or call for major changes in the distribution of wealth and resources. Yet any efforts to change the face of poverty in the United States must link a shift in representation to a demand for the redistribution of wealth and resources.

Progressive intellectuals from privileged classes who are themselves obsessed with gaining material wealth are uncomfortable with the insistence that one can be poor, yet lead a rich and meaningful life. They fear that any suggestion that poverty is acceptable may lead those who have to feel no accountability towards those who have not, even though it is unclear how they reconcile their pursuit with concern for and accountability towards the poor. Their conservative counterparts, who did much to put in place a system of representation that dehumanized the poor, fear that if poverty is seen as having no relation to value, the poor will not passively assume their role as exploited workers. That fear is masked by their insistence that the poor will not seek to work if poverty is deemed acceptable, and that the rest of us will have to support them. (Note the embedded assumption that to be poor means that one is not hardworking.) Of course, there are many more poor women and men refusing menial labor in low-paid jobs than ever before. This refusal is not rooted in laziness but in the assumption that it is not worth it to work a job where one is systematically dehumanized or exploited only to remain poor. Despite these individuals, the vast majority of poor people in our society want to work, even when jobs do not mean that they leave the ranks of the poor.

Witnessing that individuals can be poor and lead meaningful lives, I understand intimately the damage that has been done to the poor by a dehumanizing system of representation. I see the difference in self-esteem between my grandparents' and parents' generations and that of my siblings, relatives, friends and acquaintances who are poor, who suffer from a deep-seated, crippling lack of self-esteem. Ironically, despite the presence of more opportunity than that available to an older generation, low self-esteem makes it impossible for this younger generation to move forward even as it also makes their lives psychically unbearable. That psychic pain is most often relieved by some form of substance abuse. But to change the face of poverty so that it becomes, once again, a site for the formation of values, of dignity and integrity, as any other class positionality in this society, we would need to intervene in existing systems of representation.

Linking this progressive change to radical/revolutionary political movements (such as eco-feminism, for example) that urge all of us to live simply could also establish a point of connection and constructive interaction. The poor have many resources and skills for living. Those folks who are interested in sharing individual plenty as well as working politically for redistribution of wealth can work in conjunction with individuals who are materially disad-

vantaged to achieve this end. Material plenty is only one resource. Literacy skills are another. It would be exciting to see unemployed folks who lack reading and writing skills have available to them community-based literacy programs. Progressive literacy programs connected to education for critical consciousness could use popular movies as a base to begin learning and discussion. Theaters all across the United States that are not used in the day could be sites for this kind of program where college students and professors could share skills. Since many individuals who are poor, disadvantaged or destitute are already literate, reading groups could be formed to educate for critical consciousness, to help folks rethink how they can organize life both to live well in poverty and to move out of such circumstances. Many of the young women I encounter—black and white—who are poor and receiving state aid (and some of whom are students or would-be students) are intelligent, critical thinkers struggling to transform their circumstances. They are eager to work with folks who can offer guidance, know-how, concrete strategies. Freedman concludes his book with the reminder that

> it takes money, organization, and laws to maintain a social structure but none of it works if there are not opportunities for people to meet and help each other along the way. Social responsibility comes down to something simple—the ability to respond.

Constructively changing ways the poor are represented in every aspect of life is one progressive intervention that can challenge everyone to look at the face of poverty and not turn away.

Robert Reich

Secession of the Successful

R obert Reich is currently a professor at Brandeis University and a National Fellow at the Center for National Policy, having served as Secretary of Labor during President Clinton's first administration. He is the author of several books and over 200 articles and essays, most focused on the domestic and global economy. As Secretary of Labor and in his current position, Reich's specific focus has been on issues of job quality and income inequality, issues that link with those posed in the essay reprinted in this volume. In this 1991 article from the *New York Times Magazine*, Reich looks at class inequalities, not from the perspective of low-income communities like the bell hooks essay immediately preceding it, but from the perspective of what Reich calls "the fortunate fifth," those in the top 20% in terms of income earnings. What he chronicles is the increasing separation or "secession" of the most successful Americans from the social institutions and geographic neighborhoods that house the bulk of the citizenry. The challenges Reich's essay pose, for community, democracy, and service, must be faced by anyone concerned about the growing disparity between classes in the current U.S. political economy.

Secession of the Successful
Robert Reich

The noted economist argues that America's elite has retreated into a private utopia— and forsaken its stake in the national good.

The idea of "community" has always held a special attraction for Americans. In a 1984 speech, President Ronald Reagan celebrated America's "bedrock"—"its communities where neighbors help one another, where families bring up kids together, where American values are born." Gov. Mario M. Cuomo of New York, with a very different political leaning, has been almost as lyrical. "Community...is the reality on which our national life has been founded," he said in 1987.

There is only one problem with this picture. Most Americans no longer live in traditional communities. They live in suburban subdivisions bordered by highways and sprinkled with shopping malls, or in tony condominiums and residential clusters, or in ramshackle apartment buildings and housing projects. Most of them commute to work and socialize on some basis other than geographic proximity. And most people pick up and move to a different neighborhood every five years or so.

But Americans generally have one thing in common with their neighbors: they have similar incomes. And that simple fact lies at the heart of the new community. This means that their educational backgrounds are likely to be similar, that they pay roughly the same in taxes, and that they indulge in the same consumer impulses. "Tell me someone's ZIP code," the founder of a direct-mail company once bragged, "and I can predict what they eat, drink, drive—even think."

Americans who own their homes usually share one political cause with their neighbors: a near obsessive concern with maintaining or upgrading property values. And this common interest is responsible for much of what has brought neighbors together in recent years. Complete strangers, although they may live on the same street or in the same condominium complex, suddenly feel intense solidarity when it is rumored that low-income housing will be constructed in their midst or that a poorer school district will be consolidated with their own.

The renewed emphasis on "community" in American life has justified and legitimized these economic enclaves. If generosity and solidarity end at the border of similarly valued properties, then the most fortunate can be virtuous citizens at little cost. Since most people in one neighborhood or town are equally well off, there is no cause for a guilty conscience. If inhabitants of another area are poorer, let them look to one another. Why should we pay for *their* schools?

So the argument goes, without acknowledging that the critical assumption has already been made: "we" and "they" belong to fundamentally different communities. Through such reasoning, it has become possible to maintain a self-image of generosity toward, and solidarity with, one's "community" without bearing any responsibility to "them"—the other "community."

America's high earners—the fortunate top fifth—thus feel increasingly justified in paying only what is necessary to insure that everyone in their community is sufficiently well educated and has access to the public services they need to succeed.

Last year, the top fifth of working Americans took home more money than the other four-fifths put together—the highest portion in post-war history. These high earners will relinquish somewhat more of their income to the Federal Government this year than in 1990 as a result of last fall's tax changes, although considerably less than in the late 1970's, when the tax code was more progressive. But that continuing debate over whether the wealthy are paying their fair share of taxes obscures a larger issue, with more profound implications for America: the fortunate fifth is quietly seceding from the rest of the nation.

This is occurring gradually, without much awareness by members of the top group—or, for that matter, by anyone else. And the Government is speeding this process as Washington shifts responsibility for many public services to state and local governments.

The secession is taking several forms. In many cities and towns, the wealthy have in effect withdrawn their dollars from the support of public spaces and institutions shared by all and dedicated the savings to their own private services. As public parks and playgrounds deteriorate, there is a proliferation of private health clubs, golf clubs, tennis clubs, skating clubs and every other type of recreational association in which costs are shared among members. Condominiums and the omnipresent residential communities dun their members to undertake work that financially strapped local governments can no longer afford to do well—maintaining roads, mending sidewalks, pruning trees, repairing street lights, cleaning swimming pools, paying for lifeguards and, notably, hiring security guards to protect life and property. (The number of private security guards in the United States now exceeds the number of public police officers.)

Of course, wealthier Americans have been withdrawing into their own neighborhoods and clubs for generations. But the new secession is more dramatic because the highest earners now inhabit a different economy from other Americans. The new elite is linked by jet, modem, fax, satellite and fiber-optic cable to the great commercial and recreational centers of the world, but it is not particularly connected to the rest of the nation.

That is because the work this group does is becoming less tied to the activities of other Americans. Most of their jobs consist of analyzing and manipulating symbols—words, numbers or visual images. Among the most prominent of the "symbolic analysts" are management consultants, lawyers, software and design engineers, research scientists, corporate executives, financial advisers, strategic planners, advertising executives, television and movie producers, and other workers whose job titles include terms like "strategy," "planning," "consultant," "policy," "resources" or "engineer."

These workers typically spend long hours in meetings or on the telephone and even longer hours in planes or hotels—advising, making presentations, giving briefings and making deals. Periodically, they issue reports, plans, designs, drafts, briefs, blueprints, analyses, memorandums, layouts, renderings, scripts or projections. In contrast with people whose jobs tend to be tedious and repetitive, symbolic analysts find their work varied and intellectually challenging. In fact, the work is often enjoyable.

These symbolic analysts are in ever greater demand in a world market that places an increasing value on identifying and solving problems. Requests for their software designs, financial advice or engineering blueprints come from all parts of the globe. This largely explains why most (but by no means all) symbolic analysts have become wealthier, even as the ever-growing world-wide supply of unskilled labor continues to depress the wages of other Americans.

Successful Americans have not completely disengaged themselves from the lives of their less fortunate compatriots. Some devote substantial resources and energies to helping the rest of society, not through their tax payments, but through voluntary efforts. "Generosity is a reflection of what one does with his or her resources—and not what he or she advocates the government do with everyone's money," Ronald Reagan said in 1984.

The argument is fair enough. Government is not the only device for redistributing wealth. In his speech accepting the Presidential nomination at the Republican National Convention in 1988, George Bush said that the real magnanimity of America was to be found in a "brilliant diversity" of private charities, "spread like stars, like a thousand points of light in a broad and peaceful sky."

No nation congratulates itself more enthusiastically on its charitable acts than America; none engages in a greater number of charity balls, bake sales, benefit auctions and border-to-border hand holdings for good causes. Much of this is sincerely motivated and admirable.

But close examination reveals that many of these acts of benevolence do not help the needy. Particularly suspect is the private giving of those in the top income-tax bracket. Studies have revealed that their largess does not flow mainly to social services for the poor—to better schools, health clinics or recreational centers. Instead, most voluntary contributions of wealthy Americans go to the places and institutions that entertain, inspire, cure or educate wealthy Americans—art museums, opera houses, theaters, orchestras, ballet companies, private hospitals and elite universities.

And even these charitable contributions are relatively skimpy. Last year, American households with incomes of less than $10,000 gave an average of 5.5 percent of their earnings to charity or to a religious organization; those making more than $100,000 a year gave only 2.9 percent. After the 1986 tax-code overhaul reduced the benefits of charitable giving, the very rich became even stingier. According to Internal Revenue Service data, taxpayers earning $500,000 or more slashed their average donations to $16,062 in 1988 from $47,432 in 1980.

Corporate philanthropy is following the same general pattern. In recent years, the largest American corporations have been sounding the alarm about the nation's fast deteriorating primary and secondary schools. Few are more eloquent and impassioned about the need for better schools than American executives. "How well we educate all of our children will determine our competitiveness globally, and our economic health domestically, and our communities' character and vitality," said a report of The Business Roundtable, a New York-based association of top executives.

Accordingly, there are numerous "partnerships" between corporations and public schools: scholarships for poor children qualified to attend college, and programs in which businesses adopt individual schools by making conspicuous donations of computers, books and, on occasion, even money. That such activities are loudly touted by corporate public relations staffs should not detract from the good they do.

Despite the hoopla, business donations to education and charitable causes actually tapered off markedly in the 1980's, even as the economy boomed. In the 1970's, corporate giving to education jumped an average of 15 percent a year. In 1990, however, giving was only 5 percent over that in 1989; in 1989 it was 3 percent over 1988. Moreover, most of this money goes to colleges and universities—in particular, to the alma maters of symbolic analysts, who expect their children and grandchildren to follow in their footsteps. Only 1.5 percent of corporate giving in the late 1980's was to public primary and secondary schools.

Notably, these contributions have been smaller than the amounts corporations are receiving from states and communities in the form of subsidies or tax breaks. Companies are quietly procuring such deals by threatening to move their operations—and jobs—to places around the world with a more congenial tax climate. The paradoxical result has been even less corporate revenue to spend on schools and other community services than before. The executives of General Motors, for example, who have been among the loudest to proclaim the need for better schools, have also been among the most relentless in pursuing local tax abatements and in challenging their tax assessment. G.M.'s successful efforts to reduce its taxes in North Tarrytown, N.Y., where the company has had a factory since 1914, cut local revenues by $1 million in 1990, part of a larger short-fall that forced the town to lay off scores of teachers.

The secession of the fortunate fifth has been most apparent in how and where they have chosen to work and live. In effect, most of America's large urban centers have splintered into two separate cities. Once is composed of those whose symbolic and analytic services are linked to the world economy. The other consists of local service workers—custodians, security guards, taxi drivers, clerical aides, parking attendants, sales people, restaurant employees—whose jobs are dependent on the symbolic analysts. Few blue-collar manufacturing workers remain in American cities. Between 1953 and 1984, for example, New York City lost about 600,000 factory jobs; in the same interval, it added about 700,000 jobs for symbolic analysts and service workers.

The separation of symbolic analyses from local service workers within cities has been reinforced in several ways. Most large cities now possess two school systems—a private one for the children of the top-earning group and a public one for the children of service workers, the remaining blue-collar workers and the unemployed. Symbolic analysts spend considerable time and energy insuring that their children gain entrance to good private schools, and then small fortunes keeping them there—dollars that under a more progressive tax code might finance better public education.

People with high incomes live, shop and work within areas of cities that, if not beautiful, are at least aesthetically tolerable and reasonably safe; precincts not meeting these minimum standards of charm and security have been left to the less fortunate.

Here again, symbolic analysts have pooled their resources to the exclusive benefit of themselves. Public funds have been spent in earnest on downtown "revitalization" projects, entailing the construction of clusters of post-modern office buildings (complete with fiber-optic cables, private branch exchanges, satellite dishes and other communications equipment linking them to the rest of the world), multilevel parking garages, hotels with glass-enclosed atriums, upscale shopping plazas and galleries, theaters, convention centers and luxury condominiums.

Ideally, these complexes are entirely self-contained, with air-conditioned walkways linking residences, businesses and recreational space. The lucky resident is able to shop, work and attend the theater without risking direct contact with the outside world—that is, the other city.

Carrying the principle a step further, several cities have begun authorizing property owners in certain affluent districts to assess a surtax on local residents and businesses for amenities unavailable to other urban residents, services like extra garbage collections, street cleaning and security. One such New York district, between 38th and 48th Streets and Second and Fifth Avenues, raised $4.7 million from its residents in 1989, of which $1 million underwrote a private force of uniformed guards and plainclothes investigators. The new community of people with like incomes and with the power to tax and enforce the law is thus becoming a separate city within the city.

When not living in urban enclaves, symbolic analysts are increasingly congregating in suburbs and exurbs where corporate headquarters have been relocated, research parks have been created, and where bucolic universities have spawned entrepreneurial ventures. Among the most desirable of such locations are Princeton, N.J.; northern Westchester and Putnam Counties in New York; Palo Alto, Calif.; Austin, Tex.; Bethesda, Md., and Raleigh-Durham, N.C.

Engineers and strategists of American auto companies, for example, do not live in Flint or Saginaw, Mich., where the blue-collar workers reside; they cluster in their own towns of Troy, Warren and Auburn Hills. Likewise, the vast majority of the financial specialists, lawyers and executives working for the insurance companies of Hartford would never consider living there; after all, Hartford is the nation's fourth-poorest city. Instead, they flock to Windsor, Middlebury, West Hartford and other towns that are among the wealthiest in the country.

This trend, too, has been growing for decades. But technology has accelerated it. Today's symbolic analysts linked directly to the

rest of the globe can choose to live and work in the most pastoral of settings.

The secession has been encouraged by the Federal Government. For the last decade, Washington has in effect shifted responsibility for many public services to local governments. At their peak, Federal grants made up 25 percent of state and local spending in the late 1970's. Today, the Federal share has dwindled to 17 percent. Direct aid to local governments, in the form of programs introduced in the Johnson and Nixon Administrations, has been the hardest hit by budget cuts. In the 1980's, Federal dollars for clean water, job training and transfers, low-income housing, sewage treatment and garbage disposal shrank by some $50 billion a year, and Washington's share of spending on local transit declined by 50 percent. (The Bush Administration has proposed that states and localities take on even more of the costs of building and maintaining roads, and wants to cut Federal aid for mass transit.) In 1990, New York City received only 9.6 percent of all its revenue from the Federal Government, compared with 16 percent in 1981.

States have quickly transferred many of these new expenses to fiscally strapped cities and towns, with a result that by the start of the 1990's localities were bearing more than half of the cost of water and sewage, roads, parks, welfare and public schools. In New York State, the local communities' share has risen to about 75 percent of these costs.

Cities and towns with affluent inhabitants can bear these burdens relatively easily. Poorer ones, faced with the twin problems of lower incomes and greater demand for social services, have had far more difficulty. And as the gap between the richest and poorest communities has widened, the shift in responsibility for public services to cities and towns has functioned as another means of relieving wealthier Americans of the cost of aiding less fortunate citizens.

The result has been a growing inequality in basic social and community services. While the city tax rate in Philadelphia, for example, is about triple that of communities around it, the suburbs enjoy far better schools, hospitals, recreation and police protection. Eighty-five percent of the richest families in the greater Philadelphia area live outside the city limits, and 80 percent of the region's poorest live inside. The quality of a city's infrastructure—roads, bridges, sewage, water treatment—is likewise related to the average income of its inhabitants.

The growing inequality in government services has been most apparent in the public-schools. The Federal Government's share of the costs of primary and secondary education has dwindled to about 6 percent. The bulk of the cost is divided about equally between the states and local school districts. States with higher concentration of wealthy residents can afford to spend more on their schools than other states. In 1989, the average public school teacher in Arkansas, for example, received $21,700; in Connecticut, $37,300.

Even among adjoining suburban towns in the same state the differences can be quite large. Consider three Boston-area communities located within minutes of one another. All are predominantly white, and most residents within each town earn about the same as their neighbors. But the disparity of incomes between towns is substantial.

Belmont, northwest of Boston, is inhabited mainly by symbolic analysts and their families. In 1988, the average teacher in its public schools earned $36,100. Only 3 percent of Belmont's 18-year-olds dropped out of high school, and more than 80 percent of graduating seniors chose to go on to a four-year college.

Just east of Belmont is Somerville, most of whose residents are low-wage service workers. In 1988, the average Somerville teacher earned $29,400. A third of the town's 18-year-olds did not finish high school, and fewer than a third planned to attend college.

Chelsea, across the Mystic River from Somerville, is the poorest of the three towns.

Most of its inhabitants are unskilled, and many are unemployed or only employed part time. The average teacher in Chelsea, facing tougher educational challenges than his or her counterparts in Belmont, earned $26,200 in 1988, almost a third less than the average teacher in the more affluent town just a few miles away. More than half of Chelsea's 18-year-olds did not graduate from high school, and only 10 percent planned to attend college.

Similar disparities can be found all over the nation. Students at Highland Park High School in a wealthy suburb of Dallas, for example, enjoy a campus with a planetarium, indoor swimming pool, closed-circuit television studio and state-of-the-art science laboratory. Highland Park spends about $6,000 a year to educate each student. This is almost twice that spent per pupil by the towns of Wilmer and Hutchins in southern Dallas County. According to Texas education officials, the richest school district in the state spends $19,300 a year per pupil; its poorest, $2,100 a year.

The courts have become involved in trying to repair such imbalances, but the issues are not open to easy judicial remedy.

The four-fifths of Americans left in the wake of the secession of the fortunate fifth include many poor blacks, but racial exclusion is neither the primary motive for the separation nor a necessary consequence. Lower-income whites are similarly excluded, and high-income black symbolic analysts are often welcomed. The segregation is economic rather than racial, although economically motivated separation often results in de facto racial segregation. Where courts have found a pattern of racially motivated segregation, it usually has involved lower-income white communities bordering on lower-income black neighborhoods.

In states where courts have ordered equalized state spending in school districts, the vast differences in a town's property values—and thus local tax revenues—continue to result in substantial inequities. Where courts or state governments have tried to impose limits on what affluent communities can pay their teachers, not a few parents in upscale towns have simply removed their children from the public schools and applied the money they might otherwise have willingly paid in higher taxes to private school tuitions instead. And, of course, even if statewide expenditures were better equalized, poorer states would continue to be at a substantial disadvantage.

In all these ways, the gap between America's symbolic analysts and everyone else is widening into a chasm. Their secession from the rest of the population raises fundamental questions about the future of American society. In the new global economy—in which money, technologies and corporations cross borders effortlessly—a citizen's standard of living depends more and more on skills and insights, and on the infrastructure needed to link these abilities to the rest of the world. But the most skilled and insightful Americans, who are already positioned to thrive in the world market, are now able to slip the bonds of national allegiance, and by so doing disengage themselves from their less favored fellows. The stark political challenge in the decades ahead will be to reaffirm that, even though America is no longer a separate and distinct economy, it is till a society whose members have a binding obligations to one another.

Barack Obama

The Audacity of Hope:
2004 Democratic National Convention
Keynote Address

Barack Obama (1961—) is the junior United States Senator from Illinois, and candidate for the Democratic Party's 2008 presidential nomination. Born in Hawaii of a Kenyan father and a Kansan mother, Obama grew up in Hawaii and Indonesia, before attending Occidental College and Columbia University, where he received his bachelor's degree. Before attending Harvard Law School, Obama worked as a community organizer on Chicago's south side. In 1996, Obama was elected to represent the south-side Chicago neighborhood of Hyde Park in the Illinois State Senate. Following an unsuccessful attempt to run for the U.S. House of Representatives in 2000, he was elected to the U.S. Senate in 2004.

In this inspirational keynote address before the Democratic National Convention in 2004, Obama connects his own story to the story of America, and calls for an inclusive politics of democracy, hope, and social justice. He reminds us that the American story is not simply a story of rugged individualism, but of caring community, that we are our brother's and sister's keepers.

2004 Democratic National Convention Keynote Address

Barack Obama

On behalf of the great state of Illinois, crossroads of a nation, Land of Lincoln, let me express my deepest gratitude for the privilege of addressing this convention.

Tonight is a particular honor for me because, let's face it, my presence on this stage is pretty unlikely. My father was a foreign student, born and raised in a small village in Kenya. He grew up herding goats, went to school in a tin-roof shack. His father – my grandfather — was a cook, a domestic servant to the British.

But my grandfather had larger dreams for his son. Through hard work and perseverance my father got a scholarship to study in a magical place, America, that shone as a beacon of freedom and opportunity to so many who had come before.

While studying here, my father met my mother. She was born in a town on the other side of the world, in Kansas. Her father worked on oil rigs and farms through most of the Depression. The day after Pearl Harbor my grandfather signed up for duty; joined Patton's army, marched across Europe. Back home, my grandmother raised a baby and went to work on a bomber assembly line. After the war, they studied on the G.I. Bill, bought a house through F.H.A., and later moved west all the way to Hawaii in search of opportunity.

And they, too, had big dreams for their daughter. A common dream, born of two continents.

My parents shared not only an improbable love, they shared an abiding faith in the possibilities of this nation. They would give me an African name, Barack, or "blessed," believing that in a tolerant America your name is no barrier to success. They imagined — They imagined me going to the best schools in the land, even though they weren't rich, because in a generous America you don't have to be rich to achieve your potential. They're both passed away now. And yet, I know that on this night they look down on me with great pride.

They stand here – And I stand here today, grateful for the diversity of my heritage, aware that my parents' dreams live on in my two precious daughters. I stand here knowing that my story is part of the larger American story, that I owe a debt to all of those who came before me, and that, in no other country on earth, is my story even possible.

Tonight, we gather to affirm the greatness of our Nation — not because of the height of our skyscrapers, or the power of our military, or the size of our economy. Our pride is based on a very simple premise, summed up in a declaration made over two hundred years ago:

> *We hold these truths to be*
> *self-evident, that all men are*
> *created equal, that they are*
> *endowed by their Creator with*
> *certain inalienable rights, that*
> *among these are Life, Liberty*
> *and the pursuit of Happiness.*

What is the true genius of America, a faith — a faith in simple dreams, an insistence on small miracles; that we can tuck in our children at night and know that they are fed and clothed and safe from harm; that we can say what we think, write what we think, without hearing a sudden knock on the door; that we can have an idea and start our own business without paying a bribe; that we can participate in the political process without fear of retribution, and that our votes will be counted — at least most of the time.

This year, in this election we are called to reaffirm our values and our commitments, to hold them against a hard reality and see how we're measuring up to the legacy of our forbearers and the promise of future generations.

And fellow Americans, Democrats, Republicans, Independents, I say to you tonight: We have more work to do – more work to do for the workers I met in Galesburg, Illinois, who are losing their union jobs at the Maytag plant that's moving to Mexico, and now are having to compete with their own children for jobs that pay seven bucks an hour; more to do for the father that I met who was losing his job and choking back the tears, wondering how he would pay 4500 dollars a month for the drugs his son needs without the health benefits that he counted on; more to do for the young woman in East St. Louis, and thousands more like her, who has the grades, has the drive, has the will, but doesn't have the money to go to college.

Now, don't get me wrong. The people I meet — in small towns and big cities, in diners and office parks – they don't expect government to solve all their problems. They know they have to work hard to get ahead, and they want to. Go into the collar counties around Chicago, and people will tell you they don't want their tax money wasted, by a welfare agency or by the Pentagon. Go in – Go into any inner city neighborhood, and folks will tell you that government alone can't teach our kids to learn; they know that parents have to teach, that children can't achieve unless we raise their expectations and turn off the television sets and eradicate the slander that says a black youth with a book is acting white. They know those things.

People don't expect – People don't expect government to solve all their problems. But they sense, deep in their bones, that with just a slight change in priorities, we can make sure that every child in America has a decent shot at life, and that the doors of opportunity remain open to all.

They know we can do better. And they want that choice.

You know, a while back – awhile back I met a young man named Shamus in a V.F.W. Hall in East Moline, Illinois. He was a good-looking kid – six two, six three, clear eyed, with an easy smile. He told me he'd joined the Marines and was heading to Iraq the following week. And as I listened to him explain why he'd enlisted, the absolute faith he had in our country and its leaders, his devotion to duty and service, I thought this young man was all that any of us might ever hope for in a child.

But then I asked myself, "Are we serving Shamus as well as he is serving us?"

I thought of the 900 men and women – sons and daughters, husbands and wives, friends and neighbors, who won't be returning to their own hometowns. I thought of the families I've met who were struggling to get by without a loved one's full income, or whose loved ones had returned with a limb missing or nerves shattered, but still lacked long-term health benefits because they were Reservists.

When we send our young men and women info harm's way, we have a solemn obligation not to fudge the numbers or shade the truth about why they're going, to care for their families while they're gone, to tend to the soldiers upon their return, and to never ever go to war without enough troops to win the war, secure the peace, and earn the respect of the world.

Now — Now let me be clear. Let me be clear. We have real enemies in the world. These enemies must be found. They must be pursued. And they must be defeated.

It's not enough for just some of us to prosper – for alongside our famous individualism, there's another ingredient in the American saga, a belief that we're all connected as one people. If there is a child on the south side of Chicago who can't read, that matters to me, even if it's not my child. If there is a senior citizen somewhere who can't pay for their prescription drugs, and having to choose between medicine and the rent, that makes my life poorer, even if it's not my grandparent. If there's an Arab American family being rounded up without benefit of an attorney or due process, that threatens my civil liberties.

It is that fundamental belief - It is that fundamental belief: I am my brother's keeper. I am my sister's keeper that makes this country

work. It's what allows us to pursue our individual dreams and yet still come together as one American family.

E pluribus unum: "Out of many, one."

Now even as we speak, there are those who are preparing to divide us — the spin masters, the negative ad peddlers who embrace the politics of "anything goes." Well, I say to them tonight, there is not a liberal America and a conservative America –there is the United States of America. There is not a Black America and a White America and Latino America and Asian America – there's the United States of America.

The pundits, the pundits like to slice-and-dice our country into Red States and Blue States; Red States for Republicans, Blue States for Democrats. But I've got news for them, too. We worship an "awesome God" in the Blue States, and we don't like federal agents poking around in our libraries in the Red States. We coach Little League in the Blue States and yes, we've got some gay friends in the Red States. There are patriots who opposed the war in Iraq and there are patriots who supported the war in Iraq. We are one people, all of us pledging allegiance to the stars and stripes, all of us defending the United States of America.

In the end — In the end — In the end, that's what this election is about. Do we participate in a politics of cynicism or do we participate in a politics of hope?

I'm not talking about blind optimism here — the almost willful ignorance that thinks unemployment will go away if we just don't think about it, or the health care crisis will solve itself if we just ignore it. That's not what I'm talking about. I'm talking about something more substantial. It's the hope of slaves sitting around a fire singing freedom songs; the hope of immigrants setting out for distant shores; the hope of a young naval lieutenant bravely patrolling the Mekong Delta; the hope of a millworker's son who dares to defy the odds; the hope of a skinny kid with a funny name who believes that America has a place for him, too.

Hope — Hope in the face of difficulty. Hope in the face of uncertainty. The audacity of hope!

In the end, that is God's greatest gift to us, the bedrock of this nation. A belief in things not seen. A belief that there are better days ahead.

I believe that we can give our middle class relief and provide working families with a road to opportunity.

I believe we can provide jobs to the jobless, homes to the homeless, and reclaim young people in cities across America from violence and despair.

I believe that we have a righteous wind at our backs and that as we stand on the crossroads of history, we can make the right choices, and meet the challenges that face us.

America! Tonight, if you feel the same energy that I do, if you feel the same urgency that I do, if you feel the same passion that I do, if you feel the same hopefulness that I do – if we do what we must do, then I have no doubt that all across the country, from Florida to Oregon, from Washington to Maine, the people will rise up in November, and this country will reclaim its promise, and out of this long political darkness a brighter day will come.

Thank you very much everybody. God bless you. Thank you.

The Bill of Rights and Amendments XIII, *XIV, XV, United States Constitution*

The Bill of Rights is the best known feature of the U.S. Constitution; the post-Civil War amendments, especially the provisions guaranteeing equality, are currently the most litigated before the U.S. Supreme Court. Neither were contained in the original constitution, and both required a fight to be included. In fact, the major proponents of the Constitution's adoption in 1787 believed a general Bill of Rights like those attached to most of the state constitutions was unnecessary. Thomas Jefferson argued with his friend and colleague James Madison about including articles guaranteeing the basic rights of individuals against democratic majorities that might run roughshod over them (See his Letter to Madison, December 20, 1787, excerpted in Part I, Section A). The supporters of the U.S. Constitution's ratification were finally persuaded by the threat of defeat to include provisions for individual rights held against the new government, and a Bill of Rights to be added to the original constitution was the first order of business of the new Congress. The substantive provisions of the Bill of Rights are found in the first eight amendments, but Madison and others felt the Ninth and Tenth Amendments to be critical, as both stressed the limited scope of the new federal government. Madison was adamant about the inclusion of the language of the Ninth Amendment in particular, as he thought it important to state that some individual rights that may not have been enumerated in the Constitution were nevertheless guaranteed to individuals against their government.

After the Civil War, Congress passed and the states ratified the Thirteenth Amendment to the U.S. Constitution, embodying the principles of Lincoln's Emancipation Proclamation by abolishing "slavery" and "involuntary servitude." Within the next five years, two additional amendments were added to protect newly freed slaves from discrimination by state and local governments, particularly the former confederate states. The 14th Amendment begins by overturning an 1857 Supreme Court decision, *Dred Scott v. Sandford*, in which the Court had declared that black men of slave ancestry could not be citizens of the United States. It goes on to protect an individual's right to "due process of law" and "the equal protection of the laws" against state as well as federal invasion. The 15th Amendment guarantees that the right to vote shall not be denied "on account of race, color, or previous condition of servitude." These three amendments, taken together, revolutionized the American constitutional system, and changed forever the relationship between the federal government and the states. The 14th Amendment has been expanded to include groups other than those African-Americans to whom it was originally intended to apply, and has been used to "incorporate" most of the provisions of the Bill of Rights and make them applicable to all the states. The 13th Amendment, ironically, has recently been cited by students and parents opposing mandatory community service programs in public schools.

These amendments, taken together, reflect the tension in a democracy between satisfying the interests of the community, represented by a majority, and protecting the rights of a minority of individuals within a community. Most of the constitutional fights in this century have centered on this battle between responsibility to the public good and the duty to uphold the dignity and liberty of individuals.

The Bill of Rights and Amendments XIII, XIV, and XV to the U.S. Constitution

Amendment I [1791]

Congress shall make no law respecting an establishment of religion, or prohibiting the free exercise thereof; or abridging the freedom of speech, or of the press; or the right of the people peaceably to assemble, and to petition the Government for a redress of grievances.

Amendment II [1791]

A well regulated Militia, being necessary to the security of a free State, the right of the people to keep and bear Arms, shall not be infringed.

Amendment III [1791]

No Soldier shall, in time of peace be quartered in any house, without the con sent of the Owner, nor in time of war, but in a manner to be prescribed by law.

Amendment IV [1791]

The right of the people to be secure in their persons, houses, papers, and effects, against unreasonable searches and seizures, shall not be violated, and no Warrants shall issue, but upon probable cause, supported by Oath or affirmation, and particularly describing the place to be searched, and the persons or things to be seized.

Amendment V [1791]

No person shall be held to answer for a capital, or otherwise infamous crime, unless on a presentment or indictment of a Grand Jury, except in cases arising in the land or naval forces, or in the Militia, when in actual service in time of War or public danger; nor shall any person be subject for the same offence to be twice put in jeopardy of life or limb; nor shall be compelled in any criminal case to be a witness against himself, nor be deprived of life, liberty, or property, without due process of law; nor shall private property be taken for public use, without just compensation.

Amendment VI [1791]

In all criminal prosecutions, the accused shall enjoy the right to a speedy and public trial, by an impartial jury of the State and district wherein the crime shall have been committed, which district shall have been previously ascertained by law, and to be informed of the nature and cause of the accusation; to be confronted with the witnesses against him; to have compulsory process for obtaining witnesses in his favor, and to have the Assistance of Counsel for his defence.

Amendment VII [1791]

In Suits at common law, where the value in controversy shall exceed twenty dollars, the right of trial by jury shall be preserved, and no fact tried by jury, shall be otherwise re-examined in any Court of the United States, than according to the rules of the common law.

Amendment VIII [1791]

Excessive bail shall not be required, nor excessive fines imposed, nor cruel and unusual punishments inflicted.

Amendment IX [1791]

The enumeration in the Constitution, of certain rights, shall not be construed to deny or disparage others retained by the people.

Amendment X [1791]

The powers not delegated to the United States by the Constitution, nor prohibited by it to the States, are reserved to the States respectively, or to the people.

Amendment XIII [1865]

Section 1. Neither slavery nor involuntary servitude, except as a punishment for crime whereof the party shall have been duly convicted, shall exist within the United States, or any place subject to their jurisdiction.

Section 2. Congress shall have power to enforce this article by appropriate-legislation.

Amendment XIV [1868]

Section 1. All persons born or naturalized in the United States, and subject to the jurisdiction thereof, are citizens of the United States and of the State wherein they reside. No State shall make or enforce any law which shall abridge the privileges or immunities of citizens of the United States; nor shall any State deprive any person of life, liberty, or property, without due process of law; nor deny to any person within its jurisdiction the equal protection of the laws.

Section 2. Representatives shall be apportioned among the several States according to their respective numbers, counting the whole number of persons in each State, excluding Indians not taxed. But when the right to vote at any election for the choice of electors for President and Vice President of the United States, Representatives in Congress, the Executive and Judicial officers of a State, or the members of the Legislature thereof, is denied to any of the male inhabitants of such State, being twenty-one years of age, and citizens of the United States, or in any way abridged, except for participation in rebellion, or other crime, the basis of representation therein shall be reduced in the proportion which the number of such male citizens shall bear to the whole number of male citizens twenty-one years of age in such State.

Section 3. No person shall be a Senator or Representative in Congress, or elector of President and Vice President, or hold any office, civil or military, under the United States, or under any State, who having previously taken an oath, as a member of Congress, or as an officer of the United States, or as a member of any State legislature, or as an executive or judicial officer of any State, to support the Constitution of the United States, shall have engaged in insurrection or rebellion against the same, or given aid or comfort to the enemies thereof. But Congress may by a vote of two-thirds of each House, remove such disability.

Section 4. The validity of the public debt of the United States, authorized by law, including debts incurred for payment of pensions and bounties for services in suppressing insurrection or rebellion, shall not be questioned. But neither the United States nor any State shall assume or pay any debt or obligation incurred in aid of insurrection or rebellion against the United States, or any claim for the loss or emancipation of any slave; but all such debts, obligations and claims shall be held illegal and void.

Section 5. The Congress shall have power to enforce, by appropriate legislation, the provisions of this article.

Amendment XV [1870]

Section 1. The right of citizens of the United States to vote shall not be denied or abridged by the United States or by any State on account of race, color, or previous condition of servitude.

Section 2. The Congress shall have power to enforce this article by appropriate legislation.

Alexis de Tocqueville

Unlimited Power of the Majority in the United States and Its Consequences

Alexis de Tocqueville (1805–1859), French political theorist, historian, and sociologist, was born into a royalist aristocratic family. After completing his education in 1827, he was appointed magistrate in the Ministry of Justice under King Charles X. In 1831, Tocqueville and his friend Gustave de Beaumont took a leave of absence and went to the United States for nine months, ostensibly to study American penal institutions. While they did produce a study on possibilities for application of the American prison system in France, Tocqueville's stronger interests lay in the U.S. as a model of democratic stability—a stability that had eluded the French through forty years of turmoil and revolution.

In the following selection from the first volume of Tocqueville's *Democracy in America* (1835), Tocqueville discusses the possibility that the social effects of democracy could undermine its political achievements. Although the democratic form of government guarantees political liberty for all, Tocqueville sees a tyranny in the rule of public opinion that restricts—not the right—but the *ability* of individuals to think independently. When all opinions are deemed equally valid, and the majority always rules, the social pressures against differing opinions become immense. The social sanctions exercised on those who disagree with the majority lead people to believe that a dissenting opinion must also be morally wrong. Tocqueville believed that although the subjects of European absolute monarchies may live in misery, they submit nobly out of physical weakness or loyalty to the king, not out of a degrading psychological need to follow intellectual fashions.

Unlimited Power of the Majority in the United States and Its Consequences
Alexis de Tocqueville

The very essence of democratic government consists in the absolute sovereignty of the majority; for there is nothing in democratic states which is capable of resisting it. Most of the American constitutions have sought to increase this natural strength of the majority by artificial means.

The legislature is, of all political institutions, the one which is most easily swayed by the will of the majority. The Americans determined that the members of the legislature should be elected by the people *directly*, and for a *very brief term*, in order to subject them, not only to the general convictions, but even to the daily passions, of their constituents. The members of both houses are taken from the same classes in society, and nominated in the same manner; so that the movements of the legislative bodies are almost as rapid, and quite as irresistible, as those of a single assembly. It is to a legislature thus constituted, that almost all the authority of the government has been intrusted.

At the same time that the law increased the strength of those authorities which of themselves were strong, it enfeebled more and more those which were naturally weak. It deprived the representatives of the executive power of all stability and independence; and, by subjecting them completely to the caprices of legislature, it robbed them of the slender influence which the nature of a democratic government might have allowed them to exercise. In several States, the judicial power was also submitted to the election of the majority; and in all of them, its existence was made to depend on the pleasure of the legislative authority, since the representatives were empowered annually to regulate the stipend of the judges.

Custom has done even more than law. A proceeding is becoming more and more general in the United States, which will, in the end, do away with the guaranties of representative government: it frequently happens that the voters, in electing a delegate, point out a certain line of conduct to him, and impose upon him certain positive obligations which he is pledged to fulfil. With the exception of the tumult, this comes to the same thing as if the majority itself held its deliberations in the market-place.

Several other circumstances concur to render the power of the majority in America not only preponderant, but irresistible. The moral authority of the majority is partly based upon the notion, that there is more intelligence and wisdom in a number of men united than in a single individual, and that the number of the legislators is more important than their quality. The theory of equality is thus applied to the intellects of men; and human pride is thus assailed in its last retreat by a doctrine which the minority hesitate to admit, and to which they will but slowly assent. Like all other powers, and perhaps more than any other, the authority of the many requires the sanction of time in order to appear legitimate. At first, it enforces obedience by constraint; and its laws are not *respected* until they have been long maintained.

The right of governing society, which the majority supposes itself to derive from its superior intelligence, was introduced into the United States by the first settlers; and this idea, which of itself would be sufficient to create a free nation, has now been amalgamated with the manners of the people and the minor incidents of social life.

The French, under the old monarchy, held it for a maxim that the king could do no wrong; and if he did do wrong, the blame was imputed to his advisers. This notion made obedience very easy; it enabled the subject to complain of the law without ceasing to love and honor the lawgiver. The Americans entertain the same opinion with respect to the majority.

The moral power of the majority is founded upon yet another principle, which is, that the interests of the many are to be preferred to those of the few. It will readily be perceived that the respect here professed for the rights of the greater number must naturally increase or diminish according to the state of parties. When a nation is divided into several great irreconcilable interests, the privilege of the majority is often overlooked, because it is intolerable to comply with its demands.

If there existed in America a class of citizens whom the legislating majority sought to deprive of exclusive privileges which they had possessed for ages, and to bring down from an elevated station to the level of the multitude, it is probable that the minority would be less ready to submit to its laws. But as the United States were colonized by men holding equal rank, there is as yet no natural or permanent disagreement between the interests of its different inhabitants.

There are communities in which the members of the minority can never hope to draw over the majority to their side, because they must then give up the very point which is at issue between them. Thus, an aristocracy can never become a majority whilst it retains its exclusive privileges, and it cannot cede its privileges without ceasing to be an aristocracy.

In the United States, political questions cannot be taken up in so general and absolute a manner; and all parties are willing to recognize the rights of the majority, because they all hope at some time to be able to exercise them to their own advantage. The majority, therefore, in that country, exercise a prodigious actual authority, and a power of opinion which is nearly as great; no obstacles exist which can impede or even retard its progress, so as to make it heed the complaints of those whom it crushes upon its path. This state of things is harmful in itself, and dangerous for the future....

Tyranny of the Majority

I hold it to be an impious and detestable maxim, that, politically speaking, the people have a right to do anything; and yet I have asserted that all authority originates in the will of the majority. Am I, then, in contradiction with myself?

A general law, which bears the name of justice, has been made and sanctioned, not only by a majority of this or that people, but by a majority of mankind. The rights of every people are therefore confined within the limits of what is just. A nation may be considered as a jury which is empowered to represent society at large, and to apply justice, which is its law. Ought such a jury, which represents society, to have more power than the society itself, whose laws it executes?

When I refuse to obey an unjust law, I do not contest the right of the majority to command, but I simply appeal from the sovereignty of the people to the sovereignty of mankind. Some have not feared to assert that a people can never out-step the boundaries of justice and reason in those affairs which are peculiarly its own; and that consequently full power may be given to the majority by which they are represented. But this is the language of a slave.

A majority taken collectively is only an individual, whose opinions, and frequently whose interests, are opposed to those of another individual, who is styled a minority. If it be admitted that a man possessing absolute power may misuse that power by wronging his adversaries, why should not a majority be liable to the same reproach? Men do not change their characters by uniting with each other; nor does their patience in the presence of obstacles increase with their strength. For my own part, I cannot believe it; the power to do everything, which I should refuse to one of my equals, I will never grant to any number of them.

I do not think, for the sake of preserving liberty, it is possible to combine several principles in the same government so as to really oppose them to one another. The form of government which is usually termed *mixed* has always appeared to me a mere chimera. Accurately speaking, there is no such thing as a *mixed government*, in the sense usually given to that word, because, in all communities, some one principle of action may be discovered which preponderates over the others. England, in the last century,—which has been especially cited as an example of this sort of government,—was essentially an aristocratic state, although it comprised some great elements of democracy; for the laws and customs of the country were such that the aristocracy could not but preponderate in the long run, and direct public affairs according to its own will. The error arose from seeing the interests of the nobles perpetually contending with those of the people, without considering the issue of the contest, which was really the important point. When a community actually has a mixed government,—that is to say, when it is equally divided between adverse principles,—it must either experience a revolution, or fall into anarchy.

I am therefore of opinion, that social power superior to all others must always be placed somewhere; but I think that liberty is endangered when this power finds no obstacle which can retard its course, and give it time to moderate its own vehemence.

Unlimited power is in itself a bad and dangerous thing. Human beings are not competent to exercise it with discretion. God alone can be omnipotent, because his wisdom and his justice are always equal to his power. There is no power on earth so worthy of honor in itself, or clothed with rights so sacred, that I would admit its uncontrolled and all-predominant authority. When I see that the right and the means of absolute command are conferred on any power whatever, be it called a people or a king, an aristocracy or a democracy, a monarchy or a republic, I say there is the germ of tyranny, and I seek to live elsewhere, under other laws.

In my opinion, the main evil of the present democratic institutions of the United States does not arise, as is often asserted in Europe, from their weakness, but from their irresistible strength. I am not so much alarmed at the excessive liberty which reigns in that country, as at the inadequate securities which one finds there against tyranny.

When an individual or a party is wronged in the United States, to whom can he apply for redress? If to public opinion, public opinion constitutes the majority; if to the legislature, it represents the majority, and implicitly obeys it; if to the executive power, it is appointed by the majority, and serves as a passive tool in its hands. The public force consists of the majority under arms; the jury is the majority invested with the right of hearing judicial cases; and in certain States, even the judges are elected by the majority. However iniquitous or absurd the measure of which you complain, you must submit to it as well as you can.

If, on the other hand, a legislative power could be so constituted as to represent the majority without necessarily being the slave of its passions, an executive so as to retain a proper share of authority, and a judiciary so as to remain independent of the other two powers, a government would be formed which would still be democratic, without incurring hardly any risk of tyranny.

I do not say that there is a frequent use of tyranny in America, at the present day; but I maintain that there is no sure barrier against it, and that the causes which mitigate the government there are to be found in the circumstances and the manners of the country, more than in its laws.

Effects of the Omnipotence of the Majority upon the Arbitrary Authority of American Public Officers

A distinction must be drawn between tyranny and arbitrary power. Tyranny may be exercised by means of the law itself, and in that case it is not arbitrary; arbitrary power may be exercised for the public good, in which case it is not tyrannical. Tyranny usually employs arbitrary means, but, if necessary, it can do without them.

In the United States, the omnipotence of the majority, which is favorable to the legal despotism of the legislature, likewise favors the arbitrary authority of the magistrate. The majority has absolute power both to make the law and to watch over its execution; and as it has equal authority over those who are in power, and the community at large, it considers public officers as its passive agents, and readily confides to them the task of carrying out its design. The details of their office, and the privileges which they are to enjoy, are rarely defined beforehand. It treats them as a master does his servants, since they are always at work in his sight, and he can direct or reprimand them at any instant.

In general, the American functionaries are far more independent within the sphere which is prescribed to them than the French civil officers. Sometimes, even, they are allowed by the popular authority to exceed those bounds; and as they are protected by the opinion, and backed by the power, of the majority, they dare do things which even a European, accustomed as he is to arbitrary power, is astonished at. By this means, habits are formed in the heart of a free country which may some day prove fatal to its liberties.

Power Exercised by the Majority in America upon Opinion

It is in the examination of the exercise of thought in the United States, that we clearly perceive how far the power of the majority surpasses all the powers with which we are acquainted in Europe. Thought is an invisible and subtle power, that mocks all the efforts of tyranny. At the present time, the most absolute monarchs in Europe cannot prevent certain opinions hostile to their authority from circulating in secret through their dominions, and even in their courts. It is not so in America; as long as the majority is still undecided, discussion is carried on; but as soon as its decision is irrevocably pronounced, every one is silent, and the friends as well as the opponents of the measure unite in assenting to its propriety. The reason of this is perfectly clear: no monarch is so absolute as to combine all the powers of society in his own hands, and to conquer all opposition, as a majority is able to do, which has the right both of making and of executing the laws.

The authority of a king is physical, and controls the actions of men without subduing their will. But the majority possesses a power which is physical and moral at the same time, which acts upon the will as much as upon the actions, and represses not only all contest, but all controversy.

I know of no country in which there is so little independence of mind and real freedom of discussion as in America. In any constitutional state in Europe, every sort of religious and political theory may be freely preached and disseminated; for there is no country in Europe so subdued by any single authority, as not to protect the man who raises his voice in the cause of truth from the consequences of his hardihood. If he is unfortunate enough to live under an absolute government, the people are often upon his side; if he inhabits a free country, he can, if necessary, find a shelter behind the throne. The aristocratic part of society supports him in some countries, and the democracy in others. But in a nation where democratic institutions exist, organized like those of the United States, there is but one authority, one element of strength and success, with nothing beyond it.

In America, the majority raises formidable barriers around the liberty of opinion: within these barriers, an author may write what he pleases; but woe to him if he goes beyond them. Not that he is in danger of an *auto-da-fé*, but he is exposed to continued obloquy and persecution. His political career is closed forever, since he has offended the only authority which is able to open it. Every sort of compensation, even that of celebrity, is refused to him. Before publishing his opinions, he imagined that he held them in common with others; but no sooner has he declared them, than he is loudly censured by his opponents, whilst those who think like him, without having the courage to speak out, abandon him in silence. He yields at length, overcome by the daily effort which he has to make, and subsides into silence, as if he felt remorse for having spoken the truth.

Fetters and headsmen were the coarse instruments which tyranny formerly employed; but the civilization of our age has perfected despotism itself, though it seemed to have nothing to learn. Monarchs had, so to speak, materialized oppression: the democratic republics of the present day have rendered it as entirely an affair of the mind, as the will which it is intended to coerce. Under the absolute sway of one man, the body was attacked in order to subdue the soul; but the soul escaped the blows which were directed against it, and rose proudly superior. Such is not the course adopted by tyranny in democratic republics; there the body is left free, and the soul is enslaved. The master no longer says, "You shall think as I do, or you shall die"; but he says, "You are free to think differently from me, and to retain your life, your property, and all that you possess; but you are henceforth a stranger among your people. You may retain your civil rights, but they will be useless to you, for you will never be chosen by your fellow-citizens, if you solicit their votes; and they will affect to scorn you, if you ask for their esteem. You will remain among men, but you will be deprived of the rights of mankind. Your fellow-creatures will shun you like an impure being; and even those who believe in your innocence will abandon you, lest they should be shunned in their turn. Go in peace! I have given you your life, but it is an existence worse than death."

Absolute monarchies had dishonored despotism; let us beware lest democratic republics should reinstate it, and render it less odious and degrading in the eyes of the many, by making it still more onerous to the few.

Works have been published in the proudest nations of the Old World, expressly intended to censure the vices and the follies of the times: Labruyère inhabited the palace of Louis XIV., when he composed his chapter upon the Great, and Molière criticised the courtiers in the pieces which were acted before the court. But the ruling power in the United States is not to be made game of. The smallest reproach irritates its sensibility, and the slightest joke which has any foundation in truth renders it indignant; from the forms of its language up to the solid virtues of its character, everything must be made the subject of enco-mium. No writer, whatever be his eminence, can escape paying this tribute of adulation to his fel-low-citizens. The majority lives in the perpetual utterance of self-applause; and there are certain truths which the Americans can only learn from strangers or from experience.

If America has not as yet had any great writ-ers, the reason is given in these facts; there can be no literary genius without freedom of opinion, and freedom of opinion does not ex-ist in America. The Inquisition has never been able to prevent a vast number of anti-religious books from circulating in Spain. The empire of the majority succeeds much better in the United States, since it actually removes any wish to publish them. Unbelievers are to be met with in America, but there is no public organ of infidelity. Attempts have been made by some governments to protect morality by prohibiting licentious books. In the United States, no one is punished for this sort of books, but no one is in-duced to write them; not because all the citizens are immaculate in conduct, but because the ma-jority of the community is decent and orderly.

In this case the use of the power is unques-tionably good; and I am discussing the nature of the power itself. This irresistible authority is a constant fact, and its judicious exercise is only an accident.

The Greatest Dangers of the American Republics Proceed from the Omnipotence of the Majority

Governments usually perish from impotence or from tyranny. In the former case, their power

escapes from them; it is wrested from their grasp in the latter. Many observers who have witnessed the anarchy of democratic states, have imagined that the government of those states was naturally weak and impotent. The truth is, that, when war is once begun between parties, the government loses its control over society. But I do not think that a democratic power is naturally without force or resources; say, rather, that it is almost always by the abuse of its force, and the misemployment of its re-sources, that it becomes a failure. Anarchy is almost always produced by its tyranny or its mistakes, but not by its want of strength.

It is important not to confound stability with force, or the greatness of a thing with its duration. In democratic republics, the power which directs society is not stable; for it often changes hands, and assumes a new direction. But, whichever way it turns, its force is almost irresistible. The governments of the American republics appear to me to be as much central-ized as those of the absolute monarchies of Europe, and more energetic than they are. I do not, therefore, imagine that they will perish from weakness.

If ever the free institutions of America are destroyed, that event may be attributed to the omnipotence of the majority, which may at some future time urge the minorities to despera-tion, and oblige them to have recourse to physi-cal force. Anarchy will then be the result, but it will have been brought about by despotism.

Mr. Madison expresses the same opinion in the Federalist, No. 51. "It is of great impor-tance in a republic, not only to guard the society against the oppression of its rulers, but to guard one part of the society against the injustice of the other part. Justice is the end of government. It is the end of civil society. It ever has been, and ever will be, pursued until it be obtained, or until liberty be lost in the pursuit. In a society, under the forms of which the stronger faction can readily unite and oppress the weaker, an-archy may as truly be said to reign as in a state of nature, where the weaker individual is not secured against the violence of the stronger: and as, in the latter state, even the stronger individuals are prompted by the uncertainty of their condition to submit to a government which may protect the weak as well as themselves, so, in the former state, will the more powerful factions be gradually induced by a like motive to wish for a government which will protect all parties, the weaker as well as the more powerful. It can be little doubted, that, if the State of Rhode Island was separated from the Confederacy and left to itself, the insecurity of right under the popular form of government within such narrow limits would be displayed by such reiterated oppression of the factious majorities, that some power altogether independent of the people would soon be called for by the voice of the very factions whose misrule had proved the necessity of it."

Jefferson also said: "The executive power in our government is not the only, perhaps not even the principal, object of my solicitude. The tyranny of the legislature is really the danger most to be feared, and will continue to be so for many years to come. The tyranny of the executive power will come in its turn, but at a more distant period."

I am glad to cite the opinion of Jefferson upon this subject rather than that of any other, because I consider him the most powerful advocate democracy has ever had.

John Stuart Mill
On Liberty

John Stuart Mill (1806–1873), was one of the most influential thinkers of the 19th century, developing the political philosophy of liberalism inherited from Hobbes and Locke to fit the conditions of mass industrial society in his time. Mill was the eldest son of philosopher and historian James Mill, and the godson of famous utilitarian philosopher Jeremy Bentham, both of whom directed the bulk of Mill's early education. After working with his father at the British East India Company, Mill returned to London where he served a short stint as a Member of the British Parliament. He was the first MP to argue for women's suffrage, and his longstanding relationship with Harriet Taylor, who became his wife in 1851, reinforced his advocacy of women's rights, most prominently featured in his work *The Subjection of Women*.

Mill is most widely known for his work *On Liberty*, which Mill claimed owed much of its inspiration and authorship to his wife Harriet. Influenced by de Tocqueville, whose essay precedes this one, Mill was quite concerned about the protection of individual liberty in democratic societies, where the "tyranny of the majority" could restrict creativity and freedom. In the excerpt contained in this volume, Mill justifies the importance of individual liberty, and explores the nature and limits of the power that can be legitimately exercised by governments over the individual. He argues that the only legitimate authority society can have over the individual and his or her freedom is to prevent harm to others. Mill concludes: "In the part which merely concerns himself, his independence is, of right, absolute. Over himself, over his own body and mind, the individual is sovereign."

On Liberty
John Stuart Mill

Chapter I
Introductory

THE subject of this Essay is not the so-called Liberty of the Will, so unfortunately opposed to the misnamed doctrine of Philosophical Necessity; but Civil, or Social Liberty: the nature and limits of the power which can be legitimately exercised by society over the individual. A question seldom stated, and hardly ever discussed, in general terms, but which profoundly influences the practical controversies of the age by its latent presence, and is likely soon to make itself recognized as the vital question of the future. It is so far from being new, that, in a certain sense, it has divided mankind, almost from the remotest ages, but in the stage of progress into which the more civilized portions of the species have now entered, it presents itself under new conditions, and requires a different and more fundamental treatment.

The struggle between Liberty and Authority is the most conspicuous feature in the portions of history with which we are earliest familiar, particularly in that of Greece, Rome, and England. But in old times this contest was between subjects, or some classes of subjects, and the government. By liberty, was meant protection against the tyranny of the political rulers....The aim, therefore, of patriots, was to set limits to the power which the ruler should be suffered to exercise over the community; and this limitation was what they meant by liberty....

In time, however, a democratic republic came to occupy a large portion of the earth's surface, and made itself felt as one of the most powerful members of the community of nations; and elective and responsible government became subject to the observations and criticisms which wait upon a great existing fact. It was now perceived that such phrases as "self-government," and "the power of the people over themselves," do not express the true state of the case. The "people" who exercise the power, are not always the same people with those over whom it is exercised, and the "self-government" spoken of, is not the government of each by himself, but of each by all the rest. The will of the people, moreover, practically means, the will of the most numerous or the most active part of the people; the majority, or those who succeed in making themselves accepted as the majority; the people, consequently, may desire to oppress a part of their number; and precautions are as much needed against this, as against any other abuse of power. The limitation, therefore, of the power of government over individuals, loses none of its importance when the holders of power are regularly accountable to the community, that is, to the strongest party therein. This view of things, recommending itself equally to the intelligence of thinkers and to the inclination of those important classes in European society to whose real or supposed interests democracy is adverse, has had no difficulty in establishing itself; and in political speculations "the tyranny of the majority" is now generally included among the evils against which society requires to be on its guard.

Like other tyrannies, the tyranny of the majority was at first, and is still vulgarly, held in dread, chiefly as operating through the acts of the public authorities. But reflecting persons perceived that when society is itself the tyrant — society collectively, over the separate individuals who compose it — its means of tyrannizing are not restricted to the acts which it may do by the hands of its political functionaries. Society can and does execute its own mandates: and if it issues wrong mandates instead of right, or any mandates at all in things with which it ought not to meddle, it practises a social tyranny more formidable than many kinds of political oppression, since, though not usually upheld by such extreme penalties, it leaves fewer means of escape, penetrating much more deeply into the details of life, and enslaving the soul itself. Protection, therefore, against the tyranny of the magistrate is not enough; there needs protection also against the tyranny of the prevailing opinion and feeling; against the tendency of society to impose, by other means than civil penalties, its own ideas and practices as rules of conduct on those who dissent from them; to fetter the development, and, if possible, prevent the for-

mation, of any individuality not in harmony with its ways, and compel all characters to fashion themselves upon the model of its own. There is a limit to the legitimate interference of collective opinion with individual independence; and to find that limit, and maintain it against encroachment, is as indispensable to a good condition of human affairs, as protection against political despotism....

The object of this Essay is to assert one very simple principle, as entitled to govern absolutely the dealings of society with the individual in the way of compulsion and control, whether the means used be physical force in the form of legal penalties, or the moral coercion of public opinion. That principle is, that the sole end for which mankind are warranted, individually or collectively in interfering with the liberty of action of any of their number, is self-protection. That the only purpose for which power can be rightfully exercised over any member of a civilized community, against his will, is to prevent harm to others. His own good, either physical or moral, is not a sufficient warrant. He cannot rightfully be compelled to do or forbear because it will be better for him to do so, because it will make him happier, because, in the opinions of others, to do so would be wise, or even right. These are good reasons for remonstrating with him, or reasoning with him, or persuading him, or entreating him, but not for compelling him, or visiting him with any evil, in case he do otherwise. To justify that, the conduct from which it is desired to deter him must be calculated to produce evil to some one else. The only part of the conduct of any one, for which he is amenable to society, is that which concerns others. In the part which merely concerns himself, his independence is, of right, absolute. Over himself, over his own body and mind, the individual is sovereign.

It is, perhaps, hardly necessary to say that this doctrine is meant to apply only to human beings in the maturity of their faculties. We are not speaking of children, or of young persons below the age which the law may fix as that of manhood or womanhood. Those who are still in a state to require being taken care of by others, must be protected against their own actions as well as against external injury. For the same reason, we may leave out of consideration those backward states of society in which the race itself may be considered as in its nonage. The early difficulties in the way of spontaneous progress are so great, that there is seldom any choice of means for overcoming them; and a ruler full of the spirit of improvement is warranted in the use of any expedients that will attain an end, perhaps otherwise unattainable. Despotism is a legitimate mode of government in dealing with barbarians, provided the end be their improvement, and the means justified by actually effecting that end. Liberty, as a principle, has no application to any state of things anterior to the time when mankind have become capable of being improved by free and equal discussion.

[T]here is a sphere of action in which society, as distinguished from the individual, has, if any, only an indirect interest; comprehending all that portion of a person's life and conduct which affects only himself, or, if it also affects others, only with their free, voluntary, and undeceived consent and participation. When I say only himself, I mean directly, and in the first instance: for whatever affects himself, may affect others through himself; and the objection which may be grounded on this contingency, will receive consideration in the sequel. This, then, is the appropriate region of human liberty. It comprises, first, the inward domain of consciousness; demanding liberty of conscience, in the most comprehensive sense; liberty of thought and feeling; absolute freedom of opinion and sentiment on all subjects, practical or speculative, scientific, moral, or theological. The liberty of expressing and publishing opinions may seem to fall under a different principle, since it belongs to that part of the conduct of an individual which concerns other people; but, being almost of as much importance as the liberty of thought itself, and resting in great part on the same reasons, is practically inseparable from it. Secondly, the principle requires liberty of tastes and pursuits; of framing the plan of our life to suit our own character; of doing as we like, subject to such consequences as may follow; without impediment from our fellow-creatures, so long as what we do does not harm them even though they should think our conduct foolish, perverse, or wrong. Thirdly, from this liberty of each individual, follows the liberty, within the same limits, of combination among individuals; freedom to unite, for any purpose not involving harm to others: the persons combining being supposed to be of full age, and not forced or deceived.

No society in which these liberties are not, on the whole, respected, is free, whatever may be its form of government; and none is completely free in which they do not exist absolute and unqualified. The only freedom which deserves the name, is that of pursuing our own good in our own way, so long as we do not attempt to deprive others of theirs, or impede their efforts to obtain it. Each is the proper guardian of his own health, whether bodily, or mental or spiritual. Mankind are greater gainers by suffering each other to live as seems good to themselves, than by compelling each to live as seems good to the rest…

Chapter II
Of the Liberty of Thought and Discussion

THE time, it is to be hoped, is gone by when any defence would be necessary of the "liberty of the press" as one of the securities against corrupt or tyrannical government. No argument, we may suppose, can now be needed, against permitting a legislature or an executive, not identified in interest with the people, to prescribe opinions to them, and determine what doctrines or what arguments they shall be allowed to hear. This aspect of the question, besides, has been so often and so triumphantly enforced by preceding writers, that it needs not be specially insisted on in this place. [S]peaking generally, it is not, in constitutional countries, to be apprehended that the government, whether completely responsible to the people or not, will often attempt to control the expression of opinion, except when in doing so it makes itself the organ of the general intolerance of the public. Let us suppose, therefore, that the government is entirely at one with the people, and never thinks of exerting any power of coercion unless in agreement with what it conceives to be their voice. But I deny the right of the people to exercise such coercion, either by themselves or by their government. The power itself is illegitimate. The best government has no more title to it than the worst. It is as noxious, or more noxious, when exerted in accordance with public opinion, than when in opposition to it. If all mankind minus one, were of one opinion, and only one person were of the contrary opinion, mankind would be no more justified in silencing that one person, than he, if he had the power, would be justified in silencing mankind. Were an opinion a personal possession of no value except to the owner; if to be obstructed in the enjoyment of it were simply a private injury, it would make some difference whether the injury was inflicted only on a few persons or on many. But the peculiar evil of silencing the expression of an opinion is, that it is robbing the human race; posterity as well as the existing generation; those who dissent from the opinion, still more than those who hold it. If the opinion is right, they are deprived of the opportunity of exchanging error for truth: if wrong, they lose, what is almost as great a benefit, the clearer perception and livelier impression of truth, produced by its collision with error.

It is necessary to consider separately these two hypotheses, each of which has a distinct branch of the argument corresponding to it. We can never be sure that the opinion we are endeavouring to stifle is a false opinion; and if we were sure, stifling it would be an evil still.

First the opinion which it is attempted to suppress by authority may possibly be true. Those who desire to suppress it, of course deny its truth; but they are not infallible. They have no authority to decide the question for all mankind, and exclude every other person from the means of judging. To refuse a hearing to an opinion, because they are sure that it is false, is to assume that their certainty is the same thing as absolute certainty. All silencing of discussion is an assumption of infallibility. Its condemnation may be allowed to rest on this common argument, not the worse for being common....

There is the greatest difference between presuming an opinion to be true, because, with every opportunity for contesting it, it has not been refuted, and assuming its truth for the purpose of not permitting its refutation. Complete liberty of contradicting and disproving our opinion, is the very condition which justifies us in assuming its truth for purposes of action; and on no other terms can a being with human faculties have any rational assurance of being right....

The beliefs which we have most warrant for, have no safeguard to rest on, but a standing invitation to the whole world to prove them unfounded. If the challenge is not accepted, or is accepted and the attempt fails, we are far enough from certainty still; but we have done the best that the existing state of human reason admits of; we have neglected nothing that could give the truth a chance of reaching us: if the lists are kept open, we may hope that if there be a better truth, it will be found when the human mind is capable of receiving it; and in the meantime we may rely on having attained such approach to truth, as is possible in our own day. This is the amount of certainty attainable by a fallible being, and this the sole way of attaining it....

Mankind can hardly be too often reminded, that there was once a man named Socrates, between whom and the legal authorities and public opinion of his time, there took place a memorable collision. Born in an age and country abounding in individual greatness, this man has been handed down to us by those who best knew both him and the age, as the most virtuous man in it; while we know him as the head and prototype of all subsequent teachers of virtue, the source equally of the lofty inspiration of Plato and the judicious utilitarianism of Aristotle, the two headsprings of ethical as of all other philosophy. This acknowledged master of all the eminent thinkers who have since lived — whose fame, still growing after more than two thousand years, all but outweighs the whole remainder of the names which make his native city illustrious — was put to death by his countrymen, after a judicial conviction, for impiety and immorality. Impiety, in denying the gods recognized by the State; indeed his accuser asserted (see the "Apologia") that he believed in no gods at all. Immorality, in being, by his doctrines and instructions, a "corrupter of youth." Of these charges the tribunal, there is every ground for believing, honestly found him guilty, and condemned the man who probably of all then born had deserved best of mankind, to be put to death as a criminal.

To pass from this to the only other instance of judicial iniquity, the mention of which, after the condemnation of Socrates, would not be an anti-climax: the event which took place on Calvary rather more than eighteen hundred years ago. The man who left on the memory of those who witnessed his life and conversation, such an impression of his moral grandeur, that eighteen subsequent centuries have done homage to him as the Almighty in person, was ignominiously put to death, as what? As a blasphemer. Men did not merely mistake their benefactor; they mistook him for the exact contrary of what he was, and treated him as that prodigy of impiety, which they themselves are now held to be, for their treatment of him. The feelings with which mankind now regard these lamentable transactions, especially the latter of the two, render them extremely unjust in their judgment

of the unhappy actors. These were, to all appearance, not bad men — not worse than men most commonly are, but rather the contrary; men who possessed in a full, or somewhat more than a full measure, the religious, moral, and patriotic feelings of their time and people: the very kind of men who, in all times, our own included, have every chance of passing through life blameless and respected....

With us, heretical opinions do not perceptibly gain or even lose, ground in each decade or generation; they never blaze out far and wide, but continue to smoulder in the narrow circles of thinking and studious persons among whom they originate, without ever lighting up the general affairs of mankind with either a true or a deceptive light. And thus is kept up a state of things very satisfactory to some minds, because, without the unpleasant process of fining or imprisoning anybody, it maintains all prevailing opinions outwardly undisturbed, while it does not absolutely interdict the exercise of reason by dissentients afflicted with the malady of thought. A convenient plan for having peace in the intellectual world, and keeping all things going on therein very much as they do already. But the price paid for this sort of intellectual pacification, is the sacrifice of the entire moral courage of the human mind. A state of things in which a large portion of the most active and inquiring intellects find it advisable to keep the genuine principles and grounds of their convictions within their own breasts, and attempt, in what they address to the public, to fit as much as they can of their own conclusions to premises which they have internally renounced, cannot send forth the open, fearless characters, and logical, consistent intellects who once adorned the thinking world....No one can be a great thinker who does not recognize, that as a thinker it is his first duty to follow his intellect to whatever conclusions it may lead. Truth gains more even by the errors of one who, with due study and preparation, thinks for himself, than by the true opinions of those who only hold them because they do not suffer themselves to think....

Let us now pass to the second division of the argument, and dismissing the Supposition that any of the received opinions may be false, let us assume them to be true, and examine into the worth of the manner in which they are likely to be held, when their truth is not freely and openly canvassed. However unwillingly a person who has a strong opinion may admit the possibility that his opinion may be false, he ought to be moved by the consideration that however true it may be, if it is not fully, frequently, and fearlessly discussed, it will be held as a dead dogma, not a living truth....

Whatever people believe, on subjects on which it is of the first importance to believe rightly, they ought to be able to defend against at least the common objections....He who knows only his own side of the case, knows little of that. His reasons may be good, and no one may have been able to refute them. But if he is equally unable to refute the reasons on the opposite side; if he does not so much as know what they are, he has no ground for preferring either opinion....

We have now recognized the necessity to the mental well-being of mankind (on which all their other well-being depends) of freedom of opinion, and freedom of the expression of opinion, on four distinct grounds; which we will now briefly recapitulate.

First, if any opinion is compelled to silence, that opinion may, for aught we can certainly know, be true. To deny this is to assume our own infallibility.

Secondly, though the silenced opinion be an error, it may, and very commonly does, contain a portion of truth; and since the general or prevailing opinion on any object is rarely or never the whole truth, it is only by the collision of adverse opinions that the remainder of the truth has any chance of being supplied.

Thirdly, even if the received opinion be not only true, but the whole truth; unless it is suffered to be, and actually is, vigorously and earnestly contested, it will, by most of those who receive it, be held in the manner of a prejudice, with little comprehension or feeling of its rational grounds. And not only this, but, fourthly, the meaning of the doctrine itself will be in danger of being lost, or enfeebled, and deprived of its vital effect on the character and conduct: the dogma becoming a mere formal profession, inefficacious for good, but cumbering the ground, and preventing the growth of any real and heartfelt conviction, from reason or personal experience....

Chapter IV
Of the Limits of the Authority of Society Over the Individual

WHAT, then, is the rightful limit to the sovereignty of the individual over himself? Where does the authority of society begin? How much of human life should be assigned to individuality, and how much to society?

Each will receive its proper share, if each has that which more particularly concerns it. To individuality should belong the part of life in which it is chiefly the individual that is interested; to society, the part which chiefly interests society.

Though society is not founded on a contract, and though no good purpose is answered by inventing a contract in order to deduce social obligations from it, every one who receives the protection of society owes a return for the benefit, and the fact of living in society renders it indispensable that each should be bound to observe a certain line of conduct towards the rest. This conduct consists, first, in not injuring the interests of one another; or rather certain interests, which, either by express legal provision or by tacit understanding, ought to be considered as rights; and secondly, in each person's bearing his share (to be fixed on some equitable principle) of the labors and sacrifices incurred for defending the society or its members from injury and molestation. These conditions society is justified in enforcing, at all costs to those who endeavor to withhold fulfilment. Nor is this all that society may do. The acts of an individual may be hurtful to others, or wanting in due consideration for their welfare, without going the length of violating any of their constituted rights. The offender may then be justly punished by opinion, though not by law. As soon as any part of a person's conduct affects prejudicially the interests of others, society has jurisdiction over it, and the question whether the general welfare will or will not be promoted by interfering with it, becomes open to discussion. But there is no room for entertaining any such question when a person's conduct affects the interests of no persons besides himself, or needs not affect them unless they like (all the persons concerned being of full age, and the ordinary amount of understanding). In all such cases there should be perfect freedom, legal and social, to do the action and stand the consequences.

It would be a great misunderstanding of this doctrine, to suppose that it is one of selfish indifference, which pretends that human beings have no business with each other's conduct in life, and that they should not concern themselves about the well-doing or well-being of one another, unless their own interest is involved. Instead of any diminution, there is need of a great increase of disinterested exertion to promote the good of others. But disinterested benevolence can find other instruments to persuade people to their good, than whips and scourges, either of the literal or the metaphorical sort. I am the last person to undervalue the self-regarding virtues; they are only second in importance, if even second, to the social. It is equally the business of education to cultivate both. But even education works by conviction and persuasion as well as by compulsion, and it is by the former only that, when the period of education is past, the self-regarding virtues should be inculcated. Human beings owe to each other help to distinguish the better from the worse, and encouragement to choose the former

and avoid the latter. They should be forever stimulating each other to increased exercise of their higher faculties, and increased direction of their feelings and aims towards wise instead of foolish, elevating instead of degrading, objects and contemplations. But neither one person, nor any number of persons, is warranted in saying to another human creature of ripe years, that he shall not do with his life for his own benefit what he chooses to do with it. He is the person most interested in his own well-being, the interest which any other person, except in cases of strong personal attachment, can have in it, is trifling, compared with that which he himself has; the interest which society has in him individually (except as to his conduct to others) is fractional, and altogether indirect: while, with respect to his own feelings and circumstances, the most ordinary man or woman has means of knowledge immeasurably surpassing those that can be possessed by any one else. The interference of society to overrule his judgment and purposes in what only regards himself, must be grounded on general presumptions; which may be altogether wrong, and even if right, are as likely as not to be misapplied to individual cases, by persons no better acquainted with the circumstances of such cases than those are who look at them merely from without. In this department, therefore, of human affairs, Individuality has its proper field of action. In the conduct of human beings towards one another, it is necessary that general rules should for the most part be observed, in order that people may know what they have to expect; but in each person's own concerns, his individual spontaneity is entitled to free exercise. Considerations to aid his judgment, exhortations to strengthen his will, may be offered to him, even obtruded on him, by others; but he, himself, is the final judge. All errors which he is likely to commit against advice and warning, are far outweighed by the evil of allowing others to constrain him to what they deem his good.

I do not mean that the feelings with which a person is regarded by others, ought not to be in any way affected by his self-regarding qualities or deficiencies. This is neither possible nor desirable. If he is eminent in any of the qualities which conduce to his own good, he is, so far, a proper object of admiration. He is so much the nearer to the ideal perfection of human nature. If he is grossly deficient in those qualities, a sentiment the opposite of admiration will follow. There is a degree of folly, and a degree of what may be called (though the phrase is not unobjectionable) lowness or depravation of taste, which, though it cannot justify doing harm to the person who manifests it, renders him necessarily and properly a subject of distaste, or, in extreme cases, even of contempt: a person could not have the opposite qualities in due strength without entertaining these feelings. Though doing no wrong to any one, a person may so act as to compel us to judge him, and feel to him, as a fool, or as a being of an inferior order: and since this judgment and feeling are a fact which he would prefer to avoid, it is doing him a service to warn him of it beforehand, as of any other disagreeable consequence to which he exposes himself. It would be well, indeed, if this good office were much more freely rendered than the common notions of politeness at present permit, and if one person could honestly point out to another that he thinks him in fault, without being considered unmannerly or presuming. We have a right, also, in various ways, to act upon our unfavorable opinion of any one, not to the oppression of his individuality, but in the exercise of ours. We are not bound, for example, to seek his society; we have a right to avoid it (though not to parade the avoidance), for we have a right to choose the society most acceptable to us. We have a right, and it may be our duty, to caution others against him, if we think his example or conversation likely to have a pernicious effect on those with whom he associates. We may give others a preference over him in optional good offices, except those which tend to his improvement. In these various modes a person may suffer very severe penalties at the hands of others, for faults which directly concern only himself; but he suffers these penalties only in so far as they are the natural, and, as it were, the spontaneous consequences of the faults themselves, not because they are purposely inflicted on him for the sake of punishment.....

I fully admit that the mischief which a person does to himself, may seriously affect, both through their sympathies and their interests, those nearly connected with him, and in a minor degree, society at large. When, by conduct of this sort, a person is led to violate a distinct and assignable obligation to any other person or persons, the case is taken out of the self-regarding class, and becomes amenable to moral disapprobation in the proper sense of the term. If, for example, a man, through intemperance or extravagance, becomes unable to pay his debts, or, having undertaken the moral responsibility of a family, becomes from the same cause incapable of supporting or educating them, he is deservedly reprobated, and might be justly punished; but it is for the breach of duty to his family or creditors, not for the extravagance. If the resources which ought to have been devoted to them, had been diverted from them for the most prudent investment, the moral culpability would have been the same....In like manner, when a person disables himself, by conduct purely self-regarding, from the performance of some definite duty incumbent on him to the public, he is guilty of a social offence. No person ought to be punished simply for being drunk; but a soldier or a policeman should be punished for being drunk on duty. Whenever, in short, there is a definite damage, or a definite risk of damage, either to an individual or to the public, the case is taken out of the province of liberty, and placed in that of morality or law.

But with regard to the merely contingent or, as it may be called, constructive injury which a person causes to society, by conduct which neither violates any specific duty to the public, nor occasions perceptible hurt to any assignable individual except himself; the inconvenience is one which society can afford to bear, for the sake of the greater good of human freedom. If grown persons are to be punished for not taking proper care of themselves, I would rather it were for their own sake, than under pretence of preventing them from impairing their capacity of rendering to society benefits which society does not pretend it has a right to exact. But I cannot consent to argue the point as if society had no means of bringing its weaker members up to its ordinary standard of rational conduct, except waiting till they do something irrational, and then punishing them, legally or morally, for it. Society has had absolute power over them during all the early portion of their existence: it has had the whole period of childhood and nonage in which to try whether it could make them capable of rational conduct in life. The existing generation is master both of the training and the entire circumstances of the generation to come; it cannot indeed make them perfectly wise and good, because it is itself so lamentably deficient in goodness and wisdom; and its best efforts are not always, in individual cases, its most successful ones; but it is perfectly well able to make the rising generation, as a whole, as good as, and a little better than, itself. If society lets any considerable number of its members grow up mere children, incapable of being acted on by rational consideration of distant motives, society has itself to blame for the consequences....

Chapter V
Applications

THE principles asserted in these pages must be more generally admitted as the basis for discussion of details, before a consistent application of them to all the various departments of government and morals can be attempted with any prospect of advantage. The few observations I propose to make on questions of detail, are designed to illustrate the principles, rather than to follow them out to their consequences. I offer, not so much applications, as specimens of ap-

plication; which may serve to bring into greater clearness the meaning and limits of the two maxims which together form the entire doctrine of this Essay and to assist the judgment in holding the balance between them, in the cases where it appears doubtful which of them is applicable to the case.

The maxims are, first, that the individual is not accountable to society for his actions, in so far as these concern the interests of no person but himself. Advice, instruction, persuasion, and avoidance by other people, if thought necessary by them for their own good, are the only measures by which society can justifiably express its dislike or disapprobation of his conduct. Secondly, that for such actions as are prejudicial to the interests of others, the individual is accountable, and may be subjected either to social or to legal punishments, if society is of opinion that the one or the other is requisite for its protection....

Consider, for example, the case of education. Is it not almost a self-evident axiom, that the State should require and compel the education, up to a certain standard, of every human being who is born its citizen? If the government would make up its mind to require for every child a good education, it might save itself the trouble of providing one. It might leave to parents to obtain the education where and how they pleased, and content itself with helping to pay the school fees of the poorer classes of children, and defraying the entire school expenses of those who have no one else to pay for them. The objections which are urged with reason against State education, do not apply to the enforcement of education by the State, but to the State's taking upon itself to direct that education: which is a totally different thing. That the whole or any large part of the education of the people should be in State hands, I go as far as any one in deprecating. All that has been said of the importance of individuality of character, and diversity in opinions and modes of conduct, involves, as of the same unspeakable importance, diversity of education. A general State education is a mere contrivance for moulding people to be exactly like one another: and as the mould in which it casts them is that which pleases the predominant power in the government, whether this be a monarch, a priesthood, an aristocracy, or the majority of the existing generation, in proportion as it is efficient and successful, it establishes a despotism over the mind, leading by natural tendency to one over the body. An education established and controlled by the State, should only exist, if it exist at all, as one among many competing experiments, carried on for the purpose of example and stimulus, to keep the others up to a certain standard of excellence....

I have reserved for the last place a large class of questions respecting the limits of government interference, which, though closely connected with the subject of this Essay, do not, in strictness, belong to it. These are cases in which the reasons against interference do not turn upon the principle of liberty: the question is not about restraining the actions of individuals, but about helping them: it is asked whether the government should do, or cause to be done, something for their benefit, instead of leaving it to be done by themselves, individually, or in voluntary combination.

The objections to government interference, when it is not such as to involve infringement of liberty, may be of three kinds.

The first is, when the thing to be done is likely to be better done by individuals than by the government. Speaking generally, there is no one so fit to conduct any business, or to determine how or by whom it shall be conducted, as those who are personally interested in it. This principle condemns the interferences, once so common, of the legislature, or the officers of government, with the ordinary processes of industry. But this part of the subject has been sufficiently enlarged upon by political economists, and is not particularly related to the principles of this Essay.

The second objection is more nearly allied to our subject. In many cases, though individuals may not do the particular thing so well, on the average, as the officers of government, it is nevertheless desirable that it should be done by them, rather than by the government, as a means to their own mental education — a mode of strengthening their active faculties, exercising their judgment, and giving them a familiar knowledge of the subjects with which they are thus left to deal. This is a principal, though not the sole, recommendation of jury trial (in cases not political); of free and popular local and municipal institutions; of the conduct of industrial and philanthropic enterprises by voluntary associations. These are not questions of liberty, and are connected with that subject only by remote tendencies; but they are questions of development. It belongs to a different occasion from the present to dwell on these things as parts of national education; as being, in truth, the peculiar training of a citizen, the practical part of the political education of a free people, taking them out of the narrow circle of personal and family selfishness, and accustoming them to the comprehension of joint interests, the management of joint concerns — habituating them to act from public or semi-public motives, and guide their conduct by aims which unite instead of isolating them from one another. Without these habits and powers, a free constitution can neither be worked nor preserved, as is exemplified by the too-often transitory nature of political freedom in countries where it does not rest upon a sufficient basis of local liberties. The management of purely local business by the localities, and of the great enterprises of industry by the union of those who voluntarily supply the pecuniary means, is further recommended by all the advantages which have been set forth in this Essay as belonging to individuality of development, and diversity of modes of action. Government operations tend to be everywhere alike. With individuals and voluntary associations, on the contrary, there are varied experiments, and endless diversity of experience. What the State can usefully do, is to make itself a central depository, and active circulator and diffuser, of the experience resulting from many trials. Its business is to enable each experimentalist to benefit by the experiments of others, instead of tolerating no experiments but its own.

The third, and most cogent reason for restricting the interference of government, is the great evil of adding unnecessarily to its power. Every function superadded to those already exercised by the government, causes its influence over hopes and fears to be more widely diffused, and converts, more and more, the active and ambitious part of the public into hangers-on of the government, or of some party which aims at becoming the government. If the roads, the railways, the banks, the insurance offices, the great joint-stock companies, the universities, and the public charities, were all of them branches of the government; if, in addition, the municipal corporations and local boards, with all that now devolves on them, became departments of the central administration; if the employes of all these different enterprises were appointed and paid by the government, and looked to the government for every rise in life; not all the freedom of the press and popular constitution of the legislature would make this or any other country free otherwise than in name. And the evil would be greater, the more efficiently and scientifically the administrative machinery was constructed — the more skilful the arrangements for obtaining the best qualified hands and heads with which to work it....

A government cannot have too much of the kind of activity which does not impede, but aids and stimulates, individual exertion and development. The mischief begins when, instead of calling forth the activity and powers of individuals and bodies, it substitutes its own activity for theirs; when, instead of informing, advising, and upon occasion denouncing, it makes them work in fetters or bids them stand aside and does their work instead of them. The worth of a State, in the long run, is the worth of the individuals composing it; and a State which postpones the interests of their mental expansion and elevation, to a little more of administrative skill or that semblance of it which practice gives, in the details of business; a State, which dwarfs its men, in order that they may be more docile instruments in its hands even for beneficial purposes, will find that with small men no great thing can really be accomplished; and that the perfection of machinery to which it has sacrificed everything, will in the end avail it nothing, for want of the vital power which, in order that the machine might work more smoothly, it has preferred to banish.

Marge Piercy

Saille: Right to Life

Marge Piercy, American poet and novelist, was born in Detroit in 1936. She was active in the civil rights and student movements of the 1960s, and continues to be involved in feminist politics. Her critically acclaimed novels include *Woman on the Edge of Time* (1976), *Fly Away Home* (1984), *Gone to Soldiers* (1987), and *Summer People* (1989). The following selection is one of a series of poems entitled "The Lunar Cycle," published in the 1977 volume *The Moon is Always Female*.

Right to Life
Marge Piercy

A woman is not a pear tree
    thrusting her fruit in mindless fecundity
    into the world. Even pear trees bear
heavily one year and rest and grow the next
An orchard gone wild drops few warm rotting
fruit in the grass but the trees stretch
high and wiry gifting the birds forty
feet up among inch long thorns
broken atavistically from the smooth wood.

A woman is not a basket you place
your buns in to keep them warm. Not a brood
hen you can slip duck eggs under.
Not the purse holding the coins of your
descendants till you spend them in wars.
Not a bank where your genes gather interest
and interesting mutations in the tainted
rain, any more than you are.

You plant corn and you harvest
it to eat or sell. You put the lamb
in the pasture to fatten and haul it in
to butcher for chops. You slice
the mountain in two for a road and gouge
the high plains for coal and the waters
run muddy for miles and years.
Fish die but you do not call them yours
unless you wished to eat them

Now you legislate mineral rights in a woman.
You lay claim to her pastures for grazing,
fields for growing babies like iceberg
lettuce. You value children so dearly
that none ever go hungry, none weep
with no one to tend them when mothers
work, none lack fresh fruit,

none chew lead or cough to death and your
orphanages are empty. Every noon the best
restaurants serve poor children steaks.

At this moment at nine o'clock a *partera*
is performing a table top abortion on an
unwed mother in Texas who can't get Medicaid
any longer. In five days she will die
of tetanus and her little daughter will cry
and be taken away. Next door a husband
and wife are sticking pins in the son
they did not want. They will explain
for hours how wicked he is,
how he wants discipline.

We are all born of woman, in the rose
of the womb we suckled our mother's blood
and every baby born has a right to love
like a seedling to sun. Every baby born

unloved, unwanted is a bill that will come
due in twenty years with interest, an anger
that must find a target, a pain that will
beget pain. A decade downstream a child
screams, a woman falls, a synagogue is torched,
a firing squad is summoned, a button
is pushed and the world burns.

I will choose what enters me, what becomes
flesh of my flesh. Without choice, no politics,
no ethics lives. I am not your cornfield,
not your uranium mine, not your calf
for fattening, not your cow for milking.
You may not use me as your factory.
Priests and legislators do not hold
shares in my womb or my mind.
This is my body. If I give it to you
I want it back. My life
is a non-negotiable demand.

Benjamin R. Barber
The Reconstruction of Rights

In "The Reconstruction of Rights" Benjamin Barber examines the balance between rights and responsibilities in American society. He finds the scale tipped excessively toward individual rights, showing that we have neglected the historical and theoretical dependence of individual rights on the community that secures those rights. Barber argues that the very idea of rights implies the equality of citizens. And democracy is designed specifically for those who see themselves as equals. Thus, in order for rights to have any meaning, they need to be legislated and defined by an active democratic citizenry. In fact, active citizens have been the force behind the continual expansion of rights to include ever more constituents throughout American history. But this development of rights becomes endangered when we use a notion of private rights to abuse the communities enforcing our rights. When we claim our rights *against* the government rather than *through* the government, when we talk only about what the community owes us and forget what we owe the community, we forget that the community itself has rights which must be upheld by citizens rather than attacked by private individuals.

The Reconstruction of Rights
Benjamin R. Barber

If there is a single theme upon which Americans agree, it is that ours is a regime rooted in rights. Rights are how we enter our political conversation: the chips with which we bargain, the collateral in the social contract. They are the ground of both rebellion and legitimacy, of our inclinations to anarchism and our proclivities towards community.

Without coaching, any American will cry out:

"I know my rights!" or
"You got no right!" or
"What about my rights?" or
"Read him his rights!"

Corporations mimic individuals in their devotion to rights as barriers against the public regulation of private profit. The Philip Morris Company recently paid the National Archives $600,000 to associate itself with the Bill of Rights, presumably to promote its view of advertising as a First Amendment right essential to selling tobacco in an age of democratic public health advocacy. Rights are how Americans have always advanced their interests, whether as individual or corporate persons. Some might say (I will do so below) that there is even an element of obsession in the American devotion to rights, that we sometimes risk a rights absolutism as unbalanced in its political effects as the fabled "tyranny of the majority" against which rights are often deployed as the primary defense.

Yet there are good reasons for the focus on rights. The naked self comes to the bargaining table weak and puny; the language of rights clothes it. The naked self extends hardly beyond that bundle of desires and aversions that constitute its raw, pre-legitimate wants. Rights carve out a space for it to operate in—call it autonomy or dignity or, in its material incarnation, property. Wants become needs and needs acquire a moral mantle that, as rights claims, cannot be ignored. The hungry man wants to eat; the ravenous man needs to eat, the starving man has a right to eat. Rights turn the facts of want into powerful claims—powerful, at least, in civil societies that consider rights rhetoric legitimate.

Even the naked self is perforce a social self, whose claims on others imply reciprocity as well as equality. If, as this suggests, democracy is the form of governance especially suited to the language of rights, it is ironic and troubling to find the language of rights often deployed in a fashion adversarial to democracy. Perhaps this is because democracy is often understood as the rule of the majority, and rights are understood more and more as the private possessions of individuals and thus as necessarily antagonistic to majoritarian democracy. But, as I will suggest, this is to misunderstand both rights and democracy....

I mean here to advance both a logical claim and a historical claim. I want to say rights can be shown theoretically to entail equality and democracy. And at the same time, I want to argue that the actual history of rights talk in America unfolds as an increasingly progressive and democratic story. Philosophically, rights claims are always and necessarily equality claims as well. To say "I have a right" is to posit that I am the equal of others and at the same time to recognize the equality of the persons to whom, on whom, against whom the claim is made. No master ever said to a slave: "Give me my rights!" for rights can be acknowledged only by equals. Likewise, the slave who proclaims "I have the right to be free" says in the same breath "I am your equal," and hence "you are my equal." In a certain sense, in speaking of equal rights one speaks redundantly; rights are equalizers. Individuals may use rights to insulate themselves from others, to wall in their privacy, but their rights claims depend entirely on the proposition that as claimants they are the equal of all others, that no one living in a free and democratic society is privileged because of who they happen to be by virtue of race, gender, religion, and so forth.

More than anything else, this is why a constitution rooted in rights cannot systematically exclude whole classes of persons from citizenship without becoming inherently incoherent and thus unstable. Even where it is anti-democratic in its institutional provisions, it will incline to democratization, tend over time towards greater inclusiveness. This is exactly what happened to the American polity in the course of the nineteenth century. That the Constitution included provisions implicitly recognizing slavery (the three-fifths compromise for example) was a shameful comment on the Founders and perhaps on their motives. Nonetheless, such provisions sat like undigested gruel on the Constitution's rights-lined stomach and were in time regurgitated. This resulted not simply from pressures brought to bear from the outside, but arose from the inherently universalizing character of all rights talk, which pushes against artificial boundaries of every kind and makes inequalities increasingly indigestible.

If rights imply citizenship and citizenship appears as a right—the right to liberty, the right to self-legislation, the right to be included in a civic polity founded on "popular" (that-means-me!) sovereignty—the idea of the citizen will always have an aggressive, liberating, even imperial character, pushing to extend its compass to the very periphery of the universal. In Rome, early modern Europe, and America, it has been expansive in its logic and liberating in its politics. Today as rights continue to press outward, reaching the very edge of our species boundary, we can even speak of "animal rights" or "fetal rights" and still seem to be extending rather than perverting what it means for beings to have rights.

Rights are also linked logically to democracy and equality as a consequence of their essentially social character. Rousseau had already observed in *The Social Contract* that though all justice comes from God, "if we knew how to receive it from on high, we would need neither government nor laws. There is without a doubt a universal justice emanating from reason alone; but to be acknowledged among us, this justice must be reciprocal ... there must be conventions and laws to combine rights with duties and to bring justice back to its object." In a classical nineteenth-century idealist argument, the English political philosopher T. H. Green elaborates Rousseau's argument by insisting "there can be no right without a consciousness of common interest on the part of members of a society. Without this there might be certain powers on the part of individuals, but no recognition of these powers ... and without this recognition or claim to recognition there can be no right."* Recognition entails the mutuality of a common language, common conventions, and common consciousness: in other words, civility. Citizens alone possess rights, for as Green said, rights "attach to the individual...only as a member of a society." Tocqueville is, of course, right to remind us that citizens united as a majority are still capable of abusing the rights of citizens taken one by one. But Green's rejoinder is that the tyranny of the majority may be more a reflection on the inadequacies of democratic processes than the absence of rights.

Democracy as the Realm of Rights

Now if rights entail equality and require a civic context of mutual recognition to be effective, the regime form most compatible with rights is neither decentralized, limited government on the model of the Anti-Federalists, nor screened and filtered representative government on the republican model of the Federalists, but quite simply democracy—defined by universal suffrage and collective self-legislation. For democracy is the rule of equality. Limited government is indifferent to who rules so long as the rulers are constrained. Republican government elicits the consent and accountability but not the participation and judgment of the people, which is why Jefferson sometimes called representative government elective aristocracy. Rights do best, however, where those who claim them are one and the same with those upon whom the claims fall—where sovereign and subject are united in one person: a citizen. Without citizenship and participation, rights can become a charade. Without responsibility, rights may not always be enforceable. Without empowerment, rights can seem like decorative fictions. A constitution is, after all, a piece of paper, and "parchment barriers" are never much use against lead and steel and chains and guns, although they can be a significant trip-wire against majority assaults on minorities, something the Founders obviously appreciated.

In what may be the world's most effusively rights-oriented constitution, a famous document not only guarantees citizens "freedom of speech," "freedom of the press," "freedom of assembly," and "freedom of street processions and demonstrations," but also offers judges who will be constitutionally "independent and subject only to the law," "separation of church from state," as well as the "right to education," "the right to work," "the right to rest and leisure," "the right to maintenance in old age and also in case of sickness or disability," and, as if these were not enough, equal rights to women "in all spheres of economic, government, cultural, political and other public activity," and finally, guaranteeing what comes before, universal elections in which all citizens have the right to vote, "irrespective of race or nationality, sex, religion,

---

* Thomas Hill Green, Lectures on the Principles of Political Obligation (London: Longmans, 1941).

education, domicile, social origin, property status or past activities." This unprecedented fortress of human liberty was the Constitution (Fundamental Law) of the former Soviet Union, a nation in which rights have been paper parapets from which no defense of liberties can be undertaken.

As Madison observed in questioning the value of a Bill of Rights detached from the Constitution, "Repeated violations of ... parchment barriers have been committed by overbearing majorities in every state.... Whenever there is an interest and power to do wrong, wrong will generally be done and not less readily by a powerful and interested party than by a powerful and interested prince."*

Philosophical argument finds persuasive historical expression in the American setting. Successful popular movements aimed at the emancipation of slaves, the enfranchisement of women, and the remediation of the condition of the native American Indian tribes, as well as the empowerment of the poor, the working class, and others cast aside by the American market, have all had in common a devotion to the language of rights. Indeed, the single most important strategic decision faced by those who felt left out of the American way of life has been whether to mobilize against or in the name of the American Founding, understood as the Declaration of Independence, the Constitution, and the Bill of Rights. Movements that have made war on the Constitution, holding that its rights promise no salvation to the powerless, have on the whole failed. Movements that have insisted that the Founding can and must make good on the promise implicit in its universalizing rights rhetoric have succeeded.

In their explicit mimicry of the Founders' language and the citation of great rights jurists like Blackstone, the bold women at Seneca Falls in 1846 captured the logic of "entailment" with their own militant rights claims. "We hold these truths to be self-evident," they asserted, "that all men and women are created equal."** And although the radical abolitionists at times seemed to declare war on America itself, one of their most fiery leaders understood the entailments of the American tradition well enough. William Lloyd Garrison burned a copy of the Constitution in Framingham on July 4, 1854, but he nevertheless declared in *The Liberator*, in his *To the Public*, and in impassioned speeches throughout the North, that he "assented to the 'self-evident truth' maintained in the Declaration of Independence, 'that all men are created equal, and endowed by their Creator with certain inalienable rights—among which are life, liberty and the pursuit of happiness.'" On this foundation, he concluded, he would "strenuously contend for the immediate enfranchisement of our slave population."***

Some might say these radicals were trying to drive a wedge between the Declaration and the Constitution, but when John Brown went looking for legitimacy he found it in the Preamble to the Constitution as well as in the Declaration. When he offered the People of the United States a "Provisional Constitution," its preamble read: "Whereas slavery, throughout its entire existence in the United States, is none

---

*   Madison, *The Tree of Liberty: A Documentary History of Rebellion and Political Crime in America*, edited by Nicholas N. Kittrie and Eldon D. Wedlock, Jr. (Baltimore: The Johns Hopkins University Press, 1986).

** See "The Declaration of Sentiments and Resolutions of the First Women's Rights Conference," in Elizabeth Stanton, Susan B. Anthony, and Matilda Joslyn Gage, eds., *History of Woman Suffrage* (New York: Fowler & Wells, 1881), 170–173.

*** William Lloyd Garrison, in Wendell Garrison and Francis Jackson Garrison, *William Lloyd Garrison: 1805–1879* (New York: Amo Press, 1969), 408.

other than a most barbarous, unprovoked, and unjustifiable war of one portion of its citizens upon another portion ... in utter disregard and violation of those eternal and self-evident truths set forth in our Declaration of Independence, therefore we, citizens of the United States, and the oppressed people (deprived of Rights by Justice Taney) ... do ordain and establish for ourselves the following Provisional Constitution and ordinances, the better to protect our person, property, lives and liberties, and to govern our action."*

From this perspective, the Civil War and Reconstruction Amendments ending slavery and involuntary servitude and guaranteeing universal male suffrage, due process, and the equal protection of the laws to all citizens were not a reversal of America's constitutional history but the culminating event in the history of the Constitution's rights commitments as they manifested themselves in the practical politics and civic life of the nation....

Even at the time of the Founding there had been powerful opposition to slavery as an embarrassment to the language of the Declaration and the Constitution's Preamble. John Adams and John Jay were vigorously eloquent in their opposition to it (although not at the Convention), and there were a number of statesmen who would sympathize with George Mason's refusal to sign the Constitution because its twenty-year extension of the slave trade was "disgraceful to mankind."

Madison had acknowledged moral equality of blacks and in *Federalist* No. 54 had allowed that Negroes did "partake" of qualities belonging to persons as well as to property and were thus protected in the "life and limb, against the violence of all others." The slave, Madison said elsewhere, "is no less evidently regarded by the law as a member of the society, not as part of irrational creation; as a moral person, not as a mere article of property."**

Are Rights Eroding Democracy?

In our century, the powerful alliance between rights and political emancipation, between the claim to be a person and the right to be a citizen, seems in danger of coming unstuck. Increasingly, rights have retreated into the private space won for them by their civic entailments, allowing us to forget that they are secured by and only have meaning for citizens. The communities rights once created are now too often pictured as the enemies of right and the political institutions by which we secure rights are made over into external and alien adversaries—as if they had nothing to do with us. The sense of rights as a claim for political participation, and participation and civic responsibility as the foundation of rights, has yielded to peculiarly privatized notions of rights as indisputable possessions of individuals who acquire them by birth or membership in some special subgroup, and must do nothing to enforce them. Such rights exist and are efficacious as long as they are noisily promulgated.

There are multiple reasons for the new take on rights, many of which have little to do with the logic of rights itself and for which rights advocates cannot be blamed. The erosion of viable notions of the public and of a common good and the growth of interest-group liberalism in which private factions and their rights come to count as the only political entities worthy of attention has undermined citizenship and the public rights associated with it. Under conditions of privatization, consumerism,

---

*   Louis Ruchames, *John Brown: The Making of a Revolutionary* (New York: Grosset & Dunlop, 1969), 119–120.
**   James Madison to Frances Wright, Sept. 1, 1825, from James Madison, *Letters and Other Writings*, vol. 3, 495.

radical individualism, and cultural separatism, rights cease to be regarded as a civic identity to be posited and won, and are instead conceived as a natural identity to be discovered, worn, and enjoyed.

As a consequence, young people are more likely to use rights to make a case about what government owes them than to point to what they themselves might owe to the democratic government that is the guarantor of their rights ("Ask not what your country can do for you...."). Thus, for example, they may exclaim that the government has "no right" to conscript them into the army, as if it were not their government, as if there could be a democratic government in the absence of their willingness and responsibility to service it—quite literally to constitute it. Many young persons in fact do engage in community service or enlist in the armed services or participate in demonstrations and protests, but as often as not these activities are either seen as "voluntary" (it is a "volunteer army") or as a manifestation of rights and prerogatives held against government and the polity. Civic duties and social responsibilities simply do not come into it.*

The changing climate of politics is evident in the vanishing of volunteer fire departments for want of volunteers, and in the growing ungovernability of municipalities that cannot afford liability insurance against disgruntled inhabitants who conceive themselves as dissatisfied clients rather than as responsible citizens. Fire protection comes to be viewed as a service provided by government to residents rather than a service by, for and of citizens. Where Our Town becomes Their Town, rights can become a knife that severs the bonds of citizens rather than the glue that holds it together. The right to sue is a precious resource against abusive authority; yet democratic responsibility is also a powerful guarantee against abuse. We need

both. The litigious citizen expresses his rights as an individual but may be overlooking his responsibilities to the community being sued.

The precarious balance between individual and community which rights properly understood can mediate is upset, and rights are introduced on only one side of the scales, leaving the community hard pressed to advance the public good. Legal philosophers like to say that rights are trumps, which is a poignant way of underscoring the crucial subjugation of democratic government to the liberties of citizens. But there is also a sense in which, as Rousseau once wrote, citizens are trumps: "There can be no patriotism without liberty," Rousseau observes, "no liberty without virtue, no virtue without citizens; create citizens and you will have everything you need; without them you will have nothing but debased slaves from the rulers of the state on downwards."

Rights, after all, belong to individuals as citizens, and citizens belong to communities that therefore also have rights. There is no reason not to use the power of rights as legitimizers of claims in order to advance community goods. Tenants organizing against drug traffickers, victims organizing to secure their rights in a criminal justice system disposed (quite properly) to pay special attention to the rights of criminal defendants, and mothers organizing against drunk drivers (MADD) offer compelling examples of the power of rights-thinking on behalf of the community at large.

The American Civil Liberties Union has been an ardent and valuable advocate of the rights of individuals in our democracy. Yet the ACLU's conception of rights has occasionally veered towards a denial of community that may reflect the breakdown of our sense of common civic purposes as a nation. In recent years, in addition to its healthy concerns with the sanctity of political speech and the right of assembly

---

* For a provocative symposium on a "bill of duties" in which this commentator participated, see *Harper's*, February, 1991.

(both of which are important to the polity and the public good), the ACLU has dug itself into a foxhole from which it can engage in a firefight with democracy. The ACLU has opposed airport security examinations, decried sobriety checkpoints (recently declared constitutional by the Supreme Court in a 6–3 decision), argued against the voluntary fingerprinting of children in areas subject to kidnapping. By making privacy over into a supertrump card in a deck of individual rights that, with respect both to public goods and community rights, is already trump to start with, it places at risk the balance between individual and community that is the prize achievement of the history of rights in America.

In the case of the *Michigan Department of State Police* v. *Sitz*, a leading argument held that sobriety checkpoints abridged the constitutional rights of Michigan motorists by causing them "fright and surprise" in the course of ninety-second stops that were tantamount to "subjective intrusion upon liberty interests." The liberty interests of other drivers as potential victims of drunken driving usually thought of as belonging to the rights of the community, or the responsibility of the body politic, were not weighed and found wanting; they were ignored. This is a growing problem in a society where the idea of civic community has lost its resonance and interest groups such as the National Rifle Association use rights as a foil for their special pleading.

This unbalancing of the rights equation feeds into the historical mistrust some Americans still feel towards popular government. It threatens to disenfranchise the very citizenry rights were once deployed to empower. The new strategy links a Federal distrust of popular rule with a form of judicial activism that permits courts not merely to enforce rights but to legislate in their name whenever the "people" are deemed sufficiently deluded or insufficiently energetic. It is not at all clear that rights enforced on an obstinate citizen body rendered passive-aggressive (quiescent but angry) by an encroaching court

are really made more secure over the long haul. But it certainly is clear that a "democratic" government that will not permit its citizens to govern themselves when it comes to rights will soon be without either rights or democracy.

It was, of course, an original Federalist strategy aimed at curbing democracy that produced judicial review as a limit on popular legislation. In the Madisonian approach to the balance of power, the judiciary has remained a key instrument in preventing majorities from getting out of hand. Yet as Louis Hartz noticed, the majority has not really gotten out of hand very often in America. Tolerance notwithstanding, at least since *Brown* v. *Board of Education* (1954), impatient democrats seeking to secure rights that majorities sometimes neglected have allied themselves with courts willing to act as surrogate legislators where the people are found wanting. The "filtration" of the public mind favored by the Founders thus has found a modern incarnation in the not so democratic practices of judicial government.

In the recent Supreme Court case upholding a lower court decision concerning Kansas City (Missouri) school desegregation, the majority ruled in favor of a judicial intervention whose final outcome was the raising of taxes. The case is complicated, and the Missouri court did not itself directly levy taxes, but Justice Anthony Kennedy issued a sobering caution about the logic of the judiciary acting as legislative surrogate when he wrote in dissent "It is not surprising that imposition of taxes by a [judicial] authority so insulated from public communication or control can lead to deep feelings of frustration, powerlessness and anger on the part of taxpaying citizens." Frustration, powerlessness, and anger have become the currency in which many Americans have paid for the usurping of their political authority in the name of their political rights. Americans need their rights, but they need also to understand the responsibilities their rights entail. If seen solely as private things to be secured by judges rather than public things (*res publica*) to be secured by citizens, rights atrophy.

Democracies do not always do justice. Frequently they do injustice. Yet the remedy for this, as Jefferson noted a long time ago, is not to disempower citizens who have been indiscreet, but to inform their discretion, which may sometimes mean extending rather than circumscribing their power. For power teaches responsibility and responsibility limits power. Like experienced legislators, publics can and do become more discreet and competent over time. The ravages done by Proposition 13 (which initiated the tax revolt in 1978, limiting state expenditures) have gradually educated the people of California into an appreciation of their civic responsibilities. In the spring of 1990, quite on their own, and without the mandate of a court, they approved a referendum raising taxes. What America most needs just now are not more interventionist courts but more interventionist schools; not lessons in the rights of private persons but lessons in the responsibilities of public citizens; not a new view of the Bill of Rights, but a new view of the Constitution as the democratic source of all rights.

Madison might have had a better understanding of rights than the advocates of a separate Bill of Amendments when he argued for including rights in the substantive text of the constitution. For by placing them there, where they would be read in context rather than isolating them in a document that might make them seem a natural possession of passive private persons, their civic and social nature as part and parcel of the fabric of democratic republicanism might have been crystal clear.

On this two hundredth birthday of the Bill of Rights, we need to learn for ourselves what the first 75 years of American history, culminating in the Civil War, taught our ancestors in a still young America: that rights stand with, not against, democracy and if the two do not progress together, they do not progress at all.

Herman Melville
Billy Budd, Sailor

Herman Melville (1819–1891), American author, was born in New York City and drifted from job to job until 1839 when he signed aboard a trading ship bound for England. Two years later he took a job on the whaler *Acushnet*. He jumped ship in the Marquesas Islands, living a month among the natives of the Typee Valley. He took this experience as the subject of his first novel, Typee (1846). Soon after, Melville married Elizabeth Shaw, daughter of the chief justice of Massachusetts, and moved to a farm in western Massachusetts where he wrote his monumental novel, *Moby Dick* (1851). Melville wrote several other novels (*White-Jacket, Pierre, Israel, Potter, The Confidence Man*) and some short fiction, but was never widely recognized during his lifetime. The manuscript of *Billy Budd, Foretopman* was discovered among Melville's papers after his death and published in 1924.

Set in the year 1798, the story takes place in the context of naval warfare between the English and French, not long after a series of mutinies in the British fleet had given every British officer cause to intensify naval discipline. The sailor Billy Budd, impressed into service, represents the essence of childhood innocence. He is a Christ-like figure, who inspires goodwill in all who know him. John Claggart, a junior officer responsible for general discipline aboard ship, is, by contrast, spiritually corrupt. Like Billy's goodness, Claggart's evil is innate, "a depravity according to nature." Claggart's envy of Billy leads him to make unfounded accusations of treason and conspiracy which leads Billy, who speaks with difficulty, to strike out in innocent rage, inadvertently killing Claggart. Captain Vere—humane, intellectual, and a loyal military officer—is thus faced with a choice between his captain's duty to technical "justice" (the military code) and his humanity.

Billy Budd
Herman Melville

Now when the foretopman found himself closeted there, as it were, in the cabin with the captain and Claggart, he was surprised enough. But it was a surprise unaccompanied by apprehension or distrust. To an immature nature essentially honest and humane, forewarning intimations of subtler danger from one's kind come tardily if at all. The only thing that took shape in the young sailor's mind was this: Yes, the captain, I have always thought, looks kindly upon me. Wonder if he's going to make me his coxswain. I should like that. And maybe now he is going to ask the master-at-arms about me.

"Shut the door there, sentry," said the commander; "stand without and let nobody come in.—Now, Master-at-Arms, tell this man to his face what you told of him to me," and stood prepared to scrutinize the mutually confronting visages.

With the measured step and calm collected air of an asylum physician approaching in the public hall some patient beginning to show indications of a coming paroxysm, Claggart deliberately advanced within short range of Billy, and, mesmerically looking him in the eye, briefly recapitulated the accusation.

Not at first did Billy take it in. When he did, the rose-tan of his cheek looked struck as by white leprosy. He stood like one impaled and gagged. Meanwhile the accuser's eyes removing not as yet from the blue dilated ones, underwent a phenomenal change, their wonted rich violet color blurring into a muddy purple, those lights of human intelligence losing human expression, gelidly protruding like alien eyes of certain uncatalogued creatures of the deep. The first mesmeric glance was one of serpent fascination; the last was as the hungry lurch of the torpedo-fish.

"Speak, man!"—said Captain Vere to the transfixed one, struck by his aspect even more than by Claggart's. "Speak! defend yourself." Which appeal caused but a strange dumb gesturing and gurgling in Billy, amazement at such an accusation so suddenly sprung on inexperienced nonage; this, and, it may be, horror of the accuser, serving to bring out his lurking defect and in this instance for the time intensifying it into a convulsed tongue-tie; while the intent head and entire form straining forward in an agony of ineffectual eagerness to obey the injunction to speak and defend himself, gave an expression to the face like that of a condemned Vestal priestess in the moment of being buried alive, and in the first struggle against suffocation.

Though at the time Captain Vere was quite ignorant of Billy's liability to vocal impediment, he now immediately divined it, since vividly Billy's aspect recalled to him that of a bright young schoolmate of his whom he had once seen struck by much the same startling impotence in the act of eagerly rising in the class to be foremost in response to a testing question put to it by the master. Going close up to the young sailor, and laying a soothing band on his shoulder, he said: "There is no hurry, my boy. Take your time, take your time." Contrary to the effect intended, these words so fatherly in tone doubtless touching Billy's heart to the quick, prompted yet more violent efforts at utterance—efforts soon ending for the time in confirming the paralysis, and bringing to his face an expression which was as a crucifixion to behold. The next instant, quick as the flame from a discharged cannon at night, his right arm shot out, and Claggart dropped to the deck. Whether intentionally or but owing to young athlete's superior height, the blow had taken effect full upon the forehead, so shapely and intellectual looking a feature in the master-at-arms, so that the body fell over lengthwise, like a heavy plank tilted from erectness. A gasp or two, and he lay motionless.

"Fated boy," breathed Captain Vere in tone so low as to be almost a whisper, "what have you done! But here, help me."

The twain raised the felled one from the loins up into a sitting position. The spare form flexibly acquiesced, but inertly. It was like handling a dead snake. They lowered it back. Regaining erectness Captain Vere with one hand covering his face stood to all appearance as impassive as the object at his feet. Was he absorbed in taking in all the bearings of the event and what was best, not only now at once to be done, but also in the sequel? Slowly he uncovered his face, and the effect was as if the moon emerging from eclipse should reappear with quite another aspect than that which had gone into hiding. The father in him, manifested toward Billy thus far in the scene, was replaced by the military disciplinarian. In his official tone he bade the foretopman retire to a stateroom aft (pointing it out) and there remain till thence summoned. This order Billy in silence mechanically obeyed....

But Captain Vere was now again motionless, standing absorbed in thought. But again starting, he vehemently exclaimed—"Struck dead by an angel of God! Yet the angel must hang?"

That the unhappy event which has been narrated could not have happened at a worse juncture was but too true. For it was close on the heel of the suppressed insurrections, an aftertime very critical to naval authority, demanding from every English sea commander two qualities not readily interfusible—prudence and rigor. Moreover, there was something crucial in the case.

In the jugglery of circumstances preceding and attending the event on board the *Indomitable*, and in the light of that martial code whereby it was formally to be judged, innocence and guilt personified in Claggart and Budd in effect changed places. In a legal view the apparent victim of the tragedy was he who had sought to victimize a man blameless; and the indisputable deed of the latter, navally regarded, constituted the most heinous of military crimes. Yet more. The essential right and wrong involved in the matter, the clearer that might be, so much the worse for the responsibility of a loyal sea commander inasmuch as he was not authorized to determine the matter on that primitive basis.

Small wonder then that the *Indomitable*'s captain, though in general a man of rapid decision, felt that circumspectness not less than promptitude was necessary. Until he could decide upon his course, and in each detail, and not only so, but until the concluding measure was upon the point of being enacted, he deemed it advisable, in view of all the circumstances, to guard as much as possible against publicity. Here be may or may not have erred. Certain it is, however, that subsequently in the confidential talk of more than one or two gun rooms and cabins he was not a little criticized by some officers, a fact imputed by his friends and vehemently by his cousin Jack Denton to professional jealousy of "Starry Vere." Some imaginative ground for invidious comment there was. The maintenance of secrecy in the matter, the confining all knowledge of it for a time to the place where the homicide occurred, the quarter-deck cabin—in these particulars lurked some resemblance to the policy adopted in those tragedies of the palace which have occurred more than once in the capital founded by Peter the Barbarian.

The case indeed was such that fain would the *Indomitable*'s captain have deferred taking any action whatever respecting it further than to keep the foretopman a close prisoner till the ship rejoined the squadron and then submitting the matter to the judgment of his admiral.

But a true military officer is in one particular like a true monk. Not with more of self-abnegation will the latter keep his vows of monastic obedience than the former his vows of allegiance to martial duty.

Feeling that unless quick action was taken on it, the deed of the foretopman, so soon as it should be known on the gun decks, would tend to awaken any slumbering embers of the Nore among the crew, a sense of the urgency of the case overruled in Captain Vere every other consideration. But though a conscientious disciplinarian he was no lover of authority for mere authority's sake. Very far was he from embracing opportunities for monopolizing to himself the perils of moral responsibility, none at least that could properly be referred to an official superior or shared with him by his official equals or even subordinates. So thinking, he was glad it would not be at variance with usage to turn the matter over to a summary court of his own officers, reserving to himself as the one on whom the ultimate accountability would rest, the right

of maintaining a supervision of it, or formally or informally interposing at need. Accordingly a drumhead court was summarily convened, he electing the individuals composing it, the first lieutenant, the captain of marines, and the sailing master....

All being quickly in readiness, Billy Budd was arraigned, Captain Vere necessarily appearing as the sole witness in the case, and as such temporarily sinking his rank, though singularly maintaining it in a matter apparently trivial, namely, that he testified from the ship's weather side, with that object having caused the court to sit on the lee side. Concisely he narrated all that had led up to the catastrophe, omitting nothing in Claggart's accusation and deposing as to the manner in which the prisoner had received it. At this testimony the three officers glanced with no little surprise at Billy Budd, the last man they would have suspected either of the mutinous design alleged by Claggart or the undeniable deed he himself had done.

The first lieutenant, taking judicial primacy and turning toward the prisoner, said, "Captain Vere has spoken. Is it or is it not as Captain Vere says?" In response came syllables not so much impeded in the utterance as might have been anticipated. They were these: "Captain Vere tells the truth. It is just as Captain Vere says, but it is not as the master-at-arms said. I have eaten the King's bread and I am true to the King."

"I believe you, my man," said the witness, his voice indicating a suppressed emotion not otherwise betrayed.

"God will bless you for that, your honor!" not without stammering said Billy, and all but broke down. But immediately was recalled to self-control by another question, to which with the same emotional difficulty of utterance he said, "No, there was no malice between us. I never bore malice against the master-at-arms. I am sorry that he is dead. I did not mean to kill him. Could I have used my tongue I would not have struck him. But he foully lied to my face and in presence of my captain, and I had to say something, and I could only say it with a blow, God help me!"

In the impulsive aboveboard manner of the frank one the court saw confirmed all that was implied in words that just previously had perplexed them, coming as they did from the testifier to the tragedy and promptly following Billy's impassioned disclaimer of mutinous intent—Captain Vere's words, "I believe you, my man."

Next it was asked of him whether he knew of or suspected aught savoring of incipient trouble (meaning mutiny, though the explicit term was avoided) going on in any section of the ship's company.

The reply lingered. This was naturally imputed by the court to the same vocal embarrassment which had retarded or obstructed previous answers. But in main it was otherwise here, the question immediately recalling to Billy's mind the interview with the after-guardsman in the forechains. But an innate repugnance to playing a part at all approaching that of an informer against one's own shipmates—the same erring sense of uninstructed honor which had stood in the way of his reporting the matter at the time though as a loyal man-of-war-man it was incumbent on him, and failure so to do if charged against him and proven, would have subjected him to the heaviest of penalties—this, with the blind feeling now his, that nothing really was being hatched, prevailed with him. When the answer came it was a negative.

"One question more," said the officer of marines, now first speaking and with a troubled earnestness. "You tell us that what the master-at-arms said against you was a lie. Now why should he have so lied so maliciously lied, since you declare there was no malice between you?"

At that question unintentionally touching on a spiritual sphere wholly obscure to Billy's thoughts, he was nonplused, evincing a confusion indeed that some observers, such as can readily be imagined, would have construed into involuntary evidence of hidden guilt. Never-

theless he strove some way to answer, but all at once relinquished the vain endeavor, at the same time turning an appealing glance toward Captain Vere, as deeming him his best helper and friend. Captain Vere, who had been seated for a time, rose to his feet, addressing the interrogator. "The question you put to him comes naturally enough. But how can he rightly answer it? or anybody else? unless indeed it be he who lies within there," designating the compartment where lay the corpse. "But the prone one there will not rise to our summons. In effect, though, as it seems to me, the point you make is hardly material. Quite aside from any conceivable motive actuating the master-at-arms, and irrespective of the provocation to the blow, a martial court must needs in the present case confine its attention to the blow's consequence, which consequence justly is to be deemed not otherwise than as the striker's deed."

This utterance, the full significance of which it was not at all likely that Billy took in, nevertheless caused him to turn a wistful interrogative look toward the speaker, a look in its dumb expressiveness not unlike that which a dog of generous breed might turn upon his master, seeking in his face some elucidation of a previous gesture ambiguous to the canine intelligence. Nor was the same utterance without marked effect upon the three officers, more especially the soldier. Couched in it seemed to them a meaning unanticipated, involving a prejudgment on the speaker's part. It served to augment a mental disturbance previously evident enough.

The soldier once more spoke, in a tone of suggestive dubiety addressing at once his associates and Captain Vere: "Nobody is present—none of the ship's company, I mean—who might shed lateral light, if any is to be had, upon what remains mysterious in this matter."

"That is thoughtfully put," said Captain Vere; "I see your drift. Aye, there is a mystery; but, to use a Scriptural phrase, it is 'a mystery of iniquity,' a matter for psychologic theologians to discuss. But what has a military court to do with it? Not to add that for us any possible investigation of it is cut off by the lasting tongue-tie of—him—in yonder," again designating the mortuary stateroom. "The prisoner's deed—with that alone we have to do."

To this, and particularly the closing reiteration, the marine soldier, knowing not how aptly to reply, sadly abstained from saying aught. The first lieutenant, who at the outset had not unnaturally assumed primacy in the court, now overrulingly instructed by a glance from Captain Vere, a glance more effective than words, resumed that primacy. Turning to the prisoner, "Budd," he said, and scarce in equable tones, "Budd, if you have aught further to say for yourself, say it now."

Upon this the young sailor turned another quick glance toward Captain Vere; then, as taking a hint from that aspect, a hint confirming his own instinct that silence was now best, replied to the lieutenant "I have said all, sir."

The marine—the same who had been the sentinel without the cabin door at the time that the foretopman, followed by the master-at-arms, entered it—he, standing by the sailor throughout these judicial proceedings, was now directed to take him back to the after compartment originally assigned to the prisoner and his custodian. As the twain disappeared from view, the three officers, as partially liberated from some inward constraint associated with Billy's mere presence, simultaneously stirred in their seats. They exchanged looks of troubled indecision, yet feeling that decide they must and without long delay. As for Captain Vere, he for the time stood unconsciously with his back toward them, apparently in one of his absent fits, gazing out from a sashed porthole to windward upon the monotonous blank of the twilight sea. But the court's silence continuing, broken only at moments by brief consultations in low earnest tones, this seemed to arm him and energize him. Turning, he to-and-fro paced the cabin athwart, in the returning ascent to windward climbing the slant deck in the ship's lee roll, without knowing it symbolizing thus in his ac-

tion a mind resolute to surmount difficulties even if against primitive instincts strong as the wind and the sea. Presently he came to a stand before the three. After scanning their faces he stood less as mustering his thoughts for expression than as one only deliberating how best to put them to well-meaning men not intellectually mature, men with whom it was necessary to demonstrate certain principles that were axioms to himself. Similar impatience as to talking is perhaps one reason that deters some minds from addressing any popular assemblies.

When speak he did, something both in the substance of what he said and his manner of saying it, showed the influence of unshared studies modifying and tempering the practical training of an active career. This, along with his phraseology now and then, was suggestive of the grounds whereon rested that imputation of a certain pedantry socially alleged against him by certain naval men of wholly practical cast, captains who nevertheless would frankly concede that His Majesty's navy mustered no more efficient officer of their grade than "Starry Vere."

What he said was to this effect: "Hitherto I have been but the witness, little more; and I should hardly think now to take another tone, that of your coadjutor, for the time, did I not perceive in you—at the crisis too—a troubled hesitancy, proceeding, I doubt not, from the clash of military duty with moral scruple—scruple vitalized by compassion. For the compassion, how can I otherwise than share it? But, mindful of paramount obligations, I strive against scruples that may tend to enervate decision. Not, gentlemen, that I hide from myself that the case is an exceptional one. Speculatively regarded, it well might be referred to a jury of casuists. But for us here acting not as casuists or moralists, it is a case practical, and under martial law practically to be dealt with.

"But your scruples: do they move as in a dusk? Challenge them. Make them advance and declare themselves. Come now: do they import something like this: If, mindless of palliating circumstances, we are bound to regard the death of the master-at-arms as the prisoner's deed, then does that deed constitute a capital crime whereof the penalty is a mortal one? But in natural justice is nothing but the prisoner's overt act to be considered? How can we adjudge to summary and shameful death a fellow creature innocent before God, and whom we feel to be so?—Does that state it aright? You sign sad assent. Well, I too feel that, the full force of that. It is Nature. But do these buttons that we wear attest that our allegiance is to Nature? No, to the King. Though the ocean, which is inviolate Nature primeval, though this be the element where we move and have our being as sailors, yet as the King's officers lies our duty in a sphere correspondingly natural? So little is that true that, in receiving our commissions, we in the most important regards ceased to be natural free agents. When war is declared are we, the commissioned fighters, previously consulted? We fight at command. If our judgments approve the war, that is but coincidence. So in other particulars. So now. For suppose condemnation to follow these present proceedings. Would it be so much we ourselves that would condemn as it would be martial law operating through us? For that law and the rigor of it, we are not responsible. Our vowed responsibility is in this: That however pitilessly that law may operate, we nevertheless adhere to it and administer it.

"But the exceptional in the matter moves the hearts within you. Even so too is mine moved. But let not warm hearts betray heads that should be cool. Ashore in a criminal case will an upright judge allow himself off the bench to be waylaid by some tender kinswoman of the accused seeking to touch him with her tearful plea? Well the heart here denotes the feminine in man, is as that piteous woman and, hard though it be, she must here be ruled out."

He paused, earnestly studying them for a moment, then resumed.

"But something in your aspect seems to urge that it is not solely the heart that moves in you, but also the conscience, the private conscience. But tell me whether or not, occupying the position we do, private conscience should not yield to that imperial one formulated in the code under which alone we officially proceed?"

Here the three men moved in their seats, less convinced than agitated by the course of an argument troubling but the more the spontaneous conflict within.

Perceiving which, the speaker paused for a moment, then, abruptly changing his tone, went on.

"To steady us a bit, let us recur to the facts.—In wartime at sea a man-of-war's-man strikes his superior in grade, and the blow kills. Apart from its effect, the blow itself is, according to the Articles of War, a capital crime. Furthermore——"

"Aye, sir," emotionally broke in the officer of marines, "in one sense it was. But surely Budd purposed neither mutiny nor homicide."

"Surely not, my good man. And before a court less arbitrary and more merciful than a martial one that plea would largely extenuate. At the Last Assizes it shall acquit. But how here? We proceed under the law of the Mutiny Act. In feature no child can resemble his father more than that Act resembles in spirit the thing from which it derives—War. In His Majesty's service—in this ship indeed—there are Englishmen forced to fight for the King against their will. Against their conscience, for aught we know. Though as their fellow creatures some of us may appreciate their position, yet as navy officers, what reck we of it? Still less recks the enemy. Our impressed men we would fain cut down in the same swath with our volunteers. As regards the enemy's naval conscripts, some of whom may even share our own abhorrence of the regicidal French Directory, it is the same on our side. War looks but to the frontage, the appearance. And the Mutiny Act, War's child, takes after the father. Budd's intent or non-intent is nothing to the purpose.

"But while, put to it by those anxieties in you which I cannot but respect, I only repeat myself—while thus strangely we prolong proceedings that should be summary—the enemy may be sighted and an engagement result. We must do; and one of two things must we do—condemn or let go."

"Can we not convict and yet mitigate the penalty?" asked the junior lieutenant here speaking, and falteringly, for the first.

"Lieutenant, were that clearly lawful for us under the circumstances, consider the consequences of such clemency. The people" (meaning the ship's company) "have native sense; most of them are familiar with our naval usage and tradition, and how would they take it? Even could you explain to them—which our official position forbids—they, long molded by arbitrary discipline, have not that kind of intelligent responsiveness that might qualify them to comprehend and discriminate. No, to the people the foretopman's deed, however it be worded in the announcement, will be plain homicide committed in a flagrant act of mutiny. What penalty for that should follow, they know. But it does not follow. *Why?* they will ruminate. You know what sailors are. Will they not revert to the recent outbreak at the Nore? Aye. They know the well-founded alarm—the panic it struck throughout England. Your clement sentence they would account pusillanimous. They would think that we flinch, that we are afraid of them—afraid of practicing a lawful rigor singularly demanded at this juncture lest it should provoke new troubles. What shame to us such a conjecture on their part, and how deadly to discipline. You see then, whither, prompted by duty and the law, I steadfastly drive. But I beseech you, my friends, do not take me amiss. I feel as you do for this unfortunate boy. But did he know our hearts, I take him to be of that generous nature that he would feel even for us on whom in this military necessity so heavy a compulsion is laid."

With that, crossing the deck he resumed his place by the sashed porthole, tacitly leaving the three to come to a decision. On the cabin's opposite side the troubled court sat silent. Loyal lieges, plain and practical, though at bottom they dissented from some points Captain Vere had put to them, they were without the faculty, hardly had the inclination, to gainsay one whom they felt to be an earnest man, one, too, not less their superior in mind than in naval rank. But it is not improbable that even such of his words as were not without influence over them, less came home to them than his closing appeal to their instinct as sea officers in the forethought he threw out as to the practical consequences to discipline, considering the unconfirmed tone of the fleet at the time, should a man-of-war's-man's violent killing at sea of a superior in grade be allowed to pass for aught else than a capital crime demanding prompt infliction of the penalty.

Not unlikely they were brought to something more or less akin to that harassed frame of mind which in the year 1842 actuated the commander of the U.S. brig-of-war *Somers* to resolve, under the so-called Articles of War, Articles modeled upon the English Mutiny Act, to resolve upon the execution at sea of a midshipman and two petty officers as mutineers designing the seizure of the brig. Which resolution was carried out though in a time of peace and within not many days sail of home—an act vindicated by a naval court of inquiry subsequently convened ashore. History, and here cited without comment. True, the circumstances on board the *Somers* were different from those on board the *Indomitable*. But the urgency felt, well-warranted or otherwise, was much the same.

Says a writer whom few know, "Forty years after a battle it is easy for a noncombatant to reason about how it ought to have been fought. It is another thing personally and under fire to direct the fighting while involved in the obscuring smoke of it. Much so with respect to other emergencies involving considerations both practical and moral, and when it is imperative promptly to act. The greater the fog the more it imperils the steamer, and speed is put on though at the hazard of running somebody down. Little ween the snug card-players in the cabin of the responsibilities of the sleepless man on the bridge."

In brief, Billy Budd was formally convicted and sentenced to be hung at the yardarm in the early morning watch, it being now night. Otherwise, as is customary in such cases, the sentence would forthwith have been carried out. In wartime, on the field or in the fleet, a mortal punishment decreed by a drumhead court—on the field sometimes decreed by but a nod from the general—follows without delay on the heel of conviction, without appeal....

At sea in the old time, the execution by halter of a military sailor was generally from the foreyard. In the present instance, for special reasons the mainyard was assigned. Under an arm of that lee yard the prisoner was presently brought up, the chaplain attending him. It was noted at the time, and remarked upon afterwards, that in this final scene the good man evinced little or nothing of the perfunctory. Brief speech indeed he had with the condemned one, but the genuine Gospel was less on his tongue than in his aspect and manner toward him. The final preparations personal to the latter being speedily brought to an end by two boatswain's mates, the consummation impended. Billy stood facing aft. At the penultimate moment, his words, his only ones, words wholly unobstructed in the utterance, were these—"God bless Captain Vere!" Syllables so unanticipated coming from one with the ignominious hemp about his neck—a conventional felon's benediction directed aft toward the quarters of honor; syllables, too, delivered in the clear melody of a singing bird on the point of launching from the twig, had a phenomenal effect, not unenhanced by the rare personal beauty of the young sailor spiritualized now through late experience so poignantly profound.

Without volition as it were, as if indeed the ship's populace were but the vehicles of some vocal current electric, with one voice from a low and aloft came a resonant sympathetic echo—"God bless Captain Vere!" And yet at that instant Billy alone must have been in their hearts, even as he was in their eyes.

At the pronounced words and the spontaneous echo that voluminously rebounded them, Captain Vere, either through stoic self-control or a sort of momentary paralysis induced by emotional shock, stood erectly rigid as a musket in the ship-armorer's rack.

The hull deliberately recovering from the periodic roll to leeward was just regaining an even keel, when the last signal, a preconcerted dumb one, was given. At the same moment it chanced that the vapory fleece hanging low in the East was shot through with a soft glory as of the fleece of the Lamb of God seen in mystical vision, and simultaneously therewith, watched by the wedged mass of upturned faces, Billy ascended, and, ascending, took the full rose of the dawn.

Shirley Jackson
The Lottery

Shirley Jackson (1919–1965), American author, was born in San Francisco. For the last twenty years of her life she lived in North Bennington, Vermont. She received the Edgar Allen Poe Award for her short story, "Louisa, Please," and wrote many books, including *Hangsaman*, *Life Among the Savages*, and *We Have Always Lived in the Castle*. But it is her shocking nine-page tale, "The Lottery," first published in 1948, that brought her national notoriety. A metaphor for the Cold War world that followed the concentration camps and atomic bombs of World War II, "The Lottery" has been understood and interpreted in different ways by subsequent generations. First published in *The New Yorker*, the story prompted more mail than anything published in the magazine to that date.

The Lottery
Shirley Jackson

The morning of June 27th was clear and sunny, with the fresh warmth of a full-summer day; the flowers were blossoming profusely and the grass was richly green. The people of the village began to gather in the square, between the post office and the bank, around ten o'clock; in some towns there were so many people that the lottery took two days and had to be started on June 26th, but in this village, where there were only about three hundred people, the whole lottery took less than two hours, so it could begin at ten o'clock in the morning and still be through in time to allow the villagers to get home for noon dinner.

The children assembled first, of course. School was recently over for the summer, and the feeling of liberty sat uneasily on most of them; they tended to gather together quietly for a while before they broke into boisterous play, and their talk was still of the classroom and the teacher, of books and reprimands. Bobby Martin had already stuffed his pockets full of stones, and the other boys soon followed his example, selecting the smoothest and roundest stones; Bobby and Harry Jones and Dickie Delacroix—the villagers pronounced this name "Dellacroy"—eventually made a great pile of stones in one corner of the square and guarded it against the raids of the other boys. The girls stood aside, talking among themselves, looking over their shoulders at the boys, and the very small children rolled in the dust or clung to the hands of their older brothers or sisters.

Soon the men began to gather, surveying their own children, speaking of planting and rain, tractors and taxes. They stood together, away from the pile of stones in the corner, and their jokes were quiet and they smiled rather than laughed. The women, wearing faded house dresses and sweaters, came shortly after their menfolk. They greeted one another and exchanged bits of gossip as they went they to join their husbands. Soon the women, standing by their husbands, began to call to their children, and the children came reluctantly, having to be called four or five times. Bobby Martin ducked under his mother's grasping hand and ran, laughing, back to the pile of stones. His father spoke up sharply, and Bobby came quickly and took his place between his father and his oldest brother.

The lottery was conducted—as were the square dances, the teen-age club, the Halloween program—by Mr. Summers, who had time and energy to devote to civic activities. He was a round-faced, jovial man and he ran the coal business, and people were sorry for him, because be had no children and his wife was a scold. When he arrived in the square, carrying the black wooden box, there was a murmur of conversation among the villagers, and he waved and called, "Little late today, folks." The postmaster, Mr. Graves, followed him, carrying a three-legged stool, and the stool was put in the center of the square and Mr. Summers set the black box down on it. The villagers kept their distance, leaving a space between themselves and the stool, and when Mr. Summers said, "Some of you fellows want to give me a hand?" there was a hesitation before two men, Mr. Martin and his oldest son, Baxter, came forward to hold the box steady on the stool while Mr. Summers stirred up the papers inside it.

The original paraphernalia for the lottery had been lost long ago, and the black box now resting on the stool had been put into use even before Old Man Warner, the oldest man in town, was born. Mr. Summers spoke frequently to the villagers about making a new box, but no one liked to upset even as much tradition as was represented by the black box. There was a story that the present box had been made with some pieces of the box that had preceded it, the one that had been constructed when the first people settled down to make a village here. Every year, after the lottery, Mr. Summers began talking again about a new box, but every year the subject was allowed to fade off without anything's being done. The black box grew shabbier each year; by now it was no longer completely black but splintered badly along one side to show the original wood color, and in some places faded or stained.

Mr. Martin and his oldest son, Baxter, held the black box securely on the stool until Mr. Summers had stirred the papers thoroughly with his hand. Because so much of the ritual had been forgotten or discarded, Mr. Summers had been successful in having slips of paper substituted for the chips of wood that had been used for generations. Chips of wood, Mr. Summers had argued, had been all very well when the village was tiny, but now that the population was more than three hundred and likely to keep on growing, it was necessary to use something that would fit more easily into the black box. The night before the lottery, Mr. Summers and Mr. Graves made up the slips of paper and put them in the box, and it was then taken to the safe of Mr. Summers' coal company and locked up until Mr. Summers was ready to take it to the square next morning. The rest of the year, the box was put away, sometimes one place, sometimes another; it had spent one year in Mr. Graves's barn and another year underfoot in the post office, and sometimes it was set on a shelf in the Martin grocery and left there.

There was a great deal of fussing to be done before Mr. Summers declared the lottery open. There were the lists to make up—of heads of families, heads of households in each family, members of each household in each family. There was the proper swearing-in of Mr. Summers by the postmaster, as the official of the lottery; at one time, some people remembered, there had been a recital of some sort, performed by the official of the lottery, a perfunctory, tuneless chant that had been rattled off duly each year; some people believed that the official of the lottery used to stand just so when he said or sang it, others believed that he was supposed to walk among the people, but years and years ago this part of the ritual had been allowed to lapse. There had been, also, a ritual salute, which the official of the lottery had had to use in addressing each person who came up to draw from the box, but this also had changed with time, until now it was felt necessary only for the official to speak to each person approaching. Mr. Summers was very good at all this; in his clean white shirt and blue jeans, with one hand resting carelessly on the black box, he seemed very proper and important as he talked interminably to Mr. Graves and the Martins.

Just as Mr. Summers finally left off talking and turned to the assembled villagers, Mrs. Hutchinson came hurriedly along the path to the square, her sweater thrown over her shoulders, and slid into place in the back of the crowd. "'Clean forgot what day it was," she said to Mrs. Delacroix, who stood next to her, and they both laughed softly. "Thought my old man was out back stacking wood," Mrs. Hutchinson went on, "and then I looked out the window and the kids was gone, and then I remembered it was the twenty-seventh and came a-running."' She dried her hands on her apron, and Mrs. Delacroix said, "You're in time, though. They're still talking away up there."

Mrs. Hutchinson craned her neck to see through the crowd and found her husband and children standing near the front. She tapped Mrs. Delacroix on the arm as a farewell and began to make her way through the crowd. The people separated good-humoredly to let her through; two or three people said, in voices just loud enough to be heard across the crowd, "Here comes your Missus, Hutchinson," and "Bill, she made it after all." Mrs. Hutchinson reached her husband, and Mr. Summers, who had been waiting, said cheerfully, "Thought we were going to have to get on without you, Tessie." Mrs. Hutchinson said, grinning, "Wouldn't have me leave m'dishes in the sink, now, would you, Joe?," and soft laughter ran through the crowd as the people stirred back into position after Mrs. Hutchinson's arrival.

"Well, now," Mr. Summers said soberly, "guess we better get started, get this over with, so's we can go back to work. Anybody ain't here?"

"Dunbar,"' several people said. "Dunbar, Dunbar."

Mr. Summers consulted his list. "Clyde Dunbar," he said. "That's right. He's broke his leg, hasn't be? Who's drawing for him?"

"Me, I guess," a woman said, and Mr. Summers turned to look at her. "Wife draws for her husband," Mr. Summers said. "Don't you have a grown boy to do it for you, Janey?" Although Mr. Summers and everyone else in the village knew the answer perfectly well, it was the business of the official of the lottery to ask such questions formally. Mr. Summers waited with an expression of polite interest while Mrs. Dunbar answered.

"Horace's not but sixteen yet,"' Mrs. Dunbar said regretfully. "Guess I gotta fill in for the old man this year."

"Right," Mr. Summers said. He made a note on the list he was holding. Then he asked, "Watson boy drawing this year?"

A tall boy in the crowd raised his hand. "Here," he said. "I'm drawing for m'mother and me." He blinked his eyes nervously and ducked his head as several voices in the crowd said things like "Good fellow, Jack," and "Glad to see your mother's got a man to do it."

"Well," Mr. Summers said, "guess that's everyone. Old Man Warner make it?"

"Here," a voice said, and Mr. Summers nodded.

A sudden hush fell on the crowd as Mr. Summers cleared his throat and looked at the list. "All ready?" he called. "Now, I'll read the names—heads of families first—and the men come up and take a paper out of the box. Keep the paper folded in your hand without looking at it until everyone has had a turn. Everything clear?"

The people had done it so many times that they only half listened to the directions; most of them were quiet, wetting their lips, not looking around. Then Mr. Summers raised one hand high and said, "Adams." A man disengaged himself from the crowd and came forward. "Hi, Steve," Mr. Summers said, and Mr. Adams said, "Hi, Joe." They grinned at one another humorlessly and nervously. Then Mr. Adams reached into the black box and took out a folded paper. He held it firmly by one corner as he turned and went hastily back to his place in the crowd, where he stood a little apart from his family, not looking down at his hand.

"Allen," Mr. Summers said. "Anderson.... Bentham."

"Seems like there's no time at all between lotteries any more," Mrs. Delacroix said to Mrs. Graves in the back row. "Seems like we got through with the last one only last week."

"Time sure goes fast," Mrs. Graves said.

"Clark.... Delacroix."

"There goes my old man," Mrs. Delacroix said. She held her breath while her husband went forward.

"Dunbar," Mr. Summers said, and Mrs. Dunbar went steadily to the box while one of the women said, "Go on, Janey," and another said, "There she goes."

"We're next," Mrs. Graves said. She watched while Mr. Graves came around from the side of the box, greeted Mr. Summers gravely, and selected a slip of paper from the box. By now, all through the crowd there were men holding the small folded papers in their large hands, turning them over and over nervously. Mrs. Dunbar and her two sons stood together, Mrs. Dunbar holding the slip of paper.

"Harburt.... Hutchinson."

"Get up there, Bill," Mrs. Hutchinson said, and the people near her laughed.

"Jones."

"They do say," Mr. Adams said to Old Man Warner, who stood next to him, "that over in the north village they're talking of giving up the lottery."

Old Man Warner snorted. "Pack of crazy fools," he said. "Listening to the young folks, nothing's good enough for *them*. Next thing you know, they'll be wanting to go back to living in caves, nobody work any more, live *that* way for a while. Used to be a saying about 'Lottery in June, corn be heavy soon.' First thing you know, we'd all be eating stewed chickweed and acorns. There's *always* been a lottery," he added petulantly. "Bad enough to see young Joe Summers up there joking with everybody."

"Some places have already quit lotteries," Mrs. Adams said.

"Nothing but trouble in *that*," Old Man Warner said stoutly. "Pack of young fools."

"Martin." And Bobby Martin watched his father go forward. "Overdyke.... Percy."

"I wish they'd hurry," Mrs. Dunbar said to her older son. "I wish they'd hurry."

"They're almost through," her son said.

"You get ready to run tell Dad," Mrs. Dunbar said.

Mr. Summers called his own name and then stepped forward precisely and selected a slip from the box. Then he called, "Warner."

"Seventy-seventh year I been in the lottery," Old Man Warner said as he went through the crowd. "Seventy-seventh time."

"Watson." The tall boy came awkwardly through the crowd. Someone said, "Don't be nervous, Jack," and Mr. Summers said, "Take your time, son."

"Zanini."

After that, there was a long pause, a breathless pause, until Mr. Summers, holding his slip of paper in the air, said, "All right, fellows." For a minute, no one moved, and then all the slips of paper were opened. Suddenly, all the women began to speak at once, saying, "Who is it?," "Who's got it?," "Is it the Dunbars?," "Is it the Watsons?" Then the voices began to say, "It's Hutchinson. It's Bill," "Bill Hutchinson's got it."

"Go tell your father," Mrs. Dunbar said to her older son.

People began to look around to see the Hutchinsons. Bill Hutchinson was standing quiet, staring down at the paper in his hand.

Suddenly, Tessie Hutchinson shouted to Mr. Summers, "You didn't give him time enough to take any paper he wanted. I saw you. It wasn't fair!"

"Be a good sport, Tessie," Mrs. Delacroix called, and Mrs. Graves said, "All of us took the same chance."'

"Shut up, Tessie," Bill Hutchinson said.

"Well, everyone," Mr. Summers said, "that was done pretty fast, and now we've got to be hurrying a little more to get done in time." He consulted his next list. "Bill," he said, "you draw for the Hutchinson family. You got any other households in the Hutchinsons?"

"There's Don and Eva," Mrs. Hutchinson yelled. "Make *them* take their chance!"

"Daughters draw with their husbands' families, Tessie," Mr. Summers said gently. "You know that as well as anyone else."

"It wasn't *fair*," Tessie said.

"I guess not, Joe," Bill Hutchinson said regretfully. "My daughter draws with her husband's family, that's only fair. And I've got no other family except the kids."

"Then, as far as drawing for families is concerned, it's you," Mr. Summers said in explanation, "and as far as drawing for households is concerned, that's you, too. Right?"

"Right," Bill Hutchinson said.

"How many kids, Bill?" Mr. Summers asked formally.

"Three," Bill Hutchinson said. "There's Bill, Jr., and Nancy, and little Dave. And Tessie and me."

"All right, then," Mr. Summers said. "Harry, you got their tickets back?"

Mr. Graves nodded and held up the slips of paper. "Put them in the box, then," Mr. Summers directed. "Take Bill's and put it in."

"I think we ought to start over," Mrs. Hutchinson said, as quietly as she could. "I tell you it wasn't *fair*. You didn't give him time enough to choose. *Every*body saw that."

Mr. Graves had selected the five slips and put them in the box, and he dropped all the papers but those onto the ground, where the breeze caught them and lifted them off.

"Listen, everybody," Mrs. Hutchinson was saying to the people around her.

"Ready, Bill?" Mr. Summers asked, and Bill Hutchinson, with one quick glance around at his wife and children, nodded.

"Remember," Mr. Summers said, "take the slips and keep them folded until each person has taken one. Harry, you help little Dave." Mr. Graves took the hand of the little boy, who came willingly with him up to the box. "Take a paper out of the box, Davy," Mr. Summers said. Davy put his hand into the box and laughed. "Take just *one* paper," Mr. Summers said. "Harry, you hold it for him." Mr. Graves took the child's hand and removed the folded paper from the tight fist and held it while little Dave stood next to him and looked up at him wonderingly.

"Nancy next," Mr. Summers said. Nancy was twelve, and her school friends breathed heavily as she went forward, switching her skirt, and took a slip daintily from the box. "Bill, Jr.," Mr. Summers said, and Billy, his face red and his feet overlarge, nearly knocked the box over as he got a paper out. "Tessie," Mr. Summers said. She hesitated for a minute, looking around defiantly, and then set her lips and went up to the box. She snatched a paper out and held it behind her.

"Bill," Mr. Summers said, and Bill Hutchinson reached into the box and felt around, bringing his hand out at last with the slip of paper in it.

The crowd was quiet. A girl whispered, "I hope it's not Nancy," and the sound of the whisper reached the edges of the crowd.

"It's not the way it used to be," Old Man Warner said dearly. "People ain't the way they used to be."

"All right," Mr. Summers said. "Open the papers. Harry, you open little Dave's."

Mr. Graves opened the slip of paper and there was a general sigh through the crowd as he held it up and everyone could see that it was blank. Nancy and Bill, Jr., opened theirs at the same time, and both beamed and laughed, turning around to the crowd and holding their slips of paper above their heads.

"Tessie," Mr. Summers said. There was a pause, and then Mr. Summers looked at Bill Hutchinson, and Bill unfolded his paper and showed it. It was blank.

"It's Tessie," Mr. Summers said, and his voice was hushed. "Show us her paper, Bill."

Bill Hutchinson went over to his wife and forced the slip of paper out of her hand. It had a black spot on it, the black spot Mr. Summers had made the night before with the heavy pencil in the coal-company office. Bill Hutchinson held it up, and there was a stir in the crowd.

"All right, folks," Mr. Summers said. "Let's finish quickly."

Although the villagers had forgotten the ritual and lost the original black box, they still remembered to use stones. The pile of stones the boys had made earlier was ready; there were stones on the ground with the blowing scraps of paper that had come out of the box. Mrs. Delacroix selected a stone so large she had to pick it up with both hands and turned to Mrs. Dunbar. "Come on," she said. "Hurry up."

Mrs. Dunbar had small stones in both hands, and she said, gasping for breath, "I can't run at all. You'll have to go ahead and I'll catch up with you."

The children had stones already, and someone gave little Davy Hutchinson a few pebbles.

Tessie Hutchinson was in the center of a cleared space by now, and she held her hands out desperately as the villagers moved in on her. "It isn't fair," she said. A stone hit her on the side of the head.

Old Man Warner was saying, "Come on, come on, everyone." Steve Adams was in the front of the crowd of villagers, with Mrs. Graves beside him

"It isn't fair, it isn't right," Mrs. Hutchinson screamed, and then they were upon her.

Gobitis v. Minersville School District (1940) and Korematsu v. U.S. (1944)

A democratic community's commitment to diversity and toleration of minorities is most severely tested during times of war. The two Supreme Court cases that follow are good examples of the difficulties the United States has had in passing this important test.

The first case, decided one year prior to the United States' entry into World War II, involved a constitutional challenge to a compulsory flag salute regulation in the public schools. Lillian and William Gobitis, aged twelve and ten respectively, were expelled from the Minersville, Pennsylvania public schools when they refused to salute the U.S. flag as part of a compulsory daily school exercise. As Jehovah's Witnesses, the Gobitis children were taught to believe that to salute the national flag violates the commandments of Scripture, which has supreme authority for their faith. Their father Walter brought a lawsuit, charging that the compulsory aspect of the flag salute rule violated his children's rights to freedom of conscience under the First Amendment. "We show no disrespect for the flag, but we cannot salute it," Walter Gobitis said. "The Bible tells us this, and we must obey." The Supreme Court upheld the flag salute law, authorizing the state to use its power to foster patriotism in the classroom against the claims of a religious minority. Justice Felix Frankfurter, who wrote the opinion for an 8–1 majority, had himself immigrated to the United States at the age of 12, and he argued that "we live by symbols," the flag salute being one that promoted "the binding tie of cohesive sentiment," overriding the concerns for religious liberty on the behalf of Jehovah's Witnesses.

The next three years would bring a wave of persecution against Jehovah's Witnesses, with democratic majorities across the country participating in violent acts toward individuals who, in their refusal to "bow down" before the symbols of the national community, were perceived to be unpatriotic and even unAmerican. Witnesses were beaten by mobs, their Bible meetings were disrupted, and their meeting halls were burned. Finally, on June 14, 1943 (Flag Day!), the Supreme Court overturned its ruling in *Gobitis*, striking down on First Amendment grounds a West Virginia law compelling all to participate in a daily flag salute. Justice Robert Jackson's opinion in West Virginia Board of Education v. Barnette still stands as one of the most forceful defenses of the Bill of Rights against the vicissitudes of democratic majorities. He wrote: "If there is any fixed star in our constitutional constellation, it is that no official, high or petty, can prescribe what can be orthodox in politics, nationalism, religion, or other matters of opinion, or force citizens to confess by word or act their faith therein."

Our second case excerpt tells the story of Fred Korematsu, a man who challenged the constitutionality of the government's policy toward persons of Japanese ancestry during World War II. In February, 1942, two months after the bombing of Pearl Harbor, President Roosevelt issued an executive order to secure all military areas from threats of sabotage and espionage, an order quickly ratified by Congressional statute. Roosevelt's Secretary of War eventually declared the entire Pacific coast a military area, and ordered the exclusion from the West Coast of all persons of Japanese ancestry, following the urging of California congressman Leland Ford that "all Japanese, whether citizens or not, be placed in inland concentration camps." The government's exclusion order was used to take Japanese people from their homes and relocate them in detention centers in the deserts of Oregon, California, and Arizona. Over 110,000 persons were interned in these detention camps, 77,000 of them American citizens of Japanese ancestry. Japanese-Americans lost their freedom, their homes, and their livelihood; some Japanese-American parents were sent to detention centers as their sons were sent to fight for their country in Europe.

Several years after the last internment camp was closed in 1946, a presidential commission called the Japanese internment program "the most striking interference with personal freedom since slavery." The United States government finally recognized its grave mistake in 1988, when by an act of Congress it issued a formal apology and a one-time award of $20,000 to those interned who were still alive at the time. Fred Korematsu was finally vindicated in 1984, when a federal judge had his act of defying the exclusion order removed from his criminal record.

Minersville School District, Board of Education of Minersville School District, et al. *v.* Gobitis et al.

Certiorari to the Circuit Court of Appeals for the Third Circuit.

... MR. JUSTICE FRANKFURTER delivered the opinion of the Court.

A grave responsibility confronts this Court whenever in course of litigation it must reconcile the conflicting claims of liberty and authority. But when the liberty invoked is liberty of conscience, and the authority is authority to safeguard the nation's fellowship, judicial conscience is put to its severest test. Of such a nature is the present controversy.

Lillian Gobitis, aged twelve, and her brother William, aged ten, were expelled from the public schools of Minersville, Pennsylvania, for refusing to salute the national flag as part of a daily school exercise. The local Board of Education required both teachers and pupils to participate in this ceremony. The ceremony is a familiar one. The right hand is placed on the breast and the following pledge recited in unison: "I pledge allegiance to my flag, and to the Republic for which it stands; one nation indivisible, with liberty and justice for all." While the words are spoken, teachers and pupils extend their right hands in salute to the flag. The Gobitis family are affiliated with "Jehovah's Witnesses," for whom the Bible as the Word of God is the supreme authority. The children had been brought up conscientiously to believe that such a gesture of respect for the flag was forbidden by command of Scripture....

We must decide whether the requirement of participation in such a ceremony, exacted from a child who refuses upon sincere religious grounds, infringes without due process of law the liberty guaranteed by the Fourteenth Amendment....

Certainly the affirmative pursuit of one's convictions about the ultimate mystery of the universe and man's relation to it is placed beyond the reach of law. Government may not interfere with organized or individual expression of belief or disbelief....

But the manifold character of man's relations may bring his conception of religious duty into conflict with the secular interests of his fellow-men. When does the constitutional guarantee compel exemption from doing what society thinks necessary for the promotion of some great common end, or from a penalty for conduct which appears dangerous to the general good? To state the problem is to recall the truth that no single principle can answer all of life's complexities. The right to freedom of religious belief, however dissident and however obnoxious to the cherished beliefs of others—even of a majority—is itself the denial of an absolute. But to affirm that the freedom to follow conscience has itself no limits in the life of a society would deny that very plurality of principles which, as a matter of history, underlies protection of religious toleration. Our present task, then, as so often the case with courts, is to reconcile two rights in order to prevent either from destroying the other....

Conscientious scruples have not, in the course of the long struggle for religious toleration, relieved the individual from obedience to a general law not aimed at the promotion or restriction of religious beliefs. The mere possession of religious convictions which contradict the relevant concerns of a political society does not relieve the citizen from the discharge of political responsibilities.... In all these cases the general laws in question, upheld in their application to those who refused obedience from religions conviction, were manifestations of specific powers of government deemed by the legislature essential to secure and maintain that orderly, tranquil, and free society without which religious toleration itself is unattainable. Even if it were assumed that freedom of speech goes beyond the historic concept of full opportunity to utter and to disseminate views, however heretical or offensive to dominant opinion, and includes freedom from conveying what may

be deemed an implied but rejected affirmation, the question remains whether school children, like the Gobitis children, must be excused from conduct required of all the other children in the promotion of national cohesion. We are dealing with an interest inferior to none in the hierarchy of legal values. National unity is the basis of national security....

The ultimate foundation of a free society is the binding tie of cohesive sentiment. Such a sentiment is fostered by all those agencies of the mind and spirit which may serve to gather up the traditions of a people, transmit them from generation to generation, and thereby create that continuity of a treasured common life which constitutes a civilization. "We live by symbols." The flag is the symbol of our national unity, transcending all internal differences, however large, within the framework of the Constitution. This Court has had occasion to say that "... the flag is the symbol of the Nation's power, the emblem of freedom in its truest, best sense.... it signifies government resting on the consent of the governed; liberty regulated by law; the protection of the weak against the strong; security against the exercise of arbitrary power; and absolute safety for free institutions against foreign aggression."...

The wisdom of training children in patriotic impulses by those compulsions which necessarily pervade so much of the educational process is not for our independent judgment. Even were we convinced of the folly of such a measure, such belief would be no proof of its unconstitutionality. For ourselves, we might be tempted to say that the deepest patriotism is best engendered by giving unfettered scope to the most crochety beliefs. Perhaps it is best, even from the standpoint of those interests which ordinances like the one under review seek to promote, to give to the least popular sect leave from conformities like those here in issue. But the courtroom is not the arena for debating issues of educational policy. It is not our province to choose among competing considerations in the subtle process of securing ineffective loyalty to the traditional ideals of democracy, while respecting at the same time individual idiosyncracies among a people so diversified in racial origins and religious allegiances. So to hold would in effect make us the school board for the country. That authority has not been given to this Court, nor should we assume it....

Korematsu v. United States

Mr. Justice Black delivered the opinion of the Court.

The petitioner, an American citizen of Japanese descent, was convicted in a federal district court for remaining in San Leandro, California, a "Military Area," contrary to Civilian Exclusion Order No. 34 of the Commanding General of the Western Command, U.S. Army, which directed that after May 9, 1942, all persons of Japanese ancestry should be excluded from that area. No question was raised as to petitioner's loyalty to the United States....

It should be noted, to begin with, that all legal restrictions which curtail the civil rights of a single racial group are immediately suspect. That is not to say that all such restrictions are unconstitutional. It is to say that courts must subject them to the most rigid scrutiny. Pressing public necessity may sometimes justify the existence of such restrictions; racial antagonism never can....

Exclusion Order No. 34, which the petitioner knowingly and admittedly violated, was one of a number of military orders and proclamations, all of which were substantially based upon Executive Order No. 9066, 7 Fed. Reg. 1407. That order, issued after we were at war with Japan,

declared that "the successful prosecution of the war requires every possible protection against espionage and against sabotage to national-defense material, nation-defense premises, and national-defense utilities...."

In *Hirabayashi* v. *United States*, 320 U.S. 81, we sustained a conviction obtained for violation of the curfew order....

We upheld the curfew order as an exercise of the power of the government to take steps necessary to prevent espionage and sabotage in an area threatened by Japanese attack.... We are unable to conclude that it was beyond the war power of Congress and the Executive to exclude those of Japanese ancestry from the West Coast war area at the time they did. True, exclusion from the area in which one's home is located is a far greater deprivation than constant confinement to the home from 8 p.m. to 6 a.m. Nothing short of apprehension by the proper military authorities of the gravest imminent danger to the public safety can constitutionally justify either. But exclusion from a threatened area, no less than curfew, has a definite and close relationship to the prevention of espionage and sabotage. The military authorities, charged with the primary responsibility of defending our shores, concluded that curfew provided inadequate protection and ordered exclusion. They did so, as pointed out in our *Hirabayashi opinion*, in accordance with Congressional authority to the military to say who should, and who should not, remain in the threatened areas....

Here, we cannot reject as unfounded the judgment of the military authorities and of Congress that there were disloyal members of that population, whose number and strength could not be precisely and quickly ascertained....

We uphold the exclusion order as of the time it was made and when the petitioner violated it. In doing so, we are not unmindful of the hardships imposed by it upon a large group of American citizens. But hardships are part of war, and war is an aggregation of hardships. All citizens alike, both in and out of uniform, feel the impact of war in greater or lesser measure. Citizenship has its responsibilities as well as its privileges, and in time of war the burden is always heavier. Compulsory exclusion of large groups of citizens from their homes, except under circumstances of direst emergency and peril, is inconsistent with our basic governmental institutions. But when under conditions of modern warfare our shores are threatened by hostile forces, the power to protect must be commensurate with the threatened danger....

It is said that we are dealing here with the case of imprisonment of a citizen in a concentration camp solely because of his ancestry, without evidence or inquiry concerning his loyalty and good disposition towards the United States. Our task would be simple, our duty clear, were this a case involving the imprisonment of a loyal citizen in a concentration camp because of racial prejudice. Regardless of the true nature of the assembly and relocation centers—and we deem it unjustifiable to call them concentration camps with all the ugly connotations that term implies—we are dealing specifically with nothing but an exclusion order. To cast this case into outlines of racial prejudice, without reference to the real military dangers which were presented, merely confuses the issue. Korematsu was not excluded from the Military Area because of hostility to him or his race. He *was* excluded because we are at war with the Japanese Empire, because the properly constituted military authorities feared an invasion of our West Coast and felt constrained to take proper security measures, because they decided that the military urgency of the situation demanded that all citizens of Japanese ancestry be segregated from the West Coast temporarily, and finally, because Congress, reposing its confidence in this time of war in our military leaders—as inevitably it must—determined that they should have the power to do just this. There was evidence of disloyalty on the part of some, the military authorities considered that the need for action was great, and time was short. We cannot—by availing ourselves of the calm perspective of hindsight—now say that at that time these actions were unjustified.

Martin Luther King, Jr.
Letter from Birmingham Jail

M artin Luther King, Jr. (1929–1968), was born in Atlanta, Georgia and raised in a middle-class religious family. He graduated from Morehouse College in 1948 and received his doctorate from the Graduate School of Theology at Boston University in 1955. While serving as pastor of a Baptist church in Montgomery, Alabama, King became world-famous for his organization of a year-long boycott against segregated public transportation. In 1957 King founded the Southern Christian Leadership Conference which became the organizational base for his civil rights activities. King helped lead the historic 1963 March on Washington, and was awarded the Nobel Peace Prize in 1964. King often went to jail as part of his campaigns, and endured frequent threats on his life. He was assassinated in Memphis on April 4, 1968. King's tireless struggle for social justice, grounded in a broad-based religious, philosophical, and political tradition, made him one of America's great political and spiritual figures.

Dr. King wrote the following essay on April 16, 1963 while in jail for participating in civil rights demonstrations in Birmingham, Alabama. Eight prominent white clergymen had published an open letter in which they claimed to support King's fight for integration, but attacked his methods and his timing. Considering themselves "moderates," they called on King to allow the courts to advance racial integration at a moderate pace, warning that King's civil disobedience would lead to reactionary violence. In his response King fairly and conclusively refutes the eight clergymen.

But he also addresses himself to a wider audience. Drawing on a broad tradition of religious faith and social criticism (see the selections from Jefferson, Thoreau, Lincoln, and Ellison), King writes to all those concerned with the oppression of minorities.

Letter From Birmingham Jail
Martin Luther King, Jr*

April 16, 1963

My Dear Fellow Clergymen:

While confined here in the Birmingham city jail, I came across your recent statement calling my present activities "unwise and untimely." Seldom do I pause to answer criticism of my work and ideas. If I sought to answer all the criticisms that cross my desk, my secretaries would have little time for anything other than such correspondence in the course of the day, and I would have no time for constructive work.

But since I feel that you are men of genuine good will and that your criticisms are sincerely set forth, I want to try to answer your statement in what I hope will be patient and reasonable terms.

I think I should indicate why I am here in Birmingham since you have been influenced by the view which argues against "outsiders coming in." I have the honor of serving as president of the Southern Christian Leadership Conference, an organization operating in every southern state, with headquarters in Atlanta, Georgia. We have some eighty-five af-

Reprinted by arrangement with The Heirs of the Estate of Martin Luther King, Jr., c/o Writers House, Inc. as agent for the proprietor New York, New York. Copyright © 1963 by Martin Luther King, Jr., copyright renewed 1991 by Coretta Scott King.

* Author's Notes: The response to a published statement by eight fellow clergymen from Alabama (Bishop C. C. J. Carpenter, Bishop Joseph A. Durick, Rabbi Hilton L. Grafman, Bishop Paul Hardin, Bishop Holan B. Harmon, the Reverend George M. Murray, the Reverend Edward V. Ramage and the Reverend Earl Stallings) was composed under somewhat constricting circumstances. Begun on the margins of the newspaper in which the statement appeared while I was in jail, the letter was continued on scraps of writing paper supplied by a friendly Negro trusty, and concluded on a pad my attorneys were eventually permitted to leave me. Although the text remains in substance unaltered, I have indulged in the author's prerogative of polishing it for publication.

filiated organizations across the South and one of them is the Alabama Christian Movement for Human Rights. Frequently we share staff, educational and financial resources with our affiliates. Several months ago the affiliate here in Birmingham asked us to be on call to engage in a nonviolent direct-action program if such were deemed necessary. We readily consented, and when the hour came we lived up to our promise. So I, along with several members of my staff, am here because I was invited here. I am here because I have organizational ties here.

But more basically, I am in Birmingham because injustice is here. Just as the prophets of the eighth century B.C. left their villages and carried their "thus saith the Lord" far beyond the boundaries of their home towns, and just as the Apostle Paul left his village of Tarsus and carried the gospel of Jesus Christ to the far corners of the Greco-Roman world, so am I compelled to carry the gospel of freedom beyond my own home town. Like Paul, I must constantly respond to the Macedonian call for aid.

Moreover, I am cognizant of the interrelatedness of all communities and states. I cannot sit idly by in Atlanta and not be concerned about what happens in Birmingham. Injustice anywhere is a threat to justice everywhere. We are caught in an inescapable network of mutuality, tied in a single garment of destiny. Whatever affects one directly, affects all indirectly. Never again can we afford to live with the narrow, provincial "outside agitator" idea. Anyone who lives inside the United States can never be considered an outsider anywhere within its bounds.

You deplore the demonstrations taking place in Birmingham. But your statement, I am sorry to say, fails to express a similar concern for the conditions that brought about the demonstrations. I am sure that none of you would want to rest content with the superficial kind of social analysis that deals merely with effects and does not grapple with underlying causes. It is unfortunate that demonstrations are taking place in

Birmingham, but it is even more unfortunate that the city's white power structure left the Negro community with no alternative.

In any nonviolent campaign there are four basic steps: collection of the facts to determine whether injustices exist; negotiation; self-purification; and direct action. We have gone through all these steps in Birmingham. There can be no gainsaying the fact that racial injustice engulfs this community. Birmingham is probably the most thoroughly segregated city in the United States. Its ugly record of brutality is widely known. Negroes have experienced grossly unjust treatment in the courts. There have been more unsolved bombings of Negro homes and churches in Birmingham than in any other city in the nation. These are the hard, brutal facts of the case....

You may well ask: "Why direct action? Why sit-ins, marches and so forth? Isn't negotiation a better path?" You are quite right in calling for negotiation. Indeed this is the very purpose of direct action. Nonviolent direct action works to create such a crisis and foster such a tension that a community which has constantly refused to negotiate is forced to confront the issue. It seeks so to dramatize the issue that it can no longer be ignored. My citing the creation of tension as part of the work of the nonviolent-resister may sound rather shocking. But I must confess that I am not afraid of the word "tension." I have earnestly opposed violent tension, but there is a type of constructive, nonviolent tension which is necessary for growth. Just as Socrates felt that it was necessary to create a tension in the mind so that individuals could rise from the bondage of myths and half-truths to the unfettered realm of creative analysis and objective appraisal, so must we see the need for nonviolent gadflies to create the kind of tension in society that will help men rise from the dark depths of prejudice and racism to the majestic heights of understanding and brotherhood.

The purpose of our direct-action program is to create a situation so crisis-packed that it will inevitably open the door to negotiation. I therefore concur with you in your call for negotiation. Too long has our beloved Southland been bogged down in a tragic effort to live in monologue rather than dialogue....

We know through painful experience that freedom is never voluntarily given by the oppressor; it must be demanded by the oppressed. Frankly, I have yet to engage in a direct-action campaign that was "well timed" in the view of those who have not suffered unduly from the disease of segregation. For years now I have heard the word "Wait!" It rings in the ear of every Negro with piercing familiarity. This "Wait" has almost always meant "Never." We must come to see, with one of our distinguished jurists, that "justice too long delayed is justice denied."

We have waited for more than 340 years for our constitutional and God-given rights. The nations of Asia and Africa are moving with jetlike speed toward gaining political independence, but we still creep at horse-and-buggy pace toward gaining a cup of coffee at a lunch counter. Perhaps it is easy for those who have never felt the stinging darts of segregation to say, "Wait." But when you have seen vicious mobs lynch your mothers and fathers at will and drown your sisters and brothers at whim; when you have seen hate-filled policemen curse, kick and even kill your black brothers and sisters; when you see the vast majority of your twenty million Negro brothers smothering in an airtight cage of poverty in the midst of an affluent society; when you suddenly find your tongue twisted and your speech stammering as you seek to explain to your six-year-old daughter why she can't go to the public amusement park that has just been advertised on television, and see tears welling up in her eyes when she is told that Funtown is closed to colored children, and see ominous clouds of inferiority beginning to form in her little mental sky, and we are beginning to distort her personality by developing an unconscious bitterness toward white people; when you have to concoct an answer for a five-year-old son who is asking:

"Daddy, why do white people treat colored people so mean?"; when you take a cross-country drive and find it necessary to sleep night after night in the uncomfortable corners of your automobile because no motel will accept you; when you are humiliated day in and day out by nagging signs reading "white" and "colored"; when your first name becomes "nigger," your middle name becomes "boy" (however old you are) and your last name becomes "John," and your wife and mother are never given the respected title "Mrs."; when you are harried by day and haunted by night by the fact that you are a Negro, living constantly at tiptoe stance, never quite knowing what to expect next, and are plagued with inner fears and outer resentments; when you are forever fighting a degenerating sense of "nobodiness"—then you will understand why we find it difficult to wait. There comes a time when the cup of endurance runs over, and men are no longer willing to be plunged into the abyss of despair. I hope, sirs, you can understand our legitimate and unavoidable impatience.

You express a great deal of anxiety over our willingness to break laws. This is certainly a legitimate concern. Since we so diligently urge people to obey the Supreme Court's decision of 1954 outlawing segregation in the public schools, at first glance it may seem rather paradoxical for us consciously to break laws. One may well ask: "How can you advocate breaking some laws and obeying others?" The answer lies in the fact that there are two types of laws: just and unjust. I would be the first to advocate obeying just laws. One has not only a legal but a moral responsibility to obey just laws. Conversely, one has a moral responsibility to disobey unjust laws. I would agree with St. Augustine that "an unjust law is no law at all."

Now, what is the difference between the two? How does one determine whether a law is just or unjust? A just law is a man-made code that squares with the moral law or the law of God. An unjust law is a code that is out of harmony with the moral law. To put it in the terms of St.Thomas Aquinas: An unjust law is a human law that is not rooted in eternal law and natural law. Any law that uplifts human personality is just. Any law that degrades human personality is unjust. All segregation statutes are unjust because segregation distorts the soul and damages the personality. It gives the segregator a false sense of superiority and the segregated a false sense of inferiority. Segregation, to use the terminology of the Jewish philosopher Martin Buber, substitutes an "I-it" relationship for an "I-thou" relationship and ends up relegating persons to the status of things. Hence segregation is not only politically, economically and sociologically unsound, it is morally wrong and sinful. Paul Tillich has said that sin is separation. Is not segregation an existential expression of man's tragic separation, his awful estrangement, his terrible sinfulness? Thus it is that I can urge men to obey the 1954 decision of the Supreme Court, for it is morally right; and I can urge them to disobey segregation ordinances, for they are morally wrong.

Let us consider a more concrete example of just and unjust laws. An unjust law is a code that a numerical or power majority group compels a minority group to obey but does not make binding on itself. This is *difference* made legal. By the same token, a just law is a code that a majority compels a minority to follow and that it is willing to follow itself. This is *sameness* made legal.

Let me give another explanation. A law is unjust if it is inflicted on a minority that, as a result of being denied the right to vote, had no part in enacting or devising the law. Who can say that the legislature of Alabama which set up that state's segregation laws was democratically elected? Throughout Alabama all sorts of devious methods are used to prevent Negroes from becoming registered voters, and there are some counties in which, even though Negroes constitute a majority of the population, not a single Negro is registered. Can any law enacted under such circumstances be considered democratically structured?

Sometimes a law is just on its face and unjust in its application. For instance, I have been arrested on a charge of parading without a permit. Now, there is nothing wrong in having an ordinance which requires a permit for a parade. But such an ordinance becomes unjust when it is used to maintain segregation and to deny citizens the First-Amendment privilege of peaceful assembly and protest.

I hope you are able to see the distinction I am trying to point out. In no sense do I advocate evading or defying the law, as would the rabid segregationist. That would lead to anarchy. One who breaks an unjust law must do to openly, lovingly, and with a willingness to accept the penalty. I submit that an individual who breaks a law that conscience tells him is unjust, and who willingly accepts the penalty of imprisonment in order to arouse the conscience of the community over its injustice, is in reality expressing the highest respect for the law.

Of course, there is nothing new about this kind of civil disobedience. It was evidenced sublimely in the refusal of Shadrach, Meshach and Abednego to obey the laws of Nebuchadnezzar, on the ground that a higher moral law was a stake. It was practiced superbly by the early Christians, who were willing to face hungry lions and the excruciating pain of chopping blocks rather than submit to certain unjust laws of the Roman Empire. To a degree, academic freedom is a reality today because Socrates practiced civil disobedience. In our own nation, the Boston Tea Party represented a massive act of civil disobedience.

We should never forget that everything Adolf Hitler did in Germany was "legal" and everything the Hungarian freedom fighters did in Hungary was "illegal." It was "illegal" to aid and comfort a Jew in Hitler's Germany. Even so, I am sure that, had I lived in Germany at the time, I would have aided and comforted my Jewish brothers. If today I lived in a Communist country where certain principles dear to the Christian faith are suppressed, I would openly advocate the country's antireligious laws....

You speak of our activity in Birmingham as extreme. At first I was rather disappointed that fellow clergymen would see my nonviolent efforts as those of an extremist. I began thinking about the fact that I stand in the middle of two opposing forces in the Negro community. One is a force of complacency, made up in part of Negroes who, as a result of long years of oppression, are so drained of self-respect and a sense of "somebodiness" that they have adjusted to segregation; and in part of a few middle-class Negroes who, because of a degree of academic and economic security and because in some ways they profit by segregation, have become insensitive to the problems of the masses. The other force is one of bitterness and hatred, and it comes perilously close to advocating violence. It is expressed in the various black nationalist groups that are springing up across the nation, the largest and best-known being Elijah Muhammad's Muslim movement. Nourished by the Negro's frustration over the continued existence of racial discrimination, this movement is made up of people who have lost faith in America, who have absolutely repudiated Christianity, and who have concluded that the white man is an incorrigible "devil."

I have tried to stand between these two forces, saying that we need emulate neither the "do-nothingism" of the complacent nor the hatred and despair of the black nationalist. For there is the more excellent way of love and nonviolent protest. I am grateful to God that, through the influence of the Negro church, the way of nonviolence became an integral part of our struggle.

If this philosophy had not emerged, by now many streets of the South would, I am convinced, be flowing with blood. And I am further convinced that if our white brothers dismiss as "rabble-rousers" and "outside agitators" those of us who employ nonviolent direct action, and if they refuse to support our nonviolent efforts, millions of Negroes will, out of frustration and despair, seek solace and security in black-nationalist ideologies—a development that would

inevitably lead to a frightening racial nightmare.

Oppressed people cannot remain oppressed forever. The yearning for freedom eventually manifests itself, and that is what has happened to the American Negro. Something within has reminded him of his birthright of freedom, and something without has reminded him that it can be gained. Consciously or unconsciously, he has been caught up by the *Zeitgeist*, and with his black brothers of Africa and his brown and yellow brothers of Asia, South America and the Caribbean, the United States Negro is moving with a sense of great urgency toward the promised land of racial justice. If one recognizes this vital urge that has engulfed the Negro community, one should readily understand why public demonstrations are taking place. The Negro has many pent-up resentments and latent frustrations, and he must release them. So let him march; let him make prayer pilgrimages to the city hall; let him go on freedom rides—and try to understand why he must do so. If his repressed emotions are not released in nonviolent ways, they will seek expression through violence; this is not a threat but a fact of history. So I have not said to my people: "Get rid of your discontent." Rather, I have tried to say that this normal and healthy discontent can be channeled into the creative outlet of nonviolent direct action. And now this approach is being termed extremist.

But though I was initially disappointed at being categorized as an extremist, as I continued to think about the matter I gradually gained a measure of satisfaction from the label. Was not Jesus an extremist for love: "Love your enemies, bless them that curse you, do good to them that hate you, and pray for them which despitefully use you, and persecute you." Was not Amos an extremist for justice: "Let justice roll down like waters and righteousness like an ever-flowing stream." Was not Paul an extremist for the Christian gospel: "I bear in my body the marks of the Lord Jesus." Was not Martin Luther an extremist: "Here I stand; I cannot do otherwise, so help me God." And John Bunyan: "I will stay in jail to the end of my days before I make a butchery of my conscience." And Abraham Lincoln: "This nation cannot survive half slave and half free." And Thomas Jefferson: "We hold these truths to be self-evident, that all men are created equal..." So the question is not whether we will be extremists, but what kind of extremists we will be. Will we be extremists for hate or for love? Will we be extremists for the preservation of injustice or for the extension of justice? In that dramatic scene on Calvary's hill three men were crucified. We must never forget that all three were crucified for the same crime—the crime of extremism. Two were extremists for immorality, and thus fell below their environment. The other, Jesus Christ, was an extremist for love, truth and goodness, and thereby rose above his environment. Perhaps the South, the nation and the world are in dire need of creative extremists....

I have been so greatly disappointed with the white church and its leadership. I do not say this as one of those negative critics who can always find something wrong with the church. I say this as a minister of the gospel, who loves the church; who was nurtured in its bosom; who has been sustained by its spiritual blessings and who will remain true to it as long as the cord of life shall lengthen.

When I was suddenly catapulted into the leadership of the bus protest in Montgomery, Alabama, a few years ago, I felt we would be supported by the white church. I felt that the white ministers, priests and rabbis of the South would be among out strongest allies. Instead, some have been outright opponents, refusing to understand the freedom movement and misrepresenting its leaders; all too many others have been more cautious than courageous and have remained silent behind the anesthetizing security of stained-glass windows.

In spite of my shattered dreams, I came to Birmingham with the hope that the white religious leadership of this community would see the justice of our cause and, with deep moral concern, would serve as the channel through which our just grievances could reach the power structure. I had hoped that each of you would understand. But again I have been disappointed.

I have heard numerous southern religious leaders admonish their worshipers to comply with a desegregation decision because it is the law, but I have longed to hear white ministers declare: "Follow this decree because integration is morally right and because the Negro is your brother." In the midst of blatant injustices inflicted upon the Negro, I have watched white churchmen stand on the sideline and mouth pious irrelevancies and sanctimonious trivialities. In the midst of a mighty struggle to rid our nation of racial and economic injustice, I have heard many ministers say: "Those are social issues, with which the gospel has no real concern." And I have watched many churches commit themselves to a completely otherworldly religion which makes a strange, un-Biblical distinction between body and soul, between the sacred and the secular.

I have traveled the length and breadth of Alabama, Mississippi and all the other southern states. On sweltering summer days and crisp autumn mornings I have looked at the South's beautiful churches with their lofty spires pointing heavenward. I have beheld the impressive outlines of her massive religious-education buildings. Over and over I have found myself asking: "What kind of people worship here? Who is their God? Where were their voices of support when the lips of Governor Barnett dripped words of interposition and nullification? Where were they when Governor Wallace gave a clarion call for defiance and hatred? Where were their voices of support when bruised and weary Negro men and women decided to rise from the dark dungeons of complacency to the bright hills of creative protest?"

Yes, these questions are still in my mind. In deep disappointment I wept over the laxity of the church. But be assured that my tears have been tears of love. There can be no deep disappointment where there is not deep love. Yes, I love the church. How could I do otherwise? I am in the rather unique position of being the son, the grandson and the great-grandson of preachers. Yes, I see the church as the body of Christ. But, oh! How we have blemished and scarred that body through social neglect and through fear of being nonconformists.

There was a time when the church was very powerful—in the time when the early Christians rejoiced at being deemed worthy to suffer for what they believed. In those days the church was not merely a thermometer that recorded the ideas and principles of popular opinion; it was a thermostat that transformed the mores of society. Whenever the early Christians entered a town, the people in power became disturbed and immediately sought to convict the Christians for being "disturbers of the peace" and "outside agitators." But the Christians pressed on, in the conviction that they were "a colony of heaven," called to obey God rather than man. Small in number, they were big in commitment. They were too God-intoxicated to be "astronomically intimidated." By their effort and example they brought an end to such ancient evils as infanticide and gladiatorial contests.

Things are different now. So often the contemporary church is a weak, ineffectual voice with an uncertain sound. So often it is an arch-defender of the status quo. Far from being disturbed by the presence of the church, the power structure of the average community is consoled by the church's silent—and often even vocal—sanction of things as they are.

But the judgment of God is upon the church as never before. If today's church does not recapture the sacrificial spirit of the early church, it will lose its authenticity, forfeit the loyalty of millions, and be dismissed as an irrelevant social club with no meaning for the twentieth century. Every day I meet young people whose disappointment with the church has turned into outright disgust.

Perhaps I have once again been too optimistic. Is organized religion too inextricably bound to the status quo to save our nation and the world? Perhaps I must turn my faith to the inner spiritual church, the church within the church, as the true *ekklesia* and the hope of the world. But again I am thankful to God that some noble souls from the ranks of organized religion have broken loose from the paralyzing chains of conformity and joined us as active partners in the struggle for freedom. They have left their secure congregations and walked the streets of Albany, Georgia, with us. They have gone down the highways of the South on tortuous rides for freedom. Yes, they have gone to jail with us. Some have been dismissed from their churches, have lost the support of their bishops and fellow ministers. But they have acted in the faith that right defeated is stronger than evil triumphant. Their witness has been the spiritual salt that has preserved the true meaning of the gospel in these troubled times. They have carved a tunnel of hope through the dark mountain of disappointment.

I hope the church as a whole will meet the challenge of this decisive hour. But even if the church does not come to the aid of justice, I have no despair about the future. I have no fear about the outcome of our struggle in Birmingham, even if our motives are at present misunderstood. We will reach the goal of freedom in Birmingham and all over the nation, because the goal of America is freedom. Abused and scorned though we may be, our destiny is tied up with America's destiny. Before the pilgrims landed at Plymouth, we were here. Before the pen of Jefferson etched the majestic words of the Declaration of Independence across the pages of history, we were here. For more than two centuries our forebears labored in this country without wages; they made cotton king; they built the homes of their masters while suffering gross injustice and shameful humiliation—and yet out of a bottomless vitality they continued to thrive and develop. If the inexpressible cruelties of slavery could not stop us, the opposition we now face will surely fail. We will win our freedom because the sacred heritage of our nation and the eternal will of God are embodied in our echoing demands.

Before closing I feel impelled to mention one other point in your statement that has troubled me profoundly. You warmly commended the Birmingham police force for keeping "order" and "preventing violence." I doubt that you would have so warmly commended the police force if you had seen its dogs sinking their teeth into unarmed, nonviolent Negroes. I doubt that you would so quickly commend the policemen if you were to observe their ugly and inhumane treatment of Negroes here in the city jail; if you were to watch them push and curse old Negro women and young Negro girls; if you were to see them slap and kick old Negro men and young boys; if you were to observe them, as they did on two occasions, refuse to give us food because we wanted to sing our grace together. I cannot join you in your praise of the Birmingham police department.

It is true that the police have exercised a degree of discipline in handling the demonstrators. In this sense they have conducted themselves rather "nonviolently" in public. But for what purpose? To preserve the evil system of segregation. Over the past few years I have consistently preached that nonviolence demands that the means we use must be as pure as the ends we seek. I have tried to make clear that it is wrong to use immoral means to attain moral ends. But now I must affirm that it is just as wrong, or perhaps even more so, to use moral means to preserve immoral ends. Perhaps Mr. Connor and his policemen have been rather nonviolent in public, as was Chief Pritchett in Albany, Georgia, but they have used the moral means of nonviolence to maintain the immoral end of racial injustice. As T. S. Eliot has said: "The last temptation is the greatest treason: To do the right deed for the wrong reason."...

Never before have I written so long a letter. I'm afraid it is much too long to take your precious time. I can assure you that it would have been much shorter if I had been writing from a comfortable desk, but what else can one do when he is alone in a narrow jail cell, other than write long letters, think long thoughts and pray long prayers?

If I have said anything in this letter that overstates the truth and indicates an unreasonable impatience, I beg you to forgive me. If I have said anything that understates the truth and indicates my having a patience that allows me to settle for anything less than brotherhood, I beg God to forgive me.

I hope this letter finds you strong in the faith. I also hope that circumstances will soon make it possible for me to meet each of you, not as an integrationist or a civil-rights leader but as a fellow clergyman and a Christian brother. Let us all hope that the dark clouds of racial prejudice will soon pass away and the deep fog of misunderstanding will be lifted from our fear-drenched communities, and in some not too distant tomorrow the radiant stars of love and brotherhood will shine over our great nation with all their scintillating beauty.

Yours for the cause of Peace and Brotherhood,

MARTIN LUTHER KING, JR.

Henry David Thoreau
On the Duty of Civil Disobedience

Henry David Thoreau (1817–1862), American radical, graduated from Harvard in 1837 and drifted from job to job for several years until returning to his native Concord, Massachusetts where he remained the rest of his life. Through his writings and lectures, Thoreau came to be associated with the New England Transcendentalists. His thought incorporated Greek and Latin classics, Native American legend, Eastern scriptures, and his observations on the natural landscape. For two years beginning in 1845, Thoreau lived and wrote in a simple cabin in the woods beside Walden Pond. Thoreau saw this as an informal experiment in self-sufficiency and independence of the rules of society, as well as a practical activity consistent with his view that all knowledge begins with taking the time to know oneself. Thoreau's account of this experiment, published as *Walden* in 1854, reflects the apolitical, escapist aspect of Thoreau's individualism.

The following selection, "On the Duty of Civil Disobedience" (1849), takes a more explicitly political view. The essay reconciles individualism with democratic responsibility and political engagement. Thoreau's model citizen looks first to following his or her individual conscience, and by doing so that person contributes to making a more just society. In Thoreau's time, slavery and the war against Mexico represented the most prominent injustices, and he wished to have no hand in supporting them. He believed that by preserving and perfecting one's own moral integrity—acting according to one's principles in every way—a person can make a critique of society more powerful than voting or conventional political organizing allow.

Civil Disobedience
Henry David Thoreau

I heartily accept the motto,—"That government is best which governs least;" and I should like to see it acted up to more rapidly and systematically. Carried out, it finally amounts to this, which also I believe,—"That government is best which governs not at all;" and when men are prepared for it, that will be the kind of government which they will have. Government is at best but an expedient; but most governments are usually, and all governments are sometimes, inexpedient. The objections which have been brought against a standing army, and they are many and weighty, and deserve to prevail, may also at last be brought against a standing government. The standing army is only an arm of the standing government. The government itself, which is only the mode which the people have chosen to execute their will is equally liable to be abused and perverted before the people can act through it. Witness the present Mexican war, the work of comparatively a few individuals using the standing government as their tool; for, in the outset, the people would not have consented to this measure.

This American government,—what is it but a tradition, though a recent one, endeavoring to transmit itself unimpaired to posterity, but each instant losing some of its integrity? It has not the vitality and force of a single living man; for a single man can bend it to his will. It is a sort of wooden gun to the people themselves. But it is not the less necessary for this; for the people must have some complicated machinery or other, and hear its din, to satisfy that idea of government which they have. Governments show thus how successfully men can be imposed on, even impose on themselves, for their own advantage. It is excellent, we must all allow. Yet this government never of itself furthered any enterprise, but by the alacrity with which it got out of its way. *It* does not keep the country free. *It* does not settle the West. *It* does not educate. The character inherent in the American people has done all that has been accomplished; and it would have done somewhat more, if the government had not sometimes got in its way. For government is an expedient by which men would fain succeed in letting one another alone; and, as has been said, when it is most expedient, the governed are most let alone by it. Trade and commerce, if they were not made of India-rubber, would never manage to bounce over the obstacles which legislators are continually putting in their way; and, if one were to judge these men wholly by the effects of their actions and not partly by their intentions, they would deserve to be classed and punished with those mischievous persons who put obstructions on the railroads.

But, to speak practically and as a citizen, un-like those who call themselves no-government men, I ask for, not at once no government, but *at once* a better government. Let every man make known what kind of government would command his respect, and that will be one step toward obtaining it.

After all, the practical reason why, when the power is once in the hands of the people, a majority are permitted, and for a long period continue, to rule is not because they are most likely to be in the right, nor because this seems fairest to the minority, but because they are physically the strongest. But a government in which the majority rule in all cases cannot be based on justice, even as far as men understand it. Can there not be a government in which majorities do not virtually decide right and wrong, but conscience?—in which majorities decide only those questions to which the rule of expediency is applicable? Must the citizen ever for a moment, or in the least degree, resign his conscience to the legislator? Why has every man a conscience, then? I think that we should be men first, and subjects afterward. It is not desirable to cultivate a respect for the law, so much as for the right. The only obligation which I have a right to assume is to do at any time what I think right. It is truly enough said, that a corporation has no conscience; but a corporation of conscientious men is a corporation *with* a conscience. Law never made men a whit more just; and, by means of their respect for it, even the well-disposed are daily made the agents of injustice. A common and natural result of an undue respect for law is, that you may see a file of soldiers, colonel, captain, corporal privates, powder-monkeys, and all, marching in admirable order over hill and dale to the wars, against their wills, ay, against their common sense and consciences, which makes it very steep marching indeed, and produces a palpitation of the heart. They have no doubt that it is a damnable business in which they are concerned; they all are peaceably inclined. Now, what are they? Men at all? or small movable forts and magazines, at the service of some unscrupulous man in power? ...

The mass of men serve the state thus, not as men mainly, but as machines, with their bodies. They are the standing army, and the militia, jailors, constables, posse comitatus, etc. In most cases there is no free exercise whatever of the judgment or of the moral sense; but they put themselves on a level with wood and earth and stones; and wooden men can perhaps be manufactured that will serve the purpose as well. Such command no more respect than men of straw or a lump of dirt. They have the same sort of worth only as horses and dogs. Yet such as these even are commonly esteemed good citizens. Others—as most legislators, politicians, lawyers, ministers, and office-holders—serve the state chiefly with their heads; and, as they rarely make any moral distinctions, they are as likely to serve the Devil, without *intending* it, as God. A very few, as heros, patriots, martyrs, reformers in the great sense, and *men*, serve the state with their consciences also, and so necessarily resist it for the most part; and they are commonly treated as enemies by it.

He who gives himself entirely to his fellow-men appears to them useless and selfish; but he who gives himself partially to them is pronounced a benefactor and philanthropist.

How does it become a man to behave toward this American government to-day? I answer, that he cannot without disgrace be associated with it. I cannot for an instant recognize that political organization as *my* government which is the *slave's* government also.

All men recognize the right of revolution; that is, the right to refuse allegiance to, and to resist, the government, when its tyranny or its inefficiency are great and unendurable. But almost all say that such is not the case now. But such was the case, they think, in the Revolution of '75. If one were to tell me that this was a bad government because it taxed certain foreign commodities brought to its ports, it is most probable that I should not make an ado about it, for I can do without them. All machines have their friction; and possibly this does enough good to counterbalance the evil. At any rate, it is a great evil to make a stir about it. But when the friction comes to have its machine, and oppression and robbery are organized, I say, let us not have such a machine any longer. In other words, when a sixth of the population of a nation which has undertaken to be the refuge of liberty are slaves, and a whole country is unjustly overrun and conquered by a foreign army, and subjected to military law, I think that it is not too soon for honest men to rebel and revolutionize. What makes this duty the more urgent is the fact that the country so overrun is not our own, but ours is the invading army.

Unjust laws exist: shall we be content to obey them, or shall we endeavor to amend them, and obey them until we have succeeded, or shall we transgress them at once? Men generally, under such a government as this, think that they ought to wait until they have persuaded the majority to alter them. They think that, if they should resist, the remedy would be worse than the evil. But it is the fault of the government itself that the remedy *is* worse than the evil. *It* makes it worse. Why is it not more apt to anticipate and provide for reform? Why does it not cherish its wise minority? Why does it cry and resist before it is hurt? Why does it not encourage its citizens to be on the alert to point out its faults and *do* better than it would have them? Why does it always crucify Christ, and excommunicate Copernicus and Luther, and pronounce Washington and Franklin rebels?

One would think, that a deliberate and practical denial of its authority was the only offense never contemplated by government; else, why has it not assigned its definite, its suitable and proportionate penalty? If a man who has no property refuses but once to earn nine shillings for the state, he is put in prison for a period unlimited by any law that I know, and determined only by the discretion of those who placed him there; but if he should steal ninety times nine shillings from the state, he is soon permitted to go at large again.

If the injustice is part of the necessary friction of the machine of government, let it go, let it go: perchance it will wear smooth,—certainly the machine will wear out. If the injustice has a spring, or a pulley, or a rope, or a crank, exclusively for itself, then perhaps you may consider whether the remedy will not be worse than the evil; but if it is of such a nature that it requires you to be the agent of injustice to another, then, I say, break the law. Let your life be a counter friction to stop the machine. What I have to do is to see, at any rate, that I do not lend myself to the wrong which I condemn.

As for adopting the ways which the state has provided for remedying the evil, I know not of such ways. They take too much time, and a man's life will be gone. I have other affairs to attend to. I came into this world, not chiefly to make this a good place to live in, but to live in it, be it good or bad. A man has not everything to do, but something; and because he cannot do *everything*, it is not necessary that he should do *something* wrong. It is not my business to be petitioning the Governor or the Legislature any more than it is theirs to petition me; and if they should not bear my petition, what should I do then? But in this case the state has provided no way: its very Constitution is the evil. This may seem to be harsh and stubborn and unconciliatory; but it is to treat with the utmost kindness and consideration the only spirit that can appreciate or deserves it. So is all change for the better, like birth and death, which convulse the body.

I do not hesitate to say, that those who call themselves Abolitionists should at once effectually withdraw their support, both in person and property, from the government of Massachusetts and not wait till they constitute a majority of one, before they suffer the right to prevail through them. I think that it is enough if they have God on their side, without waiting for that other one. Moreover, any man more right than his neighbors constitutes a majority of one already.

I meet this American government, or its representative, the state government, directly, and face to face, once a year—no more—in the person if its tax-gatherer; this is the only mode in which a man situated as I am necessarily meets it; and it then says distinctly, Recognize me; and the simplest, most effectual, and, in the present posture of affairs, the indispensablest mode of treating with it on this head, of expressing your little satisfaction with and love for it, is to deny it then. My civil neighbor, the tax-gatherer, is the very man I have to deal with,—for it is, after all, with men and not with parchment that I quarrel,—and he has voluntarily chosen to be an agent of the government. How shall he ever know well what he is and does as an officer of the government, or as a man, until he is obliged to consider whether he shall treat me, his neighbor, for whom he has respect, as a neighbor and well-disposed man, or as a maniac and disturber of the peace, and see if he can get over this obstruction to his neighborliness without a ruder and more impetuous thought or speech corresponding with his action. I know this well, that if one thousand, if one hundred, if ten men whom I could name,—if ten *honest* men only,—ay, if *one* HONEST man, in this State of Massachusetts, *ceasing to hold slaves*, were actually to withdraw from this copartnership, and be locked up in the county jail therefor, it would be the abolition of slavery in America. For it matters not how small the beginning may seem to be: what is once well done is done forever. But we love better to talk about it: that we say is our mission. Reform keeps many scores

of newspapers in its service, but not one man. If my esteemed neighbor, the State's ambassador, who will devote his days to the settlement of the question of human rights in the Council Chamber, instead of being threatened with the prisons of Carolina, were to sit down the prisoner of Massachusetts, that State which is so anxious to foist the sin of slavery upon her sister,—though at present she can discover only an act of inhospitality to be the ground of a quarrel with her,—the Legislature would not wholly waive the subject the following winter.

Under a government which imprisons any unjustly, the true place for a just man is also a prison. The proper place to-day, the only place which Massachusetts has provided for her freer and less desponding spirits, is in her prisons, to be put out and locked out of the State by her own act, as they have already put themselves out by their principles. It is there that the fugitive slave, and the Mexican prisoner on parole, and the Indian come to plead the wrongs of his race should find them; on that separate, but more free and honorable ground, where the State Places those who are not *with* her, but *against* her,—the only house in a slave State in which a free man can abide with honor. If any think that their influence would be lost there, and their voices no longer afflict the ear of the State, that they would not be as an enemy within its walls, they do not know by how much truth is stronger than error, nor how much more eloquently and effectively he can combat injustice who has experienced a little in his own person. Cast your whole vote, not a strip of paper merely, but your whole influence. A minority is powerless while it conforms to the majority; it is not even a minority then; but it is irresistible when it clogs by its whole weight. If the alternative is to keep all just men in prison, or give up war and slavery, the State will not hesitate which to choose. If a thousand men were not to pay their tax-bills this year, that would not be a violent and bloody measure, as it would be to pay them, and enable the State to commit violence and shed innocent blood. This is, in fact, the definition of a peaceable revolution, if any such is possible. If the tax-gatherer, or any other public officer, asks me, as one has done, "But what shall I do?" my answer is, "If you really wish to do anything, resign your office." When the subject has refused allegiance, and the officer has resigned his office, then the revolution is accomplished. But even suppose blood should flow. Is there not a sort of blood shed when the conscience is wounded? Through this wound a man's real manhood and immortality flow out, and he bleeds to an everlasting death. I see this blood flowing now.

I have contemplated the imprisonment of the offender, rather than the seizure of his goods,— though both will serve the same purpose,—because they who assert the purest right, and consequently are most dangerous to a corrupt State, commonly have not spent much time in accumulating property. To such the State renders comparatively small service, and a slight tax is wont to appear exorbitant, particularly if they are obliged to earn it by special labor with their hands. If there were one who lived wholly without the use of money, the State itself would hesitate to demand it of him. But the rich man—not to make any invidious comparison—is always sold to the institution which makes him rich. Absolutely speaking, the more money, the less virtue; for money comes between a man and his objects, and obtains them for him; and it was certainly no great virtue to obtain it. It puts to rest many questions which he would otherwise be taxed to answer; while the only new question which it puts is the hard but superfluous one, how to spend it. Thus his moral ground is taken from under his feet. The opportunities of living are diminished in proportion as what are called the "means" are increased. The best thing a man can do for his culture when he is rich is to endeavor to carry out those schemes which he entertained when he was poor. Christ answered the Herodians according to their condition. "Show me the tribute-money," said he;—and one took a penny out of his pocket;—if you use money which has the image of Caesar on it and which he has made current and valuable, that is, *if you are men of the State*, and gladly enjoy the advantages of Caesar's government, then pay him back some of his own when he demands it. "Render therefore to Caesar that which is Ceasar's, and to God those things which are God's,"—leaving them no wiser than before as to which was which; for they did not wish to know... .

I have paid no poll-tax for six years. I was put into a jail once on this account, for one night; and, as I stood considering the wall of solid stone, two or three feet thick, the door of wood and iron, a foot thick, and the iron grating which strained the light, I could not help being struck with the foolishness of that institution which treated me as if I were mere flesh and blood and bones, to be locked up. I wondered that it should have concluded at length that this was the best use it could put me to, and had never thought to avail itself of my services in some way. I saw that, if there was a wall of stone between me and my townsmen, there was a still more difficult one to climb or break through before they could get to be as free as I was. I did not for a moment feel confined, and the walls seemed a great waste of stone and mortar. I felt as if I alone of all my townsmen had paid my tax. They plainly did not know how to treat me, but behaved like persons who are underbred. In every threat and in every compliment there was a blunder; for they thought that my chief desire was to stand the other side of that stone wall. I could not but smile to see how industriously they locked the door on my meditations, which followed them out again without let or hindrance, and *they* were really all that was dangerous. As they could not reach me, they had resolved to punish my body; just as boys, if they cannot come at some person against whom they have a spite, will abuse his dog. I saw that the State was half-witted, that it was timid as a lone woman with her silver spoons, and that it did not know its friends from its foes, and I lost all my remaining respect for it, and pitied it.

Thus the State never intentionally confronts a man's sense, intellectual or moral but only his body, his senses. It is not armed with superior wit or honesty, but with superior physical strength. I was not born to be forced. I will breathe after my own fashion. Let us see who is the strongest. What force has a multitude? They only can force me who obey a higher law than I. They force me to become like themselves. I do not hear of *men* being *forced* to live this way or that by masses of men. What sort of life were that to live? When I meet a government which says to me, "Your money or your life," why should I be in haste to give it my money? It may be in a great strait, and not know what to do: I cannot help that. It must help itself; do as I do. It is not worth the while to snivel about it. I am not responsible for the successful wording of the machinery of society. I am not the son of the engineer. I perceive that, when an acorn and a chestnut fall side by side, the one does not remain inert to make way for the other, but both obey their own laws, and spring and grow and flourish as best they can, till one, perchance, overshadows and destroys the other. If a plant cannot live according to its nature, it dies; and so a man....

The authority of government, even such as I am willing to submit to,—for I will cheerfully obey those who know and can do better than I, and in many things even those who neither know nor can do so well,—is still an impure one: to be strictly just, it must have the sanction and consent of the governed. It can have no pure right over my person and property but what I concede to it. The progress from an absolute to a limited monarchy, from a limited monarchy to a democracy, is a progress toward a true respect for the individual. Even the Chinese philosopher was wise enough to regard the individual as the basis of the empire. Is a democracy, such as we know it, the last improvement possible in government? Is it not possible to take a step further towards recognizing and organizing the rights of man? There will never be a really free and enlightened State until the State comes to recognize the individual as a higher and independent power, from which all its own power and authority are derived, and treats him accordingly. I please myself with imagining a State at last which can afford to be just to all men, and to treat the individual with respect as a neighbor; which even would not think it inconsistent with its own repose if a few were to live aloof from it, not meddling with it, nor embraced by it, who fulfilled all the duties of neighbors and fellow-men. A State which bore this kind of fruit, and suffered it to drop off as fast as it ripened, would prepare the way for a still more perfect and glorious State, which also I have imagined, but not yet anywhere seen.

Ayn Rand
The Fountainhead

Ayn Rand (1905–82), was born in St. Petersburg, Russia. Her family lived affluently until her father's business was nationalized by the Communist government when Rand was twelve. In 1926, two years after graduating from the University of Petrograd, Rand emigrated to the United States. She deeply admired the US for its founding principles of individual rights and freedom. Having planned to become a writer since childhood, Rand published her first novel, *We the Living*, in 1936. Her other novels include *Anthem* (1938), *The Fountainhead* (1943), and *Atlas Shrugged* (1957). In each of Rand's novels, a talented and individualistic protagonist struggles against the forces of mediocrity and collectivism. In the 1960s, Rand expanded the philosophy of her novels into an intellectual movement known as Objectivism. Objectivism derides altruism and celebrates the creativity, independence, and self-fulfillment of radically discrete individuals in capitalist society.

Rand's *The Fountainhead* tells the story of architect Howard Roark, a man of exceptional ability and integrity. Roark secretly designs a housing project for another architect of lesser ability on the condition that the plans not be changed in any way. When his plans are altered beyond recognition, Roark dynamites the completed building. At the subsequent trial, Roark conducts his own defense, presented in the following selection.

The Fountainhead
Ayn Rand

The prosecutor introduced his witnesses. The policeman who had arrested Roark took the stand to tell how he had found the defendant standing by the electric plunger. The night watchman related how he had been sent away from the scene; his testimony was brief; the prosecutor preferred not to stress the subject of Dominique. The contractor's superintendent testified about the dynamite missing from the stores on the site. Officials of Cortlandt, building inspectors, estimators took the stand to describe the building and the extent of the damage. This concluded the first day of the trial.

Peter Keating was the first witness called on the following day.

He sat on the stand, slumped forward. He looked at the prosecutor obediently. His eyes moved, once in a while. He looked at the crowd, at the jury, at Roark. It made no difference.

"Mr. Keating, will you state under oath whether you designed the project ascribed to you, known as Cortlandt Homes?"

"No. I didn't."

"Who designed it?"

"Howard Roark."

"At whose request?"

"At my request."

"Why did you call on him?"

"Because I was not capable of doing it myself."

There was no sound of honesty in the voice, because there was no sound of effort to pronounce a truth of such nature; no tone of truth or falsehood; only indifference.

...When Keating left the stand, the audience had the odd impression that no change had occurred in the act of a man's exit; as if no person had walked out.

"The prosecution rests," said the District Attorney.

The judge looked at Roark.

"Proceed," he said. His voice was gentle.

Roark got up. "Your Honor, I shall call no witnesses. This will be my testimony and my summation."

"Take the oath."

Roark took the oath. He stood by the steps of the witness stand. The audience looked at him. They felt he had no chance. They could drop the nameless resentment, the sense of insecurity which he aroused in most people. And so, for the first time, they could see him as he was: a man totally innocent of fear.

…Roark stood before them as each man stands in the innocence of his own mind. But Roark stood like that before a hostile crowd—and they knew suddenly that no hatred was possible to him. For the flash of an instant, they grasped the manner of his consciousness. Each asked himself: do I need anyone's approval?—does it matter?—am I tied? And for that instant, each man was free—free enough to feel benevolence for every other man in the room.

It was only a moment; the moment of silence when Roark was about to speak.

"Thousands of years ago, the first man discovered how to make fire. He was probably burned at the stake he had taught his brothers to light. He was considered an evildoer who had dealt with a demon mankind dreaded. But thereafter men had fire to keep them warm, to cook their food, to light their caves. He had left them a gift they had not conceived and he had lifted darkness off the earth. Centuries later, the first man invented the wheel. He was probably torn on the rack he had taught his brothers to build. He was considered a transgressor who ventured into forbidden territory. But thereafter, men could travel past any horizon. He had left them a gift they had not conceived and he had opened the roads of the world.

"That man, the unsubmissive and first, stands in the opening chapter of every legend mankind has recorded about its beginning. Prometheus was chained to a rock and torn by vultures—because he had stolen the fire of the gods. Adam was condemned to suffer—because he had eaten the fruit of the tree of knowledge. Whatever the legend, somewhere in the shadows of its memory mankind knew that its glory began with one and that one paid for his courage.

"Throughout the centuries there were men who took first steps down new roads armed with nothing but their own vision. Their goals differed, but they all had this in common: that the step was first, the road new, the vision unborrowed, and the response they received—hatred. The great creators—the thinkers, the artists, the scientists, the inventors—stood alone against the men of their time. Every great new thought was opposed. Every great new invention was denounced. The first motor was considered foolish. The airplane was considered impossible. The power loom was considered vicious. Anesthesia was considered sinful. But the men of unborrowed vision went ahead. They fought, they suffered and they paid. But they won.

"No creator was prompted by a desire to serve his brothers, for his brothers rejected the gift he offered and that gift destroyed the slothful routine of their lives. His truth was his only motive. His own truth, and his own work to achieve it in his own way…. He held his truth above all things and against all men.

"His vision, his strength, his courage came from his own spirit. A man's spirit, however, is his self. That entity which is his consciousness. To think, to feel, to judge, to act are functions of the ego.

"The creators were not selfless. It is the whole secret of their power—that it was self-sufficient, self-motivated, self-generated. A first cause, a fount of energy, a life force, a Prime Mover. The creator served nothing and no one. He lived for himself.

"And only by living for himself was he able to achieve the things which are the glory of mankind. Such is the nature of achievement.

"…There is no such thing as a collective brain. There is no such thing as a collective thought. An agreement reached by a group of men is only a compromise or an average drawn upon many individual thoughts. It is a secondary consequence. The primary act—the process of reason—must be performed by each man alone. We can divide a meal among many men. We cannot digest it in a collective stomach. No man can use his lungs to breathe for another man. No man can use his brain to think for another. All the functions of body and spirit are private. They cannot be shared or transferred.

"...The creative faculty cannot be given or received, shared or borrowed. It belongs to single, individual men. That which it creates is the property of the creator. Men learn from one another. But all learning is only the exchange of material. No man can give another the capacity to think. Yet that capacity is our only means of survival.

"Nothing is given to man on earth. Everything he needs has to be produced. And here man faces his basic alternative: he can survive in only one of two ways—by the independent work of his own mind or as a parasite fed by the minds of others. The creator originates. The parasite borrows. The creator faces nature alone. The parasite faces nature through an intermediary.

"The creator's concern is the conquest of nature. The parasite's concern is the conquest of men.

"The creator lives for his work. He needs no other men. His primary goal is within himself. The parasite lives second-hand. He needs others. Others become his prime motive.

"The basic need of the creator is independence. The reasoning mind cannot work under any form of compulsion. It cannot be curbed, sacrificed or subordinated to any consideration whatsoever. It demands total independence in function and in motive. To a creator, all relations with men are secondary.

"The basic need of the second-hander is to secure his ties with men in order to be fed. He places relations first. He declares that man exists in order to serve others. He preaches altruism.

"Altruism is the doctrine which demands that man live for others and place others above self.

"No man can live for another. He cannot share his spirit just as he cannot share his body. But the second-hander has used altruism as a weapon of exploitation and reversed the base of mankind's moral principles. Men have been taught every precept that destroys the creator. Men have been taught dependence as a virtue.

"The man who attempts to live for others is a dependent. He is a parasite in motive and makes parasites of those he serves. The relationship produces nothing but mutual corruption. It is impossible in concept. The nearest approach to it in reality—the man who lives to serve others—is the slave. If physical slavery is repulsive, how much more repulsive is the concept of servility of the spirit? The conquered slave has a vestige of honor. He has the merit of having resisted and of considering his condition evil. But the man who enslaves himself voluntarily in the name of love is the basest of creatures. He degrades the dignity of man and he degrades the conception of love. But this is the essence of altruism.

"Men have been taught that the highest virtue is not to achieve, but to give. Yet one cannot give that which has not been created. Creation comes before distribution—or there will be nothing to distribute. The need of the creator comes before the need of any possible beneficiary. Yet we are taught to admire the second-hander who dispenses gifts he has not produced above the man who made the gifts possible. We praise an act of charity. We shrug at an act of achievement.

"Men have been taught that their first concern is to relieve the suffering of others. But suffering is a disease. Should one come upon it, one tries to give relief and assistance. To make that the highest test of virtue is to make suffering the most important part of life. Then man must wish to see others suffer—in order that he may be virtuous. Such is the nature of altruism. The creator is not concerned with disease, but with life. Yet the work of the creators has eliminated one form of disease after another, in man's body and spirit, and brought more relief from suffering than any altruist could ever conceive.

"Men have been taught that it is a virtue to agree with others. But the creator is the man who disagrees. Men have been taught that it is a virtue to swim with the current. But the creator is the man who goes against the current. Men have been taught that it is a virtue to stand together. But the creator is the man who stands alone.

"Men have been taught that the ego is the synonym of evil, and selflessness the ideal of virtue. But the creator is the egotist in the absolute sense, and the selfless man is the one who does not think, feel, judge or act. These are functions of the self.

"Here the basic reversal is most deadly. The issue has been perverted and man has been left no alternative—and no freedom. As poles of good and evil, he was offered two conceptions: egotism and altruism. Egotism was held to mean the sacrifice of others to self. Altruism—the sacrifice of self to others. This tied man irrevocably to other men and left him nothing but a choice of pain: his own pain borne for the sake of others or pain inflicted upon others for the sake of self. When it was added that man must find joy in self-immolation, the trap was closed. Man was forced to accept masochism as his ideal—under the threat that sadism was his only alternative. This was the greatest fraud ever perpetrated on mankind.

"This was the device by which dependence and suffering were perpetuated as fundamentals of life.

"The choice is not self-sacrifice or domination. The choice is independence or dependence. The code of the creator or the code of the second-hander. This is the basic issue. It rests upon the alternative of life or death. The code of the creator is built on the needs of the reasoning mind which allows man to survive.

The code of the second-hander is built on the needs of a mind incapable of survival. All that which proceeds from man's independent ego is good. All that which proceeds from man's dependence upon men is evil.

"The egotist in the absolute sense is not the man who sacrifices others. He is the man who stands above the need of using others in any manner. He does not function through them. He is not concerned with them in any primary matter. Not in his aim, not in his motive, not in his thinking, not in his desires, not in the source of his energy. He does not exist for any other man—and he asks no other man to exist for him. This is the only form of brotherhood and mutual respect possible between men.

…"No work is ever done collectively, by a majority decision. Every creative job is achieved under the guidance of a single individual thought. An architect requires a great many men to erect his building. But he does not ask them to vote on his design. They work together by free agreement and each is free in his proper function. An architect uses steel, glass, concrete, produced by others. But the materials remain just so much steel, glass and concrete until he touches them. What he does with them is his individual product and his individual property. This is the only pattern for proper cooperation among men.

"The first right on earth is the right of the ego. Man's first duty is to himself. His moral law is never to place his prime goal within the persons of others. His moral obligation is to do what he wishes, provided his wish does not depend *primarily* upon other men. This includes the whole sphere of his creative faculty, his thinking, his work. But it does not include the sphere of the gangster, the altruist and the dictator.

"A man thinks and works alone. A man cannot rob, exploit or rule—alone. Robbery, exploitation and ruling presuppose victims. They imply dependence. They are the province of the second-hander.

"Rulers of men are not egotists. They create nothing. They exist entirely through the persons of others. Their goal is in their subjects, in the activity of enslaving. They are as dependent as the beggar, the social worker and the bandit. The form of dependence does not matter.

"But men were taught to regard second-handers—tyrants, emperors, dictators—as exponents of egotism. By this fraud they were made to destroy the ego, themselves and others. The purpose of the fraud was to destroy the creators. Or to harness them. Which is a synonym.

"From the beginning of history, the two antagonists have stood face to face: the creator and the second-hander. When the first creator invented the wheel, the first second-hander responded. He invented altruism.

"The creator—denied, opposed, persecuted, exploited—went on, moved forward and carried all humanity along on his energy. The second-hander contributed nothing to the process except the impediments. The contest has another name: the individual against the collective.

"The 'common good' of a collective—a race, a class, a state—was the claim and justification of every tyranny ever established over men. Every major horror of history was committed in the name of an altruistic motive. Has any act of selfishness ever equaled the carnage perpetrated by disciples of altruism? Does the fault lie in men's hypocrisy or in the nature of the principle? The most dreadful butchers were the most sincere. They believed in the perfect society reached through the guillotine and the firing squad. Nobody questioned their right to murder since they were murdering for an altruistic purpose. It was accepted that man must be sacrificed for other men. Actors change, but the course of the tragedy remains the same. A humanitarian who starts with declarations of love for mankind and ends with a sea of blood. It goes on and will go on so long as men believe that an action is good if it is unselfish. That permits the altruist to act and forces his victims to bear it. The leaders of collectivist movements ask nothing for themselves. But observe the results.

"The only good which men can do to one another and the only statement of their proper relationship is—Hands off!

…"It is an ancient conflict. Men have come close to the truth, but it was destroyed each time and one civilization fell after another. Civilization is the progress toward a society of privacy. The savage's whole existence is public, ruled by the laws of his tribe. Civilization is the process of setting man free from men.

"Now, in our age, collectivism, the rule of the second-hander and second-rater, the ancient monster, has broken loose and is running amuck. It has brought men to a level of intellectual indecency never equaled on earth. It has reached a scale of horror without precedent. It has poisoned every mind. It has swallowed most of Europe. It is engulfing our country.

…"I came here to say that I do not recognize anyone's right to one minute of my life. Nor to any part of my energy. Nor to any achievement of mine. No matter who makes the claim, how large their number or how great their need.

"I wished to come here and say that I am a man who does not exist for others.

"It had to be said. The world is perishing from an orgy of self-sacrificing.

"Conscientious" Objection to Military Service

U.S. v. Seeger (1965)

When a democratic government "of the people" decides to conscript individuals into the military in order to prepare for war, most individuals are willing to serve. But throughout the history of U.S. democracy, there has been a sizable minority who objected to military service on the grounds of individual conscience. A number of religions preach pacifism and/or the nonviolent resistance to evil, and in this century, our draft laws have reflected the presence of pacifist individuals by granting exemption to military service to "conscientious objectors," typically those who were members of "peace churches" like the Quakers and Mennonites. Conscientious objectors are required to perform alternate service "of national importance under civilian direction."

Daniel Seeger presented a classic case of individual conscience in conflict with a democratic state requiring his service in the military. Although Seeger would not connect his "objection to war in any form" to belief in a Supreme Being, he nonetheless claimed that he could not serve in the military based on his commitment to "the welfare of humanity and the preservation of the democratic values which we in the United States are struggling to maintain…I have concluded that war, from the practical standpoint, is futile and self defeating, and that from the more important moral standpoint, is unethical." But because his objection to military service was not based upon traditional religious training and belief, his draft board denied his request for conscientious objector status.

His case eventually came before the Supreme Court, which unanimously upheld Seeger's constitutional right of individual conscience against a state requirement for military service. The Court's opinion is excerpted here.

"Conscientious" Objection to Military Service

U.S. v. Seeger (1965)

Opinion of the Court
[380] US 164]

Mr. Justice Clark delivered the opinion of the court.

These cases involve claims of conscientious objectors under §6(j) of the Universal Military Training and Service Act which exempts from combatant training and service in the armed forces of the United States those persons who be reason of their religious training and belief are conscientiously opposed to participation in war in any form.

The Facts in the Cases

Seeger was convicted in the District Court for the Southern District of New York of having refused to submit to induction in the armed forces.... Although he did not adopt verbatim the printed Selective Service System form, he declared that he was conscientiously opposed to participation in war in any form by reason of his "religious" belief; that he preferred to leave the question as to his belief in a Supreme Being open, "rather than answer 'yes' or 'no'"; that his "skepticism or disbelief in the existence of God" did "not necessarily mean lack of faith in anything whatsoever"; that his was a "belief in and devotion to goodness and virtue for their own sakes, and a religious faith in a purely ethical creed." He cited such personages as Plato, Aristotle and Spinoza for support of his ethical belief in intellectual and moral integrity "without belief in God, except in the remotest sense." R. 73. His belief was found to be sincere, honest, and made in good faith; and his conscientious objection to be based upon individual training and belief, both of which included research in religious and cultural fields. Seeger's claim, however, was denied solely because it was not based upon a "belief in a relation to a Supreme Being" as required by the Act....

Chief Justice Hughes...enunciated the rationale behind the long recognition of conscientious objection to participation in war accorded by Congress in our various conscription laws when he declared that "in the forum of conscience, duty to a moral power higher than the State has always been maintained." In a similar vein Harlan Fiske Stone, later Chief Justice, drew from the Nation's past when he declared that "both morals and sound policy require that the state should not violate the conscience of the individual. All our history gives confirmation to the view that liberty of conscience has a moral and social value which makes it worthy of preservation at the hands of the state. So deep in its significance and vital, indeed, is it to the integrity of man's moral and spiritual nature that nothing short of the self preservation of the state should warrant its violation; and it may well be questioned whether the state which preserves its life by a settled policy of violation of the conscience of the individual will not in fact ultimately lose it by the process."

[I]t must be remembered that in resolving these exemption problems one deals with the beliefs of different individuals who will articulate them in a multitude of ways. In such an intensely personal area, of course, the claim of the registrant that his belief is an essential part of a religious faith must be given great weight....

In summary, Seeger professed "religious belief" and "religious faith." He decried the tremendous "spiritual" price man must pay for his willingness to destroy human life. In light of his beliefs and the unquestioned sincerity with which he held them, we think the Board, had it applied the test we propose today, would have granted him the exemption. We think it clear that the beliefs which prompted his objection occupy the same place in his life as the belief in a traditional deity holds in the lives of his friends, the Quakers....

It may be that Seeger did not demonstrate what his beliefs were with regard to the usual understanding of the term "Supreme Being." But as we have said Congress did not intend that to be the test. We therefore affirm the judgement in No. 50.

Mr. Justice Douglas, concurring.

I agree with the Court that any person opposed to war on the basis of a sincere belief, which in his life fills the same place as a belief in God fills in the life of an orthodox religionist, is entitled to exemption under the statute.

Ursula K. Le Guin

The Ones Who Walk Away from Omelas

Ursula Le Guin, American novelist, was born in Berkeley, California in 1929, received her B.A. from Radcliffe College and a Master of Arts degree in French from Columbia University in 1952. She published her first story in 1961 and has since won several major literary awards. She is best known for her science fiction novels *The Left Hand of Darkness and The Dispossessed*. She lives in Portland, Oregon.

The Ones Who Walk Away from Omelas
Ursula K. Le Guin

The central idea of this psychomyth, the scapegoat, turns up in Dostoyevsky's *Brothers Karamazov*, and several people have asked me, rather suspiciously, why I gave the credit to William James. The fact is, I haven't been able to re read Dostoyevsky, much as I loved him, since I was twenty five, and I'd simply forgotten he used the idea. But when I met it in James's "The Moral Philosopher and the Moral Life," it was with a shock of recognition. Here is how James puts it:

Or if the hypothesis were offered us of a world in which Messrs. Fourier's and Bellamy's and Morris's goes onutopias should all be outdone, and millions kept permanently happy on the one simple condition that a certain lost soul on the far off edge of things should lead a life of lonely torment, what except a specific and independent sort of emotion can it be which would make us immediately feel, even though an impulse arose within us to clutch at the hap-piness so offered, how hideous a thing would be its enjoyment when deliberately accepted as the fruit of such a bargain?

The dilemma of the American conscience can hardly be better stated. Dostoyevsky was a great artist, and a radical one, but his early social radicalism reversed itself, leaving him a violent reactionary. Whereas the American James, who seems so mild, so naïvely gentle-manly—look how he says "us," assuming all his readers are as decent as himself!—was, and remained, and remains, a genuinely radical thinker. Directly after the "lost soul" passage he goes on.

All the higher, more penetrating ideals are revolutionary. They present themselves far less in the guise of effects of past experience than in that of probable causes of future experience, factors to which the environment and the lessons it has so far taught us must learn to bend.

The application, of those two sentences to this story, and to science fiction, and to all thinking about the future, is quite direct. Ideals as "the probable causes of future experience"—that is a subtle and an exhilarating remark!

Of course I didn't read James and sit down and say, Now I'll write a story about that "lost soul." It seldom works that simply. I sat down and started a story, just because I felt like it, with nothing but the word "Omelas" in mind. It came from a road sign: Salem (Oregon) backwards. Don't you read road signs backwards? POTS. WOLS nerdlihc. Ocsicnarf Nas...Salem equals schelomo equals salaam equals Peace. Melas. O melas. Omelas. Homme hélas. "Where do you get your ideas from, Ms Le Guin?" From forgetting Dostoyevsky and reading road signs backwards, naturally. Where else?

With a clamor of bells that set the swallows soaring, the Festival of Summer came to the city Omelas, bright towered by the sea. The rigging of the boats in harbor sparkled with flags. In the streets between houses with red roofs and painted walls, between old mossgrown gardens and under avenues of trees, past great parks and public buildings, processions moved. Some were decorous: old people in long stiff robes of mauve and grey, grave master workmen, quiet, merry women carrying their babies and chatting as they walked. In other streets the music beat faster, a shimmering of gong and tambourine, and the people went dancing, the procession was a dance. Children dodged in and out, their high calls rising like the swallows' crossing flights over the music and the singing. All the processions wound towards the north side of the city, where on the great water meadow called the Green Fields boys and girls, naked in the bright air, with mud stained feet and ankles and long, lithe arms, exercised their restive horses before the race. The horses wore no gear at all but a halter without bit. Their manes were braided with streamers of silver, gold, and green. They flared their nostrils and pranced

and boasted to one another; they were vastly excited, the horse being the only animal who has adopted our ceremonies as his own. Far off to the north and west the mountains stood up half encircling Omelas on her bay. The air of morning was so clear that the snow still crowning the Eighteen Peaks burned with white gold fire across the miles of sunlit air, under the dark blue of the sky. There was just enough wind to make the banners that marked the racecourse snap and flutter now and then. In the silence of the broad green meadows one could hear the music winding through the city streets, farther and nearer and ever approaching, a cheerful faint sweetness of the air that from time to time trembled and gathered together and broke out into the great joyous clanging of the bells.

Joyous! How is one to tell about joy? How describe the citizens of Omelas?

They were not simple folk, you see, though they were happy. But we do not say the words of cheer much any more. All smiles have become archaic. Given a description such as this one tends to make certain assumptions. Given a description such as this one tends to look next for the King, mounted on a splendid stallion and surrounded by his noble knights, or perhaps in a golden litter borne by great muscled slaves. But there was no king. They did not use swords, or keep slaves. They were not barbarians. I do not know the rules and laws of their society, but I suspect that they were singularly few. As they did without monarchy and slavery, so they also got on without the stock exchange, the advertisement, the secret police, and the bomb. Yet I repeat that these were not simple folk, not dulcet shepherds, noble savages, bland utopians. They were not less complex than us. The trouble is that we have a bad habit, encouraged by pedants and sophisticates, of considering happiness as something rather stupid. Only pain is intellectual, only evil interesting. This is the treason of the artist: a refusal to admit the banality of evil and the terrible boredom of pain. If you can't lick 'em, join 'em. If it hurts, repeat it. But to praise despair is to condemn delight, to embrace violence is to lose hold of everything else. We have almost lost hold; we can no longer describe a happy man, nor make any celebration of joy. How can I tell you about the people of Omelas? They were not naïve and happy children—though their children were, in fact, happy. They were mature, intelligent, passionate adults whose lives were not wretched. O miracle! but I wish I could describe it better. I wish I could convince you. Omelas sounds in my words like a city in a fairy tale, long ago and far away, once upon a time. Perhaps it would be best if you imagined it as your own fancy bids, assuming it will rise to the occasion, for certainly I cannot suit you all. For instance, how about technology? I think that there would be no cars or helicopters in and above the streets; this follows from the fact that the people of Omelas are happy people. Happiness is based on a just discrimination of what is necessary, what is neither necessary nor destructive, and what is destructive. In the middle category, however—that of the unnecessary but undestructive, that of comfort, luxury, exuberance, etc.—they could perfectly well have central heating, subway trains, washing machines, and all kinds of marvelous devices not yet invented here, floating light sources, fuelless power, a cure for the common cold. Or they could have none of that: it doesn't matter. As you like it. I incline to think that people from towns up and down the coast have been coming in to Omelas during the last days before the Festival on very fast little trains and double decked trams, and that the train station of Omelas is actually the handsomest building in town, though plainer than the magnificent Farmers' Market. But even granted trains, I fear that Omelas so far strikes some of you as goody-goody. Smiles, bells, parades, horses, bleh. If so, please add an orgy. If an orgy would help, don't hesitate. Let us not, however, have temples from which issue beautiful nude priests and priestesses already half in ecstasy and ready to copulate with any man or woman, lover or stranger, who desires union with the deep godhead of the blood, although

that was my first idea. But really it would be better not to have any temples in Omelas—at least, not manned temples. Religion yes, clergy no. Surely the beautiful nudes can just wander about, offering themselves like divine soufflés to the hunger of the needy and the rapture of the flesh. Let them join the processions. Let tambourines be struck above the copulations, and the glory of desire be proclaimed upon the gongs, and (a not unimportant point) let the offspring of these delightful rituals be beloved and looked after by all. One thing I know there is none of in Omelas is guilt. But what else should there be? I thought at first there were no drugs, but that is puritanical. For those who like it, the faint insistent sweetness of *drooz* may perfume the ways of the city, *drooz* which first brings a great lightness and brilliance to the mind and limbs, and then after some hours a dreamy languor, and wonderful visions at last of the very arcana and inmost secrets of the Universe, as well as exciting the pleasure of sex beyond all belief; and it is not habit forming. For more modest tastes I think there ought to be beer. What else, what else belongs in the joyous city? The sense of victory, surely, the celebration of courage. But as we did without clergy, let us do without soldiers. The joy built upon successful slaughter is not the right kind of joy; it will not do; it is fearful and it is trivial. A boundless and generous contentment, a magnanimous triumph felt not against some outer enemy but in communion with the finest and fairest in the souls of all men everywhere and the splendor of the world's summer: this is what swells the hearts of the people of Omelas, and the victory they celebrate is that of life. I really don't think many of them need to take *drooz*.

Most of the processions have reached the Green Fields by now. A marvelous smell of cooking goes forth from the red and blue tents of the provisioners. The faces of small children are amiably sticky; in the benign grey beard of a man a couple of crumbs of rich pastry are entangled. The youths and girls have mounted their horses and are beginning to group around the starting line of the course. An old woman, small, fat, and laughing, is passing out flowers from a basket, and tall young men wear her flowers in their shining hair. A child of nine or ten sits at the edge of the crowd, alone, playing on a wooden flute. People pause to listen, and they smile, but they do not speak to him, for he never ceases playing and never sees them, his dark eyes wholly rapt in the sweet, thin magic of the tune.

He finishes, and slowly lowers his hands holding the wooden flute.

As if that little private silence were the signal, all at once a trumpet sounds from the pavilion near the starting line: imperious, melancholy, piercing. The horses rear on their slender legs, and some of them neigh in answer. Sober faced, the young riders stroke the horses' necks and soothe them, whispering, "Quiet, quiet, there my beauty, my hope..." They begin to form in rank along the starting line. The crowds along the racecourse are like a field of grass and flowers in the wind. The Festival of Summer has begun.

Do you believe? Do you accept the festival, the city, the joy? No? Then let me describe one more thing.

In a basement under one of the beautiful public buildings of Omelas, or perhaps in the cellar of one of its spacious private homes, there is a room. It has one locked door, and no window. A little light seeps in dustily between cracks in the boards, secondhand from a cobwebbed window somewhere across the cellar. In one corner of the little room a couple of mops, with stiff, clotted, foul smelling heads, stand near a rusty bucket. The floor is dirt, a little damp to the touch, as cellar dirt usually is. The room is about three paces long and two wide: a mere broom closet or disused tool room. In the room a child is sitting. It could be a boy or a girl. It looks about six, but actually is nearly ten. It is feeble minded. Perhaps it was born defective, or perhaps it has become imbecile through fear, malnutrition, and neglect. It picks its nose and occasionally fumbles vaguely with its toes or

genitals, as it sits hunched in the corner farthest from the bucket and the two mops. It is afraid of the mops. It finds them horrible. It shuts its eyes, but it knows the mops are still standing there; and the door is locked; and nobody win come. The door is always locked; and nobody ever comes, except that sometimes—the child has no understanding of time or interval—sometimes the door rattles terribly and opens, and a person, or several people, are there. One of them may come in and kick the child to make it stand up. The others never come close, but peer in at it with frightened, disgusted eyes. The food bowl and the water jug are hastily filled, the door is locked, the eyes disappear. The people at the door never say anything, but the child, who has not always lived in the tool room, and can remember sunlight and its mother's voice, sometimes speaks. "I will be good," it says. "Please let me out. I will be good!" They never answer. The child used to scream for help at night, and cry a good deal, but now it only makes a kind of whining, "eh haa, eh haa," and it speaks less and less often. It is so thin there are no calves to its legs; its belly protrudes; it lives on a half bowl of corn meal and grease a day. It is naked. Its buttocks and thighs are a mass of festered sores, as it sits in its own excrement continually.

They all know it is there, all the people of Omelas. Some of them have come to see it, others are content merely to know it is there. They all know that it has to be there. Some of them understand why, and some do not, but they all understand that their happiness, the beauty of their city, the tenderness of their friendships, the health of their children, the wisdom of their scholars, the skill of their makers, even the abundance of their harvest and the kindly weathers of their skies, depend wholly on this child's abominable misery.

This is usually explained to children when they are between eight and twelve, whenever they seem capable of understanding; and most of those who come to see the child are young people, though often enough an adult comes, or comes back, to see the child. No matter how well the matter has been explained to them, these young spectators are always shocked and sickened at the sight. They feel disgust, which they had thought themselves superior to. They feel anger, outrage, impotence, despite all the explanations. They would like to do something for the child. But there is nothing they can do. If the child were brought up into the sunlight out of that vile place, if it were cleaned and fed and comforted, that would be a good thing, indeed; but if it were done, in that day and hour all the prosperity and beauty and delight of Omelas would wither and be destroyed. Those are the terms. To exchange all the goodness and grace of every life in Omelas for that single, small improvement: to throw away the happiness of thousands for the chance of the happiness of one: that would be to let guilt within the walls indeed.

The terms are strict and absolute; there may not even be a kind word spoken to the child.

Often the young people go home in tears, or in a tearless rage, when they have seen the child and faced this terrible paradox. They may brood over it for weeks or years. But as time goes on they begin to realize that even if the child could be released, it would not get much good of its freedom: a little vague pleasure of warmth and food, no doubt, but little more. It is too degraded and imbecile to know any real joy. It has been afraid too long ever to be free of fear. Its habits are too uncouth for it to respond to humane treatment. Indeed, after so long it would probably be wretched without walls about it to protect it, and darkness for its eyes, and its own excrement to sit in. Their tears at the bitter injustice dry when they begin to perceive the terrible justice of reality, and to accept it. Yet it is their tears and anger, the trying of their generosity and the acceptance of their helplessness, which are perhaps the true source of the splendor of their lives. Theirs is no vapid, irresponsible happiness. They know that they, like the child, are not free. They know compassion. It is the existence of the child, and their knowledge of its existence, that makes possible the nobility of their architecture, the poignancy of their music, the profundity of their science. It is because of the child that they are so gentle with children. They know that if the wretched one were not there snivelling in the dark, the other one, the flute player, could make no joyful music as the young riders line up in their beauty for the race in the sunlight of the first morning of summer.

Now do you believe in them? Are they not more credible? But there is one more thing to tell, and this is quite incredible.

At times one of the adolescent girls or boys who go to see the child does not go home to weep or rage, does not, in fact, go home at all. Sometimes also a man or woman much older falls silent for a day or two, and then leaves home. These people go out into the street, and walk down the street alone. They keep walking, and walk straight out of the city of Omelas, through the beautiful gates. They keep walking across the farmlands of Omelas. Each one goes alone, youth or girl, man or woman. Night falls; the traveler must pass down village streets, between the houses with yellow lit windows, and on out into the darkness of the fields. Each alone, they go west or north, towards the mountains. They go on. They leave Omelas, they walk ahead into the darkness, and they do not come back. The place they go towards is a place even less imaginable to most of us than the city of happiness. I cannot describe it at all. It is possible that it does not exist. But they seem to know where they are going, the ones who walk away from Omelas.

Francis Wilkinson
The Gay Cadet

Until recently, "service" to one's country meant military service. And although the definition of "service" has broadened to include an array of nonmilitary activities, the sacrifice involved in military service and the comraderie of the platoon are still seen as a model to be emulated by civilian forms of community service. No one would argue, however, that the military is an institution that represents a model for *democratic* community, what with its hierarchical "chain of command" and its historical exclusion and/or segregation of certain citizens. The hotly debated issue of excluding gays and lesbians from the military raises a number of questions about community and "difference," about inclusion and exclusion, and about the nature of service. Differences based on sexual orientation are not the same as those based on race, gender, or class. And yet, some would argue that prejudice and discrimination against gay men and lesbians is more pervasive and destructive of democratic community. As you read about Joe Steffan, expelled from the Naval Academy in his final semester because of his sexual orientation, think about the following questions, and the implications for community and equality in the United States.

The Gay Cadet
Francis Wilkinson

The tallest building in Warren, Minnesota, is a grain elevator. So is the second tallest. A farming community of 2000 in the northwest corner of the state, Warren rests in the rich soil of the Red River Valley, one of the most productive wheat growing regions in the world, a little more than 100 miles south of Winnipeg. Many of the farmers around Warren can trace their land back to the original Scandinavian and German immigrants who first tilled it.

At the summer solstice, it is still light at 10 o'clock at night: in December, it grows dark in the afternoon. There are no hills in Warren. The only resistance to the all encompassing sky, the only stopgap to a blue devouring of the earth, is a vast and placid sea of grain cut by an occasional strip of two land highway.

This is the America heartland where Maggie and Chuck Steffan settled in to raise their son Joe and his three older sisters. It is a place of quiet ways and conservative values, sufficiently prosperous and God fearing to support seven local churches. Like his wife, Chuck Steffan is a blue eyed, fair skinned native of this region. The town pharmacist, he shares coffee and a table every morning with the same local men at Grand Central Station, the coffee shop across the street from Chuck's Rexall drug store. At tables like those at the Grand Central, in farming towns like Warren, talking of the weather is a minor art form.

Though Maggie and Chuck are less diligent about their religion these days, the Steffan children grew up regularly attending Catholic Mass, where Joe cultivated his gifted voice in the choir. A proud looking youth with sparkling blue eyes, close cropped, sandy hair, and a relentless compulsion for achievement, he graduated second in his class at Warren High School with a near perfect academic record, and was voted "most likely to succeed" by his classmates. In track, Joe set school records in the mile and two mile that still stand. "Joe is the greatest track athlete we've had in Warren in modern history," says his high school coach, John McDonald. "I probably will never be fortunate enough to coach a kid like that again."

Joe's austere self discipline was prominent early in life. He was every homeroom teacher's dream, so much a goody-goody that classmates sometimes wondered out loud if he were not some kind of alien, flawless being. In the group photographs taken for his high school yearbook, Joe is easily spotted: amidst jeans and polo shirts he alone is attired in blazer and tie. In the words of one of his high school teachers, he was "almost too perfect."

As a teen, Joe didn't go for guzzling Budweisers and cruising the empty, endless roadways around Warren as many of his peers did. He never caused problems. "We never worried about him," says his father. "If he came home an hour late, that was about the worst thing. He'd drive a little fast and stuff like that sometimes."

Joe applied for acceptance to only one college: the U.S. Naval Academy in Annapolis, Maryland. By the end of high school he had decided to trade Warren's open sky for the cramped stuffy cabin of a submarine commander, leagues beneath the surface of the sea. He would comport himself as an officer and learn the manly art of war. He would make his family, his school, and whole town proud of him.

The U.S. Naval Academy is one of the nation's most elite institutions. Founded in 1845, the historic campus on the banks of the Chesapeake has been the training ground for not only every generation of admirals and navy top brass but also for numerous captains of industry and members of Congress. The remains of the father of the American navy, John Paul Jones, are entombed beneath the academy chapel. The patron saint of the modern, nuclear navy, Admiral Hyman Rickover, was a member of the class of '22. One midshipman from a small farm town,

Jimmy Carter, became the 39th President of the United States.

Only one in 11 applicants was accepted to Joe's Class of '87 at Annapolis. (By comparison, Harvard, with one thousand few applicants that year, admitted more than one in six.) However, Joe quickly distinguished himself, finishing first in his squad in both terms of Plebe Summer. Though he never had shot a gun before, Joe was one of only two plebes in his company to earn an "expert" rating in marksmanship.

Socially, Joe was only slightly less adept: He managed well enough in the hurly burly of the academy. Although he knew how to laugh at a faggot joke or listen to his peers' tales of sexual conquest, he was unlikely to initiate such talk himself. Joe had no girlfriends. He had dated little in high school and was without a date even for the senior prom. To the formal dances occasionally held at the academy, he was most likely to bring the sister of a friend. Yet, within the intensely masculine bastion of the academy, where curfews and regulations all but foreclosed an active sex life, such details were easily overlooked.

By his second year Joe already had earned his qualification pin in submarines, a result of 10 weeks of summer work and study aboard a nuclear sub. An exceptional tenor, he was a member of the academy's famed glee club and was twice chosen to sing the national anthem at the Army Navy football game in Philadelphia. He soloed at annual Christmas concerts in Washington for the president and other distinguished guests.

"In many ways it was like a dream come true," Joe, now 25, says of his midshipman career. "By the time I was a senior I had achieve everything I had wanted to do. I was feeling on top of the world." In his final semester, the navy accepted Joe into its exclusive nuclear power program and elevated him to the rank of battalion commander. Only 22 years old, he had a staff of five first class midshipmen reporting to him and direct command over one sixth of the academy's 4,500 midshipmen—the sixth battalion. He had risen to the top of the navy's most select institution and had earned its highest accolade: leadership. It took less than a week to lose it all.

After spending more than 100,000 American tax dollars to educate, train, and equip Joe Steffan, in the winter of 1987 the navy set its investigators to work to rid the service of him.

Among other duties, the Naval Investigative Service conducts search and destroy missions on homosexual personnel. It has 1200 agents, the vast majority of them civilians, ready to check out rumors, track down anonymous tips, and interrogate friends and colleagues of alleged or suspected gays. The navy won't say who or what tipped them off about Joe. And Joe doesn't know himself. "All it takes is an anonymous letter and they'll start an investigation," Joe says. "It's really pretty much of a witch hunt."

A few months before departing the academy Joe separately had told two friends that he was gay. It is possible this disclosure was a subconscious fling at self destruction, that after playing superman for all those years, Joe secretly wanted to be found out. But it seems more likely that Joe simply tired of his role as a one dimensional man. Having portrayed for so long a rigid, ideal specimen of manhood, perhaps he wanted his friends to understand the reason behind it. Because for Joe Steffan, being superman and being gay are inextricably linked.

"The people who I have known in the military who are gay tend to be very talented and dedicated people," Joe maintains. "I don't know if it's because of a reaction to a feeling of lower self worth in their youth—which is probably what I would consider my motivation."

Joe has a way of looking you squarely in the eye at times like this, when he is most exposed. Though his soft tone remains constant, his eyes focus sharply to alert his listener to the weight of the words. At this juncture in his life, he is willing to barter raw honesty for respect.

The NIS agents never confronted Joe directly with their suspicions. But they did interview both of the friends in whom he had confided. One broke the academy's sacred honor code, lying to protect Joe's trust. The other apparently spilled the beans. Joe was not at all relieved to have his secret off his chest. "I was in shock," he says, recalling his last conversation with his former friend. "You don't even react when you hear something like that. It's like finding out that both of your parents got killed."

Overcoming a swell of anxiety, Joe responded decisively. The day after learning of his betrayal, he approached the academy's chief of chaplains Captain Byron Holderby. Seeking to salvage something of his career, he informed Holderby of the NIS investigation, admitted he was gay, and told Holderby he wished at least to graduate. The chaplain was flabbergasted. "If anybody had been asked to guess who something like this might happen to," Holderby says now, "I don't think anyone would have guessed it would be Joe." He offered to intervene with the academy's commandant in Joe's behalf.

Commandant Howard Habermeyer, Jr., was a member of the academy's class of '64. He had been a respected submarine commander in the Pacific and was stationed at the academy by way of feathering his cap, pending assignment to a more powerful post in Washington. He was noted by his charges for his insistence on going strictly by the book. In Joe's case, the book said a homosexual absolutely could not, would not, graduate from Annapolis.

As a gay brigade commander at the naval academy, Joe's position was not unlike that of a spy who rises to the top of the intelligence bureaucracy: his success stung far more than his mere presence. Had Joe been just a face in the crowd of 4500 midshipmen, his superiors would have found his homosexuality unfortunate. Since he was Joe Steffan, however, who had surpassed his peers at virtually every test and whom they themselves had nurtured and promoted to the highest level of trust and authority, his being gay served as an implacable indictment of...well, something. What made it all the more infuriating was that they couldn't begin to figure out what that something was. According to Defense Department regulations Joe should have been either a brilliantly successful midshipman *or* a homosexual. The fact that he was both left the military mindset with an impenetrable conundrum.

By now, however, Joe could see clearly how it would be resolved. In fact, his downfall was remarkably swift. On March 23, 1987, one day after his meeting with Chaplain Holderby, he marched from his first floor dorm room in the eighth wing of splendid Bancroft Hall through the sixth wing and around to the academy's administrative offices. Striding through the long, narrow hallways, he moved his athletic frame in smooth, measured clips. As always, he carried himself with a natural military bearing.

The commandant had summoned Joe to his office in order to address a memorandum Joe had written to the academy's superintendent. The memo had been routed up the command hierarchy, stopping one step short of the superintendent, at Habermeyer's office.

Seated behind an ample desk, his wiry frame centered between the flags of the United States and of the academy, Habermeyer cautiously greeted Joe. The commandant looked impassively at the younger man, a pair of wire rimmed spectacles magnifying his sober, tired eyes. Only the day before Joe had appeared well on his way to commanding a nuclear sub, following in the commandant's footsteps.

Habermeyer, who had learned of Joe's plight from the chaplain, asked why the midshipman wished to see the superintendent. "It concerns a matter about you are already aware," Joe replied with formal precision. The commandant explained that he thought it improper for the superintendent to see Joe prior to disciplinary hearings. He then flatly denied Joe's request.

A hard silence followed, seeming to confirm that there was nothing left to discuss. But Habermeyer's curiosity forced his hand.

"Well," he said, finally, "are you gay?"

Joe looked directly into Habermeyer's oncoming gaze.

"Yes," he responded.

"Well, what do you want to do about it?"

Under the circumstances, two things needed to be done immediately: "I organized a staff meeting and I called my mother," Joe says.

"What's sort of hilarious about this is that I was extremely organized in planning every single phase of my own dismissal," he recalls. "I said, 'Well, here I am. I've been trained to be organized. I've been trained to be efficient. I'm getting kicked out of the academy. What are the steps that need to be taken in order to make it as efficient as possible?'"

Along with the brigade commander and another battalion commander, Joe's sixth battalion staff assembled in the staff room in Joe's dorm at 11:30 that night. Joe stood with uncanny composure before half dozen midshipmen seated around the conference table. Earlier in the day, soon after his interview with Habermeyer, Joe had hurriedly moved his belongings out of the dorm. Now, his staff waited before him in suspense to find out why.

"First of al, I'm being kicked out of the academy," he told them. "Secondly, it's because I'm gay. And that's true. And it's important to know that no other people are involved. It was based solely on my own admission."

Stunned, the men remained seated. One midshipman at the table began quietly to cry. "You've really got balls," said another.

For nearly two years after his discharge, while Joe completed his economics degree as a transfer student at North Dakota State University in Fargo, Mr. and Mrs. Steffan told anyone who asked about their son that he had left the academy because he'd grown tired of military life. "We lied through our teeth," says Maggie, who manages to chuckle about it now. Though they did their best to be supportive of Joe, they were deeply ashamed.

"People would ask, 'Where's Joe? Where is he stationed now?' " explains Chuck, a staunchly conservative Republican who is still somewhat shell shocked from the whole ordeal.

"And you'd say, 'He quit the naval academy.' "

" 'Oh, why?' "

"And then you'd make it up as you went along."

But in December 1988, when Joe filed his lawsuit against the navy challenging his dismissal and seeking readmission, the story was in the papers and on the television news. Every adult in Warren learned that the Steffan's son had left the academy in disgrace—a homosexual.

We are on the Amtrack train bound for Annapolis, returning, in a sense, to the scene of the crime. I keep looking for a sign of what this trip might mean to Joe but none is forthcoming. His palms are dry. His expression is nontroubled. His demeanor is more nonchalant than anxious. He appears happy to be getting a break from his job at a small design firm in New York, enjoying a day trip to Annapolis.

Joe is dressed casually in a white oxford, button down shirt and khaki slacks, both of which are pressed free of wrinkles. On another man, such attire might inspire an easy weekend repose but, more than two years after leaving the academy, Joe hasn't shed the ascetic look of a navy officer. His hair is short; movements steady and precise; posture unrelentingly upright.

Leaning squarely on the armrest of his Metroliner seat, Joe answers questions about his personal life with an almost numbing directness. As he speaks, his handsome face has a simple clarity of expression that reinforces the sincerity of his calm, even toned voice. Although his words ring true, Joe's emotions are muted. He speaks of youthful libido as if it were a section of the legal code. He recounts his sexual awakening as if rendering a deposition. But then, Joe's sexuality has been on trial for some time now.

"I was tormented up until my sophomore year when I really decided that I was gay and there was nothing I was going to be able to do about it," he says flatly. "I had been involved a couple of times, but it wasn't an ongoing thing. I didn't have a lover or anything."

Homosexuality is forbidden in all the armed services, and is automatic grounds for expulsion from the academy. After he became convinced in his second year that his homosexuality was not a passing aberration, he says, he refrained from sex altogether. "At that time, in order to reconcile my feelings, I decided that the navy's (anti gay) policy was wrong and that it was contrary to human compassion and that it was also, from an economic viewpoint, not efficient," he explains.

Defense department regulations state that homosexuality is "incompatible" with military service. This applied not only to homosexual behavior, but also, as in Joe's case, to homosexual *being*. Joe could refrain from having sex if he wanted, but as long as he remained Joe Steffan, gay, he would be in flagrant violation of policy.

The defense department argues that opening the military to gay men and lesbians would increase security risks, heighten tension, and cause morale to plummet. Harry Truman rejected a similar argument based on race, nearly a half century ago when he ended segregation in the armed forces. ("The policy of the War Department is not to intermingle colored and white enlisted personnel in the same regimental organizations," said a 1940 War Department statement. "This policy has been proven satisfactory over a long period of years and to make changes would produce situations destructive to morale and detrimental to the preparations for national defense.") The Pentagon, in another instance, ultimately ignored predictions of sexual calumny in the ranks should women be permitted to serve in sexually integrated units.

But unlike the segregation of blacks and the exclusion of women, the prohibition of gays remains within the discretion of defense department policymakers. There is another difference, as well. Women and blacks could be excluded on sight from the corps of the military. Gay men and lesbians cannot be. They're already there.

"I would say that at least eight percent of the academy is gay," Joe says. "I think it's important to quantify it. The fact is there really are about 400 gay midshipman there and they are completely and utterly isolated—even within themselves in most cases—and it can be a very destructive thing to someone mentally, really strip them of their self esteem.

"I knew several gay people at the academy," he continues. "That knowledge was extremely unusual and it was on a very rare occasion that you would get someone to disclose it, because it's important stuff. A lot of times you'd be in a discussion with someone—these were people who you knew well—that by talking to them and just sort of reading how they were thinking, you knew that they were gay and they knew that you were gay. A lot of times the conservation would just evolve where the assumption would be made and, before you knew it, you'd be talking about the fact the you're both gay."

Such disclosures were safeguarded by a variation on longstanding military doctrine: Mutual Assured Destruction. If a gay midshipman exposed a fellow midshipman as gay, he could expect to be turned in, as well. Thus, the threat of mutual disclosure provided mutual deterrence.

Since seeking reinstatement in a lawsuit filed against the navy last year, Joe has received letters from dozens of gay officers and words of encouragement from countless current and former military personnel who are gay. As a grand marshal of the Minneapolis gay pride parade last summer, Joe was surrounded by gay men who wished to share their experiences with him. "There are a lot of gay officers out there that are pulling for you," one burly navy lieutenant told Joe. A former air force MP wrapped his arms around Joe in a supportive embrace. "The navy is terribly embarrassed to have to content with someone of this caliber," this veteran said later. "They can't say anything bad about him."

Of course, the navy doesn't have to. That's the beauty of this regulations; they may be justified by the most elementary tautology. "Our policy is based on many years of experience and, well, on defense policy," former Pentagon spokesman Major David Super courteously explains. "That's the way it is."

"Well, look who it is," says U.S. Navy Commander Stephen Myslinski, a longtime English teacher at the naval academy. Joe Steffan returns the commander's genuine smile and shares a round of "What have you been up to lately?"

This is not the first time Joe has been back to the Annapolis campus since his resignation, which may explain some of the ease with which he conducts his private tour. In fact, he has returned a half dozen times, most often to see the academy musicals produced in Mahan Hall. Despite all, Joe remains intensely proud of his association with the academy. It seems disgrace hasn't gone to his head.

As they stand chatting in one of the campus's antiseptically aromatic hallways, the contrast between Joe and his former teacher is striking. Nearing retirement, Myslinski displays the lumpen effects of age and weight through the bright white of his summer uniform. Joe is young, trim, strong. Married with children, Myslinski's slightly effeminate speech and soft mannerisms seem peculiarly noticeable in Joe 's presence. The two of them make for an odd juxtaposition of stereotypes; the heterosexual navy commander speaks with the homosexual's lisp, the homosexual with the commander's cocksureness.

Joe resigned from the naval academy on April 1, 1987, only weeks before the course work for his degree would have been completed and two months before he was scheduled to receive his commission as a naval officer. In the wake of his admission of homosexuality, two academy review boards unanimously concluded that Joe had "insufficient aptitude" for naval service.

The board meetings, which took place in the last week of March 1987, were cordial and perfunctory—although Performance Officer Major R.J. Funk did inform Joe only moments before his Academic Board hearings that his uniform stripes would have to be removed. The stripes were a prickly reminder of an esteem no longer afforded him.

"I told the Academic Board that I was much happier to be kicked out of the academy for having told the truth than for having lied about it," Joe recalls. "Because I retained my personal honor and I still have it. And, in many ways, I think the honor of those people involved in my discharge was diminished."

Although Joe previously had contacted the ACLU, which had agreed to represent him if he chose to challenge his dismissal, his initially decided against a lawsuit. He did not wish to turn his parents' private shame into public disgrace. And he wished to get on with his education and his life.

"But I would have dreams at night about words," Joe remembers. "I wouldn't be able to get to sleep because I would be thinking about all the things I could have said and other things I might have done to make my point better, to try to appeal in a better way, or more emotionally, whatever. It didn't go away. It just kept getting worse and worse. I finally realized after about six months that I was not going to be satisfied until I filed a lawsuit to try and get my degree and try to get back into the navy."

Joe Steffan's case is a point of extreme sensitivity to the navy, which is under increasing pressure to justify its exclusion policy. A recent study commissioned by the defense department found no rational basis for excluding homosexuals. Despite the Pentagon's attempts to keep the report secret, it was made public in October by members of Congress who had demanded its release. "The [research] material indicates a number of bases on which to question the exclusion policy," says Theodore Sarbin, a professor emeritus of psychology at the University of California who coauthored the study. "To my knowledge, there is only professional opinion—just as there was professional opinion that black and white soldiers couldn't serve together."

The Pentagon has denounced Sarbin's study for exceeding its mandate, offering more information than its sponsors wished to know. Homosexuality is not a topic the military wishes to discuss in public. One Pentagon spokesman declined even to acknowledge the existence of a previous study done on homosexuality in the navy. That study, conducted by a navy panel in 1957, reached many conclusions similar to Sarbin's. Known as the Crittenden report, it was made available in a 1977 court case but was never officially released.

Perhaps in no instance have the navy's dark fantasies of homosexuality been more spellbinding—or more grave—than in the case of the USS *Iowa* investigation. The navy alleged that the April 1989 explosion aboard the battleship *Iowa* resulted from sabotage by an allegedly disgruntled homosexual seaman. Despite having publicly terminated its investigation, the navy has yet to offer a single shred of conclusive evidence that the seaman was responsible—or even that he was gay. The dead sailor has been slandered without proof and without compunction.

The navy annually discharges upward of 700 service members for homosexuality, keeping a battery of NIS agent occupied. The army discharges far more. As society moves increasingly toward recognition of gay rights, the military's intransigence becomes more problematic. Gay congressmen Gerry Studds and Barney Frank—and a few of their colleagues still in the closet—have the power to declare war. They are not, however, permitted to fight one.

As for defining who is gay, that, too, as the *Iowa* investigation illustrates, is a discretionary call. For instance, had Joe been caught by the academy in flagrante delicto with a male janitor in the shower (as one subsequent rumor had it), it is possible—even likely—that the episode would have been attributed to youthful experimentation and labeled a harmless aberration. Joe's scrupulous adherence to the honor code by his frank admission that he was gay, however, appears to have been a more profound affront to navy values.

Marc Wolinsky, a New York lawyer who is Joe's primary legal counsel, says Joe's case is as much matter of free speech as gay rights. "You can't censor the way people think," Wolinsky says. By punishing Joe for "being" homosexual, as opposed to engaging in actual homosexual conduct, says Wolinsky, the navy has assumed the role of "thought police."

Last July, Washington D.C. federal district court judge Oliver Gasch originally declined the navy's request to dismiss Joe's suit. But in November, Justice Department lawyers taking a pretrial deposition asked Joe if he had ever had sex at the academy or since. After Wolinsky advised Joe not to answer, claiming the question was irrelevant, the judge ruled against Joe and accepted the navy's motion to dismiss the suit. Wolinsky has taken the issue to the court of appeals for the D.C. circuit and is confident of a ruling that will send the case back to district court without the requirement that Joe reveal his sexual history.

With rare exceptions the courts have upheld the military's discretion to categorically exclude homosexuals. Last week, the U.S. Supreme Court declined to hear two separate appeals challenging the military's ban on homosexuality. The high court's refusal to hear the cases of army sergeant Miriam Ben Shalom and former naval officer James Woodward does not foreclose a hearing in the Steffan case. No matter what happens at district court, the losing side will push the case to circuit court. If Steffan wins there, the Supreme Court could be forced to hear the case in order to rectify conflicting circuit court rulings.

Nevertheless, the odds of victory are long. "The law is largely on the other side," says Thomas Stoddard, executive director of the Lambda Legal Defense and Education Fund, a gay rights group that is conducting Joe's litigation. On the other hand, Stoddard reasons, Joe may be the one person whose story is compelling enough to buckle the resistance. "I would say the chances of ultimately prevailing on Joe's behalf at 40/60," says Stoddard, optimistically. "For any other claimant it would be about five to 95."

Many who knew him at the academy privately support Joe's cause. Others have begun to rethink once hardened opinions. "One day, because we found out that Joe was gay, we no longer think all these good things of him," muses a retired navy officer formerly assigned to the academy. "Because Joe is a cut above, he's willing to go through this. But should the rule be changed? I don't know what the answer to this is. I've agonized over this personally."

Joe moved to New York last June to enable him to work more readily on his case. He is planning to enter law school next fall. "If my case doesn't win," he says, "perhaps I'll litigate the one that does." There is a remarkable absence of bile in his feelings toward Annapolis. "I would say without a doubt that my experience at the naval academy has made me a more organized and capable person, and, as a result, I will be a better gay activist," Joe maintains.

Naturally, he would prefer to avert a long and nasty legal battle. "I think the best thing that could be done would be for the navy to realize and accept the fact that there are so many wonderful, successful, intelligent, competent, gay military officers—to simply accept them and let them get on with their lives—because everyone is going to be better off," Joe reasons.

But the navy will almost certainly not declare such a surrender. It is its own Mississippi, holding steadfast, vowing before God and man that integration is blasphemy. It will take years to undo.

There are not many gays in Warren. Most townspeople figure zero probably represents an accurate census of the gay population. The parents of Warren's only confirmed homosexual are thus endowed with a status unique in the community. "Their friends are very supportive of them," says one resident. "People have sympathy for the family."

The only pharmacist for miles around, Chuck Steffan is a professional in a town where there are few. He spent 10 years on the city council and has been active on a couple of other civic boards. Class gradations, even modest ones, are duly noted in a town like Warren. The Steffans have been considered by some to be, well, "standoffish," in the words of one. "The feeling was that the family thought they were better than anyone else," says this local resident. "The mighty have fallen."

Though publicity and gossip ensured that everyone at the Grand Central coffee shop was well versed in Joe's story, never a word was passed about it between Chuck and his friends. "I have coffee with him every morning," says Neil Mattson, editor of *The Warren Sheaf*, the town's weekly paper. "Never been a word about it."

The silence, however, does not indicate a vacuum of opinion. "He wanted to be a submarine commander," Mattson says of Joe. "Can you imagine a guy like that being in charge of a crew of men in that kind of space?" Mattson's head is shaking, his smile is taut with derision. "The best thing is our son beat him out for valedictorian."

One rock steady soul in Warren, however, seems to have reckoned with his conservative faith and come gingerly around to Joe's cause. "I think the naval academy has an obligation to show why homosexuals should not be in there," argues Chuck Steffan, momentarily digressing from his Republican party gospel. "A kid like Joe, he has a certain amount of ability and talent and he has certainly proved his honesty," Chuck points out. "I would think they would be looking for people like that."

Jane Addams

The Subtle Problems of Charity

Jane Addams biographical information can be found in the introduction to the excerpt from *Twenty Years at Hull House* contained in a later part of this volume ("Civic Cooperation," Part III, Neighborhood and Nation). In that excerpted article, Addams gives a largely anecdotal account of the cooperative efforts of those involved in a neighborhood settlement house in Chicago at the turn of the century. In the essay that follows, which first appeared in 1899, she raises questions about the role and perspective of the "charity visitor" within a democratic society rife with inequalities based on social class and one's position in the industrial economy. As you read her critical account here, think about how what she says might be relevant to us nearly a century later.

The Subtle Problems of Charity

Jane Addams

Probably there is no relation in life which our democracy is changing more rapidly than the charitable relation,—that relation which obtains between benefactor and beneficiary; at the same time, there is no point of contact in our modern experience which reveals more clearly the lack of that equality which democracy implies. We have reached the moment when democracy has made such inroads upon this relationship that the complacency of the old-fashioned charitable man is gone forever; while the very need and existence of charity deny us the consolation and freedom which democracy will at last give.

We find in ourselves the longing for a wider union than that of family or class, and we say that we have come to include all men in our hopes; but we fail to realize that all men are hoping, and are part of the same movement of which we are a part. Many of the difficulties in philanthropy come from an unconscious division of the world into the philanthropists and those to be helped. It is an assumption of two classes, and against this class assumption our democratic training revolts as soon as we begin to act upon it.

The trouble is that the ethics of none of us are clearly defined, and we are continually obliged to act in circles of habit based upon convictions which we no longer hold. Thus, our estimate of the effect of environment and social conditions has doubtless shifted faster than our methods of administering charity have changed. Formerly when it was believed that poverty was synonymous with vice and laziness, and that the prosperous man was the righteous man, charity was administered harshly with a good conscience; for the charitable agent really blamed the individual for his poverty, and the very fact of his own superior prosperity gave him a certain consciousness of superior morality. Since then we have learned to measure by other standards,

Jane Addams, The Subtle Problems of Charity, *Atlantic*.

and the money-earning capacity, while still rewarded out of all proportion to any other, is not respected as exclusively as it was; and its possession is by no means assumed to imply the possession of the highest moral qualities. We have learned to judge men in general by their social virtues as well as by their business capacity, by their devotion to intellectual and disinterested aims, and by their public spirit, and we naturally resent being obliged to judge certain individuals solely upon the industrial side for no other reason than that they are poor. Our democratic instinct constantly takes alarm at this consciousness of two standards.

Of the various struggles which a decade of residence in a settlement implies, none have made a more definite impression on my mind than the incredibly painful difficulties which involve both giver and recipient when one person asks charitable aid of another.

An attempt is made in this paper to show what are some of the perplexities which harass the mind of the charity worker; to trace them to ethical survivals which are held not only by the benefactor, but by the recipients of charity as well; and to suggest wherein these very perplexities may possibly be prophetic.

It is easy to see that one of the root difficulties in the charitable relationship lies in the fact that the only families who apply for aid to the charitable agencies are those who have come to grief on the industrial side; it may be through sickness, through loss of work, or for other guiltless and inevitable reasons, but the fact remains that they are industrially ailing, and must be bolstered and helped into industrial health. The charity visitor, let us assume, is a young college woman, well-bred and open-minded. When she visits the family assigned to her, she is embarrassed to find herself obliged to lay all the stress of her teaching and advice upon the industrial virtues, and to treat the members of the family almost exclusively as factors in the industrial system. She insists that they must work and be self-supporting; that the most dangerous of all situations is idleness; that seeking one's own pleasure, while ignoring claims and responsibilities, is the most ignoble of actions. The members of her assigned family may have charms and virtues,—they may possibly be kind and affectionate and considerate of one another, generous to their friends; but it is her business to stick to the industrial side. As she daily holds up these standards, it often occurs to the mind of the sensitive visitor, whose conscience has been made tender by much talk of brotherhood and equality which she has heard at college, that she has no right to say these things; that she herself has never been self-supporting; that, whatever her virtues may be, they are not the industrial virtues; that her untrained hands are no more fitted to cope with actual conditions than are those of her broken-down family.

The grandmother of the charity visitor could have done the industrial preaching very well, because she did have the industrial virtues; if not skillful in weaving and spinning, she was yet mistress of other housewifely accomplishments. In a generation our experiences have changed—our views with them; while we still keep on in the old methods, which could be applied when our consciences were in line with them, but which are daily becoming more difficult as we divide up into people who work with their hands and those who do not; and the charity visitor, belonging to the latter class, is perplexed by recognitions and suggestions which the situation forces upon her. Our democracy has taught us to apply our moral teaching all around, and the moralist is rapidly becoming so sensitive that when his life does not exemplify his ethical convictions, he finds it difficult to preach.

Added to this is a consciousness in the mind of the visitor of a genuine misunderstanding of her motives by the recipients of her charity and by their neighbors. Let us take a neighborhood of poor people, and test their ethical standards by those of the charity visitor, who comes with the best desire in the world to help them out of their distresses. A most striking incongruity, at once apparent, is the difference between the emotional kindness with which relief is given by one poor neighbor to another poor neighbor, and the guarded care with which relief is given by a charity visitor to a charity recipient. The neighborhood mind is immediately confronted not only by the difference of method, but also by an absolute clashing of two ethical standards.

A very little familiarity with the poor districts of any city is sufficient to show how primitive and frontier-like are the neighborly relations. There is the greatest willingness to lend or borrow anything, and each resident of a given tenement house knows the most intimate family affairs of all the others. The fact that the economic condition of all alike is on a most precarious level makes the ready outflow of sympathy and material assistance the most natural thing in the world. There are numberless instances of heroic self-sacrifice quite unknown in the circles where greater economic advantages make that kind of intimate knowledge of one's neighbors impossible. An Irish family, in which the man has lost his place, and the woman is struggling to eke out the scanty savings by day work, will take in a widow and her five children who have been turned into the street, without a moment's reflection upon the physical discomforts involved. The most maligned landlady is usually ready to lend a scuttleful of coal to a suffering tenant, or to share her supper. A woman for whom the writer had long tried in vain to find work failed to appear at the appointed time when a situation was found at last. Upon investigation it transpired that a neighbor further down the street was taken ill; that the children ran for the family friend, who went, of course; saying simply, when reasons for her failure to come to work were demanded, "It broke me heart to leave the place, but what could I do?"

Another woman, whose husband was sent up to the city prison for the maximum term, just three months before the birth of her child, having gradually sold her supply of household furniture, found herself penniless. She sought refuge with a friend whom she supposed to be living in three rooms in another part of the town. When she arrived, however, she discovered that her friend's husband had been out of work so long that they had been reduced to living in one room. The friend at once took her in, and the friend's husband was obliged to sleep upon a bench in the park every night for a week; which he did uncomplainingly, if not cheerfully. Fortunately it was summer, "and it only rained one night." The writer could not discover from the young mother that she had any special claim upon the "friend" beyond the fact that they had formerly worked together in the same factory. The husband she had never seen until the night of her arrival, when he at once went forth in search of a midwife who would consent to come upon his promise of future payment.

The evolutionists tell us that the instinct to pity, the impulse to aid his fellows, served man at a very early period as a rude rule of right and wrong. There is no doubt that this rude rule still holds among many people with whom charitable agencies are brought into contact, and that their ideas of right and wrong are quite honestly outraged by the methods of these agencies. When they see the delay and caution with which relief is given, these do not appear to them conscientious scruples, but the cold and calculating action of the selfish man. This is not the aid that they are accustomed to receive from their neighbors, and they do not understand why the impulse which drives people to be good to the poor should be so severely supervised. They feel, remotely, that the charity visitor is moved by motives that are alien and unreal; they may be superior motives, but they are "ag'in nature." They cannot comprehend why a person whose intellectual perceptions are stronger than his natural impulses should go into charity work at all. The only man they are accustomed so see whose intellectual perceptions are stronger than his tenderness of heart is the selfish and avaricious man, who is frankly "on the make." If the charity visitor is such a person, why does she pretend to like the poor?

Why does she not go into business at once? We may say, of course, that it is a primitive view of life which thus confuses intellectuality and business ability, but it is a view quite honestly held by many poor people who are obliged to receive charity from time to time. In moments of indignation they have been known to say, "What do you want, anyway? If you have nothing to give us, why not let us alone, and stop your questionings and investigations?" This indignation, which is for the most part taciturn, and a certain kindly contempt for her abilities often puzzle the charity visitor. The latter may be explained by the standard of world success which the visited families hold. In the minds of the poor success does not ordinarily go with charity and kind-heartedness, but rather with the opposite qualities. The rich landlord is he who collects with sternness; who accepts no excuse, and will have his own. There are moments of irritation and of real bitterness against him, but there is admiration, because he is rich and successful. The good-natured landlord, he who pities and spares his poverty-pressed tenants, is seldom rich. He often lives in the back of his house, which he has owned for a long time, perhaps has inherited; but he has been able to accumulate little. He commands the genuine love and devotion of many a poor soul, but he is treated with a certain lack of respect. In one sense he is a failure, so long have we all been accustomed to estimate success by material returns. The charity visitor, just because she is a person who concerns herself with the poor, receives a touch of this good-natured and kindly contempt, sometimes real affection, but little genuine respect. The poor are accustomed to help one another, and to respond according to their kindliness; but when it comes to worldly judgment, they are still in that stage where they use industrial success as the sole standard. In the case of the charity visitor, they are deprived of both standards: she has neither natural kindness nor dazzling riches; and they find it of course utterly impossible to judge of the motive of organized charity.

Doubtless we all find something distasteful in the juxtaposition of the two words "organized" and "charity." The idea of organizing an emotion is in itself repelling, even to those of us who feel most sorely the need of more order in altruistic effort and see the end to be desired. We say in defense that we are striving to turn this emotion into a motive: that pity is capricious, and not to be depended on; that we mean to give it the dignity of conscious duty. But at bottom we distrust a little a scheme which substitutes a theory of social conduct for the natural promptings of the heart, and we ourselves feel the complexity of the situation. The poor man who has fallen into distress, when he first asks aid, instinctively expects tenderness, consideration, and forgiveness. If it is the first time, it has taken him long to make up his mind to the step. He comes somewhat bruised and battered, and instead of being met by warmth of heart and sympathy he is at once chilled by an investigation and an intimation that he ought to work. He does not see that he is being dealt with as a child of defective will is cared for by a stern parent. There have been no years of previous intercourse and established relation, as between parents and children. He feels only the postponement or refusal, which he considers harsh. He does not "live to thank his parents for it," as the disciplined child is reported to do, but cherishes a hardness of heart to his grave. The only really popular charity is that of visiting nurses, who carry about with them a professional training, which may easily be interpreted into sympathy and kindness, in their ministration to obvious needs without investigation.

The state of mind which an investigation arouses on both sides is most unfortunate: but the perplexity and clashing of different standards, with the consequent misunderstandings, are not so bad as the moral deterioration which is almost sure to follow....

If a poor woman knows that her neighbor next door has no shoes, she is quite willing to lend her own, that her neighbor may go decently to mass or to work; for she knows the smallest item about the scanty wardrobe, and cheerfully helps out. When the charity visitor comes in, all the neighbors are baffled as to what her circumstances may be. They know she does not need a new pair of shoes, and rather suspect that she has a dozen pairs at home; which indeed she sometimes has. They imagine untold stores which they may call upon, and her most generous gift is considered niggardly, compared with what she might do. She ought to get new shoes for the family all round; "she sees well enough that they need them." It is no more than the neighbor herself would do. The charity visitor has broken through the natural rule of giving, which, in a primitive society, is bounded only by the need of the recipient and the resources of the giver; and she gets herself into untold trouble when she is judged by the ethics of the primitive society.

The neighborhood understands the selfish rich people who stay in their own part of the town, where all their associates have shoes and other things. Such people do not bother themselves about the poor; they are like the rich landlords of the neighborhood experience. But this lady visitor, who pretends to be good to the poor, and certainly does talk as though she were kind-hearted, what does she come for, if she does not intend to give them things which so plainly are needed? The visitor says, sometimes, that in holding her poor family so hard to a standard of thrift she is really breaking down a rule of higher living which they formerly possessed; that saving, which seems quite commendable in a comfortable part of town, appears almost criminal in a poorer quarter, where the next-door neighbor needs food, even if the children of the family do not....

Because of this diversity in experience the visitor is continually surprised to find that the safest platitudes may be challenged. She refers quite naturally to the "horrors of the saloon," and discovers that the head of her visited family, who knows the saloons very well, does not connect them with "horrors" at all. He remembers all the kindnesses he has received there,

the free lunch and treating which go on, even when a man is out of work and not able to pay up; the poor fellows who are allowed to sit in their warmth when every other door is closed to them; the loan of five dollars he got there, when the charity visitor was miles away, and he was threatened with eviction. He may listen politely to her reference to horrors, but considers it only "temperance talk."

The same thing happens when she urges upon him a spirit of independence, and is perhaps foolish enough to say that "every American man can find work and is bound to support his family." She soon discovers that the workingman, in the city at least, is utterly dependent for the tenure of his position upon the good will of his foreman, upon the business prosperity of the firm, or the good health of the head of it; and that, once work is lost, it may take months to secure another place. There is no use in talking independence to a man when he is going to stand in a row, hat in hand before an office desk, in the hope of getting a position. The visitor is shocked when she finds herself recommending to the head of her visited family, whom she has sent to a business friend of hers to find work, not to be too outspoken when he goes to the place, and not to tell that he has had no experience in that line unless he is asked. She has in fact come around to the view which has long been his.

The charity visitor may blame the women for lack of gentleness toward their children, for being hasty and rude to them, until she learns to reflect that the standard of breeding is not that of gentleness toward the children so much as the observance of certain conventions, such as the punctilious wearing of mourning garments after the death of a child. The standard of gentleness each mother has to work out largely by herself, assisted only by the occasional shamefaced remark of a neighbor, that "they do better when you are not too hard on them;" but the wearing of mourning garments is sustained by the definitely expressed sentiment of every woman in the street. The mother would have to bear social blame, a certain social ostracism, if she failed to comply with that requirement. It is not comfortable to outrage the conventions of those among whom we live, and if our social life be a narrow one, it is still more difficult. The visitor may choke a little when she sees the lessened supply of food and the scanty clothing provided for the remaining children, in order that one may be conventionally mourned. But she does not talk so strongly against it as she would have done during her first month of experience with the family since bereaved.

The subject of clothes, indeed, perplexes the visitor constantly, and the result of her reflections may be summed up something in this wise: The girl who has a definite social standing, who has been to a fashionable school or to a college, whose family live in a house seen and known by all her friends and associates, can afford to be very simple or even shabby as to her clothes, if she likes. But the working girl, whose family lives in a tenement or moves from one small apartment to another, who has little social standing, and has to make her own place, knows full well how much habit and style of dress have to do with her position. Her income goes into her clothing out of all proportion to that which she spends upon other things. But if social advancement is her aim, it is the most sensible thing which she can do. She is judged largely by her clothes. Her house-furnishing with its pitiful little decorations, her scanty supply of books, are never seen by the people whose social opinions she most values. Her clothes are her background, and from them she is largely judged....

The charity visitor has been rightly brought up to consider it vulgar to spend much money upon clothes, to care so much for "appearances." She realizes dimly that the care for personal decoration over that for one's home or habitat is in some way primitive and undeveloped; but she is silenced by its obvious need. She also catches a hint of the fact that the disproportionate expenditure of the poor in the matter of clothes is largely due to the exclusiveness of the

rich, who hide from them the interior of their houses and their more subtle pleasures, while of necessity exhibiting their street clothes and their street manners. Every one who goes shopping at the same time with the richest woman in town may see her clothes, but only those invited to her receptions see the Corot on her walls or the bindings in her library. The poor naturally try to bridge the difference by reproducing the street clothes which they have seen; they therefore imitate, sometimes in more showy and often in more trying colors, in cheap and flimsy material, in poor shoes and flippant hats, the extreme fashion of the well-to-do. They are striving to conform to a common standard which their democratic training presupposes belongs to us all. The charity visitor may regret that the Italian peasant woman has laid aside her picturesque kerchief, and substituted a cheap street hat. But it is easy to recognize the first attempt toward democratic expression.

The charity visitor is still more perplexed when she comes to consider such problems as those of early marriage and child labor; for she cannot deal with them according to economic theories, or according to the conventions which have regulated her own life. She finds both of these fairly upset by her intimate knowledge of the situation, and her sympathy for those into whose lives she has gained a curious insight. She discovers how incorrigibly bourgeois her standards have been, and it takes but a little time to reach the conclusion that she cannot insist so strenuously upon the conventions of her own class, which fail to fit the bigger, more emotional, and freer lives of working people. The charity visitor holds well-grounded views upon the imprudence of early marriages; quite naturally, because she comes from a family and circle of professional and business people. A professional man is scarcely equipped and started in his profession before he is thirty; a business man, if he is on the road to success, is much nearer prosperity at thirty-five than at twenty-five, and it is therefore wise for these men not to marry in the twenties. But this does not apply to the workingman. In many trades he is laid upon the shelf at thirty-five, and in nearly all trades he receives the largest wages of his life between twenty and thirty. If the young workingman has all his wages too long to himself, he will probably establish habits of personal comfort which he cannot keep up when he has to divide with a family,—habits which, perhaps, he can never overcome.

The sense of prudence, the necessity for saving, can never come to a primitive, emotional man with the force of a conviction, but the necessity of providing for his children is a powerful incentive. He naturally regards his children as his savings-bank; he expects them to care for him when he gets old, and in some trades old age comes very early. A Jewish tailor was quite lately sent to the Cook County poorhouse, paralyzed beyond recovery at the age of thirty-five. Had his little boy of nine been a few years older, the father might have been spared this sorrow of public charity. He was, in fact, better able to support a family when he was twenty than when he was thirty-five, for his wages had steadily become less as the years went on. Another tailor whom I know, a Socialist, always speaks of saving as a bourgeois virtue, one quite impossible to the genuine workingman. He supports a family, consisting of himself, a wife and three children, and his parents, on eight dollars a week. He insists that it would be criminal not to expend every penny of this amount upon food and shelter, and he expects his children later to take care of him.

This economic pressure also accounts for the tendency to put children to work over-young, and thus cripple their chances for individual development and usefulness, and with the avaricious parent it often leads to exploitation. "I have fed her for fourteen year; now she can help me pay my portage," is not an unusual reply, when a hard-working father is expostulated with because he would take his bright daughter out of school and put her into a factory. It has long been a common error for the charity visitor, who is strongly urging her family toward self-support, to suggest, or at least connive, that the children be put to work early, although she has not the excuse that the parents have. It is so easy, after one has been taking the industrial view for a long time, to forget the larger and more social claim; to urge that the boy go to work and support his parents, who are receiving charitable aid. The visitor does not realize what a cruel advantage the person who distributes charity has, when she gives advice....

The struggle for existence, which is so much harsher among people near the edge of pauperism, sometimes leaves ugly marks on character, and the charity visitor finds the indirect results most mystifying. Parents who work hard and anticipate an old age when they can no longer earn, take care that their children shall expect to divide their wages with them from the very first. Such a parent, when successful, seizes the immature nervous system of the child and hypnotizes it, so to speak, into a habit of obedience, that the nerves and will may not depart from this control when the child is older. The charity visitor, whose family relation is lifted quite out of this, does not in the least understand the industrial foundation in this family despotism.

The head of a kindergarten training class once addressed a club of working-women, and spoke of the despotism which is often established over little children. She said that the so-called determination to break a child's will many times arose from a lust of dominion, and she urged the ideal relationship founded upon love and confidence. But many of the women were puzzled. One of them remarked to the writer, as she came out of the club-room, "If you did not keep control over them from the time they were little, you would never get their wages when they were grown up." Another one said, "Ah, of course, she [meaning the speaker] doesn't have to depend upon her children's wages. She can afford to be lax with them, because, even if they don't give money to her, she can get along without it...."

The first impulse of our charity visitor is to be somewhat severe with her shiftless family for spending money on pleasures and indulging their children out of all proportion to their means. The poor family which receives beans and coal from the county, and pays for a bicycle on the installment plan, is not unknown to any of us. But as the growth of juvenile crime becomes gradually understood, and as the danger of giving no legitimate and organized pleasure to the child becomes clearer, we remember that primitive man had games long before he cared for a house or for regular meals. There are certain boys in many city neighborhoods who form themselves into little gangs with leaders somewhat more intrepid that the rest. Their favorite performance is to break into an untenanted house, to knock off the faucets and cut the lead pipe, which they sell to the nearest junk dealer. With the money thus procured they buy beer, which they drink in little freebooters' groups sitting in an alley. From beginning to end they have the excitement of knowing that they may be seen and caught by the "copper," and at times they are quite breathless with suspense. In motive and execution it is not the least unlike the practice of country boys who go forth in squads to set traps for rabbits or to round up a coon. It is characterized by a pure spirit of adventure, and the vicious training really begins when they are arrested, or when an older boy undertakes to guide them into further excitements. From the very beginning the most enticing and exciting experiences which they have seen have been connected with crime. The policeman embodies all the majesty of successful law and established government in his brass buttons and dazzlingly equipped patrol wagon. The boy who has been arrested comes back more or less a hero, with a tale to tell of the interior recesses of the mysterious police station. The earliest public excitement the child remembers is divided between the rattling fire-engines, "the time there was a fire in the next block," and the patrol wagon "the time the drunkest lady in our street was arrested." In the first year of their settlement the Hull-House residents took fifty kindergarten children to Lincoln Park, only to

be grieved by their apathetic interest in trees and flowers. On the return an omnibusful of tired and sleepy children were galvanized into sudden life because a patrol wagon rattled by. Eager little heads popped out of the windows full of questions. "Was it a man or a woman?" "How many policemen inside?" and eager little tongues began to tell experiences of arrests which baby eyes had witnessed.

The excitement of a chase, the chances of competition, and the love of a fight are all centered in the outward display of crime. The parent who receives charitable aid, and yet provides pleasures for his child and is willing to indulge him in his play, is blindly doing one of the wisest things possible; and no one is more eager for playgrounds and vacation schools than the charity visitor whose experience has brought her to this point of view....

Just when our affection becomes large and real enough to care for the unworthy among the poor as we would care for the unworthy among our own kin, is a perplexing question. To say that it should never be so is a comment upon our democratic relations to them which few of us would be willing to make.

Of what use is all this striving and perplexity? Has the experience any value? It is obviously genuine, for it induces an occasional charity visitor to live in a tenement house as simply as the other tenants do. It drives others to give up visiting the poor altogether, because, they claim, the situation is untenable unless the individual becomes a member of a sisterhood which requires, as some of the Roman Catholic sisterhoods do, that the member first take the vows of obedience and poverty, so that she can have nothing to give save as it is first given to her, and she is not thus harassed by a constant attempt at adjustment. Both the tenement house resident and the sister assume to have put themselves upon the industrial level of their neighbors. But the young charity visitor who goes from a family living upon a most precarious industrial level to her own home in a prosperous part of the city, if she is sensitive at all, is never free from perplexities which our growing democracy forces upon her.

We sometimes say that our charity is too scientific, but we should doubtless be much more correct in our estimate if we said that it is not scientific enough. We dislike the entire arrangement of cards alphabetically classified according to streets and names of families, with the unrelated and meaningless details attached to them. Our feeling of revolt is, probably, not unlike that which afflicted the students of botany and geology in the early part of this century, when flowers were tabulated in alphabetical order, when geology was taught by colored charts and thin books. No doubt the students, wearied to death, many times said that it was all too scientific, and were much perplexed and worried when they found traces of structure and physiology which their so-called scientific principles were totally unable to account for. But all this happened before science had become evolutionary and scientific at all,—before it had a principle of life from within. The very indications and discoveries which formerly perplexed, later illumined, and made the study absorbing and vital. The dry-as-dust student, who formerly excelled, is now replaced by the man who possesses insight as well as accuracy,—who holds his mind open to receive every suggestion which growth implies. He can, however, no longer use as material the dried plants of the herbariums, but is forced to go to the spots in which plants are growing. Collecting data in sociology may mean sorrow and perplexity and a pull upon one's sympathies, just as truly as collecting data in regard to the flora of the equatorial regions means heat and scratches and the test of one's endurance. Human motives have been so long a matter of dogmatism that to act upon the assumption that they are the result of growth, and to study their status with an open mind and a scientific conscience, seems wellnigh impossible to us. A man who would hesitate to pronounce an opinion upon the stones lying by the wayside because he has a suspicion that they are "geological specimens," and his

veneration for science is such that he would not venture to state to which period they belonged, will, without a moment's hesitation, dogmatize about the delicate problems of human conduct, and will assert that one man is a scoundrel and another an honorable gentleman, without in the least considering the ethical epochs to which the two belong. He disregards the temptations and environment to which they have been subjected, and requires the same human development of an Italian peasant and a New England scholar.

Is this again a mark of our democracy or of our lack of science? We are singularly slow to apply the evolutionary principle to human affairs in general, although it is fast being applied to the education of children. We are at last learning to follow the development of the child; to expect certain traits under certain conditions; to adapt methods and matter to his growing mind. No "advanced educator" can allow himself to be so absorbed in the question of what a child ought to be as to exclude the discovery of what he is. But, in our charitable efforts, we think much more of what a man ought to be than of what he is or of what he may become; and we ruthlessly force our conventions and standards upon him, with a sternness which we would consider stupid, indeed, did an educator use it in forcing his mature intellectual convictions upon an undeveloped mind.

Let us take the example of a timid child, who cries when he is put to bed, because he is afraid of the dark. The "soft-hearted" parent stays with him simply because he is sorry for him and wants to comfort him. The scientifically trained parent stays with him because he realized that the child is passing through a phase of race development, in which his imagination has the best of him. It is impossible to reason him out of demonology, because his logical faculties are not developed. After all, these two parents, wide apart in point of view, act much the same, and very differently from the pseudo-scientific parent, who acts from dogmatic conviction and is sure he is right. He talks of developing his child's self-respect and good sense, and leaves him to cry himself to sleep, demanding powers of self-control and development which the child does not possess. There is no doubt that our development of charity methods has reached this pseudo-scientific and stilted stage. We have learned to condemn unthinking, ill-regulated kind-heartedness, and we take great pride in mere repression, much as the stern parent tells the visitor below how admirably he is rearing the child who is hysterically crying upstairs, and laying the foundation for future nervous disorders. The pseudo-scientific spirit, or rather the undeveloped stage of our philanthropy, is, perhaps, most clearly revealed in this tendency to lay stress on negative action. "Don't give," "don't break down self-respect," we are constantly told. We distrust the human impulse, and in its stead substitute dogmatic rules for conduct. In spite of the proof that the philanthropic Lord Shaftesbury secured the passage of English factory laws, that the charitable Octavia Hill has brought about the reform of the London tenement houses, and of much similar concurrent testimony, we do not yet really believe that pity and sympathy, even, in point of fact quite as often precede the effort toward social amelioration as does the acceptance of a social dogma; we forget that the accumulation of knowledge and the holding of convictions must finally result in the application of that knowledge and those convictions to life itself, and that the course which begins by activity, and an appeal to the sympathies so severe that all the knowledge in the possession of the visitor is continually applied, has reasonably a greater chance for an ultimate comprehension.

For most of the years during a decade of residence in a settlement, my mind was sore and depressed over the difficulties of the charitable relationship. The incessant clashing of ethical standards, which had been honestly gained from widely varying industrial experience,—the misunderstandings inevitable between people whose conventions and mode of life had been so totally unlike,—made it seem reasonable to say that nothing could be done until industrial conditions were made absolutely democratic. The position of a settlement, which attempts at one and the same time to declare its belief in this eventual, industrial democracy, and to labor toward that end, to maintain a standard of living, and to deal humanely and simply with those in actual want, often seems utterly untenable and preposterous. Recently, however, there has come to my mind the suggestion of a principle, that while the painful condition of administering charity is the inevitable discomfort of a transition into a more democratic relation, the perplexing experiences of the actual administration have a genuine value of their own. The economist who treats the individual cases as mere data, and the social reformer who labors to make such cases impossible, solely because of the appeal to his reason, may have to share these perplexities before they feel themselves within the grasp of a principle of growth, working outward from within; before they can gain the exhilaration and uplift which come when the individual sympathy and intelligence are caught into the forward, intuitive movement of the mass. This general movement is not without its intellectual aspects, but it is seldom apprehended by the intellect alone. The social reformers who avoid the charitable relationship with any of the fellow men take a certain outside attitude toward this movement. They may analyze it and formulate it; they may be most valuable and necessary, but they are not essentially within it. The mass of men seldom move together without an emotional incentive, and the doctrinaire, in his effort to keep his mind free from the emotional quality, inevitably stands aside. He avoids the perplexity, and at the same time loses the vitality.

The Hebrew prophet made three requirements from those who would join the great forward-moving procession led by Jehovah. "To love mercy," and at the same time "to do justly," is the difficult task. To fulfill the first requirement alone is to fall into the error of indiscriminate giving, with all its disastrous results; to fulfill the second exclusively is to obtain the stern policy of withholding, and it results in such a dreary lack of sympathy and understanding that the establishment of justice is impossible. It may be that the combination of the two can never be attained save as we fulfill still the third requirement, "to walk humbly with God," which may mean to walk for many dreary miles beside the lowliest of his creatures, not even in peace of mind, that the companionship of the humble is popularly supposed to give, but rather with the pangs and misgivings to which the poor human understanding is subjected whenever it attempts to comprehend the meaning of life.

Ivan Illich

To Hell with Good Intentions

Ivan Illich (1926–1997) was born in Vienna in 1926. Expelled in 1941 because his mother was Jewish, he eventually studied theology and philosophy in Rome and obtained a Ph.D. in history at the University of Salzburg. He came to the United States in 1951, where he served as a priest in a largely Irish and Puerto Rican parish in New York City. From 1956 to 1960 he was assigned as vice-rector to the Catholic University of Puerto Rico, where he organized an intensive training center for American priests in Latin American culture. During the 1960s, Illich was co-founder of the Centre for Intercultural Documentation (CIDOC) in Cuernavaca, Mexico, where he trained missionaries for work in Latin America. In 1969, he left the priesthood, critical of the workings of the Roman Catholic Church, especially in Latin America. He is most well known for his critiques of professionalized education and medicine in *Deschooling Society* (1973) and *Medical Nemesis: The Expropriation of Health* (1982).

The address reprinted here was given by Illich to the Conference on Inter-American Student Projects (CIASP) in Cuernavaca in April, 1968. He goes directly to the heart of the dangers of paternalism and disempowerment of local communities inherent in any "service" work, but particularly when it involves travel—however distant or close by—to peoples in vastly different situations from the volunteer's own. While parts of Illich's speech are clearly dated and related to the work he was doing at CIDOC, the impact of his message should not be lost in the current era of community service work.

To Hell with Good Intentions

Ivan Illich

In the conversations which I have had today, I was impressed by two things, and I want to state them before I launch into my prepared talk.

I was impressed by your insight that the motivation of U.S. volunteers overseas springs mostly from very alienated feelings and concepts. I was equally impressed, by what I interpret as a step forward among would-be volunteers like you: openness to the idea that the only thing you can legitimately volunteer for in Latin America might be voluntary powerlessness, voluntary presence as receivers, as such, as hopefully beloved or adopted ones without any way of returning the gift.

I was equally impressed by the hypocrisy of most of you: by the hypocrisy of the atmosphere prevailing here. I say this as a brother speaking to brothers and sisters. I say it against many resistances within me; but it must be said. Your very insight, your very openness to evaluations of past programs make you hypocrites because you—or at least most of you—have decided to spend this next summer in Mexico, and therefore, you are unwilling to go far enough in your reappraisal of your program. You close your eyes because you want to go ahead and could not do so if you looked at some facts.

It is quite possible that this hypocrisy is unconscious in most of you. Intellectually, you are ready to see that the motivations which could legitimate volunteer action overseas in 1963 cannot be invoked for the same action in 1968. "Mission-vacations" among poor Mexicans were "*the thing*" to do for well-off U.S. students earlier in this decade: sentimental concern for newly-discovered poverty south of the border combined with total blindness to much worse poverty at home justified such benevolent excursions. Intellectual insight into the difficulties of fruitful volunteer action had not sobered the spirit of Peace Corps Papal-and-Self-Styled Volunteers.

Today, the existence of organizations like yours is offensive to Mexico. I wanted to make this statement in order to explain why I feel sick about it all and in order to make you aware that good intentions have not much to do with what we are discussing here. To hell with good intentions. This is a theological statement. You will not help anybody by your good intentions. There is an Irish saying that the road to hell is paved with good intentions; this sums up the same theological insight.

The very frustration which participation in CIASP programs might mean for you, could lead you to new awareness: the awareness that even North Americans can receive the gift of hospitality without the slightest ability to pay for it; the awareness that for some gifts one cannot even say "thank you."

Now to my prepared statement.

Ladies and Gentlemen:

For the past six years I have become known for my increasing opposition to the presence of any and all North American "do-gooders" in Latin America. I am sure you know of my present efforts to obtain the voluntary withdrawal of all North American volunteer armies from Latin America—missionaries, Peace Corps members and groups like yours, a "division" organized for the benevolent invasion of Mexico. You were aware of these things when you invited me—of all people—to be the main speaker at your annual convention. This is amazing! I can only conclude that your invitation means one of at least three things:

Some among you might have reached the conclusion that CIASP should either dissolve altogether, or take the promotion of voluntary aid to the Mexican poor out of its institutional purpose. Therefore you might have invited me here to help others reach this same decision.

You might also have invited me because you want to learn how to deal with people who think the way I do—how to dispute them successfully. It has now become quite common to invite Black Power spokesmen to address Lions Clubs. A "dove" must always be included in a public dispute organized to increase U.S. belligerence.

And finally, you might have invited me here hoping that you would be able to agree with most of what I say, and then go ahead in good faith and work this summer in Mexican villages. This last possibility is only open to those who do not listen, or who cannot understand me.

I did not come here to argue. I am here to tell you, if possible to convince you, and hopefully, to stop you, from pretentiously imposing yourselves on Mexicans.

I do have deep faith in the enormous good will of the U.S. volunteer. However, his good faith can usually be explained only by an abysmal lack of intuitive delicacy. By definition, you cannot help being ultimately vacationing salesmen for the middle-class "American Way of Life," since that is really the only life you know.

A group like this could not have developed unless a mood in the United States had supported it—the belief that any true American must share God's blessings with his poorer fellow men. The idea that every American has something to give, and at all times may, can and should give it, explains why it occurred to students that they could help Mexican peasants "develop" by spending a few months in their villages.

Of course, this surprising conviction was supported by members of a missionary order, who would have no reason to exist unless they had the same conviction—except a much stronger one. It is now high time to cure yourselves of this. You, like the values you carry, are the products of an American society of achievers and consumers, with its two-party system, its universal schooling, and its family-car affluence. Your are ultimately—consciously or unconsciously—"salesmen" for a delusive ballet in the ideals of democracy, equal opportunity and free enterprise among people who haven't the possibility of profiting from these.

Next to money and guns, the third largest North American export is the U.S. idealist, who turns up in every theater of the world: the teacher, the volunteer, the missionary, the community organizer, the economic developer, and the vacationing do-gooders. Ideally, these people define their role as service. Actually, they frequently wind up alleviating the damage done by money and weapons, or "seducing" the "underdeveloped" to the benefits of the world of affluence and achievement. Perhaps this is the moment to instead bring home to the people of the U.S. the knowledge that the way of life they have chosen simply is not alive enough to be shared.

By now it should be evident to all America that the U.S. is engaged in a tremendous struggle to survive. The U.S. cannot survive if the rest of the world is not convinced that here we have Heaven-on-Earth. The survival of the U.S. depends on the acceptance by all so-called "free" men that the U.S. middle-class has "made it." The U.S. way of life has become a religion which must be accepted by all those who do not want to die by the sword—or napalm. All over the globe the U.S. is fighting to protect and develop at least a minority who consume what the U.S. majority can afford. Such is the purpose of the Alliance for Progress of the middle classes which the U.S. signed with Latin America some years ago. But increasingly this commercial alliance must be protected by weapons which allow the minority who can "make it" to protect their acquisitions and achievements.

But weapons are not enough to permit minority rule. The marginal masses become rambunctious unless they are given a "Creed," or belief which explains the status quo. This task is given to the U.S. volunteer—whether he be a member of CIASP or a worker in the so-called "Pacification Programs" in Viet Nam.

The United States is currently engaged in a three-front struggle to affirm its ideals of acquisitive and achievement-oriented "Democracy." I say "three" fronts, because three great areas of the world are challenging the validity of a political and social system which makes the rich ever richer, and the poor increasingly marginal to that system.

In Asia, the U.S. is threatened by an established power—China. The U.S. opposes China with three weapons: the tiny Asian elites who could not have it any better than in an alliance with the United States; a huge war machine to stop the Chinese from "taking over" as it is usually put in this country, and; forcible re-education of the so-called "Pacified" peoples. All three of these efforts seem to be failing.

In Chicago, poverty funds, the police force and preachers seem to be no more successful in their effort s to check the unwillingness of the black community to wait for graceful integration into the system.

And finally, in Latin America the Alliance for Progress has been quite successful in increasing the number of people who could not be better off—meaning the tiny, middle-class elites—and has created ideal conditions for military dictatorships. The dictators were formerly at the service of the plantation owners, but now they protect the new industrial complexes. And finally, you come to help the underdog accept his destiny within this process!

All you will do in a Mexican village is create disorder. At best, you can try to convince Mexican girls that they should marry a young man who is self-made, rich, a consumer, and as disrespectful of tradition as one of you. At worst, in your "community development" spirit you might create just enough problems to get someone shot after your vacation ends and you rush back to your middle-class neighborhoods where your friends make jokes about "spics" and "wetbacks."

You start on your task without any training. Even the Peace Corps spends around $10,000 on each corpsmember to help him adapt to his new environment and to guard him against culture shock. How odd that nobody ever thought about spending money to educate poor Mexicans in order to prevent them from the culture shock of meeting you?

In fact, you cannot even meet the majority which you pretend to serve in Latin America—even if you could speak their language, which most of you cannot. You can only dialogue with those like you—Latin American imitations of the North American middle-class. There is no way for you to really meet with the underprivileged, since there is no common ground whatsoever for you to meet on.

Let me explain this statement, and also let me explain why most Latin Americans with whom you might be able to communicate would disagree with me.

Suppose you went to a U.S. ghetto this summer and tried to help the poor there "help themselves." Very soon you would be either spit upon or laughed at. People offended by your pretentiousness would hit or spit. People who understand that your own bad consciences push you to this gesture would laugh condescendingly. Soon you would be made aware of your irrelevance among the poor, of your status as middle class college students on a summer assignment. You would be roundly rejected, no matter if your skin is white—as most of your faces here are—or brown or black, as a few exceptions who got in here somehow.

Your reports about your work in Mexico, which you so kindly sent me, exude self-complacency. Your reports on past summers prove that you are not even capable of understanding that your do-gooding in a Mexican village is even less relevant than it would be in a U.S. ghetto. Not only is there a gulf between what you have and what others have which is much greater than the one existing between you and the poor in your own country, but there is also a gulf between what you feel and what the Mexican people feel that is incomparably greater. This gulf is so great that in a Mexican village

you, as white Americans (or cultural white Americans) can imagine yourselves exactly the way a white preacher saw himself when he offered his life preaching to the black slaves on a plantation in Alabama. The fact that you live in huts and eat tortillas for a few weeks renders your well-intentioned group only a bit more picturesque.

The only people with whom you can hope to communicate with are some members of the middle class. And here please remember that I said "some"—by which I mean a tiny elite in Latin America. You come from a country which industrialized early and which succeeded in incorporating the great majority of its citizens into the middle classes. It is no social distinction in the U.S. to have graduated from the second year of college. Indeed, most Americans now do. Anybody in this country who did not finish high school is considered underprivileged.

In Latin America the situation is quite different: 75% of all people drop out of school before they reach the sixth grade. Thus, people who have finished high school are members of a tiny minority. Then, a minority of that minority goes on for university training. It is only among these people that you will find your educational equals.

At the same time, a middle class in the United States is the majority. In Mexico, it is a tiny elite. Seven years ago your country began and financed a so-called "Alliance for Progress." This was an "Alliance" for the "Progress" of the middle class elites. Now, it is among the members of this middle class that you will find a few people who are willing to spend their time with you. And they are overwhelmingly those "nice kids" who would also like to soothe their troubled consciences by "doing something nice for the promotion of the poor Indians." Of course, when you and your middle-class Mexican counterparts meet, you will be told that you are doing something valuable, that you are "sacrificing" to help others.

And it will be the foreign priest who will especially confirm your self-image for you.

After all, his livelihood and sense of purpose depends on his firm belief in a year-round mission which is of the same type as your summer vacation-mission.

There exists the argument that some returned volunteers have gained insight into the damage they have done to others—and thus become more mature people. Yet it is less frequently stated that most of them are ridiculously proud of the "summer sacrifices." Perhaps there is also something to the argument that young men should be promiscuous for awhile in order to find out that sexual love is most beautiful in a monogamous relationship. Or that the best way to leave LSD alone is to try it for awhile—or even that the best way of understanding that your help in the ghetto is neither needed nor wanted is to try, and fail. I do not agree with this argument. The damage which volunteers do willy-nilly is too high a price for the belated insight that they shouldn't have been volunteers in the first place.

If you have any sense of responsibility at all, stay with your riots here at home. Work for the coming elections: You will know what you are doing, why you are doing it, and how to com-municate with those to whom you speak. And you will know when you fail. If you insist on working with the poor, if this is your vocation, then at least work among the poor who can tell you to go to hell. It is incredibly unfair for you to impose yourselves on a village where you are so linguistically deaf and dumb that you don't even understand what you are doing, or what people think of you. And it is profoundly damaging to yourselves when you define something that you want to do as "good," a "sacrifice" and "help."

I am here to suggest that you voluntarily renounce exercising the power which being an American gives you. I am here to entreat you to freely, consciously and humbly give up the legal right you have to impose your benevolence on Mexico. I am here to challenge you to recognize your inability, your powerlessness and your incapacity to do the "good" which you intended to do.

I am here to entreat you to use your money, your status and your education to travel in Latin America. Come to look, come to climb our mountains, to enjoy our flowers. Come to study. But do not come to help.

John McKnight
Why "Servanthood" Is Bad

John McKnight (1931–) is a professor at Northwestern University, where he also serves as Director of the Community Studies Program at the Center for Urban Affairs and Policy Research. He has worked for many years as a community organizer across the United States and Canada, and has been a proponent of what is being called "asset-based community development." In this short article, he identifies important problems with the idea of "service" that issues out of people's deficiencies and not their capacities or assets. His provocative essay should give pause to anyone motivated to "serve the needs of the community."

Why "Servanthood" Is Bad

John McKnight

John McKnight (1931–) is a professor at Northwestern University, where he also serves as Director of the Community studies Program at the Center for Urban Affairs and Policy Research. He has worked for many years as a community organizer across the United States and Canada, and has been a proponent of what is being called "asset-based community development." In this short article, he identifies important problems with the idea of "service" that issues out of people's deficiencies and not their capacities or assets. His provocative essay should give pause to anyone motivated to "serve the needs of the community."

In a small, relatively isolated community on Martha's Vineyard, about every tenth person used to be born without the ability to hear. Everybody in the community, hearing and nonhearing alike, spoke a unique sign language brought from England when they immigrated to Massachusetts in 1690. In the mid-twentieth century with increased mobility, the people ceased to intermarry, and the genetic anomaly disappeared.

But before the memory of it died—and the sign language with it—historian Nora Groce studied the community's history. She compared the experience of the nonhearing people to that of the hearing people.

She found that 80 percent of the nonhearing people graduated from high school as did 80 percent of the hearing. She found that about 90 percent of the nonhearing got married compared to about 92 percent of the hearing. They had about equal numbers of children. Their income levels were similar as were the variety and distribution of their occupations.

Then Groce did a parallel study on the Massachusetts mainland. At the time, it was considered to have the best services in the nation

Reprinted with permission from *The Other Side*, 300 W. Apsley, Philadelpia, PA 19144 (1-800-700-9280). Subscriptions $24.00 per year.

for nonhearing people. There she found that 50 percent of nonhearing people graduated from high school compared to 75 percent of the hearing. Nonhearing people married half the time while hearing people married 90 percent of the time. Forty percent of the nonhearing people had children while 80 percent of hearing people did. And nonhearing people had fewer children. They also received about one-third the income of hearing people. And their range of occupations was much more limited.

How was it, Groce wondered, that on an island with no services, nonhearing people were as much like hearing people as you could possibly measure? Yet thirty miles away, with the most advanced services available, nonhearing people lived much poorer lives than the hearing.

The one place in the United States where deafness was not a disability was a place with *no* services for deaf people. In that community all the people adapted by signing instead of handing the nonhearing people over to professionals and their services. That community wasn't just doing what was necessary to help or to serve one group. It was doing what was necessary to incorporate everyone.

I've been around neighborhoods, neighborhood organizations, and communities in big cities for thirty-six years. I have *never* seen service systems that brought people to well-being, delivered them to citizenship, or made them free.

When I'm around church people, I always check whether they are misled by the modern secular vision. Have they substituted the vision of service for the only thing that will make people whole—community? Are they service peddlers or community builders? Peddling services is unchristian—even if you're hell-bent on helping people. Peddling services instead of building communities is the one way you can be sure not to help.

We all know that at the Last Supper Jesus said, "This is my commandment: love one another as I have loved you. There is no

greater love than this: to lay down one's life for one's friends." But for mysterious reasons, I never hear the next two sentences. "You are my friends if you do what I command you. I no longer call you servants, because servants do not know the business of the one they serve. But I have called you friends because I have made known to you everything I learned from God." It's not right to be hung back by service and servantry. The goal is to be a friend.

I'm consistently impressed by how dangerous people are who want to serve others. The service ideology and its systems don't work for three reasons.

Frst, they constantly steal money from people who are poor. At the center where I work, we've added up how much money the four levels of government—federal, state, country, and city—specifically target for low-income people in Cook County. It adds up to about $6,000 for every person with an income below the poverty line. (That figure is low; not everyone below the line participates in low-income programs.) For a mother with three children, that's the equivalent of $24,000. Three years ago the median income in Cook County was $23,000. In one sense, we spend for every poor person more money than half the people in Cook County make. But Chicago still has poverty!

So I asked our researchers, "Of the money appropriated for low-income people, how much did they get in cash and how much in services?" They replied, "They got 63 percent in services and 37 percent in income." Now, if you're a family of four, that means your servants walked away with over $15,000 of the money appropriated for you while you got less than $9,000.

Bureaucracy is not the problem. (Bureaucracy eats only about 6 percent.) The money goes to health-and-human-service professionals: nurses, doctors, psychologists, psychiatrists, social workers, public-housing administrators, land-clearance officials, welfare workers. It doesn't go to poor people.

The second problem with service systems is that they base programs on "deficiencies."

I fight whenever I can—in legislatures and before policy-making bodies—against "needs surveys" in low-income neighborhoods. Here is why.

I was organizing block clubs in West Side neighborhoods. I wasn't very good. But people responded. They understood what I was saying. Then the antipoverty program came, and within three years organizing became incredibly difficult.

The antipoverty program sent people out to interview people this way:

"Mrs. Jones, we're from such-and-such. We're doing a survey. Can you tell me how far you went in school?"

She looks down a little and says, "Well, I just got through tenth grade." So they write on the clipboard, "Dropout. Two years." Not "educated ten years" but "dropout two years."

Then they say, "I wonder if you could read this to me."

She looks at it, embarrassed. "No. I can't read."

"Illiterate," they write. Then they say, "Just now you squinted your eyes. Do you have trouble seeing?"

"Yes. I think I need glasses."

"Visual deficit," they write. "Do you have any children?"

"Three daughters, ages fourteen, sixteen, and eighteen."

"Do any of them have children?"

"The fourteen-year-old has a child, and the eighteen-year-old has a child."

"Teenage pregnancy," goes on the clipboard.

Then they say, "We're going to get you some help. Just wait. We're going to make a service center here." And they cash in their needs inventory for a GED dropout training center and three people who work there, for an illiteracy program with four staff people, for a neighborhood optometrist who is responsive to the community, and for a new teenage-pregnancy counseling program that gets the schools more money.

This *poor* woman is a gold mine. That's how she ended up getting one-third what the service system got.

When I go back to this woman, organizing, I say, "Mrs. Jones, I'm organizing for the local neighborhood organization, and your neighbor told me to talk to you. She told me that when her daughter was hit by an automobile down at the corner, you took charge while she took her daughter to the emergency room. And when the tree fell down across the street, you're the one who came out and told people who to call, what to do about the tree. She told me you're the leader on this block. People trust you. People believe in you. People follow you. That's one of the most wonderful things in the world, because you have the opportunity to join with other people like yourself in the neighborhood to begin to do more things than just deal with the tree and the crisis with the little girl. So would you come with me to a meeting tonight?"

"No" she says, "I'm waiting for the people in the white coats."

Service systems teach people that their value lies in their deficiencies. They are built on "inadequacies" called illiteracy, visual deficit, and teenage pregnancy. But communities are built on the *capacities* of drop-out, illiterate, bad-scene, teenage-pregnant, battered women like Mrs. Jones. If the church is about community—not service—it's about capacity not deficiency.

Third, the service system displaces the capacity of people's organizations to solve problems. It says, "Don't form a community organization. Sit and wait for the white coat to come save you." The proliferation of an ideology of therapy and service as "what you need" has weakened associations and organizations of citizens across the United States.

Many churches and pastors have become the agents of systems. They themselves may not understand who they represent, but they refer people to systems. Instead of building community, they help take responsibility away from the community and give it to professionals. People who do this in the name of the church and of Jesus are community busters. They are not agents of Christ.

Here are five rules to protect yourself from being the agent of the devil in the middle of a church. (I could give you ten if I had more space.)

Saul Alinsky referred to the first rule as the "iron rule": Never do for others what they can do for themselves.

Second, find another's gifts, contributions, and capacities. Use them. Give them a place in the community.

Third, whenever a service is proposed, fight to get it converted into income. Don't support services. Insist that what poor people need is income.

There's a point where things called services can be useful. Most low-income communities are well beyond that point. If you improve the professional credentialing of big-city school teachers and systems, knowing and wisdom will decrease in direct relationship to the increase in that system's power. The increase in medical resources in Chicago is now decreasing the health status of poor people.

The fourth rule is a sort of subhead of the third. If those in power are hell-bent on giving poor people services rather than income, then fight for those services to come in the form of vouchers. That way the persons who must be served at least have a choice as to who will serve them. And there may be some competition.

Fifth, develop hospitality. Abraham, the head of a tribe, decided to follow a God who claimed to be the only God. That made Abraham and his people strangers in their own land. They journeyed as strangers through the world. And they developed some unique ideas about responsibilities to strangers because they were strangers themselves.

Jesus' disciples were also people who decided to become strangers—in their own land and in others. They built communities based on

their decision. That renewed their understanding of obligations to strangers, and hospitality was renewed.

In every household, in every tent, the door was open—to the stranger, the outsider, the enemy, or potential enemy. And the stranger was one with whom one acted not in service but in equality.

Then a terrible thing happened in third-century Italy. At the side of a monastery, they built a little room for strangers. And they called it a hospice. The church took over responsibility for the stranger. And Christians forgot what had been unique about their community—how to welcome the person who was outside and hungry.

The hospice took hospitality out of the community. "Hospice" became "hospital." The hospital became Humana, a for-profit corporation buying up church hospitals. Communities and churches have forgotten about hospitality. Now systems and corporations claim they can produce it and sell it and that you can consume it.

You must struggle with all your might to reclaim the central Christian act of hospitality. You will have to fight your local hospitals. You will have to fight Humana. You will have to fight the United Way. You will have to fight the social services. They have commodified hospitality and called it a service. They have made a market of the temple. And you know what you're supposed to do then. Get 'em out! Or bring into the church the hospitality that is at the center of understanding a relationship as a friend not a servant. A church's response to people without should be hospitality not services.

I met a remarkable woman in a little town in southern Georgia. She worked for a service agency responsible for mentally retarded people in a three-county area. Her agency decided it was too focused on deficiencies and needed to think about the gifts, contributions, and capacities of the people who were its charge.

So this woman began spending time with the people the agency had once called "clients" to see if she could understand—in their homes—what gifts they had to offer. She went to the home of a forty-two-year-old man who had been the victim of special education—segregated education. His name is Joe. He has one short leg (at least he limps), and he doesn't speak the way a lot of people speak. (I'm not sure what label deficiency-finding psychologists would give him. But I'm sure they would give him one.)

At age twenty-one, Joe had no place in society. So he went home to a pig farm. Every day he did two things. He fed the pigs twice a day, and he sat in the living room where he listened to the radio. (He couldn't see to watch television.)

The woman told me that after four days at Joe's house she couldn't find his gift.

"But on the fifth day," she said, "I realized what his gift was: he listens to the radio.

"I found out that three people in town spend all their time listening to the radio, and they get paid for it. One is in the sheriff's office, one in the police department, and one in the local civil-defense office. So I looked at each of these places where a person sits, listening to a radio all day. I liked the civil-defense office best. It's a voluntary organization. They have a house that somebody gave them; so the voluntary ambulance people sleep in its bedrooms. There's a desk and sitting right by the desk is a radio getting all the calls from the county. At the desk sits a twenty-seven-year-old woman who listens for calls and dispatches volunteers when someone needs an ambulance."

So she told the dispatcher, "I have somebody here who likes to listen to the radio as much as you do. I'd like to introduce you to him." And so she introduced Joe to her, and they put a chair on the other side of the desk, and he sat there every day listening to the radio.

This little house is also the neighborhood community center. Somebody is always there. People come and talk and drink coffee in the dining room. Sometimes they show movies.

Whenever anybody was there, Joe would go in. Everybody came to know Joe, and he became a part of that neighborhood. When Christmas came, the volunteers gave Joe a radio of his own to listen to at home in the evening because Joe had been with them and had shared his gifts in the face of their hospitality.

Joe began to go downtown at noon to eat at the diner. One day he went into the diner and the owner of the diner said, "Hey, Joe, what's happening?" Joe looked at him and said, "The Smith house over in Boonesville burned down this morning. And out on Route 90, at that turnoff where you can have picnics, there was a drug bust. And Mr. Schiller over in Athens had a heart attack." Everybody in the diner stopped talking and looked around at Joe. They couldn't believe it. They realized that Joe knew the answer to the question. "What's happening?" because he listened to the radio all morning.

When I went to visit this town and the woman who introduced Joe's gift of listening to the radio to the community, I saw an incredible thing. I saw, first of all, that the dispatcher and Joe were in love with each other. Then when I went with Joe to lunch, I saw that everybody who came into the diner came over to Joe first and asked, "Joe, what's happening?" And I realized that I was in the only town in the United States that now has the gift of a town crier.

The woman told me she was planning to take Joe over to the newspaper editor. It had occurred to her that in this little town with a little newspaper and one editor, the editor couldn't possibly know "what's happening." But by noon Joe knew. And if Joe would go over and talk to the editor every noon, the grasp, the breadth, the knowledge, of the newspaper and what it could report would expand mightily.

So Joe is now a stringer for the local *Gazette*. He showers his gifts on the community because somebody knew that community is about capacities, contributions, and hospitalities—not about deficiencies, needs, and services.

Matthew Spalding

Principles and Reforms for Citizen Service

Dr. Matthew Spalding is the Director of the B. Kenneth Simon Center for American Studies at the Heritage Foundation. An Adjunct Fellow with the Claremont Institute, he has taught American government at George Mason University, the Catholic University of America, Claremont McKenna College and Hillsdale College. He is the co-author of A Sacred Union of Citizens: Washington's Farewell Address and the American Character and the editor of The Founders' Almanac: A Practical Guide to the Notable Events, Greatest Leaders & Most Eloquent Words of the American Founding.

In the essay that follows, written in 2003, Spalding raises a number of serious objections to the current national service program, and makes suggestions about how to reform it. He condemns the Clinton Administration's Americorps initiative as "nothing more than a federal jobs program," and urges a return to the promotion of purely voluntary service, "done by one's own free will," without coercion or payment. Spalding wants to see a spirit of volunteerism that strengthens civil society and diminishes the role of government. He also calls upon schools and colleges to abandon service-learning, a pedagogy of "questionable value" which actually promotes advocacy and political change rather than service. As you read Spalding's critique of service-learning and current national service policies, think about how his argument applies to the work you are doing in communities connected to the classroom.

Principles and Reforms for Citizen Service
Matthew Spalding, Ph.D[1]

In his 2002 State of the Union Address, President George W Bush issued a call to all Americans to commit 4,000 hours to service and volunteerism over the course of their life-time. President Bush renewed his challenge in this year's State of the Union address and urged Congress to reconsider the Citizen Service Act of 2002, which would reform and reauthorize several programs—including AmeriCrops, VISTA and Learn & Serve America—as part of his Administration's effort to foster service, citizenship, and responsibility.

Policymakers now have an important opportunity to rethink America's national service programs as they design a reformed version of the Citizen Service Act for consideration by the new Congress. Working with the Bush Administration, lawmakers should propose a reformed legislative package that builds on the changes proposed in the 2002 legislation, takes additional steps to correct the infringement of religious liberty in existing service laws, and fundamentally transforms the current government-centered national service agenda into a true citizen service initiative that is compatible with the highest principles and traditions of American self-government.

The Wrong Direction

The idea of national service has its origins in the theories of progressive reformers at the beginning of the 20th century and is today a key aspect of modern liberalism's theory of citizenship. Progressive thinkers such as Herbert Croly and John Dewey argued that the forces of industrialism and urbanization had shattered America's traditional social order and that these conditions in the modern world required a new administrative state to better manage political life and human affairs.

[1] The author thanks Charissa Kersten and Timothy Holbert for their assistance in preparing this study.

These thinkers further argued that such an unprecedented situation required nothing less than a new relationship between citizens and the federal government that emphasized a public-spirited devotion to a collective social ideal—what Dewey called "the Great Community" and Lyndon Johnson later proclaimed a "Great Society"—and transferred the traditional, local functions of civil society to a progressive, national government focused on social reform. This new idea of citizenship, and in particular the concept of national service, was meant to replace the old-fashioned notion of an independent, self-governing citizenship with an updated civic bond to an activist nation-state.

In recent years, this national service agenda received renewed interest in the ideas and policies of former President Bill Clinton, who called for a "new covenant" that would revive a sense of national community and civic-mindedness in response to what he saw as the "gilded age" of the 1980s. The Clinton Administration used these themes as a way to make civic life an aspect of reinventing government, making government more "user-friendly" for citizens and communities while preserving—if not expanding—bureaucratic control of social programs.

This agenda was pursued within the philosophic assumptions and political goals of modern liberalism. The spirit and intentions of this paradigm were epitomized in the program Clinton proclaimed as "citizenship at its best"—AmeriCorps, the largest government program for national service since the Civilian Conservation Corps of the New Deal.[2]

Principles of Citizen Service

The government-oriented view of national service contrasts sharply with the idea of a "citizen service" that protects and strengthens civil society, focuses on service rather than social change, promotes true volunteerism, and addresses real problems—while minimizing the role of government. The following five principles of citizen service should be at the heart of the Citizen Service Act.

Principle #1: Protect and strengthen civil society

The primary goal of citizen service should be to protect and strengthen civil society, especially the non-governmental institutions at its foundation. The great social commentator Alexis de Tocqueville observed that one of the leading virtues of American society is its tendency to create local voluntary associations to meet society's most important needs. In other nations, these needs were addressed through and by government; in the United States, private individuals of all ages, all conditions, and all dispositions formed associations to deal with societal problems.

"I often admired the infinite art with which the inhabitants of the United States managed to fix a common goal to the efforts of many men and to get them to advance it freely," Tocqueville wrote in *Democracy in America*. "What political power could ever be in a state to suffice for the innumerable multitude of small

---

[2]   See John Walters, "Clinton's AmeriCorps Values: How the President Misunderstands Citizenship," *Policy Review*. No. 75 (January-February 1996).

NOTE: *Nothing written here, is to be construed as necessarily reflecting the views of The Heritage Foundation or as an attempt to aid or hinder the passage of any bill before Congress.*

undertakings that American citizens execute every day with the aid of an association?"[3]

The traditional associations of civil society – families, schools, churches, voluntary organizations, and other mediating institutions — sustain social order and public morality, moderate individualism and materialism, and cultivate the personal character that is the foundation of a self-governing society. All of this occurs without the aid of government bureaucracies or the coercive power of the law. Unlike government programs, the personal involvement, individual generosity, and consistent participation that are the hallmarks of private philanthropy have a ripple effect of further strengthening the fiber of civil society.

Policymakers must recognize that President Bush's call to service will be answered best not by a government program but by the selfless acts of millions of citizens in voluntary associations, local communities, and private organizations that are at the heart of American charity. In 2001, according to Independent Sector and the American Association of Fundraising Counsel, 83.9 million adults volunteered time to a formal charity organization and 89 percent of American households gave a total of $212 billion to chanty.[4] That same year, the Knighis of Columbus alone raised and distributed $125.6 million (half the AmeriCorps budget) and volunteered 58 million hours of service (almost 90 percent of AmeriCorps participants' service time).[5]

These private voluntary organizations thrive today precisely because their work is privately organized, highly decentralized, and directly focused on community needs and local conditions. If policymakers are serious about promoting a thriving civil society, they should emphasize not only volunteering, but also private philanthropy by promoting proposals such as the Charity Aid, Recovery, and Empowerment (CARE) Act, which would boost both private volunteerism and charitable giving.[6]

Principle #2: Focus on service

Americans have always exemplified a strong sense of civic responsibility and humane compassion toward their neighbors and the less fortunate in their communities and traditionally have supported and participated in a vast array of private service activities. The objective of citizen service legislation should be to promote a renewed commitment to this great tradition of individual service as a way of strengthening the natural grounds of citizenship and civic friendship. As Tocqueville noted, "Sentiments and ideas renew themselves, the heart is enlarged, and the human mind is developed only by the reciprocal action of men upon one another."[7]

The goal of an authentic citizen service initiative should not be to engage citizens in a government program, nor to create an artificial bond between individuals and the state or or-

3 Alexis de Tocqueville, *Democracy in America*, ed. and trans. Harvey C. Mansfield and Delba Winthrop (Chicago: University of Chicago Press, 2000), Book II, Chapter V, "The Use Which The Americans Make of Public Associations in Civil Life," pp. 489-492.

4 Independent Sector, "Giving and Volunteering in the United States 2001 — Key Findings," at *http://www.in dependentsector.org/PDFs/GV01keyfind.pdf*, and AAFRC Trust for Philanthropy, *GIVING USA 2002*; *The Annual Report on Philanthropy for the Year 2001*, "*2001* Contributions: $212.00 Billion by Source of Contributions," at *http://www.aa/rc.org/images/graphics/chait1.gif* (June 26, 2002).

5 Knights of Columbus, press release, "Knights of Columbus Reports New All-Time Highs in Charitable Giving, Volunteerism in 2001," June 7, 2002, at *http://www.kofc. org/announce.cfm?thisrecord=138* (June 19, 2002).

6 See Joseph Loconte and William W. Beach, "The Senates Response to the Presidents Faith-Based Agenda: An Analysis of the CARE Act," Heritage Foundation *Backgrounder* No. 1555, May 24, 2002.

7 Tocqueville, *Democracy in America*, p. 491.

ganization that coordinates their service, but to energize a culture of personal compassion and civic commitment to those in need of service. Citizen service should not be a tool for an educational reform agenda, a platform for political or social activism, or a method of reinventing government. A true citizen service initiative should recognize and support the dynamic and diverse nature of civil society: It should not promote one particular form of service or suggest that public service in a national, government-sponsored program is in any way better or more dignified than traditional, and nongovernmental, forms of community service.

Principle #3: Promote true volunteerism

President Bush's first objective for a Citizen Service Act is to "support and encourage greater engagement of citizens in volunteering."[8] To be truly voluntary, an action must be intentionally chosen and done by one's own free will, without compulsion or external constraint and "without profit, payment or any valuable consideration."[9] It is this altruistic process by which individuals choose—without coercion or economic benefit—to help others that has the character-forming effect of habituating and strengthening citizens' sense of duty to help their neighbors.

By contrast, "volunteerism" that is paid for and organized by the government belittles authentic volunteerism both by presenting service as an employment option rather than as the sacrificial giving of one's time and resources and by implying that money and guidance from the government is necessary if Americans are to help their neighbors. "Dependence," Thomas Jefferson noted, "begets subservience and venality, suffocates the germ of virtue, and prepares fit tools for the designs of ambition."[10] Reform of the national service laws should redesign service programs as an opportunity for true voluntary service rather than a federal jobs program. [11]

Principle #4: Address real problems

There are many social problems in America that are and will continue to be addressed most effectively by voluntary service efforts, with or without the help of government. Historically, these efforts focused primarily on helping those who could not help themselves. Rather than the handouts of charity, citizen service meant personal involvement and "suffering with" (i.e., compassion toward) the poor to provide them with opportunities through which they could rise out of poverty.[12] "I think the best way of doing good to the poor," Benjamin Franklin

---

8   The White House, Executive Office of the President, "Principles and Reforms for a Citizen Service Act," at *http//www/nation-alservice.org/about/principles/principles_reforms.html* (June 24, 2002).

9   Webster's Dictionary, Unabridged, 2nd Ed., 1958, Vol. II, p. 2049.

10 Thomas Jefferson, Notes on the State of Virginia, Query XIX, 1787, as quoted in *The Founders' Almanac: A Practical Guide to the Notable Events, Greatest Leaders & Most Eloquent Words of the American Founding*, ed. Matthew Spalding (Washington, D.C.: The Heritage Foundation, 2002), p. 184.

11 A distinction must be made between voluntary service in Americas armies of compassion—which are the backbone of the private, voluntary sector—and in the United States military. National service in the armed forces is not volumeerism, or pan of the voluntary sector, but is nevertheless voluntary in the sense that no one is conscripted. Housing, paying, feeding, and training individuals to defend the United States as part of a constitutionally authorized activity that is necessary lor national security in no way detracts from the duty and honor of voluntary military service; nor does it justify by analogy paying citizen service participants in traditional voluntary (i.e., voluntary-sector) activities.

12 For a general explanation of the virtues and history of compassion, see Marvin Olasky, *The Tragedy of American Compassion* (Wheaton, Ill.: Crossway Books, 1992).

noted, "is not making them easy in poverty, but leading or driving them out of it."[13]

If the federal government is to encourage citizen service, and if policymakers want to foster a culture of responsibility toward the less fortunate, service programs should be targeted to address serious problems where there is authentic need for assistance. In addition, such assistance should be provided in accordance with the larger traditions of compassionate service.

In determining which programs to recognize, support, and commend, policymakers should make practical distinctions between programs that meet critical needs and those that are not vital to societal well-being. Programs that help the elderly and serve the poor are on a different level from those that provide wardrobe tips,[14] dance instruction,[15] " knitting lessons,[16] art appreciation,[17] or bike clubs.[18]

Policymakers should also think twice about validating controversial activities (e.g., teaching sex education[19] or working for programs that promote abortion or refer individuals to abortion providers,[20] or that raise awareness about dating in lesbian, bisexual, transgender, and gay communities[21]). Nor should they allow as "citizen service" policy advocacy activities (such as VISTA participants' working for groups that organize opposition to welfare-reform policies,[22] or Ameri-Corps participants'

---

[13] Benjamin Franklin, "On the Price of Corn and Management of the Poor," November 1766, as quoted in *The Founders' Almanac*, pp. 183-184.

[14] AmeriCorps*VISTA participants help Dress for Success collect garments for low-income women with job interviews. See *http://www.dressforsuccess.org/who_we_are/partners.asp* (February 26, 2003).

[15] A service-learning program at Governor's School for Arts and Humanities in South Carolina uses dance to teach abused and neglected children the basics of expression. See *www.leaderschools.org/2002profiles/ south.html* (July 17, 2002).

[16] A service-learning program in a math class at Nicholas Senn High School in Chicago knits scarves and hats for a local homeless shelter. See *http://www.isbe.state.il.us/learmerve/pdf/LSWinterNews03.pdf* (January 30, 2003).

[17] AmeriCorps*VISTA participants help Art for Inner City Youth in San Francisco teach low-income students visual skills and self-esteem and "to view art with a critical eye." See *http://www.artspan.org/youth.html* (February 26, 2003)

[18] AmeriCorps participants work with JustServe in Seattle, Washington, to coordinate bike-based clubs. Program from 9/17/2001 to 8/31/2002. See *https://recruit.cns.gov/searchDetails.asp?listingid='94ASCWA0471 901-2'&* (March 31, 2003).

[19] In Houston, Texas, six AmeriCorps participants make up the "Planned Parenthood of Houston Sexuality Education Team.' which uses dance, rap, poetry, and role-playing to teach about sexuality See *www.planne dparenthood.org/education/update_dec01.html* (March 20, 2003).

[20] A simple Internet search suggests the extent to which Planned Parenthood makes use of AmeriCorps workers. The Delaware chapter of Planned Parenthood, for instance, currently advertises that it uses an AmeriCorps grant for 20 participants "to provide human sexuality education and referrals for services to teens and their parents." See Planned Parenthood of Delaware, "PPDE Partners With AmeriCorps," at *http://www.ppdd.org/ partnerships.html* (June 24, 2002).

[21] An AmeriCorps position in Seattle, Washington, organized community action teams to "build consensus, raise awareness, and develop innovative community-based solutions to dating and domestic violence in Lesbian, Bisexual, Trans and Gay communities." Program from 9/17/2001 to 8/31/2002. See *https: //recruit.cns.gov/searchDetails.asp?listingid='94ASCWA0471901-3'&* (March 31, 2003).

[22] VISTA participants work for the National Student Campaign Against Hunger and Homelessness in Amherst, Massachusetts. to "educate and expand the anti-poverty movement" through conferences, on-campus workshops, and community training sessions. See *http://www.americorps.org/joining/vista/vista_ma.html* and *www.nscahh.org* (February 12, 2003)

coordinating Peace Education camps and student activities[23] or engaging young people "in struggles against racism, sexism, meanness and meaninglessness"[24]).

Wherever possible, reform should prevent government support (and presumed public endorsement) of frivolous, controversial, and special-interest activities; it should focus instead on encouraging traditional service opportunities that address the real problems of those who are in need.

Principle #5: Minimize the role of government.

Any expanded government role in the voluntary sector is unwise and counterproductive. "The more [government] puts itself in the place of associations," Tocqueville argued, "the more particular persons, losing the idea of associating with each other, will need it to come to their aid: these are causes and effects that generate each other without rest. Will the public administration in the end direct all the industries for which an isolated citizen cannot suffice?"[25]

Citizen service that is paid for and organized by the government encourages individuals and associations to look to the state for assistance. Likewise, the government's funding of charitable organizations to pay for volunteer time reduces the need for private-sector support, making it more likely that citizens will abdicate their civic responsibilities. Institutionalized federal funding and government administration also will have the effect of further reshaping the voluntary sector, as public money and oversight inevitably pushes aside private philanthropy and sets the stage for increased lobbying and public advocacy. The long-term effect would be to shift the center of gravity within the volunteer community from civil society to the public sector.

There already exists between government and many large nonprofit organizations what Leslie Lenkowsky has called a "dysfunctional marriage," in which government money has led to a significant loss of nonprofit independence. "The partnership has been a Faustian bargain that ought to be reex-amined and renegotiated," Lenkowsky concluded.[26] Expanding this relationship to include the voluntary sector generally, and especially those smaller organizations that have thus far eluded the federal reach, would only expand and intensify the problem.

Reform should reduce govenment's financial, administrative, and regulatory role in civil socrety, Government can play an important role in revitaling citizen service, but that role, of necessity will be limited and indirect. Policymakers must keep in mind that government can best promote civil service not by creating any particular service programs (given that there is a vast network of private service activities that exist without government oversight or subsidies), but by launching a high-level bullypulpit initiative to encourage, motivate, and honor the efforts of private citizens.

---

[23] AmeriCorps participants work with the Peace Learning Center in Indianapolis, Indiana, to organize school peace activities as part of a "proactive force for transformative and positive change in the community through holistic peace education.' See *www.peacelearningcenter.org/americorps.asp* (March 20, 2003).

[24] AmeriCorps participants work with the Institute for Community Service in Seattle, Washington Program from 11/1/2002 to 8/2/2003. See *https://recruit.cns.gov/searchDetails.asp?listingid='OOASCWA470101-3'&* (March, 31, 2003).

[25] Tocqueville, *Democracy in America*, p. 491.

[26] See Leslie Lenkowsky, "Philanthropy and the Welfare State," in Peter L. Berger and Richard John Neuhaus, *To Empower People from State to Civil Society*, 2nd Ed., ed. Michael Novak (Washington, D.C.: AEI Press, 1996), pp. 85-93. Lenkowsky, who as now the Chief Executive Officer of Corporation for National and Community Service, was at the time the president of the Hudson Institute.

The Citizen Service Act 2002: A Good Start

The Citizen Service Act of 2002 (which was approved in committee but was never acted on by Congress) contained many useful and innovative changes in existing programs and should serve as the basis for future reforms.

During the Clinton Administration, AmeriCorps participants were assigned to federal agencies and departments, and grants were used to subsidize political advocacy and activities. The Citizen Service Act of 2002 would have prohibited national service grants from going to federal agencies and would not have allowed the use of non-AmeriCorps federal funds to meet AmeriCorps' matching-funds requirements. The proposal also mandated that any programs that teach sex education must not encourage sexual activity or distribute contraceptives and that they must include discussion of the health benefits of abstinence and risks of condom use.

In addition, the bill required recipients to certify that any participants who serve as tutors had earned, or were on track to obtain, a high school diploma. It further required that, to qualify, literacy programs must be rooted in scientifically based research and the essential components of reading instruction as defined in the No Child Left Behind Act of 2001.

In designing a reformed Citizen Service Act, lawmakers should go beyond these particular proposals to consider prohibiting state government and political advocacy groups from receiving service grants and to consider prohibiting sex education instruction as a valid

"service" of AmeriCorps participants. Nevertheless, lawmakers should carefully review and include as a starting point these and other useful reforms proposed in the 2002 legislation.

Removing Barriers to Religious Liberty

Regrettably the Citizen Service Act of 2002 failed to remove a fundamental obstacle to the religious liberty of faith-based organizations. Current laws for national service programs specifically prohibit any individual operating a national service project from making employment decisions or choosing volunteers on the basis of religion.[27] The Citizen Service Act of 2002 recognized that this was a problem but did not adequately address it. The bill merely proposed that faith-based organizations be given notice (and acknowledge in writing) that, by participating in national service programs, they would be subject to "anti-discriminatory" hiring policies and would not be protected by the 1964 Civil Rights Act, which grants exemptions for religious groups.

This policy undermines a faith-based organization's ability to select only staff and volunteers who strongly support the values and mission of the organization—factors that are often key to the success of an organizations outreach. This restriction on an organization's staffing decisions directly contradicts existing federal law (the 1996 Charitable Choice legislation): Its application to volunteers is equally debilitating and, in fact, may be unconstitutional.[28] Many faith-based organizations depend heavily

---

[27]   See Section 175(c) of the National and Community Service Act of 1990 (Public Law 101-610, 42 U.S.C. 12635) and Section 417(c) of the Domestic Volunteer Act of 1973 (42 U.S.C. 5057). The Citizen Service Act is intended to amend these laws.

[28]   In *Boy Scouts v. Dale*, 530 U.S. 640 (2000), the Supreme Court of the United States held that the Boy Scouts, despite access to public facilities, is a private organization and may indeed "discriminate" in choosing volunteer scout leaders that agree to the Scouts' mission statement.

on volunteer manpower, and many ask volunteers as well as paid staff to agree to a statement of faith.[29]

These provisions go against President Bush's recent executive order protecting faith-based organizations. They also conflict with regulatory language proposed by a number of federal agencies to encourage faith-based organizations' participation with social service programs and undermine efforts to reduce barriers to such participation. Allowing this language to stand in national service laws would set a disturbing precedent for other programs.[30] Any new citizen-service legislation should remove these barriers in their entirety and re-establish full legal protections for faith-based groups involved in community service.

From National Service to Citizen Serive

More fundamental changes are required, however, to transform today's national service into a true citizen service. Reforms should be implemented in the three major activities coordinated by the Corporation for National and Community Service (CNCS).

AmeriCorps

AmeriCorps was created in 1993 as a major initiative of the Clinton Administration. Today, over 50,000 individuals aged 17 and older participate in various AmeriCorps programs for 20 to 40 hours a week.[31] Most participants are selected and serve with local and national non-profit organizations, as well as smaller community organizations, in areas such as education, public safety, housing, health and nutrition, disaster relief, and environmental needs.[32]

During the Clinton Administration, AmeriCorps was essentially nothing more than a federal jobs program. The current argument on behalf of AmeriCorpsis that it is a managerial program needed to provide the infrastructure necessary to recruit other volunteers. An emphasis on the potential fruits of the program, however, does not change the basic fact that individuals are paid by the federal treasury to "volunteer" for government-approved service programs.[33]

---

[29] See, for example, "Churches, Charity and Children: How Religious Organizations Are Reaching America's At-Risk Kids," by Joseph Loconte and Lia Fantuzzo (Philadelphia: Center for Research on Religion and Urban Civil Society, 2002).

[30] Representative Barney Frank (D–MA), working with the Human Rights Campaign and the Lambda Legal Defense Fund, lobbied to add language similar to that in the national service laws to the faith-based initiative in the Senate last year. Mary Leonard, "Some Target Bias in Faith Initiative Bill," *The Boston Globe*, September 25, 2002, p. A10.

[31] A little over half of AmeriCorps participants are full-time, most are white, and 75 percent are under the age of 30. Ann Lor-deman and Alice Butler, "Community Service: A Description of AmeriCorps, Foster Grandparents, and Other Federally Funded Programs," Congressional Research Service, updated March 18, 2002.

[32] About three-quarters of AmeriCorps grant funds goes to state service commissions, which then make grants to local groups and state agencies. Most of the remainder is distributed directly by the Corporation for National and Community Service to support various service activities and national programs through a competitive grant process. In fiscal year (FY) 2002. Congress spent $257 million to support the AmeriCorps program. In 2003, the Administration asked Congress to increase the size of the program from 50,000 to 75,000 participants and increase funding for the program to $315 million, but the final budget for 2003 appropriated $275 million for the program at its current participant level. For FY 2004, the Administration has requested $364 million, as well as an additional $75 million to support education grants in the National Service Trust.

[33] For an earlier analysis, see Matthew Spalding and Krista Kafer, "AmeriCorps: Still a Bad Idea for Citizen Service," Heritage Foundation *Backgrounde*r No. 1564, June 28, 2002.

For a full term of service (1,700 hours over 10 to 12 months), AmeriCorps participants currently receive a stipend of at least $9,600 and an educational grant of $4,725. This combined income amounts to $8.43 per hour of service, which is 163 percent of the current minimum wage, and adds up to a compensation package of $14,325. This is approximately the poverty level for a two-parent family with one child[34] and is only slightly less than the annual basic pay and food allowance of an entry-grade recruit in the United States armed forces.[35]

According to the U.S. Department of Labor, the amount paid to an AmeriCorps participant in 2001 exceeded the average hourly wages of maids and housekeepers, farm workers and laborers, child-care workers and personal and home-care aides, and the nearly 10 million individuals who work in food-preparation and serving-related occupations. AmeriCorps participants also made more per hour than the majority of cashiers, retail salespersons, and everyone in personal care and service occupations.[36]

In addition, full-time AmeriCorps participants are eligible for health-care benefits (which averaged $766 but ranged as high as $2,500 per 37 eligible participant in 2002) and, as necessary, child-care benefits (which averaged $3,785 per eligible participant in 2002).[37]

Recommendations for AmeriCorps Reform

- **End AmeriCorps as a jobs program.** Policymakers should eliminate the stipends and benefits for AmeriCorps participants, thus ending the program as an employment program and reorganizing it as a true volunteer service initiative. A smaller AmeriCorps organization could become a catalyst for volunteerism by promoting and removing barriers to volunteerism, identifying needed resources and distributing important information about volunteerism, giving out service awards, and providing a clearinghouse to identify and bring volunteers together with service opportunities.[38]

- **Keep an education voucher.** Policymakers could allow AmeriCorps to continue to award modest educational grants, not as a financial incentive or an in-kind payment for volunteering, but as a nominal award for service completed. Indeed, there is

---

[34] U.S. Bureau of the Census, "Poverty Thresholds for 2002 by Size of Family and Number of Related Children Under 18 Years," updated February 3, 2003, at *http:/www.census.gov/hhes/poverty/threshold/thresh02.htm!* (February 20, 2003).

[35] An 18-year-old, single, high-school graduate, Grade E-1 recruit in the continental United States makes a basic annual pay of $13,809.60 and receives food worth $2,913.72. "Regular Military Compensation Calculator," Office oi the Secretary of Defense, at *http://militarypay.dtic.mil/militarypay/cgi-bin/rmc.pl* (February 20, 2003).

[36] U.S. Department of Labor, Bureau of Labor Statistics, "Occupational Employment Statistics," at *http://www.bls.gov/oes/2001* (February 20, 2003).

[37] "Memo on Healthcare and Childcare for Program Year 2002," prepared by the Congressional Research Service, March 11, 2003.

[38] The Administration has recently taken an important step in this direction by announcing the creation of a Presidents Council on Service and Civic Participation modeled on the President's Council on Physical Fitness and Sports.

already a separate account for Ameri-Corps education grants called the National Service Trust.[39] At current funding levels, eliminating the financial stipend and paid benefits still leaves participants with a considerable educational voucher of $4,725—nearly double the amount of the average Pell Grant in 2002.[40] This change would allow Congress to maintain the program at its current participant level while achieving a substantial budget savings or, alternatively, would allow some expansion of the program at current funding levels.

- **Invest in learning**. Rather than have the Corporation for National and Community Service hold the money and collect the interest on AmeriCorps educational grants, as is now the case, policymakers should direct that the education voucher be transferred to an individual Coverdell Education Savings Account or be used as the basis for an individual Thrift Savings Plan (similar to that which is available to federal employees) that would automatically place funds in a bond account or other sale investment. To encourage participation by individuals who have completed their education, participants could be allowed to transfer their education voucher to an education account for a family member. To retain the objective of the service award, Congress should not allow the education voucher to be traded for a smaller cash stipend (as is currently an option in VISTA) or applied to non-educational expenses or programs.

- **Increase part-time participation**. As a way to help lower-income citizens who cannot afford to participate in AmeriCorps full-time, policymakers should consider allowing a longer period of part-time service to count toward qualifying for the full educational award. They might also consider lowering the entry-level age of AmeriCorps participants to include high school students who, for part-time voluntary service, could use the education vouchers to save for college or take college prep courses outside of their schools.

Overall, it would be consistent with the principles of authentic citizen service to discontinue AmeriCorps as paid employment but continue to give participants a modest educational award in the form of a voucher. Such a reform would also have the added benefit of removing most of the rules, regulations, and problems that typically follow government money. Furthermore, by decreasing dependence on large, nationwide organizations, reforming AmeriCorps would dramatically increase the scope of service opportunities and the range of charitable locations where participants could volunteer. Both of these additional benefits would make an educational voucher program much friendlier to faith-based organizations.[41]

---

[39] Awards are made at the end of the term of service in the form of a voucher that must be used within seven years after completion of service; awards are paid directly to qualified post-secondary institutions or lenders in cases where participants have outstanding loan obligations. Awards can be used to repay existing or future qualified education loans, or to pay (or the cost of attending a qualified college or graduate school or an approved school/work program.

[40] The average Pell Grant in 2002 was $2,411, and the maximum was $4,000; 4,812 individuals received awards that year.

[41] In 2001, Senator Rick Santorum (R-PA) introduced the AmeriCorps Reform and Charitable Expansion Act (S. 1352) to voucherize the AmeriCorps program for this reason.

VISTA

President John E Kennedy first envisioned a domestic Peace Corps program in the summer of 1962. His initial proposal was for a limited program that was service-oriented, decentralized in administration; and focused on substantive, short-term projects.[42] It was President Lyndon B. Johnson who incorporated the idea into the Economic Opportunity Act of 1964 and made it part of the Great Society's broad-based "War on Poverty." Along with initiatives such as Head Start, Upward Bound, and Job Corps, the new VISTA[43] program became part of a grand strategy to address "structural poverty" through government intervention and social activism.[44]

In the 1970s, policymakers tried to de-politicize VISTA by ending its focus on community organizing and poverty policy and directing its work toward specific projects to address problems in poor communities. However, during the Carter Administration, VISTA returned to its activist culture—supporting such things as a training school for Tom Haydens Campaign for Economic Democracy a lobbying effort for the American Civil Liberties Union, and the political-activist efforts of ACORN (the Association of Community Organizations for Reform Now)—and its focus on government programs. During the 1980s, the Reagan Administration tried to focus VISTA on youth participation and traditional community service, and particular self-help programs were added in the areas of drug-abuse prevention and public literacy.[45]

Today, VISTA is operated as a subset of AmeriCorps, although it maintains an independent status by focusing on eradicating poverty and helping communities to address problems such as illiteracy, hunger, unemployment, substance abuse, homelessness, and inadequate health care. The agency-still emphasizes community organizing and supports such activities as recruiting and training, fundraising and grant writing, increasing public awareness, creating resource centers, and helping to design new programs. Currently, there are approximately 4,000 AmeriCorps*VISTA participants working in almost 900 programs.[46]

---

[42] William H. Crook and Thomas Ross, *Warriors for the Poor: The Story of VISTA* (New York: William Morrow & Co., 1969), Chapter 2. The initial study on a national service program was written by then-Attorney General Robert E Kennedy.

[43] The new program was called Volunteers in Service to America to give it the romantic acronym of VISTA, according to the House committee report, as in "the concept of a great new vista, free of poverty, which the Economic Opportunity Act seeks for all Americans." Crook and Ross, *Warriors of the Poor*, p. 45.

[44] The theory of structural poverty is that the root causes of poverty are not in barriers to opportunity, but in the inequalities and injustice systemic to capitalism and that the poor are powerless to break this cycle of poverty without government intervention and social activism. For an explanation of the shift from traditional approaches of alleviating poverty to an emphasis on structural poverty, see Charles Murray's classic *Losing Ground: American Social Policy 1950-1980* (New York: HarperCollins, 1984).

[45] By the mid-1980s, as many as one-quarter of VISTA participants focused on increasing literacy rates, most of them as reading tutors. T. Zane Reeves, *The Politics of the Peace Corps and VISTA* (Tuscaloosa: University of Alabama Press, 1988), Chapters 3–6, pp. 43-153.

[46] Participants serve full-time for at least one year (and no more than three) and receive a stipend of $9,300 and either an educational award of $4,725 or an additional stipend of up to $1,200. In addition, participants receive health insurance, training, child-care allowances, liability insurance, eligibility for student loan deferment and travel, and relocation expenses. Most participants are between 18 and 27 years old, 60 percent are white, and nearly 80 percent are women. Lordeman and Butler, "Community Service: A Description of AmeriCorps, Foster Grandparents and Other Federally Funded Programs." The program's budget for 2002 was $85 million; $94.3 million was appropriated FY 2003, and the Bush Administration has requested $95 million for FY 2004.

Recommendations for VISTA Reform

- **Focus VISTA on specific problems**. In keeping with VISTAS programmatic concentration on poverty, reform should focus VISTA on helping to solve the most important poverty-related problems of the day. One of the principal goals of the welfare reform of 1996 was to increase the number of married two-parent families. Research shows that 80 percent of poor single-parent families would escape from poverty if the single parents were married.[47] VISTA could be focused on strengthening families through groups such as Marriage Savers and the training of mentoring couples who could counsel engaged couples about key aspects of marriage. Another possibility is to focus VISTA activity on mentoring in low-income communities. The Bush Administration has proposed an additional $100 million per year to recruit and train mentors for disadvantaged children. If the need for mentors is a leading poverty-related dilemma, policymakers should consider focusing VISTA on efforts that address this need rather than creating or funding a new program. Whatever focus is selected for the agency's service activities, in keeping with renewed interest in government accountability, VISTA programs should be subject to appropriate, rigorous, and regular methods of assessment and measurement.
- **De-federalize VISTA.** Given the anti-poverty focus and longevity of the program, policymakers will probably choose to maintain VISTAs paid status and educational grant combination as an incentive to attract the skills and talents required for its particular work. Nevertheless, VISTA should be changed from a federally operated program (in which the federal government selects and supervises members) to a federally assisted program, similar to AmeriCorps. This would give sponsoring organizations greater control over recruiting and selecting participants and more flexibility in program design and delivery, as is appropriate for the civil society context in which VISTA operates, and would remove the status of VISTA participants as federal employees. It would also eliminate unfair advantages and benefits that accrue to VISTA "volunteers" but not to participants in other domestic service programs as a result of VISTAs unusual status as a federal employment program. (These benefits include worker's compensation, legal liability coverage, non-competitive hiring for federal jobs, and credit for service time toward a pension in the Federal Employees Retirement System.)

Learn & Serve America

Created in 1993, Learn & Serve America provides grants to schools, colleges, and nonprofit organizations to encourage, create, and replicate "service-learning" programs for students of ages five to 17. The Corporation for National and Community Service funds state education agencies, state commissions on national and community service, and nonprofit organiza-

---

[47] Robert Rector and Kirk A. Johnson, Ph.D., "The Effects of Marriage and Maternal Education in Reducing Child Poverty," Heritage Foundation *Center for Data Analysis Report* No. 02-05, August 2, 2002.

tions, which, in turn, select and fund local service-learning programs.[48]

The problem with Learn & Serve America is fundamental and lies in the very concept of service learning that it promotes and funds. Service learning is a particular teaching methodology in which participants engage in "thoughtfully organized service" that "is integrated into and enhances the academic curriculum of the students, or the educational components of the community service program" and provides "structured time for the students or participants to reflect on the service experience."[49]

It is certainly possible to find good projects that are being done in the name of service learning (e.g., a service-learning project that has been initiated to celebrate the Ohio state bicentennial[50]), but the vast majority of service-learning programs promote social policies, many of which are controversial. In 2002, the Corporation for National and Community Service recognized service-learning "Leader Schools" with projects that built an eagle observation site and restored wetlands to teach environmentalism,[51] used tutoring and mentoring projects to teach multiculturalism and racial diversity,[52] and invited the homeless to read their poetry in the classroom as a way to teach about the evolution of homelessness.[53] The Nicholas Senn High School in Chicago used its Learn & Serve grant money to design programs that used food banks as the basis for teaching hunger policy in history class and taught geometry by having students knit scarves and hats for the homeless during math class.[54]

Moreover, while all education is strengthened by real-world experience and service is, in itself, educational, service-learning projects by their very nature push beyond the boundaries of service into the arena of advocacy. Integrated into the curriculum along with teacher-led reflection, most of these programs place less emphasis on an individual's service (and the virtues that may be acquired through such service) and more emphasis on societal problems, social messages, and policy conclusions that can be linked to a particular service experience.

---

48 Seventy-five percent of the funding goes to school-based and community-based grants, and a smaller amount supports a higher-education program. In addition, Learn & Serve supports the National Service-Learning Clearinghouse (for information and assistance) and the National Service-Learning Exchange (a peer network of service-learning practitioners) In Fy 2002, Learn & Serve Americas budget was $43 million. Congress has appropriated the same amount for FY 2003, and the Bush Administration has asked Congress for the same amount in 2004, increasing to $65 million by 2006

49 See Section 101, Definition 23 of the National and Community Service Act of 1990 (Public Law 101-610, 42 U.S.C. 12511).

50 See "The Ohio Bicentennial Service-Learning Schools Project," at *http://www.acs.ohio-state.edu/glenninstitute/obs.htm* (August 20, 2002).

51 Wilkinson Junior High School, Middleburg, Florida, and Langley Middle School, Langley, Washington. See Corporation for National and Community Service, "List of Leader Schools: 2002 Leader Schools," at *www.feaderschools.org/2002profiles/wilkinson.html* (January 30, 2002) and *www.leaderschools.org/2002 profiles langley.html* (January 30, 2002).

52 Elida High School, Elida, Ohio, and Greely High School, Cumberland, Maine. See *ibid., www.leaderschool.org/2002profiles/elida.html* (January 30, 2003) and *www.leaderschools.org/2002profiles/greely.html* (January 30, 2003).

53 Tamanend Middle School, Warrington, Pennsylvania. See *ibid., www.leaderschools.org/2002profiles/tamanend.himl* (July 17, 2002).

54 Nicholas Senn High School, Chicago, Illinois. See *ibid., www.leaderschools.org/2002profiles/nicholas.html* and *http://www.isbe.state.il.us/learnserve/pdf/LSWinterNews03.pdf* (January 30, 2003).

Advocates of service learning speak of advancing "tolerance," "diversity," and "social justice."[55] With roots in the experiential teaching theories of John Dewey and other early education reformers, the larger objective of service learning is not learning or service but engaging individuals in social and political change.

Recommendations for Learn & Serve Reform

- **Discontinue Learn & Serve America.** Congress should end the Learn & Serve America program. If they elect to keep a smaller program that awards grants to encourage and support traditional notions of community service, lawmakers should make it clear that they do not endorse the philosophy of service learning and its strategy of pushing a particular teaching method into the academic curricula of schools and colleges. Learn & Serve should not exclusively or primarily fund service-learning programs or projects that contribute to service-learning programs in states and local school districts. To the extent that it does fund service-learning activities, these programs should "enhance" but should not be "integrated into" academic curricula. At a time when the mam focus of education reform is to improve the basics—reading, writing and arithmetic—policymakers should not be underwriting new pedagogical theories of questionable value.[56]

- **Refocus the program.** If policymakers choose to authorize a program to replace Learn & Serve America, they should make sure that it focuses on appropriate activities. One idea would be to focus on service that supports public safety, emergency response, and civil defense by educating and training students and younger Americans to teach others about the threats of terrorism and ways to defend and protect Americans from potential terrorist attacks. Another possibility would be to create a civic education and service program that would teach about citizenship as the basis of voluntary service. Given that the civic-education aspect of such a program would be of little consequence if it is badly designed (as was the case with previous pilot programs) or lost in an emphasis of service over citizenship, policymakers should consider whether the Corporation for National and Community Service is the right agency to assume this important function.

Administrative Problems

AmeriCorps has been plagued by administrative problems since its creation in 1993. During the Clinton Administration, several independent audits of the program pointed out mismanagement and serious cost overruns, with an actual per-participant cost that was considerably higher than reported.[57] Under the Bush Administration, the program has been run more

---

[55] See, for example, "Every Student a Citizen: Creating the Democratic Self," Report of the Education Commission of the States, Compact for Learning and Citizenship, Denver, Colorado, 2000.

[56] Even a recent sympathetic report notes that the claims of service learning are ahead of the scientific data, which have been short-term, have produced ambiguous results, and have not compared service learning to traditional forms of service See *The Civic Mission of the Schools* (New York: Carnegie Corporation of New York and CIRCLE: The Center for Information & Research on Civic Learning & Engagement, 2003).

[57] See Kenneth R. Weinstein and August Stofferahn, "Time to End the Troubled AmeriCorps," Heritage Foundation *Government Integrity Project Report*, May 22, 1997.

efficiently and has passed several audits, and there is much more accountability in its activities. Nevertheless, serious problems persist.

A Corporation for National and Community Service decision last November to suspend enrolling new members and reassign two managers prompted investigations by the CNCS Inspector General and the U.S. General Accounting Office.[58] In 2000 and 2001, the CNCS surpassed its enrollment target and, as determined by the Office of Management and Budget, improperly used interest on educational funds to pay for additional participant stipends, causing a $64 million shortfall in its $100 million educational trust fund for 2003.[59]

Recommendations for Administrative Reform

- **Control Spending**. As the lawmaking and appropriating branch of government, Congress has a responsibility to investigate the use of federal funds at the Corporation for National and Community Service and consider the possibility of any misconduct or wrongdoing. Until these issues are addressed and the problems are corrected, policymakers should maintain a cap on participation and neither expand existing programs nor create new national service programs. Nor should Congress provide additional funds to cover program misallocations. As a budgetary matter, spending on citizen service should not exceed, and if possible should be less than, that provided by the fiscal year (FY) 2003 budget.[60]

- **Minimize the level of bureaucracy**. In general, Congress should act to organize and minimize an increasingly complicated and confusing national service bureaucracy; consolidate duplicative programs wherever possible (e.g., the National Civilian Community Corps, which emphasizes homeland security and disaster relief, and the new Citizen Corps, which focuses on homeland security efforts in local communities); streamline programs as much as possible (e.g., consolidating various state offices to better leverage resources); and exercise greater legislative oversight over the reformed programs.[61]

- **Treat citizen service programs as a short-term stimulus**. The aftermath of September 11 has presented an important moment to encourage Americans to help their fellow citizens by participating in voluntary service programs. While there is a strong case for government involvement at this time, policymakers should regard the governments role in promoting citizen

---

[58] "AmeriCorps Freeze Draws Two Investigations," *The Washington Post*, December 14, 2002, p. A4. At its Web site, the CNCS explains that although "it appeared to those preparing the budget that the funds on hand were adequate to support the requested AmeriCorps members," enrollments were suspended because it "did not have in place adequate procedures for tracking enrollments and estimating their [cost] impact." See "Background on the AmeriCorps Enrollment Pause," at *http://www.amencorps.org/enrollmentupdateibackg round.html* (February 23, 2003).

[59] The Office of Management and Budget took the accounting move "to protect the integrity of the program" and "to operate programs within the law," according to an OM.B spokesman. "Budget Glitch Shortchanges AmeriCorps," *The Washington Post*, February 27, 2003, p. A25.

[60] For further analysis of the importance of freezing non-defense discretionary spending, see Brian M. Riedl, "Balancing the Budget by 2008 While Cutting Taxes, Funding Defense, and Creating a Prescription Drug Benefit," Heritage Foundation *Backgrounder* No. 1635, March 12, 2003.

[61] One practical problem is that no one committee has authority over all of the many national service programs, which, makes it difficult to legislate wisely and perform good oversight.

service as a short-term stimulus package for revitalizing civil society rather than as a permanent federal program. Congress should limit the number of years that organizations can take AmeriCorps and VISTA participants, and should cap the number of years and amount of funds any one organization can receive through any of the programs authorized by the Citizen Service Act. A reformed Citizen Service Act should reauthorize citizen service programs for no more than five years, and any endorsement should include a sunset clause to emphasize the non-permanent nature of these programs. The citizen service programs of the federal government should go out of existence unless Congress acts to continue the programs within 60 days of a mandated General Accounting Office report evaluating the overall success of the programs according to the principles of citizen service.

CONCLUSION

The ideas of volunteerism, civic engagement, and community service have long been a part of conservative thought, from Edmund Burkes defense of the "little platoons" as the backbone of civil society to Ronald Reagan's Private Sector Initiative. The concept of citizen service has deep roots in the principles and practices of republican self-government envisioned by the American Founding Fathers and described by Alexis de Tocqueville.

From the beginning, citizen service has been at the heart of the "compassionate conservatism" of George W Bush and the domestic policy agenda of the Bush Administration. "I ask you to be citizens," President Bush said in his inaugural address, "citizens, not spectators; citizens, not subjects; responsible citizens, building communities of service and a nation of character." The invitation acquired added meaning after September 11 as Americans throughout the nation displayed a degree of heroism, generosity, unity, and patriotism not seen in recent years.

Now, more than ever, at a time when Americans are volunteering and engaging in service to their country in unprecedented numbers and unprecedented ways, policymakers must reject the model of government-centered national service that undermines the American character and threatens to weaken the private associations that have always been the engine of moral and social reform in America. The better course is to bolster President Bush's noble call to service by creating a true citizen service that is consistent with principles of self-government, is harmonious with a vibrant civil society, and promotes a service agenda based on personal responsibility, independent citizenship, and civic volunteerism—all prerequisites for building what President Bush has called a "new culture of responsibility."

—*Matthew Spalding, Ph.D., is Director of the B. Kenneth Simon Center for American Studies ai The Heritage Foundation.*

Keith Morton

Starfish Hurling and Community Service

Formerly Director of the Feinstein Institute for Public Service, Keith Morton teaches in the Public and Community Service Studies and American Studies departments at Providence College. In this brief but provocative essay, Morton uses a commonly-told story about individuals making a difference in the lives of others to critique the often simplistic and paternalistic attitude that accompanies community service efforts.

Starfish Hurling and Community Service
Keith Morton

One of the most popular stories in community service events is that of the starfish: a (fill in your description, usually young) person is running, hurling starfish deposited on the beach by a storm back into the sea. "What are you doing," asks a (fill in your description, usually old) person, "you can't possibly throw all the starfish back. Your effort makes no difference." "It makes a difference to this one," replies the first person, who continues off down the beach.

The usual conclusions drawn from this hackneyed tale are about the importance of making a difference where you can, one person or problem at a time; about not being put off by skepticism or criticism or cynicism. The story acknowledges the relief that comes when we find a way to relieve suffering. A somewhat deeper reading is that there is merit in jumping into a situation and finding a way to act - the first step in determining what possibilities for action might exist.

But the tale is, ultimately, mis-educative and I wish people would stop using it. First, it is about a problem - starfish cast up by a storm - that is apolitical (unless you stretch for the connection between pollution and el Nino that might have precipitated the storm). There is seldom any hesitancy or moral complexity in responding to a crisis caused by natural disaster. It is the one circumstance in which charity can be an unmitigated good. The story suggests that all problems are similarly simple - that there is a path of action which is right and can avoid the traps of politics, context, or complex and contradictory human relationships.

Second, the story is about helping starfish and not about helping people. It avoids, therefore, the shadow side of service, the sticky problem of who deserves our help. The starfish are passive; they have no voice; they cannot have an opinion about their circumstances, at least not that we can hear. This one is much like that one. Their silence coincides with the fact that they can have done nothing (the story suggests) to deserve their fate. In most of the situations where this story is told, service is about people working with people: people with histories, voices, opinions, judgment, more or less power.

Third, the story avoids the possible complexity of ecology. It might be that the starfish are part of a food chain that is being interrupted as they are thrown back - birds might go hungry at a critical time of year, for example; or it might be that the starfish have been released by a storm from the ocean bottom because they have outgrown their habitat. It is never smart to intervene in an ecosystem without understanding how all of its parts are interrelated.

Fourth, the tale suggests that we should work from emotional response and not our heads, even though the problem is, in this case, knowable. As "overwhelming" as the miles of beach seem, the dilemma of the starfish is finite - this many starfish on this stretch of beach; a bit of advance organizing could result in enough volunteers to return all the starfish to the sea.

Fifth, the story privileges random, individual acts of kindness. It avoids questions of community (and we claim "community service" as our ground after all). It avoids questions of working with others. It polarizes the relationship of the two actors: how different would the story be if the second person joined in with the first?

In short, the story does nothing to teach us about community or service. This in itself is not necessarily a problem; it could be an entertaining tale, and that could be enough. What makes it a problem, however, is that the tale of the starfish pretends to teach us something about community service, even as it misdirects our sympathies, our intellects and our sense of purpose.

Don't go charging out to help. Talk, listen, build relationships, know your self, your environment; work with others where they and the situation itself can teach you how to act with more and more knowledge and effectiveness. Stop hurling starfish.

After Auschwitz

Anger,
as black as a hook,
overtakes me.
Each day,
each Nazi
took, at 8:00 A.M., a baby
and sautéed him for breakfast
in his frying pan.

And death looks on with a casual eye
and picks at the dirt under his
fingernail.

Man is evil,
I say aloud.
Man is a   ower that should be burnt,
I say aloud.
Man
is a bird full of mud,
I say aloud.

And death looks on with a casual eye
and scratches his anus.

Man with his small pink toes,
with his miraculous fingers
is not a temple
but an outhouse,
I say aloud.
Let man never again raise his teacup.
Let man never again write a book.
Let man never again put on his shoe.
Let man never again raise his eyes,
on a soft July night.
Never. Never. Never. Never. Never.
I say these things aloud.

I beg the Lord not to hear.

Anne Sexton

"Untitled"

If all who have begged help
From me in this world,
All the holy innocents,
Broken wives, and cripples,
The imprisoned, the suicidal—
If they had sent me one kopeck
I should have become 'richer
Than all Egypt'...
But they did not send me kopecks,
Instead they shared with me their strength,
And so nothing in the world
Is stronger than I,
And I can bear anything, even this.

1961

Anne Akhmatova

From *You Will Hear Thunder* by Anna Akhmatova, translated by D. M. Thomas. Published by Martin Secker & Warburg. Reprinted by permission of Random House UK Limited.

Part Three

Opportunities for Citizenship and Service

Introduction

Part III asks directly: "How can service be made a part of how we relate to our communities, at the level of the school and university, at the level of neighborhood and nation, and at the global level, where citizenship becomes an abstraction so remote from our daily lives that it has little meaning to most men and women?" An old epigram of the Green Movement says "think globally, act locally," and service certainly seems more suited to school and neighborhood than to nation or globe. Moreover, in issue areas such as education, the environment, and public health, citizens making policy are finding that solutions must be sensitive to differences in local settings and cultures. Yet power and the problems created by interdependence increasingly privilege national and planetary settings, where service is more difficult. To put it simply: participation and service tend to be local, power and policy-making central: how then can we really make a difference?

In the first section of Part III we look at the opportunities for and obstacles to citizenship and civic education on the campus. Benjamin Barber's essays explore the notion of the university as a civic community and suggest that to teach community and democracy, we must first of all see the school as a community. Rutgers University president Edward Bloustein's 1988 commencement address implements this idea, calling for community service as a prescription for the pathologies of prejudice and radical individualism that had created a sense of crisis in the society at large and had manifested themselves as particular problems for the university community. President Clinton's major policy address launching his national service initiatives connects opportunities for youth service at the local level to strategies for political and school reform. John Dewey makes the connection between the schools and a democratic social life. The remaining essays examine the contemporary realities which confront the college campus and the problems they pose for the attempt to create a democratic community within and beyond the school. The excerpt from Michael Moffatt's book dispels the myth of college as a place where serious and thoughtful students worry about society's most pressing issues, and thus challenges students directly. Dinesh D'Souza takes up the question of multiculturalism and curricular reform, contending that the current wave of "political correctness" threatens the foundations of Western democratic communities.

The second section expands the arena of citizenship beyond the school to the political boundaries of neighborhood and nation. We begin this section with Alexis de Tocqueville's historical observation about the importance of intermediary public associations in the growth and vibrancy of American democracy. Jane Addams, coming out of the settlement house and social reform traditions of the late 19th century, and Martin Luther King, coming from the civil rights movement of the mid-20th century, give practical significance to these theoretical arguments for participation in mediating public associations. Malcolm Gladwell examines the importance of relationship building in democratic communities, through the compelling story of Lois Weisberg. Evans and Boyte discuss the relationship between democracy and public spaces where citizens learn how to communicate, and deliberate, and thus acquire the capacity to engage in the messy business of democratic politics. And President Roosevelt's proposal for a Civilian Conservation Corps is excerpted as an example of the opportunities (and the limits?) national initiatives can provide for citizen service.

The final section of Part III (and of the volume) takes the arena of public participation and service one giant step further to the international, planetary level. Benjamin Barber portrays global trends, both disintegrative (tribalism) and integrative (commerce and popular culture), arguing that neither bode well for the future of democracy. When we speak of our civic responsibilities to the planet, "the environment," broadly defined, gets prime mention as an area for responsibility and service. The next two selections thus speak to issues of global responsibility for the environment and the corresponding opportunities for service. Wendell Berry attempts to link the health of the individual body and soul to that of the earth, and challenges us to take responsibility for the planet as a part of our own well-being. Excerpts from the opening statement by Secretary-General Boutros-Ghali at the United Nations 1992 "Earth Summit" in Rio de Janeiro outline a set of obligations both individuals and nation-states owe to the future generations who will inhabit the globe. We close this section and the entire volume with two pieces that provoke reflection on international service: John F. Kennedy's announcement establishing the Peace Corps in 1961, and Thich Nhat Hanh's call for mindfulness in approaching the interdependence of all life on Earth.

Benjamin R. Barber

The Civic Mission of the University

In the following essay, Benjamin Barber argues that two models of education prevail in today's universities: the vocational and the purist, neither of which is satisfactory. For neither recognizes what Barber considers the proper role of the modern university: both to serve and challenge society, and to educate the young for citizenship.

The Civic Mission of the University
Benjamin R. Barber

The modern American university is embroiled in controversy, fueled by deep uncertainty over its pedagogical purposes and its civic role in a "free" society. At times the college establishment seems to know neither what a free society is nor what the educational requisites of freedom might look like. Nonetheless, both their critics have kept administrators and busy, for like zealots (classically defined as people who redouble their efforts when they have forgotten their aims), they have covered their confusion by embellishing their hyperbole. They wring hands and rue the social crises of higher education—apathy, cynicism, careerism, prejudice, selfishness, sexism, opportunism, complacency, and substance abuse—but they hesitate when faced with hard decisions, and prefer to follow rather than challenge the national mood.

Students, reflecting the climate in which they are being educated, are, well, a mess. Minority students at Dartmouth receive anonymous hate letters from their peers, and feminists at Dartmouth are sent notes enclosed in condoms reading, "You disgust me." Students at the University of Utah are voting members of the "Who Cares?" party in student government, embracing their promises to pay their way by "panhandling, and running strip bars, raffles, and prostitution." Youthful hijinks, perhaps: after all, a decade earlier students at Wisconsin had elected the "Pail and Shovel" party into office (its platform: stealing and wasting as much money as possible); and panty raids of one kind or another have been campus staples for a century. Yet one can only feel uneasy when these newer signs of distress are read in conjunction with the wave of racism, overt sexual dis-

By permission of the author. This selection is adapted from Chapter Six of *An Aristocracy of Everyone: The Politics of Education and the Future of America*, Ballantine Books, 1992.

crimination, and homophobia that is sweeping America's campuses; or when they are correlated with national patterns of student political apathy (less than one-fifth of the 18-to-24 year-old population voted in the 1986 congressional election, less than one-half of the 37 percent of the general population that voted); or, more pointedly, when they are seen to induce paralysis among school administrators who have necessarily abjured the infantalizing tactics of "in loco parentis" without, however, having a clue about what might take its place.

The privatization and commercialization of schooling continues apace. At the college level, we still honor teaching in the abstract, but we mainly reward research. To be sure, the two should be congruent, and administrators are fond of saying that only great scholars—superb researchers toiling on the frontiers of their discipline—can be good teachers. But good teachers need to spend at least a few hours a week in the classroom. No matter how gifted, the educator cannot practice the teaching craft in front of a computer, in the laboratory, or at the library.

The reality is, as Jacques Barzun recently pointed out, that research and scholarship have not only become ever more narrow and specialized and thus remote from teaching, but they have taken the very culture which is their putative subject and held it hostage to their reflexive scholastic concerns.... Scholasticism that is academic specialization has in fact turned the study of culture into the study of the study of culture—self-conscious preoccupation with method, technique, and scholarship displacing a broad humanistic concern for culture itself. We no longer simply read books, we study what it means to read books; we do not interpret theories but develop theories of interpretation. We are awash in what W. Jackson Bate of Harvard calls "self-trivialization," pursuing an intellectual quest that takes us farther and farther from students and the world in which they are supposedly being educated to live.

Two Universities

There are two positive models of the university being purveyed today to address the current crisis in education. Mirror images of each other, one calling for a refurbished ivory tower, while the other calls for an uncritical servitude to the larger society's aims and purposes (read whims and fashions). Neither is satisfactory. We may call the first the purist model and the second the vocational model. The first is favored by academic purists and antiquarian humanists and is an embellishment on the ancient Lyceum or the medieval university. In the name of the abstract pursuit of speculative knowledge, it calls for insulating the university from the wider society. Learning for learning's own sake: not for life, not for democracy, not for money; for neither power nor happiness, neither career nor quality of life, but for its own pure sake alone. To the purist, knowledge is radically divorced from time and culture, from power and interest; above all it eschews utility. It aspires to reconstruct Aristotle's Lyceum in downtown Newark—catering, however, to the residents of New Athens rather than of New Haven or Newark.

In the Lyceum, knowledge is mined from the great intellectual veins running through the canyon of the canon. What the canon teaches is that there is a knowledge that is not conditioned by culture and interest, that is not some other century's fashion or some other culture's dominant paradigm, but which—transcending time and space—has earned the status of, if not universal truth, at least universal wisdom. This claim to universality uproots the canon from the contexts that might once have created it.... On the other hand, belief in the independent and objective veracity of the canon does not prevent purists from seeing all other knowledge, all deviations from the canon (such as feminist studies or comparative religion), as the subjective effects of contemporary cultural contexts that are transient, contingent, and subjective; that is to say, the product of liberal pedagogical conspiracies and political interest.

The vocational model abjures tradition no less decisively than the purist model abjures relevance. Indeed, it is wildly alive to the demands of the larger society it believes education must serve. Where the purist rejects even the victories of modernity (equality, social justice, universal education) as so many diseases, the advocate of education as vocational training accepts even the ravages of modernity as so many virtues—or at least as the necessary price of progress. The vocationalist wishes to see the university go prone before modernity's new gods. Service to the market, training for its professions, research in the name of its products are the hallmarks of the new full-service university, which wants nothing so much as to be counted as a peer among the nation's great corporations that serve prosperity and material happiness. Forging dubious alliances with research companies, All-American U. plies corporations for program funding, and stalks the public sector in search of public "needs" it can profitably satisfy. In each of these cases, it asks society to show the way, and it compliantly follows....

If this requires that education take on the aspect of vocational training, and that the university becomes a kindergarten for the corporate society where the young are socialized, bullied, and otherwise blackmailed into usefulness, then the curriculum must be recast in the language of opportunism, careerism, professionalism, and, in a word, commerce. Where the philosopher once said all of life is a preparation for death, the educational careerist now thinks all of life is a preparation for business—or perhaps, more bluntly, that life is business.

A Dialectic of Life and Mind

The first of our two models is aristocratic, humanistic, and poignantly nostalgic—pro-

foundly antimodern: it wishes to educate the few well and perceives in the democratic ideal an insuperable obstacle to excellence.

The vocationalist knows...education and its institutional tools are for better or worse embedded in the real world. His pedagogical tasks are socialization not insulation, integration not isolation. Education must follow where society leads.... Where once the student was taught that the unexamined life was not worth living, he is now taught that the profitably lived life is not worth examining.

Neither purist nor vocationalist recognizes that education is a dialectic of life and mind, of body and spirit, in which the two are inextricably bound together. Neither acknowledges how awkward this makes it for a liberal arts university at once to serve and challenge society, to simultaneously "transmit" fundamental values such as autonomy and free thinking, and create a climate where students are not conditioned by what is transmitted (transmission tends toward indoctrination), and where thinking is truly critical, independent, and subversive (which is what freedom means). For such a university must at once stand apart from society in order to give students room to breathe and grow free from a too insistent reality; and at the same time it must stand within the real world and its limiting conditions in order to prepare students to live real lives in a society that, if they do not mold it freely to their aspirations, will mold them to its conventions. To live eventually as effective, responsible, critical, and autonomous members of communities of discourse and activity, students must be both protected from a too precipitous engagement in them and acclimatized by responsible and critical participation in them.

If the young were born literate there would be no need to teach them literature; if they were born citizens, there would be no need to teach them civic responsibility. But of course educators know that the young are born neither wise, nor literate, nor responsible—nor, despite the great rhetoric to the contrary, are they born free. They are born at best with the potential for wisdom, literacy, and responsibility, with an aptitude for freedom which is, however, matched by an aptitude for security and thus for tyranny.

The Civic Mission

Thomas Jefferson regarded habituated belief as an enemy not only of freedom but of usable conviction, and argued that "every constitution and every law naturally expires at the end of 19 years." Canons, like constitutions, are also for the living, and if they do not expire every 19 years they surely grow tired and stale and heteronomous as time passes. Which is not to say they must be discarded: only that they must be reassessed, relegitimized, and thus reembraced by the current generation. A canon is no use if it is not ours, and it becomes ours only when we reinvent it—an act impossible without active examination, criticism, and subversion. That is why teachers cannot teach the canon properly without subverting it. Their task is not to transmit the canon but to permit their students to reinvent it. Paradoxically, only those "truths" founded on abstract reason which students can make their own, founded on their own reason, are likely to be preserved. Waving the *Republic* at the young will do nothing for restoring literacy or extending the truths of the old.

What I wish to urge is a far more dialectical model of education: one that refuses to prostrate itself, its back to the future, before the ancient gods of the canon, but is equally reluctant to throw itself uncritically, its back to the past, into the future as envisioned by the new gods of the marketplace. This argument suggests not that the university has a civic mission, but that the university is a civic mission, is civility itself, defined as the rules and conventions that permit a community to facilitate conversation and the kinds of discourse upon which all knowledge depends. On this model, learning is a social activity that can take place only within a discursive community bringing together reflection and experience. On this model, knowledge is an evolving, communal construction whose legitimacy rests directly on the character of the social process. On this model, education is everywhere and always an ineluctably communal enterprise.

I mean to suggest much more than that democracy and education are parallel activities; or that civic training and the cultivation of knowledge and judgment possess a parallel structure. I am arguing that they are the same thing: That what distinguishes truth, inasmuch as we can have it at all, from untruth, is not conformity to society's historical traditions or the standards of independent reason or the dictates of some learned canon, but conformity to communicative processes that are genuinely democratic and that occur only in free communities.

Education is above all about setting students free, but there is a great deal of difference between setting them free and leaving them alone.

The conditions of truth and the conditions of democracy are one and the same: as there is freedom, as the community is open and inclusive and the exchange of ideas thorough and spirited, so there is both more democracy and more learning, more freedom and more knowledge (which becomes, here, ideas conditionally agreed upon). And just as no argument will be privileged over other arguments simply because of how or from whom it originates, so no individual will be privileged over other individuals simply because of who he is (white or male or straight) and where he comes from (old money, good Protestant stock, the United States of America).

Once this is understood, we can move beyond the old instrumental arguments on behalf of democracy that rest the case for citizen training inside the university on the prudential need to shore up democracy outside the university. These arguments are powerful—neither education nor research can prosper in an unfree society, and schooling is the only way we are likely to be able to produce citizens who will uphold freedom but they are prudential....

However, my argument here goes well beyond Jefferson's instrumental formula making education "the guarantor of liberty." It suggests that liberty is the guarantor of education; that we not only have to educate every person to make him free, but we have to free every person to make him educable. Educated women and men make good citizens of free communities; but without a free learning community you cannot educate women and men.

The Sense of Community

Walt Whitman, who refused to wall off democracy from life, or life from poetry, or poetry from democracy, mocks those who try to cut the fabric of democracy to the sorry measure of their own tiny imaginations (he must have had the first political scientist in mind!):

Did you too, O friend, suppose democracy was only for elections, for politics, and for a party name? I say democracy is only of use there that it may pass on and come to its flower and fruits in manners, in the highest forms of interaction between men, and their beliefs—in religion, literature, colleges and schools—democracy in all public and private life....

The point where democracy and education intersect is the point we call community. For if democracy is a mode of associated living, then it is also true, Dewey [see selection above] has written, that "in the first place, the school must itself be a community life....

We should comprehend Dewey, for underlying the pathologies of our society and our schools...is a sickness of community: its corruption, its rupturing, its fragmentation, its breakdown: finally, its vanishing and its absence. We can no more learn alone than we can live alone, and if little learning is taking place in American schools and colleges it may be be-

cause there is too much solitude and too little community among the learners (and the teachers too). Schools that were once workshops of intimacy have become as alienating as welfare hotels and as lonely as suburban malls. They lack neither facilities nor resources, neither gifted teachers nor able students, but they are for the most part devoid of any sense of community. And without community, neither the almighty canon nor the almighty dollar can do much to inspire learning or promote freedom.

Common Living

We can address these troubles, both those of the purists and those of the vocationalists, by insisting on the centrality of community to both education and democracy, both convention and freedom. Where in the quest to preserve the canon is a concern for the communal conditions of learning upon which its revival (and thus its preservation) depend? In the rush to serve the society that beckons from beyond the schoolyard, what has happened to the schoolyard's own precious community?

It is not really a matter of making the liberal arts university into a community; for it already is a community, however corrupt and frangible it has become or however little it is seen as such by its privatized inhabitants (students, faculty, and administrators alike). It is a matter of recognizing the communal character of learning, and giving to community the attention and the resources it requires. Learning communities, like all free communities, function only when their members conceive of themselves as empowered to participate fully in the common activities that define the community—in this case, learning and the pursuit of knowledge in the name of common living. Learning entails communication, communication is a function of community. The equation is simple enough: no community, no communication; no communication, no learning; no learning, no education; no education, no citizens; no citizens, no freedom;

no freedom—then no culture, no democracy, no schools, no civilization. Cultures rooted in freedom do not come in fragments and pieces: you get it all, or you get nothing.

A canon is no use if it is not ours, and it becomes ours only when we reinvent it—an act impossible without active examination, criticism, and subversion.

The sociopathologies that currently afflict American universities (renewed racism, substance and alcohol abuse, alienation, suicide) are then anything but contingent features of higher education, mere symptoms that can be isolated and treated one by one like so many cuts on an otherwise healthy body. They speak rather to a disease of the whole, a systemic affliction of education's integral body, which is nothing less than the community of teachers and students in which education subsists.

Does the university have a civic mission? Of course, for it is a civic mission: the cultivation of free community; the creation of a democracy of words (knowledge) and a democracy of deeds (the democratic state). Perhaps it is time to stop complaining about the needs of society and worrying about the fate of the canon and despairing over the inadequacies of students, which after all only mirror our own [and] to start thinking about what it means to say that community is the beginning and the end of education: its indispensable condition, its ultimate object....

What Do Our Forty-Seven-Year-Olds Know?
A Multiple-Choice Test

Benjamin R. Barber

We have heard a great deal about what our 17-year-olds do and don't know. About half don't know much of anything, according to Diane Ravitch and Chester E. Finn Jr., who authored the book "What Do Our Seventeen Year Olds Know?"

We have also been lectured by E.D. Hirsch, Jr. about the decline of "cultural literacy"—the common vocabulary once provided by Homer, Shakespeare, the Bible, etc.—and by Allan Bloom about how post-Nietzschean nihilists and weak-willed college administrators have conspired with know-nothing kids to close the American mind.

Who is to blame for this alarming illiteracy? The culprit fashionable among conservatives like Secretary of Education William J. Bennett is progressive education and all those teachers of the 60's who value skills over substance, participation in learning over authority, creativity over memorization, social justice over high standards and relevance over the timeless classics.

With the complicity of the kids themselves, these dewy-eyed liberals are charged with creating a generation of cultural morons.

But there is ample to suggest that the kids are smart, not stupid—smarter than we give them credit for. They are society-smart rather than school-smart. They are adept readers—but not of books. What they read so acutely are the social signals that emanate from the world in which they have to make a living. Their teachers in this world—the nation's true pedagogues—are television, advertising, movies, politics and the celebrity domains they define.

What our 17-year-olds know is exactly what our 47-year-olds know and, by their example,

---

teach them. Thus the test we need to administer to find out whether the young are good learners is a test of what our 47-year-olds know and are teaching. To ask who wrote "The Iliad" or what the dates of the French Revolution were or the identity of the philosopher David Hume is beside the point. Rather, we should ask: What do our 47-year-olds know? This is a multiple choice-quiz.

1. One third of Yale's 1985 graduating class applied for positions as (a) kindergarten teachers (b) citizen soldiers in the volunteer army (c) doctoral students in philosophy (d) trainees at First Boston Corporation.

2. The signals coming from television and magazine advertising teach you that happiness depends on (a) the car you drive (b) the clothes you wear (c) the income you pull down (d) the way you smell (e) the books you read.

3. The American most likely to have recently read the *Iliad* and written a poem, while sitting alone listening to Palestrina, is (a) a member of Congress (b) an arbitrageur (c) a real estate developer (d) a cosmetic surgeon (e) one of those illiterate students who can't read or write.

4. The Republican administrations of 1980 to 1992 have worked to get government off the backs of the American people through deregulation and privatization in order to (a) unleash business (b) encourage market competition (c) increase productivity (d) foster trickle-down prosperity by helping the rich to get richer (e) give the young plenty of private space in which to paint, sculpt, and read the classics.

5. To be hired by a top corporation, the most important credential you can have is (a) a doctorate of divinity from Harvard (b) an honors degree in classics from Oxford (c) a Yale Younger Poets award (d) a comparative literature degree from the Sorbonne (e) an MBA from just about anywhere.

6. If you were running for president, you would devote many hours of study to (a) the Bible (b) Shakespeare's plays (c) the *Federalist Papers* (d) Plutarch's *Lives of the Romans* (e) the paperback version of *How to Master Television Makeup.*

7. To sell a screenplay to Hollywood, you should (a) adapt a play of Ibsen (b) re-tell the story of Jean Jacques Rousseau's dramatic encounter with David Hume (c) dramatize the *Aeneid*, paying careful attention to its poetic cadences (d) novelize the life story of Donald Trump, paying careful attention to its fiscal and sexual cadences.

8. Familiarity with *Henry IV, Part II* is likely to be of great importance in (a) planning a corporate takeover (b) evaluating budget cuts at the Department of Education (c) initiating a medical liability suit (d) writing an impressive job résumé (e) taking a test on "What Do Our Seventeen-Year-Olds Know."

9. Book publishers are financially rewarded today for publishing (a) cookbooks (b) cat books (c) how-to books (d) popular potboilers (e) critical editions of Immanuel Kant's early writings.

10. Universities are financially rewarded today for (a) supporting bowl-quality football teams (b) forging research relationships with large corporations (c) sustaining professional schools of law, medicine, and business (d) stroking wealthy alumni (e) developing strong philosophy departments.

11. In preparing to interrogate a Supreme Court nominee at a Judiciary Committee hearing, a senator should (a) read Laurence Tribe's *Constitutional Choices* (b) review the candidate's judicial history and job résumé (c) discuss procedure with the committee's chief counsel (d) familiarize himself with pornographic movie titles.

12. In assessing the cultural value and social significance of a new work of art, a museum committee should (a) compare the work in question with the masters (b) read a primer in aesthetics (c) develop independent critical standards (d) enroll in a college philosophy of art seminar (e) find out whether it has been funded by the National Endowment for the Arts.

13. The best way to teach critical thinking in a media-manipulated society is (a) to offer critical courses on the media (b) to increase home reading assignments so that students will be less tempted to watch television all the time (c) to read Aristotle on rhetoric (d) to place a television set in every classroom showing canned news and plenty of ads.

14. To help the young learn that "history is a living thing," Scholastic Inc., a publisher of school magazines and paperbacks aimed at adolescents, recently distributed to 40,000 junior and senior high school classrooms (a) a complimentary video of the award-winning series *The Civil War* (b) free American history textbooks (c) an abridgment of Tocqueville's *Democracy in America* (d) Billy Joel's single "We Didn't Start the Fire."

15. A major California bank that advertised "no previous credit history required" for Visa cards to Berkeley students turned down one group of applicants because (a) their parents had poor credit histories (b) they had never held jobs (c) they had outstanding student loans (d) they were humanities majors.

For extra credit: Name the ten living poets who most influenced your life, and recite a favorite stanza. Well, then, never mind the stanza, just name the poets. Okay, not ten, just five. Two? So, who's your favorite running back?

My sample of forty-seven-year olds scored extremely well on this test—as did the seventeen-year-olds who took it. (In every case the correct answer is the last, or all but the last; I think you will be able to figure out which.) Test results (nobody did the extra credit question) reveal a deep strain of hypocrisy in the lamentations of the educational and cultural critics. They want our kids to know things the country at large doesn't give a hoot about. But the illiteracy of the young is our own, reflected back at us with embarrassing force. We honor ambition, we reward greed, we celebrate materialism, we worship acquisitiveness, we commercialize art, we cherish success, and then we bark at the young about the gentle arts of the spirit. The kids know that if we really valued learning, we would pay teachers what we pay lawyers and stockbrokers; if we valued art, we would not measure it by its capacity to produce profits or to produce intolerance in prudish government funders; if we regarded literature as important, we would remove it from the celebrity sweepstakes and spend a little money on our libraries so adults could read too. If literacy were truly an issue, we would start addressing the one in five American adults who are completely illiterate—and perhaps pay some attention to the additional 34 percent who are functionally illiterate.

Kids just don't care much for hypocrisy. If they are illiterate, their illiteracy is merely ours, acquired by them with a scholarly ardor. They know what we have taught them: There is nothing in Homer, in the Bible, in Shakespeare that will benefit their climb to the top of our competitive society. While the professors argue about whether to teach the ancient history of Athens or the ancient history of Egypt, the politicians run political campaigns based on mindless image mongering and inflammatory, studiedly a historical polemics. While school teachers debate the ethics of caring, the country turns its back on the homeless. And so our students dismiss talk of civilization, whether Eurocentric or Afrocentric, and concentrate on cash-and-carry careers, a tribute not to their ignorance but to their adaptive intelligence. Although we can hardly be proud of ourselves for what we are teaching them, we should at least be proud of them for how well they have learned it.

Edward J. Bloustein

Community Service: A New Requirement for the Educated Person

E dward J. Bloustein, legal theorist and long-time President of Rutgers University, died in office a few years after delivering this inspiring commencement address in May, 1988. In it, Boustein discusses community service as a response to two destructive tendencies rampant on American campuses in the 1980s: bigotry and excessive individualism. His speech paved the way for the Rutgers Civic Education and Community Service Program, a national model for education-based community service.

Community Service
A New Requirement for the Educated Person
Edward J. Bloustein

I hope this 222d commencement of Rutgers, The State University of New Jersey, is as happy an occasion for you as it is for me. It should signify a provocative new beginning for you, another pivotal point in your life. You will now begin to employ the many gifts and talents you developed here toward the goals you choose to pursue. On behalf of all of us at Rutgers, let me congratulate you and your families on your many accomplishments and let me wish you well in your chosen pursuit.

Besides marking a new beginning for graduates, commencement provides us all with the occasion for rededication to some of the principles that enlarge and magnify what is best in each of us and in the human spirit generally. Today I want to talk about two personal and political shibboleths of the 1980s, and ask you whether they make sense for any of us or for our nation.

I must confess to begin with, however, that, of recent years, I and many other college and university presidents have hesitated to express moral convictions because we felt we would be violating the principle of the moral neutrality of the university. This is, indeed, a most important principle and I would not risk abridging it.

But some of us have mistaken teaching for preaching. We certainly should not expound a moral creed; we should not ask that what we say be believed because of the authority of our offices. We abandon our calling, however, if we neglect, as too many of us do, moral teaching. What I mean is that, as university presidents, we must invite thoughtful discussion of moral issues as we invite it of any other substantive issue. We should not exact moral conformity of our students any more than we should of our faculty, but we should express our moral concerns, and ask our students, no less than our faculty, to consider them. That, is what I intend to do now.

I put before you two tendencies of our time that I believe to be fundamentally wrong. They inhibit the satisfaction to be found in our private lives, and they also impair the attainment of our public purposes. Think about them with me.

There is a distinct sense afoot in the nation that the battle against bigotry we began to wage so intensively in the 1960s has now been won. This is partly fed by the general reaction against some of the excesses of the '60s. It expresses as well, however, some discouragement after years of effort that our exertions have not been as fruitful as we would have liked. It also reflects a return to the simplistic notion that the strains associated with the clash of cultures we find ourselves experiencing would be dissolved, and a new strength of common purpose achieved, if only everyone would adopt the ways of the dominant white, male, anglo-Christian society. Finally, I suggest that attention to bigotry has waned because many of our nation's leaders have, in effect, declared that the war against it has been won, and have displaced its position in the national consciousness with other priorities.

The bitter fact is, however, that racism, sexism, homophobia, religious intolerance, fear of and animosity toward "foreigners," and such other forms of provincialism are still very much with us. They still eat at our nation's vitals. The differences among us will not simply go away, and our failure to accommodate judiciously to them mars this nation's ability to achieve the greatness its political philosophy promises; it also impairs this university's capacity to achieve true distinction.

Declaring the war won when it has not been has had grave and unfortunate consequences.

Among other things, it has emboldened the bigots among us, and this and other campuses, as well as other communities throughout the nation, have paid a painful price as a result.

The most compelling reason to accelerate the task of rooting out bigotry is that it unjustly and cruelly encumbers the lives of people and causes them pain. We must act aggressively and affirmatively, not to give those subject to victimization some special advantage, but simply to assure surcease from neglect and deprivation.

There is another reason to do so as well, however, a reason that is frequently neglected. Our failure to redress forms of oppression is not only unjust to those who suffer it, but it also impedes the advantage we might otherwise derive from the richness and strength that the differences among us offer.

Our nation is comprised of a more imposing assemblage of races, cultures, religions, and nationalities than the world has ever known. As a result, we have people-to-people connections with virtually every life experience on the globe, linking us as no political ambassador ever could to all parts and all peoples of the world, from Africa to Europe, and now, ever more so, to Asia and South and Central America. This is surely a capability comparable in its significance for world leadership to productive factories and fertile fields, armed battalions, or nuclear warheads. Unfortunately, it has recently been gravely neglected.

In terms of the life of this university, our faculty and staff, and the men and women we enroll, come from an uncommonly broad range of backgrounds. They offer us as a university a unique strength in advancing the cause of liberal education.

Among other things, liberal education promises to overcome what the philosopher Francis Bacon called the Idols of the Den, the mistaken attachment to beliefs and values for no other reason than that they are our own. The very wide range of differences among us, enables us to appreciate a breadth of knowledge, culture, and experience which takes us beyond the narrow confines of our individual beginnings. What could be more central to our educational mission!

Let me turn next to another contemporary shibboleth, a distortion of a concept central to the nature of our democratic heritage: individualism. Of recent years it has become disturbingly fashionable for people to live as if the human condition were largely the product of personal choice and effort in the free marketplace of life, and as if greed and private wealth were sovereign virtues. The attitude is epitomized in two slang slogans. "I've got mine, Jack," and "I'm doing my own thing" have, unfortunately, found their way into our mores and gained currency as latter-day political articles of faith.

To be sure, human choice and effort are important and they do shape, to a significant degree, the human condition. And, of course, material goods contribute greatly to both the private and the public good.

But the naked pursuit of individual interest and material gain is a hopelessly inadequate source of personal satisfaction. It is also a thorough distortion of the ideal of civic virtue in the democratic state. Moreover, it is a dangerously obtuse response to the global condition in which we find ourselves.

This anemic ethic has flourished on ignorance and isolation. Born of a poverty of cultural imagination, it explains why so many among us are without material want, but are wasted and unfulfilled emotionally and spiritually. Proceeding from a xenophobic sense of self, it causes many of us to simply cut ourselves off from the poor, the dispossessed, and the downtrodden. It is that same form of self-absorption that allows us as a people to confuse those nations which recoil before our power from those which respect and admire our purposes.

All too often, as individuals and as a people, we act out the role of the Lone Ranger, riding the moral prairie alone in our righteousness, aloof from community and allies, at a remove from those who think and live differently than we do. We segregate ourselves in cocoons of homogeneity. Sometimes it takes the form of sequestered housing, sometimes that of seeking out schooling arrangements which isolate our children from the very communities they should come to understand and care for. Sometimes it takes the form of failing to consult valued allies. In some of our colleges and universities, it takes the form of neglect of the systematic study of foreign languages and culture. For individuals, colleges and universities, and for our nation, while there may be smug comfort in such isolation, it portends personal and political failure.

I believe that, as individuals and as a nation, we must substantially increase our effort to learn from and accommodate to those among us with different cultures and life styles. We who are educated must reach out to the uneducated; those of us who have a full measure of the world's wealth must hold out our hands and our hearts to those who lack even a bare portion of it. Giving is no less part of the good life than receiving. This truism is as sound a principle of foreign policy as it is of personal gratification.

Higher education already makes important contributions to teaching the virtues of sharing and caring, but I propose that we do more. I propose that we look at community service as a necessary component of the learning experiences which constitute a liberal education.

I am extremely proud of the several hundred Rutgers students who now work in the Rutgers Community Outreach program—tutoring students in the inner city schools, assisting in hospitals, serving meals to those who cannot serve themselves, acting as tour guides at local museums, and engaging in many other forms of community service. I congratulate the students at Rutgers College who have proposed community service courses that are now being adopted by our faculty. I urge that we consider going one step further by making service to others a requirement of the undergraduate liberal arts degree.

Everyone would agree, I am sure, that such service would contribute greatly to the communities in which our universities live and are nourished. In these terms, student commitment to community service would constitute a partial return to the commonweal of what they received from it.

Such service as part of an undergraduate education would have a much broader significance, however. It would constitute a valued ingredient of liberal education. It would help educate our students to the world of the sick and the aged, the world of the deprived and dispossessed, a world which looms before us and which we can no longer continue to neglect except at our moral and political peril.

This and other American universities must now explore ways to enlarge the liberal component of education by instituting a requirement of civic service. Even if we were to suppose that some portion of the student body might undertake it unwillingly, without compassion, or with disdain for its ethical quality, it would find justification in the expansion of the horizons of feeling and experience it would afford. Would it be very different from requiring our students to read and write in terms some of them will never thereafter have need or appreciation for? Why not an introduction into social and cultural literacy, reflecting our time and place, as well as an introduction into mathematical, aesthetic, or historical analysis?

I hope I have given you some season to believe that the campaign against bigotry deserves once again to be put at the very center of our national agenda, and at the very center of this university's agenda as well. Let our diversity be seen for what it is, a source of our strength, not of our weakness.

But nurturing it requires that we abandon the shallow image of individualism that has recently been in the ascendent, in favor of a more robust one. We must rediscover, as a nation and within this university, the satisfactions of caring for others as we would have them care for us; we must rediscover and teach civic responsibility as a liberalizing art. I believe that, in finding ways to modulate our individualism with altruism, we will thereby foster greater individual gratification, and bring ourselves into greater harmony with an increasingly heterogeneous and tumultuous world.

President William J. Clinton
Address on National Service,
March 1, 1993

William Jefferson Clinton became 42nd President of the United States in January, 1993. One of the major policy proposals in the political platform upon which he ran and was elected in November, 1992, was a new initiative on national service. On March 1, 1993, 32 years to the day after President Kennedy announced the formation of the Peace Corps (see Part III, Section C), President Clinton gave the following address at Rutgers, The State University of New Jersey, announcing the outlines of his national service plan. In it, he laid out the principles of a policy that would encourage more and more young Americans to serve their country through programs operated on the local level by educational institutions and grassroots community organizations. Following the formula of the old GI Bill, President Clinton proposed that young people be given opportunities to further their education in exchange for their participation in national service.

The Clinton Administration's national service initiative began with a "Summer of Service" in June, 1993, whereby 1800 young citizens worked in 16 different local community service corps across the nation for eight weeks, fulfilling a variety of educational, environmental, public health, and public safety needs. The ultimate plan is to involve over 100,000 people per year in national service, with a small federal bureaucracy administering hundreds of community service programs operated by private and public authorities on the state and local level.

Address on National Service, March 1, 1993

President William J. Clinton

I came here to ask all of you to join me in a great national adventure, for in the next few weeks I will ask the United States Congress to join me in creating a new system of voluntary national service—something that I believe in the next few years will change America forever and for the better.

My parents' generation won new dignity working their way out of the great Depression through programs that provided them the opportunity to serve and to survive. Brave men and women in my own generation waged and won peaceful revolutions here at home for civil rights and human rights, and began service around the world in the Peace Corps and here at home in Vista. Now, Americans of every generation face profound challenges in meeting the needs that have been neglected for too long in this country—from city streets plagued by crime and drugs to classrooms where girls and boys must learn the skills they need for tomorrow, to hospital wards where patients need more care. All across America we have problems that demand our common attention.

For those who answer the call and meet these challenges, I propose that our country honor your service with new opportunities for education. National service will be America at its best—building community, offering opportunity, and rewarding responsibility. National service is a challenge for Americans from every background and walk of life, and it values something far more than money. National service is nothing less than the American way to change America.

It is rooted in the concept of community: the simple idea that none of us on our own will ever have as much to cherish about our own lives if we are out here all alone as we will if we work together. That somehow a society really is an organism in which the whole can be greater than the sum of its parts. And every one of us, no matter how many privileges with which we are born, can still be enriched by the contributions of the least of us. And that we will never fulfill our individual capacities until, as Americans, we can all be what God meant for us to be.

If that is so—if that is true, my fellow Americans, and if you believe it, it must therefore follow that each of us has an obligation to serve. For it is perfectly clear that all of us cannot be what we ought to be until those of us who can help others—and that is nearly all of us—are doing something to help others live up to their potential. The concept of community and the idea of service are as old as our history. They began the moment America was literally invented.

Thomas Jefferson wrote in the Declaration of Independence, "With a firm reliance on the protection of Divine Providence, we mutually pledge to each other our lives, our fortune, and our sacred honor." In the midst of the Civil War, President Lincoln signed into law two visionary programs that helped our people come together again and build America up. The Morrill Act helped states create new land grant colleges. This is a land grant university. The university in my home state was the first land grant college west of the Mississippi River.

In these places, young people learn to make American agriculture and industry the best in the world. The legacy of the Morrill Act is not only our great colleges and universities like Rutgers, but the American tradition that merit and not money should give people a chance for a higher education.

Mr. Lincoln also signed the Homestead Act that offered 100 acres of land for families who had the courage to settle the frontier and farm the wilderness. Its legacy is a nation that stretches from coast to coast. Now we must create a new legacy that gives a new generation of Americans the right and the power to explore the frontiers of science and technology and space. The frontiers of the limitations of our knowledge must be pushed back so that we can do what we need to do. And education is the

way to do it, just as surely as it was more than 100 years ago.

Seven decades after the Civil War in the midst of the Great Depression, President Roosevelt created the Civilian Conservation Corps, which gave 2.5 million young people the opportunity to support themselves while working in disaster relief and maintaining forests, beaches, rivers, and parks. Its legacy is not only the restoration of our natural environment, but the restoration of our national spirit. Along with the Works Products Administration—the WPA—the Civilian Conservation Corps symbolized government's effort to provide a nation in depression with the opportunity to work, to build the American community through service. And all over America today, you can see projects—even today in the 1990s—built by your parents or your grandparents with the WPA plaque on it—the CCC plaque on it—the idea that people should be asked to serve and rewarded for doing it.

In the midst of World War II, President Roosevelt proposed the GI Bill of Rights, which offered returning veterans the opportunity for education in respect to their service to our country in the war. Thanks to the GI Bill, which became a living reality in President Truman's time, more than eight million veterans got advanced education. And half a century later, the enduring legacy of the GI Bill is the strongest economy in the world and the broadest, biggest middle class that any nation has ever enjoyed.

For many in my own generation, the summons to citizenship and service came on this day 32 years ago, when President Kennedy created the Peace Corps with Sargent Shriver and Harris Wofford and other dedicated Americans when President Kennedy created the Peace Corps. With Sargent Shriver and Harris, Wofford and other dedicated Americans, he enabled thousands of young men and women to serve on the leading edge of the new frontier, helping people all over the world to become what they ought to be, and bringing them the message by their very lives that America was a great country that stood for good values and human progress.

At its height, the Peace Corps enrolled 16,000 young men and women. Its legacy is not simply goodwill and good works in countries all across the globe, but a profound and lasting change in the way Americans think about their own country and the world.

Shortly after the Peace Corps, Congress, under President Johnson, created the Volunteers in Service to America. Senator Jay Rockefeller, whom I introduced a moment ago, and many thousands of other Americans went to the hills and hollows of poor places, like West Virginia and Arkansas and Mississippi, to lift up Americans through their service.

The lesson of our whole history is that honoring service and rewarding responsibility is the best investment America can make. And I have seen it today. Across this great land, through the Los Angeles Conservation Corps, which took the children who lived in the neighborhoods where the riots occurred and gave them a chance to get out into nature and to clean up their own neighborhoods and to lift themselves and their friends in the effort; in Boston with the City Year program—with all these programs represented here in this room today, the spirit of service is sweeping this country and giving us a chance to put the quilt of America together in a way that makes a strength out of diversity; that lifts us up out of our problems; and that keeps our people looking toward a better and brighter future.

National service recognizes a simple but powerful truth that we make progress not by governmental action alone, but we do best when the people and their government work at the grassroots in genuine partnership. The idea of national service permeates many other aspects of the programs I have sought to bring to America. The economic plan that I announced to Congress, for example, will offer every child the chance for a healthy start through immunization and basic health care and Head Start. But still it depends on parents doing the best they can as parents and children making the most of their opportunities.

The plan can help to rebuild our cities and our small communities through physical investments that will put people to work. But Americans still must work to restore the social fabric that has been torn in too many communities. Unless people know we can work together in our schools and our offices, in our factories, unless they believe we can walk the streets safely together, and unless we do that together, governmental action alone is doomed to fail.

The national service plan I propose will be built on the same principles as the old GI Bill—when people give something of invaluable merit to their country, they ought to be rewarded with the opportunity to further their education. National service will challenge our people to do the work that should and indeed must be done and cannot be done unless the American people voluntarily give themselves up to that work. It will invest in the future of every person who serves.

And as we rekindle the spirit of national service, I know it won't disappoint many of the students here to know that we also have to reform the whole system of student loans. We should begin by making it easier for young people to pay back their student loans and enabling them to hold jobs—enabling them to hold jobs that may accomplish much, but pay little.

Today, when students borrow money for an education, the repayment plan they make is based largely on how much they have to repay, without regard to what the jobs they take themselves pay. It is a powerful incentive, therefore, for young college graduates to do just the reverse of what we might want them to do; to take a job that pays more even if it is less rewarding because that is the job that will make the repayment of the loans possible. It is also, unfortunately, a powerful incentive for some not to make the payments at all, which is unforgivable.

So what we seek to do is to enable the American students to borrow the money they need for college and pay it back as a small percentage of their own income over time. This is especially important after a decade in which the cost of a college education has gone up even more rapidly than the cost of health care. Making a major contribution to one of the more disturbing statistics in America today, which is that the college dropout rate in this country is now 2.5 times the high school dropout rate. We can do better than that through national service and adequate financing.

The present system is unacceptable, not only for students, but for the taxpayers as well. It's complicated and it's expensive. It costs the taxpayers of our country about $4 billion every year to finance the student loan program because of loan defaults and the cost of administering the program. And I believe we can do better.

Beyond reforming this system for financing higher education, the national service program more importantly will create new opportunities for Americans to work off outstanding loans or to build up credits for future education and training opportunities.

We'll ask young people all across this country and some who aren't so young who want to further their college education to serve in our schools as teachers or tutors in reading and mathematics. We'll ask you to help our police forces across the nation, training members for a new police corps that will walk beats and work with neighborhoods and build the kind of communities ties that will prevent crime from happening in the first place so that our police officers won't have to spend all their time chasing criminals.

We'll ask young people to work, to help control pollution and recycle waste, to paint darkened buildings and clean up neighborhoods. To work with senior citizens and combat homelessness and help children in trouble get out of it and build a better life.

And these are just a few of the things that you will be able to, for most of the decisions about what you can do will be made by people like those in this room, people who run the programs represented by all of those wearing these different kinds of tee-shirts. We don't seek a national bureaucracy. I have spoken often about how we need to reinvent the government to make it more efficient and less bureaucratic, to make it more responsive to people at the grassroots level.

And I want national service to do just that. I want it to empower young people and their communities, not to empower yet another government bureaucracy in Washington. This is going to be your program at your level with your people.

And as you well know, that's what's happening all across America today. People are already serving their neighbors in their neighborhoods. Just this morning, I was inspired to see and to speak with students from Rutgers serving their community, from mentoring young people as Big Sisters, to helping older people learn new skills....

I'm impressed by the spirit behind the Rutgers civic education and community service program: the understanding that community service enriches education, that students should not only take the lessons they learn in class out into the community, but bring the lessons they learn in the community back into the classroom....

We need to begin now. We are going to be looking for the kinds of ideas that we ought to be funding. This is Monday. I ask you by Friday—every one of you—to think about what you think you can do and what we should do to be agents of renewal; to talk with your parents, your clergy, your friends, your teachers, to join the effort to renew our community and to rebuild our country; and to write to me about what you are doing. It's time for millions of us to change our country block by block, neighborhood by neighborhood—time to return to our roots an excitement, an idealism, and an energy.

I have to tell you that there are some among us who do not believe that young Americans will answer a call to action, who believe that our people now measure their success merely in the accumulation of material things. They believe this call to service will go unanswered. But I believe they are dead wrong.

And so, especially to the young Americans here, I ask you to prove that those who doubt you are wrong about your generation. And today I ask all of you who are young in spirit— whether you are a 10-year-old in a service program in our schools who reads to still younger children, or a 72-year-old who has become a foster grandparent—I ask you all to believe that you can contribute to your community and your country. And in so doing, you will find the best in yourself.

You will learn the lessons about your life that you might not ever learn any other way. You will learn again that each of us has the spark of potential to accomplish something truly and enduringly unique. You will experience the satisfaction of making a connection in a way with another person that you could do in no other way. You will learn that the joy of mastering a new skill or discovering a new insight is exceeded only by the joy of helping someone else do the same thing. You will know the satisfaction of being valued not for what you own or what you earn or what position you hold, but just because of what you have given to someone else. You will understand in personal ways the wisdom of the words spoken years ago by Martin Luther King who said "Everybody can be great because everybody can serve."

I ask you all, my fellow Americans, to support our proposal for national service and to live a proposal for national service; to learn the meaning of America at its best, and to recreate for others America at its best. We are not just another country. We have always been a special kind of community, linked by a web of rights and responsibilities, and bound together, not by bloodlines, but by beliefs. At an age in time when people all across the world are being literally torn apart by racial hatreds, by ethnic hatreds, by religious divisions, we are a nation with all of our problems, where people can come together across racial and religious lines and hold hands and work together, not just to endure our differences, but to celebrate them. I ask you to make America celebrate that again.

I ask you, in closing, to commit yourselves to this season of service because America needs it. We need every one of you to live up to the fullest of your potential, and we need you to reach those who are not here and who will never hear this talk, and who will never have the future they could otherwise have if not for something that you could do. The great challenge of your generation is to prove that every person here in this great land can live up to the fullest of their God-given capacity. If we do it, the 21st century will be the American century. The American Dream will be kept alive if you will today answer the call to service.

Thank you, and God bless you all.

John Dewey

The Democratic Conception in Education

J ohn Dewey's "The Democratic Conception in Education" (1916) is based on the
same fundamental link between democracy and community life he describes in
the selection you read in Part I of this anthology. In the following piece, Dewey
takes up his understanding of education as a social function, and considers what type
of society will support good educational practices. He establishes two criteria (which
parallel the criteria for a healthy democracy): 1) a recognition of numerous common
interests among the members of society, and 2) an ability to interact with and adapt
to other social groups. Through a look at three different epochs of educational theory,
Dewey applies these criteria both to social groups within a democratic state and to relations between states. He discusses education in terms of individual, social, national,
and humanitarian aims. The proper balance, according to Dewey, sees education as
both encouraging individual capacities and directing those capacities toward the good
of both society and humanity as a whole.

The Democratic Conception in Education
John Dewey

For the most part, save incidentally, we have hitherto been concerned with education as it may exist in any social group. We have now to make explicit the differences in the spirit, material, and method of education as it operates in different types of community life. To say that education is a social function, securing direction and development in the immature through their participation in the life of the group to which they belong, is to say in effect that education will vary with the quality of life which prevails in a group. Particularly is it true that a society which not only changes but which has the ideal of such change as will improve it, will have different standards and methods of education from one which aims simply at the perpetuation of its own customs. To make the general ideas set forth applicable to our own educational practice, it is, therefore, necessary to come to closer quarters with the nature of present social life.

1. The Implications of Human Association. Society is one word, but many things. Men associate together in all kinds of ways and for all kinds of purposes. One man is concerned in a multitude of diverse groups, in which his associates may be quite different. It often seems as if they had nothing in common except that they are modes of associated life. Within every larger social organization there are numerous minor groups: not only political subdivisions, but industrial, scientific, religious, associations. There are political parties with differing aims, social sets, cliques, gangs, corporations, partnerships, groups bound closely together by ties of blood, and so on in endless variety. In many modern states and in some ancient, there is great diversity of populations, of varying languages, religions, moral codes, and traditions. From this standpoint, many a minor political unit, one of our large cities, for example, is a congeries of loosely associated societies, rather

John Dewey, *Democracy and Education* (Macmillan, 1916).

than an inclusive and permeating community of action and thought.

The terms society, community, are thus ambiguous. They have both a eulogistic or normative sense, and a descriptive sense; a meaning *de jure* and a meaning *de facto*. In social philosophy, the former connotation is almost always uppermost. Society is conceived as one by its very nature. The qualities which accompany this unity, praiseworthy community of purpose and welfare, loyalty to public ends, mutuality of sympathy, are emphasized. But when we look at the facts which the term *denotes* instead of confining our attention to its intrinsic *connotation*, we find not unity, but a plurality of societies, good and bad. Men banded together in a criminal conspiracy, business aggregations that prey upon the public while serving it, political machines held together by the interest of plunder, are included. If it is said that such organizations are not societies because they do not meet the ideal requirements of the notion of society, the answer, in part, is that the conception of society is then made so "ideal" as to be of no use, having no reference to facts; and in part, that each of these organizations, no matter how opposed to the interests of other groups, has something of the praiseworthy qualities of "Society" which hold it together. There is honor among thieves, and a band of robbers has a common interest as respects its members. Gangs are marked by fraternal feeling, and narrow cliques by intense loyalty to their own codes. Family life may be marked by exclusiveness, suspicion, and jealousy as to those without, and yet be a model of amity and mutual aid within. Any education given by a group tends to socialize its members, but the quality and value of the socialization depends upon the habits and aims of the group.

Hence, once more, the need of a measure for the worth of any given mode of social life. In seeking this measure, we have to avoid two extremes. We cannot set up, out of our heads, something we regard as an ideal society. We must base our conception upon societies which actually exist, in order to have any assurance that our ideal is a practicable one. But, as we have just seen, the ideal cannot simply repeat the traits which are actually found. The problem is to extract the desirable traits of forms of community life which actually exist, and employ them to criticize undesirable features and suggest improvement. Now in any social group whatever, even in a gang of thieves, we find some interest held in common, and we find a certain amount of interaction and coöperative intercourse with other groups. From these two traits we derive our standard. How numerous and varied are the interests which are consciously shared? How full and free is the interplay with other forms of association? If we apply these considerations to, say, a criminal band, we find that the ties which consciously hold the members together are few in number, reducible almost to a common interest in plunder; and that they are of such a nature as to isolate the group from other groups with respect to give and take of the values of life. Hence, the education such a society gives is partial and distorted. If we take, on the other hand, the kind of family life which illustrates the standard, we find that there are material, intellectual, aesthetic interests in which all participate and that the progress of one member has worth for the experience of other members—it is readily communicable—and that the family is not an isolated whole, but enters intimately into relationships with business groups, with schools, with all the agencies of culture, as well as with other similar groups, and that it plays a due part in the political organization and in return receives support from it. In short, there are many interests consciously communicated and shared; and there are varied and free points of contact with other modes of association....

The isolation and exclusiveness of a gang or clique brings its antisocial spirit into relief. But this same spirit is found wherever one group has interests "of its own" which shut it out from full interaction with other groups, so that its prevailing purpose is the protection of what it has got, instead of reorganization and progress through wider relationships. It marks nations in their isolation from one another; families which seclude their domestic concerns as if they had no connection with a larger life; schools when separated from the interest of home and community; the divisions of rich and poor; learned and unlearned. The essential point is that isolation makes for rigidity and formal institutionalizing of life, for static and selfish ideals within the group. That savage tribes regard aliens and enemies as synonymous is not accidental. It springs from the fact that they have identified their experience with rigid adherence to their past customs. On such a basis it is wholly logical to fear intercourse with others, for such contact might dissolve custom. It would certainly occasion reconstruction. It is a commonplace that an alert and expanding mental life depends upon an enlarging range of contact with the physical environment. But the principle applies even more significantly to the field where we are apt to ignore it—the sphere of social contacts.

Every expansive era in the history of mankind has coincided with the operation of factors which have tended to eliminate distance between peoples and classes previously hemmed off from one another. Even the alleged benefits of war, so far as more than alleged, spring from the fact that conflict of peoples at least enforces intercourse between them and thus accidentally enables them to learn from one another, and thereby to expand their horizons. Travel, economic and commercial tendencies, have at present gone far to break down external barriers; to bring peoples and classes into closer and more perceptible connection with one another. It remains for the most part to secure the intellectual and emotional significance of this physical annihilation of space.

2. The Democratic Ideal. The two elements in our criterion both point to democracy. The first signifies not only more numerous and more varied points of shared common interest, but greater reliance upon the recognition of mutual interests as a factor in social control. The second means not only freer interaction between social groups (once isolated so far as intention could keep up a separation) but change in social habit—its continuous readjustment through meeting the new situations produced by varied intercourse. And these two traits are precisely what characterize the democratically constituted society.

Upon the educational side, we note first that the realization of a form of social life in which interests are mutually interpenetrating, and where progress, or readjustment, is an important consideration, makes a democratic community more interested than other communities have cause to be in deliberate and systematic education. The devotion of democracy to education is a familiar fact. The superficial explanation is that a government resting upon popular suffrage cannot be successful unless those who elect and who obey their governors are educated. Since a democratic society repudiates the principle of external authority, it must find a substitute in voluntary disposition and interest; these can be created only by education. But there is a deeper explanation. A democracy is more than a form of government; it is primarily a mode of associated living, of conjoint communicated experience. The extension in space of the number of individuals who participate in an interest so that each has to refer his own action to that of others, and to consider the action of others to give point and direction to his own, is equivalent to the breaking down of those barriers of class, race, and national territory which kept men from perceiving the full import of their activity. These more numerous and more varied points of contact denote a greater diversity of stimuli to which an individual has to respond; they consequently put a premium on variation in his action. They secure a liberation of powers which remain suppressed as long as the incitations to action are partial, as they must be in a group which in its exclusiveness shuts out many interests.

The widening of the area of shared concerns, and the liberation of a greater diversity of personal capacities which characterize a democracy, are not of course the product of deliberation and conscious effort. On the contrary, they were caused by the development of modes of manufacture and commerce, travel, migration, and intercommunication which flowed from the command of science over natural energy. But after greater individualization on one hand, and a broader community of interest on the other have come into existence, it is a matter of deliberate effort to sustain and extend them. Obviously a society to which stratification into separate classes would be fatal, must see to it that intellectual opportunities are accessible to all on equable and easy terms. A society marked off into classes need be specially attentive only to the education of its ruling elements. A society which is mobile, which is full of channels for the distribution of a change occurring anywhere, must see to it that its members are educated to personal initiative and adaptability. Otherwise, they will be overwhelmed by the changes in which they are caught and whose significance or connections they do not perceive. The result will be a confusion in which a few will appropriate to themselves the results of the blind and externally directed activities of others....

Two results should stand out from a historical survey. The first is that such terms as the individual and the social conceptions of education are quite meaningless taken at large, or apart from their context. Plato had the ideal of an education which should equate individual realization and social coherency and stability. His situation forced his ideal into the notion of a society organized in stratified classes, losing the individual in the class. The eighteenth century educational philosophy was highly individualistic in form, but this form was inspired by a noble and generous social ideal: that of a society organized to include humanity, and providing for the indefinite perfectibility of mankind. The idealistic philosophy of Germany in the early nineteenth century endeavored again to equate the ideals of a free and complete development of cultured personality with social discipline and political subordination. It made the national state an intermediary between the realization of private personality on one side and of humanity on the other. Consequently, it is equally possible to state its animating principle with equal truth either in the classic terms of "harmonious development of all the powers of personality" or in the more recent terminology of "social efficiency." All this re-ënforces the statement which opens this chapter: The conception of education as a social process and function has no definite meaning until we define the kind of society we have in mind.

These considerations pave the way for our second conclusion. One of the fundamental problems of education in and for a democratic society is set by the conflict of a nationalistic and a wider social aim. The earlier cosmopolitan and "humanitarian" conception suffered both from vagueness and from lack of definite organs of execution and agencies of administration. In Europe, in the Continental states particularly, the new idea of the importance of education for human welfare and progress was captured by national interests and harnessed to do a work whose social aim was definitely narrow and exclusive. The social aim of education and its national aim were identified, and the result was a marked obscuring of the meaning of a social aim.

This confusion corresponds to the existing situation of human intercourse. On the one hand, science, commerce, and art transcend national boundaries. They are largely international in quality and method. They involve interdependencies and cooperation among the peoples inhabiting different countries. At the same time, the idea of national sovereignty has never been as accentuated in politics as it is at the present time. Each nation lives in a state of suppressed hostility and incipient war with its neighbors. Each is supposed to be the supreme judge of its own interests, and it is assumed as matter of course that each has interests which are exclusively its own. To question this is to question the very idea of national sovereignty which is assumed to be basic to political practice and political science. This contradiction (for it is nothing less) between the wider sphere of associated and mutually helpful social life and the narrower sphere of exclusive and hence potentially hostile pursuits and purposes, exacts of educational theory a clearer conception of the meaning of "social" as a function and test of education than has yet been attained.

Is it possible for an educational system to be conducted by a national state and yet the full social ends of the educative process not be restricted, constrained, and corrupted? Internally, the question has to face the tendencies, due to present economic conditions, which split society into classes some of which are made merely tools for the higher culture of others. Externally, the question is concerned with the reconciliation of national loyalty, of patriotism, with superior devotion to the things which unite men in common ends, irrespective of national political boundaries. Neither phase of the problem can be worked out by merely negative means. It is not enough to see to it that education is not actively used as an instrument to make easier the exploitation of one class by another. School facilities must be secured of such amplitude and efficiency as will in fact and not simply in name discount the effects of economic inequalities, and secure to all the wards of the nation equality of equipment for their future careers. Accomplishment of this end demands not only adequate administrative provision of school facilities, and such supplementation of family resources as will enable youth to take advantage of them, but also such modification of traditional ideals of culture, traditional subjects of study and traditional methods of teaching and discipline as will retain all the youth under educational influences until they are equipped to be masters of their own economic and social careers. The ideal may seem remote of execution, but the democratic ideal of education is a farcical yet tragic delusion except as the ideal more and more dominates our public system of education.

The same principle has application on the side of the considerations which concern the relations of one nation to another. It is not enough to teach the horrors of war and to avoid everything which would stimulate international jealousy and animosity. The emphasis must be put upon whatever binds people together in coöperative human pursuits and results, apart from geographical limitations. The secondary and provisional character of national sovereignty in respect to the fuller, freer, and more fruitful association and intercourse of all human beings with one another must be instilled as a working disposition of mind. If these applications seem to be remote from a consideration of the philosophy of education, the impression shows that the meaning of the idea of education previously developed has not been adequately grasped. This conclusion is bound up with the very idea of education as a freeing of individual capacity in a progressive growth directed to social aims. Otherwise a democratic criterion of education can only be inconsistently applied.

Summary. Since education is a social process, and there are many kinds of societies, a criterion for educational criticism and construction implies a *particular* social ideal. The two points selected by which to measure the worth of a form of social life are the extent in which the interests of a group are shared by all its members, and the fullness and freedom with which it interacts with other groups. An undesirable society, in other words, is one which internally and externally sets up barriers to free intercourse and communication of experience. A society which makes provision for participation in its good of all its members on equal terms and which secures flexible readjustment of its institutions through interaction of the different forms of associated life is in so far democratic. Such a society must have a type of education which gives individuals a personal interest in social relationships and control, and the habits of mind which secure social changes without introducing disorder.

Three typical historic philosophies of education were considered from this point of view. The Platonic was found to have an ideal formally quite similar to that stated, but which was compromised in its working out by making a class rather than an individual the social unit. The so-called individualism of the eighteenth-century enlightenment was found to involve the notion of a society as broad as humanity, of whose progress the individual was to be the organ. But it lacked any agency for securing the development of its ideal as was evidenced in its falling back upon Nature. The institutional idealistic philosophies of the nineteenth century supplied this lack by making the national state the agency, but in so doing narrowed the conception of the social aim to those who were members of the same political unit, and reintroduced the idea of the subordination of the individual to the institution.

Michael Moffatt

"What College Is Really Like" and "Community?"

M ichael Moffatt is an anthropologist at Rutgers University who spent a semester over two different years living as a "participant observer" in a college dorm, writing about the experience as if her were a visiting anthropologist studying another culture. After careful evaluation and many conversations with the students, he attempted to evaluate the extent that the administration and faculty views of college life, perhaps like the one represented in Barber's essay in this chapter, correspond with student perspectives.

His study, which was published in 1989, concerns such issues as community, individualism, race, sex, and the life of the mind. The conclusions that he reaches mostly contradict what administrators or faculty members want to hear, and they are in some ways both a contradiction to the aims of service-learning courses, and a justification for them. For, on the one hand, he suggests that students are far less likely to learn the kinds of things adults want them to; but on the other hand, he also suggests that there is a great need for innovative forms of education that try to deal with the kinds of attitudes that Moffatt found in his study.

What College Is Really Like
Michael Moffatt

My first, most vivid impression from the dorms was how different college looked from the point of view of the undergraduates. The students' Rutgers was obviously not the same institution the professors and other campus authorities thought they knew. The college was a very complicated place, made more complicated by its inclusion in a bigger and even more confusing university. Very few administrators understood all of it—even its formal organization—let alone how it actually worked. Most campus adults did not even try; they simply did their best to grasp those small parts of the college and the university that they needed to understand. The students did the same. And the undergraduates and the professors—and the janitors and the buildings and grounds men and the campus police and the campus bus drivers and the secretaries and the graduate students and the librarians and the deans and the administrators and the public relations staff and the president—were all in contact with very different bits of institutional Rutgers.

Thus, to highlight only those differences I knew best, the students had no idea of most of what the professors spent their time doing and thinking about: research, publication, and department politics. Student friends in the dorms who knew I was a faculty member were surprised to discover that I had written a book, or even that I had my Ph.D. Two sophomore friends once admitted to me that they had always privately thought that "tenure" meant a faculty member had been around for "ten years." Most students were not sure of the relation between the two most immediate authorities in their lives, the dean of students and the dean of Rutgers College. And very few of them could name any of the higher-level university officials between these two deans at the bottom of the administration and the president of Rutgers University at the top.

Most Rutgers professors, on the other hand, would not have known how to do what the students had to accomplish successfully every semester—how to balance college and major requirements against the time and space demands of Rutgers classrooms, how to get to their classes on time on the overcrowded campus bus system, and how to push their academic needs through a half-efficient, sometimes impolite university bureaucracy. Most faculty members no longer possessed the ability to sit passively through long lectures without ever once getting a chance to open their own mouths. Few faculty members could have named the dean of students at Rutgers College. Most of them had never heard of some of the commoner terms in undergraduate slang in the 1980s. Almost all of them would have been confused and uncomfortable in the average dorm talk session, and none of them would have had any inkling of how to go about locating a good party on the College Avenue Campus on a Thursday night.

The different perspectives of the students and of campus adults were also rooted in generation, of course. Professors and other campus authorities were not in the same position in the typical American middle-class life cycle as college adolescents. College was a profession for most campus adults. It was the way station to a hoped-for profession—not to an academic one, in most cases—for most students. Presumably you had already come of age if you were a campus adult. Usually you were still coming of age if you were a student.

And generational differences, finally, were historical differences. In an effort to empathize with the students, campus authorities sometimes tried to think back to when they were college youths. They almost always got it wrong. Memory was selective, of course. But aside from this, student culture and youth culture have changed every ten or twenty years in two centuries of the history of higher education in

the United States. And the relation of every undergraduate generation to historical and social events in the wider world has always been different. One's own past student experience never serves as an adequate map for the present.

I came of age in college in the early 1960s, for example. I was on the peak of the postwar baby boom wave. Everything was always cresting for my generation. The economy was always growing; our schools were always expanding; our SATs were always going up. I knew I could study whatever I was interested in; I would always get a good job after college. In college my first year at Dartmouth, we still observed some of the old traditions established in the late nineteenth century—hats, hazing, college patriotism, and so on. I was in graduate school during the late sixties. That was the first time I had ever allowed myself to pay attention to noncollegiate youth culture, to rock-and roll. I was also grateful for the onset of the second American sexual revolution in the twentieth century during those years, my early twenties. And, though I was not particularly active politically, I found the late sixties exciting times to be young and on campus. It seemed like something new was always going on. It was difficult to be bored.

My student friends at Rutgers in the late seventies and early eighties, on the other hand, had been on the downside of the same demographic wave from which my own generation had benefited. They had grown up in much more uncertain, cynical-making times than I had, during the Vietnam collapse, Watergate, and the pallid years of Jimmy Carter's America. The economy was tighter. If your college education did not get you into the job market, what would? In high school, almost none of them would have dared to neglect the sort of universal youth culture centering on music that had thoroughly established itself in the sixties. They had also lived in a more extensively sexualized culture than I had. In college, the late sixties were ancient history to them. The occasional campus demonstrations were exciting events, part of college life as they expected to find it in the late seventies and early eighties. But students in the 1980s also expected the ambience of the typical college demonstration to be slightly archaic—to be a culture capsule from the sixties, as it were. And most of them had never heard of the quaint old customs of college life whose last vestiges I had experienced at Dartmouth in the early sixties.

There were continuities as well as changes from generation to generation in undergraduate student culture. Some aspects of the students' college as I discovered them during my dorm research were identical or similar to those from my own undergraduate days; living among the students simply served to remind me of what they were. Other things were brand new, and at first they were often very hard to see. Much of the effort involved in this research was descriptive in the most basic sense of the term: learning to notice what one did not normally notice given one's original assumptions, in this case about the students.

Thus, in my first full year in the dorms, on Erewhon Third in 1978–1979, I was most aware of what was missing from student culture in the late seventies. Student life did not remind me of the late sixties. Nor did it remind me of older, more "traditional," American college life either. After my first ethnographic year among the students, I improved my imagination about the present through historical research into past forms of student culture and western youth culture. And when I returned to the dorms in 1984–1985, I began to perceive things that I had entirely missed—that I had literally not looked at—in the late seventies.

For most faculty members, the purpose of higher education is what goes on in the classroom: learning critical thinking, how to read a text, mathematical and scientific skills, expert appreciation and technique in the arts, and so on. Some educational theorists propose broader, more humanistic goals for a college education, especially for the liberal arts: to produce "more competent, more concerned, more complete hu-

man being[s]" (Boyer 1987:1); to give students a "hope of a higher life…civilization" (Bloom 1987:336). And, almost all college authorities assume, whatever is valuable about college for the undergraduates is or ought to be the result of the deliberate impact, direct or indirect, of college adults such as themselves on the students.

Professors and other campus authorities do know, of course, that the students get up to other things in college. Many of them remember that they themselves got up to other things in college. But, in their present mature opinions, the "other things" that contemporary students are getting up to at the moment are either to be ignored or to be discouraged. Or they are, at best, the trimmings of a higher education. The main course—the essence of college—is its serious, high-minded goals as articulated and understood by its adult leaders.

The Rutgers students I knew in my research agreed that classroom learning was an important part of their college educations. College would not be college, after all, without "academics"—professors, grades, requirements, and a bachelor's degree after four years. Most students also agreed that college should be a broadening experience, that it should make you a better, more open, more liberal, more knowledgeable person. But, in the students' view of things, not all this broadening happened through the formal curriculum. At least half of college was what went on outside the classroom, among the students, with no adults around.

Beyond formal education, college as the students saw it was also about coming of age. It was where you went to break away from home, to learn responsibility and maturity, and to do some growing up. College was about being on your own, about autonomy, about freedom from the authority of adults, however benign their intentions. And last but hardly least, college was about fun, about unique forms of peer-group fun—before, in student conceptions, the grayer actualities of adult life in the real world began to close in on you.

About the middle of the nineteenth century, American undergraduates started calling this side of college — the side that belonged to them, the side that corresponded to late-adolescent development in college the way they wanted to experience it — "college life" (Horowitz 1987: 23–55, Kett 1977: 174–182, Moffatt 1985a). And so they still referred to it in the late twentieth century. American college life was originally a new adolescent culture entirely of the students' own creation, arguably the first of the modern age-graded youth cultures that were to proliferate down to preteens by the late twentieth century. It was a boisterous, pleasure-filled, group-oriented way of life: hazing and rushing, fraternities and football, class loyalty, college loyalty, and all the other "old traditions" celebrated in later alumni reminiscences.

College life had changed almost out of recognition a century later, however. By the 1980s, it was much closer to the private lives of the students. It no longer centered on the older organized extracurriculum. Nor was it an elite culture of youth any longer. Now it was populistically available to almost all students on campus, and it was for "coed" rather than for strictly masculine pleasures. But college life was still very much at the heart of college as the undergraduates thought of it in the late twentieth century. Together with the career credential conferred on them by their bachelor's degree, it was their most important reason for coming to college in the first place, their central pleasure while in it, and what they often remembered most fondly about college after they graduated. Let us look at its contours in more detail, as the students thought of it and experienced it at Rutgers in the late 1970s and mid-1980s.

Work and Play

College life, first of all, involved an understanding among the students about the proper relationship between work and play in college, about the relative value of inside-the-classroom education versus extracurricular fun. A century ago, the evaluation was a simple one. Extracurricular fun and games and the lessons learned in the vigorous student-to-student competitions that "made men" — athletics, class warfare, fraternity rushing — were obviously much more important than anything that happened to you in the classroom, as far as the students were concerned.

College students could not make the same aggressive anti-intellectual judgments in the late twentieth century, however. Most modern Rutgers students, like undergraduates elsewhere in the United States, instinctively knew what historian Helen Lefkowitz Horowitz has pointed out in an important new book on American undergraduate culture. Despite periodic crises of confidence in higher education in the United States (one is occurring as I write, in 1987), American parents have sent higher proportions of their children to college every single decade since 1890, and the trend continues in the 1980s. Why? Because, in the increasingly bureaucratic, impersonal, modern American economy, a college baccalaureate — and a good one with good grades — has become the indispensable initial qualification leading to the choicest occupations and professions via law school, business school, medical school, graduate school, and other types of professional postgraduate education. Once there were several routes to comfortable upper-middle-class status in the United States. And once, college could be a lazy affair. You could drift elegantly through Harvard as a "gentleman C" and still wind up in a prime law firm thanks to your family connections. No longer for other than a tiny portion of the American elite (Horowitz 1987: 4–10).

What was the relation between work and play in contemporary student culture, then, and what were the preferred forms of play? Consider an unsophisticated but evocative image entitled "What College is REALLY Like." It comes from a scrapbook a Rutgers freshman put together privately in 1983 for his own enjoyment and apparently for later reminiscence, one of many montages of words and pictures the student had cut out of magazines and newspapers and arranged into his own designs.

Most of the image is obviously about college fun—sexuality, drinking, and entertainment—and, implicitly, about being on one's own to enjoy such things, away from parental controls. Its exemplars, comedian Bill Murray and rock musician Billy Idol, are not collegiate types as they might have been in the early twentieth century, young men in raccoon coats or football players. They are drawn from the national and international youth culture to which most American college students orient their sense of generation in the late twentieth century, a culture that comes to them through popular music, the movies, TV, and certain mass-market magazines. The image also contains references to more local undergraduate culture at Rutgers. The Santa Claus stands for "Secret Santa," a favorite student festivity in the Rutgers dorms in the early 1980s. "TKE" is the name of the student's fraternity. One of the two references to institutional Rutgers is to its least attractive feature in student opinion, to its bureaucratic inefficiency ("RU Screw"; "Three Wrong Classes!"). The other depicts "Rutgers," together with "'83' Academics," under a mushroom-shaped cloud.

This last image needs interpretation. It did not mean, the student told me a year later, that he had wanted to "blow away" academics during his first year in college. Rather, it depicted what he had feared might happen to his grades when he decided to pledge his fraternity as a freshman. But, he told me proudly, he had kept his "cum" up to a B+. We cannot say, therefore, that the academic side of college was irrelevant to this funloving freshman. But it was obviously not a central part of college in his imagery. It was necessary but peripheral, at least at this point in his young college career.

How typical was this college youth? One way to figure out actual undergraduate priorities was to examine a crucial set of student ac-

tions: how they budgeted their time in college. Both years in the dorms, I asked hundreds of students to fill out simple time reports: "Please tell me, as precisely as possible, what things you have done, and how long each has taken, since this time twenty-four hours ago." Most of the reports were made on weekdays in the middle of the semester. On these reports, 60 to 70 percent of the students suggested that they studied about two hours a day. Another 10 to 15 percent indicated harder academic work, up to six or seven hours a day—usually, but not always, students in the more difficult majors. And the rest, about a quarter of those who filled out the time reports, hardly studied at all on a day-to-day basis, but relied on frenetic cramming before exams.

How did the students spend the rest of their time in college? They did a surprising amount of sleeping, an average of just over eight hours a day. They spent about four hours a day in classes, on buses, or dealing with Rutgers bureaucracy. A quarter of them devoted small amounts of their remaining free time, one or two hours a day, to organized extracurricular activities, mostly to fraternities or sororities, less often to other student groups. One-eighth worked at jobs between one and four hours a day. One-tenth engaged in intramural or personal athletics. And two-fifths mentioned small amounts of TV watching, less than the average for American children or adults.

The students' remaining free time was given over to friendly fun with peers, to the endless verbal banter by which maturing American youths polish their personalities all through adolescence, trying on new roles, discarding old ones, learning the amiable, flexible social skills that constitute American middle-class manners in the late twentieth century. Friendly fun was thus the bread and butter of college life as the undergraduates enjoyed it at Rutgers in the 1980s. It consisted almost entirely of spur-of-the-moment pleasures; with the exception of one type of campus organization (fraternities and sororities—see below), very little of it had to do with the older extracurriculum. Friendly fun included such easy pleasures as hanging out in a dorm lounge or a fraternity or a sorority, gossiping, wrestling and fooling around, going to dinner with friends, having a late-night pizza or a late-night chat, visiting other dorms, going out to a bar, and flirting and more serious erotic activities, usually with members of the opposite sex. And the students managed to find an impressive amount of time for such diversions in college. Across my entire sample, the average time spent on friendly fun on weekdays in the middle of the semester was a little over four hours a day.

On the face of it, then, the students were fooling around about twice as much as they were studying in college. But this is a deceptive conclusion. For from their point of view, college work also included going to classes, and the total of their classroom time plus their study time was about six hours a day. They also almost all worked more and played less around exams or when big papers or other projects were due. It was fairer to say instead that the students acted as if they assumed that academic work and friendly fun were, or ought to be, about equally important activities during one's undergraduate years.

In many ways, they also said that this was the case. Incoming freshmen usually had two goals for their first year in college: to do well in classes and to have fun (or to make friends, or to have a good social life). Older students looked back on college as either an even or a shifting mixture of work and fun. And students in college who were deviating from the ideal balance almost always knew that they were, and sounded defensive about it. Here are two female deviants, in papers written for me in 1986, confessing to the studying styles of a grind and a "blow-it-off," respectively:

The Grind: I am a little too serious about my studies…. I often give up extracurricular activities to stay home and study…. A few of my friends sent me a "personal" in

a recent [student newspaper] which read: "What's more difficult—to get Jane Doe to stop flirting or [name of writer] to stop studying?" This is not to say that I am a "nerd" or some kind of Poindexter. I have a variety of good friends, and I party as much as is feasible…. [But] I am the type of person who *has* to study…. This inner force or drive has been contained in me since childhood.

The Blow-it-off: I am a female freshman, a once level-headed, driven, and, above all, studious girl [who in college] has become a loafer…totally preoccupied with my social life…. I spend the great majority of my day in the [dorm] lounge, resulting in my nickname; "lounge lizzette."…My new, urgent goal is to combine my old, intellectual self (study habits) with my new social self so I can be a happy, well-rounded person.

What was the happy, well-rounded student in the late twentieth century, by contrast? Someone who maintained a healthy balance between academics and college life, obviously. The two halves of college ought to be *complementary* ones in the opinion of modern college students. You came to college for the challenge, for the work, and to do your best in order to qualify for a good career later in life, most students assumed. College life was the play that made the work possible and that made college personally memorable.

Autonomy

Modern college life, like college life in the mid-nineteenth century, was also about autonomy, about experiencing college ones own way, independent of the influence and the intentions of adults. At first in the dorms, however, it was more difficult to figure out where the students were not autonomous than where they were. On initial impressions, they did not really seem to be oppressed or controlled by adults in any part of their lives.

Most of them had led peer-centered existences for years before arriving at college. In their public high schools and in their homes and families, they had become masters at avoiding the close scrutiny of adults, or at manipulating adult authority when they could not avoid it. Incoming freshmen women and men also typically said that their parents had voluntarily given them more freedom—later nighttime curfews, fewer questions about their private behavior—in their last few years at home, in anticipation of their leaving daily parental authority when they did go away to college. Once they arrived at Rutgers, most of them really felt that they were on their own on a daily basis. And, in the dorms, the authority of the deans as mediated through the student preceptors did not exactly weigh heavily on their shoulders.

Looked at more carefully, however, the students actually lived in three different zones of relative autonomy and control in college in the 1980s. They were freest in their private lives. Rutgers, like other American colleges, had officially renounced in loco parentis authority over the personal conduct and moral behavior of its students in the late 1960s. Many of the other reforms that the protesting students of the sixties had tried to make in higher education had long since been rolled back by the late seventies and early eighties. But this fundamental change in college authority had endured for a generation.

It had not been an uncontested change, however. Since the sixties, adult critics had regularly deplored the new arrangements, often imagining that good old American college life had now degenerated into a noisy, dirty, hedonistic world of sex and drugs. And in the mid-1980s, with renewed public concern about teen alcoholism and, more recently, about a possible heterosexual AIDS epidemic, deans of students all over the country were thinking about new ways of intervening more directly in the personal lives of the students once again. At

Rutgers in the late 1980s, however, the basic redefinition of undergraduate autonomy arrived at in the late sixties was still holding. In the dormitories, the authority of the deans stopped at the doors to the students' rooms.

The students were least free, on the other hand, when it came to their formal education at Rutgers. Here, they had to submit in certain ways to adult authority—to professors, who gave them grades, their fundamental institutional pay. They had to sit passively in scheduled classes. They had to learn the material the professors thought was important. They often felt that they had to think like their professors to get a good grade, whether they agreed with them or not. They had to meet "requirements."

However, the students also had a degree of autonomy and of choice even in this least free side of college. College was not mandatory like high school. The undergraduates had chosen to come to college in the first place, knowing that it would be full of academic work. In college, they did not have to get to know their professors on a personal basis; they usually could not get to know them at Rutgers even if they had wanted to. So faculty authorities were not breathing down their necks. General academic requirements at Rutgers in the mid-1980s were exceptionally loose and open-ended ones. Once the students chose majors, they often had a tighter, more demanding set of academic things they had to do. But at least they had chosen those requirements. And, despite the ideal balance of work and play outlined above, there were also many ways to get through college in the 1980s with very little academic work, if that was the way you chose to balance college life against probable academic success during your four years at Rutgers.

Between their private lives, on the one hand, and academics on the other, lay a third, intermediate zone, an area where the authority of the dean of students was still intact after the liberalization of the late 1960s. The students literally walked into this zone in the dorms whenever they left the privacy of their rooms. Their dorm floors were supervised by student preceptors, at the bottom of the chain of deanly command. The dorms as a whole belonged to residence counselors, one link up the chain. Sets of dorms had full-time, adult area coordinators looking after them. Extracurricular organizations and student government were "developed" and "guided" by an associate dean with a staff of seven people, and there was an assistant dean who tried to "work with" the fraternities and sororities. A student guilty of cheating in class or a troublemaker in the dorms who could not be handled at lower levels of the system went through a judicial procedure run by yet another assistant dean. And so on up to the dean of students himself. And behind him stood the university police, wielding physical force.

How did the average student, outside a private room, experience the power of the deans at Rutgers in the 1980s? Most of the time, not at all. When they ruled India, the British used to marvel—and tremble—at having control of a nation of several hundred million peasants with a white ruling caste that numbered only in the thousands. The deans of students at Rutgers in the 1980s had the same fragile sense of their own power, for similar numerical reasons. Ultimately, about seven thousand residential students were held in check by a full-time professional staff that numbered twenty-seven individuals. Like the British in India, the deans had their own loyal natives, their hundred or so preceptors, plus other students whose "personal development" they were "fostering" by coopting them to their purposes. But they never knew just how loyal their natives were. For their part, just as Indian peasants rarely laid eyes on their white rulers, the students hardly ever saw a dean in the flesh outside of orientation and the odd official function. Consequently, most students led most of their college lives at Rutgers without thinking much about the deans at all.

But the students did know that the deans were there. And, as the residents of Hasbrouck Fourth discovered in 1984 when it came to public drinking and Secret Santa, the deans could enforce their will even within the cozy student dorm-floor groups when they really chose to do so. The students usually resented deanly power when it was directly brought to bear on them. When this happened, they typically imagined the deans as far more powerful personages than they actually were—stereotypically, as small-minded, power-hungry, dictatorial autocrats. In the fall of 1984, when the deans were insisting that some of the more run-down fraternities clean up their acts, I listened as three fraternity brothers directly compared the dean of students of Rutgers College to "Dean Wormer," the villainous college authority in that modern-college life classic *Animal House*. In the spring of 1985, as another student on the floor I had been studying confessed to me that for some months she had believed I was a spy for the deans, she added, in self-defense (perhaps revealing a post-Watergate mentality): "But when you think about it, they *could* do anything they wanted to here. I mean, they could have all these rooms wired for sound. They could be listening in on us all the time!"

Private Pleasures and the Extracurriculum

Late-nineteenth-century college life had been a group-oriented way of life. The students had claimed that college life did teach individualism, the "rugged individualism" of the era, the ability to impose one's character and one's will on other people. But it had done so through collective activities, through an extracurriculum of organized groups created and run entirely by the students: college classes, fraternities, glee clubs, campus newspapers, yearbooks, intramural and intercollegiate sports teams, and other student organizations. Not one college authority had had anything to do with these extracurricular student groups for forty or fifty years. Despite the claims of college officials that the professors and good bourgeois families in college towns kept an eye on the private lives of the undergraduates, the students in most American colleges were actually almost entirely on their own outside the classroom before about 1900. Hence the lifelong love of early-twentieth-century alumni for the old extracurriculum. It really had belonged to them (see Moffatt 1985a, 1985b: 38–99).

In the early twentieth-century, however, American social psychologists invented the modern concept of adolescence (Gillis 1974: 133–183; Kett 1977:215–244), and the leaders of American colleges borrowed from the students the notion that college was about adolescent development. They added whole new layers of staff to their burgeoning administrations: deans of students, directors of residence life, directors of student activities, athletic directors and coaches, musical directors, health specialists, psychological counselors, career counselors, and so on. They moved many of the undergraduates into newer college housing, into dormitories on the expanding campuses. The new deans of students proceeded to tame the undergraduates and college life in its original form. They made the extracurricular student their professional specialty. The nineteenth century students' "college life" became the twentieth century deans' "student life" (Moffatt 1985b: 101–169; Horowitz 1987: 118–150). As this occurred, the students progressively lost interest in the old extracurriculum they had created, and they revised their own notions of college life so that it still belonged to them. To do so, they had to move its essential pleasures closer and closer to their private lives—hence the dominance in the 1980s of informal, ad hoc forms of student fun.

Rutgers students in the 1980s gave considerably less energy to organized extracurricular groups than they did to their private pleasures. The Rutgers Student Activities Office was proud that there were 155 duly constituted student groups on the campus in 1987, not counting the fraternities and the sororities. Most undergraduates probably had a formal affiliation with one or two of them. But, according

to student time reports and the estimates of knowledgeable undergraduates, no more than one in ten of the students were really active in any of them. Freshmen often said that they intended to concentrate on their studies and their social life during their first year in college, and then possibly to "go out for something" in later years. In their accounts, an extracurricular involvement sounded like a duty that they felt might he good for them, somewhere between the fun of their private pleasures and the work of academics. Most students managed to avoid this duty entirely.

The students did make distinctions among the organized extracurricular activities in the 1980s, however. The radio station was so focal to the interests of American youth culture that it was a prestigious involvement, even if the deans ultimately oversaw its operations. So, too, was the Concerts Committee of the Program Council, the student committee that selected musical performers on campus. Another respected student organization, however, the campus newspaper, had made itself independent of college oversight. Student government, on the other hand, was a joke in the opinion of most students. The undergraduates voted for its representatives in the tiniest of turnouts. Student leaders must be lackeys of the administration, the students imagined. Even if they were not, they had no chance of accomplishing anything against the weight of deanly bureaucratic power. The only reason to become a student leader was to get to know some dean for reasons of your own, many students assumed.

The undergraduates had also invented intercollegiate athletics in the late nineteenth century. In the Original Football Game, in fact, played between Rutgers and Princeton in 1869, Rutgers undergraduates had legendarily been in on the very creation both of intercollegiate athletics and of American football (see Moffatt 1985b: 30–31, 75–81). In the twentieth century, however, following nationwide trends, the alumni and a growing professional coaching staff had taken sports out of the hands of the students. Rutgers had more recently gone big time in intercollegiate sports. By the 1980s, most students in the dorms did not know any Rutgers varsity athletes personally. (Football players were carefully housed separately from other undergraduates.) Some students enjoyed intramural athletics. Others jogged or worked out. Most of them were as likely to be fans of nearby professional teams as of any of the college teams.

There was one exception to the students' generally casual interest in the organized extra-curriculum in the late twentieth century, however, an exception that proved the rule. Rutgers students in the 1980s were strongly split in their opinions of the fraternities and the sororities. But for those of them who liked them, a quarter to a third of the students, the fraternities and sororities were going strong in the mid-1980s and getting stronger by the year. Why? Because, though the deans had attempted to "work with" the fraternities and sororities as much as with the rest of the extracurriculum, they had not really succeeded in penetrating and controlling them despite seventy years of trying. In their ritual constitutions, the fraternities were intrinsically secret, and the intense peer solidarity created by their initiations could be extended into other aspects of their operations. The members also held their houses in private ownership; the deans did not have the same right to place preceptorlike supervisors inside them as they did in the dorms. And the fraternities often produced loyal alumni who could, as influential adults in the college, counteract deans or other authorities possibly unfriendly to the Greek community.

Thus, in the late twentieth century, the fraternities still gave undergraduates an opportunity for real autonomy in a group setting rather than only in their informal private lives. Such a zone of collective autonomy had not been available elsewhere in student culture at Rutgers or at other American colleges since about 1900. What fraternity and sorority members chose to do with this autonomy, however—unfortunate-ly—was not likely to warm the hearts of many adults who believed in freedom and autonomy for college youths.

Individualism, the Real World, and the Friendly Self

The students' general preference for private pleasures over group involvements was also related to tendencies in the wider culture, to the shape of American individualism in the late twentieth century in particular. Real satisfaction and fulfillment, most middle-class Americans assume in the 1980s, are personal matters. You may choose to commit yourself to some larger social cause, but this is only one of many culturally legitimate choices you can make. There are other acceptable, more private paths to culturally meaningful fulfillment as well. And many of the students implicitly shared with their elders their sense that the American public world, which the students commonly referred to as "the *real* world," was as hopelessly complex, impersonal, and bureaucratized as, at a more local level, institutional Rutgers was. If you were capable and well-educated, you might still carve out a satisfying career in some narrow, chosen part of it, especially in one of the professions. But you rarely assumed that you could affect it or change it in any fundamental way. So if you were sensible, you learned to base your values on more private expectations and satisfactions.

The recent American individualistic self, in other words, is, as many cultural critics have observed, a "privatized" self, an inward, psychological entity of personal beliefs, values, and feelings. Unlike the rugged individualists of a century ago, Americans today do not feel that they can impose their will on the larger society. But the self still remains at the heart of their values, at the center of their felt authenticity. The true self desires or ought to desire autonomy, choice, and equal "natural" relationships with other selves, most Americans assume. And it does so by strictly sealing itself off from other known realities of the real world. As sociologist Robert Bellah and his colleagues have recently written: "We [Americans still] insist...on finding our true selves independent of any cultural or social influence...while [spending] much of our time navigating through immense bureaucratic structures...manipulating and being manipulated by others" (Bellah et al. 1985: 150).

Rutgers undergraduates did not ignore the real world in conceptualizing the self, however. They simply saw it as a different place, requiring a different, more artificial social self. The true self had to disguise itself in the wider world, they believed. It had to wear masks. It had to play roles. It had to manipulate other people. Personal development of the sort that most students expected to accomplish in college was thus a complicated business. A well-socialized current American adult was neither innerdirected nor other-directed; she or he was both. Therefore, you had to come to know, or to construct, your "real" personal identity as you came of age. At the same time, you had to polish the practical skills of masking this same true self in the public world. You had to refine your ability to influence others if you wanted to get ahead in life.

Much of what the students did among themselves in the dorms, especially in the long talk sessions held in Undergraduate Cynical, was related to the less authentic aspects of their social selves: joking, play, and ad hoc performances that taught them how to hustle and how to "operate" when necessary. Other parts of modern American college life, however, especially at more private levels with good friends and sometimes with lovers, had to do with the authentic, real self as the students thought of it in the 1980s.

And friendship as a relationship was about the self in the most fundamental way. Friendship had been the core relationship in undergraduate culture for two centuries. Since the mid-nineteenth century, the intensities of college friendships in particular have been celebrated in American culture; in the mid-1980s, the movie *The Big Chill* was their most recent sentimentalization. With your college friends, middle-class Americans believed, you left childhood behind; you became a young adult. When you graduated from college, you might never have the time or the opportunity for so many real friendships again. I noticed the centrality of friendship from my first days in the Rutgers dorms in the late 1970s—and, occasionally, the students' anticipatory nostalgia for their college friendships while they were still in the midst of them.

Though many incoming students had hometown friends at Rutgers, almost all of them believed that they would not benefit from higher education unless they also made new friends in college. And most of them did so very quickly. After a month at Rutgers, the average freshman already considered half a dozen new college acquaintances to be friends or close friends. Within two months, the average dorm resident named almost one-third of the other sixty residents on her or his dorm floor as friends or as close friends. In one longitudinal sample, freshmen and sophomores indicated that almost half of their five best friends in the world were friends they had made since they had come to college. The percentage of best college friends then rose to about three in five for juniors and seniors. And most seniors believed that they would stay in touch with their best college friends for years to come after graduation.

If anything, friendship was even more central in undergraduate culture in the 1980s than it had been in the past. For it was the only culturally unproblematic tie with another human being that still existed in the late-twentieth-century, given the fundamental assumptions of current American individualism strictly construed. All other social connections—the relationships of work, family, class, race, and ethnicity—were imposed on your true self from without (you did not choose what family you were born into, who you worked with, etc). Even love and sexual lust often chose you rather than you choosing them. (Love and lust can "overwhelm you," according to American folk psychology; see D'Andrade 1987). Your friends, on the other hand, were freely chosen, mutually chosen, egalitarian others whom you trusted with the secrets of your self. A true friend was, definitionally, someone who was close to your true self. Friendship was, in fact, simply the social side of the late twentieth century American individualistic self, which "naturally" desired to "relate" to freely chosen others.

Friendship as the students thought of it actually had its own dilemmas and uncertainties, however. Since it was about the true self, a definitionally inward entity, its ultimate proofs were entirely invisible. No external actions or rituals could constitute it. You and I are true friends if and only if both of us consider the other to be a true friend "in our hearts." And I am never entirely certain about what you really feel in your heart. The students therefore spent endless amounts of time discussing and thinking about the sincerity and authenticity of their own friendships and of those of other people whom they knew well.

Busting—aggressive mockery of one another—was important in the very definition of undergraduate friendship in the 1980s, as well as being an expression of its uncertainties. A friend was someone who knew and accepted your real self. Polite talk was inauthentic behavior appropriate to the social self. Therefore, vulgar talk and mutual mockery were natural ways in which true friends related to one another. Busting was also the way in which the undergraduates tested who their true friends really were. "Only a real friend would let you bust on them; anyone else would get mad," as one student explained it to me in 1984.

Between the two spheres into which the students (like their elders) divided life, the private world of the true self and the real world of the manipulative social self, lay a third behavior and value, perhaps the central mediating value in American daily life in the 1980s. It is one that is so taken-for-granted by most Americans that it is virtually invisible as cultural behavior. And it is virtually undescribed in analyses of contemporary American culture. It is the late-twentieth-century American social value of "friend*li*ness."

In the assumptions of most Americans, the contemporary self is neither self-contained nor exclusive in its affiliations. It is or it should be potentially open to other selves in its most authentic form; if you are a good, normal American human being in the 1980s, you should be ready, under certain unstated circumstances, to extend friendship to any other human being regardless of the artificial distinctions that divide people in the real world. To be otherwise is to be something other than a properly egalitarian American; it is to be "snobbish"; it is to "think you are better than other people." Americans know perfectly well that they cannot actually be friends with everyone, but in many daily contexts most of them still feel obliged to act as if they might be, to act friend*ly*. To act friendly is to give regular abbreviated performances of the standard behaviors of real friendship—to look pleased and happy when you meet someone, to put on the all-American friend*ly* smile, to acknowledge the person you are meeting by name (preferably by the first name, shortened version), to make casual body contact, to greet the person with one of the two or three conventional queries about the state of their 'whole self' ("How are you?" "How's it goin'?" "What's new?").

The knowledge that "friendly" is often social etiquette, that it does not always mean that the person who is acting friendly wants or expects to be friends, can be a subtle matter. Foreigners, especially from closely related Western European cultures in which similar behavior is only produced under more genuinely intimate circumstances, have to learn to distinguish American friendliness from real friendship before they can function smoothly in the United States (see Varenne 1986a). Well-raised Americans, on the other hand, usually understand the distinction without thinking about it consciously. They know that the correct response to a friendly How are you? is Fine or Not bad; only with a true friend do you perhaps sit down and talk for half an hour about how you are actually feeling at the moment. They know what five of my sophomore friends from Hasbrouck Fourth knew when, in 1985, I introduced them to the president of Rutgers University, an official so lofty that most Rutgers faculty members had never met him.

The president, in charge of a university comprising thirteen undergraduate colleges and twelve graduate schools at New Brunswick, Newark, and Camden, with a combined total of about forty-five thousand students, chose to act friendly to them for five or ten minutes: (Pointing) "There's the window to my office, over there in that next building. Stop in and visit me some time!" The sophomores knew enough not to believe him. They were impressed that he had had the good manners to act friendly, however. And for several days, back in the dorms, they bragged about their classy encounter to their real friends.

Friendliness was the fundamental code of etiquette among the students in the 1980s, the one courtesy that they expected of each other in daily life. It had its rules. You were not friendly to everyone, but you ought to be friendly to anyone you had met more than once or twice. When the students complained about the impersonality of Rutgers bureaucrats, they often meant that they treated them brusquely instead of in a friendly fashion. And, among groups of students who knew one another personally, friendliness could be virtually mandatory. To violate "friendly" in an apparently deliberate way was to arouse some of the strongest sentiments of distrust and dislike in Rutgers student culture.

Community?
Michael Moffatt

Rutgers students enjoyed much of the fun of college life, especially in their freshman and sophomore years, on their coed dorm floors among the sixty other young women and men with whom they happened to share the same level of a college residence hall in any given year. They did not need to form personal groups with these particular youths. The students could have lived anonymously in the dorms, side by side like strangers in a New York apartment house. But their own peer culture, and the deans, encouraged them to link up with everyone else on their floor. And on nearly one hundred dorm floors at Rutgers every year, they almost invariably did so.

The deans characterized these student groups in an officials that was uniquely their own. It emphasized student choice and it obfuscated deanly authority. Dorm floors should be "interdependent communities of caring individuals" who "enhanced their college experiences" together, the deans recommended. The deans "fostered" student "community-building" through the "residence life" infrastructure, through "role-models," "mediation," "program-ming," "non-credit courses," and "hall government." Power did not really exist in this voluntaristic world of deanly fantasy. Collective standards somehow emerged without agents; the deans were simply the custodians of an impersonal democratic process:

> To protect the rights of all students, community standards have been developed. The Residence Life staff strives to uphold these standards. They provide constraints for those students who demonstrate an unwillingness to monitor their own behavior without unduly inhibiting the freedoms of those students who do. With the support of all community members, behavior problems can be kept to a minimum.

The students thought about these same groups in somewhat different ways. They recognized deanly authority and power, to begin with. As my student preceptor on Gate Third in 1977 put it, "There are some mean things I have to do." But if the deans believed *that* they "developed" the undergraduates through residence life—that the shaping of the students' extracurricular values was their expert task—the undergraduates, conversely, saw the dorms at their best as places for real student autonomy. The less a given dorm activity was obviously influenced by the deans, the better the undergraduates in the residence halls tended to enjoy it.

Like the deans, the students also wanted the dorm floors to be amiable places without lots of personal conflict on them. But the term "community," like "residence hall," rarely passed from their lips. Somehow "community" made the dorm floor groups sound much more earnest and intentional than they really were in student experience. A good dorm floor, most students believed, should be a relaxed place full of girls and guys who "got along," who were able to enjoy the informal pleasures of college life in an easy, personal atmosphere of their own making. Rather than being communities, dorm floors, according to student conceptions, should simply be "friendly places."

"Community" was a suspect term for another reason: its established position in the official rhetoric of late-twentieth-century American individualism. For, in addition to being open, friendly individuals, well-socialized American adults in the 1980s are supposed to desire community. Real communities in Western or Third World societies consist of people who have to get along with one another on a daily basis. They usually do not have much choice about the matter. Real communities thus constrain or even define the individual. A village in south India is one example; a department of tenured faculty members in an American university is another. "Community," in its contemporary American ideological sense, on the other hand, is often an individualistic concept masquerading as a sociological one. It usually means something like "people who choose to live together or work together due to common interests." Moreover, it is a word used by leaders, spokespersons, and publicists much more often than it is by ordinary folk. The late-twen-

tieth-century political meaning of "community" tends to be "people who ought to choose to live or work together due to some common interest, as defined by me."

These meanings aside, "community," like "diversity" and the other key phrases of modern American individualism, is almost empty of specific content. It no longer even necessarily has to refer to a face-to-face group with a small, well-defined territorial base. Thus, cartoonist Gary Trudeau can make one of his characters belong to "the homeless community." Thus, Rutgers undergraduates can live in the "greater New York community," the "Rutgers community," the "undergraduate community" and their own "dorm communities."

Communities or not, the friendly groups of students who formed on every dorm floor every year at Rutgers did have certain recurrent sociological characteristics in common, however. Their human ingredients: undergraduates from similar provincial suburban hometowns of central and northern New Jersey. Their cultural contexts: contemporary American popular culture in its late-adolescent version, "college life" and American individualism as sources of shared interests and values among many of the residents. Their ecologies: similar spatial layouts for student sociability. Their micropolitical structures: standard bureaucratized systems of local control under the supervision of the deans (residence counselors, preceptors, and so on). And an ideal: a loosely formulated but very pervasive one concerning collective harmony or friendliness.

No two dorm floors ever worked out alike, however, and neither floor community nor floor friendliness was easily achieved. Most actual dorm floor groups amounted to varying mixes of collective success and failure. The members of every dorm floor acted out, over the course of a year of common residence and personal acquaintanceship, their own collective dramas, which they themselves reviewed and summed up now and again. This chapter is the story of one such annual student collectivity as I was able to know it, on the fourth floor of Hasbrouck Hall, where I did research a day and night a week in the academic year starting in 1984.

Who were the main actors? What was the stage on which they performed? And what collective script did they write, half-deliberately and half-accidentally, in collaboration with one another all year long?

Dinesh D'Souza
Illiberal Education

In the following three selections, Dinesh D'Souza, Catharine R. Stimpson, and Michael M. Morris describe and evaluate the recent attempts of US universities to come to grips with cultural diversity. All three authors begin with the recognition that cultural diversity is not merely a political proposal; diversity has long been a basic fact of American society, and it will become increasingly so in coming years. Diversity, however, raises many questions concerning the proper role of today's university: is it an institution responsible for spreading "cultural literacy"—the skills and knowledge necessary for participation in a democratic society—or for individual self-discovery, or both? And what books, courses, skills, or facts make a person culturally literate? All three writers walk a middle ground between those who would restrict university curriculum to the "great books" of Western culture and those who would discard the texts, institutions, and academics supportive of an imperialist Euro-American tradition. They differ in their approaches to the issue, however, as well as in their proposals for solutions.

In reading these selections, you might consider connections to the different interpretations of difference presented in Part II.A. How do you think our educational institutions can best support citizenship in a multicultural society?

Illiberal Education
Dinesh D'Souza

The Victims' Revolution

For the past decade or so the larger society has not heard much from the American university, and certainly has witnessed little of the truculence and idealistic agitation that seemed to be a campus staple in the late 1960s and early 1970s. The reason for the taciturn university atmosphere of the 1980s, commentators have generally agreed, is that the current generation of young people lacks social consciousness, and cares mainly about careers and making money. Yet in the past few years the American campus has begun to stir again. Americans have been shocked to hear of a proliferation of undergraduate bigotry; at the University of Michigan, for example, a much-publicized series of racist incidents has taken place of late. At one point someone put up posters around campus that said, "A MIND

IS A TERRIBLE THING TO WASTE—ES-PECIALLY ON A NIGGER." At Dartmouth College and elsewhere conservative groups and publications have sparked incidents involving race and ethnicity which range from the sophomoric to the deeply offensive. Ugly episodes on campus have typically been followed by noisy protest and even the seizure of college buildings by activists. Bewildered and horrified, the university leadership has typically adopted a series of measures to detoxify the atmosphere, ranging from pledges to reform the "white male curriculum" to censorship of offensive speech.

Thus, at Michigan, in response to the recent cases of insensitivity or flagrant bigotry, student and faculty activists demanded that all black professors be given immediate tenure, that admissions criteria such as standardized test scores be abolished, and that minority and female students be permitted to determine penalties for students whom they found guilty of making racially and sexually stigmatizing remarks. The university administration took these demands seriously and acquiesced in some of them, agreeing to expand preferential treatment for minority student and faculty applicants, and to adopt censorship regulations outlawing speech offensive to victimized groups such as "persons of color," women, and homosexuals.

It is not always possible in such disputes for a reasonable person, in good conscience, to take any side; there is a good deal of excess all around. The middle ground seems to have disappeared on campus, and whether it can be restored is an open question. But to those who visit virtually any American campus these days, read the student newspaper, talk with some of the undergraduates, and examine the notices for lectures and workshops posted on the bulletin board, it is clear that the heavily publicized racial confrontations on campus are mere symptoms of much deeper changes under way. These are changes in the intellectual and moral infrastructure of the American university, not in its outer trappings. They involve not only race relations or social relations of other kinds but the very substance of the curriculum, the nature of learning, and the meaning of knowledge. Within the tall gates and old buildings a new world view is being consolidated.

This alteration of the principles of liberal education—most notably the very concept of academic standards—is occurring with little public scrutiny. The outcry over the abolition of Western "great books" curricula and over the enforcement of "politically correct" speech on campus has so far been passionately superficial, posing false dichotomies (Should students read Plato or the Koran? Should universities practice censorship or tolerate blatant bigotry?) and missing the underlying principles that are shaping the dramatic changes in universities. Thus, despite the attention currently being lavished on the politics of race and sex on campus, there is, says Donald Kagan, the dean of Yale College, "a troubling ignorance outside the univer-

sity of what is going on." The transformation of American campuses is so sweeping that it is no exaggeration to call it a revolution. Its distinctive insignia can be witnessed on any major campus in America today, and in all aspects of university life.

In the Classroom

Many American universities have diluted or displaced their "core curriculum" in the great works of Western civilization to make room for new course offerings stressing non-Western cultures, African-American studies, and women's studies. There is little argument about the desirability of teaching the greatest works written by members of other cultures, by women, and by minority-group members. Many academic activists go beyond this to insist that texts be selected primarily or exclusively according to the author's race, gender, or sexual preference, and that the Western tradition be exposed in the classroom as hopelessly bigoted and oppressive in every way. "What we have now in universities is a kind of liberal closed-mindedness, a leveling impulse," says the sociologist David Riesman, of Harvard University. "Everybody is supposed to go along with the so-called virtuous positions." Because race and gender issues are so sensitive, several professors who have crossed the boundaries of what may be said in the classroom have found themselves the objects of organized vilification and administrative penalties. These curbs rarely apply to professors who are viewed as the champions of minority interests—they are permitted overtly ideological scholarship, and immunized from criticism even when they make excessive or outlandish claims with racial connotations.

- Early in 1988, in the most widely publicized of several such episodes around the country, students at Stanford University, sharing a conviction that Western culture is implacably hostile to blacks and other ethnic minorities, women, and homosexuals, gathered to demonstrate against the university's undergraduate core curriculum—a curriculum focused heavily on the philosophy, literature, and history of the Western world. The students chanted, "Hey hey, ho ho, Western culture's got to go." Ultimately, Stanford abolished its long-standing Western Culture requirement, replacing it with a program called Cultures, Ideas and Values, which stressed works on race and gender issues by Third World authors, minority-group members, and women. In practice this meant that texts such as Plato's *Republic* and Machiavelli's *Prince* would have to make way for such works as *I, Rigoberta Menchu*, the political odyssey of a Guatemalan peasant woman who discovers feminism and socialism, and Frantz Fanon's *Wretched of the Earth*, a passionate argument for violence against colonial oppression. In addition to Cultures, Ideas and Values, late last year Stanford added another requirement: a course focusing on racial, ethnic, and religious diversity in the United States.

- Core curricula at such places as Columbia University and the University of Chicago are now under attack in the aftermath of the Stanford transformation. At Mount Holyoke College students are required to take a course in Third World culture although there is no Western-culture requirement. At the University of Wisconsin students must enroll in ethnic-studies courses although they need not study Western civilization or even American history. At the University of California at Berkeley the faculty recently adopted an ethnic-course requirement, making this course one of the few that all undergraduates must take. Dartmouth College has a non-Western but no Western prerequisite for graduation. Cleveland State University requires a minimum of two courses dealing with African-Americans and one emphasizing a non-European culture.

- New approaches to teaching now enjoy prominence and acclaim on campus. These include a variety of new forms of criticism—now dominant in humanities departments around the country—that directly undermine the notion that traditional academic criteria have any validity. The result, as this point of view metastasizes, has been a kind of intellectual free fall. Speaking at a conference in Washington in October of 1989, Houston Baker, of the University of Pennsylvania, argued that the American university suffers from a crisis of too much reading and writing. Instead of "valorizing old power relations," universities should listen to the "voices of newly emerging peoples" who are challenging "Western hegemonic arrangements of knowledge." Baker emphasized the oral tradition, extolling the virtues of rap music and holding up as exemplars such groups as Public Enemy and NWA. (NWA stands for "Niggers With Attitude"; the group sings about, among other things, the desirability of killing policemen.) Baker is regarded as one of the most promising black academics in the country.

- In the winter of 1989, at the University of Virginia Law School, Professor Thomas Bergin was conducting his usually sprightly class on property. As students responded to his queries, he shot back rebuttals and gibes, egging them on to more-thoughtful answers. It is Bergin's style to employ colloquial jargon; thus, when one black student stumbled over a question, Bergin said, "Can you dig it, man?" Some students laughed, the class went on, the bell rang.

The next class day Bergin entered the room visibly shaken. "I have never been so lacerated," he said. He read from an anonymous note calling him a "racist" and a "white supremacist" on account of his remark to the black student.

Bergin did not ask who wrote the note. He did not explain his intentions and moved on to the class material. Rather, he gave the class a lengthy recital of his racial résumé: he did *pro bono* work for the civil-rights movement, he was a member of Klanwatch, which monitors hate groups, he was active in recruiting minorities to the university, and so on. Overcome with emotion, Bergin left the classroom.

- When Princeton University, in the early 1980s, debated whether to introduce a women's-studies program, which would engage in "gender scholarship" outside the traditional departments, the Dante scholar Robert Hollander expressed reservations at a faculty meeting. "I did not like the fact that this was a debate not about academic issues but about political sensitivity," Hollander says. "My colleagues were telling me that they didn't think much of the program but would vote for it anyway. I spoke out because I did not want to respond cynically."

Hollander remembers that when he voted against the proposed program for its stated political objectives, however, "I achieved instant notoriety. Even now, years later, my speech is the thing that some people remember most about me." After the motion passed, Hollander recalls, "female faculty members were embracing and kissing on the floor." This did nothing to diminish his concern that the debate was more about feelings than ideas, revealing an ideological rather than an academic agenda.

- The African-American scholar Leonard Jeffries claims in class that whites are biologically inferior to blacks and that the "ultimate culmination" of the white value system is Nazi Germany. Such statements are presented to students in the context of Jeffries's own theories about how the

Ice Ages caused the deformation of white genes, even as black genes were enhanced by "the value system of the sun." Jeffries is the chairman of the black-studies department at City College of New York and the co-author of a controversial outline of a multicultural curriculum proposed for all public schools in New York State.

- In a manual for race, class, and gender education distributed by the American Sociological Association, Becky Thompson, a sociologist, acknowledges the ideological presuppositions of her teaching methodology:

  I begin the course with the basic feminist principle that in a racist, classist and sexist society we have all swallowed oppressive ways of being, whether intentionally or not. Specifically, this means that it is not open to debate whether a white student is racist or a male student is sexist. He/she simply is. Rather, the focus is on the social forces that keep these distortions in place.

- Michael O'Brien, a professor of history at Miami University in Ohio, writes in *The Chronicle of Higher Education*, "Academe has become a kind of parliament, with each member a self-appointed delegate from a particular constituency. Each one struggles to be heard and seeks allies in an effort to attain power." O'Brien observes that "cultural egocentricity has replaced cosmopolitanism as an ethic." The quest for "diversity" thus risks its own paradoxical forms of closure and parochialism.

In Admissions Policy

Virtually all American Universities have changed their admissions rules so that they now seek to fill a sizable portion of their freshman class each year with students from certified minority groups—mainly blacks and Hispanics—who have considerably lower grade-point averages and standardized test scores than many white and Asian-American applicants who are refused admission. Since it is sometimes difficult for minority students admitted on the basis of preferential treatment to compete, most universities also offer an array of programs and incentives, including cash grants, to encourage these students to pass their courses and stay in school. The perquisites of affirmative-action policies have sometimes been extended to other groups, including Native Americans, students from Third World countries, women, Vietnam veterans, the physically disabled, homosexuals, and lesbians.

- At Berkeley black and Hispanic student applicants are up to twenty times as likely to be accepted for admission as Asian-American and white applicants who have the same academic test scores. Ernest Koenigsberg, a professor of business at Berkeley who has served on several admissions committees, asks us to imagine an applicant with a high school grade-point average of 3.5 (out of a possible 4.0) and a Scholastic Aptitude Test score of 1,200 (out of a possible 1,600). "For a black student," Koenigsberg says, "the probability of admission to Berkeley is nearly a hundred percent." However, if the same student is white or Asian-American, he says, "the probability of admission is about five percent." Koenigsberg is satisfied with such outcomes. "I suppose it's unjust, in a way, but all rules help some people and hurt others."
- At Ivy League colleges, which are among the most competitive in the nation, the typical freshman has a grade-point average close to 4.0 and an SAT score of 1,250 to 1,300. However, several of these schools admit black, Hispanic, and Native American students with grade-point averages below 3.0 and SAT aggregates under 1,000.

- A similar pattern can be found at state schools. Over the past five years the University of Virginia has virtually doubled its black freshman enrollment by accepting more than half of all blacks who apply, compared with only a quarter of whites, even though white students generally have much better academic credentials. In 1988, for example, the average white freshman at the university had scored 246 points higher on the SAT than the average black freshman. An admissions dean told *The Washington Post*, "We take more in the groups with weaker credentials and make it harder for those with stronger credentials."
- Michael Harris, a professor of history at Wesleyan University, makes the case for greater preferential treatment for minorities and loosening of academic requirements by arguing that "when you see the word 'qualifications' used, remember this is the new code word for whites."

In Life on Campus

Most Universities now seek to promote pluralism and diversity on campus by setting up and funding separate institutions for minority groups; thus one finds black student unions, black dormitories, black fraternities and sororities, black cultural centers, black dining sections, even black yearbooks. Universities also seek to mollify minority sensitivities by imposing administrative sanctions, ranging from forced apologies to expulsion, for remarks that criticize individuals or policies in terms of racial, gender, or sexual-orientation stereotypes. "Diversity" no longer refers to a range of views on a disputed question but rather entails enlisting in a whole set of ideological causes that are identified as being "for diversity."

- Jerome Pinn, a graduate student, returned to his dormitory at the University of Michigan to discover that his new roommate had pinned up several pictures of nude men. When the young man confirmed that he was gay, Pinn approached the Michigan housing office and said he wanted to move. "They were outraged," Pinn says. "They asked me what was wrong with me—what *my* problem was. Finally they agreed that I could move, but they warned me that if I told anyone the reason, I would face university charges of discrimination on the basis of sexual orientation."

- In 1987 the law school faculty of the State University of New York at Buffalo adopted a resolution that warned students not to make "remarks directed at another's race, sex, religion, national origin, age or sexual preference," including "ethnically derogatory statements, as well as other remarks based on prejudice and group stereotype." Students who violated this rule should not expect protection under the First Amendment, the faculty resolution suggested, because "our intellectual community shares values that go beyond a mere standardized commitment to open and unrestrained debate."

- According to a 1989 story in *The Wall Street Journal*, when the University of Pennsylvania was planning to require all freshmen in campus residences to participate in consciousness-raising sessions dealing with racism, sexism, and heterosexism, one undergraduate on the "diversity education" planning committee sent a note to the administration noting her reservations about the program. She expressed her "deep regard for the individual and my desire to protect the freedoms of all members of society." A university administrator sent her note back, with the word "individual" underlined and the comment, "This is a RED FLAG phrase today, which is considered by many to be RACIST. Arguments that champion the individual over the group ultimately privilege the 'individuals' belonging to the largest or dominant group."

- The *Vassar Spectator*, a student newspaper funded by the Vassar Student Association, called a black undergraduate activist, Anthony Grate, "hypocrite of the month" for espousing anti-Semitic views while publicly denouncing bigotry on campus. Reportedly, in an acrimonious outburst Grate referred to "dirty Jews" and added, "I hate Jews." Grate later apologized for his remarks. Meanwhile, apparently outraged that the newspaper had dared to criticize a black person, the Vassar Student Association attempted to ban its publication; when that failed, the VSA withdrew the paper's funding. The newspaper "unnecessarily jeopardizes an educational community based on mutual understanding," the VSA explained.

A Fervent Acquiescence

The academic and cultural revolution on campus, as suggested by these examples, is conducted in the name of those who suffer from the effects of race and gender discrimination in America, or from the effects of Western colonialism in the Third World. It is a revolution in behalf of minority victims. Its mission is to put an end to bigoted attitudes that permit perceived social injustice to continue, to rectify past and present inequities, and to advance the interests of the previously disenfranchised—unobjectionable aims, to be sure. But because the revolutionaries view xenophobia, racism, sexism, and other prejudices to be endemic and culturally sanctioned, their project seeks a fundamental restructuring of American society. It involves basic changes in the way economic rewards are distributed, and in the way cultural and political power is exercised.

Most university presidents and deans cooperate with the project to transform liberal education in the name of minority victims. This group includes an overwhelming majority of presidents of state universities and of Ivy League schools. Only a handful of college presidents have publicly voiced reservations about the course of the academic revolution.

Many university professors have qualms, because the academic revolution challenges traditional norms of scholarship and debate. But these doubts are dissipating with time, as the composition of the American faculty changes. Older, traditionally liberal professors are retiring and making way for a new generation weaned on the assorted ideologies of the late 1960s, such as the movement for black separatism and the burgeoning causes of feminism and gay rights. Many in this new generation of scholars in the humanities and social sciences have invested their energies in the contemporary incarnation of these "domestic liberation movements." At a recent conference on liberal education a reporter for *The New York Times* found the young academics in agreement that "just about everything…is an expression of race, class or gender."

Showing the frankness typical of many of the newly ascendant activists, the black scholar Henry Louis Gates, Jr., of Duke University, has written, "Ours was the generation that took over buildings in the late sixties and demanded the creation of black and women's studies programs, and now, like the return of the repressed, we have come back to challenge the traditional curriculum." Jay Parini, a professor of English at Middlebury College, writes, "After the Vietnam War, a lot of us didn't just crawl back into our library cubicles; we stepped into academic positions. With the war over, our visibility was lost, and it seemed for a while—to the unobservant—that we had disappeared. Now we have tenure, and the hard work of reshaping the universities has begun in earnest." Annette Kolodny, the dean of humanities at the University of Arizona, developed her ideological

beliefs as a leader of the Berkeley protests of the 1960s and as a worker for Cesar Chavez's United Farm Workers. "I see my scholarship as an extension of my political activism," she told a reporter. According to Kolodny, her academic work is designed to expose "the myths the U.S. has always put forward about itself as an egalitarian nation." The United States, she argues, has "taken this incredibly fertile continent and utterly destroyed it with a kind of ravaging hatred."

These academics are the bellwethers of the victims' revolution. Already their influence is in many places dominant; soon they will displace the old guard. As it is, senior members of the humanities and social science faculties frequently acquiesce in the changes, mildly protesting only when the issue engages their own concerns, such as the preservation of academic standards in their classes. Outside the mainstream of the academy a small but fast growing group called the National Association of Scholars is launching a bold but somewhat quixotic effort to arrest the pace of the revolution, an effort that has yet to show much in the way of results.

Although the revolution first shook the humanities and the social sciences, its reverberations are now being felt in law schools, medical schools, and science departments, which long considered themselves largely exempt from campus agitation. Very little seems to interrupt the revolution or stall it; changes are proposed, accepted, and implemented in broad, continuous strokes. The changes are not always indefensible; seldom, if ever, though, are they subjected to any criticism. Since the motives and the objectives of the activists seem beyond reproach, there never seems to be any need to account for the means that they employ.

There are two main reasons why the changes inside American universities are worthy of close attention. The first is that universities are facing the same questions as the rest of the country. The United States is rapidly becoming a multiracial, multicultural society in a way that it has not been before. Immigration from Asia, Latin America, and the Caribbean has populated the landscape with an array of yellow, brown, and black faces. Mine is one of them—I came to this country from India in 1978. When the United States starts to lose its predominantly white stamp, what impact will that have on its Western cultural traditions? On what terms will the evanescent majority and the emerging minorities relate to each other? How should society cope with the agendas not only of ethnic minorities but also of women and homosexuals? These challenges are currently being faced by the leadership of institutions of higher education. Universities are more than a reflection or mirror of society; they are a leading indicator and catalyst for change.

A second, related reason to examine the changes is to discover what young people are learning these days, and the likely consequences for their future and that of the country. Numerous books, studies, and surveys have documented the alarming scientific and cultural illiteracy of American students. Parents, alumni, and civic leaders are justifiably anxious. Will the new policies in academia improve or damage the prospects for American political and economic competitiveness in the world? Will they enrich or debase the minds and souls of students? Will they enhance or diminish the prospects for harmony among different groups? Will they make the United States an easier or more difficult place to govern wisely?

...Each fall some 13 million students, 2.5 million of them members of minority groups, enroll in American colleges. Most of these students are living away from home for the first time; their apprehension is mixed with excitement and anticipation. At the university they hope to shape themselves as whole human beings, both intellectually and morally. Brimming with idealism, they wish to prepare themselves for full and independent lives in the workplace, at home, and as citizens of a democratic society. In short, what they seek is liberal education.

By the time these students graduate, many colleges and universities will not have met their need for all round development. Instead, by precept and example, they will have taught them that all rules are unjust and all preferences are principled; that justice is simply the will of the stronger party; that standards and values are arbitrary, and the ideal of the educated person is largely a figment of bourgeois white male ideology; that individual rights are a red flag signaling social privilege, and should be subordinated to the claims of group interest; that all knowledge can be reduced to politics and should be pursued not for its own sake but for the political end of power; that convenient myths and well intentioned lies can substitute for truth; that double standards are acceptable as long as they are enforced to the benefit of minority victims; that disputes are best, settled not by rational and civil debate but by accusation, intimidation, and official prosecution; that the university stands for nothing in particular and has no claim to be exempt from outside pressures; and that a multiracial society cannot be based on fair rules that apply to every person but must rather be held together with a forced rationing of power among separatist racial groups. In short, instead of liberal education, what many American students are getting is its diametrical opposite: an education in closed mindedness and intolerance—which is to say, illiberal education.

Ironically, the young blacks, Hispanics, and other certified minority group members in whose name the victims' revolution is being conducted are the ones worst served by the American university's abandonment of liberal ideals. Instead of treating them as individuals, colleges typically consider minority members in terms of their group, important only insofar as their collective numbers satisfy the formulas of "diversity." Since many of these students depend on a college degree to enhance their career opportunities, their high dropout rate reflects tremendous suffering and a sense of betrayal.

Even more than others, minority students arrive on campus searching for principles of personal identity and social justice; thus they are particularly disillusioned when they leave empty handed. Moreover, most minority graduates will admit, when pressed, that if their experience in college is any indication, the prospects for race relations in the country at large are gloomy. If the university model is replicated in society at large, far from bringing ethnic harmony, it will reproduce and magnify in the broader culture the lurid bigotry, intolerance, and balkanization of campus life.

Alexis de Tocqueville

Of the Use Which the Americans Make of Public Associations in Civil Life

The first volume of Tocqueville's Democracy in America was published in 1835, the second in 1840. In this selection as with much of the rest of Volume II, Tocqueville writes not just about American democracy, but about democracy in general. His observations in this selection reflect his interest in the shift from aristocracy to democracy. Earlier in the book he discusses the problem of the tyranny of the majority in democracy; here the focus is on the role of public associations as necessary to political democracy. In his view service is related to liberty and choice. If the citizens of a democracy do not work together in shaping public life, their liberty and freedom are sacrificed to dependence on an ever increasing government. The dangers of dependence on an expanding government , he says, include the inevitable decay of the morals and intelligence of the citizenry, leading to the decline of the country as a whole.

The bonds that create community are formed through collective endeavors. Tocqueville raises the possibility that making these bonds and their implicit commitments may represent more than a loss or exchange of liberty; these bonds may be a gain of freedom.

Of the Use Which the Americans Make of Public Associations in Civil Life

Alexis de Tocqueville

I do not propose to speak of those political associations by the aid of which men endeavor to defend themselves against the despotic action of a majority or against the aggressions of regal power. That subject I have already treated. If each citizen did not learn, in proportion as he individually becomes more feeble and consequently more incapable of preserving his freedom singlehanded, to combine with his fellow citizens for the purpose of defending it, it is clear that tyranny would unavoidably increase together with equality.

Only those associations that are formed in civil life without reference to political objects are here referred to. The political associations that exist in the United States are only a single feature in the midst of the immense assemblage of associations in that country. Americans of all ages, all conditions, and all dispositions constantly form associations. They have not only commercial and manufacturing companies, in which all take part, but associations of a thousand other kinds—religious, moral, serious, futile, general or restricted, enormous or diminutive. The Americans make associations to give entertainments, to found seminaries, to build inns, to construct churches, to diffuse books, to send missionaries to the antipodes; in this manner they found hospitals, prisons, and schools. If it is proposed to inculcate some truth or to foster some feeling by the encouragement of a great example, they form a society. Wherever at the head of some new undertaking you see the government in France, or a man of rank in England, in the United States you will be sure to find an association.

I met with several kinds of associations in America of which I confess I had no previous notion; and I have often admired the extreme skill with which the inhabitants of the United States succeed in proposing a common object for the exertions of a great many men and in inducing them voluntarily to pursue it.

I have since traveled over England, from which the Americans have taken some of their laws and many of their customs; and it seemed to me that the principle of association was by no means so constantly or adroitly used in that country. The English often perform great things singly, whereas the Americans form associations for the smallest undertakings. It is evident that the former people consider association as a powerful means of action, but the latter seem to regard it as the only means they have of acting.

Thus the most democratic country on the face of the earth is that in which men have, in our time, carried to the highest perfection the art of pursuing in common the object of their common desires and have applied this new science to the greatest number of purposes. Is this the result of accident, or is there in reality any necessary connection between the principle of association and that of equality?

Aristocratic communities always contain, among a multitude of persons who by themselves are powerless, a small number of powerful and wealthy citizens, each of whom can achieve great undertakings single-handed. In aristocratic societies men do not need to combine in order to act, because they are strongly held together. Every wealthy and powerful citizen constitutes the head of a permanent and compulsory association, composed of all those who are dependent upon him or whom he makes subservient to the execution of his designs.

Among democratic nations, on the contrary, all the citizens are independent and feeble; they can do hardly anything by themselves, and none of them can oblige his fellow men to lend him their assistance. They all, therefore, become powerless if they do not learn voluntarily to help one another. If men living in democratic countries had no right and no inclination to associate for political purposes, their independence would be in great jeopardy, but they might long preserve their wealth and their cultivation: whereas if they never acquired the habit of forming associations in ordinary life, civilization itself would be endangered. A people among whom individuals lost the power of achieving great things single-handed, without acquiring the means of producing them

by united exertions, would soon relapse into barbarism.

Unhappily, the same social condition that renders associations so necessary to democratic nations renders their formation more difficult among those nations than among all others. When several members of an aristocracy agree to combine, they easily succeed in doing so; as each of them brings great strength to the partnership, the number of its members may be very limited; and when the members of an association are limited in number, they may easily become mutually acquainted, understand each other, and establish fixed regulations. The same opportunities do not occur among democratic nations, where the associated members must always be very numerous for their association to have any power.

I am aware that many of my countrymen are not in the least embarrassed by this difficulty. They contend that the more enfeebled and incompetent the citizens become, the more able and active the government ought to be rendered in order that society at large may execute what individuals can no longer accomplish. They believe this answers the whole difficulty, but I think they are mistaken.

A government might perform the part of some of the largest American companies, and several states, members of the Union, have already attempted it, but what political power could ever carry on the vast multitude of lesser undertakings which the American citizens perform every day, with the assistance of the principle of association? It is easy to foresee that the time is drawing near when man will be less and less able to produce, by himself alone, the commonest necessaries of life. The task of the governing power will therefore perpetually increase, and its very efforts will extend it every day. The more it stands in the place of associations, the more will individuals, losing the notion of combining together, require its assistance: these are causes and effects that unceasingly create each other. Will the administration of the country ultimately assume the management of all the manufactures which no single citizen is able to carry on? And if a time at length arrives when, in consequence of the extreme subdivision of landed property, the soil is split into an infinite number of parcels, so that it can be cultivated only by companies of husbandmen, will it be necessary that the head of the government should leave the helm of state to follow the plough? The morals and the intelligence of a democratic people would be as much endangered as its business and manufactures, if the government ever wholly usurped the place of private companies.

Feelings and opinions are recruited, the heart is enlarged, and the human mind is developed only by the reciprocal influence of men upon one another. I have shown that these influences are almost null in democratic countries; they must therefore be artificially created, and this can only be accomplished by associations.

When the members of an aristocratic community adopt a new opinion or conceive a new sentiment, they give it a station, as it were, beside themselves, upon the lofty platform where they stand; and opinions or sentiments so conspicuous to the eyes of the multitude are easily introduced into the minds or hearts of all around. In democratic countries the governing power alone is naturally in a condition to act in this manner, but it is easy to see that its action is always inadequate, and often dangerous. A government can no more be competent to keep alive and to renew the circulation of opinions and feelings among a great people than to manage all the speculations of productive industry. No sooner does a government attempt to go beyond its political sphere and to enter upon this new track than it exercises, even unintentionally, an insupportable tyranny; for a government can only dictate strict rules, the opinions which it favors are rigidly enforced, and it is never easy to discriminate between its advice and its commands. Worse still will be the case if the government really believes itself interested in preventing all circulation of ideas;

it will then stand motionless and oppressed by the heaviness of voluntary torpor. Governments, therefore, should not be the only active powers; associations ought, in democratic nations, to stand in lieu of those powerful private individuals whom the equality of conditions has swept away.

As soon as several of the inhabitants of the United States have taken up an opinion or a feeling which they wish to promote in the world, they look out for mutual assistance; and as soon as they have found one another out, they combine. From that moment they are no longer isolated men, but a power seen from afar, whose actions serve for an example and whose language is listened to. The first time I heard in the United States that a hundred thousand men had bound themselves publicly to abstain from spirituous liquors, it appeared to me more like a joke than a serious engagement, and I did not at once perceive why these temperate citizens could not content themselves with drinking water by their own firesides. I at last understood that these hundred thousand Americans, alarmed by the progress of drunkenness around them, had made up their minds to patronize temperance. They acted in just the same way as a man of high rank who should dress very plainly in order to inspire the humbler orders with a contempt of luxury. It is probable that if these hundred thousand men had lived in France, each of them would singly have memorialized the government to watch the public houses all over the kingdom.

Nothing, in my opinion, is more deserving of our attention than the intellectual and moral associations of America. The political and industrial associations of that country strike us forcibly; but the others elude our observation, or if we discover them, we understand them imperfectly because we have hardly ever seen anything of the kind. It must be acknowledged, however, that they are as necessary to the American people as the former, and perhaps more so. In democratic countries the science of association is the mother of science; the progress of all the rest depends upon the progress it has made.

Among the laws that rule human societies there is one which seems to be more precise and clear than all others. If men are to remain civilized or to become so, the art of associating together must grow and improve in the same ratio in which the equality of conditions is increased.

Robert D. Putman

Bowling Alone: America's Declining Social Capital

Dan Coats, Gertrude Himmelfarb, Don Eberly, and David Boaz

"Can Congress Revive Civil Society?"

In recent years, students of democratic community and politics have attempted to resuscitate the basic vision delivered by Alexis de Tocqueville (see the essay "Of the Use Which the Americans Make of Public Associations in Civil Life" that precedes these articles in this section) that vibrant networks of voluntary civic association are the foundation for a successful and stable democratic society. The two following essays are good examples of the current concern with the health of American "civil society," albeit from different perspectives. The first essay by Robert Putnam, professor and director of the Center for International Affairs at Harvard University, makes what has become a oft-cited argument about the decline in "social capital" in the United States. By using social science research data, Putnam attempts to demonstrate that we are not joining voluntary civic associations with the frequency or intensity that characterized the democratic society of de Tocqueville's days, to the detriment of our democratic political institutions and attitudes. The second essay, by

Senator Dan Coats (Republican from Indiana)—with responses by three conservative authors and social commentators—explores what role, if any, the federal government might play in reviving the institutions of local civil society, such as churches, schools, and other neighborhood associations. In the spirit of de Tocqueville, these two essays engage us in alternative visions of civil society, the "third leg"—along with the private sector of the capitalist economy and the public sector of government institutions—of the stool upon which our society rests.

Bowling Alone:
America's Declining Social CapitalRobert
D. Putman

Many students of the new democracies that have emerged over the past decade and a half have emphasized the importance of a strong and active civil society to the consolidation of democracy. Especially with regard to the postcommunist countries, scholars and democratic activists alike have lamented the absence or obliteration of traditions of independent civic engagement and a widespread tendency toward passive reliance on the state. To those concerned with the weakness of civil societies in the developing or postcommunist world, the advanced Western democracies and above all the United States have typically been taken as models to be emulated. There is striking evidence, however, that the vibrancy of American civil society has notably declined over the past several decades.

Ever since the publication of Alexis de Tocqueville's *Democracy in America*, the United States has played a central role in systematic studies of the links between democracy and civil society. Although this is in part because trends in American life are often regarded as harbingers of social modernization, it is also because America has traditionally been considered unusually "civic" (a reputation that, as we shall later see, has not been entirely unjustified).

When Tocqueville visited the United States in the 1830s, it was the Americans' propensity for civic association that most impressed him as the key to their unprecedented ability to make democracy work. "Americans of all ages, all stations in life, and all types of disposition," he observed, "are forever forming associations.

From *Journal of Democracy*, Vol. 6, No. 1, pp. 65–77. Copyright © 1995 by Robert Putnam. Reprinted by permission of the author.

There are not only commercial and industrial associations in which all take part, but others of a thousand different types—religious, moral, serious, futile, very general and very limited, immensely large and very minute.... Nothing, in my view deserves more attention than the intellectual and moral associations in America."

Recently, American social scientists of a neo-Tocquevillean bent have unearthed a wide range of empirical evidence that the quality of public life and the performance of social institutions (and not only in America) are indeed powerfully influenced by norms and networks of civic engagement. Researchers in such fields as education, urban poverty, unemployment, the control of crime and drug abuse, and even health have discovered that successful outcomes are more likely in civically engaged communities. Similarly, research on the varying economic attainments of different ethnic groups in the United States has demonstrated the importance of social bonds within each group. These results are consistent with research in a wide range of settings that demonstrates the vital importance of social networks for job placement and many other economic outcomes.

Meanwhile, a seemingly unrelated body of research on the sociology of economic development has also focused attention on the role of social networks. Some of this work is situated in the developing countries, and some of it elucidates the peculiarly successful "network capitalism" of East Asia. Even in less exotic Western economies, however, researchers have discovered highly efficient, highly flexible "industrial districts" based on networks of collaboration among workers and small entrepreneurs. Far from being paleoindustrial anachronisms, these dense interpersonal and interorganizational networks undergird ultramodern industries, from the high tech of Silicon Valley to the high fashion of Benetton.

The norms and networks of civic engagement also powerfully affect the performance of representative government. That, at least, was the central conclusion of my own 20-year, quasi-experimental study of subnational governments in different regions of Italy. Although all these regional governments seemed identical on paper, their levels of effectiveness varied dramatically. Systematic inquiry showed that the quality of governance was determined by longstanding traditions of civic engagement (or its absence). Voter turnout, newspaper readership, membership in choral societies and football clubs—these were the hallmarks of a successful region. In fact, historical analysis suggested that these networks of organized reciprocity and civic solidarity, far from being an epiphenomenon of socioeconomic modernization, were a precondition for it.

No doubt the mechanism through which civic engagement and social connectedness produce such results—better schools, faster economic development, lower crime, and more effective government—are multiple and complex. While these briefly recounted findings require further confirmation and perhaps qualification, the parallels across hundreds of empirical studies in a dozen disparate disciplines and subfields are striking. Social scientists in several fields have recently suggested a common framework for understanding these phenomena, a framework that rests on the concept of *social capital*. By analogy with notions of physical capital and human capital—tools and training that enhance individual productivity—"social capital" refers to features of social organization such as networks, norms, and social trust that facilitate coordination and cooperation for mutual benefit.

For a variety of reasons, life is easier in a community blessed with a substantial stock of social capital. In the first place, networks of civic engagement foster sturdy norms of generalized reciprocity and encourage the emergence of social trust. Such networks facilitate coordination and communication, amplify reputations, and thus allow dilemmas of collective action to be resolved. When economic and political negotiation is embedded in dense networks of social interaction, incentives for opportunism are reduced. At the same time, networks of civic engagement embody past success at collaboration, which can serve as a cultural template for future collaboration. Finally, dense networks of interaction probably broaden the participants' sense of self, developing the "I" into "we," or (in the language of rational-choice theorists) enhancing the participants' "taste" for collective benefits.

I do not intend here to survey (much less contribute to) the development of the theory of social capital. Instead, I use the central premise of the rapidly growing body of work—that social connections and civic engagement pervasively influence our public life, as well as our private prospects—as the starting point for an empirical survey of trends in social capital in contemporary America. I concentrate here entirely on the American case, although the developments I portray may in some measure characterize many contemporary societies.

Whatever Happened to Civic Engagement?

We begin with familiar evidence on changing patterns of political participation, not least because it is immediately relevant to issues of democracy in the narrow sense. Consider the well-known decline in turnout in national elections over the last three decades. From a relative high point in the early 1960s, voter turnout had by 1990 declined by nearly a quarter; tens of millions of Americans had forsaken their parents' habitual readiness to engage in the simplest act of citizenship. Broadly similar trends also characterize participation in state and local elections.

It is not just the voting booth that has been increasingly deserted by Americans. A series of identical questions posed by the Roper Organization to national samples ten times each year over the last two decades reveals that since 1973 the number of Americans who report that "in the past year" they have "attended a public meeting on town or school affairs" has fallen

by more than a third (from 22 percent in 1973 to 13 percent in 1993). Similar (or even greater) relative declines are evident in responses to questions about attending a political rally or speech, serving on a committee of some local organization, and working for a political party. By almost every measure, Americans' direct engagement in politics and government has fallen steadily and sharply over the last generation, despite the fact that average levels of education—the best individual-level predictor of political participation—have risen sharply throughout this period. Every year over the last decade or two, millions more have withdrawn from the affairs of their communities.

Not coincidentally, Americans have also disengaged psychologically from politics and government over this era. The proportion of American who reply that they "trust the government in Washington" only "some of the time" or "almost never" has risen steadily from 30 percent in 1966 to 75 percent in 1992.

These trends are well known, of course, and taken by themselves would seem amenable to a strictly political explanation. Perhaps the long litany of political tragedies and scandals since the 1960s (assassinations, Vietnam, Watergate, Irangate, and so on) has triggered an understandable disgust for politics and government among Americans, and that in turn has motivated their withdrawal. I do not doubt that this common interpretation has some merit, but its limitations become plain when we examine trends in civic engagement of a wider sort.

Our survey of organizational membership among Americans can usefully begin with a glance at the aggregate results of the General Social Survey, a scientifically conducted, national-sample survey that has been repeated 14 times over the last two decades. Church-related groups constitute the most common type of organization joined by Americans; they are especially popular with women. Other types of organizations frequently joined by women include school-service groups (mostly parent-teacher associations), sports groups, professional societies, and literary societies. Among men, sports clubs, labor unions, professional societies, fraternal groups, veterans' groups, and service clubs are all relatively popular. Religious affiliation is by far the most common associational membership among Americans. Indeed, by many measures America continues to be (even more than in Tocqueville's time) an astonishingly "churched" society. For example, the United States has more houses of worship per capita than any other nation on Earth. Yet religious sentiment in America seems to be becoming somewhat less tied to institutions and more self-defined.

How have these complex crosscurrents played out over the last three or four decades in terms of Americans' engagement with organized religion? The general pattern is clear: The 1960s witnessed a significant drop in reported weekly churchgoing—from roughly 48 percent in the late 1950s to roughly 41 percent in the early 1970s. Since then, it has stagnated or (according to some surveys) declined still further. Meanwhile, data from the General Social Survey show a modest decline in membership in all "church-related groups" over the last 20 years. It would seem, then, that net participation by Americans, both in religious services and in church-related groups, has declined modestly (by perhaps a sixth) since the 1960s.

For many years, labor unions provided one of the most common organizational affiliations among American workers. Yet union membership has been falling for nearly four decades, with the steepest decline occurring between 1975 and 1985. Since the mid-1950s, when union membership peaked, the unionized portion of the nonagricultural work force in America has dropped by more than half, falling from 32.5 percent in 1953 to 15.8 percent in 1992. By now, virtually all of the explosive growth in union membership that was associated with the New Deal has been erased. The solidarity of union halls is now mostly a fading memory of aging men.

The parent-teacher association (PTA) has been an especially important form of civic engagement in twentieth-century America because parental involvement in the educational process represents a particularly productive form of social capital. It is, therefore, dismaying to discover that participation in parent-teacher organization has dropped drastically over the last generation, from more than 12 million in 1964 to barely 5 million in 1982 before recovering to approximately 7 million now.

Next, we turn to evidence on membership in (and volunteering for) civic and fraternal organizations. These data show some striking patterns. First, membership in traditional women's groups has declined more or less steadily since the mid-1960s. For example, membership in the national Federation of Women's Clubs is down by more than half (59 percent) since 1964, while membership in the League of Women Voters (LWV) is off 42 percent since 1969.

Similar reductions are apparent in the numbers of volunteers for mainline civic organizations, such as the Boy Scouts (off by 26 percent since 1970) and the Red Cross (off 61 percent since 1970). But what about the possibility that volunteers have simply switched their loyalties to other organizations? Evidence on "regular" (as opposed to occasional or "drop-by") volunteering is available from the Labor Department's Current Population Surveys of 1974 and 1989. These estimates suggest that serious volunteering declined by roughly one-sixth over these 15 years, from 24 percent of adults in 1974 to 20 percent in 1989. The multitudes of Red Cross aides and Boy Scout troop leaders now missing in action have apparently not been offset by equal numbers of new recruits elsewhere.

Fraternal organizations have also witnessed a substantial drop in membership during the 1980s and 1990s. Membership is down significantly in such groups as the Lions (off 12 percent since 1979), the Elks (off 18 percent since 1979), the Shriners (off 27 percent since 1979), the Jaycees (off 44 percent since 1979), and the

Masons (down 39 percent since 1959). In sum, after expanding steadily throughout most of this century, many major civic organizations have experienced a sudden, substantial, and nearly simultaneous decline in membership over the last decade or two.

The most whimsical yet discomfiting bit of evidence of social disengagement in contemporary America that I have discovered is this: more Americans are bowling today than ever before, but bowling in organized leagues has plummeted in the last decade or so. Between 1980 and 1993 the total number of bowlers in America increased by 10 percent, while league bowling decreased by 40 percent. (Lest this be thought a wholly trivial example, I should note that nearly 80 million Americans went bowling at least once during 1993, *nearly a third more than voted in the 1994 congressional elections* and roughly the same number as claim to attend church regularly. Even after the 1980s' plunge in league bowling, nearly 3 percent of American adults regularly bowl in leagues.) The rise of solo bowling threatens the livelihood of bowling-lane proprietors because those who bowl as members of leagues consume three times as much beer and pizza as solo bowlers, and the money in bowling is in the beer and pizza, not the balls and shoes. The broader social significance, however, lies in the social interaction and even occasionally civic conversations over beer and pizza that solo bowlers forgo. Whether or not bowling beats balloting in the eyes of most Americans, bowling teams illustrate yet another vanishing form of social capital.

Countertrends

At this point, however, we must confront a serious counterargument. Perhaps the traditional forms of civic organization whose decay we have been tracing have been replaced by vibrant new organizations. For example, national environmental organizations (like the Sierra Club) and feminist groups (like the National Organization for Women) grew rapidly during the 1970s and 1980s and now count hundreds of thousands of dues-paying members. An even more dramatic example is the American Association of Retired Persons (AARP), which grew exponentially from 400,00 card-carrying members in 1960 to 33 million in 1993, becoming (after the Catholic Church) the largest private organization in the world. The national administrators of these organizations are among the most feared lobbyists in Washington, in large part because of their massive mailing lists of presumably loyal members.

These new mass-membership organizations are plainly of great political importance. From the point of view of social connectedness, however, they are sufficiently different from classic "secondary associations" that we need to invent a new label—perhaps "tertiary associations." For the vast majority of their members, the only act of membership consists in writing a check for dues or perhaps occasionally reading a newsletter. Few ever attend any meetings of such organizations, and most are unlikely ever (knowingly) to encounter any other member. The bond between any two members of the Sierra Club is less like the bond between any two members of a gardening club and more like the bond between any two Red Sox fans (or perhaps any two devoted Honda owners): they root for the same team and they share some of the same interests, but they are unaware of each other's existence. Their ties, in short, are to common symbols, common leaders, and perhaps common ideals, but not to one another. The theory of social capital argues that associational membership should, for example, increase social trust, but this prediction is much less straightforward with regard to membership in tertiary associations. From the point of view of social connectedness, the Environmental Defense Fund and a bowling league are just not in the same category.

If the growth of tertiary organizations represents one potential (but probably not real) counterexample to my thesis, a second counter-trend is represented by the growing prominence of nonprofit organizations, especially nonprofit service agencies. This so-called third sector includes everything from Oxfam and the Metropolitan Museum of Art to the Ford Foundation and the Mayo Clinic. In other words, although most secondary associations are nonprofits, most nonprofit agencies are not secondary associations. To identify trends in the size of the nonprofit sector with trends in social connectedness would be another fundamental conceptual mistake.

A third potential countertrend is much more relevant to an assessment of social capital and civic engagement. Some able researchers have argued that the last few decades have witnessed a rapid expansion in "support groups" of various sorts. Robert Wuthnow reports that fully 40 percent of all Americans claim to be "currently involved in [a] small group that meets regularly and provides support or caring for those who participate in it." Many of these groups are religiously affiliated, but many others are not. For example, nearly 5 percent of Wuthnow's national sample claim to participate regularly in a "self-help" group, such as Alcoholics Anonymous, and nearly as many say they belong to book-discussion groups and hobby clubs.

The groups described by Wuthnow's respondents unquestionably represent an important form of social capital, and they need to be accounted for in any serious reckoning of trends in social connectedness. On the other hand, they do not typically play the same role as traditional civic associations. As Wuthnow emphasizes,

> Small groups may not be fostering community as effectively as many of their proponents would like. Some small groups merely provide occasions for individuals to focus on themselves in the presence of others. The social contract binding members together asserts only the weakest of obligations. Come if you have time. Talk if you feel like it. Respect everyone's opinion. Never criticize. Leave quietly if you

> become dissatisfied.... We can imagine that [these small groups] really substitute for families, neighborhoods, and broader community attachments that may demand lifelong commitments, when, in fact, they do not.

All three of these potential countertrends—tertiary organizations, nonprofit organizations, and support groups—need somehow to be weighed against the erosion of conventional civic organizations. One way of doing so is to consult the General Social Survey.

Within all educational categories, total associational membership declined significantly between 1967 and 1993. Among the college-educated, the average number of group memberships per person fell from 2.8 to 2.0 (a 26-percent decline); among high-school graduates, the number fell from 1.8 to 1.2 (32 percent); and among those with fewer than 12 years of education, the number fell from 1.4 to 1.1 (25 percent). In other words, at *all* educational (and hence social) levels of American society, and counting *all* sorts of group memberships, *the average number of associational memberships has fallen by about a fourth over the last quarter-century.* Without controls for educational levels, the trend is not nearly so clear, but the central point is this: *more Americans than ever before are in social circumstances that foster associational involvement (higher education, middle age, and so on), but nevertheless aggregate associational membership appears to be stagnant or declining.*

Broken down by type of group, the downward trend is most marked for church-related groups, for labor unions, for fraternal and veterans' organizations, and for school-service groups. Conversely, membership in professional associations has risen over these years, although less than might have been predicted, given sharply rising educational and occupational levels. Essentially the same trends are evident for both men and women in the sample. In short, the available survey evidence confirms our earlier conclusion: American social capital in the form of civic associations has significantly eroded over the last generation.

Good Neighborliness and Social Trust

I noted earlier that most readily available quantitative evidence on trends in social connectedness involves formal settings, such as the voting booth, the union hall, or the PTA. One glaring exception is so widely discussed as to require little comment here: the most fundamental form of social capital is the family, and the massive evidence of the loosening of bonds within the family (both extended and nuclear) is well known. This trend, of course, is quite consistent with—and may help to explain—our theme of social decapitalization.

A second aspect of informal social capital on which we happen to have reasonably reliable time-series data involves neighborliness. In each General Social Survey since 1974 respondents have been asked, "How often do you spend a social evening with a neighbor?" The proportion of Americans who socialize with their neighbors more than once a year has slowly but steadily declined over the last two decades, from 72 percent in 1974 to 61 percent in 1993. (On the other hand, socializing with "friends who do not live in your neighborhood" appears to be on the increase, a trend that may reflect the growth of workplace-based social connections.)

Americans are also less trusting. The proportion of Americans saying that most people can be trusted fell by more than a third between 1960, when 58 percent chose that alternative, and 1993, when only 37 percent did. The same trend is apparent in all educational groups; indeed, because social trust is also correlated with education and because educational levels have risen sharply, the overall decrease in social trust is even more apparent if we control for education.

Our discussion of trends in social connectedness and civic engagement has tacitly assumed that all the forms of social capital that we have discussed are themselves coherently correlated across individuals. This is in fact true. Members of associations are much more likely than nonmembers to participate in politics, to spend time with neighbors, to express social trust, and so on.

The close correlation between social trust and associational membership is true not only across time and across individuals, but also across countries. Evidence from the 1991 World Values Survey demonstrates the following:

1) Across the 35 countries in this survey, social trust and civic engagement are strongly correlated; the greater the density of associational membership in a society, the more trusting its citizens. Trust and engagement are two facets of the same underlying factor—social capital.

2) America still ranks relatively high by cross-national standards on both these dimensions of social capital. Even in the 1990s, after several decades' erosion, Americans are more trusting and more engaged than people in most other countries of the world.

3) The trends of the past quarter-century, however, have apparently moved the United States significantly lower in the international rankings of social capital. The recent deterioration in American social capital has been sufficiently great that (if no other country changed its position in the meantime) another quarter-century of change at the same rate would bring the United States, roughly speaking, to the midpoint among all these countries, roughly equivalent to South Korea, Belgium, or Estonia today. Two generations' decline at the same rate would leave the United States at the level of today's Chile, Portugal, and Slovenia.

Why Is U.S. Social Capital Eroding?

As we have seen, something has happened in America in the last two or three decades to diminish civic engagement and social connectedness. What could that "something" be? Here are several possible explanations, along with some initial evidence on each.

The movement of women into the labor force. Over these same two or three decades, many millions of American women have moved out of the home into paid employment. This is the primary, though not the sole, reason why the weekly working hours of the average American have increased significantly during these years. It seems highly plausible that this social revolution should have reduced the time and energy available for building social capital. For certain organizations, such as the PTA, the League of Women Voters, the Federation of Women's Clubs, and the Red Cross, this is almost certainly an important part of the story. The sharpest decline in women's civic participation seems to have come in the 1970s; membership in such "women's" organizations as these has been virtually halved since the late 1960s. By contrast, most of the decline in participation in men's organizations occurred about ten years later; the total decline to date has been approximately 25 percent for the typical organization. On the other hand, the survey data imply that the aggregate declines for men are virtually as great as those for women. It is logically possible, or course, that the male declines might represent the knock-on effect of women's liberation, as dishwashing crowded out the lodge, but time-budget studies suggest that most husbands of working wives have assumed only a minor part of the housework. In short, something besides the women's revolution seems to lie behind the erosion of social capital.

Mobility: The "re-potting" hypothesis. Numerous studies of organizational involvement have shown that residential stability and such related phenomena as homeownership are clearly associated with greater civic engagement. Mobility, like frequent re-potting of plants, tends to disrupt root systems, and it takes time for an uprooted individual to put down new roots. It seems plausible that the automobile, suburbanization, and the movement to the Sun Belt have reduced the social rootedness of the average American, but one fundamental difficulty with this hypothesis is apparent: the best evidence shows that residential stability and homeownership in America have risen modestly since 1965, and are surely higher now than during the 1950s, when civic engagement and social connectedness by our measures was definitely higher.

Other demographic transformations. A range of additional changes have transformed the American family since the 1960s—fewer marriages, more divorces, fewer children, lower real wages, and so on. Each of these changes might account for some of the slackening of civic engagement, since married, middle-class parents are generally more socially involved than other people. Moreover, the changes in scale that have swept over the American economy in these years—illustrated by the replacement of the corner grocery by the supermarket and now perhaps of the supermarket by electronic shopping at home, or the replacement of community-based enterprises by outpost of distant multinational firms—may perhaps have undermined the material and even physical basis for civic engagement.

The technological transformation of leisure. There is reason to believe that deep-seated technological trends are radically "privatizing" or "individualizing" our use of leisure time and thus disrupting many opportunities for social-capital formation. The most obvious and probably the most powerful instrument of this revolution is television. Time-budget studies in the 1960s showed that the growth in time spent watching television dwarfed all other changes in the way Americans passed their days and nights. Television has made our communities (or, rather, what we experiences as our communities) wider and shallower. In the language of economics, electronic technology enables individual externalities associated with more primitive forms of entertainment. The same logic applies to the replacement of vaudeville by the movies and now of movies by the VCR. The new "virtual reality" helmets that we will soon don to be entertained in total isolation are merely the latest extension of this trend. Is technology thus driving a wedge between our individual interests and our collective interests? It is a question that seems worth exploring more systematically.

What Is To Be Done?

The last refuge of a social-scientific scoundrel is to call for more research. Nevertheless, I cannot forbear from suggesting some further lines of inquiry.

- We must sort out the dimensions of social capital, which clearly is not a unidimensional concept, despite language (even in this essay) that implies the contrary. What types of organizations and networks most effectively embody—or generate—social capital, in the sense of mutual reciprocity, the resolution of dilemmas of collective action, and the broadening of social identities? In this essay I have emphasized the density of associational life. In earlier work I stressed the structure of networks, arguing that "horizontal" ties represented more productive social capital than vertical ties.

- Another set of important issues involves macrosociological crosscurrents that might intersect with the trends described here. What will be the impact, for example, of electronic networks on social capital? My hunch is that meeting in an electronic forum is not the equivalent of meeting in a bowling alley—or even in a saloon—but hard empirical research

is needed. What about the development of social capital in the workplace? Is it growing in counterpoint to the decline of civic engagement, reflecting some social analogue of the first law of thermodynamics—social capital is neither created nor destroyed, merely redistributes? Or do the trends described int his essay represent a deadweight loss?

- A rounded assessment of changes in American social capital over the last quarter-century needs to count the costs as well as the benefits of community engagement. We must not romanticize small-town middle-class civic life in the America of the 1950s. In addition to the deleterious trends emphasized in this essay, recent decades have witnessed a substantial decline in intolerance and probably also in overt discrimination, and those beneficent trends may be related in complex ways to the erosion of traditional social capital. Moreover, a balanced accounting of the social-capital books would need to reconcile the insights of this approach with the undoubted insights offered by Mancur Olson and others who stress that closely knit social, economic, and political organizations are prone to inefficient cartelization and to what political economists term "rent seeking" and ordinary men and women call corruption.

- Finally, and perhaps most urgently, we need to explore creatively how public policy impinges on (or might impinge on) social-capital formation. In some well-known instances, public policy has destroyed highly effective social networks and norms. American slum-clearance policy of the 1950s and 1960s, for example, renovated physical capital, but at a very high cost to existing social capital. The consolidation of country post offices and small school districts has promised administrative and financial efficiencies, but full-cost accounting for the effects of these policies on social capital might produce a more negative verdict. On the other hand, such past initiatives as the county agricultural-agent system, community colleges, and tax deductions for charitable contributions illustrate that government can encourage social-capital formation. Even a recent proposal in San Luis Obispo, California, to require that all new houses have front porches illustrates the power of government to influence where and how networks are formed.

The concept of "civil society" has played a central role in the recent global debate about the preconditions for democracy and democratization. In the newer democracies this phrase has properly focused attention on the need to foster a vibrant civic life in soils traditionally inhospitable to self-government. In the established democracies, ironically, growing numbers of citizens are questioning the effectiveness of their public institutions at the very moment when liberal democracy has swept the battlefield, both ideologically and geopolitically. In America, at least, there is reason to suspect that this democratic disarray may be linked to a broad and continuing erosion of civic engagement that began a quarter-century ago. High on our scholarly agenda should be the question of whether a comparable erosion of social capital may be under way in other advanced democracies, perhaps in different institutional and behavioral guises. High on America's agenda should be the question of how to reverse these adverse trends in social connectedness, thus restoring civic engagement and civic trust.

Can Congress Revive Civil Society?

Essay by Dan Coats with responses from Gertrude Himmelfarb, Don Eberly and David Boaz[*]

In their 1975 book To Empower People, Richard John Neuhaus and Peter Berger challenged policymakers to protect and foster the "mediating structures"—neighborhood, family, church and voluntary associations—that stand between the private individual and large government institutions. "Wherever possible," they wrote, "public policy should utilize mediating structures for the realization of social purposed."

Twenty years later, Washington is heeding the call. In October 1995, Senator Dan Coats introduced a package of legislative proposals to help empower local, community-based institutions that are addressing social problems. Crafted with the help of William J. Bennett, a codirector of Empower America, the "Project for American Renewal" comprises 19 separate bills designed to use public policy—and public resources—to energize mainly private efforts to meet human needs. Coats defended his legislation at a recent symposium at The Heritage Foundation; what follows are his remarks and critiques by some of the symposium's participants.

Senator Dan Coats

Re-funding Our "Little Platoons"

An intellectual revolution is underway concerning the nature of our social crisis. It is no

From *Policy Review*, January/February 1996, pp. 24–33. Copyright © 1996 by The Heritage Foundation. Reprinted by permission.

[*]David Boaz is the executive vice president of the Cato Institute, in Washington, D.C.

longer credible to argue that rising illegitimacy, random violence, and declining values are rooted in the lack either of economic equality or of economic opportunity. These positions are still current in our political debate, but they have lost their plausibility.

America's cultural decay can be traced directly to the breakdown of certain institutions—families, churches, neighborhoods, voluntary associations—that act as an immune system against cultural disease. In nearly every community, these institutions once created an atmosphere in which most problems—a teen-age girl "in trouble," the rowdy neighborhood kids, the start of a drug problem at the local high school—could be confronted before their repetition threatened the existence of the community itself.

When civil society is strong, it infuses a community with its warmth, trains its people to be good citizens, and transmits values between generations. When it is weak, no amount of police or politics can provide a substitute. There is a growing consensus that a declining civil society undermines both civility and society.

In this discussion, the importance of civil society is something I want to assume, not argue. But it leads to another question: Does this intellectual revolution have political consequences? Should it influence the agenda of Congress, or is it irrelevant to our work?

Let me begin by saying what is *not* at issue. I do not argue that government is sufficient to the need. Nothing short of a Great Awakening, as Gertrude Himmelfarb has noted, is sufficient to the need. But I *do* argue that conservatives have duties beyond waiting for another Charles Wesley. Realism about government's limits is not a substitute for effective public policy. I am convinced that political reflection on these themes is important not only for its own sake; it provides the next, necessary stage of the conservative revolution.

Government clearly has had a role in undermining civil society. Families, churches, and community groups were forced to surrender their authority and function to bureaucratic experts. Fathers were replaced by welfare checks, private charities were displaced by government spending, religious volunteers were dismissed as "amateurs," whole communities were demolished in slum-clearance projects. The power to replace an institution is the power to destroy it.

So the first item on the political agenda is a re-limited government, leaving enough social space for civil society to resume its role.

But this brings us to a problem. The retreat of government does not automatically result in the rebirth of civil society. It is a necessary condition, but not a sufficient one. As Professor John DiIulio has observed, when a victim is stabbed, you need to remove the knife. But removing the knife will not heal the wound.

In Russia, the retreat of government has resulted in what one expert calls "anarcho-capitalism"—closer to the Mafia than the invisible hand. Even if this result had been known beforehand, it would not have been an argument to retain the communist system. But it *is* an argument for respecting the potential for social dislocation when civil society is weak. Robert Woodson of the National Center for Neighborhood Enterprise has said, "[T]he moral centers of black life were decimated by liberal policies." We should not ignore the potential for suffering, especially in our cities, when government retreats.

The decline of civil society threatens the future of our political order. It requires us to ask certain questions out of a reasonable, justified desperation. How do we creatively, but not intrusively, strengthen the safety net of civil society? How do we encourage the transfer of resources and authority, not just to state governments, but to those private and religious institutions that shape, direct, and reclaim individual lives?

There is not—and could never be—a government plan to rebuild civil society. But there must be ways to actively take the side of people

A Senator's Plan to Help Renew America

A summary of the bills Senator Coats introduced as art of his "Project for America Renewal":

Fathering, Mentoring, and Family

The Kinship Care Act Creates a $30-million demonstration program for the states to keep children out of foster care by placing them with qualified family members.

The Role Model Academy Act Establishes a residential academy for at-risk youth, offering high academic standards and job training that focuses on personal responsibility and discipline.

The Character Development Act Gives school districts three-year demonstration grants to enlist community groups to connect children with mentors and other role models.

The Mentor Schools Act Provides $1-million grants to school district willing to develop and operate single-sex schools; support mentoring of students by teachers and volunteers.

The Adoption Assistance Act Offers tax credits of $5,000 to adopting parents earning less than $60,000 and smaller credits to those earning between $60,000 and $100,000.

The Family Reconciliation Act Increases money to states under the Family Preservation and Social Service Act, to fund predivorce counseling and adopt waiting periods of at least 60 days in divorces involing children under 12.

The Family Reconciliation Act Gives a $1,000 tax credit to married couples who make at least $8,500 and receive the Earned-Income Tax Credit.

The Responsible Parenthood Act Requires that every federal dollar spent on family planning be matched by another dollar spent on abstinence education and adoption services.

Community Empowerment

The Educational Choice and Equity Act Authorizes demonstration grants for 100 school districts to give vochers for low-income families to send their children to any public or private school.

---

and institutions who are rebuilding their own communities, and who often feel isolated and poorly equipped.

This is the theory that Bill Bennett and I have adopted in the "Project for American Renewal." Government cannot directly restore what it has crippled. But we believe that deferring to and depending on these institutions in public policy would have a positive effect. As Robert Putnam of Harvard University has argued, the resources of community, unlike physical resources, become depleted when they are *not* used. They must be exercised or they atrophy.

Our goal is to exercise civil society by turning over federal roles to private institutions. In practice, we hope to tilt public policies in favor of intact families. We want to strengthen grass-roots community organizations. And we propose to shift welfare responsibilities to private and religious charities. Every dollar spent by families, community groups, and faith-based charities is more efficient and compassionate than any dollar spent by the federal government.

The Restitution and Responsibility Act Provides grants for states to strengthen the enforcement of restitution for crime victims, particularly throughtbetter data collection and stiffer sanctions.

The Assests for Independence Act Creates a $100-million demonstration program to establish savings accounts among the poor. Family deposits—used to fund housing, education, or the creation of a small business—would be matched by churches, foundations, corporations, and state and federal revenue.

The Urban Homestead Act Requires the Department of Housing and Urban Development to transfer ownership of all its unoccupied, single-family public housing within two years to local governments. Units would then be offered for sale to local community development corporations, which help low-income families find affordable housing.

The Maternity Shelter Act Provides $50 million in vouchers for women to cover their costs at private and religious maternity group homes. Also provides grants to private nonprofit groups to repair existing maternity homes.

The Neighbourhood Security Act Gives grants to community organizations that confront crime in cooperation with local police, including citizen patroles and community policing.

Effective Compassion

The Comprehensive Charity Reform Act Providers a $500 poverty tax credit ($1,000 for married couples) for donations to charitable organizations; also allows non itemizing taxpayers to deduct their charitable contributions.

The Compassion Credit Act Creates a $500 tax credit for those who provide home care for the needy, including the homeless, abused women with children, unmarried pregnant women, and hospice patients such as AIDS and cancer sufferers.

The Medical Volunteer Act Extends federal insurance against liability suits to any health-care professional who provides free medical service to a "medically underserved" person.

The Community Partnership Act Provides demonstration grants for programs that match welfare recipients and nonviolent criminals with religious communities willing to offer moral guidance and practical help.

The centerpiece and symbol of the package is the "Comprehensive Charity Reform Act." It would allow individuals to donate $500 of their tax liability to private, antipoverty organizations. This measure would take about 8 percent of federal welfare spending and provide it directly to institutions actually winning their war on poverty, armed with spiritual vitality, tough love, and true compassion.

My objective is to promote a new ethic of giving in America. When individuals make these contributions to effective charities, it is a form of involvement beyond writing a check to the federal government. It encourages a new definition of citizenship—one in which men and women examine and support the programs in their own communities that serve the poor.

This is exactly how I came to be involved in these issues. My initial interest was not academic, I had the experience of seeing how religious charities not only feed the body but touch the soul. They are dramatically effective, while the programs I reauthorized year after year in Congress did not even bother to keep track of their dismal results.

One of my favorite examples is the Gospel Mission in Washington, D.C. It provides one of the most vivid contrasts to government failure I have ever seen. It has a 12-month drug rehabilitation rate of 66 percent, while a once-heralded government program just three blocks away rehabilitates less than 10 percent of those it serves. Yet the government program spends many times more per person.

To explain the difference you need to talk to those the Gospel Mission has served. One addict who came to the shelter after failing in several government programs says, "Those programs generally take addiction from you, but don't place anything within you. I needed a spiritual lifting. People like those at the mission are like God walking into your life. Not only am I drug-free, but more than that, I can be a person again."

Marvin Olasky has talked about the need to "defund" government and "refund" those faith-based institutions that actually work. Bill Bennett and I have taken this not merely as an interesting observation but as a challenge. The Project for American Renewal is not the definitive answer, but it is the beginning of a debate we can no longer avoid.

Naturally we've encountered criticism, which has centered around three questions. First, is the project a violation of the letter and spirit of devolution? Nothing could be further from the truth. What we advocate is a particularly radical form of devolution. Some conservatives only seem comfortable transferring federal resources and authority to state bureaucracies. Our package would redistribute power directly to families, grass-roots community organizations, and private and religious charities. It is hardly a conservative position to argue that, of all the institutions of American society, only state governments merit our trust.

Our goal should not only be to redistribute power *within* government, but to spread power *beyond* government.

Second, should there be *any* role for the federal government in these matters?

My response is that conservatives need to pick their fights. States are better positioned to do many things—but not to do everything.

Federalism is useful, but we need to avoid a 10th Amendment utopianism. Bill Bennett tells the story of a governor who sought a series of federal waivers from him when he was President Reagan's education secretary. Bennett responded that they would be granted, but only if the governor also sent a list of state obstacles to reform. The state regulations far outnumbered the federal one.

State officials can repeat the same mistakes as their federal counterparts. State welfare bureaucracies can be just as strong and wrong as federal programs. We need the wisdom to concentrate on those areas where we can be most effective, even if it means a federal role in jump-starting reform. It is a paradox that it takes an active federal government to divest itself of its own power. Federal inertia serves the cause of bureaucratic centralization.

Third, does the project—with its tax credits—contradict the Republican economic agenda, particularly the flat tax?

I support a flatter, fairer, simpler tax code. But I am convinced that eliminating the charitable deduction would be social engineering on massive scale. The level of charitable giving is closely correlated with the treatment of charitable contributions in tax law. Abandoning this commitment would invoke the law of unintended consequences with a vengeance.

There are many in the Congress who could not and would not support such a reform. And many of the most serious flat-tax proposals now recognize this fact, carving out an exception for charitable giving. Those are the only initiatives with a political future.

I believe we are led by policy to creatively surrender federal authority to civil society. But there is a political point to be made as well.

There is only one thing more important than what Republicans do in the budget debate. It is what they say the day after it has ended. If our only appeal to Americans is a balanced budget and devolution to state bureaucracies, the Republican revolution is likely to falter.

No lasting political realignment can occur without an element of vision and hope—a message that our worst social problems, while persistent, are not permanent. Hope is what turns a sociological debate into a compelling political theme. If we do not develop such a theme, Republicans will become social Darwinists by default—accepting the survival of the fittest. But we know where that hope is kindled—among individuals and groups engaged in the hard, noble work of restoration. Their victories are among America's great, untold stories. No alternative approach to our cultural crisis holds as much promise as the success of these "little platoons," precisely because they have qualities not found in government at any level—spiritual renewal and authentic compassion. As a matter of public policy, and as a matter of prudent politics, it is time to aggressively take their side in the battle to recivilize American society.

Gertrude Himmelfarb

Remoralizing Civil Society

I have never been beguiled by the idea of devolution. Like Senator Coats, I believe that devolution—the transfer of power from the federal government to local and state government—is a necessary but not a sufficient step in the reform of our society. I also believe that the next stage of devolution—the transfer of power from government at all levels to civil society—is necessary—but again not sufficient.

In recent time, civil society has had many of its functions usurped by an overweening government. Welfare has displaced a good deal of charity. Families have been relieved of the obligation to care for their aged and incapacitated members. Communities can no longer stigmatize behavior such as illegitimacy that the government subsidizes and, in effect, legitimizes—rhetorically as well as practically. (While researching my last book, I wrote a federal agency to inquire about the latest statistics on illegitimacy. I received a letter firmly rebuking me for using that term; the proper term, I was told, is either "nontraditional child bearing" or "alternative modes of parenting"—hence, legitimizing illegitimacy).

Civil society has thus been severely weakened by government. But it also has been weakened by the culture in general. More important, it has been corrupted by the culture. In fact, some of the institutions in civil society are thriving as never before. There are powerful philanthropies and foundations, more than we've ever had before, and some have unprecedented wealth; there are private schools and colleges, social agencies, civic institutions, cultural organizations, and churches of all kinds. And all are flourishing in civil society.

But not always to good effect. Senator Coats describes civil society as an "immune system" against social disease. But civil society has been infected by the same virus that has afflicted the culture in general. The theories and practices that have been so detrimental to our educational system—affirmative action, multiculturalism, outcome-based education—have been initiated and promoted by private foundations and universities. Some of the most egregious projects funded by the National Endowment for the Arts have been proudly exhibited in local museums supported by the cultural elites of those communities. Even the churches, both mainstream and New Age churches, have contributed to what I would call the "de-moralization" of society, the kind of permissiveness and self-indulgence that is so conspicuous in our culture at large. The family is the bedrock of civil society. But it, too, is in a bad state—witness the prevalence of illegitimacy, divorce, transient "relationships," neglected children, households where the main cultural vehicle is television, with its incessant messages of promiscuity and violence.

It is not enough, then to revitalize civil society. We have to start thinking about "remoralizing" civil society. And that is a far, far more difficult task. And here—paradoxically—is where the government can be helpful. Unlike some of my conservative friends, I've never been a libertarian in economic affairs; nor am I much of a libertarian in social and cultural affairs. In our present situation, it seems to me, the remoralization of society requires that we avail ourselves of all of the resources that we can command—public and private, religious and secular, governmental as well as civil.

This may be the most important lesson I learned from the Victorians: They did not bifurcate their lives. They did not distinguish between private virtue and public virtue. Nor did they try to keep religion out of the public square. The Dissenters, for example, had no objection to the established Church of England (there was no serious movement for the disestablishment of the Church throughout the entire Victorian period). Secularists habitually joined with religious groups—utilitarians with Evangelicals—in promoting various measures of social reform. Government officials responsible for the distribution of public relief cooperated with private charities, their common purpose being to prevent the "de-moralization of the poor" —what we more politely call the "culture of dependency." They used, in short, whatever resources were available, in civil society and in the polity, to help stabilize and remoralize society.

It's often said that you can't legislate morality. But we have, in fact, done just that. The civil-rights legislation in the 1960s had the effect not only of legally proscribing racial discrimination but also of proscribing it morally. The fact is that individuals, communities, families, neighborhoods, and churches do not function in isolation. They cannot sustain traditional values that are at odds with those being promoted by

the government, by the courts, and by the culture. All values, even traditional values, have to be legitimized. And in a secular society, the main organs of legitimization are government, law, and the culture.

Conservatives, then, must not only eliminate laws and social policies that have illegitimatized traditional values. They also must devise laws and social policies that will legitimize traditional values. One might say that our legislators and policymakers are as much our moral instructors as are our teachers and preachers. This is why the Project for American Renewal is an important document—not only for the specific measures it proposes, but also for the principle it conveys: that government—responsible, modest, self-critical government—may be a useful ally of civil society in the remoralization of society.

Gertrude Himmelfarb is professor emeritus of history at the Graduate School of the City University of New York. Her most recent book is *The De-Moralization of Society: From Victorian Virtues to Modern Values* (Knopf, 1995).

Don Eberly

The New Demands of Citizenship

Dan Coats has issued a challenge for us to join in a new intellectual revolution, and join it we must. The most promising aspect of this revolution is that its recovery of the term "civil society" suggests that this concept may once again take deep root in our policy debates and in the public imagination. Civil society may very well supply the framework for a promising new social policy for the 21st century.

In his book *The Quest for Community*, Robert Nisbet suggested that the great challenge of modern society is "protecting, reinforcing, nurturing where necessary, the varied groups and associations which form the true building blocks of the social order." Nisbet's concern at the time (the 1950s) was that the human yearning for community, which is rooted in our social nature, would likely feed the hunger for a pervasive centralized government if not properly directed toward the restoration of real, functioning local communities. Our failure to heed his warning has left us with precisely the dangerous combination he feared—a powerful central state combined with radically weakened social institutions. In considering solutions to America's cultural decline, we would do well to keep in mind an ancient Chinese proverb: The possibility of progress begins when you call a problem by its right name. The present crisis in America is a crisis not merely of political and governmental dysfunction, but of societal disintegration.

We are witnessing today a dangerous depletion of the spiritual and psychological qualities upon which democracy and limited government depend. Out character-shaping institutions are collapsing in the face of a hedonistic mass culture increasingly characterized by violence, incivility, and a flagrant disregard for human dignity. We Americans are in rapid retreat from the very idea of society.

If we are to reverse this trend, we must change our conversation, and quickly, from the deterministic logic of the social sciences, which shift responsibility for antisocial behavior from the individual to the larger society. And we must move beyond our preoccupation with governmentalism—that is, what government does, how it does it, or what it stops doing.

Can Congress restore civil society? No one here believes that Congress can do more than help to set the conditions for such a recovery. But we should question whether Congress is prepared to do this much. Politicians must recognize that their ultimate success in policy reform depends precisely upon a deeper social renewal that can only originate in our hearts, homes, and local communities. The real question, then, is how do we, as a political community, respond to Nisbet's challenge to nurture the varied groups and associations of civil society.

There are many positive contributions that social policy reforms can make toward this end. Peter Berger and Richard John Neuhaus, in their classic wok *To Empower People*, urged that the intermediary institutions and associations of civil society be recognized in policy reforms. They offered two primary principles to guide public policy formulation: first, that public policy should protect and foster mediating structures; and second, that wherever possible, public policy should encourage mediating structures to address social concerns. This is essentially what the Coats bill is attempting to do. Finally, there is much the individual politician can contribute to the recovery of foundational solutions: Elected officials can lead in rebuilding civic community and recovering effective charity in their districts.

The most important thing is that we get the intellectual revolution right. That requires understanding what civil society is, why it matters, and what we Americans can do to recover it. The debate that lies ahead may indeed spark one of the most consequential shifts in social policy we have ever witnessed. The bill signals a departure from our current obsession with either the state or the market as instrument for social progress. Civil society is a different sphere. It is an intermediary sector, where private individuals join voluntarily in associations that operate neither on the principle of coercion, nor entirely on the principle of rational self-interest. In fact, the *modus operandi* of life in civil society gives expression to the pursuit of the common good, where actions are animated by a spirit of trust and collaboration.

If I have a caution here, it is that civil society not simply be embraced mostly for its utilitarian value in replacing the central welfare state. The stakes in recovering civil society go far beyond the replacement of the welfare state, as important as that is.

The mediating associations of civil society, as Alexis de Tocqueville tells us, are essential to both our democratic and economic systems.

He noted that "feelings and opinions are recruited, the heart is enlarged, and the human mind is developed only by the reciprocal influence of men upon one anther" operating in civil society. This sector generates the social capital—responsible citizens capable of self-governance and trust toward others—upon which our economic and democratic life depend. Lose this third sector, and you end up not with two sectors but eventually with only one: the bureaucratic state. The reason for this is that a society of isolated, atomized individuals is simply no match for the power and expansive ambition of the omnicompetent state. In fact, individuals who are cut off from the problem-solving, order-creating realm of civil society will almost certainly turn to government for order and safety, and yes, even for a sense of belonging and purpose. The result is a politically organized society which is held together mainly by force of state authority. Anyone who thinks that the monster of statism has been slain by the mere adoption of the policies of political devolution should think again.

Civil society, by definition, embraces institutions, groups, and associations, not individuals. It frustrates our dominant cultural impulse, which is to assert that the autonomous self is the only sovereign, and it grates against our dominant political reflex, which celebrates boundless individual choice as the highest good. The realm of civil society is free and largely autonomous, but it nevertheless imposes constraints and obligations on the individual and limits his choices. In other words, talk of civil society implies a return to authority and order. Many Western liberals—whether in political or economic terms—have embraced a notion of absolute freedom that is simply not self-sustaining.

So as we evaluate this legislation, we must remember what has happened in our political culture even as we discuss the need for mentoring, fathering, character-shaping charity, community empowerment, and curbing divorce. Public policy has shifted away from our decades-long impulse to empower isolated individuals. Policies are now being directed at asserting institutional authority, social obligations, and moral requirements over the individual. We must be clear: We are talking about restoring authority in the noncoercive realm of civil society, not the coercive realm of the state.

Freedom from the suffocating clutches of the social-service state is not simply a freedom to be left alone, as the latest conservative mantra has it. It is a freedom to become American again—compassionate, civic minded, and committed to rebuilding the good society.

The risk of the present revolution in Washington is that it simply replaces a sterile statism with an equally sterile antistatism, which does little to give life to a dying society. Dismantling ineffective and costly government is important work, but it does not constitute by itself a social or political philosophy. Freeing up the market is a splendid idea, but it does not constitute by itself a vision for a well-ordered society, and the market contributes little by itself to the recovery of community. (Some would argue that its effects are precisely the opposite.)

If civil society reappears, it will have been due to two events. First, we will have taken seriously the coherent moral vision reflected in this bill and worked to lodge it deeply within our public imagination, using it as the framework for rebuilding institutions, renewing human dignity, and restoring a functional society. Second, we will have directed our politics to the task of mobilizing Americans to do what politicians cannot.

We must applaud the Coats initiative without raising a new round of false expectations. The legislation should be accompanied by the issuing of greater demands—yes, *demands*—on American citizens. We're reminded daily that they apparently want power back. Well, this means helping them recover an awareness of their own social duties. With its emphasis on localism, citizenship, and networks of civic engagement, this bill issues a bold moral challenge to every American, one that should not be dismissed.

The great question of our time is, "How do we renew, regenerate, re-energize civil society?" There is no compulsory program for civil society; it must be summoned forth. It will happen as we tap into the currents that have always renewed human society: religious revival, the quest for transcendence, moral order, and membership in community. This is important work, and work that every American citizen must embrace.

Don Eberly is the director of the Civil Society Project and founder of the National Fatherhood Initiative. He is also the author of *Restoring the Good Society* (Hourglass Books, 1994).

David Boaz

Conservative Social Engineering

Senator Coats is to be commended for recognizing that devolution of power from the federal government to state governments is not a sufficient answer to America's problems. He correctly notes that many of our problems require "the recovery of families, neighborhoods, churches, schools, and voluntary associations...an influence that is literally 'civilizing.'" He rightly point out that "even if government directly undermined civil society, it cannot directly reconstruct it."

It is important, as Senator Coats argues, to demonstrate that faith in limited government is not just a negative attitude toward government; rather, it is rooted in an appreciation of the complicated network of institutions and associations that bind us together and provide us with much of what makes life worthwhile. Unfortunately, while the senator has correctly identified the problem—the decline of civil society—he doesn't seem to understand the reasons for the decline. Despite his rhetorical skepticism about the efficacy of government, his 19-bill legislative package, dubbed the Project for American Renewal, shows a faith in government almost as breathtaking as that of the architects of the Great Society.

First the good news: The centerpiece of Coats's plan is the Comprehensive Charity Reform Act, which would provide a $500-per-person tax credit for charitable contributions to groups helping the poor. That approach—also found in legislation introduced by Senator John Ashcroft and Representatives Jim Kolbe and Joseph Knollenberg—would shift charitable spending from government to millions of individuals and private organizations, and we can expect entirely exemplary results. Private charitable groups have a far better record than government agencies at getting people back on their feet, off welfare, and into stable work and family lives.

Now for the rest of the story. Coats says that the Project for American Renewal "is not a government plan to rebuild civil society" and that he favors "a radical form of devolution [that] would redistribute power directly to families, grass-roots community organizations, and private and religious charities." But in practice he apparently believes that the federal government should tax American citizens, bring their money to Washington, and then dole it out to sensible state and local programs and responsible private institutions. Surely we have learned that government grants do not create strong, creative, vibrant private organizations. Rather, organizations that depend on government funding will have to follow government rules, will be unable to respond effectively to changing needs, and will get caught up in games of grantsmanship and bureaucratic empire-building.

Moreover, nearly every one of his bills would further entangle the federal government in the institutions of civil society. Under the Role Model Academy Act, the federal government would "establish an innovative residential academy for at-risk youth." Under the Mentor Schools Act, the feds would provide grants to school districts wanting to develop and operate "same gender" schools. The Character Development Act would give school districts demonstration grants to work with community groups to develop mentoring programs. The Family Reconciliation Act would "provide additional federal funding...to implement a waiting period and pre-divorce counseling" for couples with children.

Many of these bills are intended to address real problems, such as the effects of divorce on children and the terrible plight of children trapped in fatherless, crime-ridden, inner-city neighborhoods. But why is it appropriate or effective for the federal government to intrude into these problems? Surely local school districts should decide whether to build same-sex schools or residential academies for at-risk youth; and if the people of, say, Detroit decide that such options would make sense, any theory of responsible, accountable government would suggest that the local city council or school board both make that decision and raise the funds to carry it out.

Many of Coats's bills deal with symptoms—they try to reform public housing by setting aside units for married couples or to provide mentors for children without fathers—rather than dealing with the real problem, a welfare system that guarantees every teenager her choice of an abortion or an apartment if she gets pregnant. Some of the bills accept the federal Leviathan as a given and tinker with it—for instance, by requiring that every federal dollar spent on family planning be matched by another dollar spent on abstinence education and adoption services. Others just follow the failed liberal policy of handing out federal dollars for whatever Congress thinks is a good idea—school choice, restitution to crime victims, maternity homes, community crime-watch programs.

Over the past 60 years, we've watched the federal government intrude more and more deeply into our lives. We've seen well-intentioned government programs become corrupted by the ideologues and bureaucrats placed in charge. We've seen schools and charities get hooked on federal dollars. The nature of government doesn't change when it is charged with carrying out conservative social engineering rather than liberal social engineering.

Let's not forget that if, say, Coats's Maternity Shelter Act were implemented next year, Donna Shalala, the secretary of health and human services, would be charged with implementing it. She might appoint HUD assistant secretary Andrew Cuomo to run it, or maybe unemployed excongressman Mel Reynolds, or maybe just some Harvard professor who thinks single motherhood is a viable lifestyle option for poor young women. One reason conservatives shouldn't set up well-intentioned government programs is that they won't always be in power to run them.

In *Democracy in America*, Alexis de Tocqueville noted that "Americans of all ages, all conditions, and all dispositions constantly form associations...to give entertainments, to found seminaries, to build inns, to construct churches, to diffuse books, to send missionaries to the antipodes; in this manner they found hospitals, prisons, and schools."

So why have families, churches, and neighborhood associations atrophied? Government, especially federal government, is a big part of the reason. Programs from Social Security to school breakfasts make family members less dependent on each other. Bureaucratic welfare programs not only encourage unwed motherhood and fatherlessness, they usurp a traditional role of churches. Governments promise to feed babies, teach children about sex, build playgrounds, run museums, provide job training, rehabilitate drug and alcohol abusers, and care for the elderly. Little is left for mediating institutions.

How do we get back to the healthy civil society that Tocqueville observed? Here's a program: First, reaffirm the constitutional mandate of the Tenth Amendment. That means the federal government should withdraw from areas in which it has no powers under Article I, Section 8 of the Constitution.

Second, cut federal taxes—not by $500, but by a lot—so that people have more money to spend, both on their own families and on charitable efforts. An important side effect of a large tax cut might be that more families discover they can live on one income and choose to have one parent stay home to care for children.

Third, under the principle of subsidiarity, return all the functions of civil society to the lowest level at which they can be adequately performed—the individual, the family, the church, the neighborhood, the school, the community, if necessary the state government. Advocates of limited government need to emphasize that the absence of government is not nothing: it's individual initiative and creativity and the vast array of associations that make up civil society.

Despite all we've learned about the failure of government, Coats just doesn't seem to get it. His proposals reflect the Washington that Roosevelt built, the Washington where, if you think of a good idea, you create a government program.

But ultimately, you either believe in individual liberty, limited government, and free markets, or you end up inviting the coercive state into every nook and cranny of civil society.

Jane Addams
Civic Cooperation

Jane Addams (1860–1935), US social reformer, was born in Cedarville, Illinois. In 1889, after breaking off her studies due to health problems and then spending several years in Europe, Addams co-founded Hull House, a community center for the poor in Chicago. Serving a largely immigrant population, Hull House soon blossomed into a dynamic center of community life and social reform. Among other activities, Hull House initiated a home for working girls, a day care program, a Labor Museum, a club for boys, and a Little Theater. Addams became an active figure in urban politics, speaking and writing on legislative reforms to improve the lives of the working poor. Addams's publications on urban life include *Hull House Maps and Papers* (1895), *Democracy and Social Ethics* (1902), and *The Spirit of Youth* and the *City Streets* (1909). In *A New Conscience and an Ancient Evil* (1912) Addams argued for women's suffrage as a way to combat prostitution.

In addition to her activities in support of women's suffrage, Addams was prominent in the international peace movement, helping to found the Women's International League for Peace and Freedom in 1919, and serving as its president for the rest of her life. Addams was co-recipient of the Nobel Peace prize in 1931. The following selection comes from her autobiographical *Twenty Years at Hull-House* (1910), an international classic.

Civic Cooperation
Jane Addams

One of the first lessons we learned at Hull-House was that private beneficence is totally inadequate to deal with the vast numbers of the city's disinherited. We also quickly came to realize that there are certain types of wretchedness from which every private philanthropy shrinks and which are cared for only in those wards of the County Hospital provided for the wrecks of vicious living or in the city's isolation hospital for smallpox patients.

I have heard a broken-hearted mother exclaim when her erring daughter came home at last too broken and diseased to be taken into the family she had disgraced, "There is no place for her but the top floor of the County Hospital; they will have to take her there," and this only after every possible expedient had been tried or suggested. This aspect of governmental responsibility was unforgettably borne in upon me during the smallpox epidemic following the World's Fair, when one of the residents, Mrs. Kelley, as state factory inspector was much concerned in discovering and destroying clothing which was being finished in houses containing unreported cases of smallpox. The deputy most successful in locating such cases lived at Hull-House during the epidemic because he did not wish to expose his own family. Another resident, Miss Lathrop, as a member of the State Board of Charities, went back and forth to the crowded pest house which had been hastily constructed on a stretch of prairie west of the city. As Hull-House was already so exposed, it seemed best for the special smallpox inspectors from the Board of Health to take their meals and change their clothing there before they went to their respective homes. All of these

From *Twenty Years at Hull House* by Jane Addams. (Macmillan Publishing Company, 1910.)

officials had accepted without question and as implicit in public office, the obligation to carry on the dangerous and difficult undertakings for which private philanthropy is unfitted, as if the commonalty of compassion represented by the state was more comprehending than that of any individual group....

In our first two summers we had maintained three baths in the basement of our own house for the use of the neighborhood and they afforded some experience and argument for the erection of the first public bathhouse in Chicago, which was built on a neighboring street and opened under the City Board of Health. The lot upon which it was erected belonged to a friend of Hull-House who offered it to the city without rent, and this enabled the city to erect the first public bath from the small appropriation of ten thousand dollars. Great fear was expressed by the public authorities that the baths would not be used and the old story of the bathtubs in model tenements which had been turned into coal bins was often quoted to us. We were supplied, however, with the incontrovertible argument that in our adjacent third square mile there were in 1892 but three bathtubs and that this fact was much complained of by many of the tenement-house dwellers. Our contention was justified by the immediate and overflowing use of the public baths, as we had before been sustained in the contention that an immigrant population would respond to opportunities for reading when the Public Library Board had established a branch reading room at Hull-House.

We also quickly discovered that nothing brought us so absolutely into comradeship with our neighbors as mutual and sustained effort such as the paving of a street, the closing of a gambling house, or the restoration of a veteran police sergeant....

Many subsequent years of living in kindly neighborhood fashion with the people of the nineteenth ward, has produced upon my memory the soothing effect of the second-class railroad carriage and many of these political experiences have not only become remote

but already seem improbable. On the other hand, these campaigns were not without their rewards; one of them was a quickened friendship both with the more substantial citizens in the ward and with a group of fine young voters whose devotion to Hull-House has never since failed; another was a sense of identification with public-spirited men throughout the city who contributed money and time to what they considered a gallant effort against political corruption. I remember a young professor from the University of Chicago who with his wife came to live at Hull-House, traveling the long distance every day throughout the autumn and winter that he might qualify as a nineteenth-ward voter in the spring campaign. He served as a watcher at the polls and it was but a poor reward for his devotion that he was literally set upon and beaten up, for in those good old days such things frequently occurred. Many another case of devotion to our standard so recklessly raised might be cited but perhaps more valuable than any of these was the sense of identification we obtained with the rest of Chicago.

So far as a Settlement can discern and bring to local consciousness neighborhood needs which are common needs, and can give vigorous help to the municipal measures through which such needs shall be met, it fulfills its most valuable function. To illustrate from our first effort to improve the street paving in the vicinity, we found that when we had secured the consent of the majority of the property owners on a given street for a new paving, the alderman checked the entire plan through his kindly service to one man who had appealed to him to keep the assessments down. The street long remained a shocking mass of wet, dilapidated cedar blocks, where children were sometimes mired as they floated a surviving block in the water which speedily filled the holes whence other blocks had been extracted for fuel. And yet when we were able to demonstrate that the street paving had thus been reduced into cedar pulp by the heavily loaded wagons of an adjacent factory, that the expense of its repaving should be borne from a general fund and not by the poor property owners, we found that we could all unite in advocating reform in the method of repaving assessments, and the alderman himself was obliged to come into such a popular movement. The Nineteenth Ward Improvement Association which met at Hull-House during two winters, was the first body of citizens able to make a real impression upon the local paving situation. They secured an expert to watch the paving as it went down to be sure that their half of the paving money was well expended. In the belief that property values would be thus enhanced, the common aim brought together the more prosperous people of the vicinity, somewhat as the Hull-House Coöperative Coal Association brought together the poorer ones....

Certainly the need for civic coöperation was obvious in many directions, and in none more strikingly than in that organized effort which must be carried on unceasingly if young people are to be protected from the darker and coarser dangers of the city. The coöperation between Hull-House and the Juvenile Protective Association came about gradually, and it seems now almost inevitably. From our earliest days we saw many boys constantly arrested, and I had a number of most enlightening experiences in the police station with an Irish lad whose mother upon her deathbed had begged me "to look after him." We were distressed by the gangs of very little boys who would sally forth with an enterprising leader in search of old brass and iron, sometimes breaking into empty houses for the sake of the faucets or lead pipe which they would sell for a good price to a junk dealer. With the money thus obtained they would buy cigarettes and beer or even candy, which could be conspicuously consumed in the alleys where they might enjoy the excitement of being seen and suspected by the "coppers." From the third year of Hull-House, one of the residents held a semiofficial position in the nearest police station, at least the sergeant agreed to give her provisional charge of every boy and girl under arrest for a trivial offense.

Mrs. Stevens, who performed this work for several years, became the first probation officer of the Juvenile Court when it was established in Cook County in 1899. She was the sole probation officer at first, but at the time of her death, which occurred at Hull-House in 1900, she was the senior officer of a corps of six. Her entire experience had fitted her to deal wisely with wayward children. She had gone into a New England cotton mill at the age of thirteen, where she had promptly lost the index finger of her right hand through "carelessness," she was told, and no one then seemed to understand that freedom from care was the prerogative of childhood. Later she became a typesetter and was one of the first women in America to become a member of the typographical union, retaining her "card" through all the later years of editorial work. As the Juvenile Court developed, the committee of public-spirited citizens who first supplied only Mrs. Stevens's salary, later maintained a corps of twenty-two such officers; several of these were Hull-House residents who brought to the house for many years a sad little procession of children struggling against all sorts of handicaps. When legislation was secured which placed the probation officers upon the pay roll of the county, it was a challenge to the efficiency of the civil service method of appointment to obtain by examination, men and women fitted for this delicate human task. As one of five people asked by the Civil Service Commission to conduct this first examination for probation officers, I became convinced that we were but at the beginning of the nonpolitical method of selecting public servants, but even stiff and unbending as the examination may be, it is still our hope of political salvation.

In 1907 the Juvenile Court was housed in a model court building of its own, containing a detention home and equipped with a competent staff. The committee of citizens largely responsible for this result, thereupon turned their attention to the conditions which the records of the court indicated had led to the alarming amount of juvenile delinquency and crime.

They organized the Juvenile Protective Association, whose twenty-two officers meet weekly at Hull-House with their executive committee to report what they have found and to discuss city conditions affecting the lives of children and young people.

The association discovers that there are certain temptations into which children so habitually fall that it is evident that the average child cannot withstand them. An overwhelming mass of data is accumulated showing the need of enforcing existing legislation and of securing new legislation, but it also indicates a hundred other directions in which the young people who so gayly walk our streets, often to their own destruction, need safeguarding and protection.

The effort of the association to treat the youth of the city with consideration and understanding, has rallied the most unexpected forces to its standard. Quite as the basic needs of life are supplied solely by those who make money out of the business, so the modern city has assumed that the craving for pleasure must be ministered to only by the sordid. This assumption, however, in a large measure broke down as soon as the Juvenile Protective Association courageously put it to the test. After persistent prosecutions, but also after many friendly interviews, the Druggists' Association itself prosecutes those of its members who sell indecent postal cards; the Saloon Keepers' Protective Association not only declines to protect members who sell liquor to minors, but now takes drastic action to prevent such sales; the Retail Grocers' Association forbids the selling of tobacco to minors; the Association of Department Store Managers not only increased the vigilance in their waiting rooms by supplying more matrons, but as a body they have become regular contributors to the association; the special watchmen in all the railroad yards agree not to arrest trespassing boys but to report them to the association; the firms manufacturing moving picture films not only submit their films to a volunteer inspection committee, but ask for suggestions in regard to new matter; and

the five-cent theaters arrange for "stunts" which shall deal with the subject of public health and morals when the lecturers provided are entertaining as well as instructive.

It is not difficult to arouse the impulse of protection for the young, which would doubtless dictate the daily acts of many a bartender and pool-room keeper if they could only indulge it without thereby giving their rivals an advantage. When this difficulty is removed by an evenhanded enforcement of the law, that simple kindliness which the innocent always evoke goes from one to another like a slowly spreading flame of good will. Doubtless the most rewarding experience in any such undertaking as that of the Juvenile Protective Association, is the warm and intelligent coöperation coming from unexpected sources—official and commercial as well as philanthropic. Upon the suggestion of the association, social centers have been opened in various parts of the city, disused buildings turned into recreation rooms, vacant lots made into gardens, hiking parties organized for country excursions, bathing beaches established on the lake front, and public schools opened for social purposes. Through the efforts of public-spirited citizens a medical clinic and a Psychopathic Institute have become associated with the Juvenile Court of Chicago, in addition to which an exhaustive study of court-records has just been completed. To this carefully collected data concerning the abnormal child, the Juvenile Protective Association hopes in time to add knowledge of the normal child who lives under the most adverse city conditions....

It is difficult to close this chapter without a reference to the efforts made in Chicago to secure the municipal franchise for women. During two long periods of agitation for a new City Charter, a representative body of women appealed to the public, to the Charter Convention, and to the Illinois Legislature for this very reasonable provision. During the campaign when I acted as chairman of the federation of a hundred women's organizations, nothing impressed me so forcibly as the fact that the response came from bodies of women representing the most varied traditions. We were joined by a church society of hundreds of Lutheran women, because Scandinavian women had exercised the municipal franchise since the seventeenth century and had found American cities strangely conservative; by organizations of working women who had keenly felt the need of the municipal franchise in order to secure for their workshops the most rudimentary sanitation and the consideration which the vote alone obtains for workingmen; by federations of mothers' meetings, who were interested in clean milk and the extension of kindergartens; by property-owning women, who had been powerless to protest against unjust taxation; by organizations of professional women, of university students, and of collegiate alumnae; and by women's clubs interested in municipal reforms. There was a complete absence of the traditional women's rights clamor, but much impressive testimony from busy and useful women that they had reached the place where they needed the franchise in order to carry on their own affairs. A striking witness as to the need of the ballot, even for the women who are restricted to the most primitive and traditional activities, occurred when some Russian women waited upon

me to ask whether under the new charter, they could vote for covered markets and so get rid of the shocking Chicago grime upon all their food; and when some neighboring Italian women sent me word that they would certainly vote for public washhouses if they ever had the chance to vote at all. It was all so human, so spontaneous, and so direct that it really seemed as if the time must be ripe for political expression of that public concern on the part of women which has so long been forced to seek indirection. None of these busy women wished to take the place of men nor to influence them in the direction of men's affairs, but they did seek an opportunity to coöperate directly in civic life through the use of the ballot in regard to their own affairs.

A Municipal Museum which was established in the Chicago Public Library building several years ago, largely through the activity of a group of women who had served as jurors in the departments of social economy, of education, and of sanitation in the World's Fair at St. Louis, showed nothing more clearly than that it is impossible to divide any of these departments from the political life of the modern city which is constantly forced to enlarge the boundary of its activity.

Martin Luther King, Jr.

On Being a Good Neighbor

In his "Letter from Birmingham Jail" (see Part II.B), Martin Luther King, Jr., had refuted the charge that he came to Birmingham as an "outside agitator." Like Paul the Apostle, he wrote, "I too am compelled to carry the gospel of freedom beyond my particular hometown." King expressed this idea more fully in his sermon "On Being a Good Neighbor," published with a collection of his most memorable sermons in *Strength to Love* (1963). King was one of our century's great orators, and his sermon appeals to both common folks and intellectuals, using arguments both spiritual and worldly. King preached almost every week, usually at Ebenezer Baptist Church in Atlanta, Georgia, where he served as co-pastor with his father.

On Being a Good Neighbor
Martin Luther King, Jr.

And who is my neighbour?

Luke 10:29

I Should like to talk with you about a good man, whose exemplary life will always be a flashing light to plague the dozing conscience of mankind. His goodness was not found in a passive commitment to a particular creed, but in his active participation in a life-saving deed; not in a moral pilgrimage that reached its destination point, but in the love ethic by which he journeyed life's highway. He was good because he was a good neighbor.

The ethical concern of this man is expressed in a magnificent little story, which begins with a theological discussion on the meaning of eternal life and concludes in a concrete expression of compassion on a dangerous road. Jesus is asked a question by a man who had been trained in the details of Jewish law: "Master, what shall I do to inherit eternal life." The retort is prompt: "What is written in the law? how readest thou?" After a moment the lawyer recites articulately: "Thou shalt love the Lord thy God with all thy heart, and with all thy soul, and with all thy strength, and with all thy mind; and thy neighbour as thyself." Then comes the decisive word from Jesus: "Thou hast answered right: this do, and thou shalt live."

The lawyer was chagrined. "Why," the people might ask, "would an expert in law raise a question that even the novice can answer?" Desiring to justify himself and to show that Jesus' reply was far from conclusive, the lawyer asks, "And who is my neighbour?" The lawyer was now taking up the cudgels of debate that might have turned the conversation into an abstract theological discussion. But Jesus, determined not to be caught in the "paralysis of analysis," pulls the question from mid-air and places it on a dangerous curve between Jerusalem and Jericho.

He told the story of "a certain man" who went down from Jerusalem to Jericho and fell among robbers who stripped him, beat him, and, departing, left him half dead. By chance a certain priest appeared, but he passed by on the other side, and later a Levite also passed by. Finally, a certain Samaritan, a half-breed from a people with whom the Jews had no dealings, appeared. When he saw the wounded man, he was moved with compassion, administered first aid, placed him on his beast, "and brought him to an inn, and took care of him."

Who is my neighbor? "I do not know his name," says Jesus in essence. "He is anyone toward whom you are neighborly. He is anyone who lies in need at life's roadside. He is neither Jew nor Gentile; he is neither Russian nor American; he is neither Negro nor white. He is 'a certain man'—any needy man—on one of the numerous Jericho roads of life." So Jesus defines a neighbor, not in a theological definition, but in a life situation.

What constituted the goodness of the good Samaritan? Why will he always be an inspiring paragon of neighborly virtue? It seems to me that this man's goodness may be described in one word—altruism. The good Samaritan was altruistic to the core. What is altruism? The dictionary defines altruism as "regard for, and devotion to, the interest of others." The Samaritan was good because he made concern for others the first law of his life.

The Samaritan had the capacity for a *universal altruism*. He had a piercing insight into that which is beyond the eternal accidents of race, religion, and nationality. One of the great tragedies of man's long trek along the highway of history has been the limiting of neighborly concern to tribe, race, class, or nation. The God of early Old Testament days was a tribal god and the ethic was tribal. "Thou shalt not kill" meant "Thou shalt not kill a fellow Israelite, but for God's sake, kill a Philistine." Greek democracy embraced a certain aristocracy, but not the hordes of Greek slaves whose labors built the city-states. The universalism at the center of the Declaration of Independence has been shamefully negated by America's appalling tendency to substitute "some" for "all." Numerous people in the North and South still believe that the affirmation, "All men are created equal," means "All white men are created equal." Our unswerving devotion to monopolistic capitalism makes us more concerned about the economic security of the captains of industry than for the laboring men whose sweat and skills keep industry functioning.

What are the devastating consequences of this narrow, group-centered attitude? It means that one does not really mind what happens to the people outside his group. If an American is concerned only about his nation, he will not be concerned about the peoples of Asia, Africa, or South America. Is this not why nations engage in the madness of war without the slightest sense of penitence? Is this not why the murder of a citizen of your own nation is a crime, but the murder of the citizens of another nation in war is an act of heroic virtue? If manufacturers are concerned only in their personal interests, they will pass by on the other side while thousands of working people are stripped of their jobs and left displaced on some Jericho road as a result of automation, and they will judge every move toward a better distribution of wealth and a better life for the working man to be socialistic. If a white man is concerned only about his race, he will casually pass by the Negro who has been robbed of his personhood, stripped of his sense of dignity, and left dying on some wayside road.

A few years ago, when an automobile carrying several members of a Negro college basketball team had an accident on a Southern highway, three of the young men were severely injured. An ambulance was immediately called, but on arriving at the place of the accident, the driver, who was white, said without apology that it was not his policy to service Negroes, and he drove away. The driver of a passing automobile graciously drove the boys to the nearest hospital, but the attending physician belligerently said, "We don't take niggers in this hospital." When the boys finally arrived at a "colored" hospital in a town some fifty miles from the scene of the accident, one was dead and the other two died thirty and fifty minutes later respectively. Probably all three could have been saved if they had been given immediate treatment. This is only one of thousands of inhuman incidents that occur daily in the South, an unbelievable expression of the barbaric consequences of any tribal-centered, national-centered, or racial-centered ethic.

The real tragedy of such narrow provincialism is that we see people as entities or merely as things. Too seldom do we see people in their true *humanness*. A spiritual myopia limits our vision to external accidents. We see men as Jews or Gentiles, Catholics or protestants, Chinese or American, Negroes or whites. We fail to think of them as fellow human beings made from the same basic stuff as we, molded in the same divine image. The priest and the Levite saw only a bleeding body, not a human being like themselves. But the good Samaritan will always remind us to remove the cataracts of provincialism from our spiritual eyes and see men as men. If the Samaritan had considered the wounded man as a Jew first, he would not have stopped, for the Jews and the Samaritans had no dealings. He saw him as a human being first, who was a Jew only by accident. The good neighbor looks beyond the external accidents and discerns those inner qualities that make all men human and, therefore, brothers.

The Samaritan possessed the capacity for a *dangerous altruism*. He risked his life to save a brother. When we ask why the priest and the Levite did not stop to help the wounded man, numerous suggestions come to mind. Perhaps they could not delay their arrival at an important ecclesiastical meeting. Perhaps religious regulations demanded that they touch no human body for several hours prior to the performing of their temple functions. Or perhaps they were on their way to an organizational meeting of a Jericho Road Improvement Association. Certainly this would have been a real need, for it is not enough to aid a wounded man on the Jericho Road; it is also important to change the conditions which make robbery possible. Philanthropy is commendable, but it must not cause the philanthropist to overlook the circumstances of economic injustice which make philanthropy necessary. Maybe the priest and the Levite believed that it is better to cure injustice at the causal source than to get bogged down with a single individual effect.

These are probable reasons for their failure to stop, yet there is another possibility, often overlooked, that they were afraid. The Jericho Road was a dangerous road. When Mrs. King and I visited the Holy Land, we rented a car and drove from Jerusalem to Jericho. As we traveled slowly down that meandering, mountainous road, I said to my wife, "I can now understand why Jesus chose this road as the setting for his parable." Jerusalem is some two thousand feet above and Jericho one thousand feet below sea level. The descent is made in less than twenty miles. Many sudden curves provide likely places for ambushing and exposes the traveler to unforeseen attacks. Long ago the road was known as the Bloody Pass. So it is possible that the Priest and the Levite were afraid that if they stopped, they too would be beaten. Perhaps the robbers were still nearby. Or maybe the wounded man on the ground was a faker, who wished to draw passing travelers to his side for quick and easy seizure. I imagine that the first question which the priest and the Levite asked was: "If I stop to help this man, what will happen to me?" But by the very nature of his concern, the good Samaritan reversed the question: "If I do not stop to help this man, what will happen to him?" The good Samaritan engaged in a dangerous altruism.

We so often ask, "What will happen to my job, my prestige, or my status if I take a stand on this issue? Will my home be bombed, will my life be threatened, or will I be jailed?" The good man always reverses the question. Albert Schweitzer did not ask, "What will happen to my prestige and security as a university professor and to my status as a Bach organist, if I work with the people of Africa?" but rather he asked, "What will happen to these millions of people who have been wounded by the forces of injustice, if I do not go to them?" Abraham Lincoln did not ask, "What will happen to me if I issue the Emancipation Proclamation and bring an end to chattel slavery?" but he asked, "What will happen to the Union and to millions of Negro people, if I fail to do it?" The Negro professional does not ask, "What will happen to my secure position, my middle-class status, or my personal safety, if I participate in the movement to end the system of segregation?" but "What will happen to the cause of justice and the masses of Negro people who have never experienced the warmth of economic security, if I do not participate actively and courageously in the movement?"

The ultimate measure of a man is not where he stands in moments of comfort and convenience, but where he stands at times of challenge and controversy. The true neighbor will risk his position, his prestige, and even his life for the welfare of others. In dangerous valleys and hazardous pathways, he will lift some bruised and beaten brother to a higher and more noble life.

The Samaritan also possessed *excessive altruism*. With his own hands he bound the wounds of the man and then set him on his own beast. It would have been easier to pay an ambulance to take the unfortunate man to the hospital, rather than risk having his neatly trimmed suit stained with blood.

True altruism is more than the capacity to pity; it is the capacity to sympathize. Pity may represent little more than the impersonal concern which prompts the mailing of a check, but true sympathy is the personal concern which demands the giving of one's soul. Pity may arise from interest in an abstraction called humanity, but sympathy grows out of a concern for a par-

ticular needy human being who lies at life's roadside. Sympathy is fellow feeling for the person in need—his pain, agony, and burdens. Our missionary efforts fail when they are based on pity, rather than true compassion. Instead of seeking to do something *with* the African and Asian peoples, we have too often sought only to do something *for* them. An expression of pity, devoid of genuine sympathy, leads to a new form of paternalism which no self-respecting person can accept. Dollars possess the potential for helping wounded children of God on life's Jericho Road, but unless those dollars are distributed by compassionate fingers they will enrich neither the giver nor the receiver. Millions of missionary dollars have gone to Africa from the hands of church people who would die a million deaths before they would permit a single African the privilege of worshiping in their congregation. Millions of Peace Corps dollars are being invested in Africa because of the votes of some men who fight unrelentingly to prevent African ambassadors from holding membership in their diplomatic clubs or establish residency in their particular neighborhoods. The Peace Corps will fail if it seeks to do something *for* the underprivileged peoples of the world; it will succeed if it seeks creatively to do something *with* them. It will fail as a negative gesture to defeat Communism; it will succeed only as, a positive effort to wipe poverty, ignorance, and disease from the earth. Money devoid of love is like salt devoid of savor, good for nothing except to be trodden under the foot of men. True neighborliness requires personal concern. The Samaritan used his hands to bind up the wounds of the robbed man's body, and he also released an overflowing love to bind up the wounds of his broken spirit.

Another expression of the excessive altruism on the part of the Samaritan was his willingness to go far beyond the call of duty. After tending to the man's wounds, he put him on his beast, carried him to an inn, and left money for his care, making clear that if further financial needs arose he would gladly meet them. "Whatsoever thou spendest more, when I come again, I will repay thee." Stopping short of this, he would have more than fulfilled any possible rule concerning one's duty to a wounded stranger. He went beyond the second mile. His love was complete.

Dr. Harry Emerson Fosdick has made an impressive distinction between enforceable and unenforceable obligations. The former are regulated by the codes of society and the vigorous implementation of law-enforcement agencies. Breaking these obligations, spelled out on thousands of pages in law books, has filled numerous prisons. But unenforceable obligations are beyond the reach of the laws of society. They concern inner attitudes, genuine person-to-person relations, and expressions of compassion which law books cannot regulate and jails cannot rectify. Such obligations are met by one's commitment to an inner law, written on the heart. Man-made laws assure justice, but a higher law produces love. No code of conduct ever persuaded a father to love his children or a husband to show affection to his wife. The law court may force him to provide bread for the family, but it cannot make him provide the bread of love. A good father is obedient to the unenforceable. The good Samaritan represents the conscience of mankind because he also was obedient to that which could not be enforced. No law in the world could have produced such unalloyed compassion, such genuine love, such thorough altruism.

In our nation today a mighty struggle is taking place. It is a struggle to conquer the reign of an evil monster called segregation and its inseparable twin called discrimination—a monster that has wandered through this land for well-nigh one hundred years, stripping millions of Negro people of their sense of dignity and robbing them of their birthright of freedom.

Let us never succumb to the temptation of believing that legislation and judicial decrees play only minor roles in solving this problem. Morality cannot be legislated, but behavior can be regulated. Judicial decrees may not change

the heart, but they can restrain the heartless. The law cannot make an employer love an employee, but it can prevent him from refusing to hire me because of the color of my skin. The habits, if not the hearts, of people have been and are being altered every day by legislative acts, judicial decisions, and executive orders. Let us not be misled by those who argue that segregation cannot be ended by the force of law.

But acknowledging this, we must admit that the ultimate solution to the race problem lies in the willingness of men to obey the unenforceable. Court orders and federal enforcement agencies are of inestimable value in achieving desegregation, but desegregation is only a partial, though necessary, step toward the final goal which we seek to realize, genuine intergroup and interpersonal living. Desegregation will break down the legal barriers and bring men together physically, but something must touch the hearts and souls of men so that they will come together spiritually because it is natural and right. A vigorous enforcement of civil rights laws will bring an end to segregated public facilities which are barriers to a truly desegregated society, but it cannot bring an end to fears, prejudice, pride, and irrationality, which are the barriers to a truly integrated society. These dark and demonic responses will be removed only as men are possessed by the invisible, inner law which etches on their hearts the conviction that all men are brothers and that love is mankind's most potent weapon for personal and social transformation. True integration will be achieved by true neighbors who are willingly obedient to unenforceable obligations.

More than ever before, my friends, men of all races and nations are today challenged to be neighborly. The call for a worldwide good-neighbor policy is more than an ephemeral shibboleth; it is the call to a way of life which will transform our imminent cosmic elegy into a psalm of creative fulfillment. No longer can we afford the luxury of passing by on the other side. Such folly was once called moral failure;

today it will lead to universal suicide. We cannot long survive spiritually separated in a world that is geographically together. In the final analysis, I must not ignore the wounded man on life's Jericho Road, because he is a part of me and I am a part of him. His agony diminishes me, and his salvation enlarges me.

In our quest to make neighborly love a reality, we have, in addition to the inspiring example of the good Samaritan, the magnanimous life of our Christ to guide us. His altruism was universal, for he thought of all men, even publicans and sinners, as brothers. His altruism was dangerous, for he willingly traveled hazardous roads in a cause he knew was right. His altruism was excessive, for he chose to die on Calvary, history's most magnificent expression of obedience to the unenforceable.

Malcolm Gladwell

Six Degrees of Lois Weisberg

Malcolm Gladwell (1963--) is a journalist based in New York City who has been a staff writer for *The New Yorker* since 1996. From 1987 to 1996, he was a science writer, and later the New York bureau chief, for the *Washington Post*. He was born in the United Kingdom but raised in rural Canada. He is best known as the author of the best-selling books *The Tipping Point: How Little Things Can Make a Big Difference* (2000) and *Blink: The Power of Thinking Without Thinking* (2005). In 2005, Time Magazine named Gladwell one of its 100 Most Influential People.

In "Six Degrees of Lois Weisberg," originally published in *The New Yorker* in 1999, Gladwell tells the story of a woman who fits his personality type of a "Connector," someone who knows lots of people. As the story unfolds, the reader will find that Lois Weisberg doesn't know and network with people just for the sake of networking, but rather, to bring them together to create positive change for communities. Her story reinforces the importance of relationship building in public life, and raises a number of critical questions for anyone involved in community service or social change efforts.

Six Degrees of Lois Weisberg
Malcolm Gladwell

*She's a grandmother, she lives in a
big house in Chicago, and you've never
heard of her. Does she run the world?*

1

Everyone who knows Lois Weisberg has
a story about meeting Lois Weisberg,
and although she has done thousands of
things in her life and met thousands of people,
all the stories are pretty much the same. Lois
(everyone calls her Lois) is invariably smoking
a cigarette and drinking one of her dozen or so
daily cups of coffee. She will have been up until
two or three the previous morning, and up again
at seven or seven-thirty, because she hardly
seems to sleep. In some accounts — particularly
if the meeting took place in the winter — she'll
be wearing her white, furtopped Dr. Zhivago
boots with gold tights; but she may have on her
platform tennis shoes, or the leather jacket with
the little studs on it, or maybe an outrageous
piece of costume jewelry, and, always, those
huge, rhinestone-studded glasses that make her
big eyes look positively enormous. "I have no
idea why I asked you to come here, I have no
job for you," Lois told Wendy Willrich when
Willrich went to Lois's office in downtown
Chicago a few years ago for an interview. But
by the end of the interview Lois did have a job
for her, because for Lois meeting someone is
never just about meeting someone. If she likes
you, she wants to recruit you into one of her
grand schemes — to sweep you up into her
world. A while back, Lois called up Helen
Doria, who was then working for someone on
Chicago's city council, and said, "I don't have
a job for you. Well, I might have a little job. I
need someone to come over and help me clean

up my office." By this, she meant that she had a big job for Helen but just didn't know what it was yet. Helen came, and, sure enough, Lois got her a big job.

Cindy Mitchell first met Lois twenty-three years ago, when she bundled up her baby and ran outside into one of those frigid Chicago winter mornings because some people from the Chicago Park District were about to cart away a beautiful sculpture of Carl von Linné from the park across the street. Lois happened to be driving by at the time, and, seeing all the commotion, she slammed on her brakes, charged out of her car – all five feet of her – and began asking Cindy questions, rat-a-tat-tat: "Who are you? What's going on here? Why do you care?" By the next morning, Lois had persuaded two Chicago Tribune reporters to interview Cindy and turn the whole incident into a cause célèbre, and she had recruited Cindy to join an organization she'd just started called Friends of the Parks, and then, when she found out that Cindy was a young mother at home who was too new in town to have many friends, she told her, "I've found a friend for you. Her name is Helen, and she has a little boy your kid's age, and you will meet her next week and the two of you will be best friends." That's exactly what happened, and, what's more, Cindy went on to spend ten years as president of Friends of the Park. "Almost everything that I do today and eighty to ninety per cent of my friends came about because of her, because of that one little chance meeting," Cindy says. "That's a scary thing. Try to imagine what would have happened if she had come by five minutes earlier."

It could be argued, of course, that even if Cindy hadn't met Lois on the street twenty-three years ago she would have met her somewhere else, maybe a year later or two years later or ten years later, or, at least, she would have met someone who knew Lois or would have met someone who knew someone who knew Lois, since Lois Weisberg is connected, by a very short chain, to nearly everyone. Weisberg is now the Commissioner of Cultural Affairs

for the City of Chicago. But in the course of her seventy-three years she has hung out with actors and musicians and doctors and lawyers and politicians and activists and environmentalists, and once, on a whim, she opened a secondhand-jewelry store named for her granddaughter Becky Fyffe, and every step of the way Lois has made friends and recruited people, and a great many of those people have stayed with her to this day. "When we were doing the jazz festival, it turned out – surprise, surprise – that she was buddies with Dizzy Gillespie," one of her friends recalls. "This is a woman who cannot carry a tune. She has no sense of rhythm. One night Tony Bennett was in town, and so we hang out with Tony Bennett, hearing about the old days with him and Lois."

Once, in the mid-fifties, on a whim, Lois took the train to New York to attend the World Science Fiction Convention and there she met a young writer by the name of Arthur C. Clarke. Clarke took a shine to Lois, and next time he was in Chicago he called her up. "He was at a pay phone," Lois recalls. "He said, 'Is there anyone in Chicago I should meet?' I told him to come over to my house." Lois has a throaty voice, baked hard by half a century of nicotine, and she pauses between sentences to give herself the opportunity for a quick puff. Even when she's not smoking, she pauses anyway, as if to keep in practice. "I called Bob Hughes, one of the people who wrote for my paper." Pause. "I said, 'Do you know anyone in Chicago interested in talking to Arthur Clarke?' He said, 'Yeah, Isaac Asimov is in town. And this guy Robert, Robert... Robert Heinlein.' So they all came over and sat in my study." Pause. "Then they called over to me and they said, 'Lois' — I can't remember the word they used. They had some word for me. It was something about how I was the kind of person who brings people together."

This is in some ways the archetypal Lois Weisberg story. First, she reaches out to somebody — somebody outside her world. (At the time, she was running a drama troupe, whereas

Arthur C. Clarke wrote science fiction.) Equally important, that person responds to her. Then there's the fact that when Arthur Clarke came to Chicago and wanted to meet someone Lois came up with Isaac Asimov. She says it was a fluke that Asimov was in town. But if it hadn't been Asimov it would have been someone else. Lois ran a salon out of her house on the North Side in the late nineteen-fifties, and one of the things that people remember about it is that it was always, effortlessly, integrated. Without that salon, blacks would still have socialized with whites on the North Side — though it was rare back then, it happened. But it didn't happen by accident: it happened because a certain kind of person made it happen. That's what Asimov and Clarke meant when they said that Lois has this thing — whatever it is — that brings people together.

2

Lois is a type — a particularly rare and extraordinary type, but a type nonetheless. She's the type of person who seems to know everybody, and this type can be found in every walk of life. Someone I met at a wedding (actually, the wedding of the daughter of Lois's neighbors, the Newbergers) told me that if I ever went to Massapequa I should look up a woman named Marsha, because Marsha was the type of person who knew everybody. In Cambridge, Massachusetts, the word is that a tailor named Charlie Davidson knows everybody. In Houston, I'm told, there is an attorney named Harry Reasoner who knows everybody. There are probably Lois Weisbergs in Akron and Tucson and Paris and in some little town in the Yukon Territory, up by the Arctic Circle. We've all met someone like Lois Weisberg. Yet, although we all know a Lois Weisberg type, we don't know much about the Lois Weisberg type. Why is it, for example, that these few, select people seem to know everyone and the rest of us don't? And how important are the people who know everyone? This second question is critical, because

once you begin even a cursory examination of the life of someone like Lois Weisberg you start to suspect that he or she may be far more important than we would ever have imagined – that the people who know everyone, in some oblique way, may actually run the world. I don't mean that they are the sort who head up the Fed or General Motors or Microsoft, but that, in a very down-to-earth, day-to-day way, they make the world work. They spread ideas and information. They connect varied and isolated parts of society. Helen Doria says someone high up in the Chicago government told her that Lois is "the epicenter of the city administration," which is the right way to put it. Lois is far from being the most important or the most powerful person in Chicago. But if you connect all the dots that constitute the vast apparatus of government and influence and interest groups in the city of Chicago you'll end up coming back to Lois again and again. Lois is a connector.

Lois, it must be said, did not set out to know everyone. "She doesn't network for the sake of networking," says Gary Johnson, who was Lois's boss years ago, when she was executive director of the Chicago Council of Lawyers. "I just think she has the confidence that all the people in the world, whether she's met them or not, are in her Rolodex already, and that all she has to do is figure out how to reach them and she'll be able to connect with them."

Nor is Lois charismatic — at least, not in the way that we think of extroverts and public figures as being charismatic. She doesn't fill a room; eyes don't swivel toward her as she makes her entrance. Lois has frizzy blond hair, and when she's thinking — between her coffee and her cigarette — she kneads the hair on the top of her head, so that by the end of a particularly difficult meeting it will be standing almost straight up. "She's not like the image of the Washington society doyenne," Gary Johnson says. "You know, one of those people who identify you, take you to lunch, give you the treatment. Her social life is very different. When I bump into her and she says, 'Oh, we should catch up,' what she means is that someday I should go with her to her office, and we'd go down to the snack bar and buy a muffin and then sit in her office while she answered the phone. For a real treat, when I worked with her at the Council of Lawyers she would take me to the dining room in the Wieboldt's department store." Johnson is an old-school Chicago intellectual who works at a fancy law firm and has a corner office with one of those Midwestern views in which, if you look hard enough, you can almost see Nebraska, and the memory of those lunches at Wieboldt's seems to fill him with delight. "Now, you've got to understand that the Wieboldt's department store – which doesn't exist anymore – was a notch below Field's, where the suburban society ladies have their lunch, and it's also a notch below Carson's," he says. "There was a kind of room there where people who bring their own string bags to go shopping would have a quick lunch. This was her idea of a lunch out. We're not talking Pamela Harriman here."

In the mid-eighties, Lois quit a job she'd had for four years, as director of special events in the administration of Harold Washington, and somehow hooked up with a group of itinerant peddlers who ran the city's flea markets. "There was this lady who sold jewelry," Lois said. "She was a person out of Dickens. She was bedraggled. She had a houseful of cats. But she knew how to buy jewelry, and I wanted her to teach me. I met her whole circle of friends, all these old gay men who had antique stores. Once a week, we would go to the Salvation Army." Lois was arguably the most important civic activist in the city. Her husband was a judge. She lived in a huge house in one of Chicago's nicest neighborhoods. Yet somehow she managed to be plausible as a flea-market peddler to a bunch of flea-market peddlers, the same way she managed to be plausible as a music lover to a musician like Tony Bennett. It doesn't matter who she's with or what she's doing; she always manages to be in the thick of things. "There was a woman I knew – Sandra – who had a kid in

school with my son Joseph," Lois told me. Lois has a habit of telling stories that appear to be tangential and digressive but, on reflection, turn out to be parables of a sort. "She helped all these Asians living uptown. One day, she came over here and said there was this young Chinese man who wanted to meet an American family and learn to speak English better and was willing to cook for his room and board. Well, I'm always eager to have a cook, and especially a Chinese cook, because my family loves Chinese food. They could eat it seven days a week. So Sandra brought this man over here. His name was Shi Young. He was a graduate student at the Art Institute of Chicago." Shi Young lived with Lois and her family for two years, and during that time Chicago was in the midst of political turmoil. Harold Washington, who would later become the first black mayor of the city, was attempting to unseat the remains of the Daley political machine, and Lois's house, naturally, was the site of late-night, top-secret strategy sessions for the pro-Washington reformers of Chicago's North Side. "We'd have all these important people here, and Shi Young would come down and listen," Lois recalls. "I didn't think anything of it." But Shi Young, as it turns out, was going back up to his room and writing up what he heard for the China Youth Daily, a newspaper with a circulation in the tens of millions. Somehow, in the improbable way that the world works, a portal was opened up, connecting Chicago's North Side reform politics and the readers of the China Youth Daily, and that link was Lois's living room. You could argue that this was just a fluke — just as it was a fluke that Isaac Asimov was in town and that Lois happened to be driving by when Cindy Mitchell came running out of her apartment. But sooner or later all those flukes begin to form a pattern.

3

In the late nineteen-sixties, a Harvard social psychologist named Stanley Milgram conducted an experiment in an effort to find an answer to what is known as the small-world problem, though it could also be called the Lois Weisberg problem. It is this: How are human beings connected? Do we belong to separate worlds, operating simultaneously but autonomously, so that the links between any two people, anywhere in the world, are few and distant? Or are we all bound up together in a grand, interlocking web? Milgram's idea was to test this question with a chain letter. For one experiment, he got the names of a hundred and sixty people, at random, who lived in Omaha, Nebraska, and he mailed each of them a packet. In the packet was the name and address of a stockbroker who worked in Boston and lived in Sharon, Massachusetts. Each person was instructed to write his name on a roster in the packet and send it on to a friend or acquaintance who he thought would get it closer to the stockbroker. The idea was that when the letters finally arrived at the stockbroker's house Milgram could look at the roster of names and establish how closely connected someone chosen at random from one part of the country was to another person chosen at random in another part. Milgram found that most of the letters reached the stockbroker in five or six steps. It is from this experiment that we got the concept of six degrees of separation.

That phrase is now so familiar that it is easy to lose sight of how surprising Milgram's finding was. Most of us don't have particularly diverse groups of friends. In one well-known study, two psychologists asked people living in the Dyckman public-housing project, in uptown Manhattan, about their closest friend in the project; almost ninety per cent of the friends lived in the same building, and half lived on the same floor. In general, people chose friends of similar age and race. But if the friend lived down the hall, both age and race became a lot less important. Proximity overpowered similarity. Another study, involving students at the University of Utah, found that if you ask someone why he is friendly with someone else

he'll say that it is because they share similar attitudes. But if you actually quiz the pairs of students on their attitudes you'll find out that this is an illusion, and that what friends really tend to have in common are activities. We're friends with the people we do things with, not necessarily with the people we resemble. We don't seek out friends; we simply associate with the people who occupy the same physical places that we do: People in Omaha are not, as a rule, friends with people who live in Sharon, Massachusetts. So how did the packets get halfway across the country in just five steps? "When I asked an intelligent friend of mine how many steps he thought it would take, he estimated that it would require 100 intermediate persons or more to move from Nebraska to Sharon," Milgram wrote. "Many people make somewhat similar estimates, and are surprised to learn that only five intermediaries will – on the average – suffice. Somehow it does not accord with intuition."

The explanation is that in the six degrees of separation not all degrees are equal. When Milgram analyzed his experiments, for example, he found that many of the chains reaching to Sharon followed the same asymmetrical pattern. Twenty-four packets reached the stockbroker at his home, in Sharon, and sixteen of those were given to him by the same person, a clothing merchant whom Milgram calls Mr. Jacobs. The rest of the packets were sent to the stockbroker at his office, and of those the majority came through just two men, whom Milgram calls Mr. Brown and Mr. Jones. In all, half of the responses that got to the stockbroker were delivered to him by these three people. Think of it. Dozens of people, chosen at random from a large Midwestern city, sent out packets independently. Some went through college acquaintances. Some sent their packets to relatives. Some sent them to old workmates. Yet in the end, when all those idiosyncratic chains were completed, half of the packets passed through the hands of Jacobs, Jones, and Brown. Six degrees of separation doesn't simply mean that everyone is linked to everyone else in just six steps. It means that a very small number of people are linked to everyone else in a few steps, and the rest of us are linked to the world through those few.

There's an easy way to explore this idea. Suppose that you made a list of forty people whom you would call your circle of friends (not including family members or co-workers), and you worked backward from each person until you could identify who was ultimately responsible for setting in motion the series of connections which led to that friendship. I met my oldest friend, Bruce, for example, in first grade, so I'm the responsible party. That's easy. I met my college friend Nigel because he lived down the hall in the dormitory from Tom, whom I had met because in my freshman year he invited me to play touch football. Tom, then, is responsible for Nigel. Once you've made all the connections, you will find the same names coming up again and again. I met my friend Amy when she and her friend Katie came to a restaurant where I was having dinner. I know Katie because she is best friends with my friend Larissa, whom I know because I was told to look her up by a mutual friend, Mike A., whom I know because he went to school with another friend of mine, Mike H., who used to work at a political weekly with my friend Jacob. No Jacob, no Amy. Similarly, I met my friend Sarah S. at a birthday party a year ago because she was there with a writer named David, who was there at the invitation of his agent, Tina, whom I met through my friend Leslie, whom I know because her sister Nina is best friends with my friend Ann, whom I met through my old roommate Maura, who was my roommate because she had worked with a writer named Sarah L., who was a college friend of my friend Jacob. No Jacob, no Sarah S. In fact, when I go down my list of forty friends, thirty of them, in one way or another, lead back to Jacob. My social circle is really not a circle but an inverted pyramid. And the capstone of the pyramid is a single person, Jacob, who is responsible for an overwhelming majority of my relationships. Jacob's full name, incidentally, is Jacob Weisberg. He is Lois Weisberg's son.

This isn't to say, though, that Jacob is just like Lois. Jacob may be the capstone of my pyramid, but Lois is the capstone of lots and lots of people's pyramids, and that makes her social role different. In Milgram's experiment, Mr. Jacobs the clothing merchant was the person to go through to get to the stockbroker. Lois is the kind of person you would use to get to the stockbrokers of Sharon and also the cabaret singers of Sharon and the barkeeps of Sharon and the guy who gave up a thriving career in orthodontics to open a small vegetarian falafel hut.

4

There is another way to look at this question, and that's through the popular parlor game Six Degrees of Kevin Bacon. The idea behind the game is to try to link in fewer than six steps any actor or actress, through the movies they've been in, to the actor Kevin Bacon. For example, O. J. Simpson was in "Naked Gun" with Priscilla Presley, who was in "The Adventures of Ford Fairlane" with Gilbert Gottfried, who was in "Beverly Hills Cop II" with Paul Reiser, who was in "Diner" with Kevin Bacon. That's four steps. Mary Pickford was in "Screen Snapshots" with Clark Gable, who was in "Combat America" with Tony Romano, who, thirty-five years later, was in "Starting Over" with Bacon. That's three steps. What's funny about the game is that Bacon, although he is a fairly young actor, has already been in so many movies with so many people that there is almost no one to whom he can't be easily connected. Recently, a computer scientist at the University of Virginia by the name of Brett Tjaden actually sat down and figured out what the average degree of connectedness is for the quarter million or so actors and actresses listed in the Internet Movie Database: he came up with 2.8312 steps.

That sounds impressive, except that Tjaden then went back and performed an even more heroic calculation, figuring out what the average degree of connectedness was for everyone in the database. Bacon, it turns out, ranks only six hundred and sixty-eighth. Martin Sheen, by contrast, can be connected, on average, to every other actor, in 2.63681 steps, which puts him almost six hundred and fifty places higher than Bacon. Elliott Gould can be connected even more quickly, in 2.63601. Among the top fifteen are people like Robert Mitchum, Gene Hackman, Donald Sutherland, Rod Steiger, Shelley Winters, and Burgess Meredith.

Why is Kevin Bacon so far behind these actors? Recently, in the journal Nature, the mathematicians Duncan Watts and Steven Strogatz published a dazzling theoretical explanation of connectedness, but a simpler way to understand this question is to look at who Bacon is. Obviously, he is a lot younger than the people at the top of the list are and has made fewer movies. But that accounts for only some of the difference. A top-twenty person, like Burgess Meredith, made a hundred and fourteen movies in the course of his career. Gary Cooper, though, starred in about the same number of films and ranks only eight hundred and seventy-eighth, with a 2.85075 score. John Wayne made a hundred and eighty-three movies in his fifty-year career and still ranks only a hundred and sixteenth, at 2.7173. What sets someone like Meredith apart is his range. More than half of John Wayne's movies were Westerns, and that means he made the same kind of movie with the same kind of actors over and over again. Burgess Meredith, by contrast, was in great movies, like the Oscar-winning "Of Mice and Men" (1939), and in dreadful movies, like "Beware! The Blob" (1972). He was nominated for an Oscar for his role in "The Day of the Locust" and also made TV commercials for Skippy peanut butter. He was in four "Rocky" movies, and also played Don Learo in Godard's "King Lear." He was in schlocky made-for-TV movies, in B movies that pretty much went straight to video, and in pictures considered modern classics. He was in forty-two dramas, twenty-two comedies, eight adventure films, seven action films, five sci-fi films, five horror flicks, five Westerns, five documentaries, four crime movies, four thrillers, three war movies, three films noir, two children's films, two romances, two mysteries, one musical, and one animated film. Burgess Meredith was the kind of actor who was connected to everyone because he managed to move up and down and back and forth among all the different worlds and subcultures that the acting profession has to offer. When we say, then, that Lois Weisberg is the kind of person who "knows everyone," we mean it in precisely this way. It is not merely that she knows lots of people. It is that she belongs to lots of different worlds.

In the nineteen-fifties, Lois started her drama troupe in Chicago. The daughter of a prominent attorney, she was then in her twenties, living in one of the suburbs north of the city with two small children. In 1956, she decided to stage a festival to mark the centenary of George Bernard Shaw's birth. She hit up the reclusive billionaire John D. MacArthur for money. ("I go to the Pump Room for lunch. Booth One. There is a man, lurking around a pillar, with a cowboy hat and dirty, dusty boots. It's him.") She invited William Saroyan and Norman Thomas to speak on Shaw's legacy; she put on Shaw plays in theatres around the city; and she got written up in Life. She then began putting out a newspaper devoted to Shaw, which mutated into an underground alternative weekly called the Paper. By then, Lois was living in a big house on Chicago's near North Side, and on Friday nights people from the Paper gathered there for editorial meetings. William Friedkin, who went on to direct "The French Connection" and "The Exorcist," was a regular, and so were the attorney Elmer Gertz (who won parole for Nathan Leopold) and some of the editors from Playboy, which was just up the street. People like Art Farmer and Thelonious Monk and Dizzy Gillespie and Lenny Bruce would stop by when they were in town. Bruce actually lived in Lois's house for a while. "My mother was hysterical about it, especially one day when she rang the doorbell and he answered in a bath towel," Lois told me. "We had a window on the porch, and he didn't have a key, so the window was always left open for him. There were a lot of rooms in that house, and a lot of people stayed there and I didn't know they were there." Pause. Puff. "I never could stand his jokes. I didn't really like his act. I couldn't stand all the words he was using."

Lois's first marriage – to a drugstore owner named Leonard Solomon – was breaking up around this time, so she took a job doing public relations for an injury-rehabilitation institute. From there, she went to work for a public-interest law firm called B.P.I., and while she was at B.P.I, she became concerned about the fact that Chicago's parks were neglected and crumbling, so she gathered together a motley collection of nature lovers, historians, civic activists, and housewives, and founded the lobbying group Friends of the Parks. Then she became alarmed on discovering that a commuter railroad that ran along the south shore of Lake Michigan – from South Bend to Chicago – was about to shut down, so she gathered together a motley collection of railroad enthusiasts and environmentalists and commuters, and founded South Shore Recreation, thereby saving the railroad. Lois loved the railroad buffs. "They were all good friends of mine," she says. "They all wrote to me. They came from California. They came from everywhere. We had meetings. They were really interesting. I came this close" – and here she held her index finger half an inch above her thumb – "to becoming one of them." Instead, though, she became the executive director of the Chicago Council of Lawyers, a progressive bar association. Then she ran Congressman Sidney Yates's reelection campaign. Then her sister June introduced her to someone who got her the job with Mayor Washington. Then she had her flea-market period. Finally, she went to work for Mayor Daley as Chicago's Commissioner of Cultural Affairs.

If you go through that history and keep count, the number of worlds that Lois has belonged to comes to eight: the actors, the writers, the doctors, the lawyers, the park lovers, the politicians, the railroad buffs, and the flea-market aficionados. When I asked Lois to make her own list, she added musicians and the visual artists and architects and hospitality-industry people whom she works with in her current job. But if you looked harder at Lois's life you could probably subdivide her experiences into fifteen or twenty worlds. She has the same ability to move among different subcultures and niches that the busiest actors do. Lois is to Chicago what Burgess Meredith is to the movies.

Lois was, in fact, a friend of Burgess Meredith. I learned this by accident, which is the way I learned about most of the strange celebrity details of Lois's life, since she doesn't tend to drop names. It was when I was with her at her house one night, a big, rambling affair just off the lakeshore, with room after room filled with odds and ends and old photographs and dusty furniture and weird bric-a-brac, such as a collection of four hundred antique egg cups. She was wearing bluejeans and a flowery-print top and she was smoking Carlton Menthol 100s and cooking pasta and holding forth to her son Joe on the subject of George Bernard Shaw, when she started talking about Burgess Meredith. "He was in Chicago in a play called 'Teahouse of the August Moon,' in 1956," she said, "and he came to see my production of 'Back to Methuselah,' and after the play he came up to me and said he was teaching acting classes, and asked would I come and talk to his class about Shaw. Well, I couldn't say no." Meredith liked Lois, and when she was running her alternative newspaper he would write letters and send in little doodles, and later she helped him raise money for a play he was doing called "Kicks and Company." It starred a woman named Nichelle Nichols, who lived at Lois's house for a while. "Nichelle was a marvellous singer and dancer," Lois said. "She was the lead. She was also the lady on the first..." Lois was doing so many things at once — chopping and stirring and smoking and eating and talking — that she couldn't remember the name of the show that made Nichols a star. "What's that space thing?" She looked toward Joe for help. He started laughing. "Star something," she said. "'Star...Star Trek'! Nichelle was Lieutenant Uhura!"

5

On a sunny morning not long ago, Lois went to a little café just off the Magnificent Mile, in downtown Chicago, to have breakfast with Mayor Daley. Lois drove there in a big black Mercury, a city car. Lois always drives big cars, and, because she is so short and the cars are so big, all that you can see when she drives by is the top of her frizzy blond head and the lighted ember of her cigarette. She was wearing a short skirt and a white vest and was carrying a white cloth shopping bag. Just what was in the bag was unclear, since Lois doesn't have a traditional relationship to the trappings of bureaucracy. Her office, for example, does not have a desk in it, only a sofa and chairs and a coffee table. At meetings, she sits at the head of a conference table in the adjoining room, and, as often as not, has nothing in front of her except a lighter, a pack of Carltons, a cup of coffee, and an octagonal orange ceramic ashtray, which she moves a few inches forward or a few inches back when she's making an important point, or moves a few inches to the side when she is laughing at something really funny and feels the need to put her head down on the table.

Breakfast was at one of the city's tourist centers. The Mayor was there in a blue suit, and he had two city officials by his side and a very serious and thoughtful expression on his face. Next to him was a Chicago developer named Al Friedman, a tall and slender and very handsome man who is the chairman of the Commission on Chicago Landmarks. Lois sat across from them, and they all drank coffee and ate muffins and batted ideas back and forth in the way that people do when they know each other very well. It was a "power breakfast," although if you went around the table you'd find that the word "power" meant something very different to everyone there. Al Friedman is a rich developer. The Mayor, of course, is the administrative leader of one of the largest cities in the country. When we talk about power, this is usually what we're talking about: money and authority. But there is a third kind of power as well — the kind Lois has — which is a little less straightforward. It's social power.

At the end of the nineteen-eighties, for example, the City of Chicago razed an entire block in the heart of downtown and then sold it to a developer. But before he could build on it the real-estate market crashed. The lot was an eyesore. The Mayor asked for ideas about what to do with it. Lois suggested that they cover the block with tents. Then she heard that Keith Haring had come to Chicago in 1989 and worked with Chicago high-school students to create a giant five-hundred-foot-long mural. Lois loved the mural. She began to think. She'd long had a problem with the federal money that Chicago got every year to pay for summer jobs for disadvantaged kids. She didn't think it helped any kid to be put to work picking up garbage. So why not pay the kids to do arts projects like the Haring mural, and put the whole program in the tents? She called the program Gallery 37, after the number of the block. She enlisted the help of the Mayor's wife, Maggie Daley, whose energy and clout were essential in order to make the program a success. Lois hired artists to teach the kids. She realized, though, that the federal money was available only for poor kids, and, Lois says, "I don't believe poor kids can advance in any way by being lumped together with other poor kids." So Lois raised money privately to bring in middle-income kids, to mix with the poor kids and be put in the tents with the artists. She started small, with two hundred and sixty "apprentices" the first year, 1990. This year, there were more than three thousand.

The kids study sculpture, painting, drawing, poetry, theatre, graphic design, dance, textile design, jewelry-making, and music. Lois opened a store downtown, where students' works of art are sold. She has since bought two buildings to house the project full time. She got the Parks Department to run Gallery 37 in neighborhoods around the city, and the Board of Education to let them run it as an after-school program in public high schools. It has been copied all around the world. Last year, it was given the Innovations in American Government Award by the Ford Foundation and the Harvard school of government.

Gallery 37 is at once a jobs program, an arts program, a real-estate fix, a schools program, and a parks program. It involves federal money and city money and private money, stores and buildings and tents, Maggie Daley and Keith Haring, poor kids and middle-class kids. It is everything, all at once — a jumble of ideas and people and places which Lois somehow managed to make sense of. The ability to assemble all these disparate parts is, as should be obvious, a completely different kind of power from the sort held by the Mayor and Al Friedman. The Mayor has key allies on the city council or in the statehouse. Al Friedman can do what he does because, no doubt, he has a banker who believes in him, or maybe a lawyer whom he trusts to negotiate the twists and turns of the zoning process. Their influence is based on close relationships. But when Lois calls someone to help her put together one of her projects, chances are she's not calling someone she knows particularly well. Her influence suggests something a little surprising — that there is also power in relationships that are not close at all.

6

The sociologist Mark Granovetter examined this question in his classic 1974 book "Getting a Job." Granovetter interviewed several hundred professional and technical workers from the Boston suburb of Newton, asking them in detail about their employment history. He found that almost fifty-six per cent of those he talked to had found their jobs through a personal connection, about twenty per cent had used formal means (advertisements, headhunters), and another twenty per cent had applied directly. This much is not surprising: the best way to get in the door is through a personal contact. But the majority of those personal connections, Granovetter found, did not involve close friends. They were what he called "weak ties." Of those who used a contact to find a job, for example, only 16.7 per cent saw that contact "often," as they would have if the contact had been a good friend; 55.6 per cent saw their contact only "occasionally"; and 27.8 per cent saw the contact "rarely." People were getting their jobs not through their friends but through acquaintances.

Granovetter argues that when it comes to finding out about new jobs – or, for that matter, gaining new information, or looking for new ideas – weak ties tend to be more important than strong ties. Your friends, after all, occupy the same world that you do. They work with you, or live near you, and go to the same churches, schools, or parties. How much, then, do they know that you don't know? Mere acquaintances, on the other hand, are much more likely to know something that you don't. To capture this apparent paradox, Granovetter coined a marvellous phrase: "the strength of weak ties." The most important people in your life are, in certain critical realms, the people who aren't closest to you, and the more people you know who aren't close to you the stronger your position becomes.

Granovetter then looked at what he called "chain lengths" — that is, the number of people who had to pass along the news about your job before it got to you. A chain length of zero means that you learned about your job from the person offering it. A chain length of one means that you heard about the job from someone who had heard about the job from the employer. The people who got their jobs from a zero chain were the most satisfied, made the most money, and were unemployed for the shortest amount of time between jobs. People with a chain of one stood second in the amount of money they made, in their satisfaction with their jobs, and in the speed with which they got their jobs. People with a chain of two stood third in all three categories, and so on. If you know someone who knows someone who knows someone who has lots of acquaintances, in other words, you have a leg up. If you know someone who knows someone who has lots of acquaintances, your chances are that much better. But if you know someone who has lots of acquaintances – if you know someone like Lois – you are still more fortunate, because suddenly you are just one step away from musicians and actors and doctors and lawyers and park lovers and politicians and railroad buffs and flea-market aficionados and all the other weak ties that make Lois so strong.

This sounds like a reformulation of the old saw that it's not what you know, it's who you know. It's much more radical than that, though. The old idea was that people got ahead by being friends with rich and powerful people – which is true, in a limited way, but as a practical lesson in how the world works is all but useless. You can expect that Bill Gates's godson is going to get into Harvard and have a fabulous job waiting for him when he gets out. And, of course, if you play poker with the Mayor and Al Friedman it is going to be a little easier to get ahead in Chicago. But how many godsons can Bill Gates have? And how many people can fit around a poker table? This is why affirmative action seems pointless to so many people: It appears to promise something – entry to the old-boy network – that it can't possibly deliver. The old-boy network is always going to be just for the old boys.

Granovetter, by contrast, argues that what matters in getting ahead is not the quality of your relationships but the quantity – not how close you are to those you know but, paradoxi-

cally, how many people you know whom you aren't particularly close to. What he's saying is that the key person at that breakfast in downtown Chicago is not the Mayor or Al Friedman but Lois Weisberg, because Lois is the kind of person who it really is possible for most o f us to know. If you think about the world in this way, the whole project of affirmative action suddenly starts to make a lot more sense. Minority-admissions programs work not because they give black students access to the same superior educational resources as white students, or access to the same rich cultural environment as white students, or any other formal or grandiose vision of engineered equality. They work by giving black students access to the same white students as white students — by allowing them to make acquaintances outside their own social world and so shortening the chain lengths between them and the best jobs.

This idea should also change the way we think about helping the poor. When we're faced with an eighteen-year-old high-school dropout whose only career option is making five dollars and fifty cents an hour in front of the deep fryer at Burger King, we usually talk about the importance of rebuilding inner-city communities, attracting new jobs to depressed areas, and re-investing in neglected neighborhoods. We want to give that kid the option of another, better-paying job, right down the street. But does that really solve his problem? Surely what that eighteen-year-old really needs is not another marginal inducement to stay in his neighborhood but a way to get out of his neighborhood altogether. He needs a school system that provides him with the skills to compete for jobs with middle-class kids. He needs a mass-transit system to take him to the suburbs, where the real employment opportunities are. And, most of all, he needs to know someone who knows someone who knows where all those good jobs are. If the world really is held together by people like Lois Weisberg, in other words, how poor you are can be defined quite simply as how far you have to go to get to someone like her. Wendy Willrich and Helen Doria and all the countless other people in Lois's circle needed to make only one phone call. They are well-off. The dropout wouldn't even know where to start. That's why he's poor. Poverty is not deprivation. It is isolation.

7

I once met a man named Roger Horchow. If you ever go to Dallas and ask around about who is the kind of person who might know everyone, chances are you will be given his name. Roger is slender and composed. He talks slowly, with a slight Texas drawl. He has a kind of wry, ironic charm that is utterly winning. If you sat next to him on a plane ride across the Atlantic, he would start talking as the plane taxied to the runway, you would be laughing by the time the seat-belt sign was turned off, and when you landed at the other end you'd wonder where the time had gone.

I met Roger through his daughter Sally, whose sister Lizzie went to high school in Dallas with my friend Sara M., whom I know because she used to work with Jacob Weisberg. (No Jacob, no Roger.) Roger spent at least part of his childhood in Ohio, which is where Lois's second husband, Bernie Weisberg, grew up, so I asked Roger if he knew Bernie. It would have been a little too apt if he did – that would have made it all something out of "The X-Files" — but instead of just answering, "Sorry, I don't," which is what most of us would have done, he paused for a long time, as if to flip through the "W"s in his head, and then said, "No, but I'm sure if I made two phone calls..."

Roger has a very good memory for names. One time, he says, someone was trying to talk him into investing his money in a business venture in Spain, and when he asked the names of the other investors he recognized one of them as the same man with whom one of his ex-girl-friends had had a fling during her junior year abroad, fifty years before. Roger sends people

cards on their birthdays: he has a computerized Rolodex with sixteen hundred names on it. When I met him, I became convinced that these techniques were central to the fact that he knew everyone — that knowing everyone was a kind of skill. Horchow is the founder of the Horchow Collection, the first high-end mail-order catalogue, and I kept asking him how all the connections in his life had helped him in the business world, because I thought that this particular skill had to have been cultivated for a reason. But the question seemed to puzzle him. He didn't think of his people collection as a business strategy, or even as something deliberate. He just thought of it as something he did — as who he was. One time, Horchow said, a close friend from childhood suddenly resurfaced. "He saw my catalogue and knew it had to be me, and when he was out here he showed up on my doorstep. I hadn't seen him since I was seven. We had zero in common. It was wonderful." The juxtaposition of those last two sentences was not ironic; he meant it.

In the book "The Language Instinct," the psychologist Steven Pinker argues against the idea that language is a cultural artifact – something that we learn "the way we learn to tell time." Rather, he says, it is innate. Language evelops "spontaneously," he writes, "without conscious effort or formal instruction," and "is deployed without awareness of its underlying logic.... People know how to talk in more or less the sense that spiders know how to spin webs." The secret to Roger Horchow and Lois Weisberg is, I think, that they have a kind of social equivalent of that instinct – an innate and spontaneous and entirely involuntary affinity for people. They know everyone because – in some deep and less than conscious way – they can't help it.

8

Once, in the very early nineteen-sixties, after Lois had broken up with her first husband, she went to a party for Ralph Ellison, who was then teaching at the University of Chicago. There she spotted a young lawyer from the South Side named Bernie Weisberg. Lois liked him. He didn't notice her, though, so she decided to write a profile of him for the Hyde Park Herald. It ran with a huge headline. Bernie still didn't call. "I had to figure out how I was going to get to meet him again, so I remembered that he was standing in line at the reception with Ralph Ellison," Lois says. "So I called up Ralph Ellison" – whom she had never met – "and said, 'It's so wonderful that you are in Chicago. You really should meet some people on the North Side. Would it be O.K. if I have a party for you?'" He said yes, and Lois sent out a hundred invitations, including one to Bernie. He came. He saw Dizzy Gillespie in the kitchen and Ralph Ellison in the living room. He was impressed. He asked Lois to go with him to see Lenny Bruce. Lois was mortified; she didn't want this nice Jewish lawyer from the South Side to know that she knew Lenny Bruce, who was, after all, a drug addict. "I couldn't get out of it," she said. "They sat us down at a table right at the front, and Lenny keeps coming over to the edge of the stage and saying" – here Lois dropped her voice down very low – "'Hello, Lois. 'I was sitting there like this." Lois put her hands on either side of her face. "Finally I said to Bernie, 'There are some things I should tell you about. Lenny Bruce is a friend of mine. He's staying at my house. The second thing is I'm defending a murderer. '"(But that's another story.) Lois and Bernie were married a year later.

The lesson of this story isn't obvious until you diagram it culturally: Lois got to Bernie through her connections with Ralph Ellison and Lenny Bruce, one of whom she didn't know (although later, naturally, they became great friends) and one of whom she was afraid to say that she knew, and neither of whom, it is safe to speculate, had ever really been connected with each other before. It seems like an absurdly roundabout way to meet someone. Here was

a thirtyish liberal Jewish intellectual from the North Side of Chicago trying to meet a thirtyish liberal Jewish intellectual from the South Side of Chicago, and to get there she charted a cross-cultural social course through a black literary lion and an avant-garde standup comic. Yet that's a roundabout journey only if you perceive the worlds of Lenny Bruce and Ralph Ellison and Bernie Weisberg to be impossibly isolated. If you don't – if, like Lois, you see them all as three points of an equilateral triangle – then it makes perfect sense. The social instinct makes everyone seem like part of a whole, and there is something very appealing about this, because it means that people like Lois aren't bound by the same categories and partitions that defeat the rest of us. This is what the power of the people who know everyone comes down to in the end. It is not – as much as we would like to believe otherwise something rich and complex, some potent mixture of ambition and energy and smarts and vision and insecurity. It's much simpler than that. It's the same lesson they teach in Sunday school. Lois knows lots of people because she likes lots of people. And all those people Lois knows and likes invariably like her, too, because there is nothing more irresistible to a human being than to be unqualifiedly liked by another.

Not long ago, Lois took me to a reception at the Museum of Contemporary Art, in Chicago – a brand-new, Bauhaus-inspired building just north of the Loop. The gallery space was impossibly beautiful – cool, airy, high-ceilinged. The artist on display was Chuck Close. The crowd was sleek and well groomed. Black- clad young waiters carried pesto canapés and glasses of white wine. Lois seemed a bit lost. She can be a little shy sometimes, and at first she stayed on the fringes of the room, standing back, observing. Someone important came over to talk to her. She glanced up uncomfortably. I walked away for a moment to look at the show, and when I came back her little corner had become a crowd. There was her friend from the state legislature. A friend in the Chicago Park District. A friend from her neighborhood. A friend in the consulting business. A friend from Gallery 37. A friend from the local business- development group. And on and on. They were of all ages and all colors, talking and laughing, swirling and turning in a loose circle, and in the middle, nearly hidden by the commotion, was Lois, clutching her white bag, tiny and large-eyed, at that moment the happiest person in the room.

Sara Evans and Harry Boyte
The People Shall Rule

Sara Evans is Chair of the History Department at the University of Minnesota. She is perhaps best known for her book *Personal Politics*, an historical study of the continuity between the women's movement and the Southern civil rights movement. Harry Boyte, whose essay "Practical Politics" appears in Part I, Section C of this volume, is Director of Project Public Life at the University of Minnesota's Hubert Humphrey Institute for Public Affairs. In their book *Free Spaces*, originally published in 1986, Evans and Boyte examine the major democratic movements in United States history, focusing on the role of autonomous institutions such as churches, clubs, and other voluntary associations in teaching political and participatory skills. According to the authors, these institutions have served as "free spaces," places where those seeking democratic rights could learn the political arts and develop strategies for change. In the following selection, the authors contrast free spaces with those reform movements prominent since the Progressive era when citizen involvement shifted from communal organizations to the more anonymous realm of national politics. This shift represented a decline in participatory democracy as citizens became increasingly alienated from the political forces shaping their lives. Popular democratic movements were understood simply in the terms of egoistic interest group politics. An often neglected group of social movements, however, have gathered strength through their appeals to the American republican tradition with its emphasis on the public obligations of democratic citizens. Based on the establishment of "free spaces," movements for racial justice, gender equality, and workers's rights have all found success in nurturing a notion of citizenship as commitment to the good of the community.

The People Shall Rule
Sara Evans and Harry Boyte

The genius of the United States is not best or most in its executives or legislatures, nor in its ambassadors or authors or colleges or churches or parlors, nor even in its newspapers or inventors...but always most in the common people...their good temper and openhandedness—the terrible significance of their elections—the President's taking off his hat to them not they to him—these too are unrhymed poetry.... The largeness of nature or the nation were monstrous without a corresponding largeness and generosity of the spirit of the citizen.

Walt Whitman, *Leaves of Grass, 1855*

On June 28, 1822, Denmark Vesey stood before a Charleston, South Carolina, court for sentencing. The white judge addressed the silent black man with incredulity: "It is difficult to imagine what infatuation could have prompted you to attempt an enterprise so wild and visionary. You were a free man; were comparatively wealthy; and enjoyed every comfort compatible with your situation."

Vesey embodied white southerners' deepest fears. An investigation of rumored plots among the slaves had uncovered a vast, well-planned conspiracy across hundreds of square miles. Vesey, a free carpenter and devout Christian, a man with apparently everything to lose and little to gain, was a key leader.

Vesey remained quiet before the bewildered judge, obedient to the injunction of his compatriot, Peter Royas, who said, "Do not open your lips! Die silent, as you shall see me do." He and thirty-six others were sentenced to death. Forty-three were forced into exile. Forty-eight more were whipped before being released for lack of evidence. Most were silent to the end.

620 ❖ OPPORTUNITIES FOR CITIZENSHIP AND SERVICE

White Charlestonians constantly feared an eruption of murderous rage from their slaves. But they did not comprehend the complex realities of a man like Vesey, whose passionate religious convictions and leadership in a long struggle to maintain black churches' independence from white control had led directly to his leadership of the plot. Though southern whites worried about what went on in black worship services and periodically sought to control them, they had convinced themselves that Christianity pacified the black population. Black religion was thought to be "childlike" and otherworldly. Indeed, Christian conversion had been a mode of "root[ing] out all living connection with the [African] homeland," as black historian Vincent Harding has observed.

The paradox is that, far from succeeding, Christianity furnished the basic language of freedom for black Americans. And the places where it was practiced, from hidden services at the margins of plantations to black churches struggling to survive in southern cities, proved the staging areas for action. "The religion of white America," said Harding, "was insistently, continually wrested from the white mediators by black hands and minds and transformed into an instrument of struggle." Put simply, blacks, like the first Christians themselves, forged a religion of and by the slaves and the dispossessed. They found in the insights, language, and communion of religion a transformative source of self-affirmation. In doing so, they turned questions like those of the incredulous judge back on themselves, and challenged the very values that he equated with contentment and happiness.

How is such radical transformation of value and culture possible? Where do ordinary people, steeped in lifelong experiences of humiliation, barred from acquisition of basic skills of citizenship—from running meetings to speaking in public—gain the courage, the self-confidence, and above all the hope to take action in their own behalf? What are the structures of support, the resources, and the experiences that gener-

ate the capacity and the inspiration to challenge "the way things are" and imagine a different world? To ask such questions is to challenge the fundamentals of conventional wisdom—and to pose in new ways the meaning and possibility of democracy in the modern world.

Democracy: "The People Shall Rule"

In 1975, a writer for *Business Week* magazine sounded a theme heard often in the business press during the decade. What previously people had accepted with gratitude, the man complained, now were assumed to be rights. The Sixties' social unrest had made the American public all too demanding and self-assertive about concerns that ranged from taxes to the environment. But the problem was not new. Current unruliness brought to the surface "a conflict as old as the American republic: the conflict between a political democracy and a capitalist economy."

To say a fundamental conflict exists between capitalism and democracy sounds odd. The two are entwined in most people's minds, supposedly inseparable. But in fact up until the late nineteenth century, "democracy" was seen as a disturbing, even as a subversive, idea in polite society. The source of unease was obvious enough. From antiquity, democracy—simply, the notion that "the people shall rule"—had been associated with a constellation of ideas that accompanied wide-ranging efforts at social change.

Indeed, both subject and verb of the formulation that "the people shall rule" held unsettling implications. In the first instance, the meaning of "the people" denoted the idea of *popular power:* locating control over the institutions of society and government in the majority of the population, the common people. As Aristotle defined it, "a democracy is a state where the freemen and the poor, being in the majority, are invested with the power of the state." According to Plato, Socrates predicted that violence would inevitably accompany the transition to such government: "Democracy comes into being after the poor have conquered their opponents, slaughtering some and banishing others, while to the remainder they give an equal share of freedom and power."

The insurgent content of the term, with its implications of a "world turned upside down," asserted itself repeatedly in democratic popular uprisings. One can imagine the terror which John Ball, leader of a fourteenth century English peasant revolt, struck in the hearts of the powerful when he orated: "Things cannot go well in England, nor ever will, until all goods are held in common and until there will be neither serfs nor gentlemen, and we shall be equal." For subsequent democratic rebels in English history, the vision of a far-reaching "commonwealth" proved a recurring pattern. Thus Gerrard Winstanley, theoretician of a radical faction of the seventeenth-century English Civil War, which had in fact established what was called "The Commonwealth," took the term with a shocking literalness: "The whole earth shall be a common treasury," Winstanley wrote. "For the earth is the Lord's.... There shall be no lords over others, but everyone shall be a lord of himself, subject to the law of righteousness, reason and equity."

If the concept of "the people" embodied in democracy was troubling, the prospect of direct "rule" was at least as bothersome for those who believed society was best governed by a few. Again dating from ancient Greece, the concept of direct rule involved the idea of free and active participation (albeit a limited franchise) by those defined as citizens. As G. Lowes Dickinson has described the Greek polis, "to be a citizen of a state did not merely imply the payment of taxes and the possession of a vote; it implied a direct and active cooperation in all the functions of civil and military life. A citizen was normally a soldier, a judge, and a member of the governing assembly; and all his public duties he performed not by deputy, but in person." Even in the Middle Ages, when feudal relationships characterized political life, an occasional political theorist ruminated upon the benefits that direct participation might produce. Thus, for example, Marsiglio of Padua wrote in the early fourteenth century that "a law made by the hearing or consent of the whole multitude, even though it were less useful, would be readily observed and endured by every one of the citizens, because then each would seem to have set the law upon himself and hence would have no protest against it, but would rather tolerate it with equanimity."

With the settlement of the New World, a laboratory existed for putting such ideas into practice. Thus, the first political constitution to use the term democracy—Rhode Island's in 1641—meant "popular government; that is to say it is the power of the body of freemen orderly assembled, or major part of them, to make or constitute just Lawes, by which they will be regulated."

Finally, the notion of democracy entailed not only rights to participate, but the responsibilities of citizenship. The concept of "the citizen" suggested one who was able to put aside at times immediate and personal interests and focus on public affairs. Such a trait amounted to civic virtue, suggested by Walt Whitman's observation in 1855 that a nation the size and extent of America "were monstrous" without a citizenry of correspondingly large and generous spirit. The values associated with citizenship included a concern for the common good, the welfare of the community as a whole, willingness to honor the same rights for others that one possesses, tolerance of diverse religious, political, and social beliefs, acceptance of the primacy of the community's decisions over one's own private inclinations, and a recognition of one's obligations to defend and serve the public....

Free Spaces

To understand the inner life of democratic movements, one must rethink such traditional categories as "politics," "private life," "public activity," "reaction," and "progress." Only then can we hope to fathom how people draw upon their past for strength, create out of traditions—which may seem on their face simply to reinforce the status quo—new visions of the future, gain out of the experience of their daily lives new public skills and a broader sense of hope and responsibility.

The central argument of this book is that particular sorts of public places in the community, what we call free spaces, are the environments in which people are able to learn a new self-respect, a deeper and more assertive group identity, public skills, and values of cooperation and civic virtue. Put simply, free spaces are settings between private lives and large-scale institutions where ordinary citizens can act with dignity, independence, and vision. These are, in the main, voluntary forms of association with a relatively open and participatory character—many religious organizations, clubs, self-help and mutual aid societies, reform groups, neighborhood, civic, and ethnic groups, and a host of other associations grounded in the fabric of community life. The sustained public vitality and egalitarianism of free spaces are strikingly unlike the "public" face of reactionary or backward-looking protests. Democratic action depends upon these free spaces, where people experience a schooling in citizenship and learn a vision of the common good in the course of struggling for change.

Free spaces are never a pure phenomenon. In the real world, they are always complex, shifting, and dynamic—partial in their freedom and democratic participation, marked by parochialism of class, gender, race, and other biases of the groups which maintain them. There are no easy or simple ways to sustain experiences of democratic participation and values of civic virtue in the heart of broader environments that undermine them and demand, at least on the face of it, very different sorts of values. Democratic movements have had varying degrees of success in sustaining themselves, in spreading their values, symbols, and ideas to larger audiences, in changing the world. They have in different ways and with different outcomes addressed issues such as the bureaucratic state, the problem of size in organization, the role of experts, the power of conventional media. They have sought to hold leaders accountable through a variety of measures—from direct election and recall to frequent turnover in top leadership, and widespread dissemination of information—or they have failed to develop such measures. And they have drawn upon and transformed threads in peoples' cultures and traditions, weaving ideas, into new sets of values, beliefs and interpretations of the world, codes of behavior, and visions of the future. Together, these new elements make up, in democratic movements, basic alternatives to the conventional ways of the world, what might be called "movement cultures," that suggest a different way of living.

Free spaces are the foundations for such movement counter-cultures. And for all their variations, free spaces have certain common features, observable in movements varying widely in time, aims, composition, and social environment. They are defined by their roots in community, the dense, rich networks of daily life; by their autonomy; and by their public or quasi-public character as participatory environments which nurture values associated with citizenship and a vision of the common good. In a full way, the spirit, dynamics, and character of free spaces can only be understood in the concreteness of particular stories, where people gain new skills, a new sense of possibility, and a broadened understanding of whom "the people" include.

Imagine a large assembly hall, festooned with symbols and signs, in Hamilton, Ontario, early October 1885. Several hundred delegates to the ninth annual convention of the Noble

Order of the Knights of Labor assembled from Arkansas, New York, Missouri, Maryland, Illinois, Louisiana, Pennsylvania, Connecticut, Virginia, and a dozen other states. Old-timers from Union battles of the late 1860s mingled with young immigrant men and women, part of that vast wave of five million people who came to America from cities like Glasgow, Liverpool, Vienna, and Minsk during the 1880s. Confederate veterans gave the secret sign of recognition. Former soldiers of the Union Army responded in kind. Signaling with hand across forehead, they showed that they, too, worked by "the sweat of our brow."

They were full of rising confidence. The growing movement had generated hopes that the overwhelming power of the new economic cartels and monopolies in America might be broken. Strikes and boycotts, spreading across the country, had achieved significant victories against the new breed of industrialists like Jay Gould, the railroad magnate who boasted that he could "hire one half of the working class to kill the other half." In keeping with the mood of the occasion, Master Workman William Mullen, Knights leader from Richmond, Virginia, convened the meeting.

"I have here a gavel to present this General Assembly," Mullen began, with modest disclaimers. "It is as plain a gavel as I have ever seen, in fitful keeping with the plain but beautiful workings of our honored Order." As he described how his District Assembly of white working men and women had put it together, the audience listened, transfixed.

"The handle of this gavel is made from a piece of the sounding board that stood in old St. John's Church at the time that Patrick Henry made his famous speech. [It is] therefore a piece of the instrument that echoed and re-echoed the patriotic words, 'give me liberty or give me death!' The handle of this gavel is, as you can see, topped with a piece of wood of a different kind, cut at Yorktown, Virginia, as near as possible to the scene of the surrender of Cornwallis to Washington, and therefore repre-sents the close of the first Revolution." Thus Mullen drew on the legacy which northerners and southerners shared. As he described the ball, he turned to the issue which had torn the nation apart. "It is," he explained, "from one of the pillars of the old Libby prison that the ball of this gavel is made. This building has been made historic by the part it played in the second Revolution. In this house of ancient architectural design were confined true and patriotic sons of our common country as prisoners of war for being engaged in a struggle to liberate a race of people from the galling yoke of slavery."

Finally, with the evangelical fervor that ignited audiences in Richmond time after time, Mullen turned to the future. "There still remains a battle to be fought for the establishment of universal freedom. Can those who are now the slaves of monopoly and oppression be liberated as easily as was the African race in America?" He answered himself as he passed the gavel to Grandmaster Workman Terence Powderly, leader of the national movement. "Yea, even more easily! To accomplish the second requires only organization, education and cooperation. To you, sir," he concluded, "as the representative of that grand army that is to work the third Revolution in which all the nations of the earth are to be liberated, I present you with this gavel, clothed with so much of our past history. God grant that this gavel may, in your hands, preside over in the future many happy gatherings of the noble-hearted sons of toil to celebrate the holiday of the establishment of these grand principles—a fair day's pay for a fair day's work, and an injury to one is the concern of all!"

Mullen's enthusiasm reflected the excitement of the convention. But it also grew from changes in towns like Richmond. An interracial movement had rapidly emerged in the city, addressing not only specific issues of wages and jobs but also the most revolutionary of cultural issues in that former capital of the Confederacy. As historian Peter Rachleff described, "a new movement culture [developed], centered on the Knights, which not only supported a revitalized labor movement but also promoted a biracial popular movement which threatened to turn Southern society upside down." The ultimate purpose of the Knights was expressed in the solemnly intoned hope that "the day will come when men of all the nations of the earth shall govern themselves." Every initiate into the Order heard the words as they joined.

The experiment in interracial cooperation and workers' self-organization ultimately failed in Richmond in the 1880s. And the day when people "of all the nations of the earth shall govern themselves" remains yet a distant goal. But both their achievement and their sentiments reach across time and space. For decades afterwards, in Richmond and across the South, white youngsters growing up with games of "Johnny Reb" and songs of Dixie's faded glory would fail to understand the common ties binding North and South together which those doughty laboring men and women had symbolized with their careful handicraft. And it would be generations before black and white workers would again make common cause in the old Confederacy's capital on such a scale.

When listened to attentively, the members of the Richmond Knights of Labor have a contemporary impact with peculiar parallel to their challenge to the culture of the Old South. Put simply, their endeavors turn our modern, up-to-date, and sophisticated ways of thinking about things like democracy and self-government upside down, as well.

The Richmond Knights' achievements were a testimony to hard work and spirited leadership, but they were possible because of the particular features of the voluntary associations and community roots from which the Knights emerged, and the nature of the institution itself as it flourished and expanded. The Knights drew their power from religious and democratic traditions deeply embedded in both white and black communities of Richmond. A reinterpretation of such traditions in ways that furthered working people's self-assertion and even common action between black and white

communities was possible because the Knights' assemblies were autonomous institutions—that is, they were voluntary organizations that working people controlled themselves, relatively free of outside sanction. Finally, for a time, the Knights created a remarkable "public" environment where workers from different communities—and most amazingly, even different races—could come together, forge relationships that had never been imagined, and develop regular communications with other communities of working people in northern states once simply stereotyped as "damn Yankees." Such new relationships, emerging from particular community histories, created simultaneously an enlarged vision of community, a sense of the common good that had never before existed in the South in this way.

In sum, the free spaces at the heart of the Richmond Knights of Labor were schools for citizenship that made "democracy" come alive with a powerful, heady sense of possibility. Such schooling in citizenship has proven indispensable for democratic movements in widely varying times and places. In turn, a more detailed understanding of the ways in which free spaces are crucial to the revitalization and sustenance of democratic vision and activity requires a look at different democratic movements.

This study will explore the major democratic movements in United States history, movements for the rights, dignity, and voice of blacks, women, workers, and farmers. In each case, we trace the ebb and flow of social protest across time, noting the characteristics of the free spaces that nourished them and the influence of broader historical and social settings.

A broadly comparative approach demonstrates the common elements which make these movements democratic. It also clarifies the limitations of particular movements' vision. Despite dramatic differences, in each case we find the common characteristics of free spaces which we have identified: communal roots, autonomy, and public character. At the same time, the specific features of different movements allow us to explore how free spaces shape the structure, leadership, and ideology of each.

For example, under slavery, the very possibility of thinking and speaking in ways that opposed the dominant culture depended upon the creation of autonomous institutions—churches—about which white slaveowners had little knowledge and over which they had little control. The charismatic leadership of black ministers, in turn, shaped a leadership style which persists to the present. Thus the black church is an especially clear illustration of free space....

One could make a similar argument about the importance of autonomous institutions such as churches, clubs, and saloons for the emergence of working-class culture. But for a highly mobile and culturally uprooted American work force, the issue of autonomy has been inseparably connected with the question of community. Indeed, in the case of American workers' movements, the possibility of group action has depended crucially upon the survival, sustenance, and sometimes the retrieval of historical memories and the re-creation of voluntary associations that bridge segmented worlds of work and community. An exploration of the theme of community, in turn, leads to some thoughts about the need to reevaluate widely used concepts such as "class consciousness."

The history of feminism shifts the primary focus to the public aspects of free spaces. For women to claim their citizenship rights, they required environments in which they could develop public identities and skills, simultaneously drawing upon and changing traditions that defined women in terms of family and personal worlds. In the process, women redefined the meaning of "public" and "common good." Yet the fact that those environments were also shaped by the realities of class and race ultimately limited both the claim to female citizenship and the constituency that could be mobilized in its name. Finally, populist movements rooted in rural America illustrate the powerful and complex role of traditional ideologies. And they highlight in particular the importance of democratic participation that teaches values of citizenship, racial tolerance, and the common good to any inclusive vision of "the people."

Free spaces, then, are the places in which the pieties we learn in school or hear in Fourth of July speeches take on living substance and meaning. A deeper understanding of them recasts the role of voluntary associations—considered, for example, in current neoconservative thought to be the main barrier against an all-encompassing modern state—from that of defensive refuge to active source of change. And it suggests, finally, the need to rethink our contemporary approaches to public life and politics, social change, and democracy itself.

Franklin Delano Roosevelt
The Civilian Conservation Corps

Franklin Delano Roosevelt (1882–1945), four-term president of the United States from 1933 to 1945, was born in Hyde Park, NY. He graduated from Harvard University in 1904, and was admitted to the New York bar. Though suffering the aftereffects of polio, he was elected governor of New York in 1928 and United States president in 1932. Taking office in the midst of the Great Depression, Roosevelt immediately instituted his New Deal, a comprehensive reform program for economic recovery. The various New Deal programs revolutionized US economic, political, and social life. Roosevelt was elected for an unprecedented third term in 1940. His remaining years in office were dominated by US involvement in World War II. He died during his fourth term in 1945, before the end of the war.

As part of the his New Deal, Roosevelt called for the establishment of a Civilian Conservation Corps. In the spring of 1933 hundreds of thousands of young men were faced with little opportunity for employment. The Corps was designed to both provide jobs and stimulate the national economy. Additionally, Roosevelt saw the Corps as a moral antidote to the degrading experience of prolonged unemployment. The Corps engaged over 2,000,000 men in 1,500 camps in outdoor work such as flood control, reforestation, and road maintenance.

The Civilian Conservation Corps Is Started

Franklin Delano Roosevelt

Executive Order No. 6101.
April 5, 1933

By virtue of the authority vested in me by the Act of Congress entitled "An Act for the relief of unemployment through the performance of useful public work, and for other purposes," approved March 31, 1933 (Public No. 5, 73d Congress), it is hereby ordered that:

(1) For the purpose of carrying out the provisions of said Act Robert Fechner is hereby appointed Director of Emergency Conservation Work at an annual rate of compensation of $12,000, less the reduction prescribed in subparagraph (b), Section 2, Title II, of the Act of Congress entitled "An Act to maintain the credit of the United States Government" (Public No. 2, 73d Congress), approved March 20, 1933.

(2) The Secretary of War, the Secretary of Agriculture, the Secretary of the Interior, and the Secretary of Labor each shall appoint a representative, and said representatives shall constitute an Advisory Council to the Directory of Emergency Conservation Work.

(3) There is hereby established in the Treasury a fund of $10,000,000 by the transfer of an equal amount from the unobligated balances of the appropriation for emergency construction of public buildings contained in the act approved July 21, 1932, as authorized by Section 4 of the said Act of March 31, 1933, which fund shall be subject to requisition by the said Robert Fechner, as Director of Emergency Conservation Work, on the approval of the President.

(4) Subject to direction by the President, supplies and materials of the several departments or establishments shall be furnished on the requisition of the Director of Emergency Conservation Work, and the departments and establishments fur-

nishing such supplies and materials shall be reimbursed therefor in accordance with instructions of the President.

(5) Reimbursement, if any, to the departments or establishments for other services rendered shall be made in accordance with instructions of the President.

An act for the relief of unemployment through the performance of useful public work, and for other purposes, approved March 31, 1933

Be it enacted by the Senate and House of Representatives of the United States of America in Congress assembled, That for the purpose of relieving the acute condition of widespread distress and unemployment now existing in the United States, and in order to provide for the restoration of the country's depleted natural resources and the advancement of an orderly program of useful public works, the President is authorized, under such rules and regulations as he may prescribe and by utilizing such existing departments or agencies as he may designate, to provide for employing citizens of the United States who are unemployed, in the construction, maintenance and carrying on of works of a public nature in connection with the forestation of lands belonging to the United States or to the several States which are suitable for timber production, the prevention of forest fires, floods and soil erosion, plant pest and disease control, the construction, maintenance or repair of paths, trails and firelanes in the national parks and national forests, and such other work on the public domain, national and State, and Government reservations incidental to or necessary in connection with any projects of the character enumerated, as the President may determine to be desirable: *Provided,* That the President may in his discretion extend the provisions of this Act to lands owned by counties and municipalities and lands in private ownership, but only for the purpose of doing thereon such kinds of cooperative work as are now provided for by Acts of Congress in preventing and controlling

forest fires and the attacks of forest tree pests and diseases and such work as is necessary in the public interest to control floods. The President is further authorized, by regulation, to provide for housing the persons so employed and for furnishing them with such subsistence, clothing, medical attendance and hospitalization, and cash allowance, as may be necessary, during the period they are so employed, and, in his discretion, to provide for the transportation of such persons to and from the places of employment. That in employing citizens for the purposes of this Act no discrimination shall be made on account of race, color, or creed; and no person under conviction for crime and serving sentence therefor shall be employed under the provisions of this Act. The President is further authorized to allocate funds available for the purposes of this Act, for forest research, including forest products investigations, by the Forest Products Laboratory.

Sec. 2. For the purpose of carrying out the provisions of this Act the President is authorized to enter into such contracts or agreements with States as may be necessary, including provisions for utilization of existing State administrative agencies, and the President, or the head of any department or agency authorized by him to construct any project or to carry on any such public works, shall be authorized to acquire real property by purchase, donation, condemnation, or otherwise, but the provisions of section 355 Of the Revised Statutes shall not apply to any property so acquired.

Sec. 3. Insofar as applicable, the benefits of the Act entitled "An Act to provide compensation for employees of the United States suffering injuries while in the performance of their duties, and for other purposes," approved September 7, 1916, as amended, shall extend to persons given employment under the provisions of this Act.

Sec. 4. For the purpose of carrying out the provisions of this Act, there is hereby authorized to be expended, under the direction of the President, out of any unobligated moneys heretofore appropriated for public works (except for projects on which actual construction has been commenced or may be commenced within ninety days, and except maintenance funds for river and harbor improvements already allocated), such sums as may be necessary; and an amount equal to the amount so expended is hereby authorized to be appropriated for the same purposes for which such moneys were originally appropriated.

Sec. 5. That the unexpended and unallotted balance of the sum of $300,000,000 made available under the terms and conditions of the Act approved July 21, 1932, entitled "An Act to relieve destitution," and so forth, may be made available, or any portion thereof, to any State or Territory or States or Territories without regard to the limitation of 15 per centum or other limitations as to per centum.

Sec. 6. The authority of the President under this Act shall continue for the period of two years next after the date of the passage hereof and no longer.

Approved, March 31st 1933.

Benjamin R. Barber

Jihad vs. McWorld

In this essay, Benjamin Barber addresses questions of community and democracy as they relate to global trends—none of which, he argues, are disposed to enhance citizenship. It is at the planetary level that participation and service become most problematic.

Jihad vs McWorld
Benjamin R. Barber

Just beyond the horizon of current events lie two possible political futures—both bleak, neither democratic. The first is a retribalization of large swaths of human mankind by war and bloodshed: a threatened Lebanonization of national states in which culture is pitted against culture, people against people, tribe against tribe—a Jihad in the name of a hundred narrowly conceived faiths against every kind of interdependence, every kind of artificial social cooperation and civic mutuality. The second is being borne in on us by the onrush of economic and ecological forces that demand integration and uniformity and that mesmerize the world with fast music, fast computers, and fast food—with MTV, Macintosh, and McDonald's, pressing nations into one commercially homogenous global network: one McWorld tied together by technology, ecology, communications, and commerce. The planet is falling precipitantly apart and coming reluctantly together at the very same moment.

These two tendencies are sometimes visible in the same countries at the same instant: thus Yugoslavia, clamoring just recently to join the New Europe, is exploding into fragments; India is trying to live up to its reputation as the world's largest integral democracy while powerful new fundamentalist parties like the Hindu nationalist Bharatiya Janata Party, along with nationalist assassins, are imperiling its hard-won unity. States are breaking up or joining up: the Soviet Union has disappeared almost overnight, its parts forming new unions with one another or with like-minded nationalities in neighboring states. The old interwar national state based on territory and political sovereignty looks to be a mere transitional development.

The tendencies of what I am here calling the forces of Jihad and the forces of McWorld

By permission of the author. This selection is adapted from "Jihad vs. McWorld," cover essay, *The Atlantic*, March 1992.

operate with equal strength in opposite directions, the one driven by parochial hatreds, the other by universalizing markets, the one re-creating ancient subnational and ethnic borders from within, the other making national borders porous from without. They have one thing in common: neither offers much hope to citizens looking for practical ways to govern themselves democratically. If the global future is to pit Jihad's centrifugal whirlwind against McWorld's centripetal black hole, the outcome is unlikely to be democratic—or so I will argue.

McWorld, or the Globalization of Politics

Four imperatives make up the dynamic of McWorld: a market imperative, a resource imperative, an information-technology imperative, and an ecological imperative. By shrinking the world and diminishing the salience of national borders, these imperatives have in combination achieved a considerable victory over factiousness and particularism, and not least of all over their most virulent traditional form—nationalism. It is the realists who are now Europeans, the utopians who dream nostalgically of a resurgent England or Germany, perhaps even a resurgent Wales or Saxony. Yesterday's wishful cry for one world has yielded to the reality of McWorld.

The market imperative. Marxist and Leninist theories of imperialism assumed that the quest for ever-expanding markets would in time compel nation-based capitalist economies to push against national boundaries in search of an international economic imperium. Whatever else has happened to the scientistic predictions of Marxism, in this domain they have proved farsighted. All national economies are now vulnerable to the inroads of larger, transnational markets within which trade is free, currencies are convertible, access to banking is open, and contracts are enforceable under law. In Europe, Asia, Africa, the South Pacific, and the Ameri-

cas such markets are eroding national sovereignty and giving rise to entities—international banks, trade associations, transnational lobbies like OPEC and Greenpeace, world news services like CNN and the BBC, and multinational corporations that increasingly lack a meaningful national identity—that neither reflect nor respect nationhood as an organizing or regulative principle.

The market imperative has also reinforced the quest for international peace and stability, requisites of an efficient international economy. Markets are enemies of parochialism, isolation, fractiousness, war. Market psychology attenuates the psychology of ideological and religious cleavages and assumes a concord among producers and consumers—categories that ill fit narrowly conceived national or religious cultures. Shopping has little tolerance for blue laws, whether dictated by pub-closing British paternalism, Sabbath-observing Jewish Orthodox fundamentalism, or no-Sunday-liquor-sales Massachusetts Puritanism. In the context of common markets, international law ceases to be a vision of justice and becomes a workaday framework for getting things done—enforcing contracts, ensuring that governments abide by deals, regulating trade and currency relations, and so forth.

Common markets demand a common language, as well as a common currency, and they produce common behaviors of the kind bred by cosmopolitan city life everywhere. Commercial pilots, computer programmers, international bankers, media specialists, oil riggers, entertainment celebrities, ecology experts, demographers, accountants, professors, athletes—these compose a new breed of men and women for whom religion, culture, and nationality can seem only marginal elements in a working identity. Shopping has a common signature throughout the world. Cynics might even say that some of the recent revolutions in Eastern Europe have had as their true goal not liberty and the right to vote but well-paying jobs and the right to shop (although the vote is proving easier to acquire than consumer goods). The market imperative is, then, plenty powerful; but, notwithstanding some of the claims made for "democratic capitalism," it is not identical with the democratic imperative.

The resource imperative. Democrats once dreamed of societies whose political autonomy rested firmly on economic independence. The Athenians idealized what they called autarky, and [t]he dream of autarky briefly engrossed nineteenth-century America as well, for the underpopulated, endlessly bountiful land, the cornucopia of natural resources, and the natural barriers of a continent walled in by two great seas led many to believe that America could be a world unto itself. Given this past, it has been harder for Americans than for most to accept the inevitability of interdependence. But the rapid depletion of resources even in a country like ours, where they once seemed inexhaustible, and the maldistribution of arable soil and mineral resources on the planet, leave even the wealthiest societies ever more resource-dependent and many other nations in permanently desperate straits.

Every nation, it turns out, needs something another nation has; some nations have almost nothing they need.

The information-technology imperative. Enlightenment science and the technologies derived from it are inherently universalizing. They entail a quest for descriptive principles of general application, a search for universal solutions to particular problems, and an unswerving embrace of objectivity and impartiality.

Scientific progress embodies and depends on open communication, a common discourse rooted in rationality, collaboration, and an easy and regular flow and exchange of information. Such ideals can be hypocritical covers for power-mongering by elites, and they may be shown to be wanting in many other ways, but they are entailed by the very idea of science and they make science and globalization practical allies.

Business, banking, and commerce all depend on information flow and are facilitated by new communication technologies. The hardware of these technologies tends to be systemic and integrated—computer, television, cable, satellite, laser, fiber-optic, and microchip technologies combining to create a vast interactive communications and information network that can potentially give every person on earth access to every other person, and make every datum, every byte, available to every set of eyes. If the automobile was, as George Ball once said (when he gave his blessing to a Fiat factory in the Soviet Union during the Cold War), "an ideology on four wheels," then electronic telecommunication and information systems are an ideology at 186,000 miles per second—which makes for a very small planet in a very big hurry. Individual cultures speak particular languages; commerce and science increasingly speak English; the whole world speaks logarithms and binary mathematics.

Moreover, the pursuit of science and technology asks for, even compels, open societies. Satellite footprints do not respect national borders; telephone wires penetrate the most closed societies. With photocopying and then fax machines having infiltrated Soviet universities and *samizdat* literary circles in the eighties, and computer modems having multiplied like rabbits in communism's bureaucratic warrens thereafter, *glasnost* could not be far behind. In their social requisites, secrecy and science are enemies.

The new technology's software is perhaps even more globalizing than its hardware. The information arm of international commerce's sprawling body reaches out and couches distinct nations and parochial cultures, and gives them a common face chiseled in Hollywood, on Madison Avenue, and in Silicon Valley. Throughout the 1980S one of the most-watched television programs in South Africa was *The Cosby Show.* The demise of apartheid was already in production. Exhibitors at the 1991 Cannes film festival expressed growing anxiety over the "homogenization" and "Americanization" of the global film industry when, for the third year running, American films dominated the awards ceremonies. America has dominated the world's popular culture for much longer, and much more decisively. In November of 1991 Switzerland's once insular culture boasted best-seller lists featuring *Terminator 2* as the No. 1 movie, *Scarlett* as the No. 1 book, and Prince's *Diamonds and Pearls* as the No. 1 record album. No wonder the Japanese are buying Hollywood film studios even faster than Americans are buying Japanese television sets. This kind of software supremacy may in the long term be far more important than hardware superiority, because culture has become more potent than armaments. What is the power of the Pentagon compared with Disneyland? Can the Sixth Fleet keep up with CNN? McDonald's in Moscow and Coke in China will do more to create a global culture than military colonization ever could....

Yet in all this high-tech commercial world there is nothing that looks particularly democratic. It lends itself to surveillance as well as liberty, to new forms of manipulation and covert control as well as new kinds of participation, to skewed, unjust market outcomes as well as greater productivity. The consumer society and the open society are not quite synonymous. Capitalism and democracy have a relationship, but it is something less than a marriage. An efficient free market after all requires that consumers be free to vote their dollars on competing goods, not that citizens be free to vote their values and beliefs on competing political candidates and programs. The free market flourished in junta-run Chile, in military-governed Taiwan and Korea, and, earlier, in a variety of autocratic European empires as well as their colonial possessions.

The ecological imperative. The impact of globalization on ecology is a cliché even to world leaders who ignore it. We know well enough that the German forests can be destroyed by Swiss and Italians driving gas-guzzlers fueled by leaded gas. We also know that the planet can be asphyxiated by greenhouse gases because Brazilian farmers want to be part of the twentieth century and are burning down tropical rain forests to clear a little land to plough, and because Indonesians make a living out of converting their lush jungle into toothpicks for fastidious Japanese diners, upsetting the delicate oxygen balance and in effect puncturing our global lungs. Yet this ecological consciousness has meant not only greater awareness but also greater inequality, as modernized nations try to slam the door behind them, saying to developing nations, "The world cannot afford *your* modernization; ours has wrung it dry!"

Each of the four imperatives just cited is transnational, transideological, and transcultural. Each applies impartially to Catholics, Jews, Muslims, Hindus, and Buddhists; to democrats and totalitarians; to capitalists and socialists. The Enlightenment dream of a universal rational society has to a remarkable degree been realized—but in a form that is commercialized, homogenized, depoliticized, bureaucratized, and, of course, radically incomplete, for the movement toward McWorld is in competition with forces of global breakdown, national dissolution, and centrifugal corruption. These forces, working in the opposite direction, are the essence of what I call Jihad.

Jihad, or the Lebanonization of the World

OPEC, the World Bank, the United Nations, the International Red Cross, the multinational corporation...there are scores of institutions that reflect globalization. But they often appear as ineffective reactors to the world's real actors: national states and, to an ever greater degree, subnational factions in permanent rebellion against uniformity and integration—even the kind represented by universal law and justice. The headlines feature these players regularly: they are cultures, not countries; parts, not wholes; sects, not religions; rebellious factions and dissenting minorities at war not just with globalism but with the traditional nation-state. Kurds, Basques, Puerto Ricans, Ossetians, East Timoreans, Quebecois, the Catholics of Northern Ireland, Abkhasians, Kurile Islander Japanese, the Zulus of Inkatha, Catalonians, Tamils, and, of course, Palestinians—people without countries, inhabiting nations not their own, seeking smaller worlds within borders that will seal them off from modernity....

This mania has left the post-Cold War world smoldering with hot wars; the international scene is little more unified than it was at the end of the Great War. There were more than thirty wars in progress last year, most of them ethnic, racial, tribal, or religious in character, and the list of unsafe regions doesn't seem to be getting any shorter. Some new world order!

The aim of many of these small-scale wars is to redraw boundaries, to implode states and resecure parochial identities: to escape McWorld's dully insistent imperatives. The mood is that of Jihad: war not as an instrument of policy but as an emblem of identity, an expression of community, an end in itself. Even where there is no shooting war, there is fractiousness, secession, and the quest for ever smaller communities. Add to the list of dangerous countries those at risk: In Switzerland and Spain, Jurassian and Basque separatists still argue the virtues of ancient identities, sometimes in the language of bombs. Hyperdisintegration in the former Soviet Union may well continue unabated—not just a Ukraine independent from the Soviet Union but a Bessarabian Ukraine independent from the Ukrainian republic; not just Russia severed from the defunct union but Tatarstan severed from Russia. Yugoslavia makes even the disunited, ex-Soviet, nonsocialist republics that were once the Soviet Union look integrated, its sectarian fatherlands springing up within factional motherlands like weeds within weeds within weeds. Kurdish independence would threaten the territorial integrity of four Middle Eastern nations. Well before the current cataclysm Soviet Georgia made a claim

for autonomy from the Soviet Union, only to be faced with its Ossetians (164,000 in a republic of 3.5 million) demanding their own self-determination within Georgia. The Abkhasian minority in Georgia has followed suit. Even the good will established by Canada's once promising Meech Lake protocols is in danger, with Francophone Quebec again threatening the dissolution of the federation. In South Africa the emergence from apartheid was hardly achieved when friction between Inkatha's Zulus and the African National Congress's tribally identified members threatened to replace Europeans' racism with an indigenous tribal war....

The passing of communism has torn away the thin veneer of internationalism (workers of the world unite!) to reveal ethnic prejudices that are not only ugly and deepseated but increasingly murderous. Europe's old scourge, anti-Semitism, is back with a vengeance, but it is only one of many antagonisms. It appears all too easy to throw the historical gears into reverse and pass from a Communist dictatorship back into a tribal state.

Among the tribes, religion is also a battlefield. ("Jihad" is a rich word whose generic meaning is "struggle"—usually the struggle of the soul to avert evil. Strictly applied to religious war, it is used only in reference to battles where the faith is under assault, or battles against a government that denies the practice of Islam. My use here is rhetorical, but does follow both journalistic practice and history.) Remember the Thirty Years War? Whatever forms of Enlightenment universalism might once have come to grace such historically related forms of monotheism as Judaism, Christianity, and Islam, in many of their modern incarnations they are parochial rather than cosmopolitan, angry rather than loving, proselytizing rather than ecumenical, zealous rather than rationalist, sectarian rather than deistic, ethnocentric rather than universalizing. As a result, like the new forms of hypernationalism, the new expressions of religious fundamentalism are fractious and pulverizing, never integrating. This is religion as the Crusaders knew it: a battle to the death for souls that if not saved will be forever lost.

The atmospherics of Jihad have resulted in a breakdown of civility in the name of identity, of comity in the name of community. International relations have sometimes taken on the aspect of gang war—cultural turf battles featuring tribal factions that were supposed to be sublimated as integral parts of large national, economic, post-colonial, and constitutional entities.

The Darkening Future of Democracy

These rather melodramatic tableaux vivants do not tell the whole story, however. For all their defects, Jihad and McWorld have their attractions. Yet, to repeat and insist, the attractions are unrelated to democracy. Neither McWorld nor Jihad is remotely democratic in impulse. Neither needs democracy; neither promotes democracy....

To the extent that either McWorld or Jihad has a *natural* politics, it has turned out to be more of an antipolitics. For McWorld, it is the antipolitics of globalism: bureaucratic, technocratic, and meritocratic, focused (as Marx predicted it would be) on the administration of things—with people, however, among the chief things to be administered. In its politico-economic imperatives McWorld has been guided by laissez-faire market principles that privilege efficiency, productivity, and beneficence at the expense of civic liberty and self-government.

For Jihad, the antipolitics of tribalization has been explicitly antidemocratic: one-party dictatorship, government by military junta, theocratic fundamentalism—often associated with a version of the *Führerprinzip* that empowers an individual to rule on behalf of a people. Even the government of India, struggling for decades to model democracy for a people who will soon number a billion, longs for great leaders; and for every Mahatma Gandhi, Indira Gandhi, or Rajiv Gandhi taken from them by zealous as-sassins, the Indians appear to seek a replacement who will deliver them from the lengthy travail of their freedom.

The Confederal Option

How can democracy be secured and spread in a world whose primary tendencies are at best indifferent to it (McWorld) and at worst deeply antithetical to it (Jihad)? My guess is that globalization will eventually vanquish retribalization. The ethos of material "civilization" has not yet encountered an obstacle it has been unable to thrust aside....

Jihad may be a last deep sigh before the eternal yawn of McWorld.... Yet democracy is how we remonstrate with reality, the rebuke our aspirations offer to history. And if retribalization is inhospitable to democracy, there is nonetheless a form of democratic government that can accommodate parochialism and communitarianism, one that can even save them from their defects and make them more tolerant and participatory: decentralized participatory democracy. And if McWorld is indifferent to democracy, there is nonetheless a form of democratic government that suits global markets passably well—representative government in its federal or, better still, confederal variation.

With its concern for accountability, the protection of minorities, and the universal rule of law, a confederalized representative system would serve the political needs of McWorld as well as oligarchic bureaucratism or meritocratic elitism is currently doing. As we are already beginning to see, many nations may survive in the long term only as confederations that afford local regions smaller than "nations" extensive jurisdiction. Recommended reading for democrats of the twenty-first century is not the U.S. Constitution or the French Declaration of Rights of Man and Citizen but the Articles of Confederation, that suddenly pertinent document that stitched together the thirteen American colonies into what then seemed a too loose confederation of independent states but now appears a new form of political realism, as veterans of Yeltsin's new Russia and the new Europe created at Maastricht will attest.

By the same token, the participatory and direct form of democracy that engages citizens in civic activity and civic judgment and goes well beyond just voting and accountability—the system I have called "strong democracy"—suits the political needs of decentralized communities as well as theocratic and nationalist party dictatorships have done. Local neighborhoods need not be democratic, but they can be. Real democracy has flourished in diminutive settings: the spirit of liberty, Tocqueville said, is local. Participatory democracy, if not naturally apposite to tribalism, has an undeniable attractiveness under conditions of parochialism....

For democracy to persist in our brave new McWorld, we will have to commit acts of conscious political will. Political will requires much more than the quick fix of the transfer of institutions. Like technology transfer, institution transfer rests on foolish assumptions about a uniform world of the kind that once fired the imagination of colonial administrators.... Today's well-intentioned quick fixers...are hoping to democratize by long distance. Post Bulgaria a parliament by first-class mail. Fed Ex the Bill of Rights to Sri Lanka. Cable Cambodia some common law.

Yet Eastern Europe has already demonstrated that importing free political parties, parliaments, and presses cannot establish a democratic civil society; imposing a free market may even have the opposite effect. Democracy grows from the bottom up and cannot be imposed from the top down. Civil society has to be built from the inside out. The institutional superstructure comes last....

Democrats need to seek out indigenous democratic impulses. There is always a desire for self-government, always some expression of participation, accountability, consent, and representation, even in traditional hierarchical societies. These need to be identified, tapped, modified, and incorporated into new democratic practices with an indigenous flavor. The tortoises among the democratizers may ultimately outlive or outpace the hares, for they will have the time and patience to explore conditions along the way, and to adapt their gait to changing circumstances. Tragically, democracy in a hurry often looks something like France in 1794 or China in 1989.

It certainly seems possible that the most attractive democratic ideal in the face of the brutal realities of Jihad and the dull realities of McWorld will be a confederal union of semi-autonomous communities smaller than nation-states, tied together into regional economic associations and markets larger than nation-states—participatory and self-determining in local matters at the bottom, representative and accountable at the top. The nation-state would play a diminished role, and sovereignty would lose some of its political potency. The Green movement adage "Think globally, act locally" would actually come to describe the conduct of politics.

This vision reflects only an ideal, however—one that is not terribly likely to be realized. Freedom, Jean-Jacques Rousseau once wrote, is a food easy to eat but hard to digest. Still, democracy has always played itself out against the odds. And democracy remains both a form of coherence as binding as McWorld and a secular faith potentially as inspiriting as Jihad.

Wendell Berry
The Body and the Earth

Wendell Berry was born in Kentucky in 1934, and his life work has dealt primarily with his native state and region. A professor of English at the University of Kentucky, Berry's poetry, novels, and essays all reflect a concern with the despoilation of the land and culture of Kentucky. Still, his ability to connect the individual self and its sustenance to land and earth make him a universalist rather than a mere regionalist. His 1977 book, *The Unsettling of America*, offers a critique of modern agricultural practices which becomes a general examination of society's understanding of our planet. In the following selection from that book, Berry argues that although modern agriculture can feed more people than ever before, our understanding of food production shows a fragmented, deficient, and destructive conception of the human body and soul. Human health, for Berry, is not only the absence of illness, but a state of wholeness. To be healthy is to live within the cycles of nature. While Western culture and religion have given the soul dominance over the body, and placed both body and soul in competition with nature, true health requires a recognition of the interconnectedness of these aspects of life.

The Body and the Earth
Wendell Berry

On the Cliff

The question of human limits, of the proper definition and place of human beings within the order of Creation, finally rests upon our attitude toward our biological existence, the life of the body in this world. What value and respect do we give to our bodies? What uses do we have for them? What relation do we see, if any, between body and mind, or body and soul? What connections or responsibilities do we maintain between our bodies and the earth? These are religious questions, obviously, for our bodies are part of the Creation, and they involve us in all the issues of mystery. But the questions are also agricultural, for no matter how urban our life, our bodies live by farming; we come from the earth and return to it, and so we live in agriculture as we live in flesh. While we live our bodies are moving particles of the earth, joined inextricably both to the soil and to the bodies of other living creatures. It is hardly surprising, then, that there should be some profound resemblances between our treatment of our bodies and our treatment of the earth.

That humans are small within the Creation is an ancient perception, represented often enough in art that it must be supposed to have an elemental importance. On one of the painted walls of the Lascaux cave (20,000–15,000 B.C.), surrounded by the exquisitely shaped, shaded, and colored bodies of animals, there is the childish stick figure of a man, a huntsman who, having cast his spear into the guts of a bison, is now weaponless and vulnerable, poignantly frail, exposed, and incomplete. The message seems essentially that of the voice out of the whirlwind in the Book of Job: the Creation is bounteous and mysterious, and humanity is only a part of it—not its equal, much less its master.

Old Chinese landscape paintings reveal, among towering mountains, the frail outline of a roof or a tiny human figure passing along a road on foot or horseback. These landscapes are almost always populated. There is no implication of a dehumanized interest in nature "for its own sake." What is represented is a world in which humans belong, but which does not belong to humans in any tidy economic sense; the Creation provides a place for humans, but it is greater than humanity and within it even great men are small. Such humility is the consequence of an accurate insight, ecological in its bearing, not a pious deference to "spiritual" value....

Until modern times, we focused a great deal of the best of our thought upon such rituals of return to the human condition. Seeking enlightenment or the Promised Land or the way home, a man would go or be forced to go into the wilderness, measure himself against the Creation, recognize finally his true place within it, and thus be saved both from pride and from despair. Seeing himself as a tiny member of a world he cannot comprehend or master or in any final sense possess, he cannot possibly think of himself as a god. And by the same token, since he shares in, depends upon, and is graced by all of which he is a part, neither can be become a fiend; he cannot descend into the final despair of destructiveness. Returning from the wilderness, he becomes a restorer of order, a preserver. He sees the truth, recognizes his true heir, honors his forebears and his heritage, and gives his blessing to his successors. He embodies the passing of human time, living and dying within the human limits of grief and joy.

On the Tower

Apparently with the rise of industry, we began to romanticize the wilderness—which is to say we began to institutionalize it within the concept of the "scenic." Because of railroads and improved highways, the wilderness was no longer an arduous passage for the traveler, but something to be looked at as grand or beautiful from the high vantages of the roadside. We became viewers of "views." And because we no longer traveled in the wilderness as a matter of course, we forgot that wilderness still circumscribed civilization and persisted in domesticity. We forgot, indeed, that the civilized and the domestic continued to *depend* upon wilderness—that is, upon natural forces within the climate and within the soil that have never in any meaningful sense been controlled or conquered. Modern civilization has been built largely in this forgetfulness.

And as we transformed the wilderness into scenery, we began to feel in the presence of "nature" an awe that was increasingly statistical. We would not become appreciators of the Creation until we had taken its measure. Once we had climbed or driven to the mountain top, we were awed by the view, but it was an awe that we felt compelled to validate or prove by the knowledge of how high we stood and how far we saw. We are invited to "see seven states from atop Lookout Mountain," as if our political boundaries had been drawn in red on the third morning of Creation.

We became less and less capable of sensing ourselves as small within Creation, partly because we thought we could comprehend it statistically, but also because we were becoming creators, ourselves, of a mechanical creation by which we felt ourselves greatly magnified. We built bridges that stood imposingly in titanic settings, towers that stood around us like geologic presences, single machines that could do the work of hundreds of people. Why, after all, should one get excited about a mountain when one can see almost as far from the top of a building, much farther from an airplane, farther still from a space capsule? We have learned to be fascinated by the statistics of magnitude and power. There is apparently no limit in sight, no end, and so it is no wonder that our minds, dizzy with numbers, take refuge in a yearning for infinitudes of energy and materials.

And yet these works that so magnify us also dwarf us, reduce us to insignificance. They magnify us because we are capable of them. They diminish us because, say what we will, once we build beyond a human scale, once we conceive ourselves as Titans or as gods, we are lost in magnitude; we cannot control or limit what we do. The statistics of magnitude call out like Sirens to the statistics of destruction. If we have built towering cities, we have raised even higher the cloud of megadeath. If people are as grass before God, they are as nothing before their machines.

If we are fascinated by the statistics of magnitude, we are no less fascinated by the statistics of our insignificance. We never tire of repeating the commonizing figures of population and population growth. We are entranced to think of ourselves as specks on the pages of our own overwhelming history. I remember that my high-school biology text dealt with the human body by listing its constituent elements, measuring their quantities, and giving their monetary worth—at that time a little less than a dollar. That was a bit of the typical fodder of the modern mind, at once sensational and belittling—no accidental product of the age of Dachau and Hiroshima....

Health

After I had begun to think about these things, I received a letter containing an account of a more recent suicide:

"My friend _____ jumped off the Golden Gate Bridge two months ago.... She had been terribly depressed for years. There was no help for her. None that she could find that was sufficient. She was trying to get from one phase of her life to another, and couldn't make it. She had been terribly wounded as a child....

Her wound could not be healed. She destroyed herself."

The letter had already asked, "How does a human pass through youth to maturity without 'breaking down'?" And it had answered: "help from tradition, through ceremonies and rituals, rites of passage at the most difficult stages."

My correspondent went on to say: "Healing, it seems to me, is a necessary and useful word when we talk about agriculture." And a few paragraphs later he wrote: "The theme of suicide belongs in a book about agriculture..."

I agree. But I am also aware that many people will find it exceedingly strange that these themes should enter so forcibly into this book. It will be thought that I am off the subject. And so I want to take pains to show that I am *on* the subject—and on it, moreover, in the only way most people have of getting on it: by way of the issue of their own health. Indeed, it is when one approaches agriculture from any *other* issue than that of health that one may be said to be off the subject.

The difficulty probably lies in our narrowed understanding of the word *health*. That there is some connection between how we feel and what we eat, between our bodies and the earth, is acknowledged when we say that we must "eat right to keep fit" or that we should eat "a balanced diet." But by health we mean little more than how we feel. We are healthy, we think, if we do not feel any pain or too much pain, and if we are strong enough to do our work. If we become unhealthy, then we go to a doctor who we hope will "cure" us and restore us to health. By health, in other words, we mean merely the absence of disease. Our health professionals are interested almost exclusively in preventing disease (mainly by destroying germs) and in curing disease (mainly by surgery and by destroying germs).

But the concept of health is rooted in the concept of wholeness. To be healthy is to be whole. The word *health* belongs to a family of words, a listing of which will suggest how far the consideration of health must carry us: *heal*, *whole*, *wholesome*, *hale*, *hallow*, *holy*. And so it is possible to give a definition to health that is positive and far more elaborate than that given to it by most medical doctors and the officers of public health.

If the body is healthy, then it is whole. But how can it be whole and yet be dependent, as it obviously is, upon other bodies and upon the earth, upon all the rest of Creation, in fact? It immediately becomes clear that the health or wholeness of the body is a vast subject, and that to preserve it calls for a vast enterprise. Blake said that "Man has no Body distinct from his Soul..." and thus acknowledged the convergence of health and holiness. In that, all the convergences and dependences of Creation are surely implied. Our bodies are also not distinct from the bodies of other people, on which they depend in a complexity of ways from biological to spiritual. They are not distinct from the bodies of plants and animals, with which we are involved in the cycles of feeding and in the intricate companionships of ecological systems and of the spirit. They are not distinct from the earth, the sun and moon, and the other heavenly bodies.

It is therefore absurd to approach the subject of health piecemeal with a departmentalized band of specialists. A medical doctor uninterested in nutrition, in agriculture, in the wholesomeness of mind and spirit is as absurd as a farmer who is uninterested in health. Our fragmentation of this subject cannot be our cure, because it is our disease. The body cannot be whole alone. Persons cannot be whole alone. It is wrong to think that bodily health is compatible with spiritual confusion or cultural disorder, or with polluted air and water or impoverished soil. Intellectually, we know that these patterns of interdependence exist; we understand them better now perhaps than we ever have before; yet modern social and cultural patterns contradict them and make it difficult or impossible to honor them in practice.

To try to heal the body alone is to collaborate in the destruction of the body. Healing is impossible in loneliness; it is the opposite of loneliness. Conviviality is healing. To be healed we must come with all the other creatures to the feast of Creation. Together, the above two descriptions of suicides suggest this very powerfully. The setting of both is urban, amid the gigantic works of modern humanity. The fatal sickness is despair, a wound that cannot be healed because it is encapsulated in loneliness, surrounded by speechlessness. Past the scale of the human, our works do not liberate us—they confine us. They cut off access to the wilderness of Creation where we must go to be reborn—to receive the awareness, at once humbling and exhilarating, grievous and joyful, that we are a part of Creation, one with all that we live from and all that, in turn, lives from us. They destroy the communal rites of passage that turn us toward the wilderness and bring us home again.

The Isolation of the Body

Perhaps the fundamental damage of the specialist system—the damage from which all other damages issue—has been the isolation of the body. At some point we began to assume that the life of the body would be the business of grocers and medical doctors, who need take no interest in the spirit, whereas the life of the spirit would be the business of churches, which would have at best only a negative interest in the body. In the same way we began to see nothing wrong with putting the body—most often somebody else's body, but frequently our own—to a task that insulted the mind and demeaned the spirit. And we began to find it easier than ever to prefer our own bodies to the bodies of other creatures and to abuse, exploit, and otherwise hold in contempt those other bodies for the greater good or comfort of our own.

The isolation of the body sets it into direct conflict with everything else in Creation. It gives it a value that is destructive of every other value. That this has happened is paradoxical, for the body was set apart from the soul in order that the soul should triumph over the body. The aim is stated in Shakespeare's Sonnet 146 as plainly as anywhere:

> Poor soul, the center of my sinful earth,
> Lord of these rebel powers that thee array,
> Why dost thou pine within and suffer dearth,
> Painting thy outward walls so costly gay?
> Why so large cost, having so short a lease,
> Dost thou upon thy fading mansion spend?
> Shall worms, inheritors of this excess,
> Eat up thy charge? Is this thy body's end?
> Then, soul, live thou upon thy servant's loss,
> And let that pine to aggravate thy store;
> Buy terms divine in selling hours of dross;
> Within be fed, without be rich no more.
> So shalt thou feed on death, that feeds on men,
> And death once dead, there's no more dying then.

The soul is thus set against the body, to thrive at the body's expense. And so a spiritual economy is devised within which the only law is competition. If the soul is to live in this world only by denying the body, then its relation to worldly life becomes extremely simple and superficial. Too simple and superficial, in fact, to cope in any meaningful or useful way with the world. Spiritual value ceases to have any worldly purpose or force. To fail to employ the body in this world at once for its own good and the good of the soul is to issue an invitation to disorder of the most serious kind.

What was not foreseen in this simple-minded economics of religion was that it is not possible to devalue the body and value the soul. The body, cast loose from the soul, is on its own. Devalued and cast out of the temple, the body does not skulk off like a sick dog to die in the bushes. It sets up a counterpart economy of its own, based also on the law of competition, in which it devalues and exploits the spirit. These two economies maintain themselves at each other's expense, living upon each other's loss, collaborating without cease in mutual futility and absurdity.

You cannot devalue the body and value the soul—or value anything else. The prototypical act issuing from this division was to make a person a slave and then instruct him in religion—a "charity" more damaging to the master than to the slave. Contempt for the body is invariably manifested in contempt for other bodies—the bodies of slaves, laborers, women, animals, plants, the earth itself. Relationships with all other creatures become competitive and exploitive rather than collaborative and convivial. The world is seen and dealt with, not as an ecological community, but as a stock exchange, the ethics of which are based on the tragically misnamed "law of the jungle." This "jungle" law is a basic fallacy of modern culture. The body is degraded and saddened by being set in conflict against the Creation itself, of which all bodies are members, therefore members of each other. The body is thus sent to war against itself.

Divided, set against each other, body and soul drive each other to extremes of misapprehension and folly. Nothing could be more absurd than to despise the body and yet yearn for its resurrection. In reaction to this supposedly religious attitude, we get, not reverence or respect for the body, but another kind of contempt: the desire to comfort and indulge the body with equal disregard for its health. The "dialogue of body and soul" in our time is being carried on between those who despise the body for the sake of its resurrection and those, diseased by bodily extravagance and lack of exercise, who nevertheless desire longevity above all things. These think that they oppose each other, and yet they could not exist apart. They are locked in a conflict that is really their collaboration in the destruction of soul and body both.

What this conflict has done, among other things, is to make it extremely difficult to set a proper value on the life of the body in this world—to believe that it is good, howbeit short and imperfect. Until we are able to say this and know what we mean by it, we will not be able to live our lives in the human estate of grief and joy, but repeatedly will be cast outside in violent swings between pride and despair. Desires that cannot be fulfilled in health will keep us hopelessly restless and unsatisfied.

Competition

By dividing body and soul, we divide both from all else. We thus condemn ourselves to a loneliness for which the only compensation is violence—against other creatures, against the earth, against ourselves. For no matter the distinctions we draw between body and soul, body and earth, ourselves and others—the connections, the dependences, the identities remain. And so we fail to contain or control our violence. It gets loose. Though there are categories of violence, or so we think, there are no categories of victims. Violence against one is ultimately violence against all. The willingness to abuse other bodies is the willingness to abuse one's own. To damage the earth is to damage your children. To despise the ground is to despise its fruit; to despise the fruit is to despise its eaters. The wholeness of health is broken by despite.

If competition is the correct relation of creatures to one another and to the earth, then we must ask why exploitation is not more successful than it is. Why, having lived so long at the expense of other creatures and the earth, are we not healthier and happier than we are? Why does modern society exist under constant threat of the same suffering, deprivation, spite, contempt, and obliteration that it has imposed on other people and other creatures? Why do the health of the body and the health of the earth decline together? And why, in consideration of this decline of our worldly flesh and household, our "sinful earth," are we not healthier in spirit?

It is not necessary to have recourse to statistics to see that the human estate is declining with the estate of nature, and that the corruption of the body is the corruption of the soul. I know that the country is full of "leaders" and experts of various sorts who are using statistics to prove the opposite: that we have more cars, more super-highways, more TV sets, motorboats, prepared foods, etc., than any people ever had before—and are therefore better off than any people ever were before. I can see the burgeoning of this "consumer economy," and can appreciate some of its attractions and comforts. But that economy has an inside and an outside; from the outside there are other things to be seen.

I am writing this in the north-central part of Kentucky on a morning near the end of June. We have had rain for two days, hard rain during the last several hours. From where I sit I can see the Kentucky River swiftening and rising, the water already yellow with mud. I know that inside this city-oriented consumer economy there are many people who will never see this muddy rise and many who will see it without knowing what it means. I know also that there are many who will see it, and know what it means, and not care. If it lasts until the weekend there will be people who will find it as good as clear water for motor-boating and waterskiing.

In the past several days I have seen some of the worst-eroded corn fields that I have seen in this country in my life. This erosion is occurring on the cash-rented farms of farmers' widows and city farmers, absentee owners, the doctors and businessmen who buy a farm for the tax breaks or to have "a quiet place in the country" for the weekends. It is the direct result of economic and agricultural policy; it might be said to *be* an economic and agricultural policy. The signs of the "agridollar," big-business fantasy of the Butz mentality are all present: the absenteeism, the temporary and shallow interest of the land-renter, the row-cropping of slopes, the lack of rotation, the plowed-out waterways, the rows running up and down the hills. Looked at from the field's edge, this is ruin, criminal folly, moral idiocy. Looked at from Washington, D.C., from inside the "economy" it is called "free enterprise" and "full production."

And around me here, as everywhere else I have been in this country—in Nebraska, Iowa, Indiana, New York, New England, Tennessee—the farmland is in general decline: fields and whole farms abandoned, given up with their scars unmended, washing away under the weeds and bushes; fine land put to row crops year after year, without rest or rotation; buildings and fences going down; good houses standing empty, unpainted, their windows broken.

And it is clear to anyone who looks carefully at any crowd that we are wasting our bodies exactly as we are wasting our land. Our bodies are fat, weak, joyless, sickly, ugly, the virtual prey of the manufacturers of medicine and cosmetics. Our bodies have become marginal; they are growing useless like our "marginal" land because we have less and less use for them. After the games and idle flourishes of modern youth, we use them only as shipping cartons to transport our brains and our few employable muscles back and forth to work.

As for our spirits, they seem more and more to comfort themselves by buying things. No longer in need of the exalted drama of grief and joy, they feed now on little shocks of greed, scandal, and violence. For many of the churchly, the life of the spirit is reduced to dull preoccupation with getting to Heaven. At best, the world is no more than an embarrassment and a trial to the spirit, which is otherwise radically separated from it. The true lover of God must not be burdened with any care or respect for His works. While the body goes about its business of destroying the earth, the soul is to lie back and wait for Sunday, keeping itself free of earthly contaminants. While the body exploits other bodies, the soul stands aloof, free from sin, crying to the gawking bystanders: "I am not enjoying it!" As far as this sort of "religion" is concerned, the body is no more than the luster-less container of the soul, a mere "package," that will nevertheless light up in eternity, forever cool and shiny as a neon cross. This separation of the soul from the body and from the world is no disease of the fringe, no aberration, but a fracture that runs through the mentality of institutional religion like a geologic fault. And this rift in the mentality of religion continues to characterize the modern mind, no matter how secular or worldly it becomes.

But I have not stated my point exactly enough. This rift is not *like* a geologic fault; it *is* a geologic fault. It is a flaw in the mind that runs inevitably into the earth. Thought affects or afflicts substance neither by intention nor by accident, but because, occurring in the Creation that is unified and whole, it must; there is no help for it.

The soul, in its loneliness, hopes only for "salvation." And yet what is the burden of the Bible if not a sense of the mutuality of influence, rising out of an essential unity, among soul and body and community and world? These are all the works of God, and it is therefore the work of virtue to make or restore harmony among them. The world is certainly thought of as a place of spiritual trial, but it is also the confluence of soul and body, word and flesh, where thoughts must become deeds, where goodness is to be enacted. This is the great meeting place, the narrow passage where spirit and flesh, word and world, pass into each other. The Bible's aim, as I read it, is not the freeing of the spirit from the world. It is the handbook of their interaction. It says that they cannot be divided; that their mutuality, their unity, is inescapable; that they are not reconciled in division, but in harmony. What else can be meant by the resurrection of the body? The body should be "filled with light," perfected in understanding. And so everywhere there is the sense of consequence, fear and desire, grief and joy. What is desirable is repeatedly defined in the tensions of the sense of consequence. False prophets are to be known "by their fruits." We are to treat others as we would be treated; thought is thus barred from any easy escape into aspiration or ideal, is turned around and forced into action. The following verses from Proverbs are not very likely the original work of a philosopher-king; they are overheard from generations of agrarian grandparents whose experience taught them that spiritual qualities become earthly events:

I went by the field of the slothful, and by the vineyard of the man void of understanding;

And, lo, it was all grown over with thorns, and nettles had covered the face thereof, and the stone wall thereof was broken down.

Then I saw, and considered it well. I looked upon it, and received instruction.

Yet a little sleep, a little slumber, a little folding of the hands to sleep:

So shall thy poverty come as one that traveleth; and they want as an armed man.

Fertility as Waste

But there is yet another and more direct way in which the isolation of the body has serious agricultural effects. That is in our society's extreme oversimplification of the relation between the body and its food. By regarding it as merely a consumer of food, we reduce the function of the body to that of a conduit which channels the nutrients of the earth from the supermarket to the sewer. Or we make it a little factory which transforms fertility into pollution—to the enormous profit of "agribusiness" and to the impoverishment of the earth. This is another technological and economic interruption of the cycle of fertility.

Much has already been said here about the division between the body and its food in the productive phase of the cycle. It is the alleged wonder of the Modern World that so many people take energy from food in which they have invested no energy, or very little. Ninety-five percent of our people, boasted the former deputy assistant secretary of agriculture, are now free of the "drudgery" of food production. The meanings of that division, as I have been trying to show, are intricate and degenerative. But that is only half of it. Ninety-five percent (at least) of our people are also free of any involvement or interest in the maintenance phase of the cycle. As their bodies take in and use the nutrients of the soil, those nutrients are transformed into what we are pleased to regard as "wastes"—and are duly wasted.

This waste also has its cause in the old "religious" division between body and soul, by which the body and its products are judged offensive. Once, living with this offensiveness was considered a condemnation, and that was bad enough. But modern technology "saved" us with the flush toilet and the water-borne sewage system. These devices deal with the "wastes" of our bodies by simply removing them from consideration. The irony is that this technological purification of the body requires the pollution of the rivers and the starvation of the fields. It makes the alleged offensiveness of the body truly and inescapably offensive and blinds an entire society to the knowledge that these "offensive wastes" are readily purified in the topsoil—that, indeed, from an ecological point of view, these are not wastes and are not offensive, but are valuable agricultural products essential both to the health of the land and to that of the "consumers."

Our system of agriculture, by modeling itself on economics rather than biology, thus removes food from the *cycle* of its production and puts it into a finite, linear process that in effect destroys it by transforming it into waste. That is, it transforms food into fuel, a form of energy that is usable only once, and in doing so it transforms the body into a consumptive machine.

It is strange, but only apparently so, that this system of agriculture is institutionalized, not in any form of rural life or culture, but in what we call our "urban civilization." The cities subsist in competition with the country; they live upon a one-way movement of energies out of the countryside—food and fuel, manufacturing materials, human labor, intelligence, and talent. Very little of this energy is ever returned. Instead of gathering these energies up into coherence, a cultural consummation that would not only return to the countryside what belongs to it, but also give back generosities of learning and art, conviviality and order, the modern city dissipates and wastes them. Along with its glittering "consumer goods," the modern city produces an equally characteristic outpouring of garbage and pollution—just as it produces and/or collects unemployed, unemployable, and otherwise wasted people.

Once again it must be asked, if competition is the appropriate relationship, then why, after generations of this inpouring of rural wealth, materials, and humanity into the cities, are the cities and the countryside in equal states of disintegration and disrepair? Why have the rural and urban communities *both* fallen to pieces?

Health and Work

The modern urban-industrial society is based on a series of radical disconnections between body and soul, husband and wife, marriage and community, community and the earth. At each of these points of disconnection the collaboration of corporation, government, and expert sets up a profit-making enterprise that results in the further dismemberment and impoverishment of the Creation.

Together, these disconnections add up to a condition of critical ill health, which we suffer in common—not just with each other, but with all other creatures. Our economy is based upon this disease. Its aim is to separate us as far as possible from the sources of life (material, social, and spiritual), to put these sources under the control of corporations and specialized professionals, and to sell them to us at the highest profit. It fragments the Creation and sets the fragments into conflict with one another. For the relief of the suffering that comes of this fragmentation and conflict, our economy proposes, not health, but vast "cures" that further centralize power and increase profits: wars, wars on crime, wars on poverty, national schemes of medical aid, insurance, immunization, further industrial and economic "growth," etc.; and these, of course, are followed by more regulatory laws and agencies to see that our health is protected, our freedom preserved, and our money well spent. Although there may be some "good intention" in this, there is little honesty and no hope.

Only by restoring the broken connections can we be healed. Connection *is* health. And what our society does its best to disguise from us is how ordinary, how commonly attainable, health is. We lose our health—and create profitable diseases and dependences—by failing to see the direct connections between living and eating, eating and working, working and loving. In gardening, for instance, one works with the body to feed the body. The work, if it is knowledgeable, makes for excellent food. And it makes one hungry. The work thus makes eating both nourishing and joyful, not consumptive, and keeps the eater from getting fat and weak. This is health, wholeness, a source of delight. And such a solution, unlike the typical industrial solution, does not cause new problems.

The "drudgery" of growing one's own food, then, is not drudgery at all. (If we make the growing of food a drudgery, which is what "agribusiness" does make of it, then we also make a drudgery of eating and of living.) It is—in addition to being the appropriate fulfillment of a practical need—a sacrament, as eating is also, by which we enact and understand our oneness with the Creation, the conviviality of one body with all bodies. This is what we learn from the hunting and farming rituals of tribal cultures.

THE WORLD ❖ 649

As the connections have been broken by the fragmentation and isolation of work, they can be restored by restoring the wholeness of work. There is work that is isolating, harsh, destructive, specialized or trivialized into meaninglessness. And there is work that is restorative, convivial, dignified and dignifying, and pleasing. Good work is not just the maintenance of connections—as one is now said to work "for a living" or "to support a family"—but the *enactment* of connections. It *is* living, and a way of living; it is not support for a family in the sense of an exterior brace or prop, but is one of the forms and acts of love.

To boast that now "95 percent of the people can be freed from the drudgery of preparing their own food" is possible only to one who cannot distinguish between these kinds of work. The former deputy assistant secretary cannot see work as a vital connection; he can see it only as a trade of time for money, and so of course he believes in doing as little of it as possible, especially if it involves the use of the body. His ideal is apparently the same as that of a real-estate agency which promotes a rural subdivision by advertising "A homelife of endless vacation." But the society that is so glad to be free of the drudgery of growing and preparing food also boasts a thriving medical industry to which it is paying $500 per person per year. And that is only the down payment.

We embrace this curious freedom and pay its exorbitant cost because of our hatred of bodily labor. We do not want to work "like a dog" or "like an ox" or "like a horse"—that is , we do not want to use ourselves as beasts. This as much as anything is the cause of our disrespect for farming and our abandonment of it to businessmen and experts. We remember, as we should, that there have been agricultural economies that used people as beasts. But that cannot be remedied, as we have attempted to do, by using people as machines, or by not using them at all.

Perhaps the trouble began when we started using animals disrespectfully: as "beasts"—that is, as if they had no more feeling than a machine. Perhaps the destructiveness of our use of machines was prepared in our willingness to abuse animals. That it was never necessary to abuse animals in order to use them is suggested by a passage in *The Horse in the Furrow*, by George Ewart Evans. He is speaking of how the medieval ox teams were worked at the plow: "...the ploughman at the handles, the team of oxen—yoked in pairs or four abreast—and the driver who walked alongside with his goad." And then he says: "It is also worth noting that in the Welsh organization...the counterpart of the driver was termed *y geilwad or the caller*. He walked *backwards* in front of the oxen singing to them as they worked. Songs were specially composed to suit the rhythm of the oxen's work..."

That seems to me to differ radically from our customary use of any living thing. The oxen were not used as beasts or machines, but as fellow creatures. It may be presumed that this work used people the same way. It is possible, then, to believe that there is a kind of work that does not require abuse or misuse, that does not use anything as a substitute for anything else. We are working well when we use ourselves as the fellow creatures of the plants, animals, materials, and other people we are working with. Such work is unifying, healing. It brings us home from pride and from despair, and places us responsibly within the human estate. It defines us as we are: not too good to work with our bodies, but too good to work poorly or joylessly or selfishly or alone.

Boutros Boutros-Ghali

Opening Statement at the United Nations Conference on Environment and Development Rio de Janeiro, 3–14 June 1992

The United Nations Conference on Environment and Development (UNCED), held in Rio de Janeiro, Brazil, June 4–14, 1992, brought together representatives from 177 nations, including 120 heads of state, and several hundred nongovernmental organizations. The Conference represented an unprecedented manifestation of public concern for the natural environment, and specifically addressed the question of how to help the Southern countries avoid the environmental degradation caused by industrialization in the North. Although it stimulated international concern, some criticized the "Earth Summit" for addressing only the obvious effects of poor environmental practices without seriously confronting the underlying social, political, and economic causes.

The agreements reached at UNCED were compiled in the UN document, *Agenda 21*. The UN subsequently established the UN Commission on Sustainable Development, a consultative body consisting of 53 member states with the objective of supervising the implementation of *Agenda 21*. In the United States, 650 non-governmental organizations formed the U.S. Citizens Network on UNCED. A number of U.S. cities also established "sustainability committees" to undertake evaluation of their local environmental practices. UNCED's ultimate success may depend in part on the ability of individual citizens and the international community to foster the vision eloquently presented by the UN Secretary General, Boutros Boutros-Ghali, at the opening of the Conference and reprinted here.

Report of the United Nations Conference on Environment and Development

Boutros Boutros-Ghali

In the subjects we shall discuss during the Conference which I have the great honour to open at this moment, nothing could be more risky than to succumb to the power of words and to limit ourselves to that. Nothing would be more dangerous than to believe or to give the impression that just because things are said, the challenges have been met. And yet I do not think that I am succumbing to the power of words in saying that this is an historic moment. Historic—yes, I believe that it is, and I would put forward three reasons for this—each one in itself capable of moving us greatly as this Conference, which the entire world will follow, begins.

Let us try to grasp, first of all, what this Earth Summit means: here we have a gathering of nations, united before us, represented at the highest level by their leaders, supported by an exceptional rallying of peoples, and determined to reflect—and then act—in concert to protect their planet. This meeting is proof that we have understood how very fragile our

Earth—and the life it shelters—is: this is the first reason, then, why it is historic and reflects a radical change in the way man looks at himself.

In the past, the individual was surrounded by nature so abundant that its immensity was terrifying. This was still true at the beginning of this century. All victories have been victories over nature, from the wild beasts menacing the cavemen to the distances separating communities. The wild beasts have been conquered, and so have the distances, and taking both these conquests into account, we can say that all of science has grown out of the conflict between man and nature, with man moving forward by gradually taming an infinite nature.

Yet, "the time of the finite world" has come, a world in which we are "under house arrest": what this means is simply that nature no longer exists in the classic sense of the term, and that henceforth nature lies within the hands of man. It also means that man has triumphed over his environment, a triumph nevertheless fraught with danger. Finally, it means that there are no more cases to discover, no more "new frontiers," and that every new triumph over nature will in fact be a triumph over ourselves. Progress, then, is not necessarily compatible with life; we may no longer take the logic of the infinite for granted. It is this great epistemological break which the Earth Summit may ultimately symbolize for historians.

This meeting is historic for a second, no less exalting, reason: we are looking at a time-frame that extends far beyond the span of our individual lives. The reflection and, especially the action for which we are to lay the political foundation here will not be undertaken for ourselves, or even for our contemporaries. For we can still waste the planet's resources, at our current pace, for a few decades more. We can still live, for a few years or a few decades more, with the acid rain that is only gradually destroying our forests, lakes, works of architecture and even ourselves; we can stand it if the climate heats up by a few degrees, if the biological diversity of our planet diminishes, if the pollution of our waters continues, if the desertification of the planet accelerates—we will always have enough forests, enough water, enough natural resources. But we must realize that one day, when we as individuals have ceased to exist, it will no longer be possible to let things go on, or let things go, and that, ultimately, the storm will break on the heads of future generations. For them, it will be too late.

What we do here, then, we do for our grandchildren and, beyond, for future generations. Our presence here is proof that we intend to give precedence to time in the political sense—that is, history—over our own personal history. We are here for the long term, which is calculated in decades and centuries. This is the noblest aspect of our collective efforts at Rio.

This moment is historic for a third reason, which derives from the other two and has to do with the United Nations, which it is my honour to head. It is a huge task which the Organiza-

tion, together with all those who have placed their hope in universalism, is tackling here. Will we be able to show that men are capable of rising above the conflicts of a different era to work together to tackle the immense challenges that have been handed them? "The worst is always certain," quipped the Spanish writer Unamuno. This might be true if we were to leave in a week's time without having taken the difficult but crucial decisions that are expected of us. We must therefore go beyond the norm and bring our system to a higher plane. By whatever means, we are in a sense condemned here to moving closer, even if by only a step, to the virtuous planet, "al-ma'mura al-fadila," anticipated by the Islamic philosopher Al Farabi....

I do not know whether ideas make the world go round; in any event, nothing is possible without them. We must begin, then, by an act of collective reflection, which is also part of the work of the United Nations, and we must equip ourselves with courage, for reflection entails a risk: the risk that we will be forced to give up myths, comfortable ways of thinking, sacred economic principles. Our reflection has a common denominator, which is the central concept of our Conference, and that is development. Development! The term has enjoyed unprecedented glory. Yet, it has been through the preparatory work for this Conference that the term has taken on its full meaning. We now know that if we prove unable to expand the concept of development further, we will find ourselves confronted with a paradox that would make us smile if it did not mask so much suffering and danger: the Earth is simultaneously suffering from underdevelopment and from overdevelopment.

We must therefore expand the meaning of the term "development" as we know it in the light of scientific developments and the challenges that face us today. I believe that in the future, this expansion will take place in two directions: the first is towards what we now call "sustainable development"; the second is towards what I propose to call "planetary development." Once again, in my mind these concepts concern the entire world, North and South, East and West.

Let us take sustainable development first: it may be defined as development that meets the needs of the present as long as resources are renewed or, in other words, that does not compromise the development of future generations. This is a new way of looking at development, one which takes into account its persistence. It forces us to realize that, just as the countries of the South face problems in protecting the environment, the countries of the North must likewise deal with the problems of overdevelopment. The countries of the North, like the countries of the South, fail to respect the spirit of sustainable development. We know, for example, that global warming is caused by the gases which constitute the very underpinnings of industrialized societies. This means that the lifestyle of rich countries is ecologically unsound, and that their development cannot, at the present stage, be considered "sustainable." We also know that it is in the poor countries that the depletion of resources is most serious, given that those countries are obliged to overwork the natural resources on which their survival depends. They are compelled to sacrifice their future to eke out a precarious daily existence in the present.

Thus, one point must be clearly stated: one cannot protect a natural resource by denying its use to those who depend on it for survival: the link between environmental protection and poverty does not only concern large scale production, but also everyday life, particularly that of women, who have to provide for domestic needs, for water or wood. That is why, in many countries action against poverty helps protect the environment.

Let us stop, then, making a distinction between two aspects of the same question—economy on the one hand and ecology on the other. Any ecological disaster is an economic disas-

ter. Moreover, the two words have a common Greek root, "*oiko*," meaning "home." Mr. Gorbachev suggested that Europe should become a "common home." Yet, the entire universe is our "common home." Ecology comes from the Greek "*oikos logos*," that is, "the science of the home"; economy comes from the Greek "*oikonomia*," that is, "good management of the home." They amount to the same thing; ecology is, by its very nature, part of economy.

This principle has both micro and macroeconomic implications. It has consequences for pricing in particular: since environmental degradation entails a loss of social capital, as well as social costs, this loss must be taken into account in the same way that an investment is amortized. As nature is now entirely in man's hands, it is quite normal to consider it, no longer as a given but as an acquisition, an investment which must constantly be rolled over, amortized just like other costs, salaries, financial expenditures and raw materials. By including "nature costs," we are doing more than protecting resources in the long term; we are enhancing the quality and durability of goods, we are recycling waste and, ultimately, we are saving. Produce, consume, but recycle, too: these are three key concepts for the future.

I should like to emphasize this second theoretical advance, which follows from the first, whether we call it "the new collective security" or "planetary development."

Since time immemorial, mankind has had to face threats to its security. Security evolves, however. To put it simply, I would say that it is now becoming less and less a military matter—since in a world in the process of unification any war is, in a way, a kind of civil war—and is, instead acquiring an economic and ecological dimension. Let us see what this means. First of all, it means that a portion of so called "security" spending in the old sense of the word, in other words military spending, must be redirected towards planetary development projects. Secondly, planetary development means debt for environment swaps. Lastly, planetary development involves a third level of effort: transfers of technology and financing, based, *inter alia*, on the "polluter pays" principle. Here, projects abound which sometimes include the creation or strengthening of institutions or, at the least, of distribution mechanisms. It is not up to me to indicate a preference among them, but their advantages and drawbacks must be discussed, keeping ever present the need to arrive at clear and concrete results.

For we absolutely must achieve concrete results. I realize, of course, that some at least of these results may occasionally clash with powerful vested interests. Let me say, however, that these interests, like the others, must show concern for the long term future and take into account the inherent force of the feeling of equality that moves all peoples of the planet and, quite simply, the force of necessity. There can be no question that the wealthier one is, the more responsibilities one has, and that the countries of the North, first and foremost public opinion in those countries—and it is to that public opinion that I am now talking—must realize that their efforts are essential as regards both financing and technology. This is what I meant by planetary development, the complement to sustainable development, and the "new development" is all this: a spirit and certain working principles. This new spirit must infuse the way in which human beings look at things, at plants, at animals, from the glassful of water discarded after a casual sip to the animals whose species are dwindling rapidly in number. All these, the world's riches, are not something we own but, as Saint Exupéry wrote, something we have on loan from our children....

I cannot emphasize too strongly that States will be the principal instruments for the implementation of the decisions and guidelines adopted here. Moreover, the protection of the planet must be a universal effort involving all those living on it.

In this context, it is especially encouraging that the preparatory work for this Conference has been characterized by such close cooperation between countries at different stages of development and between Governments and the scientific and academic communities and non governmental actors. These networks will have to be maintained and strengthened.

In this area of sustainable development, more than in other areas, we are in a situation where we have to take action in the face of uncertainty. This is because we do not fully understand how ecosystems function, because we have sometimes to work to a very long time scale, and because cause and effect are often separated in space. It will therefore be important to ensure that emerging opinions among scientists and experts receive full attention in decision making processes. We have to find innovative ways of promoting a dialogue between science and politics in the context of the follow up to this Conference.

I wish in the same context to pay special tribute to the non governmental community. Over a thousand non governmental organizations are accredited to the Conference. They have contributed a great deal to the preparatory process—they have worked hard and expect a lot from your deliberations. They should also have a critical role in the follow up.

These organizations represent the peoples of the world whose voice is so clearly heard in the Preamble to the Charter of the United Nations. They represent men and women—and I note that there is an article 20 of the draft Declaration which rightly focuses on women—managers and workers, writers and artists, and individuals from all walks of life.

I see this Conference as a vast planet wide endeavour. During the preparatory process, actors of all kinds—national and local authorities, producers and consumers, community groups and many more—were involved in forging the consensus which this Conference must now cement. It is only through action by every one of us living on this planet that we will succeed in achieving our goals.

Our Rio meeting has already aroused unprecedented interest throughout the world. It has captured the imagination of people everywhere.

As Secretary General, new to the job but none the less well aware of the constraints on the powers of Governments, and indeed of international organizations, my hope is that what I may call the "spirit of Rio"—that is, the spirit of Planet Earth—will spread throughout the world. The spirit of Rio must embody the full awareness of the fragility of our planet. The spirit of Rio must lead us to think constantly of the future, our children's future.

That is why, in opening this Conference, I am very moved when I wish you success in your work. Let me end with these few simple words: never will so much depend on what you do or do not do here—for yourselves, for others, for your children and grandchildren, for the planet—for life in all its interdependent forms.

---- ❖ ----

John Fitzgerald Kennedy

Special Message to Congress on the Peace Corps
March 1, 1961

---- ❖ ----

John Fitzgerald Kennedy (1917–63), president of the United States from 1961 to his assassination on November 23, 1963, was born in Brookline, Massachusetts. He graduated from Harvard University in 1940. After serving in the Navy during World War II, he was elected as a Democrat to the House of Representatives in 1946 and to the Senate in 1953. In 1960, Kennedy was elected president by a small margin over Richard M. Nixon. Kennedy's domestic program, named the New Frontier, called for increased federal involvement in civil rights, education, medicine, urban renewal, and medical insurance. Kennedy was assassinated in Dallas, Texas in November 1963.

In March 1961, Kennedy signed an executive order establishing a volunteer Peace Corps. A U.S. government agency, the Peace Corps was intended to promote world peace and understanding by sending trained U.S. volunteers to developing countries to provide needed skills and assistance. It still exists today.

Special Message to Congress on the Peace Corps March 1, 1961

John Fitzgerald Kennedy

I recommend to the Congress the establishment of a permanent Peace Corps—a pool of trained American men and women sent overseas by the U. S. Government or through private organizations and institutions to help foreign countries meet their urgent needs for skilled manpower....

Throughout the world the people of the newly developing nations are struggling for economic and social progress which reflects their deepest desires. Our own freedom, and the future of freedom around the world, depend, in a very real sense, on their ability to build growing and independent nations where men can live in dignity, liberated from the bonds of hunger, ignorance and poverty.

One of the greatest obstacles to the achievement of this goal is the lack of trained men and women with the skill to teach the young and assist in the operation of development projects—men and women with the capacity to cope with the demands of swiftly evolving economies, and with the dedication to put that capacity to work in the villages, the mountains, the towns and the factories of dozens of struggling nations.

The vast task of economic development urgently requires skilled people to do the work of the society—to help teach in the schools, construct development projects, demonstrate modern methods of sanitation in the villages, and perform a hundred other tasks calling for training and advanced knowledge.

To meet this urgent need for skilled manpower we are proposing the establishment of a Peace Corps—an organization which will recruit and train American volunteers, sending them abroad to work with the people of other nations.

This organization will differ from existing assistance programs in that its members will supplement technical advisers by offering the specific skills needed by developing nations if they are to put technical advice to work. They will help provide the skilled manpower necessary to carry out the development projects planned by the host governments, acting at a working level and serving at great personal sacrifice. There is little doubt that the number of those who wish to serve will be far greater than our capacity to absorb them.

Among the specific programs to which Peace Corps members can contribute are: teaching in primary and secondary schools, especially as part of national English language teaching programs; participation in the worldwide program of malaria eradication; instruction and operation of public health and sanitation projects; aiding in village development through school construction and other programs; increasing rural agricultural productivity by assisting local farmers to use modern implements and techniques. The initial emphasis of these programs will be on teaching. Thus the Peace Corps members will be an effective means of implementing the development programs of the host countries—programs which our technical assistance operations have helped to formulate.

The Peace Corps will not be limited to the young, or to college graduates. All Americans who are qualified will be welcome to join this effort. But undoubtedly the Corps will be made up primarily of young people as they complete their formal education.

Because one of the greatest resources of a free society is the strength and diversity of its private organizations and institutions much of the Peace Corps program will be carried out by these groups, financially assisted by the Federal Government.

Peace Corps personnel will be made available to developing nations in the following ways:

1. Through private voluntary agencies carrying on international assistance programs.
2. Through overseas programs of colleges and universities.
3. Through assistance programs of international agencies.
4. Through assistance programs of the United States government.
5. Through new programs which the Peace Corps itself directly administers.

...The benefits of the Peace Corps will not be limited to the countries in which it serves. Our own young men and women will be enriched by the experience of living and working in foreign lands. They will have acquired new skills and experience which will aid them in their future careers and add to our own country's supply of trained personnel and teachers. They will return better able to assume the responsibilities of American citizenship and with greater understanding of our global responsibilities.

Although this is an American Peace Corps, the problem of world development is not just an American problem. Let us hope that other nations will mobilize the spirit and energies and skill of their people in some form of Peace Corps—making our own effort only one step in a major international effort to increase the welfare of all men and improve understanding among nations.

Thich Nhat Hanh
Being Peace

Thich Nhat Hanh (1926–) is a Vietnamese Buddhist Monk who has lived in exile from his native country since the end of the Vietnam War. A monk since the age of 16, his efforts at reconciliation between North and South during the Vietnam War caused Martin Luther King to nominate him for the Nobel Peace Prize in 1967. Founder of the Plum Village Buddhist Center in southern France, Thich Nhat Hanh has been an influential figure in translating ideas and practices of Buddhism for the West.

In this brief excerpt from Being Peace, Thich Nhat Hanh calls his readers to a different kind of global awareness, one based on the interdependence of all being. He alerts us to the need for constant "mindfulness" in the face of the fast-paced and destructive character of modern life.

Being Peace
Thich Nhat Hanh

There is a Zen story about a man riding a horse which is galloping very quickly. Another man, standing alongside the road, yells at him, "Where are you going?" and the man on the horse yells back, "I don't know. Ask the horse." I think that is our situation. We are riding many horses that we cannot control. The proliferation of armaments, for instance, is a horse. We have tried our best, but we cannot control these horses. Our lives are so busy.

In Buddhism, the most important precept of all is to live in awareness, to know what is going on. To know what is going on, not only here, but there. For instance, when you eat a piece of bread, you may choose to be aware that our farmers, in growing the wheat, use chemical poisons a little too much. Eating the bread, we are somehow co-responsible for the destruction of our ecology. When we eat a piece of meat or drink alcohol, we can produce awareness that 40,000 children die *each day* in the third world from hunger and that in order to produce a piece of meat or a bottle of liquor, we have to use a lot of grain. Eating a bowl of cereal may be more reconciling with the suffering of the world than eating a piece of meat. An authority on economics who lives in France told me that if only the people in Western countries would reduce the eating of meat and the drinking of alcohol by 50%, that would be enough to change the situation of the world. Only 50% less.

Every day we do things, we are things, that have to do with peace. If we are aware of our lifestyle, our way of consuming, of looking at things, we will know how to make peace right in the moment we are alive, the present moment. When we pick up the Sunday newspaper, for instance, we may be aware that it is a very heavy edition, maybe three or four pounds. To print such a paper, a whole forest may be need-

Reprinted from *Being Peace* (1987, 2005) by Thich Nhat Hanh with permission of Parallax Press, Berkeley, California www.parallax.org.

ed. When we pick up the paper, we should be aware. If we are very aware, we can do something to change the course of things.

In my temple, I was the first monk to ride a bicycle. At that time, there were no gathas to recite while riding on a bicycle. We have to practice intelligently, to keep the practice up to date, so recently I wrote a gatha you can use before you start your car. I hope you will find it helpful:

> *Before starting the car,*
> *I know where I am going.*
> *The car and I are one.*
> If the car goes fast, 1 go fast.

Sometimes we don't really need to use the car, but because we want to get away from ourselves, we go down and start the car. If we recite the gatha, "Before starting the car, I know where I am going," it can be like a flashlight—we may see that we don't need to go anywhere. Anywhere we go, we will have our self with us; we cannot escape ourselves. Sometimes it is better to turn the engine off and go out for a walking meditation. It may be more pleasant to do that.

It is said that in the last few years, two million square miles of forest land have been destroyed by acid rain, and that is partly because of our cars. "Before starting the car, I know where I am going," is a very deep question. "Where shall 1 go? To my own destruction?" If the trees die, humans are going to die also. If trees and animals are not alive, how can we be alive?

"The car and I are one." We have the impression that we are the boss, and the car is only an instrument, but that is not true. With the car, we become something different. With a gun, we become very dangerous. With a flute, we become pleasant. With 50,000 atomic bombs, humankind has become the most dangerous species on earth. We were never so dangerous as we are now. We should be aware. The most basic precept of all is to be aware of what we do, what we are, each minute. Every other precept will follow from that.

We have to look deeply at things in order to see. When a swimmer enjoys the clear water of the river, he or she should also be able to be the river. One day I was having lunch at Boston University with some friends, and I looked down at the Charles River. I had been away from home for quite a long lime, and seeing the river, I found it very beautiful. So 1 left my friends and went down to wash my face and dip my feet in the water, as we used to do in our country. When I returned, a professor said, 'That's a very dangerous thing to do. Did you rinse your mouth in the river?" When I told him, "Yes," he said, "You should see a doctor and get a shot."

I was shocked. I didn't know that the rivers here are so polluted. You may call them dead rivers. In our country the rivers get very muddy sometimes, but not that kind of dirt. Someone told me that there are so many chemicals in the Rhine River in Germany that it is possible to develop photographs in it. We can be good swimmers, but can we be a river and experience the fears and hopes of a river? If we cannot, then we do not have the chance for peace. If all the rivers are dead, then the joy of swimming in the river will no longer exist.

If you are a mountain climber or someone who enjoys the countryside, or the green forest, you know that the forests are our lungs outside of our bodies. Yet we have been acting in a way that has allowed two million square miles of forest land to be destroyed by acid rain. We are imprisoned in our small selves, thinking only of the comfortable conditions for this small self, while we destroy our large self. One day I suddenly saw that the sun is my heart, my heart outside of this body. If my body's heart ceases to function I cannot survive; but if the sun, my other heart, ceases to function, I will also die immediately. We should be able to be our true self. That means we should be able to be the river, we should be able to be the forest, we should be able to be a Soviet citizen. We must do this to understand, and to have hope for the future. That is the non-dualistic way of seeing.

Over the Carnage Rose
Prophetic a Voice

Over the carnage rose prophetic a voice,
Be not dishearten'd, affection shall solve the problems of freedom yet,
Those who love each other shall become invincible,
They shall yet make Columbia victorious.
Sons of the Mother of All, you shall yet be victorious,
You shall yet laugh to scorn the attacks of all the remainder of the earth.
No danger shall balk Columbia's lovers,
If need be a thousand shall sternly immolate themselves for one.
One from Massachusetts shall be a Missourian's comrade.
From Maine and from hot Carolina, and another an Oregonese, shall be friends triune,
More precious to each other than all the riches of the earth.
To Michigan, Florida perfumes shall tenderly come,
Not the perfumes of owers, but sweeter, and wafted beyond death.
It shall be customary in the houses and streets to see manly affection,
The most dauntless and rude shall touch face to face lightly,
The dependence of Liberty shall be lovers,
The continuance of Equality shall be comrades.
These shall tie you and band you stronger than hoops of iron,
I, ecstatic, O partners! O lands! with the love of lovers tie you.
(Were you looking to be held together by lawyers?
Or by an agreement on a paper? or by arms?
Nay, nor the world, nor any living thing, will so cohere.)

Walt Whitman

Instructions on the Use of the Enclosed CD

The CD included with this book contains questions from each of the articles excerpted in the anthology. These questions are meant to bridge classroom and community, and can be used in preparation for class discussion or as a guide in formal written assignments or journals. In addition, there are two folders on the CD: one which contains a number of classroom activities and exercises that can be used in conjunction with concepts in the readings and that can enhance a service-learning course using this anthology; and one with a series of internet links to important service-learning resources and materials.

To make your way through the CD, we have separated the questions by entry, so that each set of questions following an essay has its own document saved on the enclosed disk. In order to easily identify and access a particular set of questions corresponding to one of the essay entries in the anthology, look for a document containing the last name of the author of the particular essay, and then open it. For example, the set of questions following "The Garden Party" is saved as "Mansfield." In the case of more than one essay by a particular author, we have named the first essay "1," the second "2," and so on (e.g., addams1 and addams2 for the questions related to the two Jane Addams essays in the anthology). In some cases, the question document may be saved by a name other than an author's name (e.g., "federalist," "community, citizenship, and service," or "civil society," in reference to those collected essays in the anthology).

The "classroom exercises" folder will allow you to get ideas about how to link this anthology to skills and values of democratic citizenship. Each activity has its own page in the folder, with directions and accompanying materials needed to perform it.